T0329467

1

ETERNAL INEQUALITY

ETERNAL INEQUALITY

A History of
Humanity and Hierarchy
during the Last 4 Million Years

by Christopher Cumo

Algora Publishing
New York

Library of Congress Cataloging-in-Publication Data

Names: Cumo, Christopher, author.
Title: Eternal inequality : a history of humanity and hierarchy during the last 4
   million years / Christopher Cumo.
Description: New York : Algora Publishing, 2023. | Includes bibliographical
   references and index. | Summary: "Money, land, and other
   commodities—aggregated and passed to heirs—heighten inequality and stoke
   animus against it. Cumo describes the sweep of this dynamic over a vast
   expanse of time and territory, showing that colossal fortunes provoked
   warfare, rebellion, and revolution. Violence emerged both to challenge
   and to enforce inequality"— Provided by publisher.
Identifiers: LCCN 2022053211 (print) | LCCN 2022053212 (ebook) | ISBN
   9781628944976 (trade paperback) | ISBN 9781628944983 (hardcover) | ISBN
   9781628944990 (pdf)
Subjects: LCSH: Equality. | Social structure. | Revolutions.
Classification: LCC HM821 .C8994 2023 (print) | LCC HM821 (ebook) | DDC
   305—dc23/eng/20221222
LC record available at https://lccn.loc.gov/2022053211
LC ebook record available at https://lccn.loc.gov/2022053212

TABLE OF CONTENTS

INTRODUCTION

0.1 Abstract

Eternal Inequality argues that humans have an impulse to organize, and have always organized, what zoologists, psychologists, and anthropologists call dominance hierarchies, peck orders or pecking orders, and that elites have always enforced inequality.[1] "Despotism is the basic idea of the world, indissolubly bound up with all life and existence. On it rests the meaning of the struggle for existence," wrote Norwegian zoologist and ethologist Thorleif Schjelderup-Ebbe (1894–1976) in encapsulating this viewpoint.[2]

Evolution shapes behavior, including hierarchization and violence, a view fundamental to science. Observing a restaurant's managers and workers, British geneticist Adam Rutherford (b. 1975) remarked that evolution molded their interactions, which were not random but occurred within hierarchy.[3] The owner hierarchizing them and their actions, they occupied the same building, commanded or obeyed one another, and obeyed customers.

Eternal Inequality argues further that the past was a Newtonian system of action and reaction whereby vast inequality sparked backlash from the

---

[1] Porter G. Perrin, "'Pecking Order' 1927-54," *American Speech* 30, no. 4 (December 1955): 265-266; Robert Jurmain, Lynn Kilgore, Wenda Trevathan, and Russell L. Ciochon. *Introduction to Physical Anthropology*, 2013-2014 ed. (Belmont, CA: Wadsworth Cengage Learning, 2014), 212-213.

[2] W. C. Allee, *The Social Life of Animals* (Ann Arbor: University of Michigan Libraries, 1958), accessed April 15, 2022, ‹https://babel.hathitrust.org/cgi/pt?id=mdp.39015064489134&view=1up&seq=2&skin=2021,› 136; John Price, "A Remembrance of Thorleif Schjelderup-Ebbe," *Human Ethology Bulletin* 10, no. 1 (March 1995): 3.

[3] Adam Rutherford, *Humanimal: How Homo sapiens Became Nature's Most Paradoxical Creature* (New York: The Experiment, 2019), 209.

underclass. This dynamic structured prehistory and history and this book's parts and chapters.

Shifting the metaphor from physics to ecology, elites preyed on commoners. Understanding this fact, English Irish author and cleric Jonathan Swift (1667–1745) stated that England's absentee landlords, having "devoured" Irish laborers, might as well eat the children.[4] "Rich people...are often angry because they suspect that the poor want to seize their wealth," wrote British author and "female Marx" Virginia Woolf (1882–1941).[5] Oppressing everyone else, rich men "control everything," she remarked.[6] Emphasizing violence as impulse, Austrian zoologist and "ethologist of world repute" Konrad Lorenz (1903–1989) labelled it "a spontaneous instinctive drive" that civilization will never eradicate.[7]

0.2 Inequality's Persistence

"Inequality has become a much more important topic in the press, social networks and academic publications over the last 3 or 4 years," wrote Serbian American economist Branko Milanovic (b. 1953) in 2015.[8] Interest is understandable given current disparities, huge by any reckoning, which the next chapter overviews. The world's six richest magnates owned more than the poorest 4 billion people in 2017.[9]

Inequality outlasted myriad events, including revolutions: Neolithic, scientific, industrial, French, Russian, and Chinese. Unable to eradicate inequality, we invoked gods. Religions waxed and waned as prophets defended the poor. Amos (c. 750 BCE) condemned the wealthy who "sell the just man for silver, and the poor man for a pair of sandals. They trample the heads of the weak into the dust of the earth and force the lowly out of

---

[4] Jonathan Swift, "A Modest Proposal for Preventing the Children of Poor People in Ireland from Being a Burden to Their Parents or Country, and for Making Them Beneficial to the Public," in *Student's Book of College English*, ed. David Skwire, Frances Chitwood, Raymond Ackley, and Raymond Fredman (Beverly Hills, CA: Glencoe Press, 1975), 198.

[5] Virginia Woolf, *A Room of One's Own* (San Diego: Harcourt Brace Jovanovich, 1981), 33-34; Jane Marcus, "Introduction," in *Three Guineas* (Orlando, FL: Harvest Book, 2006), lii.

[6] Ibid., 34.

[7] Robert Ardrey, *The Territorial Imperative: A Personal Inquiry into the Animal Origins of Property and Nations* (New York: Atheneum, 1966), 302; Sally Carrighar, "War Is Not in Our Genes," in *Man and Aggression*, 2d ed., ed. Ashley Montagu (New York: Oxford University Press, 1973), 129.

[8] Branko Milanovic, "Pareto to Piketty CUNY 15 Spring," 2015, accessed April 19, 2022, ‹https://www.scribd.com/document/256716727/Pareto-to-Piketty-Cuny-15-Spring.›

[9] Greg Robb, "The Harsh Truth about Economic Inequality, Based on Thousands of Years of Evidence," Market Watch, September 19, 2017, accessed April 19, 2022, ‹https://www.marketwatch.com/story/want-to-level-income-inequality-so-far-only-war-and-disease-have-worked-2017-09-18.›

the way."[10] Micah (c. 700 BCE) denounced elites whose oppression of the underclass resembled metaphorical attempts to "eat the flesh of my people."[11] Isaiah criticized "elders and princes" who hoarded "loot wrested from the poor."[12]

Mercantilism, capitalism, and communism organized economies. In African American author Richard Wright's (1908–1960) *Native Son* (1940), Marxist organizer Jan Erlone envisioned a future with "no rich and no poor."[13] Believing communism inevitable, Wright, "the greatest black writer in the world," nonetheless criticized its over simplicity.[14] Encircling the planet, capitalism, "the greatest of all evolutionary developments," precluded Marxism's global triumph.[15] Capitalism's corollary, inequality too resulted from natural selection.

Progressive Era America, Wright's milieu at birth, created the Country Life Commission to reduce inequality between city and countryside and recruited social workers to uplift slums.[16] Activists established Chicago's Hull House in 1889, Boston's Andover House in 1891, New York City's Henry Street Settlement in 1893 and Lenox Hill Neighborhood House in 1894, Cleveland, Ohio's Hiram House in 1896, El Paso's Houchen House in 1912, and hundreds of similar agencies. Combining the Protestant ethic, education, optimism, and the belief that science and technology fostered progress, these enterprises battled penury by Americanizing immigrants and teaching indigents to emulate their betters.

Yet nothing equalized rich and poor. Inequality enlarged, diminished, or remained static throughout time and place but never vanished, *Eternal Inequality* shows. Political promises and efforts at social engineering littered the past without ending inequality. Reformers advocated equality while elites prospered and paupers languished. Examining the disconnect between

---

[10] Amos 2:6-7 (New American Bible).

[11] Micah 3:3.

[12] Isaiah 3:14.

[13] Richard Wright, *Native Son* (New York: Harper Perennial/Modern Classics, 2005), 68.

[14] Richard Wright, *Black Boy (American Hunger): A Record of Childhood and Youth* (New York: Harper Collins, 2005), 372; James Baldwin, *Collected Essays: Notes of a Native Son, Nobody Knows My Name, The First Next Time, No Name in the Street, The Devil Finds Work, and Other Essays* (New York: Library of America, 1984), 253.

[15] Ralph Holloway, "Territory and Aggression in Man: A Look at Ardrey's *Territorial Imperative*," in *Man and Aggression*, 2d ed., ed. Ashley Montagu (New York: Oxford University Press, 1973), 182.

[16] Scott J. Peters and Paul A. Morgan, "The Country Life Commission: Reconsidering a Milestone in American Agricultural History," *Agricultural History* 78, no. 3 (Summer 2004): 302; Nancy A. Hewitt and Steven F. Lawson, *Exploring American Histories: A Brief Survey with Sources* (Boston and New York: Bedford/St. Martin's, 2013), 579-580.

rhetoric and reality, this book contends that inequality persisted because humans always hierarchized and violently perpetuated it.

Eternal Inequality acknowledges this thesis' contentiousness. Chapter 1 pits scholars and scientists who believed we always hierarchized against those who supposed the first communities egalitarian only to degenerate into hierarchies. Devolution implies a garden-of-Eden syndrome. Genesis (c. 550 BCE) put the first people in utopia, where disease, senescence, warfare, famine, and death were nonexistent.[17] Conditions worsened only afterwards, Genesis' fourth chapter affirmed by narrating the hypothetical first murder.[18] Elsewhere the Tanakh mentioned unpleasantries like deceit, theft, idolatry, incest, rape, sodomy, bestiality, and human sacrifice.[19]

Our evolution appears to confirm deterioration in that *Homo erectus*, *Homo heidelbergensis*, and *Homo neanderthalensis* had larger bones and muscles than we.[20] Likewise emphasizing decline, Swiss philosopher Jean-Jacques Rousseau (1712–1778), articulating "the foundations of human rights and democratic principles," asserted that humankind lost its original purity and vitality by surrendering equality for hierarchy and enslavement.[21] This belief populated literature with the noble savage uncorrupted by civilization. Rejecting this claim, this book argues—like English philosopher Thomas Hobbes (1588–1679), "whose uncompromising pronouncements on the fate of human communities continue to haunt political science to this day," and kindred scholars—that people always hierarchized.[22] Inequality, hierarchy, stratification, or whatever noun is preferred, shaped our evolution, prehistory, and history.

Enforcing inequality, elites acknowledged that nobody wants to be poor. Absent acquiescence, coercion commands obedience, stated Hobbes.[23] Consequently, roughly 1.6 million Africans perished during the Middle Passage.[24] Other events included Rome's 71 BCE crucifixion of about 6,000

---

[17] Gen. 2:8-25.

[18] Gen. 4:8

[19] Examples are Gen. 19: 1-5; Exodus 22:19; Exodus 32:1-6; Lev. 20:15-16; Joshua 7:1; 2 Sam. 11:2-17; 2 Sam. 13:1-14; Judges 11:29-40

[20] Jurmain, Kilgore, Trevathan, and Ciochon, 311, 344; Chris Stringer and Peter Andrews, *The Complete World of Human Evolution* (London: Thames & Hudson, 2005), 149.

[21] Jean-Jacques Rousseau, *A Discourse on Inequality*, trans. Maurice Cranston (London: Penguin Books, 1984), 57, 67-68, 109; Paul Kleinman, *Philosophy 101: From Plato and Socrates to Ethics and Metaphysics, An Essential Primer on the History of Thought* (New York: Adams Media, 2013), 73.

[22] Martyn Oliver, *History of Philosophy: Great Thinkers from 600 B.C. to the Present Day* (New York: Barnes & Noble, 1999(, 68.

[23] Thomas Hobbes, *Leviathan* (Oxford and New York: Oxford University Press, 1998), 18.

[24] Johannes Postma, *The Atlantic Slave Trade* (Westport, CT and London: Greenwood Press, 2003), 35.

slaves who joined slave and gladiator Spartacus (c. 110–71 BCE) in rebellion, Hungary's 1514 execution of some 70,000 poor after soldier Gyorgy Dozsa's (1470–1514) rebellion (Gheorghe Doja in Romanian), and China's slaughter of perhaps 30 million desperate peasants during the Taiping rebellion (1850–1865).[25] Indifference to the homeless in our times is violence that drags their life expectancy roughly 25 years below the national average.[26]

Causing premature death, inequality makes destitution a capital crime. A 2016 Massachusetts Institute of Technology study showed that the richest centile of U.S. men outlived the poorest centile nearly 15 years on average.[27] The gap exceeded 10 years for U.S. women in these centiles. Inequality being violence enforced by violence, the backlash against it is violent, indicate chapters 13, 16, 18, and 19 in treating late medieval revolts and the French, Russian, and Chinese revolutions. Barbarism required prey to defend themselves.[28]

Use of the words "enslavement," "slavery," and "slave" throughout this book requires commentary. First, in these pages I do not term any slave an "enslaved person." The adjective and noun are thought to convey a person's humanity better than the terse "slave," but for the purposes of this book I have given priority to concision and consistency.[29] After all, English avoids designating pianists "pianistic people" or politicians "political people," or warriors "war-making people."

Second, some scholars insist that "enslavement," "slavery," and "slave" are difficult to define because exploitation's magnitude changed over time and place. Moreover, neither complete unfreedom nor absolute freedom ever existed, nullifying any a priori attempt to equate slave and chattel.

---

[25] Mary T. Boatwright, Daniel J. Gargola, and Richard J. A. Talbert, *The Romans: From Village to Empire* (New York and Oxford: Oxford University Press, 2004), 207; Paul Freedman, "A Dossier of Peasant and Seigneurial Violence," in *The Routledge History Handbook of Medieval Revolt*, ed. Justine Firnhaber-Baker and Dirk Schoenaers (London and New York: Routledge, 2017), 267; Robert W. Strayer, Edwin Hirschmann, Robert B. Marks, Robert J. Smith, James J. Horn, and Lynn H. Parsons, *The Making of the Modern World: Connected Histories, Divergent Paths (1500 to the Present)* (New York: St. Martin's Press, 1989), 370.

[26] Sabrina Hennecke, "Living and Dying on the Street, across from a Hospital: How to Better Help the Homeless," *Miami Herald*, July 19, 2021, accessed April 16, 2022, ‹https://www.yahoo.com/news/living-dying-street-across-hospital-213303274.html?.tsrc=fp_deeplink.›

[27] Peter Dizikes, "New Study Shows Rich, Poor Have Huge Mortality Gap in U.S." MIT News, April 11, 2016, accessed July 3, 2022, ‹http://news.mit.edu/2016/study-rich-poor-huge-mortality-gap-us-0411.›

[28] Edward O. Wilson, *On Human Nature* (Cambridge, MA and London: Harvard University Press, 2004), 101-102.

[29] Nikole Hannah-Jones, Caitlin Roper, Ilena Silverman, and Jake Silverstein, "A Note about This Book," in *The 1619 Project: A New Origin Story*, ed. Nikole Hannah-Jones, Caitlin Roper, Ilena Silverman, and Jake Silverstein (New York: One World, 2021), xiii.

Eternal Inequality affirms the need for care in defining any noun while rejecting attempts to finesse the concept of slave. This book aims to understand unfreedom from the perspective of omegas. The claim, for example, that indenture was not slavery is correct, though it obscures the reality that underlings lost an unrecoverable portion of their lives during a period of unfreedom. Failure to acknowledge this fact diminishes their sacrifice. Moreover, indenture was permanent when a person died before the contract's completion. Consequently, in these pages serfdom, peonage, slavery, corvée, conscription, and other coercions are unified as one category of powerlessness. Differences among these abuses were less important than recognition that they were abuses.

The noun "peasant" also requires clarification. Scholars use it to designate farmworkers at or near hierarchy's bottom. Accepting this definition, *Eternal Inequality* equates "peasant," "farmworker," and "farmhand" such that none owned land or had freedom to use it as they wished. Instead, tenancy prevailed, with rent in cash or more often in kind. Some farmworkers were hired by the day or task. When their status degenerated into slavery, serfdom, peonage, or another category of unfreedom, this book designates them accordingly.

The term "farmer" will be used when repetition of "peasant," "farmworker," or "farmhand" risks monotony, while acknowledging its defects. Today, the use of "farmer" assumes landownership and ability to decide what to raise, though since chapter 5's Neolithic revolution few who tilled land enjoyed these privileges. They had to obey the landowner.

Mindful of Milanovic's remark, this book uses curiosity about inequality to explore prehistory and history's chasm between rich and poor. Inequality as concept and actuality permits scholars and scientists to study the past by mining insights from history, sociology, economics, biology, anthropology, and political science. Biology contextualizes us as one of several social animals. Establishing that such species, notably our closest relatives the chimpanzee, bonobo, and gorilla, hierarchize, *Eternal Inequality* uses Occam's rule to argue that the common ancestor of all three and humankind ranked its members.

Named after English philosopher and theologian William of Occam (1285–1347), Occam's rule, also termed the principle of parsimony, states that whenever two hypotheses satisfactorily explain a phenomenon, the simpler is preferable.[30] In this case, the simpler is that the behavior hierarchization arose once in our lineage, namely in the common ancestor of us, the

---

[30] Robert C. Solomon and Kathleen M. Higgins, *A Short History of Philosophy* (New York and Oxford: Oxford University Press, 1996), 149.

chimpanzee, bonobo, and gorilla, rather than not in the common progenitor but separately in all four. Eschewing needless complexity, Occam's rule and this book seek epistemological economy.

0.3 Eternal Inequality's Interdisciplinary and Evolutionary Approach to the Past

Considering that interdisciplinary treatment yields the greatest insights about the past, this book differs from traditional scholarship by investigating not just history, anthropology, demography, sociology, biology, epidemiology, climatology, or economics, "the Dismal Science," but instead marshals multiple perspectives to understand the last 4 million years.[31] Detractors might oppose this duration because our species may be no older than 200,000 years. But this criticism ignores that no sharp boundary separates us from our predecessor, *H. erectus*, whose hierarchy anticipated ours.

Heeding evolutionary thinkers, my argument interprets the past conservatively. Just as the anatomical innovations that made us human, for example bipedalism, grasping hands, big brains, flat faces, and binocular vision, were complete at our origin, our behaviors, including hierarchization, emerged early in our lineage. Just as we cannot change our anatomical hallmarks, we likely cannot alter our penchant for ranking everybody. Encapsulating the matter, American paleontologist, zoologist and geologist George Gaylord Simpson (1902–1984), who integrated "paleontology into the mainstream of biological research," wrote, "man himself can be considered as a biological phenomenon."[32]

Surveying our ancestry, chapter 3 describes australopithecine and *Homo* hierarchies. Hierarchization intensified when *H. erectus* mastered fire and formed campsites. Evaluating talents, aspirations, and motivations while gathered around the hearth, these people formed and refined hierarchy. Once established, divisions into superior and inferior deepened over time as humans elaborated culture.

The title *Eternal Inequality: Humanity and Hierarchy during the Last 4 Million Years* links rather than divides us and our forebears. "Humanity" includes not just our species but all members of *Homo*. Indeed, *homo*, "man" understood apart from gender, loses meaning unless humanity is a big enough tent to

---

[31] Jacques Barzun, *Darwin, Marx, Wagner: Critique of a Heritage*, 2d ed. (Chicago and London: University of Chicago Press, 1981), 135.
[32] George Gaylord Simpson, *Biology and Man* (New York: Harcourt, Brace & World, 1969), vii; Leo F. Laporte, *George Gaylord Simpson: Paleontologist and Evolutionist* (New York: Columbia University Press, 2000), 2.

house every member of our genus. The word "eternal," emphasizing that we always hierarchized, does not treat unbounded time.

With inequality an evolutionary outcome, *Eternal Inequality* suspects that had our ancestors created hierarchies and egalitarian communities, the first better amassed resources to support large populations. An advantage being leadership, a chief or council could make decisions and mobilize people quicker and more efficiently than a democracy. Over time, hierarchies prevailed as competition extinguished egalitarians.

0.4 The Past's Newtonian System

Besides premodern humans, *Eternal Inequality* traces *Homo sapiens'* prehistory and history. Roughly the last 5,000 years, history adds an important dimension to this analysis by supplying written accounts, which help identify past inequality, its magnitude, and the above Newtonian system.

Aggregated and passed to heirs, the means of production—land, serfs, servants, and slaves in agrarian communities, shops and ships in commercial economies, and factories in industrial societies—intensified, and stoked animus against, inequality.[33] Describing the sweep of these forces, *Eternal Inequality* shows that fortunes provoked warfare, rebellion, and revolution such that violence enforced and challenged inequality. This book demonstrates that plutocrats oppressed the underclass across time and place. While sometimes retaliating, underlings often lacked the wherewithal to resist.

Like a textbook, *Eternal Inequality* narrates events. By arranging them as occurrences that inflamed or provoked reaction against inequality, it identifies patterns in humankind's effort to construct or challenge inequalities inherent in social animals. The past yields no welter of people, dates, and events but intelligibility.

0.5 The Past's Universal Law

An attempt to make inequality our motivator resembles an effort to construct a universal law of history. Conceived in these terms, my approach resurrects the nineteenth century, when German philosopher and historian Georg Wilhelm Friedrich Hegel (1770–1831) and German economists Karl Marx (1818–1883) and Friedrich Engels (1820–1895) searched for laws

---

[33] Karl Marx and Friedrich Engels, *Communist Manifesto*, trans. Samuel Moore (Chicago: Great Books Foundation, 1955), 8-16.

that governed the past.[34] This comparison may make *Eternal Inequality* seem atavistic to historians who reject lawlike descriptions of the past as over-simple because history's particulars, unique to place and time, are unrepeatable and so resist distillation into a law.

This perspective deserves consideration, though Taiwanese historian Mu-Chou Poo (b. 1952) stated that attempts to derive "the law of history" help us understand the past.[35] This author agrees, seeing humans as sufficiently predictable to allow us to summarize behavior in a law. Natural selection has given us a suite of anatomical traits and tendencies, as noted. Anatomy plus behavior shaped the past, defined in *Eternal Inequality* as the aggregate of our responses to stimuli. Prehistory and history thus exhibit lawlike regularity. Instructive in this regard is our quest to describe the cosmos, as the word implies, in terms of laws. Peculiar would we be to have pursued this knowledge for millennia without ourselves being subject to laws that describe us and the past.

Revisiting interdisciplinarity, *Eternal Inequality*'s uniqueness stems, first, from its integration of insights from the natural sciences, social sciences, and humanities to systematize history. Inequality and the backlash against it shaped this system. Second, this book, emphasizing our impulse to hierarchize everywhere always, regresses this instinct 4 million years, eternalizing inequality from the perspective of a species that originated some 200,000 years ago.

0.6 The Book's Parts and Chapters

These insights organize *Eternal Inequality* into six parts. The first, Inequality Drove Evolution, overviews our development over the last 4 million years and ends with early differential burials and Upper Paleolithic (c. 43,000–c. 8000 BCE) achievements. The second, Inequality Enlarged, describes the wealth gap circa 8000 BCE to 1400 CE. The third, Inequality and Its Discontents, examines medieval inequality and the fourteenth-century backlash against it. Afterwards, inequality intensified, notes Part IV, Inequality Again on the Rise. Part V, Another Backlash against Inequality, treats French, Russian, and Chinese revolutions. But this class war failed as the last half century enlarged inequality, the subject of Part VI, Toward an Increasingly Unequal Present.

---

[34] Henry D. Aiken, *The Age of Ideology: The 19th Century Philosophers* (New York: New American Library, 1956), 190.

[35] Mu-Chou Poo, *Daily Life in Ancient China* (Cambridge, UK: Cambridge University Press, 2018), xi.

These six parts comprise 20 chapters. The first four locate inequality within our biological, social, and cultural evolution. Chapter 5 describes how agriculture and pastoralism, originating before 8000 BCE in Southwest Asia, worsened inequality. Chapters 5 through 11 document inequality in agrarian Mediterranean, Indian, Chinese, and American societies. Chapters 12 and 13 survey medieval inequality and rural and urban reactions against it. Heeding French economist Thomas Piketty (b. 1971) that slavery was "without a doubt the most extreme type of inequality," chapter 14 notes the enslavement of over 10 million Africans, their transatlantic journey, and their work on New World plantations.[36] Slaves lacked even identity because masters, never bothering to learn their birth names, instead assigned them.[37] This system that enriched few while denying millions their humanity created modernity. Marx and the Trinidadian historian, prime minister, and "*social-movement intellectual*" Eric Williams (1911–1981) believed slavery and the slave trade bankrolled chapter 15's industrialization.[38] Bondage and industry rewarded elites, who faced backlash through the revolutions treated in chapters 16–19. The final chapter approaches the present.

0.7 Review and Preview

Evolution led us to hierarchize everywhere always, elites enforced inequality, and commoners reacted against it. The tension between elites who favored, and underlings who opposed, inequality shaped prehistory and history and constituted their law. Chapter 1 contextualizes this thesis within a debate between thinkers who believed we were originally egalitarian but later became unequal and those who identified inequality as our permanent condition.

---

[36] John P. McKay, Bennett D. Hill, John Buckler, Clare Haru Crowston, Merry E. Wiesner-Hanks, and Joe Perry, *Understanding Western Society: A Brief History* (Boston and New York: Bedford/St. Martin's, 2012), 441; Thomas Piketty, *Capital and Ideology*, trans. Arthur Goldhammer (Cambridge, MA and London: Belknap Press of Harvard University Press, 2020), 203.

[37] Piketty, 206.

[38] Karl Marx, *Capital: A Critique of Political Economy*, vol. 1, trans. Ben Fowkes (London: Penguin Books, 1990), 924-925; William A. Darity Jr., "Foreword," in *Capitalism and Slavery*, Eric Williams, 3d ed. (Chapel Hill: University of North Carolina Press, 2021), xii; Eric Williams, *Capitalism and Slavery*, 3d ed. (Chapel Hill: University of North Carolina Press, 2021), 77, 83-84; Maurice St. Pierre, *Eric Williams and the Anticolonial Tradition: The Making of a Diasporan Intellectual* (Charlottesville and London: University of Virginia Press, 2015), 2; the italics duplicate the original.

Chapter 1 Debate over Inequality's Origin and Relation to Violence

1.1 Abstract

Current inequality elicits commentary from journalists, humanists, social scientists, and natural scientists. Much of the literature transcends description by attempting to explain why inequality is so stark, to predict how it might affect the future, and to suggest ways to lessen it. Joining this discussion, chapter 1, first, puts current inequality at roughly 50 years' gestation, though inequality itself is much older, prompting inquiry into whether humans always hierarchized or were once egalitarian only to become unequal. Second, this chapter, examining the relationship between inequality and violence, contends that elites enforced hierarchy.

1.2 Current Inequality

Little reflection is necessary to appreciate humankind's habit of creating dominance hierarchies, peck orders, or pecking orders. More than abstractions, these rankings calibrate society through money, which quantifies status by helping people within and outside a community sort individuals quickly and precisely. For example, neighbors compare homes, cars, boats, and other belongings that wealth purchases. Therein lies consumerism's allure. Pervading existence, inequality, as inescapable as death, fixes everyone's social and economic position.

Elemental to humankind, inequality, enlarging over the last half century, produced another Gilded Age, the name American authors Mark Twain (1835–1910) and Charles Dudley Warner (1829–1900) gave the late nineteenth century, when magnates amassed gargantuan profits while impoverishing everyone else.[39] In today's Gilded Age, American socialite Kylie Jenner (b. 1997) purchased a $72 million jet, plus $5 million annual maintenance, in 2020.[40] Clothes cost $300,000 monthly, an amount that, adjusted for different times and currencies, is at least that of chapter 16's French queen Marie Antoinette (1755–1793).[41] Security adds $300,000 to $400,000 to monthly expenses. Another $80 million bought properties throughout California.

Today's technological and information revolution intensified inequality. During the last half century, a "global plutocracy" that pits workers against one another everywhere decreased wages in rich nations like the United States.[42] The top centile of incomes worldwide in 2008 surpassed the poorest decile roughly 160 times.[43] That year American bank Goldman Sachs exceeded $1 trillion in assets whereas almost 1 billion people worldwide earned no more than $1 daily.[44]

Inequality grew faster in the United States than in other modern economies after 2010.[45] The world's 1,426 billionaires more than doubled Africa's wealth in 2013.[46] Six magnates owned more than the poorest 4 billion people in 2017.[47] That year, 12.3 percent of Americans—13 million children and 27 million adults—fell below the poverty line.[48] In 2020, indigenes, 5

[39] Nancy A. Hewitt and Steven F. Lawson, *Exploring American Histories: A Brief Survey with Sources* (Boston and New York: Bedford/St. Martin's, 2013), 505.

[40] Mehera Bonner, "Kris Jenner Is 'Worried' that Kylie Jenner's Spending Her Money too Fast," *Cosmopolitan*, July 21, 2022, accessed July 21, 2022, ‹Kris Jenner Is "Worried" That Kylie Jenner's Spending Her Money Too Fast (yahoo.com);› Jennifer Hassan, "Kylie Jenner Gets Roasted for Flaunting Private Jet in Climate Crisis," *Washington Post*, July 21, 2022, accessed July 21, 2022, ‹Kylie Jenner gets roasted for flaunting private jet in climate crisis (msn.com).›

[41] Bonner; Hassan; Rachel Burrow, "A Look at Marie-Antoinette's Breathtaking Jewelry Collection: The Controversial Queen of France Spared No Expense When It Came to Her Trousseau," *Veranda*, June 16, 2020, accessed September 10, 2022, ‹Marie-Antionette's Prized Jewelry Collection (veranda.com).›

[42] Branko Milanovic, *Global Inequality: A New Approach for the Age of Globalization* (Cambridge, MA and London: Belknap Press of Harvard University Press, 2016), 3.

[43] Ibid., 25.

[44] Niall Ferguson, *The Ascent of Money: A Financial History of the World* (New York: Penguin Press, 2008), 1-2.

[45] Karen Petrou, *Engine of Inequality: The Fed and the Future of Wealth in America* (Hoboken, NJ: Wiley, 2021), 2.

[46] Milanovic, *Global Inequality*, 41.

[47] Greg Robb, "The Harsh Truth about Economic Inequality, Based on Thousands of Years of Evidence," Market Watch, September 19, 2017, accessed April 19, 2022, ‹https://www.marketwatch.com/story/want-to-level-income-inequality-so-far-only-war-and-disease-have-worked-2017-09-18.›

[48] Tim Cooke, *Working toward Abolishing Poverty* (Catharines, ON and New York: Crabtree, 2020), 29; Ashley Nicole, *Poverty and Welfare* (Philadelphia and Miami: Mason Crest, 2020), 10.

percent of global population, totaled 15 percent of paupers.[49] Roughly one fifth of aborigines were poor and one third had been homeless at least once. At the other pole that year, billionaire assets surpassed $10 trillion for the first time.[50] Even before chapter 20's COVID-19 profited elites while the downtrodden faced eviction, U.S. wealth distribution was the most lopsided among modern nations.[51]

1.3 Equality v. Inequality

1.3.1 Equality Posited as Humanity's Original State

Inequality is old, though onlookers might wonder whether it is immutable. Two possibilities exist; either humans always hierarchized, or they did not, in which case the past had egalitarian communities absent today. Emphasizing change, this possibility understands nature and humankind as variable. Empiricism demonstrates change. For instance, our eyes witness plant and animal growth over time. A tomato seedling without flowers matures into a vine with yellow blooms that, upon pollination, develop fruit of a color that varies by cultivar.

In Greece and its colonies, the first natural philosophers appreciated what nature taught them. Greek scientist Anaximenes (c. 585–c. 526 BCE) and Greek philosopher and poet Heraclitus (c. 540–c. 480 BCE) asserted that the universe, never static, changed predictably.[52] Echoing this idea, Egyptian philosopher Plotinus (204–270 CE), aiming "to awaken the eye of wisdom," described a "kosmos" in "ceaseless flux."[53]

Describing plants new to France's countryside, observing how trees shed leaves as winter approached, and watching laborers harvest grapes and return home when vines were bare, Swiss philosopher Jean-Jacques Rousseau (1712–1778) likewise understood nature as changeable.[54] Applying change to

---

[49] Cooke, 35.

[50] Igor Derysh, "Billionaire Wealth Rises to More Than $10 Trillion for the First Time Ever Amid Pandemic: Analysis," Salon, October 17, 2020, accessed April 8, 2022, ‹https://www.salon.com/2020/10/17/billionaire-wealth-rises-to-more-than-10-trillion-for-first-time-ever-amid-pandemic-analysis-2.›

[51] Petrou, 2; Michelle Conlin, "The Great Divergence: U.S. COVID-19 Economy Has Delivered Luxury Homes for Some, Evictions for Others," Reuters, October 31, 2020, accessed April 9, 2022, ‹https://www.yahoo.com/news/great-divergence-u-covid-19-110903275.html.›

[52] Robert S. Brumbaugh, *The Philosophers of Greece* (Albany: State University of New York Press, 1981), 26, 43.

[53] Plotinus, *The Six Enneads*, trans. Stephen MacKenna and B. S. Page (Chicago: Encyclopaedia Britannica, 1988), 35; Stephen R. L. Clark, *Plotinus: Myth, Metaphor, and Philosophical Practice* (Chicago and London: University of Chicago Press, 2016), xi.

[54] Jean-Jacques Rousseau, *Reveries of the Solitary Walker*, trans. Peter France (Middlesex, UK: Penguin Books, 1979), 36-37.

us, he believed the earliest societies lacked gradations because private property was unknown.[55] Its invention created inequality as the lucky and ruthless monopolized land. Similarly German economists Karl Marx (1818–1883)
and Friedrich Engels (1820–1895), "by far the better writer," thought the first
tribes shared land.[56] Private property again inaugurated inequality.

Property's treatment as human construct, however, ignores territoriality
in other animals.[57] Invertebrates and vertebrates that perceive space as theirs
repulse invaders. This behavior implies recognition of trespass. If property is
biological and predated us, we neither invented it nor once enjoyed proper-
tyless equality. Among forebears, chapter 3's *Australopithecus* and early *Homo*
may have been territorial.[58]

In his 1888 preface to a *Communist Manifesto* reprint, Engels, identifying
"economic factors [as] the basic cause of the clash between different classes,"
hoped Marxism would revolutionize history as Darwinism had biology.[59]
In *The Descent of Man* (1871), British naturalist Charles Darwin (1809–1882),
"the most influential biologist to have lived," contrasted primitivism and
civilization, declaring hunter-gatherers more equal physically, behavior-
ally, economically, and socially than their sedentary counterparts.[60] Defining
neither primitivism nor civilization, he remarked that the second arose from
the first and that hunter-gatherers were undifferentiated whereas civilization hierarchized.[61]

Absent definition or chronology, *The Descent of Man* pinpointed neither
where nor when egalitarianism became inequality. Equating civilization and
urbanism, French paleontologist Frederic-Marie Bergounioux (1900–1983)
estimated that cities emerged about 6000 BCE.[62] Later scholars refined

---

[55] Jean-Jacques Rousseau, *A Discourse on Inequality*, trans. Maurice Cranston (London: Penguin Books, 1984), 57, 67-68, 109.

[56] Karl Marx and Friedrich Engels, *Communist Manifesto*, trans. Samuel Moore (Chicago: Great Books Foundation, 1955), 8; Larry Ceplair, *Revolutionary Pairs: Marx and Engels, Lenin and Trotsky, Gandhi and Nehru, Mao and Zhou, Castro and Guevara* (Lexington: University Press of Kentucky, 2020), 9.

[57] Edward O. Wilson, *Sociobiology: The New Synthesis*, 25th anniversary ed. (Cambridge, MA and London: Belknap Press of Harvard University Press, 2000), 256.

[58] Ibid., 565.

[59] Friedrich Engels, "Preface," in *Communist Manifesto*, Karl Marx and Friedrich Engels, trans. Samuel Moore (Chicago: Great Books Foundation, 1955), 5; Ceplair, 14.

[60] Charles Darwin, *The Descent of Man, and Selection in Relation to Sex* (London: Penguin Books, 2004), 46; John Bowlby, *Charles Darwin: A New Life* (New York and London: Norton, 1990), 1.

[61] Darwin, 160, 170.

[62] F. M. Bergounioux, "Notes on the Mentality of Primitive Man," in *Social Life of Early Man*, ed. Sherwood L. Washburn (Chicago: Aldine Publishing, 1961), 106.

the date between roughly 5800 and 3750 BCE in Mesopotamia.[63] Darwin's opinion, therefore, originated inequality then and there.

Like Darwin, German philosopher and philologist Friedrich Nietzsche (1844–1900), among "the most iconic thinkers of our time," did not date inequality's emergence.[64] His philological training leading him to seek this event in language, he argued that elites defined "good" as what benefited them and "evil" as what harmed them.[65] Arising in prehistory, these definitions made "good" nobility and "evil" commonness.[66] This dichotomy divided aristocrat from everyone else and master from slave, though inequality preceded the words "good" and "evil" because the rich overshadowed the underclass before inventing language to contrast elite superiority and pleb inferiority.[67]

Nietzsche omitted when elites first set good against evil and master against slave, understandable vagueness for a preliterate event involving speech's formation. American anthropologist Clark Spencer Larsen (b. 1952) estimated that speech arose as early as 2 million year ago.[68] British geneticist Adam Rutherford (b. 1975) dated the event 600,000 to 70,000 years ago.[69] Austrian American historian Walter Scheidel (b. 1966) suggested 300,000 to 100,000 years ago.[70] American anthropologist Robert Jurmain (1948–2021) and coauthors favored 200,000 to 100,000 years ago.[71] These ranges overlap our predecessor *Homo erectus* and raise the possibility that we spoke from the outset. Even so, speech's origin does not pinpoint society's bifurcation into masters and slaves. Despite cleverness and originality, Nietzsche speculated.

German physicist, 1921 Nobel laureate in physics, and *"greatest genius of all time"* Albert Einstein (1879–1955) attributed inequality to state formation

---

[63] Stephen Bertman, *Handbook to Life in Ancient Mesopotamia* (New York: Facts on File, 2003), 55.

[64] Lucy Huskinson, An Introduction to Nietzsche (Peabody, MA: Hendrickson Publishers, 2009), xiii.

[65] Friedrich Nietzsche, *On the Genealogy of Morals*, trans. Walter Kaufman and R. J. Hollingdale (New York: Viking Books, 1969), 25–29.

[66] Friedrich Nietzsche, *Human, All Too Human, I*, trans. Gary Handwerk (Stanford, CA: Stanford University Press, 1995), 16, 51.

[67] Nietzsche, *On the Genealogy of Morals*, 26.

[68] Clark Spencer Larsen. *Our Origins: Discovering Physical Anthropology* (New York and London: Norton, 2008), 270.

[69] Adam Rutherford, *Humanimal: How Homo sapiens Became Nature's Most Paradoxical Creature* (New York: The Experiment, 2019), 177.

[70] Walter Scheidel, *The Great Leveler: Violence and the History of Inequality from the Stone Age to the Twenty-First Century* (Princeton, NJ and Oxford: Princeton University Press, 2017), 28.

[71] Robert Jurmain, Lynn Kilgore, Wenda Trevathan, and Russell L. Ciochon. *Introduction to Physical Anthropology*, 2013-2014 ed. (Belmont, CA: Wadsworth Cengage Learning, 2014), 352.

and warfare.[72] Only polities could raise, equip, feed, pay, and command an army. Victors impoverished losers by taking resources like land. Conquerors enacted laws to privilege themselves while disadvantaging their subjects. Priests, government, or both established schools to teach that elites were virtuous and earned eminence whereas sloth pauperized the underclass. "Every human society must justify its inequalities," wrote French economist Thomas Piketty (b. 1971) in summarizing this deceit.[73]

The belief that warfare caused inequality ignores that we invented neither, states chapter 3. Below, English philosopher Thomas Hobbes (1588–1679) described war as innately human. Anything inborn is biological and arose gradually by natural selection. Chapter 3's Australian physician and anatomist Raymond Dart (1893–1988) and American playwright and science writer Robert Ardrey (1908–1980), believing war predated us, made *Australopithecus* its architect, though it probably arose in the common ancestor of chimpanzees and us because they also form groups that kill enemies.[74]

Like Rousseau, Marx, and Engels, American geographer Jared Diamond (b. 1937) in 1999, Spanish American political scientist Carles Boix (b. 1962) in 2010, Serbian American economist Branko Milanovic (b. 1953) in 2011, and American author Jeffrey Moussaieff Masson (b. 1941) in 2014, emphasizing our relationship with land, wrote that equality prevailed before agriculture and pastoralism.[75]

Eternal Inequality disagrees. Where rich, predictable resources permitted sedentism, hunter-gatherers, bifurcating into aristocrats and slaves, were as unequal as farmers and herders.[76] Among hunter-gatherers, Chinook elites

---

[72] Albert Einstein, *Ideas and Opinions*, trans. Sonja Bargmann (New York: Modern Library, 1994), 166; Jurgen Neffe, *Einstein: A Biography*, trans. Shelley Frisch (New York: Farrar, Straus and Giroux, 2007), 4. The italics duplicate the original.

[73] Thomas Piketty, *Capital and Ideology*, trans. Arthur Goldhammer (Cambridge, MA and London: Belknap Press of Harvard University Press, 2020), 1.

[74] Jurmain, Kilgore, Trevathan, and Ciochon, 207-209.

[75] Jared Diamond, "The Worst Mistake in History of the Human Race," *Discover Magazine*, May 1, 1999, accessed April 19, 2022, ⟨https://www.discovermagazine.com/planet-earth/the-worst-mistake-in-the-history-of-the-human-race⟩; Carles Boix, "Origins and Persistence of Economic Inequality," *Annual Review of Political Science* 13 (2010): 489-516, accessed April 19, 2022, ⟨Origins and Persistence of Economic Inequality | Annual Review of Political Science (annualreviews.org).⟩; Branko Milanovic, *The Haves and the Have-Nots: A Brief and Idiosyncratic History of Global Inequality* (New York: Basic Books, 2011), 217; Jeffrey Moussaieff Masson, *Beasts: What Animals Can Teach Us about the Origins of Good and Evil* (New York: Bloomsbury, 2014), 45-46.

[76] Eric Alden Smith, Kim Hill, Frank Marlowe, David Nolin, Polly Wiessner, Michael Gurven, Samuel Bowles, Monique Borgerhoff Mulder, Tom Hertz, and Adrian Bell. "Wealth Transmission and Inequality among Hunter-Gatherers." *Current Anthropology* 51, no. 1 (February 2010): 23.

---

confiscated paupers' food when shortage threatened the Pacific Northwest.[77] This theft mirrored elite macaque females that stole food from subordinates' mouths.[78] Such ruthlessness persisted wherever regressive taxation imperiled the underclass. California's hunter-gatherers reserved the honor of cremation for decedents, especially men, who had prospered while alive.[79] Post-contact Great Plains nomads measured wealth in horses.[80] Prominent men owned up to 40 mounts. Before and after 1492, master–slave inequality pitted power against powerlessness among North and South American hunter-gatherers and farmers, disqualifying agriculture and animal husbandry as inequality's cause.

American anthropologist Siobhan Mattison and coauthors in 2016 judged early communities "relatively egalitarian."[81] Inequality required people, first, to amass defensible resources.[82] The geographic density of crops and livestock satisfied this criterion. Docile sheep that congregated among one another could be protected, unlike wild animals that fled humans. Second, people had to invent laws that defined resources as property, Rousseau's requisite, and that eased their passage to heirs.[83] As mentioned above, however, some theories dispute that we ever held resources in common.

American Australian historian David Christian (b. 1946) averred in 2018 that hunter-gatherers enjoyed rough equality; their surroundings, filling their needs, obviated hoarding.[84] This claim supported Diamond, Boix, Milanovic, and Masson because egalitarianism ended with farming and herding. This new relationship with land and biota produced food that enlarged population. Elites emerged to manage this bounty and labor.

Christian's opinion required that subsistence made hunter-gatherers egalitarian. Meeting but not exceeding needs, nature prevented anyone from taking or desiring more. Yet nature blunts no billionaire's greed amid super-

---

[77] Wayne Suttles, "Coping with Abundance: Subsistence on the Northwest Coast," in *Man the Hunter*, ed. Richard B. Lee and Irven DeVore (Chicago: Aldine Publishing, 1968), 59.

[78] Jurmain, Kilgore, Trevathan, and Ciochon, 186.

[79] David N. Dickel, Peter D. Schulz, and Henry M. McHenry, "Central California: Prehistoric Subsistence Changes and Health," in *Paleopathology at the Origins of Agriculture*, ed. Mark Nathan Cohen and George J. Armelagos (Orlando, FL: Academic Press, 1984), 453.

[80] Joseph M. Prince and Richard H. Steckel, *Tallest in the World: Native Americans of the Great Plains in the Nineteenth Century* (Cambridge, MA: National Bureau of Economic Research, 1998), 8-9.

[81] Siobhan M. Mattison, Eric A. Smith, Mary K. Shenk, and Ethan E. Cochrane, "The Evolution of Inequality," *Evolutionary Anthropology Issues, News and Reviews* 25, no. 4 (July 2016): 184.

[82] Ibid., 187.

[83] Ibid., 189.

[84] David Christian, *Origin Story: A Big History of Everything* (London: Allen Lane, 2018), 187, 212.

abundance. Moreover, Pacific Northwest kleptocrats, exhibiting greed by stealing indigents' food, had enough to divide into nobles and commoners.

1.3.2 Inequality Posited as Humanity's Original State

Heraclitus' maxim that "the only constant is change" was opposed by the steady-state philosophy of Ecclesiastes (c. 250 BCE), which exposed "the fragility of traditional wisdom."[85] "Nothing is new under the sun," lamented Qoheleth after a lifelong quest for wisdom.[86] This language countered the author's description of impermanence elsewhere. People worked, aged, died, and were forgotten. A new generation arose only to suffer the same fate.

Despite appearing to contradict empirical evidence of change, the static model influenced science. Before 1859 most scientists thought species unchangeable. *Dionaea muscipula*, for example, had never been, and would never become, anything but the Venus flytrap. Encapsulating this opinion, French botanist Michel Adanson (1727–1806) stated "that the transmutation of species does not happen among plants, no more than among animals."[87] Biologists and anthropologists attributed this error to Greek philosopher Plato (c. 428–c. 348 BCE), among "the most dazzling writers in the Western literary tradition and one of the most penetrating, wide-ranging, and influential authors in the history of philosophy," Christianity, conservatism, or their combination.[88]

Stasis as concept affected science, and Plato's pupil Greek philosopher Aristotle (384–322 BCE), whom Italian "*philosophical* theologian" and Christian saint Thomas Aquinas (1225–1274) esteemed "the Philosopher" and whose treatises shaped biology, astronomy, physics, and chemistry for centuries, defined inequality as innate and unalterable: "For that some should rule and others be ruled is a thing not only necessary, but expedient; from the hour of their birth, some are marked out for subjection, others for

---

[85] The statement is "the apparent constant in the universe in change" in Robert C. Solomon and Kathleen M. Higgins, *A Short History of Philosophy* (New York and Oxford: Oxford University Press, 1996), 33; Gianfranco Ravasi, "Foreword," in *The Living Dead: Ecclesiastes through Art*, ed. Corinna Ricasoli (Paderborn, Germany: Ferdinand Schoeningh, 2018), 9; Luca Mazzinghi, "The Book of Ecclesiastes," in *The Living Dead: Ecclesiastes through Art*, ed. Corinna Ricasoli (Paderborn, Germany: Ferdinand Schoeningh, 2018), 19.

[86] Ecclesiastes 1:9 (New American Bible).

[87] Ernst Mayr, *The Growth of Biological Thought: Diversity, Evolution, and Inheritance* (Cambridge, MA and London: Belknap Press of Harvard University Press, 1982), 260.

[88] Ibid., 38, 87, 307-309; Jurmain, Kilgore, Trevathan, and Ciochon, 26-27; Richard Kraut, "Plato," in Stanford Encyclopedia of Philosophy, last modified February 12, 2022, accessed June 18, 2022, ‹Plato (Stanford Encyclopedia of Philosophy).›

rule."[89] Equality nonexistent, the art of governance required the multitude to obey the lawgiver.

Equality was no more real in the American colonies. "God Almighty... hath so disposed of the condition of mankind, as in all times some must be rich, some poor, some high and eminent in power and dignity; others mean and in subjection," remarked English lawyer and first Massachusetts Bay Colony governor John Winthrop (1588–1649) who, having eight servants, "was among those whom God had designated for power and dignity."[90] This language implied not only that God always hierarchized people but that inequality, as his will, benefited everyone. In this context, third U.S. president Thomas Jefferson's (1743–1826) statement of equality in the *Declaration of Independence* (1776) illustrated Piketty's deceit because Jefferson owned over 600 slaves.[91]

Humanity's division into "rich and poor" diffused tension by obliging the "inferior sort" to obey superiors, whose abuse of the lowly, Winthrop believed, God checked.[92] He thus created a fantasy whereby God, taming "the law of nature," eliminated oppression.[93]

Although concluding similarly about inequality, Hobbes demolished this fiction. Rather than theologize, he posited our original lifeways, a time before government, as the "state of nature."[94] Technology was primitive, laws nonexistent, and privation and danger ubiquitous. A person could rely on only brawn and wit, however great or meager. These hypotheticals influenced philosophers and political theorists like Rousseau, English philosopher John Locke (1632–1704), French philosopher Voltaire (1694–1778), and German philosopher and historian Georg Wilhelm Friedrich Hegel (1770–1831).

---

[89] Aristotle, *Politics*, trans. Benjamin Jowett (New York: Modern Library, 1943), 58; Arthur Herman, *The Cave and the Light: Plato Versus Aristotle, and the Struggle for the Soul of Western Civilization* (New York: Random House, 2013), 235; Brian Leftow, "Introduction," in *Summa Theologiae: Questions on God*, Thomas Aquinas, ed. Brian Davies and Brian Leftow (Cambridge, UK: Cambridge University Press, 2006), ix. The italics duplicate the original.

[90] John Winthrop, "From *A Model of Christian Charity*," in *The Norton Anthology of American Literature*, 2d ed., Nina Baym, Francis Murphy, Ronald Gottesman, Hershel Parker, Laurence B. Holland, William H. Pritchard, and David Kalstone (New York and London: Norton, 1986), 11-12; Daniel T. Rodgers, *As a City on a Hill: The Story of America's Most Famous Lay Sermon* (Princeton, NJ and Oxford: Princeton University Press, 2018), 20-21.

[91] Thomas Piketty, *Capital in the Twenty-First Century*, trans. Arthur Goldhammer (Cambridge, MA and London: Belknap Press of Harvard University Press, 2014), 158.

[92] Winthrop, 12.

[93] Ibid., 13.

[94] Bertrand Russell, *A History of Western Philosophy: And Its Connection with Political and Social Circumstances from the Earliest Times to the Present Day*, 14th ed. (New York: Simon & Schuster, 1964), 550.

A realist, Hobbes observed selfishness, aggression, and disparities in wealth, status, privilege, and power.[95] Unchecked by government, selfishness and aggression "render men apt to invade, and destroy one another."[96] The result "is called war, and such a war, as is of every man, against every man" whereby "every man is enemy to every man."[97] As Einstein noted, war yields inequality.

Grounding his logic in empiricism, Hobbes watched his contemporaries lock doors and belongings and travel armed and with others in recognition of danger.[98] This reasoning modeled the introduction's Occam's rule. In this instance, the simpler explanation of why people imperil one another is that they have always enforced inequality. An onlooker need explain no putative transition from equality and decency to inequality and depravity.

As stated, Hobbes influenced Hegel who, articulating "one of the most influential systems of thought," agreed that "The state of nature, therefore, is rather the state of injustice, violence, untamed natural impulses, of inhuman deeds and emotions."[99] Arising to restrain humanity, government normalized and intensified inequality by compelling obedience through fear.[100]

Bergounioux, mentioned earlier, identified inequality throughout prehistory and history. He believed the earliest people formed clans governed by a chief, whose wife and children occupied the second tier whereas everyone else populated the bottom.[101] Government hardened, bureaucratized, and multiplied gradations.

Like Hobbes and Hegel, Ardrey, "the most influential writer in English dealing with the innate or instinctive attributes of human nature," found ferocity, enforcing inequality, at our core.[102] The instinct to dominate weaklings, which he designated a "fundamental life force," intensified disparity.[103]

---

[95] Thomas Hobbes, *Leviathan* (Oxford and New York: Oxford University Press, 1998), 45.
[96] Ibid., 84.
[97] Ibid.
[98] Ibid.
[99] G. W. F. Hegel, *Reason in History: A General Introduction to the Philosophy of History*, trans. Robert S. Hartman (Indianapolis and New York: Bobbs-Merrill, 1953), 54; Henry D. Aiken, *The Age of Ideology: The 19th Century Philosophers* (New York: New American Library, 1956), 71.
[100] Ibid., 60.
[101] Bergounioux, 107, 112.
[102] Robert Ardrey, *African Genesis: A Personal Investigation into the Animal Origins and Nature of Man* (New York: Atheneum, 1970), 11, 89; Geoffrey Gorer, "Ardrey on Human Nature: Animals, Nations, Imperatives," in *Man and Aggression*, 2d ed., ed. Ashley Montagu (New York: Oxford University Press, 1973), 159.
[103] Ardrey, 112.

Hierarchy's early evolution in our lineage suggests that we always ranked one another.[104]

Arguing that natural selection bequeathed inequality and aggression, America's Edward Wilson (b. 1929), among "the half dozen greatest biologists of the twentieth century," described us as products of innovation and stasis.[105] For example, we alone among primates walk on two legs by default whereas apes, though capable of awkward bipedalism for short distances, favor quadrupedality.[106] Inequality and violence, however, typify primates such that our lineage conserved these traits "in relatively unaltered form."[107] Rather than invent these attributes, we inherited them from ancestors.

Jurmain and colleagues likewise treated inequality as evolutionary. Noting its prevalence in primates, they remarked that we and chimpanzees behave in ways that differ in degree, not kind.[108] Our behaviors, rooted in biology, are modifications of how other primates and our ancestors acted. These insights indicate that our predilection for inequality and its enforcement are inborn and characterized us from our origin.

Occam's rule and evolution also guided Scheidel, who stated that humans and our closest kin—chimpanzee, bonobo, and gorilla—hierarchize.[109] Rather than suppose independent evolution in each, he believed all four's common ancestor hierarchized, the introduction noted. Inequality thus predated us and structured our entirety on earth.

1.4 Inequality and Violence

Underlings sometimes revolted against elites.[110] When vast, such turmoil threatened hierarchy. The French, Russian, and Chinese revolutions discussed in chapters 16, 18 and 19, for example, harnessed class warfare to overthrow the old order, though violence—a product of "Stone Age emotions"—was usually elites' prerogative.[111] Paupers lacked the wherewithal to harm their aggressors. Rather than a two-way street, brutality was

---

[104] Ibid., 89.
[105] Wilson, *Sociobiology*, 547-551; Richard Rhodes, *Scientist: E. O. Wilson: A Life in Nature* (New York: Doubleday, 2021), 2.
[106] Robert McNeill Alexander, "Bipedal Animals, and Their Differences from Humans," *Journal of Anatomy* 204, no. 5 (May 2004): 321-330, accessed April 19, 2022, ‹https://www.ncbi.nlm.nih.gov/pmc/articles/PMC1571302.›
[107] Wilson, *Sociobiology*, 551.
[108] Jurmain, Kilgore, Trevathan, and Ciochon, 182, 213.
[109] Scheidel, 25-26.
[110] Ibid., 7.
[111] Edward O. Wilson, *The Social Conquest of Earth* (New York and London: Liveright Publishing, 2012), 7.

chiefly unidirectional, with momentum toward one destination: inequality's perpetuation.

Understanding this tendency, the gospels depicted Jesus (c. 5 BCE–c. 30 CE), "a great world teacher," as inegalitarian despite his critique of riches.[112] Roman society was markedly unequal, chapter 8 emphasizes. Yet in Mark (c. 70), Matthew (c. 90), and Luke (c. 90) he is portrayed as acknowledging imperial authority.[113] Rather than oppose inequality, Jesus disliked its configuration, seeking to reverse first and last.[114]

In *Strange Case of Dr. Jekyll and Mr. Hyde* (1886), Scottish author Robert Louis Stevenson (1850–1894), "a consummate technician and professional man of letters," demonstrated the reality that elites were prehistory and history's thugs, contradicting the notion of a gentleman.[115] The villain appeared to be Edward Hyde, an ugly brute who inexplicably trampled a girl and killed a man. Mentioning Hyde's shortness and deformation, Stevenson signaled his low status.[116] Designating him a caveman, the author accentuated his primitiveness and seemed to evoke a Hobbesian past when life was "solitary, poor, nasty, brutish, and short."[117]

Although the reader learns that Hyde occupied Henry Jekyll's home, suspicion was slow to confront the doctor, who had an enviable education and whose home "wore a great air of wealth and comfort."[118] Stevenson valued Jekyll's wealth at 250,000 pounds sterling.[119] Anchoring this amount to the year of publication permits comparison of Jekyll's fictitious wealth with real contemporaries.

His riches seem unimpressive at under 1/16th those of English banker and rentier Samuel Jones Loyd (1796–1883), who crowned England's apex as possibly the wealthiest of its 25 millionaires to die between 1880 and 1893.[120] His fortune placing him in a club too exclusive for Jekyll, Loyd had few if any peers.

---

[112] Mohandas K. Gandhi, "Jesus: The Man Who Belongs to the Whole World," in *The Story of Jesus*, ed. Gardner Associates (Pleasantville, NY and Montreal: Reader's Digest, 1993), 360.

[113] Mark 12:14-17; Matt. 22:17-21; Luke 20:22-25.

[114] Matt. 20:1-16.

[115] Annette R. Federico, *Thus I Lived with Words: Robert Louis Stevenson and the Writer's Craft* (Iowa City: University of Iowa Press, 2017), xii.

[116] Robert Louis Stevenson, *Strange Case of Dr. Jekyll and Mr. Hyde*, in *Dr. Jekyll and Mr. Hyde and Other Stories* (New York: Knopf, 1992), 5, 8.

[117] Ibid., 16; Hobbes, 84.

[118] Stevenson, 10, 16.

[119] Ibid., 25.

[120] Martin Daunton, *Wealth and Welfare: An Economic and Social History of Britain, 1851-1951* (Oxford and New York: Oxford University Press, 2007), 38-39.

Jekyll shined brighter amid lesser luminaries. Each of 29 English land-owners averaged 17,241 acres in the 1890s.[121] The prices of five Irish estates sold between 1886 and 1889 yields a mean value of 12.7 pounds sterling per acre.[122] Ireland was not England, of course, but the fact that the sellers were English lords indicates that the average price satisfied English standards. An estimate of 12.7 pounds sterling may undervalue an acre, whose sale in 1880, the latest year in *Essays in Economic History* (1966), averaged 34 pounds sterling in England and Wales.[123] But prices were falling and would rebound only slowly. As late as 1914, an English acre averaged just 25 pounds sterling.[124] Accepting 12.7 pounds sterling per acre yields 218,961 pounds sterling, which Jekyll surpassed, for 17,241 acres. My calculation underreports value if these men held more than land, though debts lowered net worth.[125]

Besides these comparisons, Jekyll outshone the masses. The third Earl of Yarborough's (1835–1875) farmhands would have needed almost two decades' frugality to save 850 pounds sterling, his cigars' price upon death.[126] It follows that he prized his cigars over the toilers who created his wealth and privilege. Roughly one tenth York's 1899 population earned under subsistence.[127] Food and lodging cost up to four fifths of their income, thwarting efforts to save.[128] Penury kept commoners below Jekyll.

The upshot is that Jekyll's eminence precluded suspicion. Yet *Strange Case of Dr. Jekyll and Mr. Hyde* made the two one. Repeated transmutation into Hyde enabled Jekyll to commit crimes, elude detection, and celebrate "his pleasure" at hoodwinking everyone.[129] "Violence guarantee[s] success," enthused billionaire and former Uber CEO Travis Kalanick (b. 1976) in affirming Stevenson in 2016.[130]

---

[121] Michael Turner, "Agriculture, 1860-1914," in *The Cambridge Economic History of Modern Britain: Vol II: Economic Maturity, 1860-1939*, ed. Roderick Floud and Paul Johnson (Cambridge, UK: Cambridge University Press, 2004), 154.

[122] David Cannadine, *The Decline and Fall of the British Aristocracy* (New York: Vintage Books, 1999), 104, 737.

[123] "A Century of Land Values: England and Wales," in *Essays in Economic History*, ed. E. M. Carus-Wilson (London: Edward Arnold, 1966), 131.

[124] Cannadine, *Decline and Fall of the British Aristocracy*, 110.

[125] David Cannadine, "The Landowner as Millionaire: The Finances of the Dukes of Devonshire, c. 1800-c. 1926," *Agricultural History Review* 25, no. 2 (1977): 77-97.

[126] Alan Armstrong, *Farmworkers in England and Wales: A Social and Economic History, 1770-1980* (Ames: Iowa State University Press, 1988), 133.

[127] Daunton, 389.

[128] Ibid., 399; Robert C. Allen, "Real Incomes in the English-Speaking World, 1879-1913," in *Labour Market Evolution: The Economic History of Market Integration, Wage Flexibility and the Employment Relation*, ed. George Grantham and Mary MacKinnon (London and New York: Routledge, 1994), 109.

[129] Stevenson, 66.

[130] Igor Bonifacic, "Uber Co-Founder Travis Kalanick Reportedly Saw Violence against Drivers as a Tool for Growth," Engadget, July 10, 2022, accessed July 11, 2022, ‹Uber

---

The past likewise corroborates Stevenson, though space accommodates few of innumerable aggressions against commoners. Shaping civilization in several ways, Greece hardened the divide between rich and poor. Between roughly 1100 and 500 BCE, aristocrats expanded control of Greek cities.[131] Holding wealth in the form of land, livestock, and slaves, nobles managed society, religion, economy, and military. Medium and smallholders subsisted rather than prospered. Movement up or down the economic ladder was rare.

Disregarding commoners, the *Iliad*, "a somberly magnificent tragic poem" attributed to Greek poet Homer, whose authorship and existence are uncertain but who may have lived about 800 BCE, exalted elites from the first verses.[132] Fighting for honor and women, nobles confirmed their superiority with such grandeur that gods could not ignore them and proved *Eternal Inequality*'s contention that elites monopolized violence.

Rigidity and militarism characterized Sparta, where population growth circa 800 to 500 BCE increased competition for land.[133] Enlarging territory through conquest, warrior aristocrats reduced competition. Archon Lycurgus (c. 800–c. 730), whom Aristotle and Greek historian and philosopher Plutarch (46–124 CE) described as an actual person despite scholars' doubts, helped militarize Sparta and declared all legally equal while nobles protected their power and scotched upward mobility.[134] Suppressing individuality and disrupting families, authorities barracked boys at age seven to prepare for military life.[135] Turning them against luxury, this indoctrination diffused class tensions by prizing austerity.

Greece's adoption of coinage after 600 BCE permitted wealth to rival birth in conferring power, prestige, and privilege.[136] The *nouveaux riches* neared the economic and social apex whereas the poor suffered as money's influx from trade caused inflation. Unable to afford wealth creators like olive

---

co-founder Travis Kalanick reportedly saw violence against drivers as a tool for growth | Engadget.⟩

[131] Robert J. Littman, *The Greek Experiment: Imperialism and Social Conflict, 800-400 BC* (New York: Harcourt Brace Jovanovich, 1974), 99-102.

[132] W. B. Stanford, "Homer," in *Ancient Writers: Greece and Rome, Vol. I: Homer to Caesar*, ed. T. James Luce (New York: Charles Scribner's Sons, 1982), 3; Roy T. Matthews and F. DeWitt Platt, *The Western Humanities*, 3d ed. (Mountain View, CA: Mayfield Publishing, 1998), 39; Homer, *The Iliad*, trans. E. V. Rieu (London: Penguin Books, 2003), 4.

[133] John P. McKay, Bennett D. Hill, John Buckler, Clare Haru Crowston, Merry E. Wiesner-Hanks, and Joe Perry, *Understanding Western Society: A Brief History* (Boston and New York: Bedford/St. Martin's, 2012), 63-64.

[134] Ibid.; Plutarch, *Lycurgus*, trans. Arthur Hugh Clough (Chicago: Great Books Foundation, 1955), 1-44; Aristotle, *Politics*, trans. Benjamin Jowett (New York: Modern Library, 1943), 114, 121, 122, 192.

[135] McKay, Hill, Buckler, Crowston, Wiesner-Hanks, and Perry, 64.

[136] Littman, 103-114.

trees or grapevines, smallholders suffered as inequality widened between the "very rich" and the "very poor."[137]

Even before these problems climaxed, Athenian archon Draco had exacerbated poverty by preventing debtors from selling land, crops, or livestock, all of which the creditor took.[138] This requirement made them, their families, and heirs peons. Draco's 621 BCE laws "were written not in ink but in blood," wrote Plutarch.[139] For this reason, his name persists as the adjective "draconian."

With rich against poor, Sparta, Athens, and their allies fought Persia and then themselves from 499 to 404 BCE.[140] Sacrificing commoners in battle, warrior aristocrats unleashed famine, disease, and destruction. Expressing class war's evils after this strife, Plato lamented in *Republic* (c. 380 BCE): "Cities, cities everywhere, but city none for me! Each is at least two cities, one of the poor and one of the rich, enemies to each other."[141]

In this dialogue and others, Plato expressed ideas through his mentor Socrates (469–399 BCE), "the noblest and the wisest and the most just" man, he wrote.[142] In *Phaedo* (c. 360 BCE), Plato had Socrates discuss several issues, including greed, which he blamed on what we would call materialism.[143] Conceiving the individual as mind and body, Socrates elevated the mind and likened the body to prison. Greed thus imprisoned one in perpetual servitude to corporeal needs and wants, which Socrates blamed for causing "all wars."[144]

Readers might think commoners as bellicose as elites because everyone has needs and wants. But this interpretation ignores Socrates', and by extension Plato's, audience, whom this section specifies by noting, first, Plato's description of Socrates' protégés as boys.[145] Most boys lacked leisure for Socratic disputation, leaving only elite sons in attendance. Second, commoners' workaday lives were remote from Plato's epistemological concerns. Third, using Socrates as his mouthpiece, Plato called a slave "boy,"

---

[137] Ibid., 123.

[138] Robin W. Winks, Crane Brinton, John B. Christopher, and Robert Lee Wolff, *A History of Civilization, Vol. I: Prehistory to 1715*, 7th ed. (Englewood Cliffs, NJ: Prentice Hall, 1988), 37.

[139] Littman, 121.

[140] McKay, Hill, Buckler, Crowston, Wiesner-Hanks, and Perry, 57, 68.

[141] Plato, *Republic*, in *Great Dialogues of Plato*, trans. W. H. D. Rouse (New York and Scarborough, ON: New American Library, 1956), 220.

[142] Plato, *Phaedo*, in *Great Dialogues of Plato*, trans. W. H. D. Rouse (New York and Scarborough, ON: New American Library, 1956), 521.

[143] Ibid., 469-470.

[144] Ibid., 469.

[145] Plato, *Apology*, in *Great Dialogues of Plato*, trans. W. H. D. Rouse (New York and Scarborough, ON: New American Library, 1956), 424.

language he might have avoided had he wished to attract non-elites.[146] Fourth, he traced his paternal ancestry to an eleventh-century Athenian king and his maternal lineage to Athenian archon Solon (c. 630–c. 560 BCE).[147] His stepfather and two uncles were prominent politicians.[148] Family and friends urged his entry into politics, but Socrates' execution drove Plato from public life.

The point is that Plato addressed his peers, judging them greedy and warlike. Although distancing himself from Socrates, and by implication Plato, Nietzsche made similar linkages by characterizing prehistory's German elites as warriors, thereby bundling wealth, power, privilege, inequality, and violence.[149]

Juxtaposing these traits before Nietzsche, Rousseau described society as a vehicle for letting the rich violate the masses, who consented to inequality.[150] But this conjecture is illogical. Violence compels whereas consent renders compulsion unnecessary.

Attuned to Plato's description of class war, Marx and Engels described rich and poor in endless conflict.[151] Eager for profit, elites used government to conquer new lands and enslave indigenes.[152] Factories minimized pay and made workers commodities, slaves, and units of production.[153] Too meager to allow for savings, their wages flowed to landlord, creditor, and grocer. Greed and ego led magnates to venerate materialism and practice "naked, shameless, direct, brutal exploitation."[154]

Also linking wealth, power, privilege, inequality, and violence, American anthropologist David Graeber (1961–2020) pitted creditor against debtor.[155] Default threatened borrowers, their families, or both with slavery. Throughout the past, he wrote, most people confronted "the terrifying prospect of one's sons and daughters being carried off to the homes of repulsive strangers to clean their pots and provide occasional sexual services, to be

---

[146] Plato, *Meno*, in *Great Dialogues of Plato*, trans. W. H. D. Rouse (New York and Scarborough, ON: New American Library, 1956), 42-43.

[147] Francis MacDonald Cornford, *Before and after Socrates* (Cambridge, UK: Cambridge University Press, 1932), 55; C. D. C. Reeve, "Introduction," in *Republic*, Plato, trans. C. D. C. Reeve (Indianapolis and Cambridge, MA: Hackett Publishing, 2004), ix.

[148] Cornford, 57-58; Brumbaugh, 135.

[149] Friedrich Nietzsche, *The Birth of Tragedy*, trans. Douglas Smith (Oxford and New York: Oxford University Press, 2000), 3-4; Nietzsche, *Genealogy of Morals*, 28-31.

[150] Rousseau, *Discourse on Inequality*, 71, 77.

[151] Marx and Engels, 8.

[152] Ibid., 10-11.

[153] Ibid., 16-18.

[154] Ibid., 11.

[155] David Graeber, *Debt: The First 5,000 Years* (Brooklyn and London: Melville House, 2014), 8.

subject to every conceivable form of violence and abuse, possibly for years, conceivably forever."[156]

Animus also attended famine, which haunted Greece during the Peloponnesian War (431–404 BCE), which French historian Fernand Braudel (1902–1985) judged so frequent "for centuries on end that it became incorporated into man's biological regime and built into his daily life," and which turned bestial wherever elites starved indigents.[157] In Ireland, which Marx and Engels believed originally classless, landlords extorted inordinate rent, which made tenants plant almost all acreage to cash crops or convert it to pasture.[158] With little land for their own needs, tenants grew potatoes for maximum sustenance per acre. When disease destroyed the tuber in 1845 and 1846, hungry people ate bark, soil, weeds, leather, insects, rodents, and feces.[159] Too weak to leave their beds, families perished in their hovels. Dogs, cats, pigs, and rats devoured corpses, too numerous for burial, that clogged gutters and streets. Over 1 million starved and 1.5 million fled the island while well-fed plutocrats debated, delayed, and worsened tragedy by taking crops and livestock as rent.

Across the Atlantic Ocean, U.S. businesses slashed pay and jobs during the 1873 to 1879 depression.[160] Railroads repeatedly cut wages and fired everyone suspected of union sympathies in "a fight to the death between labor and capital."[161] Low pay kept workers from affording dues. Under assault and underfunded, unions collapsed. In March 1877, the four largest railroads, sensing labor's vulnerability, agreed to coordinate pay cuts. "The great principle upon which we joined to act was to earn more and to spend less," enthused Baltimore and Ohio (B & O) railroad president John Garrett (1820–1884) in summarizing capitalism's logic.[162] Martinsburg, West

---

[156] Ibid., 85.

[157] McKay, Hill, Buckler, Crowston, Wiesner-Hanks, and Perry, 68; Fernand Braudel, *Capitalism and Material Life, 1400-1800*, trans. Miriam Kochan (New York: Harper Colophon Books, 1973), 38.

[158] Marx and Engels, 8.

[159] Cecil Woodham-Smith, "The Great Hunger: Ireland, 1845-1849," in *European Diet from Pre-Industrial to Modern Times*, ed. Elborg Forster and Robert Forster (New York: Harper Torchbooks, 1975), 10-18; Gail L. Schumann and Cleora J. D'Arcy, *Hungry Planet: Stories of Plant Diseases* (St. Paul, MN: American Phytopathological Society, 2012), 12.

[160] Joshua Freeman, Nelson Lichtenstein, Stephen Brier, David Bensman, Susan Porter Benson, David Brundage, Bret Eynon, Bruce Levine, and Bryan Palmer, *Who Built America?: Working People and the Nation's Economy, Politics, Culture, and Society* (New York: Pantheon Books, 1992), xxiv.

[161] Ibid.; James L. Hunt, review of *The Great Industrial War: Framing Class Conflict in the Media, 1865-1950*, by Troy Rondinone, *The Historian* 73, no. 3 (Fall 2011): 579-580.

[162] Freeman, Lichtenstein, Brier, Bensman, Benson, Brundage, Eynon, Levine, and Palmer, xxiv.

Virginia, workers struck in July after B & O decreased wages 10 percent. Pittsburgh railroad and iron workers followed their example.

Although the walkouts were peaceful, President Rutherford Hayes (1822–1893), declaring them "unlawful and insurrectionary," sent soldiers to Martinsburg, emboldening governors.[163] The Maryland National Guard slaughtered 11 strikers and wounded 40. But Pittsburgh guardsmen, themselves workers, joined the strike. On July 20, reserves arriving from Philadelphia bayoneted 20 protestors including three toddlers. Another 25 died next day. Chicago bankers, lawyers, and merchants gathered mercenaries against "tramps."[164] Xenophobia engulfing San Francisco, strikers killed immigrants and destroyed property.

During a turbulent fortnight, the strikes grew into the first nationwide work stoppage.[165] Conflict, begun by plutocrats, ended over 100 lives and wrecked property worth millions of dollars. Class war, perpetrated by elites and resisted by Marxists, anarchists, laborers, and people of conscience, cleaved the United States, "the most capitalist of all countries."[166]

1.5 Review and Preview

This chapter pitted the opinion that the first societies were egalitarian but later became unequal against belief in inequality's immutability. Affirming the second, next chapter contextualizes our inequality within nonhuman hierarchies. Attention focuses on the bumblebee, honeybee, chicken, bonobo, and chimpanzee. Anticipating our inequality instinct, bees, chickens, and chimpanzees, like us, enforce inequality.

---

[163] Ibid., xxv–xxvii; Jonathan Levy, *Ages of American Capitalism: A History of the United States* (New York: Random House, 2021), 266.

[164] Freeman, Lichtenstein, Brier, Bensman, Benson, Brundage, Eynon, Levine, and Palmer, xxvii–xxviii.

[165] Ibid, xxviii.

[166] Levy, 740.

CHAPTER 2 NONHUMAN INEQUALITY AND VIOLENCE

2.1 Abstract

We understand ourselves best within the context of sociality's evolution, averred American biologist Edward Wilson (b. 1929).[167] The first creatures being solitary, sociality originated in insects during the Mesozoic era, bookended by mass extinctions 225 million and 65 million years ago. Stratification and specialization helped them amass and maintain communities that out-competed isolates for resources. Moreover, groups were safer than loners from predators. Also hierarchical, we domesticated social animals that accepted or tolerated us as alpha. Discussing honeybees and chickens as examples, this chapter, turning to primates, examines our closest kin, the bonobo and chimpanzee, contending that chimpanzee inequality resembles ours.

2.2 Sociality in Humans and Kindred Animals

Greek philosopher Aristotle (384–322 BCE), "for so many centuries...a dominant force, if not the dominant force, in Western philosophy and in Western culture," identified us as animals.[168] Seeking our uniqueness, he deemed only us rational, an opinion that ignores chimpanzee, bonobo, and

---

[167] Edward O. Wilson, *The Social Conquest of Earth* (New York and London: Liveright Publishing, 2012), 109.

[168] Aristotle, *Nicomachean Ethics*, trans. Martin Ostwald (Indianapolis and New York: Bobbs-Merrill, 1962), 16-17; Henry B. Veatch, *Aristotle: A Contemporary Appreciation* (Bloomington and London: Indiana University Press, 1974), 3.

gorilla communication through symbols.[169] Moreover, they, monkeys, otters, finches, and crows use tools. Disproving Aristotle, these achievements demonstrate that we differ from other animals in degree, not kind.

Our distinctiveness questionable, our sociality, shared with kindred animals, informs this book's understanding of us. For example, late antiquity's Egyptian and Syrian Christians unhappy with taxes, rent, corvée, conscription, poverty, disorder, and the absence of upward mobility, abandoned farms.[170] Their desert isolation may appear to repudiate sociality, but their holiness attracted followers who formed chapter 12's monasteries. Even solitude thus created community.

Sociality makes us a minority. Against French philosopher and sociologist Alfred Espinas' (1844–1922) opinion that all animals are social, "perhaps several tens of thousands" among earth's over 1 million species congregate.[171] Wilson attributed this uncommonness to "millions of years of evolution" in numerous steps.[172] The greater a species' evolutionary complexity, the more improbable its development. Extinction might have eliminated its succession of forebears at any juncture along the way.

Despite infrequent evolution, collectivists dominate terrestrial life.[173] Aiding evolution, we duplicated our sociality in prehistory by molding similar animals into livestock. For example, the chicken, examined later, was domesticated around 8000 BCE, a date near agriculture's invention.[174] Just when farming encouraged sedentism, we tamed a bird that stayed near home.[175] Like us, it was diurnal and hierarchical. This relationship's durability implies that chickens added us to the flock as alpha and that we chose to reconfigure nature by bringing within our orbit animals that mirrored our

[169] Robert Jurmain, Lynn Kilgore, Wenda Trevathan, and Russell L. Ciochon, *Introduction to Physical Anthropology*, 2013-2014 ed. (Belmont, CA: Wadsworth Cengage Learning, 2014), 200, 204-206; Ruth Moore, *Evolution*, rev. ed. (New York: Time-Life Books, 1968), 31.

[170] Robin W. Winks, Crane Brinton, John B. Christopher, and Robert Lee Wolff, *A History of Civilization, Vol. I: Prehistory to 1715*, 7th ed. (Englewood Cliffs, NJ: Prentice Hall, 1988), 111; John P. McKay, Bennett D. Hill, John Buckler, Clare Haru Crowston, Merry E. Wiesner-Hanks, and Joe Perry, *Understanding Western Society: A Brief History* (Boston and New York: Bedford/St, Martin's, 2012), 162.

[171] W. C. Allee, *The Social Life of Animals* (Ann Arbor: University of Michigan Libraries, 1958), accessed April 21, 2022, ‹https://babel.hathitrust.org/cgi/pt?id=mdp.39015064489134&view=1up&seq=2&skin=2021,› 10-11; Katharine Faust, "Animal Social Networks," in *The SAGE Handbook of Social Network Analysis*, ed. John Scott and Peter J. Carrington (Los Angeles: SAGE, 2011), 148.

[172] Wilson, *Social Conquest of Earth*, 109.

[173] Ibid.

[174] Eric Chaline, *Fifty Animals that Changed the Course of History* (New York: Firefly Books, 2011), 90-91.

[175] Andrew Lawler, *Why Did the Chicken Cross the World? The Epic Saga of the Bird that Powers Civilization* (New York: Atria Books, 2014), 13.

hierarchy and habits. Humans and livestock thus combined inequality and mutualism throughout their long association.

2.3 Sociality's Origin and Evolution

Shaping our evolution and lifeways, sociality originated in insects, which likely evolved from crustaceans 480 million years ago.[176] In the order Hymenoptera, which emerged 270 million years ago, Mesozoic eusocial bees and ants evolved from wasps, all hierarchical, though the original wasp was solitary.[177] Bees, which American entomologist William Wheeler (1865–1937) judged vegetarian variants of wasps and which British entomologist Paul Williams (b. 1959) and coauthors termed "essentially hairy wasps," arose 125 million years ago.[178] Revealing insects with wasp and ant traits, 90 million-year-old fossils captured a moment in the transition from wasp to ant.[179] In the order Isoptera, eusocial termites evolved from cockroaches 175 million years ago.[180]

These insects, particularly bees, intrigued Greek philosopher Plato (c. 428–c. 348 BCE), Aristotle, Roman poet Virgil (70 BCE–19 CE), English poet Geoffrey Chaucer (c. 1343–1400), English poet and playwright William Shakespeare (1564–1616), and German economist Karl Marx (1818–1883).[181] German philosopher and philologist Friedrich Nietzsche (1844–1900) likened us to bees that make knowledge our honey.[182] We desire facts as they seek nectar and pollen.

Few other insects became eusocial, though nature, where organisms competed for resources and mates, favored the trait by advantaging social

---

[176] Anne Sverdrup-Thygeson, *Extraordinary Insects: The Fabulous Indispensable Creatures Who Run Our World*, trans. Lucy Moffatt (New York: Simon & Schuster, 2018), xvii; Wilson, *Social Conquest of Earth*, 114; Hayley Dunning, "Intricacies of Insect Evolution Revealed," London Natural History Museum, November 7, 2014, accessed April 22, 2022, ‹https://www.nhm.ac.uk/discover/news/2014/november/intricacies-insect-evolution-revealed.html.›

[177] Wilson, *Social Conquest of Earth*, 110, 115; Faust, 149; Fergus Chadwick, Steve Alton, Emma Sarah Tennant, Bill Fitzmaurice, and Judy Earl, *The Bee Book* (New York: DK, 2016), 14.

[178] O. E. Plath, "Insect Societies," in A Handbook of Social Psychology, vol. 1, ed. Carl Murchison (New York: Russell & Russell, 1935), 94; Paul H. Williams, Robbin W. Thorp, Leif L. Richardson, and Sheila R. Colla, *Bumblebees of North America: An Identification Guide* (Princeton, NJ and Oxford: Princeton University Press, 2014), 9; Lucy M. Long, *Honey: A Global History* (London: Reaktion Books, 2017), 15.

[179] Wilson, *Social Conquest of Earth*, 121-122.

[180] Ibid., 136; Faust, 149.

[181] Dave Goulson, *A Sting in the Tale: My Adventures with Bumblebees* (New York: Picador, 2013), 107; Thor Hanson, *Buzz: The Nature and Necessity of Bees* (New York: Basic Books, 2018), ix; Mark L. Winston, *Bee Time: Lessons from the Hive* (Cambridge, MA and London: Harvard University Press, 2014), 174.

[182] Friedrich Nietzsche, *On the Genealogy of Morals*, trans. Walter Kaufmann and R. J. Hollingdale (New York: Vintage Books, 1967), 15.

animals' survival and reproduction. For example, two solitary female bees hierarchize if forced into one cell.[183] One is queen, reproducing and guarding eggs and larvae. Subordinating herself by surrendering the opportunity to transmit genes to the next generation, the other gathers food for all. Bees appearing to lack volition, instinct must drive behavior such that even loners hierarchize if grouped.

Not every individual in a social species prospers. For example, chapter 13's commoners, not the rich, starved.[184] Famine presaged the Black Death (1347–1351), which killed peasants and workmen whereas elites sequestered in country estates.[185] Recounting contagion's 1348 appearance, Florentine author Giovanni Boccaccio (1313–1375) mentioned a dead pauper, whose rags spread disease and death to pigs, whereas the wealthy fled, and others profited by selling nostrums and whatever else desperate people would buy.[186]

Loners are also disadvantaged. Revisiting the two solitary females, if each had its own cell in which to lay eggs, each foraged for herself and larvae. Her absence for this purpose exposed larvae to predation. If each instead devoted every moment to guarding progeny, all starved. But if both females hierarchized as above, all were likelier to survive, though one sacrificed her chance to transmit genes by ceaselessly foraging, as mentioned.

Subordinating her to the colony, natural selection operated on the collective as it continued to sort individuals such that those best adapted to their surroundings survived in greatest numbers to swamp the next generation with their, or alpha's, genes. Reproductive success is dominance's ultimate expression.

Selective pressure on the group diminished where progeny left upon maturation to form their own communities. One gene's mutation, however, suppressed the dispersal instinct in eusocial insects' ancestors.[187] Multiple generations crowded a colony absent outmigration. Risk grew as misfortune killed not few but scads. Large groups, and numerous genes, competed for resources to sustain populations. Colonies that evolved the best specialists—workers that gathered the most food and best defended everyone—prospered. Inadequate food and protection imperiled less successful colonies.

---

[183] Wilson, *Social Conquest of Earth*, 136-137, 142.

[184] McKay, Hill, Buckler, Crowston, Wiesner-Hanks, and Perry, 322-323.

[185] Ibid., 327.

[186] Giovanni Boccaccio, *The Decameron*, trans. Wayne A. Rebhorn (New York and London: Norton, 2013), 6-7; "Marchionne di Coppo di Stefano Buonaiuti," trans. Jonathan Usher, Brown University, Decameron Web, last modified February 18, 2010, accessed April 22, 2022, ‹https://www.brown.edu/Departments/Italian_Studies/dweb/plague/perspectives/marchionne.php.›

[187] Wilson, *Social Conquest of Earth*, 142.

2.4 Social Insects, Inequality, and Violence

2.4.1 The Bumblebee

Wilson credited Swiss entomologist Pierre Huber (1777–1840) with inaugurating the study of nonhuman hierarchies in 1802 by publishing an article on bumblebees, which arose 25 million years ago to become North America's only native hierarchical bee.[188] Each community's queen reproduces. Although a worker, being female, may lay eggs, the queen's larvae eat them.[189]

Transition from bumblebees to us underscores cannibalism's unpleasantness. With Irish laborers "every day dying and rotting by cold and famine," English Irish author and cleric Jonathan Swift (1667–1745), estimating over 85 percent of parents too poor to support their children, offered the faux remedy, mentioned in the introduction, of letting the wealthy eat these young."[190]

Entomophagy threatened whenever a worker tried to eat a queen's egg, behavior which natural selection may have favored to prevent overpopulation.[191] Perceiving this danger in humans, whom war, famine, and disease culled, English demographer and cleric Thomas Malthus (1766–1834) authored "the first great analysis of the interconnectedness of population, environment, and the economy."[192]

A cannibalistic worker violated hierarchy, causing the queen to bite and kick it.[193] Enforcing inequality, this violence informs *Eternal Inequality* and our past. The queen bee's retaliation is echoed in the record of a Caribbean master who hanged a slave in the 1690s for stealing two turkeys.[194] In both

---

[188] Wilson, *Sociobiology*, 281, 625; Chadwick, Alton, Tennant, Fitzmaurice, and Earl, 15; "About Bumblebees," Xerces Society for Invertebrate Conservation, 2006-2021, accessed April 22, 2022, ‹https://www.xerces.org/bumblebees/about#:~:text=Bumble%20bees%20 are%20the%20only,spring%2C%20summer%2C%20and%20fall.›

[189] Wilson, *Sociobiology*, 281.

[190] Jonathan Swift, "A Modest Proposal for Preventing the Children of Poor People in Ireland from Being a Burden to Their Parents or Country, and for Making Them Beneficial to the Public," in *Student's Book of College English*, ed. David Skwire, Frances Chitwood, Raymond Ackley, and Raymond Fredman (Beverly Hills, CA: Glencoe Press, 1975), 198, 200.

[191] Wilson, *Sociobiology*, 281.

[192] Thomas Malthus, *An Essay on the Principle of Population* (Amherst, New York: Prometheus Books, 1998), 13-14, 100, 139-140; Robert J. Mayhew, *Malthus: The Life and Legacies of an Untimely Prophet* (Cambridge, MA and London: Belknap Press of Harvard University Press, 2014), 3.

[193] Wilson, *Sociobiology*, 281.

[194] Richard S. Dunn, *Sugar and Slaves: The Rise of the Planter Class in the English West Indies, 1624-1713* (Chapel Hill: University of North Carolina Press, 1972), 244.

---

cases, hunger must have motivated the transgression, which elites punished, affirming inequality's inviolability.

Bumblebee cannibals do not fight the queen but seek escape with minimal injuries.[195] Workers unable to flee perish. Chastened survivors stop trying to eat eggs, but instead guard the queen, her eggs, and larvae, and feed and warm all.

Turning to heredity, all offspring are arrangements of the queen's genes. Being diploid, each female has two sets of chromosomes, one from the queen and one from a drone, because she develops from a fertilized egg.[196] But haploid drones, hatching from unfertilized eggs, inherit only one set of chromosomes from the queen, the lone gene donor. Inheriting the same set of chromosomes from her, all drones are clones. No nest occupant hatches from an outsider's egg.

All being kin, each benefits by prioritizing the hive over her or his interests. Subordinating everyone to the queen, this imperative perpetuates hierarchy. But it is imperfect; a worker resists rearing drones, which are less closely related to her than she is to her sisters because, as mentioned, females are diploid whereas males are haploid.[197] Preferring to raise her own daughters, which would be more closely related to her than she is to drones, she lays eggs to compete with the queen, who in late summer starts laying unfertilized eggs. But worker eggs are also unfertilized, so only drones would result, frustrating the desire for daughters. As before, the queen retaliates by attacking the worker, and queen larvae eat worker eggs. But the tide turns as more workers challenge the queen. Food diminishes as they fight rather than forage. This Hobbesian "war of every one against every one" dooms the colony.[198]

"Within the shadowy confines of the nest fights do occur, and cannibalism, infanticide and murder are rife," wrote British biologist Dave Goulson (b. 1965) in summarizing this denouement.[199] Such misdeeds typify us and evince the introduction's Newtonian backlash against inequality, whether by worker bees or farmhands and workmen. Revolution becomes necessary.

2.4.2 The Honeybee

As noted, humans created livestock by domesticating kindred animals during the Neolithic period. Among domesticates, the honeybee originated

---

[195] Wilson, *Sociobiology*, 281.
[196] Goulson, 110.
[197] Ibid., 112-114.
[198] Thomas Hobbes, *Leviathan* (Oxford and New York: Oxford University Press, 1998), 86.
[199] Goulson, 107.

before 40 million years ago.[200] Southwest Asia, Egypt, or North Africa tamed it around 5500 to 2000 BCE.

Like bumblebees, honeybees display haplodiploidy and occupy one of three castes.[201] Although Aristotle thought a king ruled the hive, Pierre Huber's father Swiss entomologist François Huber (1750–1831) found a queen atop the summit. Both queen and workers are female, but more and better food throughout life enlarges her and concretizes her superiority over them. A hive may exceed 50,000 workers, the second caste, which outnumber other residents.[202] Earth has some 83 billion honeybee workers.[203] The third caste, drones, living only to impregnate the queen, hatch and die in autumn.[204] Intercourse kills a drone, who loses genitals and guts upon leaving her.[205]

Workers sustain the hive. Living 25 to 35 days, they begin adulthood as "janitors" that clean cells.[206] About day five they graduate to feeding larvae. Around seven days later they start building new honeycomb, heating or cooling the hive to optimal temperature, and guarding the entrance. Demotion to gatherer follows. A forager may visit 2,000 flowers daily, dying afterwards. When population diminishes, workers forage earlier and perish younger. Sacrificing themselves through strenuous, early exertions, they prove that inequality harms the underclass.

Human worker bees, slaves likewise suffered. Arduous labor truncating lives, their price diminished within a decade after puberty. The sale of over 135,000 men, women, and children from 1804 to 1862 in New Orleans, "the Walmart of people-selling," indicated that men fetched the highest price, which peaked at age 22.[207] They were healthy enough to have survived diseases that killed half the population, slave and free, before puberty.[208] Such mortality explains why a vigorous man sometimes quintupled a child

---

[200] Winston, 9; Henry Hobhouse, *Seeds of Change: Six Plants That Transformed Mankind* (Washington, DC: Shoemaker & Hoard, 2005), 54; Long, 16.

[201] Winston, 11-13; Goulson, 110.

[202] Goulson, 83.

[203] Sverdrup-Thygeson, 42.

[204] Ibid., 39.

[205] Michael S. Engel, *Innumerable Insects: The Story of the Most Diverse and Myriad Animals on Earth* (New York: Sterling, 2018), 130.

[206] Winston, 175-178; Wilson, *Sociobiology*, 282; Chadwick, Alton, Tennant, Fitzmaurice, and Earl, 28.

[207] Laurence J. Kotlikoff, "The Structure of Slave Prices in New Orleans, 1804 to 1862," *Economic Inquiry* 17, no. 4 (October 1979): 497, 502; Kahalil Gibran Muhammad, "Sugar," in *The 1619 Project: A New Origin Story*, ed. Nikole Hannah-Jones, Caitlin Roper, Ilena Silverman, and Jake Silverstein (New York: One World, 2021), 83.

[208] Edward S. Deevey Jr., "The Human Population," *Scientific American* 203, no. 3 (September 1, 1960): 202.

in price.[209] Toil thereafter undermined vitality. A former South Carolina rice plantation and a former Texas sugarcane estate's slave skeletons exhibited osteoarthritis, spinal degeneration, and bones thickened where tendons once attached.[210]

A forager tells hive mates the distance, direction, and amount of a location's nectar and pollen through a dance at least 35 million years old that Aristotle first described.[211] Her movements, informing others that surround and point their antennae at her, help them decide whether nectar and pollen are abundant enough to justify journey to the location. Hierarchy and specialization benefit a hive by thus streamlining the search for food.

Geography and climate rigidified honeybee inequality more than that of bumblebees. Adapted to a temperate climate, they formed 50 to 500 member communities that died each autumn.[212] Honeybees, however, originated in the tropics or subtropics.[213] Year-round warmth supported huge populations that required control through inflexible hierarchy.

Rigidity is evident in honeybee workers' inability to lay eggs if their ovaries remain immature whereas bumblebee workers' ovaries mature during metamorphosis.[214] But if a honeybee queen dies unexpectedly, workers try to rear a new queen from larvae within hours of her demise.[215] If the attempt fails, several workers may enlarge their ovaries to lay eggs. But these unfertilized eggs become drones, not females that might compete for the throne. Absent leadership, workers, vying to lay and guard the most eggs while fighting rivals, die within weeks.

Hostility also erupts when queen and workers leave to form a new colony.[216] The remaining larvae pupate. The first adult to emerge slaughters as many rivals as she can before they complete pupation. Those she cannot

[209] Stephan Thernstrom, *A History of the American People, Vol. I: To 1877*, 2d ed. (San Diego: Harcourt Brace Jovanovich, 1989), 272.

[210] Ted A. Rathbun and Richard H. Steckel, "The Health of Slaves and Free Blacks in the East," in *The Backbone of History: Health and Nutrition in the Western Hemisphere*, ed. Richard H. Steckel and Jerome C. Rose (Cambridge, UK: Cambridge University Press, 2002), 214, 220; Jessica Campisi and Brandon Griggs, "Nearly 100 Bodies Found at a Texas Construction Site Were Probably Black People Forced into Labor—after Slavery Ended," CNN, July 19, 2018, accessed April 22, 2022, ‹https://www.cnn.com/2018/07/18/us/bodies-found-construction-site-slavery-trnd/index.html.›

[211] Engel, 159, 161-162.

[212] Wilson, *Sociobiology*, 429-430; Alina Bradford, "Facts about Bumblebees," Live Science, January 13, 2017, accessed April 22, 2022, ‹https://www.livescience.com/57509-bumblebee-facts.html.›

[213] Wilson, *Sociobiology*, 430-433.

[214] Engel, 128.

[215] Winston, 194.

[216] Ibid., 12.

kill before emergence fight her to the death. The survivor becomes the new queen.

As the Romans observed, another atrocity follows mating. A queen copulating with one drone, most males avoid death from sex, though their fate is no better as workers expel them from the hive.[217] Having specialized as sperm donors, drones perish from inability to forage or, without the hive's warmth, from hypothermia.

2.5 The Chicken, Inequality, and Violence

Movement from eusocial insects to chickens advanced inequality from Mesozoic to Cenozoic era, which began 65 million years ago, when extinction eradicated about 10 percent of freshwater species, over half the marine life, and some 90 percent of terrestrial florae and faunae, including dinosaurs, opening niches for new species.[218] Among survivors, birds colonized every continent. Although humans hunted them early on, domestication was gradual and shaped few species, including chicken, turkey, duck, and pigeon. An outcome of artificial selection, the first, deriving from red junglefowl, entered life's pageant late.

The ancestor ranges from northern India east and south through Southeast Asia, including Indonesia.[219] Hierarchy puts one male over several females. If present, subordinate cocks trail the cohort. Helping alpha monopolize mating, this arrangement ensures his genes' prevalence in the next generation.

Unlike bumblebees and honeybees, red junglefowl and chickens, allowing all hens to reproduce, better approximate us. Moreover, *Gallus gallus domesticus* evinces our proclivity for domesticating kindred animals, as noted.

Chickens led Norwegian zoologist and ethologist Thorleif Schjelderup-Ebbe (1894–1976) to study nonhuman hierarchies.[220] Spurring research in inequality and aggression, his "seminal work" led the introduction's zoologists, psychologists, and anthropologists to designate these traits in congregants, including us, as dominance hierarchies, peck orders, or pecking orders.[221] A hen's pecking a subordinate resembled a master's whipping a

---

[217] Ibid., 13; Plath, 107.

[218] Jurmain, Kilgore, Trevathan, and Ciochon, 125; Stanley A. Rice, *Encyclopedia of Evolution* (New York: Facts on File, 2007), 99; Michael C. Gerald with Gloria E. Gerald, *The Biology Book: From the Origin of Life to Epigenetics, 250 Milestones in the History of Biology* (New York: Sterling, 2015), 510.

[219] Wilson, *Sociobiology*, 283-284.

[220] Ibid., 281.

[221] Ibid.; Ivan D. Chase, "Models of Hierarchy Formation in Animal Societies," *Behavioral Science* 19, no. 6 (November 1974): 374.

slave. Both caused injury or death. Cannibalism sometimes befell dead chickens.[222]

A "law of nature," the peck order lets the leader peck all flock mates with impunity.[223] Beta may peck anyone but alpha. This scheme continues to the bottom, where the lowest, pecking none, must endure all pecks. Although pitiless, this arrangement precludes ceaseless harassment. Chickens that accept their status receive fewer pecks than those that seek upward mobility.

Set in the 1930s' South, *Hymn to the Rising Sun* (1936) by American playwright Paul Green (1894–1981), "a genius at the task of showing ideals in conflict," dramatized our peck order.[224] While preparing prisoners for labor on July 4, the warden admonished them to obey authority there and upon rejoining society.[225] The convicts being blacks and poor whites, his advice affirmed U.S. racial and economic inequality. At hierarchy's nadir, inmate Runt, dying from dehydration, evinced underlings' disposability.[226]

The peck order assigns roles. As protector, the rooster watches for predators, crows to warn of their approach, and fights them where retreat is impossible.[227] He resolves quarrels, enforces hierarchy, and prioritizes hens for copulation. Deciding where to forage, the dominant hen leads others there. She maintains order while the rooster, or another hen absent him, is sentinel. Leading the flock to the coop in evening, she roosts only after all are safe inside.

As in us, inequality emerges early. Within three days of hatching, peeps begin to compete for supremacy, implying an inequality instinct that the present work extends to us.[228] The bravest, most curious female asserts dominance absent a male.[229] She tastes new or strange edibles first, eats before others and until full, lets others near food only afterwards, and rebuffs underlings' attempts to crowd her.

One male in a brooder with females is dominant.[230] Two or more males spar by circling one another, glaring at each other, stretching their necks to

---

[222] Lucie B. Amundsen, *Locally Laid: How We Built a Plucky, Industry-Changing Egg Farm—From Scratch* (New York: Avery, 2016), 145.

[223] Ibid., 102; Freeman, 36-37.

[224] John Herbert Roper, *Paul Green: Playwright of the Real South* (Athens and London: University of Georgia Press, 2003), xi.

[225] Paul Green, *Hymn to the Rising Sun* (New York: Samuel French, 1936), 19-21.

[226] Ibid., 31-32.

[227] Melissa Caughey, *How to Speak Chicken: Why Your Chickens Do What They Do and Say What They Say* (North Adams, MA: Storey Publishing, 2017), 60, 70.

[228] Pam Freeman, *Backyard Chickens: Beyond the Basics* (Minneapolis, MN: Voyageur Press, 2017), 37.

[229] Caughey, 58.

[230] Johannes Paul and William Windham, *Keeping Pet Chickens: Bring Your Backyard to Life and Enjoy the Bounty of Fresh Eggs from Your Own Small Flock of Happy Hens* (Hauppauge, NJ:

appear larger, and bumping chests.[231] More bellicose than hens, cocks prize size, strength, and belligerence.[232] Combat ensues when two meet unless one surrenders beforehand.[233] The rooster hierarchy tops the hens' such that omega rooster outranks alpha hen.[234]

When hierarchizing, chickens contest food, water, roosts, nesting boxes, dustbathing areas, and priority in entering and exiting the coop.[235] Superiors most peck subordinates when eating.[236] Hobbyists lessen disputes by spacing several food and water dispensers so alpha cannot stop inferiors from eating or drinking.[237] Chickens with few diversions, an autumn and winter predicament as coop confinement lengthens, peck subordinates.[238] Hostility pervades crowded farms, which debeak hens to lessen injuries.[239] Absent this precaution, pecking may cause death by drawing blood, which incites others to attack the victim.

One fight nearly killed a rooster after another pecked an eye.[240] Rescuing it and treating the wound for two weeks, the owner reintroduced the bird, but the puncture demoted it to omega. Unable to eat or drink for fear of being pecked, it would have perished without permanent removal from the flock.

Like inferior chickens' "semistarvation," slaves, being omegas, suffered greatest privation.[241] Skeletons of Barbadian slaves who lived circa 1660 to 1820 revealed undernutrition.[242] Mortality spiked upon weaning, when infants starved without mother's milk. Owners throughout the Americas cut expenses by underfeeding the young, old, and infirm.[243] Meager diets encour-

---

Barron's, 2005), 52; Allee, 141.

[231] Caughey, 58.

[232] Allee, 132, 141.

[233] Ibid., 130.

[234] Wilson, *Sociobiology*, 283.

[235] Lissa Lucas and Traci Torres, *My Pet Chicken Handbook: Sensible Advice and Savvy Answers for Raising Backyard Chickens* (Emmaus, PA: Rodale, 2013), 176-177; Freeman, 35.

[236] Allee, 133.

[237] Brian Barth, "The Secrets of Chicken Flocks' Pecking Order," Modern Farmer, March 16, 2016, accessed April 22, 2022, ‹https://modernfarmer.com/2016/03/pecking-order.›

[238] Lucas and Torres, 147.

[239] Amundsen, 63-64; Caughey, 63-64.

[240] Allee, 133-134.

[241] Ibid., 208.

[242] Jerome S. Handler and Robert S. Corruccini, "Plantation Slave Life in Barbados: A Physical Anthropological Analysis," *Journal of Interdisciplinary History* 14, no. 1 (Summer 1983): 79.

[243] Dunn, 320.

aged geophagy, which may have caused half of all deaths on some planta-tions.[244]

Studying the peck order, American psychologist Carl Murchison (1887–1961) grouped six roosters unfamiliar with one another.[245] Their tussle lasted 32 weeks, though alpha asserted immediate superiority, and beta faced no challenger by week 20. The final ranking was linear, an arrangement common in birds, mammals, autocracies, militaries, and corporations.[246]

Once established, hierarchy—stemming from fear, chickens' intuition of rank, and their memory of one another, which may persist two or three weeks—endures until interrupted by a new arrival, death, or a chicken's departure.[247] Underlings vocalize distress upon seeing a superior and flee at his or her approach, sometimes hiding until he or she is otherwise occupied.[248] Superiors enjoy intimidating inferiors.[249] A chicken's removal disrupting hierarchy, reintroduction renews or heightens tensions. A returnee must reassert status, which others contest.

A flock may have subpopulations with their own hierarchies. For example, one hobbyist added bantam silkies to a larger population.[250] Forming their own peck order, they ate, drank, roosted, nested, and dustbathed together and apart from the rest. Subhierarchies destabilize a flock when others chal-lenge their legitimacy.

Like other congregants, chickens dislike solitude. For instance, an owner isolated a hatchling too slow and weak to compete for food and water.[251] Although the action saved her, she wailed at the seclusion. To quiet her, the owner divided the brooder with a mesh, preventing others from harming her while allowing her to see and sleep next to them as everyone huddled at the partition. Once vigorous, she joined her companions.

---

[244] Handler and Corruccini, 77; Kenneth F. Kiple and Virginia H. Kiple, "Deficiency Diseases in the Caribbean," in *Caribbean Slavery in the Atlantic World: A Student Reader*, ed. Verene A. Shepherd and Hilary McD. Beckles (Princeton, NJ: Markus Wiener Publishers, 2000), 789; Margaret J. Weinberger, "Pica," in *The Cambridge World History of Food*, vol. 1, ed. Kenneth F. Kiple and Kriemhild Conee Ornelas (Cambridge, UK: Cambridge University Press, 2000), 969, 971.

[245] Wilson, *Sociobiology*, 280.

[246] Ibid.; Chase, 374; Frans De Waal, *Mama's Last Hug: Animal Emotions and What They Tell Us about Ourselves* (New York and London: Norton, 2019), 181; Allee, 129.

[247] Lucas and Torres, 49-50; Andy Schneider, *Chicken Fact or Chicken Poop: The Chicken Whisperer's Guide to the Facts and Fictions You Need to Know to Keep Your Flock Healthy and Happy* (Beverly, MA: Quarry Books, 2018), 81; Wilson, *Sociobiology*, 281; Thorleif Schjelderup-Ebbe, "Social Behavior of Birds," in *A Handbook of Social Psychology*, vol. 2, ed. Carl Murchison (New York: Russell & Russell, 1935), 949.

[248] Schjelderup-Ebbe, 949; Allee, 134.

[249] Schjelderup-Ebbe, 950.

[250] Caughey, 57.

[251] Lucas and Torres, 124-125.

Soothing her, these interactions demonstrated her preference for community even though disability disadvantaged her. Conferring survival and reproductive advantages, the peck order imprinted on red junglefowl and persists in her and all chickens.[252] Rather than alert predators by wrangling over food, chickens evolved to stay quiet while waiting their turn to eat. Alpha ate first, ensuring the best genes' propagation. Weaklings' death distressing the flock less than the leader's demise, chickens will kill a frail cohabitant.[253]

Inequality, where stable, benefits them.[254] Hens lay more eggs, eat more, weigh more, and suffer fewer pecks absent tension than amid fights for dominance. Alpha controls reproduction by copulating more often with more hens than do inferior males. Fecundity and stability, whereby the most prolific breeds are fiercest, demonstrate the link between belligerence and reproduction. Now estimated at a population of around 8 billion, humanity proves violence's advantages.[255]

2.6 Primate Inequality and Violence

2.6.1 Evolution of Primate Hierarchy

Evincing and intensifying mammalian gregariousness, our social and behavioral complexity grew with encephalization, a feature of primates and an outcome of their evolution.[256] Emerging early, diurnal habit prioritized vision and vocalization over chemical secretions to communicate. Anticipating speech, vocalization helped them forge alliances. Dexterity, vision, and vocalization favored brainy individuals that increased social complexity by adroitly manipulated their surroundings and one another. As gatherers or hunters, primates congregated to control an area and its resources. Fostering internal loyalty and suspicion of outsiders, the group projected hierarchy beyond a community by downgrading strangers.

These dynamics hierarchized most primates.[257] Several, for example baboons and macaques, form hierarchies that scientists study for insight into human sociality. They scrutinize the chimpanzee given its kinship with us. Until 1933, they divided it into two subspecies, the common chimpanzee

---

[252] Freeman, 35-36.
[253] Amundsen, 63-64.
[254] Wilson, *Sociobiology*, 283-284; Allee, 135.
[255] "Current World Population," Worldometer, 2022, accessed July 7, 2022, ⟨https://www.worldometers.info/world-population.⟩
[256] Wilson, *Sociobiology*, 514-516.
[257] Ibid., 283.

and the pygmy chimpanzee or bonobo, though taxonomy now recognizes separate species.[258] With over 98 percent of our DNA, both merit comparison with us.[259]

2.6.2 The Bonobo and Inequality

Confinement to the Democratic Republic of the Congo, where disorder and war hindered research, made bonobos, discovered in 1929, less familiar to us than chimpanzees.[260] Warfare, hunting, and habitat destruction imperil a population of some 29,000 to 50,000 bonobos. Resembling the chimpanzee, they are nonetheless slenderer, lighter, more arboreal, and have smaller heads and ears, higher foreheads, and flatter, darker faces.[261] Among apes, the bonobo best approximates our anatomy.

Females governing groups, bonobo hierarchy deviates from ours. Skillful coalition building helps them dominate males, which form weaker alliances than chimpanzee and human males.[262] Being larger and stronger and having longer canines than a female bonobo, he dominates her in a dyad, but larger groups empower females, which share choice fruits among themselves but seldom with a male, even when he begs.[263] Males accept this imbalance rather than fight females for food. Backlash's absence The absence of backlash implies that females govern bonobo society more autocratically than despots rule humankind.

Violence's infrequency does not preclude tension, which intercourse reduces.[264] Although many primates and other animals confine sex to reproduction, bonobos, like us, copulate for pleasure, embodying the slogan "make love, not war."[265] Also humanlike is bonobo adoption of the missionary position. Unlike us, however, females initiate sex even with infants.[266] Sibling incest may be the only taboo.

---

[258] Ibid., 539; Jurmain, Kilgore, Trevathan, and Ciochon, 162, 164; Buffy Silverman, *Bonobos* (Chicago: Heinemann Library, 2012), 9.

[259] Waal, *Mama's Last Hug*, 124; Frans B. M. De Waal, "Bonobo Sex and Society: The Behavior of a Close Relative Challenges Assumptions about Male Supremacy in Human Evolution," *Scientific American*, June 1, 2006, accessed April 22, 2022, ‹https://www.scientificamerican.com/article/bonobo-sex-and-society-2006-06/#›; Silverman, 8.

[260] Waal, "Bonobo Sex and Society."

[261] Ibid.; Jurmain, Kilgore, Trevathan, and Ciochon, 164-165; Waal, *Mama's Last Hug*, 193; Silverman, 9.

[262] Waal, *Mama's Last Hug*, 197-198.

[263] Ibid., 197.

[264] Jurmain, Kilgore, Trevathan, and Ciochon, 165; Waal, "Bonobo Sex and Society."

[265] Jurmain, Kilgore, Trevathan, and Ciochon, 165.

[266] Meredith F. Small, "Casual Sex Play Common among Bonobos: Sex among Our Closest Relatives Is a Rather Open Affair," *Discover Magazine*, May 31, 1992, accessed April 23, 2022, ‹Casual Sex Play Common Among Bonobos | Discover Magazine›; Vanessa Woods and Brian Hare, "Bonobo But Not Chimpanzee Infants Use Socio-Sexual Contact with

Despite differences between bonobos and us, their hierarchies resemble ours where offspring inherit status, usually from the mother.[267] This circumstance may elevate a dominant female's mediocre daughter above peers. Inept rulers likewise litter our past. Neither they nor we create meritocracies.[268]

2.6.3 The Chimpanzee, Inequality, and Violence

The bonobo aside, chimpanzees construct inequality almost as complex as ours.[269] They inhabit 30 to 80 member groups that patrol territory. Affection links mother and offspring. Even adult children remain loyal to her. Like humans, chimpanzees mature slowly. Long adolescence helps them learn status and social nuances. For example, inferiors learn to avoid confrontation by walking around, not toward, a superior.[270] They cede a branch or food to him and may touch his lips, thighs, or genitals to signal submission.

Unlike bonobos and like us, chimpanzee males rule. Size determines which male governs several primate species, notes chapter 3, though not chimpanzees. Alpha relies more on shrewdness than physicality to promote peace and stability, make allies, and protect those at or near hierarchy's nadir.[271] When a chimpanzee surrenders rank by losing a fight or quarrel, females usually outnumber males in consoling him or her, though no one is quicker to hug the loser than alpha. Rather than inflame disputes, "the healer-in-chief" intervenes with arms raised until calm prevails.[272]

Such males enjoy long tenures, whereas tyrants fail within one or two years.[273] Other males may challenge a popular leader, though they seldom succeed because the community favors him. Females know he promotes stability conducive to rearing offspring. But an oppressor pushes others toward a rival in hopes of better governance.

A deposed autocrat may suffer ambush or assassination. For example, Ntologi held power through bribes and theft.[274] Stealing monkey meat and styling himself hunter and provider, he fed supporters, not detractors. Initially successful, favoritism provoked an attack that nearly crippled him. Unable to muster sympathy, he lived alone while convalescing. Incomplete

---

Peers," NIH, National Library of Medicine, April 2011, accessed April 23, 2022, ‹Bonobo but not chimpanzee infants use socio-sexual contact with peers - PubMed (nih.gov).›
[267] Waal, "Bonobo Sex and Society."
[268] Allee, 159.
[269] Wilson, *Sociobiology*, 539.
[270] Ibid., 546.
[271] Waal, *Mama's Last Hug*, 175-176.
[272] Ibid., 175.
[273] Ibid., 187-188.
[274] Ibid., 185-186.

recovery forced him to hierarchy's cellar upon rejoining the group. Juveniles frightened him by feigning attack. This vulnerability led others to kill him.

Hostility intensified at a zoo, where inequality and antagonism were easier to observe than in the wild.[275] Luit formed alliances with cohabitants while awaiting opportunity to challenge two males who shared power. When their partnership deteriorated, he ascended, causing the two to revive their pact and plot against him. Fearing violence, primatologists tried to separate the three, who resisted by embracing one another. This maneuver successful, the two attacked Luit at night, biting him hundreds of times, castrating him, and severing toes and fingers. Although still alive at dawn, he died during surgery. Barely hurt, the aggressors likely coordinated an ambush. Having inflicting most of Luit's wounds, the younger became chief.

Because chimpanzees, like us, decode subtle gestures, intuit intentions, and create and manipulate coalitions, Luit must have suspected danger before primatologists tried to intervene.[276] Frustrating them, Luit risked his life in the conviction he could mend relations given his skill as reconciler. He also understood separation would have let the two plot against him while preventing his diffusing tensions on the spot. The gamble precipitated his dethronement, mutilation, and death.

2.7 Inequality, Misery, Violence, and Death

Inequality shortened nonelite lives throughout the animal kingdom while elites lived long and produced many offspring.[277] This disparity characterizes us, reveals that biology is destiny, and reiterates that we differ from other animals only in degree. English philosopher Thomas Hobbes (1588–1679) described existence during prehistory, when penury debilitated nearly everyone, as "solitary, poor, nasty, brutish, and short."[278] Such misfortune made poverty "dishonourable" and wealth "honourable."[279]

Humankind encouraged this dichotomy. Ramses II (c. 1303–1213 BCE), "Egypt's greatest king," sired over 100 children.[280] Three millennia later at hierarchy's other pole, Caribbean slaves, suffering "frightfully high" mortality, "died much faster than they were born."[281] From 1850 to 1870,

---

[275] Ibid., 181-184.
[276] Ibid., 183-184.
[277] Wilson, *Social Conquest of Earth*, 109.
[278] Hobbes, 84.
[279] Ibid., 61-62.
[280] Bob Brier and Hoyt Hobbs, *Ancient Egypt: Everyday Life in the Land of the Nile* (New York: Sterling, 2009), 36; Steven Snape, *Ancient Egypt: The Definitive Visual History* (London: DK, 2021), 212.
[281] Dunn, 301.

Manchester and Liverpool, England's slums pulled life expectancy a decade below the national average.[282] Across the Atlantic Ocean, homelessness truncated lives 25 years sooner than the U.S. average. The wealthiest centile of U.S. men outlived the poorest centile almost 15 years. The divide exceeded a decade for women in these centiles. These particulars suggest that elites have long condemned indigents to premature death and that inequality and indifference to misery are violence.

Our patrimony, inequality and violence link us with other animals, notably chimpanzees, and with next chapter's *Australopithecus* and premodern *Homo*. "Chimpanzee-like violence preceded and paved the way for human war, making modern humans the dazed survivors of a continuous, 5-million-year habit of lethal aggression," wrote British anthropologist and primatologist Richard Wrangham (b. 1948) and American author Dale Peterson (b. 1944).[283] These words echo next chapter's Australian physician and anatomist Raymond Dart (1893–1988) and American playwright and science writer Robert Ardrey (1908–1980).

2.8 Review and Preview

This chapter described sociality's genesis and operation. Stratification and specialization helped communities outcompete loners for resources. Arising in Mesozoic insects and spreading to Cenozoic vertebrates including birds and mammals, inequality, specialization, and violence anticipated us. Next chapter identifies these traits in our lineage. Australopithecines may have ranked one another 4 million years ago. Inequality and aggression persisted in *Homo*, with *Homo erectus* displaying both in ways we would amplify.

---

[282] Simon Szreter and Graham Mooney, "Urbanization, Mortality, and the Standard of Living Debate: New Estimates of the Expectation of Life at Birth in Nineteenth-Century British Cities," *The Economic History Review* 51, no. 1 (February 1998): 88-89.

[283] Richard Wrangham and Dale Peterson, *Demonic Males: Apes and the Evolution of Human Aggression* (Boston: Houghton Mifflin, 1996), 63.

Chapter 3 Human Origins, Inequality, and Violence

3.1 Abstract and Introduction

The primate order, introduced last chapter and to which we belong, originated about 55 million years ago.[284] Over time, primates colonized and adapted to localities. In Africa, apes diversified into numerous genera and species before 15 million years ago.[285] Arising from an African ape, our lineage diverged from those of the chimpanzee, bonobo, and gorilla about 8 million years ago.[286] Orangutan and gibbon ancestors settled Asia and shaped neither our origin nor evolution. Our genus, *Homo*, emerged in eastern or southern Africa around 2.8 million years ago.[287] *Homo sapiens* may be 200,000 years old.[288]

This book argues that inequality and its enforcement, emerging in our lineage some 4 million years ago, antedated us. Australian physician and anatomist Raymond Dart (1893–1988) and American playwright and science writer Robert Ardrey (1908–1980) traced hierarchy and aggression

---

[284] Clark Spencer Larsen, *Our Origins: Discovering Physical Anthropology* (New York and London: Norton, 2008), 238-239.

[285] Ibid., 279.

[286] Ibid., 282.

[287] Evan Hadingham, "Where Is the Birthplace of Humankind? South Africa and East Africa Both Lay Claims," *National Geographic*, September 11, 2015, accessed April 25, 2022, https://www.nationalgeographic.com/history/article/150911-hominin-hominid-berger-homo-naledi-fossils-ancestor-rising-star-human-origins; Bonnie Yoshida-Levine, "Early Members of the Genus *Homo*," Pressbooks, 2019, accessed April 25, 2022, ‹Early Members of the Genus Homo–Explorations (hawaii.edu).›

[288] Robert Jurmain, Lynn Kilgore, Wenda Trevathan, and Russell L. Ciochon, *Introduction to Physical Anthropology*, 2013-2014 ed. (Belmont, CA: Wadsworth Cengage Learning, 2014), 364.

to *Australopithecus, Homo*'s predecessor. Their opinion omitted that ferocity began almost as early as life because some bacteria emit toxins against rivals.[289] An impulse as old as aggression and the inequality it enforces must be biological.

This argument rejects English philosopher John Locke's (1632–1704) claim that we are born "white paper, void of all characters," a belief that lingered into the 1970s, when sociobiologists countered that natural selection gave us instincts.[290] Amplifying this position, *Eternal Inequality* deems us gene assemblages. Genes construct the paper and marks: traits like eye and hair color. Natural selection discriminates among genes, which influence our tendencies, by acting on phenotype. Conception finalizes genes' arrangement by fixing a zygote's chromosomes.

Excepting identical twins, each person receives a unique package of genes, which variegate individuals from conception. Environmental differences amplify inequality throughout life, precluding equal outcomes. At most, a society may aspire to equalize opportunities.

Discriminating among genes, natural selection bequeathed us anatomy and behavior. This behavioral bundle—human nature—emerges early. The authors of a 2001 study, dividing a group of five-year-olds into pairs and offering everyone two tokens, found participants were willing to accept only 1 if the partner received none.[291] Rather than equality at 2 tokens, each child preferred inequality with 1 token as long as he or she outranked the partner. Moreover, children assert dominance from the outset at daycare.[292] The yearning for superiority is rooted in emotions, whose power to leave us speechless implies origin in our lineage before the brain evolved language.[293] Such longevity must be biological, and biology predisposes social animals toward inequality, last chapter argued.

Revisiting Locke, his concern was ideas, not biology. He thought newborns lacked them, which experience taught.[294] *Eternal Inequality* tests this belief by acknowledging that I perceive nothing with limitless mass,

---

[289] Arik Kershenbaum, *The Zoologist's Guide to the Galaxy: What Animals on Earth Reveal about Aliens—and Ourselves* (New York: Penguin Press, 2021), 169.

[290] John Locke, *An Essay Concerning Human Understanding*, ed. Roger Woolhouse (London: Penguin Books, 2004), 109; Edward O. Wilson, *On Human Nature* (Cambridge, MA and London: Harvard University Press, 2004), ix–x.

[291] Christina Starmans, Mark Sheskin, and Paul Bloom, "Why People Prefer Unequal Societies," *Nature Human Behaviour* 1 (April 7, 2017), accessed April 25, 2022, ‹http://starlab. utoronto.ca/papers/2017%20Starmans%20Sheskin%20Bloom%20Inequality.pdf›, 4.

[292] Frans De Waal, *Mama's Last Hug: Animal Emotions and What They Tell Us about Ourselves* (New York and London: Norton, 2019), 177.

[293] Ibid., 178; Noel T. Boaz and Russell L. Ciochon, *Dragon Bone Hill: An Ice-Age Saga of Homo erectus* (Oxford: Oxford University Press, 2004), 172.

[294] Locke, 109.

---

dimensions, or duration. I am finite, and everything my senses detect is finite. Yet I understand infinity well enough to grasp that the infinity of integers doubles that of even integers. This chapter does not claim that genes programmed infinity as concept in me. Nonetheless, they directed my brain's development such that it has a priori ideas. Rejecting Locke, this book seeks a biological understanding of us grounded in our evolution.

3.2 Humankind's African Origin

Myth expressed the earliest attempts to identify our origin. Influential in the West, Genesis (c. 550 BCE) pinpointed neither place nor time of our putative creation. Mention of the Tigris and Euphrates rivers indicated Southwest Asia, but "the land of Cush" referenced eastern or northeastern Africa, perhaps Ethiopia or Egypt, a regional power ambitious to conquer the Levant or at least dictate terms of trade.[295] The "east" implied Asia, though this imprecision muddled rather than clarified our beginning.[296]

Against myth, British naturalist Charles Darwin (1809–1882), noting our resemblance to the chimpanzee and gorilla and their habitation of only Africa, put our origins there, though evidence seemed to point elsewhere.[297] Indeed, Darwin lived amid Neanderthal discoveries in Europe, not Africa.

Examining an 1856 find, Rudolf Virchow (1821–1902), "the most important German physician, biologist, social scientist, and anthropologist of the nineteenth century," dismissed its antiquity.[298] Judging it a modern "pathological idiot" deformed by rickets during childhood and arthritis in adulthood, he tainted Neanderthal for decades.[299] Irish geologist William King (1809–1886), coining the name *Homo neanderthalensis*, supposed that "thoughts and desires which once dwelt within it never soared beyond those of a brute."[300] Reconstructing a 1908 discovery, paleontologist and "leading French theorist of human evolution" Marcellin Boule (1861–1942) declared

---

[295] Gen. 2:13-14 (New American Bible).

[296] Gen. 2:8.

[297] Charles Darwin, *The Descent of Man, and Selection in Relation to Sex* (London: Penguin Books, 2004), 182.

[298] Ruth Moore, *Evolution*, rev. ed. (New York: Time-Life Books, 1968), 130; Friedrich C. Luft, "Rudolf Virchow and the Anthropology of Race," *Hektoen International: A Journal of Medical Humanities* 14, no. 1 (Winter 2022), ‹Rudolf Virchow and the anthropology of race (hekint.org).›

[299] Moore.

[300] Ralf W. Schmitz, "Neandertal (Feldhofer Grotte)," in *History of Physical Anthropology, Vol. 2: M-Z*, ed. Frank Spencer (New York & London: Garland Publishing, 1997), 710; Myron Schultz, "Rudolf Virchow," *Emerging Infectious Diseases* 14, no. 9 (September 2008), accessed April 25, 2022, ‹https://www.ncbi.nlm.nih.gov/pmc/articles/PMC2603088›; Leon Jaroff, "The Neanderthal Mystery," *Time*, June 24, 2001, accessed April 25, 2022, ‹http://content.time.com/time/magazine/article/0,9171,163991,00.html.›

it unable to stand fully erect.[301] Such denigration downgraded Europe as humankind's cradle.

Proposing Asia, German physician, zoologist, and "Darwin's great champion" Ernst Haeckel (1834–1919) heeded Swedish physician, naturalist, and "father of modern taxonomy" Carl von Linne (1707–1778) by linking us with Indonesian and Malaysian orangutans.[302] Seemingly confirming Haeckel, Dutch physician and anatomist Eugene Dubois (1858–1940), among "the founding fathers of paleoanthropology," discovered the first *Homo erectus'* femur, skullcap, and two teeth between 1890 and 1892 on Indonesian island Java.[303] He named it *Pithecanthropus erectus*, an obsolete designation, to emphasize not only its simian traits but its fully upright bipedalism. Defending its place in our lineage, he opposed the species' characterization as primitive and unimportant. Ridiculed by ministers and scientists, he hid the fossils nearly 30 years to deny critics access to them.[304] Although Haeckel credited Dubois with finding the "missing link," Virchow wrongly criticized his failure to notice the skullcap belonged to an ape and the femur to a man.[305]

While Dubois and Haeckel battled detractors, Europe regained the spotlight. British lawyer, amateur archaeologist, and "serial liar" Charles Dawson (1864–1916) in 1912 claimed discovery of an ancestral cranium and mandible, dubbed Piltdown Man, in Sussex, England.[306] Its large skull pleased scientists who thought cognition directed our evolution whereas *H. erectus* disquieted them. Although its femur was humanlike, its cranium suggested an ape's low dome. But later finds, resembling *H. erectus*, undermined Piltdown Man. British geologist and anthropologist Kenneth Oakley (1911–1981), British

---

[301] Michael Hammond, "The Expulsion of the Neanderthals from Human Ancestry: Marcellin Boule and the Social Context of Scientific Research," *Social Studies of Science* 12, no. 1 (February 1982): 2; Michael Hammond, "Boule, Marcellin (1861-1942)," in *History of Physical Anthropology, Vol. 1: A-L*, ed. Frank Spencer (New York & London: Garland Publishing, 1997), 203.

[302] Larsen, *Our Origins*, 303-304; Glenn C. Conroy, *Reconstructing Human Origins: A Modern Synthesis* (New York and London: Norton, 1997), 5; Robert J. Richards, *The Tragic Sense of Life: Ernst Haeckel and the Struggle over Evolutionary Thought* (Chicago and London: University of Chicago Press, 2008), xvii; Charles H. Calisher, "Taxonomy: What's in a Name? Doesn't a Rose by Any Other Name Smell as Sweet?" *Croatian Medical Journal* 48, no. 2 (April 2007): 268-270. Accessed August 21, 2022. ‹Taxonomy: What's in a name? Doesn't a rose by any other name smell as sweet? - PMC (nih.gov)›.

[303] Richards, 253; Pat Shipman and Paul Storm, "Missing Links: Eugene Dubois and the Origins of Paleoanthropology," *Evolutionary Anthropology* 11 (2002): 108, accessed August 8, 2022, ‹(PDF) Missing Links: Eugène Dubois and the Origins of Paleoanthropology (researchgate.net).›

[304] Moore, 131-132; Conroy, 290.

[305] Richards, 253-254.

[306] F. Clark Howell, *Early Man*, rev. ed. (New York: Time-Life Books, 1968), 24-25; Larsen, *Our Origins*, 274-275.

---

biologist Joseph Weiner (1915–1982), and British anatomist, surgeon, and anthropologist Wilfrid Le Gros Clark (1895–1971) proved it fraud in 1953.

3.3 *Australopithecus*

3.3.1 *Africa and Australopithecus*

While Piltdown Man limped toward oblivion, the drama returned to Africa. Zambia in 1921 yielded the first *Homo heidelbergensis*.[307] Three years later, Dart, confirming our African origin and inaugurating "a new era in paleoanthropology," discovered South Africa's Taung Child, the first *Australopithecus africanus* and the oldest hominin to that date.[308] Dart's publications and lectures popularized the species, which existed roughly 3.5 million to 2.1 million years ago.[309] Later discoveries buttressed Africa's priority.

About six years old at death, the child lived around 3 million to 2.4 million years ago amid a hominin radiation.[310] By 2 million years ago, *Australopithecus* coexisted with related genera *Paranthropus* and *Homo*.[311] *Eternal Inequality* judges *Paranthropus* outside its scope, scrutinizes *Homo* throughout the text, and overviews australopithecine distribution, anatomy, inequality, and violence in this section and the next.

Australopithecus' eight species inhabited southern and eastern Africa 4.2 million to 2 million years ago as climate changed.[312] Trees and rainfall

[307] Chris Stringer and Peter Andrews, *The Complete World of Human Evolution* (London: Thames & Hudson, 2005), 8, 148-149; Miles Russell, *The Piltdown Man Hoax: Case Closed* (Stroud, UK: History Press, 2012), 8.

[308] Howell, 48; Dean Falk, "Hominin Brain Evolution, 1925-2011: An Emerging Overview," in *African Genesis: Perspectives on Hominin Evolution*, ed. Sally C. Reynolds and Andrew Gallagher (Cambridge, UK: Cambridge University Press, 2012), 145-146.

[309] "*Australopithecus africanus*," Smithsonian National Museum of Natural History, last modified January 22, 2021, accessed June 29, 2022, https://humanorigins.si.edu/evidence/human-fossils/species/australopithecus-africanus;› Leo Sands, "Fossils: Cave Woman One Million Years Older Than Previously Thought," BBC News, June 29, 2022, accessed June 29, 2022, ‹Fossils: Cave woman one million years older than thought (yahoo.com).›

[310] Larsen, *Our Origins*, 275; Bernard Wood, *Human Evolution: A Very Short Introduction* (Oxford and New York: Oxford University Press, 2005), 47.

[311] Andy I. R. Herries, Jesse M. Martin, A. B. Leece, Justin W. Adams, Giovanni Boschian, Renaud Joannes-Boyau, Tara R. Edwards, Tom Mallett, Jason Massey, Ashleigh Murszewski, Simon Neubauer, Robyn Pickering, David S. Strait, Brian J. Armstrong, Stephanie Baker, Matthew V. Caruana, Tim Denham, John Hellstrom, Jacopo Moggi-Cecchi, Simon Mokobane, Paul Penzo-Kajewski, Douglass S. Rovinsky, Gary T. Schwartz, Rhiannon C. Stammers, Coen Wilson, Jon Woodhead, and Colin Menter, "Contemporaneity of *Australopithecus*, *Paranthropus*, and Early *Homo erectus* in South Africa," *Science* 368, no. 6486 (April 3, 2020), accessed April 25, 2022, ‹https://science.sciencemag.org/content/368/6486/eaaw7293?rss=1.›

[312] Carol V. Ward and Ashley S. Hammond, "*Australopithecus* and Kin," *Nature Education Knowledge* 7, no. 3 (2016), accessed April 25, 2022, ‹https://www.nature.com/scitable/

decreased, opening space to herbs like grasses. Although thick forest had favored arboreality, its patchy replacements required terrestrialism where trees were sparse and arboreality where they prevailed.

Australopithecus exploited these habitats. Long, apelike fingers and arms relative to torso and legs eased movement through trees.[313] An opposable thumb helped other fingers grasp branches. Long, flexible toes did likewise. Arboreality helped the genus evade terrestrial predators. When it descended to the ground, perhaps to seek food after depleting a locale, erectness enabled bipedalism, which is more efficient than quadrupedality. Natural selection adapted pelvis, knees, and feet for walking. For example, fossil footmarks reveal arches like ours in australopithecine feet.

Nearly 3.7 million years old, Laetoli, Tanzania's footprints imply sexual dimorphism, which typifies primates and increases with rivalry for females as strong males with large bodies and canines deter weaklings from mating.[314] Investing less energy than females in rearing young, males have more for quarrels over estrous females. Alpha males mating indiscriminately, all females pass their genes to offspring. Selection for size is thus unidirectional only in males. Competitive and aggressive, mandrill, baboon, gorilla, and orangutan males at least double females in size.[315]

Monogamy may lessen competition, aggression, and dimorphism by letting each male pair with a female. Among less dimorphic primates, male chimpanzees are about 50 percent larger than females.[316] This reduction is important because chimpanzees—chapter 2 examined their inequality and aggression—are, along with bonobos, the best proxy for humans.[317] Chimps and people share over 98 percent of DNA, noted the previous chapter, and behave similarly. Like gibbons, however, men outweigh women by only 15 percent.[318]

Eternal Inequality emphasizes humans and apes' similitude. Linne put us and orangutans in *Homo*, Dubois made the gibbon our forebear, American

---

knowledge/library/australopithecus-and-kin-145077614›; "Climate Effects on Human Evolution," Smithsonian National Museum of Natural History, last modified February 3, 2022, accessed April 25, 2022, ‹https://humanorigins.si.edu/research/climate-and-human-evolution/climate-effects-human-evolution.›

[313] Larsen, *Our Origins*, 290; Conroy, 190.

[314] Larsen, *Our Origins*, 184-185.

[315] Lisa Hendry, "*Australopithecus afarensis*, Lucy's Species," London Natural History Museum, accessed April 25, 2022, ‹https://www.nhm.ac.uk/discover/australopithecus-afarensis-lucy-species.html›; Jurmain, Kilgore, Trevathan, and Ciochon, 157, 160-161, 190.

[316] Jurmain, Kilgore, Trevathan, and Ciochon, 163.

[317] Larsen, *Our Origins*, 52.

[318] Jurmain, Kilgore, Trevathan, and Ciochon, 158; J. Michael Plavcan, "Body Size, Size Variation, and Sexual Size Dimorphism in Early *Homo*," *Current Anthropology* 53, Supplement 6 (December 2012): S411.

journalist and science writer Ruth Moore (1909–1989) grouped us among apes, British zoologist Desmond Morris (b. 1928) titled his "landmark" book *The Naked Ape*, and American geographer Jared Diamond (b. 1937) named his 2014 study *The Third Chimpanzee for Young People: On the Evolution and Future of the Human Animal.*[319]

Revisiting Laetoli, a male over 5.5 feet tall likely made the large tracks whereas two or three adult females and another two or three children left the small ones.[320] The arrangement resembles a gorilla troop of one large male and several females. Mountain gorilla males outweigh females 2 to 2.5 times, a disparity that might have characterized *Australopithecus*.[321]

Inequality and competition for females transcend primates. For example, a male sheet-web spider asserts dominance by being first to enter a female's web.[322] Interlopers risk attack from his fangs, corroborating *Eternal Inequality*'s thesis that elites enforce inequality. Conflict drives her to the web's edge. Moreover, her tendency to leave the web's hub upon his entrance famishes her because she can no longer detect prey. Surrendering a web to him, she subordinates her interests to his.

3.3.2 Australopithecines, Inequality, and Violence

The attempt to describe australopithecine inequality, a task the previous section began, may seem daunting. The genus left no incontrovertible artifacts, though 3.4-million-year-old cuts on bones indicate tool use.[323] It lacked money and status symbols. Only footprints and skeletal fragments, not whole individuals, exist. With two fifths of its skeleton intact, *Australopithecus afarensis* specimen Lucy is the most complete of over 300 found.[324]

---

[319] Conroy, 5, 290; Moore, 185; "The Naked Ape at 50: 'Its Central Claim Has Surely Stood the Test of Time,'" *The Guardian*, September 24, 2017, accessed April 25, 2022, ‹The Naked Ape at 50: 'Its central claim has surely stood the test of time ' | Evolution | The Guardian;› Jared Diamond, *The Third Chimpanzee for Young People: On the Evolution and Future of the Human Animal* (New York and Oakland, CA: Seven Stories Press, 2014), viii.

[320] Michael Greshko, "Newfound Footprints Stir Debate over Our Ancestors' Sex Lives," *National Geographic*, December 14, 2016, accessed April 25, 2022, ‹https://www.nationalgeographic.com/history/article/oldest-human-footprints-australopithecus-lucy-tanzania-science.›

[321] Ibid.; Jurmain, Kilgore, Trevathan, and Ciochon, 161.

[322] Edward O. Wilson, *Sociobiology: The New Synthesis*, 25th anniversary ed. (Cambridge, MA and London: Belknap Press of Harvard University Press, 2000), 282; Leilani A. Walker and Gregory I. Holwell, "Bad Tenants: Female Sheet-Web Spiders, *Cambridgea foliata* (Araneae: Desidae), Lose Feeding Opportunities When Cohabiting with Males," *Journal of Arachnology* 46, no. 3 (2018): 392.

[323] "Oldest Evidence of Human Stone Tool Use and Meat Eating Found," Max-Planck-Gesellschaft, August 12, 2010, accessed April 25, 2022, ‹https://www.mpg.de/research/oldest-evidence-human-stone-tool-use.›

[324] Wood, 71-72; "*Australopithecus afarensis*," Smithsonian National Museum of Natural History, last modified January 22, 2021, accessed April 25, 2022, ‹https://humanorigins.

Suggesting that males more than doubled females in size, these remains reinforce the notion of competition for females.[325]

This chapter gauges inequality by comparing courtship—a word for australopithecine amorousness, absent a better noun—and wealth. Both are competitions, a fact evident to suitors who spend lavishly on dates in hopes of sex. Pursuing many women, former U.S. president Donald Trump (b. 1946), highlighting competitiveness, remarked that money was unimportant "except as a way to keep score."[326] Wealth purchases scarce resources. The greater the affluence, the scarcer the item it affords. Largeness paralleled riches in nonhuman primates—australopithecine, chimpanzee, bonobo, gorilla, or other—giving powerful males ovulating females, the scarce resource.

Enforcing inequality, violence, which Ardrey traced to African "killer apes," typified last chapter's social animals like primates.[327] Through natural selection, Africa, full of danger, harshened us. Far from an evolutionary afterthought, aggression permeates our genes such that "Man takes deeper delight in his weapons than in his women."[328]

Hunting stimulated this pleasure by requiring our ancestors to kill.[329] Cowards retreated, losing sustenance and an opportunity to impress potential mates.[330] Hunters attracted women, fed progeny, and turned spears on each other after perfecting the hunt. Enlarging the brain over time, weapons hastened our evolution.[331] Nature thus favored "the efficient capacity for violence, the enjoyment of violence," Ardrey remarked.[332]

Barbarousness evoked fear, which he made the glue that cemented people in place within hierarchy.[333] Fear and intuition of status crystallized early in life, making them inborn. A "fundamental life force," the urge to domi-

---

si.edu/evidence/human-fossils/species/australopithecus-afarensis.›

[325] Hendry.

[326] Donald J. Trump with Tony Schwartz, *Trump: The Art of the Deal* (New York: Ballantine Books, 1987), 63.

[327] Robert Ardrey, *African Genesis: A Personal Investigation into the Animal Origins and Nature of Man* (New York: Atheneum, 1970), 1.

[328] Ibid., 204.

[329] "Aggression and Violence in Man—A Dialogue," L. S. B. Leakey Foundation for Research Related to Man's Origin, November 1971, accessed April 25, 2022, ‹https://authors.library.caltech.edu/25660/1/Munger_Africana_Library__Notes.9.pdf,› 10.

[330] Ibid., 20.

[331] Ardrey, *African Genesis*, 105, 312.

[332] "Aggression and Violence in Man," 20.

[333] Ardrey, *African Genesis*, 89.

nate subjugated weaklings.[334] Our fraught origin and evolution in predatory Africa destined us to murder "each other for fun," he wrote.[335]

Ardrey borrowed these ideas from Dart, whom he met in 1955.[336] Friendship blossomed as Ardrey studied Dart's fossils and artifacts. Their association, born of shared ideas and interests, made the dramatist Dart's protégé. In this role, Ardrey amplified his mentor's message that biology coarsened us.

Dart reached this conclusion in the 1940s after pondering australopithecine and baboon fossils in the caves of South Africa's Makapansgat Valley.[337] Baboon skulls bore injuries he attributed to *Australopithecus*, believing it bashed them with antelope humeri as prelude to eating the carcasses. A pitiless environment honed its survival instincts, leading it to destroy and devour remorselessly. Australopithecines, he wrote in *The International Anthropological and Linguistic Review*, smashed bones to extract marrow and "tore the battered bodies of their quarries apart limb from limbs and slaked their thirst with blood, consuming the flesh raw like every other carnivorous beast."[338] This hypothesis made carnivory, hunting, and violence evolution's drivers.

A. africanus' depiction as first biped and hunter amplified Darwin's belief that erectness encouraged hunting by freeing the hands for weapons.[339] Darwin, Dart, and Ardrey acknowledged that it became warfare when our ancestors aimed stones and spears at one another.[340] Encapsulating this view, American biologist Edward Wilson (b. 1929) wrote in 1978 that "warfare... has been endemic to every form of society, from hunter-gatherer bands to industrial states."[341] "War in one form or another appeared with the first man," remarked former U.S. president and 2009 Nobel Peace Prize recipient Barack Obama (b. 1961), "our crown jewel" to black supporters, in echoing him.[342]

Denying "that man is a rational animal," American anthropologist Sherwood Washburn (1911–2000) believed hunting grafted enthusiasm for

---

[334] Ibid., 112.

[335] Robert Ardrey, *The Territorial Imperative: A Personal Inquiry into the Animal Origins of Property and Nations* (New York: Atheneum, 1966), vii.

[336] Ibid.; Nadine Weidman, "Popularizing the Ancestry of Man: Robert Ardrey and the Killer Instinct," *Isis* 102, no. 2 (June 2011): 282-285.

[337] Weidman, 281-282; Robin Derricourt, "The Enigma of Raymond Dart," *The International Journal of African Historical Studies* 42, no. 2 (2009): 264.

[338] Raymond A. Dart, "The Predatory Transition from Ape to Man," *International Anthropological and Linguistic Review* 1, no. 4 (1953), accessed April 25, 2022, ‹the-predatory-transition-from-ape-to-man.pdf (wordpress.com).›

[339] Darwin, 71-72.

[340] Ibid.; Dart; "Aggression and Violence in Man," 20.

[341] Wilson, *On Human Nature*, 99.

[342] Jeffrey Moussaieff Masson, *Beasts: What Animals Can Teach Us about the Origins of Good and Evil* (New York: Bloomsbury, 2014), 2; Ta-Nehisi Coates, *We Were Eight Years in Power: An American Tragedy* (New York: One World, 2017), 295.

killing onto an older instinct to dominate.[343] Coupling sadism and inequality, natural selection fashioned us to enjoy watching criminals suffer torture and execution.

Such behavior predated us. Cranial trauma convinced Dart that australopithecines massacred and ate each other.[344] "The loathsome cruelty of mankind to man forms one of his inescapable, characteristic, and differentiative features; and it is explicable only in terms of his carnivorous and cannibalistic origin," he wrote. Evolution made us brutes.

Dart's stridency discomforted the *Review* editor, who supposed *Australopithecus* "only the ancestors of the modern Bushman and Negro, and of *nobody else.*"[345] This belief saw blacks as atavisms that retained australopithecine behaviors. Their putative primitiveness put them beneath whites, who supposedly evolved from a superior hominin. Evolution thus produced Greek philosopher Aristotle's (384–322 BCE) chain of being, which arranged all matter including life from nadir to apex.[346] Haeckel modified this arrangement in 1867, drawing a succession of forms from protoplasm to Papuan.[347] None looked modern, questioning the notion of advancement for black and brown people.

Conferees at the 1955 Pan-African Congress on Prehistory criticized Dart, a reproach that continued decades.[348] South African paleontologist Charles Brain (b. 1931) demonstrated in 1967 that animals other than *Australopithecus* gnawed the baboon skulls.[349] Rather than predator, it was prey to leopards, cheetahs, and lions. Far from bellicose, it seemed hapless and incapable of defending itself let alone killing wantonly. Rejecting Dart and Ardrey's belief that Africa's harsh environment coarsened australopithecines, Wilson denied in 1978 that an unpleasant upbringing inevitably made someone violent.[350] Absent environment as cause, biology must be destiny.

Predation selected social animals over isolates for survival, chapter 2 noted. Safety from predators increased with group size. The need for protection encouraged *Australopithecus*, anticipating *Homo*, to aggregate, though

---

[343] Ardrey, *The Territorial Imperative*, 258-259; Rosalind Ribnick, "A Short History of Primate Field Studies: Old World Monkeys and Apes," in *A History of American Physical Anthropology, 1930-1980*, ed. Frank Spencer (New York: Academic Press, 1982) 60.

[344] Dart.

[345] Ardrey, *African Genesis*, 29. This quote duplicates the original italics.

[346] Henry B. Veatch, *Aristotle: A Contemporary Appreciation* (Bloomington and London: Indiana University Press, 1974), 73-74.

[347] Howell, 20.

[348] Weidman, 282-283.

[349] Henry T. Bunn, "Meat Made Us Human," in *Evolution of the Human Diet: The Known, the Unknown, and the Unknowable*, ed. Peter S. Ungar (Oxford and New York: Oxford University Press, 2007), 191.

[350] Wilson, *On Human Nature*, 119.

Dart and Ardrey, understanding australopithecines as aggressors, envisioned these proto societies as abettors of hunting and war.

Their language is easier to dismiss as hyperbole than to acknowledge as insight into our behavior. For example, a 1950s Malayan soldier's hematophagy supports Dart's conviction that australopithecines did so.[351] Vampire folklore may stem from the belief that Romanian prince Vlad III (c. 1430–c. 1476) likewise practiced hematophagy.[352] Witnesses accused Hungarian countess Elizabeth Bathory (1560–1614) of drinking girls' blood to preserve her youth.[353] Rhetoric aside, Dart and Ardrey's position aligned with Italian philosopher Niccolò Machiavelli (1469–1527) and English philosopher Thomas Hobbes' (1588–1679) evaluation of humankind. Depravity reigns absent civilization's veneer.

3.4 *Homo*

3.4.1 Homo's Origin and Onset of Reduction in Sexual Dimorphism

Dimorphism shrank in *Homo*, though premodern fossils indicate that differences between men and women surpassed those in extant people.[354] *H. heidelbergensis* from Argo, France and *H. heidelbergensis* or Neanderthals from Sima de los Huesos, Spain show dimorphism 400,000 to 300,000 years ago. The Spanish crania imply that men were about a quarter larger than women, an amount above us but beneath australopithecines, chimpanzees, gorillas, and baboons.

Homo likely evolved about 2.8 million years ago from *A. africanus*, *A. afarensis*, or *Australopithecus garhi*, though the fossil record's discontinuities complicate efforts to identify our genus' immediate precursor.[355] Moreover, species like *Australopithecus sediba*, with australopithecine and human features, hamper genealogical reconstruction by resisting categorization.[356]

---

[351] Ibid., 100-101.

[352] "Vampire History," A & E Television, September 13, 2017, last modified February 21, 2020, accessed April 25, 2022, ‹https://www.history.com/topics/folklore/vampire-history.›

[353] Richard Cavendish, "Death of Countess Elizabeth Bathory," *History Today* 64, no. 8 (August 2014), accessed April 25, 2022, ‹https://www.historytoday.com/archive/months-past/death-countess-elizabeth-bathory.›

[354] Conroy, 279, 354, 359, 361, 369; Plavcan, S417.

[355] Edward O. Wilson, *The Social Conquest of Earth* (New York and London: Liveright Publishing, 2012), 109, 114; Ernst Mayr, *The Growth of Biological Thought: Diversity, Evolution, and Inheritance* (Cambridge, MA and London: Belknap Press of Harvard University Press, 1982), 621; Yoshida-Levine; Larsen, *Our Origins*, 293.

[356] Jurmain, Kilgore, Trevathan, and Ciochon, 297-299.

Anthropologists named Dubois' discovery *H. erectus* in the 1950s, though *Homo*'s earliest species may have been *Homo habilis*, which Kenyan British anthropologist Louis Leakey (1903–1972), South African physician and "paleoanthropologist of international stature" Phillip Tobias (1925–2012), and British physician and "primate paleobiologist" John Napier (1917–1987) named and described in 1964.[357] Tobias and Napier envisioned it the link between *Australopithecus* and *H. erectus* whereas Leakey, denying the second as our ancestor, thought *H. habilis* evolved into us.

Critics rejected, first, his name. Meaning "handy man," the moniker indicated Leakey, Tobias, and Napier's belief that it had fashioned the first tools.[358] But tool making, a behavior, was irrelevant; only anatomy identified a species.[359] Second, detractors thought his brain too small for inclusion in *Homo*. *H. erectus*' brain marked the threshold for admission. Third, both species were estimated to have originated 1.8 million years ago, refuting Tobias and Napier's decision to make *H. habilis H. erectus*' predecessor because natural selection had insufficient time to grade the first into the second.[360] "Passionate, impetuous, volatile and always larger than life," Leakey circumvented the difficulty by making *H. habilis* rather than *H. erectus* our ancestor, as noted, but this claim was implausible because *H. erectus* looked much more human than *H. habilis*.[361] American anthropologist Francis Clark Howell (1925–2007), "principal architect and prime mover of the multidisciplinary study of human evolution," avoided the problem of how to characterize this new hominin and where it belonged in our phylogeny by omitting it from his popular *Early Man*, published in 1965 and updated in 1968, and by designating *H. erectus* "a true man at last."[362]

Unlike us, *H. habilis* had *Australopithecus*' height, build, short gait, and arboreal-terrestrial mobility.[363] Australopithecine traits implied inequality through competition for mates and dimorphism. This impression strength-

---

[357] Boaz and Ciochon, 67; Jurmain, Kilgore, Trevathan, and Ciochon, 303; Conroy, 255, 257; Geoffrey H. Sperber, "Tobias, Phillip V(allentine) (1925-)," in *History of Physical Anthropology, Vol. 2: M-Z*, ed. Frank Spencer (New York & London: Garland Publishing, 1997), 1037; Leslie Aiello, "Napier, John Russell (1917-1987)," in *History of Physical Anthropology, Vol. 2: M-Z*, ed. Frank Spencer (New York & London: Garland Publishing, 1997), 705.

[358] Larsen, *Our Origins*, 306; Phillip V. Tobias, "The Species *Homo habilis*: Example of a Premature Discovery," *Annales Zoologici Fennici* 28, no. 3/4 (February 19, 1992): 372.

[359] Conroy, 260; Tobias, 372.

[360] Conroy, 264; Jurmain, Kilgore, Trevathan, and Ciochon, 299; Larsen, *Our Origins*, 309.

[361] Brian Fagan, "Louis Leakey & Mary Leakey," in *The Great Archaeologists*, ed. Brian Fagan (London: Thames & Hudson, 2014), 215.

[362] Howell, 77; Tim D. White, "Clark Howell (1925-2007)," *Nature* 447, no. 52 (2007), May 2, 2007, accessed September 23, 2022, ‹F. Clark Howell (1925–2007) | Nature.›

[363] Larsen, *Our Origins*, 307-308.

ened upon comparison with baboons, which join humans as the "most successful" extant terrestrial primate.[364] Like our ancestors, baboons, whose males double females in size noted an earlier section, inhabit patchy woodlands.

Yet this comparison is questionable. Baboon males weaponize their long canines when competing for females.[365] But *H. habilis* lacked such canines, implying less competition for mates and reduction in dimorphism. Over millennia, this trend yielded slightly dimorphic modern humans.

3.4.2 Diversity in Premodern Homo

Temptation exists to conceive evolution as the above chain of being. But linearity oversimplifies an evolution that produced five hominin species 3 to 1 million years ago.[366] An attempt to understand this complexity starts with chronology. As noted, an early assumption crowded *H. habilis* and *H. erectus* by originating both 1.8 million years ago. This compression is incorrect. Arising almost 3 million years ago, *H. habilis* had enough time to become *H. erectus*.[367]

Among the other three species, *Homo rudolfensis* lived 1.9 to 1.8 million years ago.[368] The name memorializes his discovery near Kenya and Ethiopia's Lake Rudolf, now Lake Turkana, which early peoples probably visited for water and food, and which also yielded *H. habilis*. Although likely favoring plants, early *Homo* probably also ate aquatic insects, amphibians, and fish.

H. habilis and *H. rudolfensis*' coexistence and similarities complicate their classification. The debate concerns how taxonomists interpret differences within a population. Those who divide members into two or more species are known as "splitters" whereas consolidators favor a single species and are known as "lumpers."[369] Splitters emphasized that *H. rudolfensis*' cranium

---

[364] Conroy, 273.

[365] Carlos Drews, "Contexts and Patterns of Injuries in Free-Ranging Male Baboons (*Papio cynocephalus*)," *Behaviour* 133, no. 5/6 (May 1996): 443-444.

[366] "Human Evolution Interactive Timeline," Smithsonian National Museum of Natural History, last modified April 27, 2021, accessed April 25, 2022, ‹https://humanorigins.si.edu/evidence/human-evolution-interactive-timeline.›

[367] Larsen, *Our Origins*, 293; "*Homo ergaster/erectus*: Down from the Trees," The Human Journey, Institute for the Study of Human Knowledge, 2022, accessed July 9, 2022, ‹https://humanjourney.us/discovering-our-distant-ancestors-section/homo-erectus/?gclid=CjwKCAjwgISIBhBfEiwALE19SdTETP7AMBUrGthzLUM4a6XYM34Gu0tVFFiBh-T6oIWPUPgUWVNIo5hoCh_oQAvD_BwE›; "Homo habilis," Smithsonian National Museum of Natural History, last modified July 1, 2022, accessed July 9, 2022, ‹Homo habilis | The Smithsonian Institution's Human Origins Program (si.edu).›

[368] "Homo rudolfensis," Smithsonian National Museum of Natural History, last modified July 7, 2022, accessed July 9, 2022, ‹https://humanorigins.si.edu/evidence/human-fossils/species/homo-rudolfensis.›

[369] George Gaylord Simpson, *The Principles of Classification and a Classification of Mammals* (New York: Bulletin of the American Museum of Natural History, 1945), 22-23.

exceeded *H. habilis*' by nearly 25 percent, an important difference given interest in cognition's evolutionary role.[370]

Preoccupation with intellect predated anthropology's study of human origins and persists among scholars and scientists. Greek philosopher Plato (c. 428–c. 348 BCE) prioritized mind over body.[371] His pupil Aristotle believed rationality alone differentiated us from other animals, stated last chapter. Egyptian philosopher Plotinus (204–270 CE), "ashamed of being in a body," reiterated Plato's tenet that cognition transcended corporeality.[372] French mathematician, scientist, and "Father of Modern Philosophy" Rene Descartes (1596–1650), defined himself, and by extension everyone, as "a thinking thing; that is, a mind, or intellect, or understanding, or reason."[373] "All our dignity...consists in thought," wrote French mathematician, scientist, and philosopher Blaise Pascal (1623–1662).[374] Among "the geniuses of the age," he termed us "a thinking reed."[375] Naming us *H. sapiens*, Linne likewise made reason our hallmark.[376] Designating us "intelligent machines," American physicist Frank Tipler (b. 1947) asserted that someone with ten times more thoughts than another lived tenfold longer.[377]

Revisiting *H. habilis* and *H. rudolfensis*, splitters noted the second's larger leg bones and inferred a physique less simian than *H. habilis*.[378] *H. habilis* and *H. rudolfensis*' status as two species, implying other Lake Turkana fossils' division into multiple genera and species, unsettled lumpers by creating an untidy phylogeny. An alternative classified all as *H. habilis* or *Homo ergaster*, a name for African *H. erectus*.[379] Eliminating *H. rudolfensis*, this bifurcation assigned its remains to *H. habilis*. The surmise that no *H. habilis* or *H. rudolfensis* man was shorter than a woman strengthened belief in "strong" dimorphism,

---

[370] Conroy, 267.

[371] Plato, *Phaedo*, in *Great Dialogues of Plato*, trans. W. H. D. Rouse (New York and Scarborough, ON: New American Library, 1956), 467-468.

[372] Plotinus, *The Six Enneads*, trans. Stephen MacKenna and B. S. Page (Chicago: Encyclopaedia Britannica, 1988), 200-201; Stephen R. L. Clark, *Plotinus: Myth, Metaphor, and Philosophical Practice* (Chicago and London: University of Chicago Press, 2016), 5.

[373] Rene Descartes, *Mediations on First Philosophy*, 3d ed., trans. Donald A. Cress (Indianapolis and Cambridge: Hackett Publishing, 1993), 19; Richard Watson, *Cogito, Ergo Sum: The Life of Rene Descartes* (Boston: David R. Godine, 2002), 3.

[374] Blaise Pascal, *Pensees*, trans. W. F. Trotter (Mineola, MN: Dover Publications, 2003), 97.

[375] Ibid.; William C. Placher, *A History of Christian Theology: An Introduction* (Philadelphia: Westminster Press, 1983), 212.

[376] Conroy, 375.

[377] Frank J. Tipler, *The Physics of Immortality: Modern Cosmology, God and the Resurrection of the Dead* (New York: Doubleday, 1994), 43, 134.

[378] Stringer and Andrews, 135.

[379] Conroy, 266.

though definition of all large remains as male and all small ones as female guaranteed this outcome.[380]

Circularity aside, early *Homo* poses other problems. First, fossils are difficult to assign to a species and sex because anthropologists found no postcranial and cranial fragments together.[381] Second, fossils' dearth weakens generalizations. Third, biologists often use body mass to calculate dimorphism in living organisms, but bones neither pinpoint a vertebrate's mass while alive nor guarantee accurate estimation of dimorphism when compared with another. Any two *Homo* men, for example, would have illustrated that bone and body masses correlate poorly if the lighter man had more massive bones, but emaciation wasted his body. Correlation aside, bone and body masses vary throughout life in response to factors like growth, food quantity and quality, disease, parasitism, injury, and senescence.

Yet early *Homo* was probably dimorphic because, as noted, modern people and apes display this trait to lesser or greater degree. Resulting from competition for mates, dimorphism evolved separately in each or only once: in the common ancestor. The introduction's Occam's rule favoring the second, inequality predated us and shaped our entirety on earth. Only the magnitude of our ancestors' dimorphism, competition, and inequality remains debatable.

3.4.3 Homo erectus, Sexual Dimorphism, and Inequality

Besides *H. habilis* and *H. rudolfensis*, *H. erectus/H. ergaster* visited Lake Turkana.[382] Originating around 1.9 million year ago, he justified Howell's enthusiasm by resembling us more than his forerunners had.[383] Whereas they looked more simian than human, he had our proportions, indicating full terrestrialism.[384] Whereas australopithecines and early peoples seldom stood 4 feet, *H. erectus* averaged 5.5 feet, with men 5.9 feet and women 5.3 feet.[385] American anthropologist Clark Spencer Larsen (b. 1952) attributed the enlargement, occurring within 200,000 years, to an increase in meat intake.[386]

His numbers, putting *H. erectus* men around 11 percent taller than women, compare with the earlier statistic that modern men outweigh women by 15

---

[380] Plavcan, S417.

[381] Ibid.

[382] Larsen, *Our Origins*, 309-310.

[383] "*Homo erectus*," Smithsonian National Museum of Natural History, last modified January 22, 2021, accessed April 25, 2022, ‹https://humanorigins.si.edu/evidence/human-fossils/species/homo-erectus›; Jurmain, Kilgore, Trevathan, and Ciochon, 310.

[384] Larsen, *Our Origins*, 311, 322.

[385] Ibid., 321; Jurmain, Kilgore, Trevathan, and Ciochon, 311.

[386] Larsen, *Our Origins*, 321.

percent.[387] Were *H. erectus* men heavier than women, as was likely, the species and modern people probably exhibited equal dimorphism, which undershot *Australopithecus* and early *Homo*. Dimorphism shrank from *H. habilis* to *H. erectus* as female stature grew more than men's, bringing the sexes near parity.[388]

Parity implies that competition for mates lessened from australopithecines and early peoples to *H. erectus*. If present, monogamy gave more men opportunity to mate than was possible earlier. With large men unable to monopolize women, societies approached reproductive, though not social, equality.

Description of *H. erectus'* inequality requires culture's examination. By culture, this book means that people, including *Homo's* extinct members, differ from most animals in passing more than genes to offspring. The extras—like ideas, art, music, language, drama, agriculture, pastoralism, industry, sports, mathematics, science, and technology—are culture. This package being huge, complex, and changeable, humans invented schools, also part of culture, to institutionalize its transmission across generations.

Less elaborate than ours, *H. erectus'* culture no less decisively shaped inequality. This cultural chronology begins with hunting, which influenced hierarchy and whose invention Dart and Ardrey attributed to australopithecines. Although surely opportunists that ate insects, amphibians, and other small prey, *Australopithecus* and early *Homo* probably scavenged more than hunted.[389]

British primatologist Jane Goodall (b. 1934), laying "the foundation for understanding chimpanzee behaviors and similarities to humans," proved that chimpanzees hunt.[390] This activity characterizing them and us before farming and herding, Occam's rule suggests that the common ancestor of both pursued game and that australopithecines and early peoples hunted if sporadically. *Homo* hunted from its inception, asserted South African archeologist Glynn Isaac (1937–1985).[391] Shaping inequality and gender roles, elites may have assigned men to hunt and women to collect plants and rear children. Were this scenario correct, men returned to camp with the kill, which nourished them, women, and children.

---

[387] Ibid.

[388] Ibid.; Plavcan, S417.

[389] Clark Spencer Larsen, "Dietary Reconstruction and Nutritional Assessment of Past Peoples: The Bioanthropological Record," in *The Cambridge World History of Food*, vol. 1., ed. Kenneth F. Kiple and Kriemhild Conee Ornelas (Cambridge, UK: Cambridge University Press, 2000), 13-14.

[390] Larsen, *Our Origins*, 189; Megan Mitchell, *Jane Goodall: Primatologist and UN Messenger of Peace* (New York: Cavendish Square, 2017), 101, 103.

[391] Bunn, 191-192.

Adding meat to the diet about 1.5 million years ago, *H. erectus*, began hunting habitually around 800,000 years later.[392] Although critics disagreed, Howell believed the species improved hunting with fire, a "hallmark of humanity," by igniting vegetation in Torralba and Ambrona, Spain 300,000 years ago to drive elephants into mud, where he butchered them and broke the bones for marrow.[393] Howell speculated that these hunters, occupying groups of roughly 30 people, joined neighbors when herds were numerous to increase probability of success.[394] Planning implied hierarchy as someone took charge.[395]

Details aside, Howell rightly linked *H. erectus* and fire. The first human outside Africa, he moved east, south, and north through Asia and west and north through Europe.[396] Although Dubois' Indonesian discovery stirred controversy, its tropical location made sense. Helping the body shed heat, numerous sweat glands and sparse hair adapted the species to warmth.[397] Upright posture minimized skin exposed to the sun's most direct rays. Dark pigmentation, inferred from hair's paucity, reduced skin-cancer risk.

Despite these adaptations, *H. erectus* braved cold as far north as Zhoukoudian, China and Boxgrove, England.[398] These migrations required mastering fire, given the absence of warm clothes, which *H. sapiens* invented about 170,000 years ago.[399] Anthropologists once thought Zhoukoudian caves had hearths, but the putative ash is organic debris unassociated with fire.[400] Evidence instead came from South Africa's Wonderwerk Cave, where *H. erectus* cooked with fire 1 million years ago.[401]

---

[392] Larsen, "Dietary Reconstruction and Nutritional Assessment of Past Peoples," 13-14.

[393] Howell, 83-84; Boaz and Ciochon, 100; Manuel Santonja, Alfredo Perez-Gonzalez, Joaquin Panera, Susana Rubio-Jara, Carmen Sese, Enrique Soto, and Laura Sanchez-Romero, "Ambrona and Torralba Archaeological and Palaeontological Sites, Soria Province," in *Pleistocene and Holocene Hunter-Gatherers in Iberia and the Gibraltar Strait: The Current Archaeological Record*, ed. Robert Sala Ramos (Universidad de Burgos, 2014), accessed April 25, 2022, ‹https://www.researchgate.net/publication/269702592_Ambrona_and_Torralba_archaeological_and_palaeontological_sites_Soria_Province,› 518-519.

[394] Howell, 92-93.

[395] Ardrey, *The Territorial Imperative*, 263.

[396] Larsen, *Our Origins*, 316.

[397] Andrei Tapalaga, "Why Humans Lost Most of Their Body Hair," History of Yesterday, February 3, 2021, accessed April 25, 2022, ‹Why Humans Lost Most of Their Body Hair | by Andrei Tapalaga | History of Yesterday.›

[398] Larsen, *Our Origins*, 310.

[399] Boaz and Ciochon, 103-104, 120; Danielle Torrent, "Lice DNA Study Shows Humans First Wore Clothes 170,000 Years Ago," ScienceDaily, January 7, 2011, accessed April 25, 2022, ‹https://www.sciencedaily.com/releases/2011/01/110106164616.htm.›

[400] Jurmain, Kilgore, Trevathan, and Ciochon, 320-321.

[401] Ibid.; Matt Kaplan, "Million-Year-Old Ash Hints at Origins of Cooking: South African Cave Yields Earliest Evidence for Human Use of Fire," *Nature* (April 2, 2012), accessed

The campsite, fire and cooking intensified inequality.[402] Supplying warmth and food, campsites enticed people to occupy an area longer than their antecedents had. Although *H. erectus* remained nomadic, campsites, having nursing women and children, required protection. All animals with campsite equivalents (nests) defend them with ferocity that increases with time and labor invested in their construction.[403] The need to repel invaders made some nesters specialize as defenders who subordinated themselves to the group by risking their lives fighting enemies. Others prioritized the group by foraging for all.

A nester, *H. erectus* behaved likewise.[404] Whether he, like us, esteemed warriors is unknown, though earlier paragraphs emphasized his hierarchy and specialization. Judging campmates by personal attributes, he selected those most suitable for leadership, hunting, gathering, defense, and childrearing. When a group absorbed new members, elites, quickly and accurately evaluating them, required everyone's acquiescence. Inequality and compulsion thus preceded us.

These abilities implied a "highly intelligent and intensely social" brain, encephalization's gift.[405] Whereas australopithecine brains were 410 to 530 cubic centimeters and early *Homo* averaged 631, *H. erectus* had a mean 900, with the brainiest at 1,250.[406] Ranging from 1,150 to 1,750, modern people average 1,325. Enlargement from *Australopithecus* and early *Homo* to *H. erectus* resulted from the third's greater height and mass than his predecessors. Scaled to body size, *H. erectus'* brain roughly equaled early *Homo* but undershot *H. neanderthalensis* and *H. sapiens*.

H. erectus used his brain to perpetuate and enforce hierarchy. Solidarity within groups heightened internal cohesion, outsiders' denigration, and warfare between tribes.[407] Rather than australopithecines, *H. erectus* was a "bloodthirsty killer" whose brutishness endured so long that he evolved a thick cranium to protect against trauma.[408] Like last chapter's chickens, *H. erectus* sometimes ate his own.[409]

April 25, 2022, <https://www.nature.com/articles/nature.2012.10372.pdf,> 1.

[402] Wilson, *Social Conquest of Earth*, 47-48.

[403] Ibid., 148-157.

[404] Ibid., 41-44.

[405] Ibid., 17, 47-48.

[406] Jurmain, Kilgore, Trevathan, and Ciochon, 293, 311.

[407] Boaz and Ciochon, 170-172.

[408] Ibid.

[409] Larsen, 320.

3.5 Review and Preview

Like chapter 2, this chapter described inequality and violence as evolutionary outcomes that anticipated our behaviors. Dart and Ardrey traced both traits to *Australopithecus*, whose dimorphism diminished in *Homo*, making *H. erectus* no more dimorphic than us. Perpetuating inequality at campsites, which developed from fire's control and cooking, he birthed us. Next chapter overviews *H. erectus'* evolution into *H. heidelbergensis*, who preceded *H. neanderthalensis* in Europe and *H. sapiens* in Africa. The last two heightened inequality through religion and differential burials.

Chapter 4 Paleolithic Burials, Religion, and Inequality

4.1 Abstract

Our lineage's inequality began in australopithecines about 4 million years ago and persisted in *Homo*, with *Homo erectus* ranking one another by personal qualities. Originating in Africa and migrating to Eurasia, he evolved into *Homo heidelbergensis*, the first species to cache the dead, perhaps to deter scavengers. Absent solicitude and ritual, this behavior was not burial, though it transcended many animals' indifference toward the dead. His successors, Neanderthals and *Homo sapiens*, buried the dead in ways that stir our emotions. Neanderthal burials implied spirituality that enlarged inequality. Upper Paleolithic abundance permitted *H. sapiens* elites to amass unprecedented wealth and display it through burial. These opulent inhumations intimated inequality's magnitude.

4.2 Awareness of Death

This chapter searches the biota for behavior toward the dead that illuminates inequality. Showing no awareness of death, many animals do not pause when another perishes but abandon it. Indifference may benefit creatures like mosquitoes and houseflies, which have offspring that die in ghastly numbers, and which might grieve ceaselessly were they introspective. "The real importance of a large number of eggs or seeds is to make up for much destruction at some period of life," British naturalist Charles Darwin (1809–

1882) wrote in expressing death's arithmetic.[410] Nature inured unfortunates to kins' massacre.

Unlike insects, all mammals and birds mourn a companion's demise, averred Dutch American primatologist Frans De Waal (b. 1948).[411] Elephants examine a dead cohabitant, silently touching it with their trunk as though caressing it.[412] They identify its skeleton among many bones, vocalize distress, and emit liquid via facial glands that resembles tears when they sense a friend or kin's imminent death and after its passing. A mother may trail the herd for days after her calf dies. A herd may revisit the place where a companion died for years and may cover the remains with soil or leaves, a burial-like behavior. They extend this treatment to human corpses but to nothing else.

Chimpanzees—which chapter 2 identified, like bonobos, as our closest relative—behave similarly. They vocalize sorrow with humanlike intensity when a companion dies.[413] One mother carried a dead infant 27 days.[414] When a matriarch died, her adopted daughter refused to eat or leave the corpse for days as though holding a wake. Waal speculated that survivors evolved such conduct, which amplified chapter 2's discussion of chimpanzee sociality, to confirm decedents' death.

Regression from chimpanzees to *Australopithecus* may maintain cognitive continuity. Chapter 3 put its brain between 410 and 530 cubic centimeters, overlapping chimpanzees' 285 to 500.[415] Like chimpanzees, australopithecines must have had some awareness of death. Their behavior toward decedents may be glimpsed from *Australopithecus afarensis'* 3.2-million-year-old remains of 13 to 22 individuals in Hadar, Ethiopia.[416]

Chapter 3 introduced the famous *A. afarensis* specimen Lucy, which American anthropologist and "trailblazer" Donald Johanson (b. 1943) discovered

---

[410] Charles Darwin, *The Origin of Species by Means of Natural Selection or the Preservation of Favored Races in the Struggle for Life* (New York: Modern Library, 1993), 93-94.

[411] Frans De Waal, *Mama's Last Hug: Animal Emotions and What They Tell Us about Ourselves* (New York and London: Norton, 2019), 41.

[412] Carl Safina, *Beyond Words: What Animals Think and Feel* (New York: Henry Holt, 2015), 67-69.

[413] Ibid., 70-71.

[414] Waal, 39-41.

[415] Robert Jurmain, Lynn Kilgore, Wenda Trevathan, and Russell L. Ciochon, *Introduction to Physical Anthropology*, 2013-2014 ed. (Belmont, CA: Wadsworth Cengage Learning, 2014), 293.

[416] John Relethford, *The Human Species: An Introduction to Biological Anthropology* (Mountain View, CA: Mayfield Publishing, 1990), 308; Brian Switek, "What Killed the Hominins of AL 333?" *Wired*, January 10, 2011, accessed February 19, 2022, ‹https://www.wired.com/2011/01/what-killed-the-hominins-of-al-333.›

---

in 1974.[417] Unearthing the above fossils the next year, he judged them kin— "the 'first family'"—who died together, possibly in a flash flood.[418] Although the region's geology supported the idea of a flood, its waters were sluggish. Moreover, the fragments were on a hill, suggesting the australopithecines would have had time to leave as water rose.

Perhaps the pre-humans climbed the hill after a flood, became trapped in mud, and could not escape predators like sabertoothed tigers, lions, or leopards. The remains, however, displayed few teeth marks.[419] This result made sense had carnivores slaughtered too many australopithecines to permit all victims' consumption, but too many assumptions bloat this explanation.

Supposing the individuals lived at different times and were unrelated, British biochemist Roger Lewin (b. 1944) thought the remains accumulated over an unknown duration.[420] Beset by rival hypotheses, American paleontologist Brian Switek (b. 1983) designated the fossils among prehistory's "most mysterious."[421]

These scenarios aside, British archaeologist Paul Pettitt proposed that, whatever caused death, survivors, moving decedents to the hill, hid them "in tall grass" from scavengers.[422] Such behavior indicated awareness of death and perhaps desire to prevent corpse desecration. Were the hill a camp or lookout, australopithecines must have prioritized predator deterrence.

4.3 From *Homo erectus* to *Homo heidelbergensis*

Sketching *Australopithecus*' evolution into *Homo*, chapter 3 identified *H. erectus* as the first human outside Africa. Migrants went as far east and south as tropical Indonesia 2 million to 1 million years ago whereas fire's control let others move north to Zhoukoudian near Beijing, China.[423] Other temperate Asian settlements included Majuangou, China and Dmanisi, Georgia. European *H. erectus* penetrated north to Boxgrove, England, and Heidelberg,

---

[417] Lydia Pyne, *Seven Skeletons: The Evolution of the World's Most Famous Human Fossils* (New York: Viking, 2016), 153; C. A. P. Saucier, *The Lucy Man: The Scientist Who Found the Most Famous Fossil Ever!* (Amherst: NY: Prometheus Books, 2011), 110.

[418] Relethford, 308; Switek; Tim D. White, "Afar Triangle," in *History of Physical Anthropology, Vol. 1: A-L*, ed. Frank Spencer (New York & London: Garland Publishing, 1997), 13.

[419] Switek; Paul Pettitt, *The Palaeolithic Origins of Human Burial* (London and New York: Routledge, 2011), 43-44.

[420] Pettitt, 44.

[421] Switek.

[422] Pettitt, 45.

[423] Peter Bellwood, "Archaeology of Southeast Asian Hunters and Gatherers," in *The Cambridge Encyclopedia of Hunters and Gatherers*, ed. Richard B. Lee and Richard Daly (Cambridge, UK: Cambridge University Press, 1999), 284; Clark Spencer Larsen, *Our Origins: Discovering Physical Anthropology* (New York and London: Norton, 2008), 316-317.

Germany. The Heidelberg specimen provoked disagreement over its classification as *H. erectus* or *H. heidelbergensis*.

Occupying three continents, *H. erectus* adapted to localities by evolving
diverse phenotypes.[424] Although variation was large, trends emerged over
time, including encephalization by roughly 30 percent while the cranium
lightened, and teeth shrank.[425] These humans endured in Africa until roughly
300,000 years ago, in Europe until after 98,000 BCE, and in Asia as late as
23,000 BCE.[426]

Retaining *H. erectus* features, later species descended from it, though
anthropologists debate the path toward *H. sapiens*.[427] Although unable to
settle the issue, *Eternal Inequality* notes that perhaps 800,000 years ago Afro-
Eurasians resembled *H. erectus* while having unique traits.[428] These innovations 850,000 to 200,000 years ago anticipated a new species, *H. heidelbergensis* in Africa and Europe. Asian populations defied easy categorization,
though *H. heidelbergensis* may have inhabited China about 230,000 years ago.
It retained *H. erectus*' postcranial robusticity, though the skull lightened and
grew to house a brain about 1,100 cubic centimeters on average whereas *H.
erectus* averaged 900, noted last chapter.[429]

4.4 *Homo heidelbergensis* or *Homo neanderthalensis* and Corpse Disposal at Sima de los Huesos

Although this book emphasizes similarities between nonhumans, especially apes, and humanity, people may have regarded the dead in a new way
at Sima de los Huesos, Spain over 400,000 years ago.[430] The cave yielded over
4,000 bones from at least 32 people. This abundance detailed an anatomy
that combined *H. heidelbergensis* and *H. neanderthalensis* traits. Spanish excavators assigned the fossils to the former whereas British anthropologists Chris
Stringer (b. 1947) and Peter Andrews (b. 1940) designated them Neanderthals.

Below a 43-foot shaft was the past's densest clump of human fossils.[431]
Absent evidence of fire or food scraps and containing only one stone tool,
the cramped space was never a home. The remains accumulated because
people deposited them in the "earliest evidence of deliberate body disposal

---

[424] Jurmain, Kilgore, Trevathan, and Ciochon, 328.

[425] Larsen, 326-327.

[426] Ibid., 309; Jurmain, Kilgore, Trevathan, and Ciochon, 318, 329.

[427] Jurmain, Kilgore, Trevathan, and Ciochon, 337, 340.

[428] Ibid., 332-334, 337, 340.

[429] Ibid., 311, 356.

[430] Ibid., 336; Stringer and Andrews, 152-153.

[431] Stringer and Andrews, 152.

of the dead," stated American anthropologist Robert Jurmain (1948–2021) and coauthors.[432] Resembling burial, these actions lacked evidence of ritual. Survivors may have intended not memorialization but separation of themselves from corpses whose decay would attract scavengers.

Never stationary long enough to face this problem, other primates lack this behavior.[433] Although not burial, corpse disposal, requiring interaction with the dead, seems unusual when contrasted, for example, with mosquitoes. Someone harassed by them might kill several without affecting survivors' pursuit of blood. Their persistence seems sensible; their eggs cannot develop without blood, and they gain nothing by pausing to mourn others' death. Neither alive nor haunting the memory, dead mosquitoes suffer annihilation in a fundamental way.

Yet, as mentioned, elephants and chimpanzees grieve the dead. The mother that carried her expired infant 27 days, for example, displayed solicitude. Whether the above corpse disposal met this threshold of concern is unclear, though it demonstrated awareness of death's finality and required survivors to acknowledge through their actions a corpse's continued existence. Even so, its consignment to space apart from the living may not differ radically from food scraps' placement in middens.

Burial surpasses such behavior. Although eager to demonstrate continuity between other animals and us, Waal noted our uniqueness in burying the dead, often with grave goods, and in envisioning an afterlife.[434] Such thinking transcends empiricism by believing someone's essence endures forever despite the body's decay.

Speculation about beliefs acknowledges the difficulty of understanding what premodern humans thought about death. At a minimum, corpse disposal revealed that people memorialized its humanity. Then and now, burial derives power from silent communication of this truth. Indeed, death and interment evoke emotions beyond language. Burial lies in the realm of action, not platitude.

Revisiting Sima de los Huesos, its remains indicated neither forethought nor special treatment. Every corpse receiving the same attention, survivors did not privilege some over others. But *H. heidelbergensis'* successors, occupying this chapter's remainder, designated few as elites through elaborate burial and most as ordinary through spare interment.

Eternal Inequality heeds American anthropologists Robert Jurmain, Lynn Kilgore, Wenda Trevathan, and Russell Ciochon (b. 1948), Kenyan anthro-

---

[432] Jurmain, Kilgore, Trevathan, and Ciochon, 336.
[433] Waal, 45.
[434] Ibid., 44.

pologist and "expert fossil hunter" Richard Leakey (1944–2022), British archaeologist Chantal Conneller, Austrian American historian Walter Scheidel (b. 1966), Israeli anthropologists Erella Hovers (b. 1956) and Anna Belfer-Cohen (b. 1949), British biochemist Roger Lewin, and British anthropologists Chris Stringer and Peter Andrews in positing that a person's status continued after death such that elites, unlike commoners, received sumptuous burials.[435] That is, grave goods revealed a decedent's status while alive. The masses outnumbering chieftains, simple burials swamped elaborate ones. Stringer, Andrews, Conneller, and Scheidel asserted that lavish child burials implied privilege's inheritance, a feature of premodern and modern societies.[436]

Of course, burial may misrepresent status. Chapter 6's Job (c. 550 BCE) permits a thought experiment. Its protagonist, Asia's richest man, had thousands of livestock, vast pasturage, and many servants.[437] Yet calamity, destroying his property and children, must have compelled the now destitute stockman to bury them simply, understating their status while alive. Such reversals, imaginary or real, do not disqualify burial as status indicator because elites protected their fortunes. When it struck, misfortune harmed paupers more than plutocrats.

4.5 Neanderthals

4.5.1 Classification, Origin, and Dispersal

Since Neanderthals' nineteenth-century discovery, scientists have debated whether they are enough like us to merit inclusion in our species. A species is the group of individuals whose mating produces fertile offspring. This definition includes Neanderthals in *H. sapiens* because both mated to

---

[435] Jurmain, Kilgore, Trevathan, and Ciochon, 385; Chantal Conneller, "Power and Society: Mesolithic Europe," in *The Oxford Handbook of the Archaeology of Death and Burial* (Oxford: Oxford University Press, 2013), 347-348; Erella Hovers and Anna Belfer-Cohen, "Insights into Early Mortuary Practices of *Homo*," in *The Oxford Handbook of the Archaeology of Death and Burial* (Oxford: Oxford University Press, 2013), 632; Richard Leakey and Roger Lewin, *Origins Reconsidered: In Search of What Makes Us Human* (New York: Anchor Books/Doubleday, 1992), 269-270; Walter Scheidel, *The Great Leveler: Violence and the History of Inequality from the Stone Age to the Twenty-First Century* (Princeton, NJ and Oxford: Princeton University Press, 2017), 40; Chris Stringer and Peter Andrews, *The Complete World of Human Evolution* (London: Thames & Hudson, 2005), 214-215; Roger Lewin, "The Old Man of Olduvai Gorge: Irrepressible Louis Leakey, Patriarch of the Fossil-Hunting Family, Championed the Search for Human Origins in Africa, Attracting Criticism and Praise," *Smithsonian Magazine*, October 2002, accessed September 10, 2022, ‹The Old Man of Olduvai Gorge | History| Smithsonian Magazine.›

[436] Stringer and Andrews, 214-215; Scheidel, 40; Conneller, 347-348.

[437] Job 1:3 (New American Bible).

yield children that could reproduce upon maturation. Neanderthals are thus a subspecies of us: *H. sapiens neanderthalensis*. We, the lone extant human, are *H. sapiens sapiens*. Yet the Smithsonian Institution rejects this categorization, making Neanderthals a separate species: *H. neanderthalensis*.[438]

Unable to settle the issue, this book concludes that Neanderthals and we mated because we retain their genes. If, from the common ancestor of Neanderthals and us, these genes were distributed evenly throughout current populations, scientists would not need to infer sex between the two.[439] Yet sub-Saharan peoples have few or no such genes because Neanderthals, evolving in Eurasia rather than Africa, never encountered them. Neanderthal genes, however, did enter North Africa and Egypt. Although Neanderthals occupied neither region, both, long exchanging people and commodities throughout the Mediterranean, acquired Neanderthal genes from southern Europe and the Levant. Moderns with Eurasian lineage have Neanderthal genes because Neanderthals, settling the region, mated with them. Although Neanderthals belonged to our species, this book designates them *H. neanderthalensis* and us *H. sapiens* for simplicity and in deference to the Smithsonian Institution.

Originating around 200,000 years ago in East Africa, *H. sapiens* may have bred with Neanderthals in Asia before 98,000 BCE.[440] This mating, "effectively the norm," may have peaked around 73,000 to 53,000 BCE.[441] Moderns with Asian lineage—notably Asian mainlanders, Indonesians, Papuans, aborigines, and Amerindians—have up to one fifth of genes from Neanderthals. Besides sub-Saharans, Europeans, at or under 2 percent, have the least.

The primary coupling was a Neanderthal man and a *H. sapiens* woman.[442] Without evidence, some scientists, pitting a muscular man against a weak woman, suspected rape. To be sure, chimpanzee males sometimes rape females, though not outsiders. Bonobos resemble us in copulating for reasons besides reproduction or violence, chapter 2 indicated. Neanderthals and *H. sapiens* probably acted likewise.

Sima de los Huesos may have the earliest Neanderthal fossils. Their transitional status implies Neanderthal evolution from *H. heidelbergensis* before

---

[438] Jurmain, Kilgore, Trevathan, and Ciochon, 331.
[439] Rebecca Wragg Sykes, *Kindred: Neanderthal Life, Love, Death and Art* (London: Bloomsbury Sigma, 2020), 323.
[440] Ibid., 323-325.
[441] Ibid., 325.
[442] Ibid., 328.

400,000 years ago.[443] From Europe, they colonized western Asia around 150,000 years ago and central Asia before 98,000 BCE.[444]

4.5.2 Anatomy, Religion, and Burial

Western Asia's Neanderthals were more gracile than Europe's, though robustness defined a people whose fossils first emerged in Europe.[445] A thick physique conserved heat in a cold climate.[446] Large muscles moving stout bones, American anthropologist Francis Clark Howell (1925–2007) imagined Neanderthals "a formidable opponent in a college wrestling tournament."[447] Stringer and Andrews supposed them wrestlers and marathoners, though their anatomy favored neither speed nor endurance.[448]

Against their image as idiots, Neanderthals' brain averaged 1,520 cubic centimeters whereas ours averaged 1,325, noted in the previous chapter.[449] A large body and cold climate, favoring braininess' efficiency at low temperature, encephalized them. The skull that housed this brain differed from ours in robusticity and shape. In profile, the head, having little forehead, spanned horizontal space rather than took our globular form.[450] Above the eyes, a brow ridge exceeded ours. Projecting forward, the face had a large, long nose. The teeth were bigger than ours, and Neanderthals lacked a chin.

Braininess may have evoked "the first stirrings of a social and religious sense."[451] Diagraming six 40,000-year-old burials at La Ferrassie, France's "prehistoric cemetery," Howell noted their east-west orientation in alignment with the sun's apparent path across the sky.[452] Neanderthals may have thought the sun—luminous, above them, and warmth's provider—the alpha

[443] Jurmain, Kilgore, Trevathan, and Ciochon, 385; Johannes Kraus, Ludovic Orlando, David Serre, Bence Viola, Kay Prufer, Michael P. Richards, Jean-Jacques Hublin, Catherine Haani, Anatoly P. Derevianko, and Svante Paabo, "Neanderthals in Central Asia and Siberia," *Nature* 449 (September 30, 2007): 902-904, accessed April 28, 2022, ⟨https://www.nature.com/articles/nature06193?proof=t%253B.⟩

[444] Jurmain, Kilgore, Trevathan, and Ciochon, 385; Kseniya A. Kolobova, Richard G. Roberts, Victor P. Chabai, Zenobia Jacobs, Maciej T. Krajcarz, Alena V. Shalagina, Andrey I. Krivoshapkin, Bo Li, Thorsten Uthmeier, Sergey V. Markin, Mike V. Morley, Kieran O'Gorman, Natalia A. Rudaya, Sahra Talamo, Bence Viola, and Anatoly P. Derevianko, "Archaeological Evidence for Two Separate Dispersals of Neanderthals into Southern Siberia," *Proceedings of the National Academy of Sciences* 117, no. 6 (January 27, 2020): 2879-2885, accessed April 28, 2022, ⟨https://www.pnas.org/content/117/6/2879.⟩

[445] Jurmain, Kilgore, Trevathan, and Ciochon, 347.

[446] Wragg Sykes, 49; Larsen, 348-349.

[447] F. Clark Howell, *Early Man*, rev. ed. (New York: Time-Life Books, 1968), 126.

[448] Stringer and Andrews, 157; Wragg Sykes, 65.

[449] Larsen, 342.

[450] Wragg Sykes, 49.

[451] Howell, 130.

[452] Ibid., 128, 130.

object and life's source because the body is warm when alive and cool when dead and because of vegetation's autumn death and spring regeneration. Such thinking may have spiritualized Neanderthals, who may have imagined an afterlife like earthly existence.

If associating the sun with hierarchy, Neanderthals may have anticipated Platonism. Depicting humanity imprisoned in a dim cave, Greek philosopher Plato (c. 428–c. 348 BCE) described a man's struggle up and out into light.[453] This enlightenment gave him truth everyone else lacked. Truth's source, the sun, furnishing certainty, crowned Plato's epistemology.

The sun was important to chapter 7's Egypt, which Plato visited according to Roman statesman Marcus Cicero (106–43 BCE).[454] Power emanated from sun god Ra or Re, whose son was the god Horus.[455] Representing Horus, pharaoh held authority through connection to Ra. The upshot is that Neanderthals, like Plato and the Egyptians, may have concretized and enlarged hierarchy by topping it with the sun.

This chapter infers inequality from Neanderthals' 30 to 40 nearly complete skeletons out of 200 to 300 individuals.[456] Relative intactness implied burial of these few as protection against scavengers and the rest's abandonment. The numbers, suggesting interment of 10 to 20 percent of persons, identified their high status. Burial's restriction to them approximated wealth distribution over time. For example, the richest 10 percent of Europeans held 90 percent of assets until roughly 1900 CE.[457]

Affirming "human dignity," evoking spirituality, and ranking decedents, the oldest true burials, of some six Neanderthals and 30 *H. sapiens*, were in Israel 130,000 to 100,000 years ago, averred Israeli archaeologist Avraham Ronen (1935–2018).[458] They included two with large animal bones, though he judged only one, a *H. sapiens* adolescent grasping deer antlers, deliberate. Size signifying the decedent's eminence, supposed Ronen, only one (2.8 percent) of the roughly 36 decedents was elite. Three others had grave goods like flint, stones, and pierced snail shells as beads. One stone, the lone

[453] Plato, *Republic*, in *The Great Dialogues of Plato*, trans. W. H. D. Rouse (New York and Scarborough, ON: New American Library, 1956), 312-315.

[454] Whitney M. Davis, "Plato on Egyptian Art," *The Journal of Egyptian Archaeology* 65, no. 1 (August 1979): 122; Robert N. Bellah, *Religion in Human Evolution: From the Paleolithic to the Axial Age* (Cambridge, MA and London: Belknap Press of Harvard University Press, 2011), 227.

[455] Chris Gosden, *Magic: A History from Alchemy to Witchcraft, from the Ice Age to the Present* (New York: Farrar, Straus and Giroux, 2020), 93.

[456] Wragg Sykes, 48.

[457] David Christian, *Origin Story: A Big History of Everything* (London: Allen Lane, 2018), 234.

[458] Avraham Ronen, "The Oldest Burials and Their Significance," in *African Genesis: Perspectives on Hominin Evolution*, ed. Sally C. Reynolds and Andrew Gallagher (Cambridge, UK: Cambridge University Press, 2012), 554, 558, 560.

with engravings that implied language, may also have signaled eminence, raising the percentage to 5.6.[459] The rest, unadorned in death, may have been commoners.

Scientists debate burials' details. For instance, Shanidar, Iraq's at least 11 decedents, most intact before excavation, ignited controversy.[460] Finding pollen, American archaeologist Ralph Solecki (1917–2019) surmised that survivors adorned one corpse with flowers about 58,000 BCE.[461] Labeling the decedent a shaman or chief, Leakey and Lewin wrote that "his burial befitted an important member of the group."[462] Reinforcing the notion of hierarchy, American biologist Edward Wilson (b. 1929) judged shamans "special people" with enormous prestige.[463] Rejecting elite interment, opinion now credits wind or another natural process with depositing pollen.[464]

Disagreement aside, Neanderthal burials evinced deep emotions.[465] For example, Mezmaiskaya cave in Russia's Adygea Republic held the remains of a newborn no more than two weeks old at death about 68,000 BCE. Months too young to be able to roll over on its own, survivors must have placed it on its right side in a flexed position as though asleep. No pre-Neanderthal exhibited such tenderness toward the dead.

4.6 *Homo sapiens*

4.6.1 *Origin* and *Dispersal*

Around 68,000 BCE, our genus included at least five species, though extinction would claim all but us.[466] Likely evolving from *H. heidelbergensis* in East Africa, we entered Asia before 38,000 BCE.[467] Another opinion avers that East Asian *H. sapiens* evolved from *H. erectus* during the last 200,000 years. During the ice age, land connected mainland Asia with Indonesia, from where *H. sapiens* colonized New Guinea and Australia, possibly by bamboo raft.[468] *H.*

---

[459] Ibid., 561.

[460] Wragg Sykes, 296.

[461] Leakey and Lewin, 269-270; Richard E. Leakey, *The Making of Mankind* (New York: E. P. Dutton, 1981), 153.

[462] Leakey and Lewin, 269-270.

[463] Edward O. Wilson, *On Human Nature* (Cambridge, MA and London: Harvard University Press, 2004), 180-181.

[464] Wragg Sykes, 296.

[465] Ibid., 290-291.

[466] David Reich, *Who We Are and How We Got Here: Ancient DNA and the New Science of the Human Past* (New York: Pantheon Books, 2018), 64.

[467] Jurmain, Kilgore, Trevathan, and Ciochon, 364, 373.

[468] Ibid., 375.

sapiens entered Europe around 38,000 BCE. Chapters 11 and 14 discuss the western hemisphere's settlement.

4.6.2 Upper Paleolithic Period

4.6.2.1 Chronology, Economy, and Culture

Prehistory unfolded during the Paleolithic period, which began with stone tool manufacture and had three parts: Lower (c. 3.4 million years ago–c. 250,000 years ago), Middle (c. 250,000 years ago–c. 38,000 BCE), and Upper (c. 38,000 BCE–c. 8000 BCE).[469] Prosperity undergirded Upper Paleolithic technology, economy, and art. Eurasia's cold, aridity, and wind around 38,000 BCE favored grasses over trees.[470] Preserving florae, warmth about 28,000 BCE benefited us given our tropical origin.[471] We hunted reindeer, mammoth, bison, horse, antelope, fox, wolf, cave lion, and bear from Spain in the west to Russia in the east.[472] Besides hunting mammals, we fished and caught birds more than in the past. This "time of relative abundance" peaked European and African Paleolithic populations.[473]

Plenitude intensified specialization as some people became artists.[474] Art's prevalence then is difficult to gauge. Most rock shelter paintings vanished over time, leaving those deep inside caves. Perhaps for this reason, art at Altamira and El Castillo, Spain and Lascaux and Grotte Chauvet, France endures as "the culmination of 2 million years of cultural development."[475] The images climaxed prehistory, believed American playwright and science writer Robert Ardrey (1908–1980).[476] American archaeologist Alexander Marshack (1918–2004) compared them with Italian sculptor and painter Michelangelo Buonarroti (1475–1564) and Austrian composer Wolfgang Amadeus Mozart's (1756–1791) accomplishments.[477] Howell described them as "so powerfully conceived and executed as to rank among mankind's great artistic achievements."[478] Stringer and Andrews judged them part of

---

[469] Ibid., 380; "Oldest Evidence of Human Stone Tool Use and Meat Eating Found," Max-Planck-Gesellschaft, August 12, 2010, accessed April 25, 2022, ‹https://www.mpg. de/research/oldest-evidence-human-stone-tool-use.›

[470] R. Dale Guthrie, *The Nature of Paleolithic Art* (Chicago and London: University of Chicago Press, 2005), 18.

[471] Jurmain, Kilgore, Trevathan, and Ciochon, 380-381.

[472] Ibid., 381; Scheidel, 31.

[473] Jurmain, Kilgore, Trevathan, and Ciochon, 381.

[474] Howell, 158-159.

[475] Jurmain, Kilgore, Trevathan, and Ciochon, 382-383, 385.

[476] Robert Ardrey, *The Hunting Hypothesis: A Personal Conclusion Concerning the Evolutionary Nature of Man* (New York: Atheneum, 1976), 182.

[477] Leakey, 176-177.

[478] Howell, 155.

a "'creative explosion'...seen by many archaeologists as marking the definite arrival of fully modern minds."[479]

Besides paintings, people crafted statuettes, often of women.[480] Some were realistic whereas others enlarged breasts, buttocks, and belly, perhaps to symbolize fertility. These evocations of "lovely lipids" and of "erotic love via images focused on sexually charged features of (mostly) female anatomy" and both sexes' genitals trod "the trail of lust."[481] Eight bone flutes at Blaubeuren, Germany's Geissenklosterle cave, implied musicality.[482]

Besides art and music, Upper Paleolithic people invented techniques for making long flake tools, fashioned the first rope and baskets, and may have invented the bow and arrow.[483] Ceramic animal figurines predated pottery by over 15,000 years. Jewelry ornamented the body in life and death. The atlatl increased the range of spears and with the barbed harpoon targeted fish, especially salmon. These attainments evinced "a distinct leap in manipulative and organizational abilities."[484]

4.6.2.2 Death and Burial

Anthropologists Erella Hovers and Anna Belfer-Cohen detected no opulent burials before roughly 48,000 BCE.[485] Their judgment depended partly on opulence's definition, though this chapter pinpoints resources' availability as the primary factor. As noted, the climate warmed around 28,000 BCE. Likely yielding more kills than in colder millennia, hunting gave elites wealth for display in burial. This circumstance explains grand burials' prevalence circa 27,000 to 19,000 BCE.[486] While the next chapter describes how cooling around 18,000 BCE influenced subsistence, this paragraph emphasizes that warmth about 28,000 to 18,000 BCE enriched elites, who had less to splurge on burial outside these millennia.

As in other times and places, Upper Paleolithic elites monopolized resources, which made their graves far grander than commoners'.[487] Sungir, some 120 miles east of Moscow, Russia, housed the most extravagant Paleolithic burials dated to about 32,000 to 22,000 BCE, anticipated monumental tombs from the pharaohs to today, and supplied the "most famous example of unearned status and inequality."[488] Two decedents, a nine- or ten-year-old

---

[479] Stringer and Andrews, 213.
[480] Howell, 150-151; Jurmain, Kilgore, Trevathan, and Ciochon, 382.
[481] Guthrie, 303-304.
[482] Jurmain, Kilgore, Trevathan, and Ciochon, 382.
[483] Ibid., 380-383; Stringer and Andrews, 212-213.
[484] Leakey, 159.
[485] Hovers and Belfer-Cohen, 632.
[486] Pettitt, 142.
[487] Jurmain, Kilgore, Trevathan, and Ciochon, 381; Scheidel, 31.
[488] Jurmain, Kilgore, Trevathan, and Ciochon, 384; Scheidel, 31.

girl and a 12- or 13-year-old boy, displayed "a wide range of prestige items."[489] Stringer and Andrews ranked them "the offspring of an important individual—perhaps a chief."[490] Buried head to head in one grave, their bodies paralleled two spears, each a straightened mammoth tusk, one longer than six feet.[491] The pit held over 10,000 mammoth ivory beads, likely sewn onto their garments, work American zoologist Russell Dale Guthrie (b. 1936) deemed "women's art."[492] Roughly 300 fox canine teeth had holes to permit their assembly into headbands and belts. Deer antlers were likewise pierced, probably for the same purpose. Also present were ivory animal carvings, pins, and pendants.

Besides these two, a man around age 40 was buried with some 3,000 beads, likely sewn onto his fur coat and hat.[493] With him were about 20 pendants and 25 ivory rings. He wore ivory armbands. Fox canines may have been strung together in a necklace.

The three rested on hematite (ferric oxide).[494] Iron's oxidation reddened it, bestowing the name red ochre. Numerous burials had the pigment, suggesting widespread ritual. Applied atop a grave, it may have warned against digging there.[495] Survivors often applied it to decedents' head and pelvis. These burials overlapping Upper Paleolithic art, aesthetics may have determined use. Applied to the body, for example, it simulated animation by darkening death's pallor.

These burials required time and effort. At 15 to 45 minutes to carve one bead, the total would have required a person to devote 1.6 to 4.7 years of 40-hour weeks to Sungir's trio.[496] Many in the tribe must have joined this work to permit timely inhumation. The juvenile grave's 300 canines came from at least 75 foxes. Teeth broken during extraction would have raised the number. Worn in life, these items would not have been fashioned in death, saving time and exertion. But the beads, sized to the individual, led Scheidel to suppose manufacture for interment.

---

[489] Scheidel, 31.
[490] Stringer and Andrews, 214-215.
[491] Jurmain, Kilgore, Trevathan, and Ciochon, 384.
[492] Guthrie, 205.
[493] Ibid.; Scheidel, 31; Alun Harvey, "Ancient Burial Practices at Sunghir in Russia," Hunebed Nieuwscafe, February 2019, accessed February 19, 2022, ‹https://www.hunebednieuws-cafe.nl/2019/02/ancient-burial-practices-at-sunghir-in-russia/?cn-reloaded=1.›
[494] Jurmain, Kilgore, Trevathan, and Ciochon, 384.
[495] "Why Is Ochre Found in Some Graves?" Nationalmuseet, accessed February 19, 2022, ‹https://en.natmus.dk/historical-knowledge/denmark/prehistoric-period-until-1050-ad/the-mesolithic-period/a-woman-and-a-child-from-goengehusvej/why-is-ochre-found-in-some-graves.›
[496] Scheidel, 31.

Unlike the three elites, a femur on the ground implied an unburied corpse disarticulated by scavengers.[497] Yet it lacked carnivore teeth marks and may have been unburied if winter froze the soil.[498] Such behavior, whereby some received lavish attention and others nothing, implied vast inequality.

Believing elites totaled all or almost all Upper Paleolithic inhumations, favoritism that resembled Egypt, where only the wealthy afforded mummification, Canadian archaeologist Julien Riel-Salvatore and American anthropologist Claudine Gravel-Miguel judged Sungir "atypical."[499] Jurmain and coauthors described it "a somewhat extraordinary exception."[500] Scheidel thought it "without parallel in the Paleolithic record."[501] Rarity confirms that elites, monopolizing wealth, restricted conspicuousness to few. Were Sungir burials common, this book would acknowledge that humans distributed wealth widely.

The Arene Candide cave of Liguria, Italy, housed another rich burial. Arrangement and adornment of the roughly 28,000-year-old remains of a teenager, the "Young Prince of the Arene Candide," implied prestige.[502] His sturdy bones suggested a strong, active youth.[503] His right hand held a 9-inch blade made of French flint, implying that this hunter, who might have killed prey by hurling spears at them, was right-handed. Craftsmanship and the flint's distant source intimated elite status. Like Sungir's dead, he rested on hematite. Survivors covered him with it. Hundreds of shells and deer canines adorned his cap. Near his knees were four pierced deer antlers, which

---

[497] Lea Surugue, "Why this Paleolithic Burial Site Is So Strange (and So Important)," *Sapiens Anthropology Magazine*, February 22, 2018, accessed February 19, 2022, ‹https://www.sapiens.org/archaeology/paleolithic-burial-sunghir.›

[498] Erik Trinkaus and Alexandra P. Buzhilova, "Diversity and Differential Disposal of the Dead at Sunghir," *Antiquity* 92, no. 361 (February 9, 2018): 7-21, accessed April 28, 2022, ‹https://www.cambridge.org/core/journals/antiquity/article/diversity-and-differential-disposal-of-the-dead-at-sunghir/B7672FB594E94A505A35E10C869F3808.›

[499] Julien Riel-Salvatore and Claudine Gravel-Miguel, "Upper Paleolithic Mortuary Practices in Eurasia," in *The Oxford Handbook of the Archaeology of Death and Burial* (Oxford: Oxford University Press, 2013), 304, 333; Tim Sandle, "Pharaohs and Mummies: Diseases of Ancient Egypt and Modern Approaches," *Journal of Infectious Diseases and Preventive Remedies* 1, no. 4 (November 2013), accessed April 28, 2022, ‹https://www.researchgate.net/publication/258842087_Pharaohs_and_Mummies_Diseases_of_Ancient_Egypt_and_Modern_Approaches.›

[500] Jurmain, Kilgore, Trevathan, and Ciochon, 384.

[501] Scheidel, 32.

[502] Ibid.; "The Young Prince of the Arene Candide," *Museo Diffuso del Finale*, 2019, accessed July 13, 2022, ‹https://www.mudifinale.com/en/il-giovane-principe.›

[503] "The Prince of Arene Candide," Ligurian Archaeological Museum, accessed February 19, 2022, ‹https://www.museidigenova.it/en/prince-arene-candide;› Scheidel, 32; P. B. Pettitt, M. Richards, R. Maggi, and V. Formicola, "The Gravettian Burial Known as the Prince ("Il Principe"): New Evidence for His Age and Diet," *Antiquity* 77, no. 295 (March 2003): 15, accessed April 28, 2022, ‹https://dro.dur.ac.uk/5846/1.›

archaeologist Paul Pettitt and coauthors made symbols of power as *batons de commandement*, and two mammoth ivory pendants.[504]

Besides fish and mollusks, the teen "ate a lot of meat," an agrarian elite's diet, later chapters note.[505] In this context, however, interpretation is difficult. Were meat plentiful, his diet would not have differentiated him from others. But if scarce, it would have signaled privilege. About one fifth to one quarter fish and shellfish, his diet, approximating Eurasian contemporaries, was unexceptional in this respect.[506]

A 6,500-year-old burial in Bihor, Romania, housed an "extremely rich" woman's skeleton and grave goods including a copper bracelet, some 800 pearls, and over 200 grams of gold.[507] Fashioned into strands, the metal likely adorned her hair in life and death. One gram being worth $55.17 on September 10, 2022, the grave held over $11,034 of gold.[508] By comparison, Pharaoh Tutankhamen's (r. 1334–1325 BCE) tomb had around 110 kilograms of it worth over $6 million, 550 times hers. Chapter 16's French queen Marie Antoinette (1755–1793) had a diamond and pearl pendant worth $36 million at auction.[509] Although no grave item, its use as jewelry paralleled the Romanian woman's gold. The trend from her through Tutankhamen to Marie Antoinette implies growth in elite wealth and inequality over time.

4.7 Review and Preview

Neanderthals and *H. sapiens* exhibited inequality through religion and burial. Next chapter moves from Paleolithic to Neolithic, when Southwest Asians invented agriculture and pastoralism, which, replacing hunting and gathering over millennia, gave elites new opportunities for wealth. Early farming, herding, land maldistribution, elite control of economy, religion,

---

[504] Pettitt, Richards, Maggi, and Formicola, 15.

[505] "The Prince of Arene Candide."

[506] Pettitt, Richards, Maggi, and Formicola, 17.

[507] Bethany Dawson, "Trove of Ancient Gold Rings Buried with 'Extremely Rich' Woman Who Lived 6,500 Years Ago Discovered in Romania," *Business Insider*, August 28, 2022, accessed September 10, 2022, ‹Trove of ancient gold rings buried with 'extremely rich' woman who lived 6,500 years ago discovered in Romania (yahoo.com);› Eugenia Pasca, "Bihor: Golden Treasure, with 169 Rings, Unique in Europe—Discovered by MTC Archaeologists," Agerpres, August 11, 2022, accessed September 10, 2022, ‹Bihor: Golden treasure, with 169 rings, unique in Europe - discovered by archaeologists MTC | AGERPRES.›

[508] "Gold Price in US Today," GoldPriceZ, September 10, 2022, accessed September 10, 2022, ‹Gold Price in USA - Today Gold Rate per Gram in US Dollars ($) (goldpricez.com).›

[509] Rachel Burrow, "A Look at Marie-Antoinette's Breathtaking Jewelry Collection: The Controversial Queen of France Spared No Expense When It Came to Her Trousseau," *Veranda*, June 16, 2020, accessed September 10, 2022, ‹Marie-Antionette's Prized Jewelry Collection (veranda.com).›

and government, paupers' destitution and impotence, taxation, tenancy, peonage, corvée, conscription, and slavery intensified inequality.

CHAPTER 5 SOUTHWEST ASIAN INEQUALITY

5.1 Abstract

Southwest Asian farming and herding began about 9500 BCE as climate changed and population rose. American anthropologist Clark Spencer Larsen (b. 1952) compared their advent to bipedalism and speech's evolution in importance.[510] American Australian historian David Christian (b. 1946) ranked these Neolithic milestones with photosynthesis and multicellularity.[511] Despite their novelty and significance, agriculture and pastoralism perpetuated rather than invented inequality, which intensified as elites monopolized land and subjugated commoners, who fled to the hinterland to escape taxes, rent, usury, corvée, conscription, and servitude. Contagion killed underfed, overworked, overcrowded urbanites while class antagonism grew.

5.2 Foraging's End

Chapters 3 and 4 overviewed foragers, scavengers, hunters, and fishers' evolution and lifeways. Like its predecessors, *Homo sapiens* obtained rather than produced food during the entire Paleolithic period. Current plenitude and convenience make this approach seem inadequate. American archaeologist Robert Braidwood (1907–2003), pioneering "the multidisciplinary

---

[510] Clark Spencer Larsen, *Our Origins: Discovering Physical Anthropology* (New York and London: Norton, 2008), 382.

[511] David Christian, *Origin Story: A Big History of Everything* (London: Allen Lane, 2018), 188.

archaeology of today," deemed hunting and gathering "a savage's existence, and a very tough one."[512]

Canadian anthropologist Richard Lee (b. 1937) demonstrated, however, that Namibia and Angola's San had light workloads and much leisure.[513] This revelation upended the narrative such that farmers now led "the tough life" at an occupation "far more onerous than hunting and gathering."[514]

But this belief does not nullify Braidwood. First, foraging's ease, even if true in some situations, may not mirror extinct people's lives. Second, past hunter-gatherers occupied diverse ecosystems. Regular, abundant resources required less exertion to collect than sparse ones. Third, climate change, degrading even fecund areas, weakened generalizations about foraging or farming over time and space.

As mentioned, climate, which varied more in the Paleolithic than in the Neolithic, may have pushed hunter-gatherers toward farming and herding.[515] Around 18,000 BCE, abundance shrank as Eurasia cooled to produce the glacial maximum.[516] Large prey less numerous, humans, targeting small mammals, birds, fish, and shellfish, expended more time and effort per calorie gained.

Gathering, hunting, and fishing sustained populations only 1/100th as dense as later agrarian communities.[517] Hunter-gatherers reproduced slowly because food was scarcer than in agriculture and pastoralism, because they seldom surpassed age 20, because they curbed their numbers through abortion, infanticide, and geronticide, because they delayed weaning to inhibit ovulation, and because half of all newborns perished before puberty.[518] Deaths spiked at weaning, when infants starved without mother's milk. Mothers postponed this event, again, by prolonging nursing. Between 28,000 and 8000 BCE, world population grew under 0.01 percent annually, doubling the

---

[512] Larsen, 401; Mehmet Ozdogan, "Robert Braidwood," in *The Great Archaeologists*, ed. Brian Fagan (London: Thames & Hudson, 2014), 229.

[513] Larsen, 401.

[514] Christian, *Origin Story*, 198; Kevin M. McGeough, "The Origins of Agriculture," in *World History Encyclopedia, Vol. 1: An Introduction to World History*, ed. Carolyn Neel and Alfred J. Andrea (Santa Barbara, CA: ABC-CLIO, 2011), 215; James C. Scott, *Against the Grain: A Deep History of the Earliest States* (New Haven, CT and London: Yale University Press, 2017), 20.

[515] Larsen, 382, 385; Siobhan M. Mattison, Eric A. Smith, Mary K. Shenk, and Ethan E. Cochrane, "The Evolution of Inequality," *Evolutionary Anthropology Issues, News and Reviews* 25, no. 4 (July 2016): 184.

[516] David Christian, "Acceleration: The Agrarian Era," in *Berkshire Encyclopedia of World History*, vol. 1, ed. William H. McNeill, Jerry H. Bentley, David Christian, David Levinson, J. R. McNeill, Heidi Roupp, and Judith P. Zinsser (Great Barrington, MA: Berkshire Publishing Group, 2005), TWF18-19; Larsen, 364-365.

[517] Christian, *Origin Story*, 203.

[518] Ibid., 312; Christian, "Acceleration: The Agrarian Era," TWF19; Edward S. Deevey Jr., "The Human Population," *Scientific American* 203, no. 3 (September 1, 1960), 202.

---

total every 8,000 to 9,000 years.[519] Growth must have been uneven, decelerating near the glacial maximum.

5.3 Southwest Asia, Agriculture, Pastoralism, and Diets

Southwest Asian hunter-gatherers ate grass seeds before 20,500 BCE.[520] Twenty-thousand-year-old millstones imply their consumption's enlargement. Rainfall, greater than today, supported vegetation, including wheat, rye, and barley's precursors.[521] The twelfth millennium BCE Younger Dryas, cooling and drying the climate, decreased plants.[522]

Southwest Asians termed Natufians, perhaps observing the germination of uneaten seeds, compensated for dearth around 9500 BCE by planting them in the Levant's Jordan Valley to grow food rather than simply relying on nature.[523] Deepening the association between plants and people, this behavior made barley, rye, and wheat's domesticators participants in floral evolution. Of the three, wheat now dominates, though this supremacy was untrue before modernity.[524] Better tolerating cold, salinity, drought, and excessive moisture, barley and rye were safer options. Moreover, beer

---

[519] David Christian, "Beginnings: The Era of Foragers," in *Berkshire Encyclopedia of World History*, vol. 1, ed. William H. McNeill, Jerry H. Bentley, David Christian, *et al.* (Great Barrington, MA: Berkshire Publishing Group, 2005), TWF10.

[520] William Rubel, *Bread: A Global History* (London: Reaktion Books, 2011), 11-12.

[521] Naomi F. Miller and Wilma Wetterstrom, "The Beginnings of Agriculture: The Ancient Near East and North Africa," in *The Cambridge World History of Food*, vol. 2, ed. Kenneth F. Kiple and Kriemhild Conee Ornelas (Cambridge, UK: Cambridge University Press, 2000), 1123-1124; Joy McCorriston, "Wheat," in *The Cambridge World History of Food*, vol. 1, ed. Kenneth F. Kiple and Kriemhild Conee Ornelas (Cambridge, UK: Cambridge University Press, 2000), 162.

[522] Harald Haarmann, "Foraging to Farming—The Neolithic Revolution," in *World History Encyclopedia, Vol. 2, Era 1: Beginnings of Human Society*, ed. Alfred J. Andrea, Carolyn Neel, and Mark Aldenderfer (Santa Barbara, CA: ABC-CLIO, 2011), 131; David R. Harris, "Origins and Spread of Agriculture," in *The Cultural History of Plants*, ed. Ghillean Prance and Mark Nesbitt (New York and London: Routledge, 2005), 15.

[523] Jared Diamond, *The Third Chimpanzee for Young People: On the Evolution and Future of the Human Animal* (New York and Oakland, CA: Seven Stories Press, 2014), 169; Larsen, 386-387; Don Nardo, *The Greenhaven Encyclopedia of Ancient Mesopotamia* (Detroit: Greenhaven Press, 2007), 121.

[524] Mark Nesbitt, "Grains," in *The Cultural History of Plants*, ed. Ghillean Prance and Mark Nesbitt (New York and London: Routledge, 2005), 49.

---

making, spurring farming, guaranteed barley acres.[525] Millet and rice were later additions.[526]

Other crops included legumes pea, chickpea, lentil, and fava bean, vegetables garlic, onion, leek, turnip, radish, beet, cabbage, carrot, mustard, and lettuce, and fruits olive, cucumber, date, fig, pear, peach, apple, apricot, quince, cherry, plum, grape, and pomegranate.[527] Those unable to afford meat obtained all essential amino acids by combining legumes with barley, rye, or wheat. This plant protein complex abetted Neolithic inequality whereby well-fed elites oppressed laborers whose poverty made them vegetarians.[528] Besides crops, Southwest Asians domesticated or adopted sheep, goats, cattle, pigs, ducks, geese, and chickens between the sixth and first millennia BCE.[529]

Elites advertised eminence by eating a richer, more varied diet than commoners. More than any other food, meat differentiated plutocrats from paupers, who subsisted on porridge or gruel that, depending on the harvest, featured peas or another legume and barley. Wheat, especially as bread, was too expensive for them. Commoners kept a garden for vegetables. Among fruits, dates gave people unable to afford honey sweetness.[530] Southwest Asia lacked sugar before the seventh century CE.[531]

"In strongly hierarchical and status-conscious societies, rich men use food as one of a number of ways of signaling their wealth and winning or maintaining prestige in the sight of the world. Food in pre-industrial society was the more effective as a marker of economic and social distinction for the fact that it consumed the greater proportion (perhaps 66–75%) of family income," wrote British classicist Peter Garnsey (b. 1938).[532]

---

[525] Phillip A. Cantrell II, "Beer and Ale," in *The Cambridge World History of Food*, vol. 1, ed. Kenneth F. Kiple and Kriemhild Conee Ornelas (Cambridge, UK: Cambridge University Press, 2000), 619-620; Joy McCorriston, "Barley," in *The Cambridge World History of Food*, vol. 1, ed. Kenneth F. Kiple and Kriemhild Conee Ornelas (Cambridge, UK: Cambridge University Press, 2000), 81-82.

[526] Karen Rhea Nemet-Nejat, *Daily Life in Ancient Mesopotamia* (Westport, CT and London: Greenwood Press, 1998), 247; Delphine Roger, "The Middle East and South Asia," in *The Cambridge World History of Food*, vol. 2, ed. Kenneth F. Kiple and Kriemhild Conee Ornelas (Cambridge, UK: Cambridge University Press, 2000), 1142.

[527] Nemet-Nejat, 247, 255; Nardo, 121; Stephen Bertman, *Handbook to Life in Ancient Mesopotamia* (New York: Facts on File, 2003), 245.

[528] James C. Whorton, "Vegetarianism," in *The Cambridge World History of Food*, vol. 2, ed. Kenneth F. Kiple and Kriemhild Conee Ornelas (Cambridge, UK: Cambridge University Press, 2000), 1553.

[529] Nemet-Nejat, 249-253; Bertman, 246; Nardo, 120-121.

[530] Miller and Wetterstrom, 1135; Nardo, 121.

[531] Henry Hobhouse, *Seeds of Change: Six Plants that Transformed Mankind* (Washington, DC: Shoemaker & Hoard, 2005), 56.

[532] Peter Garnsey, *Food and Society in Classical Antiquity* (Cambridge, UK: Cambridge University Press, 1999), 113.

Historians call the earliest agricultural region the Fertile Crescent to denote its productivity and shape.[533] At the northern end of the Persian Gulf, its easternmost protrusion moved northwest along the Tigris and Euphrates rivers, then southwest along the eastern shore of the Mediterranean Sea, and south along the Nile River through Egypt. In tracing this path, the Fertile Crescent overlapped today's Turkey, Iraq, Syria, Lebanon, Jordan, Israel, the West Bank, and Egypt.

The Tigris, Euphrates, and Nile underpinned Fertile Crescent farming. Leaving the Nile for chapter 7, this paragraph mentions the Tigris and Euphrates, which, originating in eastern Turkey's mountains, flow southeast to the Persian Gulf. Rain and melting snow swell them in spring. Overflowing their banks, they silt the ground. This cycle, repeated annually long before human habitation, created alluvium.[534] Greeks designated land between the rivers Mesopotamia.[535]

Scholars term agriculture and pastoralism's advent, early spread, and initial effects the Neolithic Revolution. If the word "revolution" conveys rapidity, its use here is misleading. Hunting, fishing, and gathering's transition to farming and herding took millennia. Even today, wild fish consumption continues our original food acquisition rather than production.

5.4 Land and Inequality

5.4.1 Landowner and Farmworker

The Neolithic did not invent inequality but it did make more people unequal than hunting and gathering by increasing population. Moreover, the Neolithic, molding inequality into an intuitive and obvious form, bifurcated the economy into few landowners—who controlled the means of production: land, crops, livestock, and labor—and innumerable landless, who enriched them. Makers created, but never enjoyed, the wealth takers seized.

Opulent child burials by 5000 BCE near the Tigris River's Tell es-Sawwan and Yarim Tepe signaled wealth and rank's inheritance, a topic treated last chapter.[536] About the same time, a wealthy home near Mosul, Iraq's Tell Arpachiyah had fine pottery, alabaster cups, and obsidian ornaments.

---

[533] Joseph R. Strayer and Hans W. Gatzke, *The Mainstream of Civilization*, 3d ed. (New York: Harcourt Brace Jovanovich, 1979), 7.

[534] Christian, *Origin Story*, 201.

[535] Bertman, 2.

[536] Walter Scheidel, *The Great Leveler: Violence and the History of Inequality from the Stone Age to the Twenty-First Century* (Princeton, NJ and Oxford: Princeton University Press, 2017), 40.

"The most striking organizational characteristic of Mesopotamian society in all periods was its economic division into have and have-nots, into those who held land and those dependent on the landholders," wrote Near Eastern scholar Karen Rhea Nemet-Nejat.[537] The code attributed to Babylonian king Hammurabi (r. 1792–1750 BCE) recognized three classes.[538] At the top, elites owned all land. Second were nominally free citizens without land, though elites circumscribed everyone's freedom but theirs. Third, slaves lacked freedom and land. These divisions widened over time as slaves grew more numerous and vital to the economy.[539] Roughly doubling about 2000 to 600 BCE for the wealthiest decile of urban families' daughters, dowries evinced growing inequality.[540]

Emphasizing steep inequality, Roman naturalist Pliny the Elder (23–79 CE) later criticized six men for owning "half of Africa" during Emperor Nero's (37–68) reign.[541] Although hyperbole, this claim, examined in chapter 8, highlighted agrarian disparities. Expressing a similar sentiment two millennia later, American geographer Jared Diamond (b. 1937) faulted the Neolithic for "deep class divisions."[542]

Inequality disadvantaged Mesopotamian hirelings, who in the second and first millennia BCE earned daily one-quarter bushel of barley, 4.5 pounds of bread, over one gallon of beer, and enough wool, if saved a year, to make one garment.[543] Although the food and beverage may seem generous, they barely fed a family. Moreover, inflation eroded purchasing power as compensation stagnated. "If you're poor, you're better dead than alive; if you've got bread, you can't afford salt; if you've got salt, you can't afford bread," stated a second or first millennium BCE adage.[544]

In contrast, elites had the advantages. In twenty-fourth century BCE Lagash, Sumer, monarchs absorbed temples, land, and farmhands.[545] Nobles took debtors' farms. Not paying laborers, officials overcharged for funerals

---

[537] Nemet-Nejat, 263.

[538] Bertman, 62.

[539] Ibid.; Hans Neumann, "Slavery in Private Households toward the End of the Third Millennium B.C.," in *Slaves and Households in the Near East*, ed. Laura Culbertson (Chicago: Oriental Institute of the University of Chicago, 2011), 21.

[540] Scheidel, 48.

[541] Elio Lo Cascio, "The Early Roman Empire: The State and the Economy," in *The Cambridge Economic History of the Greco-Roman World*, ed. Walter Scheidel, Ian Morris, and Richard Saller (Cambridge, UK: Cambridge University Press, 2007), 640.

[542] Jared Diamond, "The Worst Mistake in the History of the Human Race," *Discover Magazine*, May 1, 1999, accessed May 3, 2022, ‹https://www.discovermagazine.com/planet-earth/the-worst-mistake-in-the-history-of-the-human-race.›

[543] Bertman, 249; Nemet-Nejat, 264.

[544] Bertman, 179.

[545] Scheidel, 54-58.

and sheep shearing. Akkadian kings circa 2400 to 2200 BCE confiscated temple property or appointed family or friends to manage it. These practices concentrated thousands of acres per elite. A Babylonian axiom acknowledged before 1000 BCE that "the king is the one at whose side wealth walks."[546]

Even before the formation of the state, slaves walked behind, not beside, plutocrats.[547] Defining slavery as compulsory altruism, *Eternal Inequality* asserts that sociality, discussed in chapter 2, favored it in us as in bumblebees and honeybees. Anticipating English lawyer and first governor of Massachusetts Bay Colony John Winthrop (1588–1649), quoted in chapter 1, Mesopotamians thought gods ordained slavery. Although scholars differentiate bondage and lesser coercions, this book treats all as freedom's denial because a person resents even temporary unfreedom. This book neither minimizes this experience nor contrasts slavery and its approximations.

Warfare from roughly 3500 BCE generated captives.[548] Nemet-Nejat averred that officials executed those the economy could not use, but this policy should not be overstated.[549] More populous and organized than villages, the earliest states conquered and enslaved northern Mesopotamians and people east of the Tigris.[550] These raids recurred often. First, the state hemorrhaged residents, who fled to the hinterland to escape exploitation. Second, mortality may have exceeded birthrate, requiring additions through conquest.

Elites understood that their privilege necessitated everyone else's maltreatment.[551] Unwilling to work, aristocrats off-loaded toil on underlings. This circumstance made war less land grab than labor's acquisition and compulsion. Warfare intensified inequality by producing winners and losers, noted chapter 1. Describing Mesopotamia in these terms, American political scientist James Scott (b. 1936) concluded that "It would be almost impossible to exaggerate the centrality of bondage."[552] This viewpoint challenged American historian Don Nardo's (b. 1947) opinion of it as "an important but not necessarily essential element of domestic life and public institutions."[553]

Warfare and the state inflamed class conflict. Amassing fortunes, elites provoked the introduction's Newtonian backlash from commoners who fled

---

[546] Ibid., 58.
[547] Scott, 155; Nardo, 267.
[548] Scott, 154; Nemet-Nejat, 117.
[549] Nemet-Nejat, 117.
[550] Scott, 154-155, 158; Bertman, 274.
[551] Scott, 150-151.
[552] Ibid., 155.
[553] Nardo, 265.

beyond aristocrats or retaliated when unable to escape. Despite opposition, government, enduring and enlarging, benefited the wealthy, who won class warfare by imposing taxes, corvée, conscription, rent, peonage, usury, and slavery.

Controlling the military and courts, they enforced their will then and now. Under plutocratic sway, schools propagate the fiction that the ruling class earned the right to command because the state is a meritocracy.[554] Underlings must venerate authority.

War prompted Sumer's Uruk, possibly the first city, to create a "house of prisoners" which distributed captives to landowners, temples, and the military.[555] Restricting slaves to small groups and frequently moving them, officials lessened the likelihood of revolt. Owners enforced servility through beating and disfigurement. Texts listed dead slaves who suffered abuse, overwork, and undernutrition. Yielding countless captives, war made them disposable. Callousness made slaves abscond, causing bounty hunters after 3000 BCE to specialize in capturing and returning runaways.

War targeted young adults whose homeland had borne the expense of rearing them, letting masters exploit them at least cost until death or sale.[556] Putative submissiveness made women and children, listed by thousands in documents, ideal slaves.[557] The true number must have been larger because few primary texts survived the millennia. Owners bred women, "the early state's manpower machines," like livestock.[558] As during chapter 15's Industrial Revolution, management preferred children, who were vulnerable and needed fewer provisions than adults, as clothmakers. Like chapter 2's omega hens, orphans especially lacked protectors.

Abuse, ruthlessness, overwork, undernutrition, high mortality, and unfreedom made Mesopotamia "an early gulag."[559] Assigning slaves the worst work, masters disincentivized revolt among the technically free who, no matter how poor, avoided such labor.

Given class antagonism, Nemet-Nejat must be right that elites executed some prisoners, a wartime practice that justified peacetime killings. The first

---

[554] Thomas Piketty, *Capital and Ideology*, trans. Arthur Goldhammer (Cambridge, MA and London: Belknap Press of Harvard University Press, 2020), 1.

[555] Scott, 160-161; Department of Ancient Near Eastern Art, "Uruk: The First City," Heilbrunn Timeline of Art History, New York Metropolitan Museum of Art, October 2003, accessed May 3, 2022, ‹https://www.metmuseum.org/toah/hd/uruk/hd_uruk.htm›; Nardo, 265.

[556] Scott, 167.

[557] Laura Culbertson, "A Life-Course Approach to Household Slaves in the Late Third Millennium B.C.," in *Slaves and Households in the Near East*, ed. Laura Culbertson (Chicago: Oriental Institute of the University of Chicago, 2011), 37.

[558] Scott, 168-169.

[559] Ibid., 170.

owners were military officers whose slaves tilled land, as mentioned. Taking the same form, Uruk slave and livestock lists indicated that elites equated both as farm property.[560] Like livestock and tools, slaves helped masters gain wealth, Greek philosopher Aristotle (384–322 BCE) asserted next chapter.[561]

From the third millennium BCE, default justified peonage.[562] Paupers sometimes surrendered their children or themselves as slaves. Famine enlarged bondage as temples enslaved those with nowhere else to turn for food. Enslaving criminals, courts further augmented unfreedom's roster. Babylonian merchants bought foreigners. A clay cast of a child's foot and a cuneiform receipt recorded one sale about 1200 BCE.[563]

Slaves populated the home, where first millennium BCE affluent families owned one to four on average, though Mesopotamia's total is unknown.[564] A legal document from Nippur, Sumer listed 27 slaves, 17 men and 10 women, whose inheritance a brother and sister contested. Rich urbanites owned at least 40. Most domestics, singers, and entertainers were slave women.[565] Men expected sex from young, attractive ones. Wealthy women sometimes gifted girls to husbands for this purpose.

The foregoing indicated slaves' status as property, subject to branding and sale anytime and inheritance upon an owner's death.[566] Hammurabi's code compensated possessors, not slaves, upon their injury. Their children were unfree unless one parent was free. Whether this policy conferred advantages is unknown. Runaways were punished if caught, and abettors faced execution. Anyone who cut the lock of hair that identified slaves lost a hand whereas the slave suffered impalement. Theft of a slave was also a crime. Authorities hoped to deter people from aiding slaves through public torture and execution.

Absent enslavement by war, debt, or heredity, slaves might be purchased, as mentioned. Mesopotamian texts valued commodities, including slaves, in shekels of silver such that one shekel purchased one bushel of barley.[567] A slave cost 20 to 90 shekels in about 2000 BCE.[568] A document from Babylonian king Nebuchadnezzar I's (r. 1124–1103 BCE) reign valued a slave at 40

---

[560] Ibid., 160.
[561] Aristotle, *Politics*, trans. Benjamin Jowett (New York: Modern Library, 1943), 56-57.
[562] Nemet-Nejat, 117; Neumann, 23.
[563] Bertman, 275.
[564] Neumann, 22; Nardo, 266.
[565] Nemet-Nejat, 117, 126; Neumann, 24.
[566] Neumann, 24; Bertman, 275.
[567] David Graeber, *Debt: The First 5,000 Years* (Brooklyn and London: Melville House, 2014), 39.
[568] Nemet-Nejat, xx, 257.

shekels whereas a ram or goat cost 2, an ox 20 to 30, and a donkey 30.[569] At roughly 10 shekels' pay annually, a laborer underpriced a slave.[570] An owner had to provision chattel, who might die before profiting him.

Slavery grew over time, especially after roughly 2000 BCE.[571] The south's Babylon and the north's Assyria "built their empires on the backs of slaves."[572] To satisfy demand, Assyria established markets near the Persian Gulf and throughout the Mediterranean. Assyrian king Ashurbanipal II (r. 883–859 BCE) boasted of enslaving 15,000 captives during one war. Slaves erected the Assyrian capital Nimrud in the ninth and eighth centuries BCE. Summarizing unfreedom's ubiquity, American British classicist Moses Finley (1912–1986) judged Mesopotamia "a world without free men."[573]

5.4.2 Taxes and Rent

"Macroparasities" and "tribute takers" maltreated the first farmers and stockmen.[574] Animus between taxpayer and collector worsened conflict between maker and taker. Taxation intensified when authorities auctioned the role of collector to the highest bidder.[575] Once the quota was delivered the taxman was free to extort and keep everything extra.

Mesopotamian barley, rye, and wheat abetted taxation by being determinate plants,[576] meaning that vegetative growth ceases upon flowering and seeding. If fields were planted at a customary time, the harvest was easy to predict. The time for reaping being simultaneous and brief, taxmen were able to swarm farms at harvest's completion. Indeterminate plants like New World tomato, however, continue vegetative growth even after the first flowers emerge. Letting the plant flower and fruit throughout its life extends the harvest through continuous growth so there would be no optimal time for an agent's arrival. Second, grains, being mostly dry matter, could be stored longer and were easier to transport to cities than tomato, Africa's watermelon, or another hydrous crop. Third, farmers who produced subterranean edibles like western hemisphere potato, sweet potato, or cassava might resist taxation by harvesting piecemeal to feed their families. Publicans who wanted the entire crop dug it themselves or made peasants do the

---

569 Bertman, 249.
570 Nemet-Nejat, 257.
571 Ibid., xx; Marjorie Gann and Janet Willen, *Five Thousand Years of Slavery* (Toronto, ON: Tundra Books, 2011), 4.
572 Gann and Willen, 4-5.
573 M. I. Finley, "Was Greek Civilization Based on Slave Labour?" *Historia: Zietschrift fur alte geschichte* 8, no. 2 (April 1959): 164.
574 Christian, "Acceleration: The Agrarian Era," TWF23.
575 Bertman, 68.
576 Scott, 21-22.

job. But grains, producing food above ground, supplied no such hindrance. Officials simply seized what was stored.

Even when the harvest failed, taxmen demanded payment and beat, enslaved, or killed those unable to comply.[577] This "looting" typified many "crude forms of coercion."[578] Indeed, the state arose to enforce inequality.[579] "There are lords and there are kings, but the real person to fear is the tax collector," stated a second or first millennium BCE Mesopotamian maxim.[580]

Taxation weakened agriculture. Low productivity—each seed produced just five seeds at harvest on average—yielded just a 10 percent surplus, enough for 10 farmers to feed themselves plus one nonfarmer.[581] Southwest Asian and Egyptian shortages from roughly 4000 to 500 BCE destroyed this remnant.[582] Summarizing its ubiquity, French historian Fernand Braudel (1902–1985), quoted in chapter 1, judged famine inseparable from our existence.[583]

Taxes devoured even adequate harvests. Sumer amassed a huge bureaucracy before 2000 BCE to collect taxes.[584] Its existence and activity indicate government's abandonment of tax farming, perhaps because private citizens could not be trusted to deliver their quota. Around this time, two documents, whose interpretation is contested, appear to have taxed barley at 48 percent of the harvest and livestock and other items similarly.[585]

If this percentage is accurate, Sumer taxed more than chapter 7's Egypt and chapters 10 and 19's China. Hebrews in Egypt owed pharaoh a quintile of the harvest.[586] China's taxes diminished from 15–20 percent of the harvest in the fourteenth century CE to 5 percent in the eighteenth century.[587]

---

[577] Christian, *Origin Story*, 216.

[578] Ibid., 212; Christian, "Acceleration: The Agrarian Era," TWF27.

[579] Howard Spodek, "Urbanization," in *World History Encyclopedia, Vol. 1: An Introduction to World History*, ed. Carolyn Neel and Alfred J. Andrea (Santa Barbara, CA: ABC-CLIO, 2011), 221; Christian, *Origin Story*, 216.

[580] Bertman, 178-179.

[581] Nemet-Nejat, 254; Christian, *Origin Story*, 214.

[582] Donald J. Ortner and Gretchen Theobald, "Paleopathological Evidence of Malnutrition," in *The Cambridge World History of Food*, vol. 1, ed. Kenneth F. Kiple and Kriemhild Conee Ornelas (Cambridge, UK: Cambridge University Press, 2000), 41.

[583] Fernand Braudel, *Capitalism and Material Life, 1400-1800*, trans. Miriam Kochan (New York: Harper Colophon Books, 1973), 38.

[584] Jacob L. Dahl, "Revisiting Bala," *Journal of the American Oriental Society* 126, no. 1 (January-March 2006): 77.

[585] Ibid., 78, 83.

[586] Gen. 47:23-24 (New American Bible).

[587] Robert W. Strayer, Edwin Hirschmann, Robert B. Marks, Robert J. Smith, James J. Horn, and Lynn H. Parsons, *The Making of the Modern World: Connected Histories, Divergent Paths (1500 to the Present)* (New York: St. Martin's Press, 1989), 350.

Besides taxes, Sumer required corvée several months annually, often on state farms, though canals, dikes, aqueducts, roads, bridges, grain bins, fortifications, palaces, and temples also siphoned labor for construction and maintenance.[588] These exertions involved "dirt work, brick-making, towing, and a great deal of carrying."[589] Drudgery aside, government conscripted farmworkers, though the wealthy hired substitutes or sent slaves.[590]

These practices imperiled agriculture by demanding too much of the harvest and diverting labor elsewhere, including to state farms, too long and at harvest time.[591] Meanwhile nobles, growing "fat off the work of others," widened the gulf between "disease ridden masses and a healthy elite class that is rich or powerful but produces nothing."[592]

The temptation is to designate Mesopotamia a command economy. Officials sought this goal, but premodern states lacked technologies like surveillance equipment and instantaneous communication to micromanage affairs. Absent such advances, Mesopotamia's bureaucracy required innumerable agents to penetrate the countryside as best they could. The point is that government could not collect all taxes, whether over, under, or at 48 percent. A high rate was wishful rather than a reckoning of what was possible.

Unable to collect every shekel, government had to aim high. About 3000 BCE, for example, Uruk enslaved about 9,000 of 40,000 to 45,000 residents to make cloth.[593] At least 20 percent of the population, these slaves underrepresented the total because farming, construction, and maintenance required more. Whatever the number, only agricultural slaves produced food. Uruk must have levied high crop taxes to feed nonfarm slaves plus unproductive elites.

An exorbitant rate heightened apprehension about the taxman, as mentioned. Although taxes befell farmers, they were not the lone victims. High duties led merchants to smuggle goods.[594]

Moderns may under appreciate the early agrarian tax burden. Farmers created all wealth through strenuous, unremitting labor; they endured privation, undertook a risky occupation absent insurance, and paid nearly

---

[588] Piotr Steinkeller, "Corvee Labor in Ur III Times," in *From the 21st Century B.C. to the 21st Century A.D.: Proceedings of the International Conference on Sumerian Studies Held in Madrid 22-24 July 2010*, ed. Steven Garfinkle and Manuel Molina (Winona Lake, IN: Eisenbrauns, 2013), 348, 364.

[589] Ibid., 348.

[590] Ibid., 367; Dahl, 83.

[591] Nemet-Nejat, 257-258.

[592] Diamond, *The Third Chimpanzee*, 181.

[593] Scott, 157, 159-160.

[594] Mathilde Touillon-Rici, "Trade and Contraband in Ancient Assyria," The British Museum, April 2, 2018, accessed February 21, 2022, ‹https://blog.britishmuseum.org/trade-and-contraband-in-ancient-assyria.›

---

all taxes. Even the greatest exertions never guaranteed success. Locusts, drought, flooding from a broken dike, or another catastrophe often destroyed crops. Despite perils, farmers knew that nothing delayed the taxman, who contributed nothing to the farm.

Taxes aside, rent was more burdensome where tenancy prevailed. Landlords took two thirds to three quarters of the harvest when paying taxes and supplying implements, seeds, and livestock.[595] Even when contributing only land, they took one third to half the produce.

5.4.3 Debt, Inequality, and Peonage

5.4.3.1 Mesopotamia

Debt shaped Mesopotamia, which invented usury about 3500 BCE.[596] Temples charged interest on loans to merchants who undertook distant trade. Interest reflected the risk that bandits might steal goods or kill merchants. In other instances, the other party, weary of awaiting a merchant, finalized a deal with someone else. In yet other cases, disease killed a participant during the journey. Although temples lost money when misfortune struck, interest recouped losses by profiting on successes.

Usury entered farming and herding before 2400 BCE.[597] Tenants borrowed against a future harvest, which jeopardized repayment when inadequate. Scarcity forced many into debt to afford food.[598] Twelve to 20 percent interest rates imperiled repayment given the 0.1 percent annual economic growth between roughly 1 and 1820 CE.[599] Hammurabi's code tried to lessen exploitation by canceling debts every third year, though creditors objected.[600]

Default justified enslavement, as mentioned. Chapter 1 quoted American anthropologist David Graeber (1961–2020), who described a past when debtors lost their children to creditors and when the tussle between debtor and creditor was the primary class antagonism.[601] Antiquity's rebellions aimed to nullify debts and break elite power by redistributing land.[602]

---

[595] Nemet-Nejat, 266.

[596] Graeber, 64.

[597] Ibid., 64-65.

[598] Ibid., 81.

[599] Nemet-Nejat, 265; Branko Milanovic, *The Haves and the Have-Nots: A Brief and Idiosyncratic History of Global Inequality* (New York: Basic Books, 2011), 49; Alan Greenspan and Adrian Woodridge, *Capitalism in America: A History* (New York: Penguin Press, 2018), 6.

[600] Niall Ferguson, *The Ascent of Money: A Financial History of the World* (New York: Penguin Press, 2008), 30.

[601] Graeber, 8.

[602] Moses Finley, *Slavery in Classical Antiquity: Views and Controversies* (Cambridge, UK: W. Heffer, 1960), 63.

Historian Don Nardo thought serfs a separate caste, which Babylonian texts supposedly recognized about 2000 BCE.[603] He assumed they, numerous on royal and temple farms, produced the surplus that enriched elites. His description of these farmworkers, however, reveals them as tenants, whose ubiquity this chapter affirms.

5.4.3.2 The Levant

Inequality, defined by landowners' power and commoners' impotence, shaped Judaism. If Greece tried to craft political solutions to problems, Judaism sought resolution through submission to God. Originally nomads, Hebrews settled Palestine, where transition to pastoralism and agriculture exacerbated inequality.[604] Monopolizing land, elites enslaved debtors and their families. Attempting to curb inequality, Deuteronomy (c. 650 BCE) voided debts every seventh year, a variation on Hammurabi's code, and freed peons.[605] Likely proposed when the prophets were active, these remedies must have failed because those quoted in the introduction repeated the assault against inequality.

While the next chapter revisits biblical attitudes toward inequality, this section affirms that Hebrews, having been slaves in Egypt, accepted bondage as inevitable.[606] Escape took them in the thirteenth century BCE to Palestine, where they united under a series of kings.[607] After Solomon's (c. 965–c. 925 BCE) death, the kingdom split into the north's Israel, destroyed by Assyria in 722 BCE, and the south's Judah, conquered by Babylon in 587 BCE.

Babylon resettled survivors east and southeast of Nippur and north of Uruk, an area depopulated by war, in hopes of reviving the economy.[608] Although Nehemiah (c. 400 BCE) described them as slaves, their status was ambiguous.[609] If Babylon deemed the settlement permanent, Hebrews could not move. They owed part of the harvest as tax plus labor and military service, but these widespread burdens did not constitute slavery. Corvée required

---

[603] Nardo, 255.

[604] Graeber, 81.

[605] Deuteronomy 15:1-3; Gordon Wenham, "The Date of Deuteronomy: Linch-pin of Old Testament Criticism," *Themelios* 10, no. 3, accessed September 6, 2021, ‹https://www.thegospelcoalition.org/themelios/article/the-date-of-deuteronomy-linch-pin-of-old-testament-criticism.›

[606] Exodus 1:8-14.

[607] John P. McKay, Bennett D. Hill, John Buckler, Clare Haru Crowston, Merry E. Wiesner-Hanks, and Joe Perry, *Understanding Western Society: A Brief History* (Boston and New York: Bedford/St. Martin's, 2012), 37-38.

[608] F. Rachel Magdalene and Cornelia Wunsch, "Slavery between Judah and Babylon: The Exilic Experience," in *Slaves and Households in the Near East*, ed. Laura Culbertson (Chicago: Oriental Institute of the University of Chicago, 2011), 116.

[609] Ibid.; Nehemiah 7:6.

their digging irrigation canals and building roads and edifices. Besides these duties, they grew grain and dates.

During this Babylonian captivity (586–538 BCE), Hebrews documented their experiences.[610] Some 200 texts survive, though only seven mentioned bondage. Paucity weakens generalizations, though all seven revealed Hebrew ownership of slaves. Their names suggested Hebraic, Akkadian, and Egyptian origins unless masters renamed them upon acquisition.

The seven emphasized slaves as property. One owner obtained a woman from another, though by what means is unknown.[611] Indebted to another man, this master rented her to him to retire the obligation. In another instance, siblings went to Babylon's royal court after their father's death to formalize the division of slaves and other property.[612] The transaction must have been important to motivate travel to the capital and might have been part of a larger deal. Other texts referenced slaves' sale, sometimes more than once, or passage to an heir.

Within three generations of Hebrews' arrival, stratification, abetted by farming and herding, arose as some prospered while others failed.[613] Like their peers elsewhere, Hebrew elites hired substitutes for corvée and military service.[614] Far above slaves, these wealthy emulated the native aristocracy, though outsider status prevented their summiting the hierarchy.

5.5 Cities and Inequality

Agriculture and pastoralism supported urbanization, which Mesopotamia began around 4000 BCE and which crowded people for the first time.[615] Indeed, Mesopotamian metropolises may have had antiquity's densest populations.[616] Sumer totaled roughly 10,000 to 100,000 inhabitants per city, where "wretched" conditions and inequality prevailed.[617] Ordinary houses had a floor of roughly 144 square feet whereas Greek geographer Strabo (c. 64 BCE–c. 24 CE) put the base of Babylon's Hanging Gardens, which king Nebuchadnezzar II (c. 630–c. 562 BCE) designed for a wife or courtesan, at 242,400 square feet.[618] At these figures, the gardens would have encom-

[610] Magdalene and Wunsch, 113-128.

[611] Ibid., 119-120.

[612] Ibid., 122-123.

[613] Ibid., 117.

[614] Ibid., 128.

[615] Nemet-Nejat, xviii.

[616] Bertman, 201.

[617] Nemet-Nejat, 100, 105.

[618] Nardo, 135, 142; Bertman, 201; Tom Head, *Ancient Mesopotamia* (North Mankato, MN: Essential Library, 2015), 52-53.

passed over 1,680 houses. At three persons—husband, wife, and child—per dwelling, over 5,040 people would have filled the area, which Nebuchadnezzar intended to pleasure rather than house one individual.

Such aggregations dwarfed hunter-gatherers, who numbered up to roughly 150 members per group.[619] Small, mobile populations accumulated little waste in one locale, seldom suffered contagion, and had little immunity to it. Mesopotamia's cities, however, had garbage in the streets.[620] Rats, insects, parasites, and pathogens proliferated. Striking virgin populations, epidemics may have killed a greater fraction during farming and herding's first five millennia, around 9500 to 4500 BCE, than in any subsequent 5,000 years.[621] Farmers, pastoralists, and urbanites, like foragers, seldom surpassed age 20 and saw half their newborns die before puberty.[622]

Contagion disproportionately killed paupers weakened by undernutrition and overwork. Worsening illness and mortality, herding gave Southwest Asians zoonoses. Mesopotamian texts mentioned tuberculosis, typhus, pneumonic and bubonic plague, smallpox, and leprosy, all virulent amid the underclass.[623] Making food dear, diseases destroyed crops and livestock.

5.6 Review and Preview

Southwest Asia invented agriculture and pastoralism, heightened inequality, and pitted landowners against laborers. Elites exploited underlings through tenancy, slavery, peonage, usury, taxes, corvée, and conscription. Oppression prompted commoners to migrate beyond the state, which enslaved foreigners to replenish loses. Among slaves, Hebrews toiled in Egypt and Babylon. Next chapter examines Hebraic, early Christian, and Hellenic attitudes toward inequality.

---

[619] Christian, *Origin Story*, 204.
[620] Nemet-Nejat, 103.
[621] Scott, 97.
[622] Deevey, 202; Christian, *Origin Story*, 312.
[623] Nemet-Nejat, 146; Bertman, 306.

Chapter 6 Inequality in Ancient Thought

6.1 Abstract

Like us, ancient Jews, Christians, and Greeks had disparate attitudes toward wealth and its distribution. Judaism and Christianity vacillated about affluence and inequality. Greek philosophers Plato (c. 428–c. 348 BCE) and Aristotle (384–322 BCE) thought inequality and slavery innately human. These authors belonging to the elites, leisure and privilege shaped their attitudes. Drudgery denied everyone else time and energy to write, so that textual analysis biases history by overrepresenting elites and their ideas.

6.2 Religion and Inequality

6.2.1 Judaism and Inequality

6.2.1.1 Hebrews and Slavery

Bondage shaped identity because Hebrews, believing the god Yahweh commanded the prophet Moses to lead them to freedom, began worshiping this deity while fleeing enslavement in Egypt.[624] Moses was so important to Judaism that legends embellished his memory.[625]

Although Yahweh worship began with the exodus, Genesis (c. 550 BCE) purported to narrate events from time's beginning. From putative origin in

---

[624] William C. Placher, *A History of Christian Theology: An Introduction* (Philadelphia: Westminster Press, 1983), 19-20; Exodus 3:1-10 (New American Bible).

[625] Gary Glassman, "Moses and the Exodus," NOVA, August 2007, accessed February 24, 2022, <https://www.pbs.org/wgbh/nova/bible/meyers.html.>

Eden, Hebrews were nomads driven by famine into Egypt.[626] This circumstance disadvantaged them as tenants who owed 20 percent—a double tithe—of the harvest to pharaoh, though agriculture yielded only 10 percent surplus. Recurrent famine destroyed more than the surplus, endangering those unable to afford high prices. Absent famine, 20 percent tax eliminated the surplus plus another 10 percent. Egypt's farmworkers, including Hebrews, hungered while the rich ate well.

The Hebrew plight devolved into slavery, which Exodus (c. 600 BCE) blamed for overworking chattel and murdering Hebrew sons.[627] Unhappy with their lot, Hebrews confronted authority. Exodus recounted a series of clashes between them and pharaoh, possibly Seti I (r. c. 1294–1279), his son Ramses II (r. 1279–1237 BCE) or his grandson Merenptah (r. 1236–1223 BCE), culminating in Yahweh's massacre of every Egyptian family's eldest son and oldest male livestock offspring.[628]

Describing events, replete with Yahweh's intervention in history, from a religious perspective, Exodus, advocating class struggle, inspired slave resistance throughout history. In principle, pharaoh owned all land, crops, livestock, and labor.[629] This arrangement, or any wealth distribution, may be expressed from zero to one on the Gini continuum, named after its inventor Italian statistician and economist Corrado Gini (1884–1965). A Gini of zero indicates maximum equality such that everyone in a society has identical wealth. The larger the Gini the greater is inequality such that at one, one person has all wealth, leaving everybody else none.

Gini coefficients express hypotheticals. No community distributes lifelong identical wealth among everyone; equality was "infeasible in practice," and no community can endure when one person, hoarding everything, condemns the rest to die from privation.[630] Unable to reproduce without a mate, the lone survivor would extirpate humanity upon death.

The hypothetical of pharaoh with all the wealth yielded a Gini of one, though next chapter proves he owned not everything. At hierarchy's other end, Hebrews were chattel whose children could be killed with impunity.

---

[626] Gen. 47:1-5.

[627] Exodus 1:8-22.

[628] Exodus 5:1-12:30; Rosalie David, *Handbook to Life in Ancient Egypt*, rev. ed. (New York: Facts on File, 2003), 92-93; Theodore Burgh, "Ramses II," in *Berkshire Encyclopedia of World History*, vol. 4, ed. William H. McNeill, Jerry H. Bentley, David Christian, David Levinson, J. R. McNeill, Heidi Roupp, and Judith P. Zinsser (Great Barrington, MA: Berkshire Publishing Group, 2005), 1549.

[629] Bob Brier and Hoyt Hobbs, *Ancient Egypt: Everyday Life in the Land of the Nile* (New York: Sterling, 2009), 77.

[630] Walter Scheidel, *The Great Leveler: Violence and the History of Inequality from the Stone Age to the Twenty-First Century* (Princeton, NJ and Oxford: Princeton University Press, 2017), 224.

This dichotomy should have guaranteed pharaoh's triumph, but Yahweh upended hierarchy by sparking the Hebrew backlash against oppression. Scholars debate these events, which this chapter envisions as wishful enact-ment of the introduction's Newtonian system. Egypt's vast inequality caused Hebrews to retaliate by fashioning a god that destroyed oppressors and by defining such action as justice. German philosopher and philologist Friedrich Nietzsche (1844–1900) disparaged this righteousness as slave morality.[631]

6.2.1.2 Hebrews, Sedentism, and Inequality

Escape from Egypt spurred Hebrews in the thirteenth century BCE to settle last chapter's Palestine, where agriculture and pastoralism intensified inequality.[632] Few amassed land and oppressed the landless through usury, servitude, tenancy, taxation, corvée, and conscription.

The Tanakh examined the agrarian elite, nowhere more enigmatically than in Job (c. 550 BCE), "the most radical wisdom text in the Bible."[633] Most commentators pondering theology or philosophy, this chapter considers economics. The book's eponym, "greater than any of the men of the East," had thousands of livestock and many acres and laborers.[634] The text judged him "a blameless and upright man...who feared God and avoided evil."[635]

But ambiguity emerged at the outset; Job, a common name, originally meant "enemy."[636] Perhaps the author or authors implied that Job exploited underlings, a leitmotif articulated by Plato, who described rich and poor as enemies. Satan declared Job faithful only because Yahweh enriched and protected him and his family.[637] Moreover, magnates gain nothing through generosity. "No one ever makes a billion dollars," remarked New York congresswoman Alexandria Ocasio-Cortez (b. 1989).[638] "You take a billion dollars." Job must therefore have prospered by subjugating labor.

This maltreatment initially seems not to have troubled Yahweh, who lauded Job.[639] Yet he must have had reservations to let Satan destroy Job's

---

[631] Friedrich Nietzsche, *On the Genealogy of Morals*, trans. Walter Kaufman and R. J. Hollingdale (New York: Viking Books, 1969), 36.

[632] David Graeber, *Debt: The First 5,000 Years* (Brooklyn and London: Melville House, 2014), 81.

[633] Robert Alter, "The Poetic and Wisdom Books," in *The Cambridge Companion to Biblical Interpretation*, ed. John Barton (Cambridge, UK: Cambridge University Press, 2003), 235.

[634] Job 1:3.

[635] Job 1:1.

[636] Notes on Job, New American Bible (Camden, NJ: Thomas Nelson, 1971), 564.

[637] Job 1:9-11.

[638] Theron Mohamed, "'No One Ever Makes a Billion Dollars. You Take a Billion Dollars': Alexandria Ocasio-Cortez Slams Billionaires for Exploiting Workers," Markets Insider, January 24, 2020, accessed February 24, 2022, ‹https://markets.businessinsider.com/news/stocks/aoc-accuses-billionaires-exploiting-workers-paying-slave-wages-2020-1.›

[639] Job 1:8.

ranch and children.[640] But Satan's culpability is unclear because the text states that "lightning...from heaven" killed the sheep and shepherds and because Yahweh faulted Satan not for the calamities but for causing him to harm Job.[641]

Admiring elites and ignoring servants, the scripture repeated that Job's children spent their days feasting with each other rather than working.[642] Nowhere did scripture indicate that Job or his family toiled on their estate. His piety involved the proper rituals.[643] Whether it included charity is unclear. He never pinpointed instances of almsgiving, though he challenged Yahweh to destroy his arm if he had denied paupers anything.[644]

After the tragedy, three friends traveled an unspecified distance to console him.[645] They too were elites. First, stratification must have confined fraternity to his peers. Second, they had leisure to travel to him and commiserate a week before speaking. Conversation lengthened their stay. Workers lacked such freedom. Job's twenty-third chapter introduced a fourth traveler, whose silence had hidden him from readers.[646] The text mentioned his youth and named his father, perhaps implying that his eminence, inherited and unearned, derived from kinship.

Throughout the narrative, Job, declaring innocence, demanded explanation from Yahweh, whose appearance in chapters 38 through 41 neither specified Job's sin nor justified the punishment.[647] Instead Yahweh, emphasizing omnipotence, owed nobody explanation for condemning underlings to "lives of quiet desperation."[648] Job retracted his plea and Yahweh doubled his original plenitude as reward.[649]

This resolution may dissatisfy. Enjoying affluence, privilege, and leisure unknown to slaves, servants, or laborers, Job may have been less guiltless than he supposed. His assertion of innocence self-serving, his suffering might have pleased farmworkers. Finally, Yahweh humbled an elite. Perhaps the scripture criticized inordinate wealth, which injured Job by arousing Satan's envy.

---

[640] Job 1:12-19.
[641] Job 1:16; Job 2:3.
[642] Job 1:4; 1:13-19.
[643] Job 1:5.
[644] Job 31:16-23.
[645] Job 2:11-13.
[646] Job 23:2-6.
[647] Job 6:1-7:21; Job 9:1-35; Job 10:1-22; Job 13:23-27; Job 16:12-17:16; Job 19:6-29; Job 23: 1-17; Job 32:30-37; Job 38:1-41:26.
[648] Henry David Thoreau, *Walden* (Chicago: Great Books Foundation, 1955), 33.
[649] Job 42:1-6; Job 42:10

American philosopher Kenneth Seeskin (b. 1947), grouping Job among the prophets, dated their origin to the eighth century BCE.[650] The introduction quoting Amos (c. 750 BCE), Micah (c. 700 BCE), and Isaiah, last chapter mentioned their repetitiveness as evidence that elites ignored them. Indeed, the prophets acknowledged that few heeded them.[651]

Prophecy ended in the sixth century BCE, remarked Seeskin, though American theologian William Placher (1948–2008) believed it dwindled and then ended after chapter 5's Babylonian captivity (586–538 BCE).[652] If Jewish messianic precursor John the Baptist (c. 5 BCE–c. 30 CE) and Jesus (c. 5 BCE–c. 30 CE) are considered prophets, however, the activity entered the first century CE. The next sections concern Jesus.

6.2.2 Early Christianity and Inequality

6.2.2.1 Jesus' Historicity and the Gospels

Early Christian views about inequality begin with Jesus. An attempt to reconstruct him and his opinions may seem straightforward. One need only assemble information about him as a writer might for U.S. president Joe Biden (b. 1942). A September 13, 2022, Google search of the words "president Joe Biden" yielded roughly 219 million websites. Augmenting these materials, a biographer might interview the president and people close to him, read his speeches over his decades in public office, and consult media reports by journalists who interviewed him or an associate.

Antiquity cannot duplicate this thoroughness. First, documents are less plentiful. For example, few details exist about Greek mathematician Euclid (c. 325–c. 265 BCE) despite his renown as a founder of geometry.[653] Having about 40 versions of his life by the Middle Ages, a biographer might appear more fortunate with Jesus.[654] But inconsistencies create the second impediment to understanding him and his ideas. For example, several accounts, including the canonical gospels, recounted miracles. By contrast, the Gospel of Thomas mentioned no miracle, not even the resurrection.[655] The similarly

---

[650] Kenneth Seeskin, *Thinking about the Prophets: A Philosopher Reads the Bible* (Philadelphia: Jewish Publication Society, 2020), xi.

[651] Placher, 22.

[652] Ibid., 24-25; Seeskin, xi.

[653] "Euclid," in *Top 101 Mathematicians*, ed. Louis C. Coakley (New York: Britannica, 2017), 43; Josette Campbell and Chris Hayhurst, *Euclid: The Father of Geometry* (New York: Rosen Publishing, 2016), 45.

[654] "Preface," in *The Other Gospels: Accounts of Jesus from outside the New Testament*, ed. and trans. Bart D. Ehrman and Zlatko Plese (Oxford: Oxford University Press, 2014), xi.

[655] *The Gospel According to Thomas*, in *The Other Gospels: Accounts of Jesus from outside the New Testament*, ed. and trans. Bart D. Ehrman and Zlatko Plese (Oxford: Oxford University Press, 2014), 161-173.

named Infancy Gospel of Thomas, unique among texts, described Jesus' murder of three people.[656] Among canonical accounts, only John (c. 100 CE) included Lazarus' resurrection and omitted Satan's temptation of Jesus.[657] Luke (c. 90) alone detailed 12-year-old Jesus' trip to Jerusalem.[658] Only Matthew (c. 90) and Luke described Jesus' birth, and their versions differ.[659] These discrepancies affirm that the writers never met him.[660] Their identity unknown, their gospels dated decades after Jesus' death. The absence of eyewitness testimony constitutes the third barrier.

Jesus' historicity being unrecoverable, this chapter seeks the canonical gospels' attitudes about inequality. Likely written late in the first century, they, though not biographies of Jesus, supplied information about inequality, economics, and society.

Although not historical, these accounts likely center on a real person. Otherwise, ancient authors would not have written some 40 hagiographies about him. Like Moses, Jesus was so consequential that legends enlarged his exploits. The distinction between fact and embellishment uncertain, this chapter, rather than trying to differentiate the two, seeks the canonical gospels' perspectives about inequality, as mentioned.

6.2.2.2 Condemnation of Wealth

A Jew who chose Jewish apostles, Jesus may have wanted to reform Judaism, not invent a religion. After his death, Jewish convert to Christianity Paul (c. 5–c. 65 CE), "the most important Christian thinker of all time," helped shape Jesus' message into a new faith.[661] The time, near the High Roman Empire's (c. 200 BCE–c. 200 CE) midpoint, suited proselytizing. Having made the Mediterranean a commercial zone, Rome eased the exchange of commodities, people, and ideas. Using maritime routes, Paul spread Christianity to eastern Mediterranean ports, which, like other cities, had numerous poor.[662]

---

[656] *The Infancy Gospel of Thomas*, in *The Other Gospels: Accounts of Jesus from outside the New Testament*, ed. and trans. Bart D. Ehrman and Zlatko Plese (Oxford: Oxford University Press, 2014), 8, 11.

[657] John 11:1-44.

[658] Luke 2:41-52.

[659] Matt 1:18-2:18; Luke 2:1-20.

[660] Robin W. Winks, Crane Brinton, John B. Christopher, and Robert Lee Wolff, *A History of Civilization, Vol. I: Prehistory to 1715*, 7th ed. (Englewood Cliffs, NJ: Prentice Hall, 1988), 101-103.

[661] James Dunn, "The Pauline Letters," in *The Cambridge Companion to Biblical Interpretation*, ed. John Barton (Cambridge, UK: Cambridge University Press, 2003), 276; John P. McKay, Bennett D. Hill, John Buckler, Clare Haru Crowston, Merry E. Wiesner-Hanks, and Joe Perry, *Understanding Western Society: A Brief History* (Boston and New York: Bedford/St. Martin's, 2012), 159.

[662] Joseph R. Strayer and Hans W. Gatzke, *The Mainstream of Civilization*, 3d ed. (New York: Harcourt Brace Jovanich, 1979), 90.

Written for them, the gospels sometimes denounced riches, a message Jesus must have embraced. As noted, the prophets castigated elites for oppressing the multitude. The earliest gospel, Mark (c. 70 CE) began by linking Jesus with Isaiah, calling readers to renounce sin, and introducing John the Baptist, whose meager attire and diet of "grasshoppers and wild honey" signaled asceticism and opposition to wealth.[663]

Connecting himself and his message to Jesus by baptizing him, John implied that Jesus was his follower.[664] Beginning his ministry then or after John's death, Jesus attacked luxury and indifference to the underclass. For example, Luke stated that a man, wanting his portion of an inheritance, asked Jesus' intercession.[665] The fact that he was due property indicated affluence in a world of indigents. Refusing the request, Jesus told of a man who, building a bin to store bountiful crops, expected to live well for years. But he died that night, and Jesus branded him a "fool!"[666] Eschewing money, Jesus advised listeners to amass spiritual treasure, which suffered neither decay nor theft.[667]

The story of a rich man who ignored homeless Lazarus, a different person than the man in John, also criticized wealth.[668] The magnate died, was buried, and entered hell. In contrast, Luke implies burial's absence when Lazarus died. In one sense, this circumstance is understandable for someone penniless who may have lacked family. Unburied, his fate might have resembled chapter 4's Sungir, Russia. Although three persons received elaborate interments, a femur on the ground from a fourth corpse implied non-burial and disarticulation by scavengers. In Luke, however, Lazarus was unburied because angels took him to heaven.

First and last's reversal underscored that the gospels condemned elites and comforted paupers. Although critical of riches, Jesus may not have advocated equality. Chapter 8's Rome was markedly unequal. Yet Mark, Matthew, and Luke had him acknowledge Roman authority.[669] Rather than oppose inequality, Jesus disliked its configuration, seeking, the parable of Lazarus and the rich man emphasized, to upend first and last.[670]

Now an omega in hell, the former magnate, no longer commanding others, begged Hebrew patriarch Abraham in heaven to let Lazarus cool him with a water droplet.[671] Abraham refused because the man had neglected Lazarus and

---

[663] Mark 1:1-6.

[664] Mark 1:9.

[665] Luke 12:13-21.

[666] Luke 12:20.

[667] Luke 12:32-34.

[668] Luke 16:19-31.

[669] Mark 12:14-17; Matt. 22:17-21; Luke 20:22-25.

[670] Matt. 20:16.

[671] Luke 16:24-31.

because nobody could cross the boundary between hell and heaven. He then beseeched Abraham to let Lazarus warn his brothers. Again refusing because nothing could reform them, Abraham affirmed that inequality is permanent (and, this book contends, apparently biological) and that elites have always oppressed underlings.

6.2.2.3 Ambiguity toward Wealth

Not all commentary about wealth and inequality echoed these parables. For example, Matthew related the story of a vineyard owner who hired laborers at dawn after agreeing to "the usual daily wage."[672] This language indicates that the parties negotiated pay, though workers could seldom influence it before the nineteenth century.[673] Implying as much, Matthew noted that the owner hired men into late afternoon because labor's surfeit, which would have discouraged generosity, idled them.[674]

Moreover, "the usual daily wage," though imprecise, must have been low. During Jesus' ministry, Palestine was in the Roman Empire, which, like other polities, perpetuated steep inequality. Disparities persisted because, as Ocasio-Cortez noted, the exploitation of workers created fortunes. During the high empire, those who qualified for the Senate had incomes roughly 500 times above commoners' earnings.[675] A Roman soldier earned about 1,000 sesterces annually against the 12 million of land speculator and slave trader Marcus Crassus (115–53 BCE).[676] Workers being powerless and poor, Roman statesman Marcus Cicero (106–43 BCE) likened labor—arduous, sporadic, and underpaid—to slavery.[677]

The owner augmented the initial workforce with more men throughout the day.[678] Paying everybody identically, he disappointed those who toiled all day "in the scorching heat."[679] Equal pay for unequal work would have preserved inequality with landowners still atop the hierarchy. Retaining the economy's bifurcation into rich and poor, Matthew affirmed "equality in poverty."[680] Equal pay would have worsened injustice by rewarding under-achievement while underpaying those who worked longest and hardest, Aris-

---

[672] Matt. 20: 2.

[673] McKay, Hill, Buckler, Crowston, Wiesner-Hanks, and Perry, 730.

[674] Matt 20:6-7.

[675] Branko Milanovic, *The Haves and the Have-Nots: A Brief and Idiosyncratic History of Global Inequality* (New York: Basic Books, 2011), 49.

[676] Ibid., 42; Mary Beard, *SPQR: A History of Ancient Rome* (New York and London: Liveright Publishing, 2015), 461.

[677] Beard, 441, 446-448.

[678] Matt. 20:3-7.

[679] Matt. 20:8-12.

[680] Milanovic, 50.

totle indicated later. Emphasizing inequality, Matthew ended the lesson by writing that "the last shall be first and the first shall be last."[681]

Yet this anecdote defended rather than overturned the status quo. Telling complainers to return home, the owner stated that wealth let him do whatever he wanted.[682] Obviating reproof, money kept the first atop hierarchy and the last at bottom.

Matthew reaffirmed this message five chapters later when a wealthy man gave three servants coins to invest.[683] The first doubled the 5,000 he received. The second did likewise with 2,000 whereas the third invested none of the 1,000 entrusted him. Rewarding the two usurers but punishing the third, the man gave his 1,000 to the servant with 10,000.

Rather than reverse first and last, this narrative widened the gap; the first not only doubled his money but received 1,000 coins from the servant who earned nothing. Rather than 1,000, he, becoming homeless upon banishment to "the darkness outside," lost everything.[684] Defending inaction, the servant expressed fear of a master who harvested what he did not plant.[685] This statement implied that the master's riches came from theft. "Those who have will get more until they grow rich, while those who have not will lose even the little they have," remarked Matthew in defending this behavior.[686]

6.3 Greek Thought and Inequality

6.3.1 Plato and Hierarchy

Transition from Judaism and Christianity to Hellenism, which perceived inequality less a matter for believers to resolve with their god than for people to negotiate among themselves, moved from faith to philosophy. Aware that philosophy and religion differed, Plato announced that "we must trust our reasoning."[687] Philosophy, which some scholars trace to Greek scientist, mathematician, and philosopher Thales (c. 624–c. 545 BCE), may be as old as religion, or it may have emerged from religion.[688]

---

[681] Matt 20:16.

[682] Matt 20:14-15.

[683] Matt 25:14-30.

[684] Matt 25:30.

[685] Matt 25:24-25.

[686] Matt 25:29.

[687] Plato, *Republic*, in *Great Dialogues of Plato*, trans. W. H. D. Rouse (New York and Scarborough, ON: New American Library, 1956), 185.

[688] Demetris Nicolaides, *In the Light of Science: Our Ancient Quest for Knowledge and the Measure of Modern Physics* (Amherst, NY: Prometheus Books, 2014), 71; Francis MacDonald Cornford, *Before and after Socrates* (Cambridge, UK: Cambridge University Press, 1932), 5; Robert S.

Early philosophers sought to describe the universe's origin, the substance or substances that constituted it, and the relationship between change and stasis.[689] Ridiculing this inquiry and wanting self-knowledge as prelude to proper conduct, Plato expressed his mentor Greek philosopher Socrates' (469–399 BCE) dissatisfaction with purely physical descriptions of reality.[690]

Humans being social, chapter 2 noted, Plato aimed to prescribe communal conduct.[691] Understanding community as hierarchical, he equated egalitarianism with anarchy. But he also knew, as mentioned, that inequality, pitting rich against poor, provoked class antagonism. That is, elites oppressed laborers, who resented abuse and sometimes retaliated in Newtonian fashion. Society again risked anarchy.

In *Republic* (c. 380 BCE), Plato made the city the archetypal community.[692] Although villages were no less communal, he probably preferred to examine cities because he inhabited one. People formed the first city, he imagined, because success was likelier together than alone. Nobody satisfying all needs and wants on his own, individuals congregated. None mastering every occupation, the city attracted specialists, each able to contribute a good or service. This view of city as synergy made urbanites "partners and helpers."[693]

Plato ignored the city's criminals and vagrants who diminished its appeal. The losers tended to be last chapter's farmers whose produce, sustaining metropolises, flowed as taxes and rent to urban bureaucrats and rentiers. City parasitizing farm, countryfolk fled beyond government to escape oppression.

Plato's tripartite city ranked producers like shoemakers and weavers at the bottom.[694] He added farmers to this class, though they inhabited the countryside and suffered rather than profited from urbanism, as noted. Atop hierarchy, lawgivers, who were "perfect," ruled the city.[695] Between the two, soldiers, enforcing laws, protected the city from outside invaders and internal malcontents.

Although this structure seems straightforward, he attached conditions to it. The previous paragraph mentioned, for example, the ruler's perfec-

---

Brumbaugh, *The Philosophers of Greece* (Albany: State University of New York Press, 1981), 12.

[689] Cornford, 2, 18-27.

[690] Plato, *Phaedo*, in *Great Dialogues of Plato*, trans. W. H. D. Rouse (New York and Scarborough, ON: New American Library, 1956), 500-503; Plato, *Apology*, in *Great Dialogues of Plato*, trans. W. H. D. Rouse (New York and Scarborough, ON: New American Library, 1956), 434-443.

[691] Plato, *Republic*, 128-154.

[692] Ibid., 165-171.

[693] Ibid., 165.

[694] Ibid., 166, 215.

[695] Ibid., 171, 214-215.

tion. Plato envisioned him an incorruptible philosopher.[696] Trustworthiness gave him freedoms denied others. For example, he alone could lie but only to advantage the city.

This thinking seems naïve. People dissemble for many reasons, not just to further the collective. Indeed, ambition, not selflessness, motivates dishonesty. Praising honesty as abstraction, Italian philosopher Nicolo Machiavelli (1469–1527), who "exerted an extraordinary influence on modern thought and practice throughout the world," believed leaders, violating agreements against their interests, achieved greatness through deceit.[697] "If men were all good, this precept would not be a good one; but as they are bad, and would not observe their faith with you, so you are not bound to keep faith with them."[698] This logic requires habitual duplicity.

Aiming to shrink the divide between ruler and subject by abolishing private property beyond "what is absolutely necessary," Plato wanted all buildings to admit the public.[699] Nobody could hoard surplus, which corrupted its possessor. "Wealth creates luxury and idleness and faction, and poverty adds meanness and bad work to the faction," he warned.[700]

But inequality's reduction displeased authorities accustomed to profiting from their position, remarked *Republic* participant Adeimantus.[701] Humans always bifurcating into magnates and underlings, elites never surrendered wealth and privilege or debased themselves through equality with commoners.

Although egalitarianism was naïve, Plato aimed to benefit the group rather than privilege one class over another.[702] The collective would fail amid class conflict, whereby plutocrats, masters rather than public servants, angered everyone else. Thus rent, the city pitted elites against commoners, factions "always plotting against each other."[703]

Disliking true egalitarianism, Plato criticized democracy for feigning "equality of a sort, distributed to equal and unequal alike."[704] Differences in

---

[696] Ibid., 173-186.

[697] Nicolo Machiavelli, *The Prince*, trans. Luigi Ricci (Chicago: Great Books Foundation, 1955), 57-58; Elisa Carrillo, "Machiavelli, Niccolò," in *Berkshire Encyclopedia of World History*, vol. 3, ed. William H. McNeill, Jerry H. Bentley, David Christian, David Levinson, J. R. McNeill, Heidi Roupp, and Judith P. Zinsser (Great Barrington, MA: Berkshire Publishing Group, 2005), 1169.

[698] Machiavelli, 58.

[699] Plato, *Republic*, 216-217.

[700] Ibid., 219.

[701] Ibid., 217.

[702] Ibid., 349.

[703] Ibid.

[704] Ibid., 357.

worth and ability elevated free persons above slaves.[705] Although violence against slaves was wrong, citizens should disdain them.

Disliking inferiors, Plato distrusted indigents. With nothing to lose as the chasm widened between them and elites, paupers might risk revolution in hopes of overthrowing oppressors.[706] He feared "Violence and Anarchy" whereby "the poor conquer and kill some of the other party and banish others."[707] This outcome anathema, Plato upheld inequality's inviolability.

6.3.2 Aristotle: Inequality as Innately Human

6.3.2.1 Slavery

Although contradicting his mentor Plato on several issues, Aristotle likewise judged people inherently unequal in chapter 1.[708] Plato wanted to diminish inequality, the previous section indicated, whereas Aristotle, believing any attempt to achieve equality or privilege commoners harmed everyone, wished to preserve its magnitude to avert anarchy.[709]

Relationships created community throughout nature, Aristotle asserted.[710] For example, male and female plants and animals coupled to reproduce. This association transcending volition, nature mandated reproduction, else a species vanished. Equally necessary, the superior-subordinate pairing underpinned society, produced hierarchy, and precluded equality.

Inequality pervaded home, village, and city.[711] Putting husband above wife, owner over slave, and father before child, the home evinced superiors' control of inferiors. Aristotle acknowledged that critics thought bondage, presumably absent elsewhere in the biota, unnatural. Rather than part of nature, it was a construct. Unnaturalness was evident in coercion, which was unnecessary to make someone breathe, sleep, drink, or eat. Failure to refute this point weakened Aristotle's defense of slavery.

Yet bondage, defined last chapter as compulsory altruism, transcends us as demonstrated by chapter 2's worker bees who resemble slaves. Privileging the group over the individual, sociality disadvantaged omegas.

Rather than try to decouple bondage and force, Aristotle admitted that governments enslaved people through war, a practice last chapter noted in Southwest Asia.[712] On one hand, he, believing a conqueror demonstrated superiority by enslaving infe-

---

[705] Ibid., 347.

[706] Ibid., 354.

[707] Ibid., 355-359.

[708] Henry B. Veatch, *Aristotle: A Contemporary Appreciation* (Bloomington and London: Indiana University Press, 1974), 5; Brumbaugh, 173.

[709] Aristotle, *Politics*, trans. Benjamin Jowett (New York: Modern Library, 1943), 62.

[710] Ibid., 52.

[711] Ibid., 53-56.

[712] Ibid., 60-61.

riors, linked violence and virtue. His opinion that the strong should rule parroted the doctrine of *Republic* participant Thrasymachus that the powerful govern by making and enforcing laws.[713] On the other hand, force discomforted Aristotle, who conceived master and slave as "friends" with "a common interest."[714] Realizing this language's absurdity, Aristotle deemed an owner's duties irksome enough to prompt his hiring an overseer.

Aristotle defined a slave as property that helped owners gain necessities.[715] As "a living possession," he resembled livestock rather than a plow, spade, or other tool.[716] Repeating that "he who is by nature not his own...is also a possession," Aristotle wrote that "the use made of slaves and of tame animals is not very different."[717] Nature fitted slaves, like livestock, for labor by giving them strong bodies but only enough reason to understand their chores whereas masters had physiques unsuited for labor but intellects ideal for command. Through careful management, an owner protected slaves, like livestock, from danger. Bondage thus advantaged everyone.

Demonstrating elitism in a man who benefited from antiquity's inequality, Aristotle defended slavery with the dispassion of someone detached from its consequences. In a zero-sum economy and society, his prestige and privilege would have diminished had paupers gained status. Revolution, Plato warned earlier, threatened elites.

Like Plato, birth into a prominent family privileged Aristotle. His father was physician to Macedonian king Amyntas III (420–370 BCE).[718] Leisure enabling lifelong study, Aristotle attended Plato's Academy in Athens, thereafter joining friends at Assos (in today's Turkey) to concentrate on marine biology. At Macedonian king Philip II's (382–336 BCE) invitation, he tutored Philip's son, Alexander the Great (356–323 BCE).

6.3.2.2 Wealth Distribution

Beyond slavery as an aspect of inequality, Aristotle listed three wealth distributions.[719] Quantifying his typology, a community might exhibit maximum inequality with a Gini of one, maximum equality with a Gini of zero, or inequality between these opposites with a Gini between zero and one.

The Gini maximum and minimum express hypotheticals. Disbelieving that Gini was ever zero, this book maintains that humans always hierarchized. The issue is inequality's magnitude, not existence. Inequality ranging between zero and one, myriad possibilities exist because the disparity may vary almost infinitely.

---

[713] Ibid., 72; Plato, *Republic*, 137.
[714] Aristotle, *Politics*, 62-63.
[715] Ibid., 56-57.
[716] Ibid., 57.
[717] Ibid., 58-60.
[718] T. A. Sinclair, "Translator's Introduction," in *The Politics*, Aristotle, trans. T. A. Sinclair (London: Penguin Books, 1981), 13.
[719] Aristotle, *Politics*, 80.

Despite variability, history reveals trends. The maximum Gini of one being impossible, Branko Milanovic calculated that after 2010 the most unequal nations were Brazil and South Africa at roughly 0.6.[720] Also markedly unequal, China, Malaysia, the Philippines, and most of Africa and Latin America were between 0.5 and 0.6.[721] Russia and the United States, between 0.4 and 0.5, approximated Rome's republic over two millennia earlier.[722] Affirming inequality's persistence, stasis over this duration supports the leitmotif that it is permanent and innate in us.

Although inequality unsettles some economists, Aristotle justified it, first, as an outcome of private property's unequal distribution.[723] All polities favoring private over communal property, privatization trumped socialism. Second, contradicting Matthew's parable of the vineyard, he made inequality an outcome of linking pay and productivity; those who worked harder and longer than others deserved greater compensation. Third, equality, not promoting happiness, was bad policy.

Aristotle faulted inordinate inequality for class conflict in Sparta and northern Greece.[724] As in *Nicomachean Ethics*, he advocated moderation.[725] Moderate inequality trumped an extreme and untenable Gini near zero or one. Landowners might cushion inequality by sharing food, slaves, dogs, and horses with others.[726] Such generosity was not socialism. These items, belonging to the owner, never became communal property.

6.4 Review and Preview

Ancient religion and philosophy vacillated about inequality, though authors, being elites, often defended the status quo. Next chapter treats ancient Egyptian inequality, which reflected the chasm between landowners and landless. The sumptuous tombs of the pharaohs, among the past's grandest, persist as symbols of opulence. By contrast, nobody memorialized Egypt's indigents.

---

[720] Milanovic, 30-31.

[721] Ibid.; Thomas Piketty, *Capital and Ideology*, trans. Arthur Goldhammer (Cambridge, MA and London: Belknap Press of Harvard University Press, 2020), 623; Scheidel, 227.

[722] Milanovic, 30-31.

[723] Aristotle, *Politics*, 87-89.

[724] Ibid., 107-108.

[725] Aristotle, *Nicomachean Ethics*, trans. Martin Ostwald (Indianapolis and New York: Bobbs-Merrill, 1962), 42-43.

[726] Aristotle, *Politics*, 88.

CHAPTER 7. EGYPTIAN INEQUALITY

7.1 Abstract

Egypt, "the world's first superpower," perpetuated gargantuan inequality.[727] In principle, pharaoh owned all land, livestock, labor, and crops, yielding a Gini, a measure of inequality defined last chapter, of one. Negating pharaoh's monopoly, priests and local elites, exploiting underlings through tenancy, taxation, corvée, conscription, usury, serfdom, and slavery, had large estates. Beset by these demands, peasants suffered overwork, undernutrition, injury, and early death. Elites feared retaliation from them and understood that class antagonism threatened upheaval.

7.2 Gift of the Nile

The Fertile Crescent discussed in chapter 5 included Egypt's Nile Valley. As the Tigris and Euphrates rivers nourished Mesopotamia, the Nile underpinned Egyptian agriculture. Understanding the river's importance, Greek historian Herodotus (c. 485–c. 425 BCE) declared Egypt the "gift of the Nile."[728]

The world's longest river, it originates in Uganda, flows north over 4,100 miles, and enters the Mediterranean Sea.[729] Occupying part of the river, Egypt stretched from the Mediterranean coast in the north to the first cataract at Aswan in the south. Deterring invaders, deserts west and east of the

---

[727] Douglas J. Brewer, *Ancient Egypt: Foundations of a Civilization* (Harlow, UK: Pearson Longman, 2005), 156.

[728] J. Gwyn Griffiths, "Hecataeus and Herodotus on 'a Gift of the River'," *Journal of Near Eastern Studies* 25, no. 1 (January 1966): 57.

[729] Brewer, 28; Nel Yomtov, *Ancient Egypt* (New York: Scholastic, 2013), 10.

Nile let Egypt develop without continual interference. The Sinai Peninsula extended Egypt northeast into Asia, whose empires occasionally conquered Egypt, which at other times penetrated northeast to amass territory. South of the first cataract, Nubia traded with and fought Egypt.

Movement south through Egypt necessitates travel up the Nile. The southernmost part is Upper Egypt, from where the Nile flows north to the delta near Giza and Cairo, dividing into smaller streams that branch west and east on the journey north to the Mediterranean. The delta separates the north's Lower Egypt from Upper Egypt.

With water and edible aquatic creatures, the Nile attracted settlers over 300,000 years ago.[730] These inhabitants were premodern people, whose evolution chapter 3 overviewed. Displaying modern features, Egypt's oldest skeletons approximated 68,000 BCE.[731] Given modern humans' African origin around 200,000 years ago, 130 millennia appear to have elapsed before Egypt's colonization, though their early presence in Morocco should have permitted equally early residence in Egypt because only 2,300 miles separated the two. Continuously occupying Egypt during the last 250,000 years, premodern and thereafter modern people ate plants, fish, and game whose thirst brought them to the Nile.[732] Southwest Asian crop and livestock adoption around 5000 BCE deepened dependence on the river.[733]

Unlike the Tigris and Euphrates, the Nile's predictability made Egypt stabler than Mesopotamia. Ethiopia's rainfall and melting snow swelled the Nile, which flooded Egypt annually between June and October.[734] Its silt made the Nile Valley "one of the most fertile strips of land in the world."[735] But fertility extended only as far as the river widened at maximum inundation. West and east of this area, desert prohibited farming. Egypt's geography, hydrology, and climate thus confined civilization to lands adjacent the Nile.

An advantage of studying Egypt is its literature and art as sources of evidence. Not only locals documented Egypt's past; neighbors described a civilization they often esteemed above theirs. Old even by Greek and Roman

---

[730] Beatrix Midant-Reynes, *The Prehistory of Egypt: From the First Egyptians to the First Pharaohs*, trans. Ian Shaw (Oxford, UK and Malden, MA: Blackwell, 2000), 25.

[731] Chris Stringer and Peter Andrews, *The Complete World of Human Evolution* (London: Thames & Hudson, 2005), 161.

[732] Brewer, 44-60.

[733] Naomi F. Miller and Wilma Wetterstrom, "The Beginnings of Agriculture," in *The Cambridge World History of Food*, vol. 2, ed. Kenneth F. Kiple and Kriemhild Coneè Ornelas (Cambridge, UK: Cambridge University Press, 2000), 1129-1130.

[734] Brewer, 38, 40.

[735] Robert N. Bellah, *Religion in Human Evolution: From the Paleolithic to the Axial Age* (Cambridge, MA and London: Belknap Press of Harvard University Press, 2011), 228.

standards, Egypt's durability comforted onlookers who revered constancy and feared change as misfortune's harbinger.

7.3 Castes

7.3.1 Elites

Evincing stark inequality that epitomized Greek philosopher Plato's (c. 428–c. 348 BCE) discussion in chapters 1 and 6 of the tension between elites and laborers, Egypt corroborated *Eternal Inequality*'s contention that the first subjugated the second. Nobody who studied it could think humankind egalitarian.

Religion crowned Egypt with chapter 4's sun god Ra or Re. Life's creator, he ruled earth, sky, and underworld.[736] Descending to earth incarnate, Ra became the first pharaoh and appointed son Horus as successor.[737] Styling themselves Horus, pharaohs linked themselves to Ra and solidified their status as gods.

Although this mythology regressed pharaoh far into prehistory, most of Egypt's past lacked centralism. The Nile valley's Neolithic villages were independent into the fourth millennium, when Upper Egyptian rentiers began accumulating enough wealth to erect monumental tombs.[738] Tradition credited Upper Egypt's ruler Menes, whose historicity is debatable, with conquering Lower Egypt to unite the Nile valley between the first cataract and the Mediterranean around 3100 BCE. Establishing the capital in Memphis roughly 12 miles south of Cairo, the first pharaohs inaugurated dynasticism.

They claimed all land and everything on it, as mentioned. This pretension, necessitating absolute authority and wealth, culminated the innate longing to top humanity's hierarchy. The elite tradition of building enormous tombs incentivized construction of ever larger monuments as pharaohs sought to eclipse their predecessors. These structures awed visitors and perpetuated a decedent's eminence into eternity.

These efforts climaxed during the Old Kingdom's fourth dynasty (c. 2613–c. 2494 BCE), "the age of pyramids."[739] "Nothing in Egyptian history or

---

[736] John P. McKay, Bennett D. Hill, John Buckler, Clare Haru Crowston, Merry E. Wiesner-Hanks, and Joe Perry, *Understanding Western Society: A Brief History* (Boston and New York: Bedford/St. Martin's, 2012), 19.

[737] Bob Brier and Hoyt Hobbs, *Ancient Egypt: Everyday Life in the Land of the Nile* (New York: Sterling, 2009), 73-75.

[738] Bellah, 229; Yomtov, 10-14.

[739] Yomtov, 16; Bellah, 234-235; Rosalie David, *Handbook to Life in Ancient Egypt*, rev. ed. (New York: Facts on File, 2003), 63.

---

that of any other archaic society comes near to equaling the colossal under-taking involved in the construction of the great pyramids of Cheops and Khephren at Giza in the middle of the third millennium BCE, engineering feats not equaled again in human history until the twentieth century," enthused American sociologist Robert Bellah (1927–2013).[740] Although Giza's three pyramids memorialized pharaohs, anonymous workers toiled decades to erect them. Celebrated over the millennia, these edifices would not exist without the men and women whose exertions created all wealth.

The largest of the trio, Cheops' Great Pyramid, approximating 2589 to 2566 BCE, had a 13.1-acre base and 481-foot apex that crowned the world's tallest structure until French engineer Gustave Eiffel (1832–1923) completed his 1889 tower.[741] One hundred thousand slaves built the Great Pyramid over two decades, estimated Herodotus.[742] American Egyptologist Barbara Mertz (1927–2013) and American anthropologist Douglas Brewer (b. 1954) reduced the workforce to roughly 20,000, none slaves.[743] Instead, farmworkers assembled it in increments when the annual inundation delayed agriculture.

Misinterpretations cloud the pyramids and kindred structures. First, belief that patriotism inspired workers is incorrect.[744] Like Mesopotamia, Egypt used corvée, which involved everyone in principle, though as in Meso-potamia the rich sent substitutes.[745] Second, the claim that government fed workers is misleading.[746] They fed themselves with the previous year's harvest, which they produced. Government was the distributor not wealth's creator or people's provider.

Monuments aside, pharaohs symbolized order, which meant the status quo.[747] "Every town says let us suppress the powerful among us," feared a First Intermediate Period (c. 2181–c. 1991 BCE) document.[748] Threatening at any moment, class conflict was a slippery slope toward a nadir where, evincing the introduction's Newtonian backlash, "The children of princes are dashed against the walls."[749]

---

[740] Bellah, 235.

[741] Bellah, 235; Brier and Hobbs, 14; Mertz, 227; David, 63.

[742] Mertz, 238; Yomtov, 19.

[743] Mertz, 238; Brewer, 200.

[744] Yomtov, 19.

[745] Marjorie Gann and Janet Willen, *Five Thousand Years of Slavery* (Toronto, ON: Tundra Books, 2011), 6; David, 142.

[746] Brier and Hobbs, 18.

[747] Ibid., 74; David, 63.

[748] Brier and Hobbs, 74.

[749] Ibid.

The danger was real because workers swamped the rich. Egypt's 1 million to 1.5 million people included only "a few hundred" nobles.[750] Addition of their families raised the total to 2,000 or 3,000. Inclusion of local landowners made the percentage 3 to 5. The mean of 1 million and 1.5 million yielded around 1.25 million commoners. The mean percentage of 4 yielded 50,000 elites against these 1.25 million.

These 50,000 prevented pharaoh's hoarding everything. Unlike the United States millennia later, Egypt united government and religion. As civil and religious leader, pharaoh gave temples and their priests land. Appointing kin and confidants priests, he strengthened the link between government and religion. As landholders, priests helped him preserve stasis in the country-side. By New Kingdom's end about 1070 BCE, temples collectively had more land than pharaoh, who remained the largest individual landowner.[751]

Equally important, neither Egypt nor any premodern polity could micromanage society.[752] Despite projecting power by owning property in all Egypt's 44 districts, pharaoh lacked instantaneous communication and surveillance equipment to monitor and respond to events.[753] Absent a police state, power devolved to local elites, as in chapters 10 and 19's China, who rivaled priests and pharaoh.

Class antagonism may explain the pyramids and other tombs' fate. Over decades of discovery and publicity, scholars and public celebrated Egypt's treasures and regretted what was stolen. For example, American Egyptologist Robert Brier (b. 1943) and American philosopher Hoyt Hobbs rued that the Great Pyramid's "anti-burglary systems...sadly proved to no avail: the pyramid was picked clean in ancient times."[754]

Another outcome is unimaginable in the Newtonian system. Cheating labor, pharaohs and other elites seized the harvest. Retaliating by looting tombs, the underclass retook the wealth they had produced over a lifetime.

7.3.2 Commoners

Chapter 5's 10 percent surplus spared few of these proletarians from agriculture. Brier and Hobbs estimated taxes at a decile of the harvest, a claim evaluated later.[755] Confiscating the surplus, this rate freed only elites from drudgery.

---

[750] Bellah, 234.
[751] Brier and Hobbs, 78.
[752] Ibid., 77.
[753] David, 146; Nardo, 16.
[754] Brier and Hobbs, 14.
[755] Ibid., 81.

As noted, Egyptian agriculture began around 5000 BCE. The surplus let elites ornament tombs beyond anything possible for underlings within 600 years.[756] Differentiating among grave goods, Brewer divided early Egypt into nobles and senior officials, midgrade bureaucrats and craftspeople, and farmworkers.[757]

Doubting that a middle class existed, last chapter quoted Serbian American economist Branko Milanovic's (b. 1953) observation that premodern economies displayed "equality in poverty."[758] From the earliest dynasties, landless farmhands were tenants, laborers, serfs, slaves, or *hemw*, a category overviewed later.[759]

Coinage absent until the sixth century BCE, compensation consisted of part of the harvest.[760] Some landowners let workers keep what they gleaned in one day after the harvest. Common by late dynasties, tenancy often involved a contract between landowner and renter, who hired laborers. Owner and tenant splitting the harvest, the latter decided how much to give hirelings.

Pharaoh's hypothetical ownership of everything enslaved labor. American British classicist Moses Finley (1912–1986) deemed Egypt's farmhands unfree.[761] Brier and Hobbs labeled them serfs rather than slaves; attached to land, they were not sold individually but changed owners upon its sale or inheritance.[762] This logic made all commoners, roughly 1.25 million by the earlier calculation, serfs.

Eternal Inequality doubts Egypt ever lacked slaves. Although serfs might have outnumbered them, bondage grew over time.[763] Like Mesopotamia, Egypt acquired them through war. A commander enslaved over 10,000 captives in one campaign, bragged one text. A roughly 500 BCE stone carving showed black Africans' enslavement, which chapters 9, 12, and 14 examine.

Besides warfare, courts could enslave anyone who shirked corvée or conscription.[764] As in Mesopotamia, default enslaved debtors. In other cases, officials beat them. One decree ordered 100 lashes upon default.[765] Punishment did not prevent indebtedness' increase, especially during the New

---

[756] Brewer, 77-81.

[757] Ibid., 144-145.

[758] Branko Milanovic, *The Haves and the Have-Nots: A Brief and Idiosyncratic History of Global Inequality* (New York: Basic Books, 2011), 50.

[759] Brewer, 156.

[760] Ibid., 156, 158; David, 319.

[761] M. I. Finley, *The Ancient Economy* (Berkeley: University of California Press, 1999), 98.

[762] Brier and Hobbs, 90.

[763] Ibid., 90-91; Gann and Willen, 6-7.

[764] Gann and Willen, 6-7.

[765] David Graeber, *Debt: The First 5,000 Years* (Brooklyn and London: Melville House, 2014), 218-219.

Kingdom (c. 1570–c. 1070 BCE). Later pharaohs attempted to counteract this trend. Bakenranef (r. 720–715 BCE), for example, copied Mesopotamia by cancelling debts and freeing peons for fear that indebted soldiers might be jailed when Egypt needed them to defend the fatherland. His decree was among the earliest to mention debt imprisonment. Macedonian king Alexander the Great's (356–323 BCE) successors in Egypt, identifying debt as a persistent problem, regularized its cancellation.

The wealthy bought slaves from beyond Egypt's deserts. Crossing the Sahara from south to north, chapter 15's caravan routes fostered blacks' enslavement. Apprehensiveness about bondage was so pervasive that elites, fearing enslavement in the afterlife, entombed laborers' statuettes with them so these men and women would toil in their place.[766]

Besides serfs and slaves, American historian Don Nardo (b. 1947) described *hemw*, a category difficult to define.[767] Unfree to work as they pleased, they obeyed the master. This restriction abounded; non-slaves, free in a narrow sense, heeded the owner whose land they worked. *Hemw* could be bought, sold, rented, inherited, gifted, or otherwise transferred, and their children were unfree, all slave characteristics. Yet they earned wages below what free people expected, married anyone irrespective of status, owned property, and bequeathed it to heirs, all attributes of freedom that led British Egyptologist Ann Rosalie David (b. 1946) to deny slavery's existence.[768]

Eternal Inequality disagrees. *Hemw*'s putative rights expressed aspiration over actuality because rank preoccupied Egyptians. Like Americans, they embraced upward mobility despite its nonexistence.[769] Whatever this category's supposed benefits, *hemw* disliked their status. Coercion ubiquitous, unfree Egyptians always outnumbered their free compatriots.[770]

7.4 Dietary Inequality

7.4.1 Elites

Rich and poor ate different diets, with meat marking the divide. Elites consumed beef, pork, mutton, lamb, chevon, capretto, rabbit, hare, antelope, donkey, hedgehog, catfish, perch, mullet, tilapia, carp, eel, turtle, clams, crocodile, goose, duck, pigeon, dove, heron, quail, pelican, and chicken by

---

[766] Ibid.
[767] Nardo, 38-39.
[768] David, 361.
[769] Brewer, 158.
[770] Brier and Hobbs, 90.

the fourth century BCE.[771] Introduction of horse and chariot after the Second Intermediate Period (c. 1782–c. 1570 BCE) helped hunters add lion, leopard, ostrich, and elephant to elite diets.

New Kingdom priests at a temple to Amun, Amen, or Amon, another solar deity, managed a ranch with over 400,000 cattle.[772] Another employed nearly 1,000 men to tend numerous herds. Other evidence that priests favored beef came from middens near their dwellings at South Abydos, Upper Egypt. Approximating 95 percent cow bones, trash proved beef the chief meat.[773] "Meat was a luxury dish in Egypt," affirmed French historian Pierre Tallet (b. 1966).[774] The poor afforded none, except perhaps during an occasional festival when they indulged beyond their means.

Brier and Hobbs thought bread ubiquitous, though *Eternal Inequality* disagrees.[775] Next chapter's elites of first century CE Herculaneum, in Italy, ate bread whereas commoners afforded only gruel or porridge. Chapter 7 regresses this pattern to pre-Roman Egypt. Honey or other additives priced bread further beyond workers. Bread was chapter 5's barley, which was safer than wheat to grow. Wheat's uncommonness made it dear, though the wealthy did not balk.

Mortuary texts stated decedents' preference for bread. These inscriptions in burial chambers, which only the wealthy afforded, confirmed bread's eminence.[776] Mummies' teeth exhibited abrasions from sand in bread.[777] Only the rich afforded mummification, mentioned chapter 4. Evincing fondness for bread, one Second Intermediate Period pharaoh and family ate some 2,000 loaves daily.[778] The wealthy ate few African millets like sorghum.[779]

[771] Barbara Mertz, *Red Land, Black Land: Daily Life in Ancient Egypt*, 2d ed. (New York: William Morrow, 2008), 108-109; Brier and Hobbs, 119-131; David, 365; Don Nardo, *Life in Ancient Egypt* (San Diego: Reference Point Press, 2015), 25.

[772] Lionel Casson, *Everyday Life in Ancient Egypt*, rev. ed. (Baltimore and London: Johns Hopkins University Press, 2001), 39.

[773] Lisa Sabbahy, "A Decade of Advances in the Paleopathology of the Ancient Egyptians," in *Egyptian Bioarchaeology: Humans, Animals, and the Environment*, ed. Salima Ikram, Jessica Kaiser, and Roxie Walker (Leiden: Sidestone Press, 2015), 116; Pierre Tallet, "Food in Ancient Egypt," in *A Companion to Food in the Ancient World*, ed. John Wilkins and Robin Nadeau (Chichester, UK: Wiley Blackwell, 2015), 321.

[774] Tallet, 321.

[775] Brier and Hobbs, 121.

[776] Mertz, 108.

[777] Brier and Hobbs, 135.

[778] Ibid., 86.

[779] Alexandra Touzeau, Romain Amiot, Janne Blichert-Toft, Jean-Pierre Flandrois, François Fourel, Vincent Grossi, François Martineau, Pascale Richardin, and Christoph Lecuyer, "Diet of Ancient Egyptians Inferred from Stable Isotope Systematics," *Journal of Archaeological Science* 46, no. 1 (June 2014): 120.

They consumed imports like almonds and cinnamon.[780] Augmenting elite menus around 400 CE, Rome imported Asia's oranges, lemons, peaches, and bananas into Egypt. Egyptians grew coconuts for magnates, who used honey as a sweetener whereas underlings relied on dates.[781] American anthropologists Naomi Miller and Wilma Wetterstrom doubted the "lower classes ever saw honey."[782] Sugar was unknown in ancient Egypt.[783]

Elites ate three, and everyone else two, meals daily.[784] The best vintages accompanied feasts.[785] The delta yielded the best grapes, whose wines cost most. Tutankhamen's (r. 1334–1325 BCE) tomb held 26 jars of delta wine.[786] Figs, dates, and pomegranates also made wine. Elites disparaged beer as ordinary, a judgment that persists. Commoners sometimes drank wine at festivals, though cheapness recommended beer.

The wealthy ate not only more meals but more food than indigents. Art depicted mounds of edibles, which servants brought guests in bowls.[787] Overindulgence, which writers thought improper, sickened gluttons and drunks.[788] Abetting decadence, topless women gyrated to music. Feasts thus let elites advertise rank through conspicuous consumption and debasement of servants and harlots.

7.4.2 Commoners

As noted, the rich owned many cattle. Pricing beef beyond him, one cow cost a smallholder's harvest or a workman's yearly wages.[789] A reconstruction of his foods listed barley gruel or porridge, lettuce, celery, parsley, turnip, beet, radish, fava bean, pea, lentil, chickpea, garlic, onion, leek, cucumber, papyrus root, lotus root, nuts, juniper berry, doum palm fruit, carob, jujube, pomegranate, watermelon, fig, date, grape, raisin, plum, and possibly apple.[790] Rome introduced olives into Egypt after 30 BCE, though sesame rivaled them for oil.[791] Elite and commoner diets surpassed others in variety before modernity, believed Brier and Hobbs.[792]

---

[780] Brier and Hobbs, 124-125.

[781] Nardo, 26.

[782] Miller and Wetterstrom, 1135.

[783] Brier and Hobbs, 131.

[784] Nardo, 27.

[785] Ibid.; Brier and Hobbs, 125; Mertz, 109.

[786] Brier and Hobbs, 127.

[787] Ibid., 132-133.

[788] Ibid., 122, 133-134; Mertz, 111.

[789] Brier and Hobbs, 119.

[790] Ibid., 124, 135; Nardo, 25.

[791] Peter Garnsey, *Food and Society in Classical Antiquity* (Cambridge, UK: Cambridge University Press, 1999), 14.

[792] Brier and Hobbs, 119.

Recalling their diet as slaves in Egypt, Numbers (c. 500 BCE) stated that Hebrews ate cucumber, watermelon, leek, garlic, onion, and fish but no meat.[793] Curious is the intimation that they consumed abundant fish given animal protein's rarity among paupers. Written around a millennium after the events they purported to narrate, these reminiscences may have been exaggerations. Numbers listed these foods amid Hebrew dissatisfaction with homelessness as people in a new neighborhood might want old acquaintances and familiar surroundings even when their former lives had been unpleasant.

7.5 Unequal Workload and Health

7.5.1 Elites

7.5.1.1 Indolence

Elites pursued hedonism, which government guaranteed through lifetime pensions.[794] Largess was possible because government taxed the harvest.[795] Nowadays conservatives oppose taxation because money might flow from rich to poor, though Egypt taxed commoners to support elites. Redistributing wealth upward, taxation oppressed underlings.

American anthropologist David Graeber (1961–2020) blamed this ruthlessness on bureaucrats who "had their hands in everything: there was a dazzling array of taxes and a continual distribution of allotments, wages, and payments from the state" and who based taxes on the Nile's inundation.[796] If it covered 2 percent more land than the previous year, for example, taxes increased 2 percent irrespective of the harvest. As in Mesopotamia, agents swarmed the countryside when grain ripened to take their portion.[797]

A second millennium BCE account stated that a taxman, tying, beating, and drowning a farmworker for nonpayment, enslaved the wife and children as onlookers fled the village.[798]

As mentioned, Brier and Hobbs believed Egyptian taxes took a decile of the harvest. This estimate seems doubtful, as it halved the quintile quoted in chapter 5 for Hebrews in Egypt. That chapter put Sumer's barley tax at 48 percent of the harvest, though full collection must have been impossible.

---

[793] Num. 11:5 (New American Bible).
[794] Brier and Hobbs, 87.
[795] Ibid., 81-83.
[796] Ibid., 81; Graeber, 217-218.
[797] Brier and Hobbs, 102.
[798] David Christian, *Origin Story: A Big History of Everything* (London: Allen Lane, 2018), 216.

Additionally, chapter 5 estimated fourteenth century CE China's rural taxes at 15–20 percent of the harvest.

Even 10 percent tax, eliminating agriculture's 10 percent surplus, left farmers only enough for food and next year's seed. Although the Nile benefited Egypt, surplus was never certain. Pharaoh's dream of seven years' plenty and seven years' dearth implied that half of Egypt's crops failed.[799] Insects, diseases, and hail killed its livestock and crops.[800] Taxation amid ruination anticipated U.S. Supreme Court chief justice John Marshall's (1755–1835) warning that "the power to tax involves the power to destroy."[801]

7.5.1.2 Gluttony

An earlier section described elite overindulgence, which weakened health. Researchers examining 137 Egyptian, Peruvian, American Southwestern, and Aleutian Island mummies for atherosclerosis, the last two, with just five individuals each, are omitted.[802] Twenty-nine of the 76 (38.2 percent) Egyptians displayed the condition, which meat overconsumption likely caused, compared with 13 of the 51 (25.5 percent) Peruvians.

These Egyptians were typical. Forty-four of 52 mummies (84.6 percent) in Cairo's Egyptian Museum evinced atherosclerosis or another cardiovascular disease.[803] Another sample revealed it in nine of 16 (56.3 percent) mummies.[804]

Overconsumption and inactivity harming Egypt's wealthy, atherosclerosis troubled Ramses II (r. 1279–1237 BCE), may have killed thirteenth son and successor Merenptah (r. 1236–1223 BCE), ailed diabetic priest Inemakhet, and clogged five arteries in princess Ahmose Meryet Amon (c.

---

[799] Gen. 41:1-31.

[800] Exodus 8:13-14; Exodus 9:3-6; Exodus 9:8-10; Exodus 9:18-31; Exodus 10:4-15.

[801] Stephan Thernstrom, *A History of the American People, Vol. I: To 1877*, 2d ed. (San Diego: Harcourt Brace Jovanovich, 1989), 319.

[802] R. C. Thompson, A. H. Allam, G. P. Lombardi, L. S. Wann, M. L. Sutherland, J. D. Sutherland, M. A. Soliman, B. Frohlich, D. T. Mininberg, J. M. Monge, C. M. Vallodolid, S. L. Cox, G. Abd el-Maksoud, I. Badr, M. I. Miyamoto, A. el-Halim Nur el-Din, J. Narula, C. E. Finch, and G. S. Thomas, "Atherosclerosis across 4000 Years of Human History: The Horus Study of Four Ancient Populations," *Lancet* 381 (April 6, 2013): 1211-1222, accessed May 10, 2022, ‹https://www.ncbi.nlm.nih.gov/pubmed/23489753.›

[803] Sabbahy, 116.

[804] Colleen M. Story, "The History of Heart Disease," Healthline, last modified September 21, 2019, accessed February 28, 2022, ‹https://www.healthline.com/health/heart-disease/history.›

1580–c. 1550 BCE), whose heart attack was fatal.[805] Overindulgence and idleness fattened diabetic Hatshepsut (c. 1508–c. 1458 BCE).[806]

Illuminating elite lives and deaths, mummies indicated that most perished in their thirties.[807] Of 30 whose lifespan could be estimated from a collection in Lyon, France's Museum of Natural History, 24 died before age 40 including seven before age 20.[808] Six, one fifth of this sample, surpassed 40 years, longevity few matched into the Middle Ages.[809]

Despite drawbacks, plenitude protected Egypt's plutocrats from hunger, though they may not have suffered fewer infections and infestations amid rampant contagion and parasites.[810] Abundance was not their only edge because they avoided overwork and injuries that debilitated commoners. Exhaustion, which killed Caribbean slaves, also slew Egypt's poor.

7.5.2 Commoners

Unlike elites, the underclass suffered undernutrition, which afflicted Tell el-Amarna, the capital under early monotheist Akhenaten (r. 1350–1334 BCE).[811] Its South Tombs Cemetery had 274 partial and complete skeletons. Remains of 95 adults and 64 youths, at least half complete, allowed study. Grave goods' paucity or absence identified commoners. The 64 pre-adults displayed stunting as early as 7.5 months, near weaning's start.[812] Transition to solids brought chronic undernutrition. Adults remained stunted, with women on average shorter than elsewhere in Egypt. Men were shorter than their counterparts except those around 4200 BCE. Cribra orbitalia, porous-

---

[805] Ibid.; Sabbahy, 117; Renate Germer, *Mummies: Life after Death in Ancient Egypt* (Munich and New York: Prestel, 1997), 127; James Owen, "Egyptian Princess Mummy Had Oldest Known Heart Disease," *National Geographic News*, April 15, 2011, accessed February 28, 2022, ‹Egyptian Princess Mummy Had Oldest Known Heart Disease (nationalgeographic.com).›

[806] Meredith F. Small, "Mummy Reveals Egyptian Queen Was Fat, Balding and Bearded," Live Science, July 6, 2007, accessed February 28, 2022, ‹https://www.livescience.com/7336-mummy-reveals-egyptian-queen-fat-balding-bearded.html.›

[807] Germer, 128.

[808] Guillaume Herzberg and Raoul Perrot, "*Paleopathologie de 31 Cranes Egyptiens Momifies du Museum d'Histoire Naturelle de Lyon*," *Paleobios* 1, no. 1-2 (1983): 105.

[809] McKay, Hill, Buckler, Crowston, Wiesner-Hanks, and Perry, 212; Edward S. Deevey Jr., "The Human Population," *Scientific American* 203, no. 3 (September 1, 1960): 200.

[810] Walter Scheidel, *Death on the Nile: Disease and the Demography of Roman Egypt* (Leiden: Brill, 2001), 59-95; Germer, 127-128.

[811] Barry Kemp, Anna Stevens, Gretchen R. Dobbs, Melissa Zabecki, and Jerome C. Rose, "Life, Death and beyond in Akhenaten's Egypt: Excavating the South Tombs Cemetery at Amarna," *Antiquity* 87, no. 335 (March 1, 2013): 67-68; Kevin M. McGeough, "Akhenaten," in *World History Encyclopedia, Vol. 4, Era 2: Early Civilizations, 4000-1000 BCE*, ed. Kevin M. McGeough, Alfred J. Andrea, and Carolyn Neel (Santa Barbara, CA: ABC-CLIO, 2011), 619-620.

[812] Ibid., 71-72.

---

ness in the upper eye orbits, indicated anemia. Although pathogens and parasites may cause it, researchers implicated diets deficient in iron or, less often, vitamin B9 or B12. The body absorbing iron better from animals than plants, insufficient meat was likely culpable.

Roughly 5 percent of juvenile remains, exhibiting porousness in cranial sphenoid, temporal, or occipital bones, evinced scurvy.[813] The actual percentage of vitamin C deficient children must have been larger because scurvy must be severe and prolonged to deform bones. Many vegetables and fruits having the vitamin, the masses must have lacked a varied diet, rebutting Brier and Hobbs' opinion that they ate many foods. With scant meat, vegetables, and fruits, they must have eaten barley, chickpea, fava bean, and lentil, none having adequate vitamin C. They must have eaten few peas, a vitamin C rich legume.[814]

Insufficiency fortified nobody for drudgery. Over three quarters of adult skeletons had osteoarthritis in the ankle, knee, hip, spine, elbow, shoulder, wrist, or their combination.[815] Adult bones thickened where tendons attached. The condition, worse than in other Egyptians but milder than in Levantines and Amerindians, revealed strenuousness, probably carrying or dragging heavy stone blocks while building the city. Amarna's opulence crippled workers; over two thirds of adults had at least one fracture.

Amarna may be compared with other Egyptian sites, including Tell Ibrahim Awad, Lower Egypt, whose poor may have fared better. Only one (1.3 percent) of its 77 partial skeletons from the Old Kingdom, First Intermediate Period, and Middle Kingdom (c. 2040–c. 1700 BCE) displayed cribra orbitalia. In contrast, it afflicted over a quartile of Tell el-Daba, Lower Egypt crania and nearly two fifths in Elephantine, an Upper Egyptian island. Tell Ibrahim Awad might, however, have mirrored Amarna and Elephantine had centuries of irrigation not degraded so many skeletons.

Better preserved than bones, teeth revealed undernutrition. Thirty-eight percent of Tell Ibrahim Awad crania had teeth with thin enamel, betraying the body's attempt, especially when young, to conserve energy and nutrients during privation.[816] Percentages in predynastic Egypt and Nubia at 40 and in Tell el-Daba at 46 imply undernutrition severe enough to impair devel-

---

[813] Ibid., 72.

[814] "Peas, Green, Raw," USDA FoodData Central, April 1, 2019, accessed February 28, 2022, ‹https://fdc.nal.usda.gov/fdc-app.html#/food-details/170419/nutrients›; Anitra C. Carr and Balz Frei, "Toward a New Recommended Dietary Allowance for Vitamin C Based on Antioxidant and Health Effects in Humans," The American Journal of Clinical Nutrition 69, no. 6 (June 1, 1999): 1086.

[815] Kemp, Stevens, Dobbs, Zabecki, and Rose, 73-74.

[816] Ibid., 164-165.

opment in nearly half these populations. Had commoners afforded it, meat might have improved health.

Egypt's masses died young. A Tell Ibrahim Awad lifespan estimate of 32.1 years omitted youth mortality because the cemetery lacked juvenile remains.[817] Egyptian life expectancy at birth around 19 years, half Roman Egypt's population died before age 10.[818] Half these deaths occurred in the first year. Adolescence alone evading high mortality, almost nobody surpassed 50 years.[819]

7.6 Review and Preview

This chapter furthers a larger investigation over several chapters of agriculture's tendency to worsen inequality by bifurcating society into landowners and landless. This lopsidedness recurs next chapter in Rome, where elites parasitized countryside and provinces. Roman inequality grew as land concentrated among few, fortunes increased among the uberwealthy, and slavery prevailed.

---

[817] Phillips, Rose, and Haarlem, 161, 163.

[818] Scheidel, 30-31; Ann E. M. Liljas, "Old Age in Ancient Egypt," University College London, March 2, 2015, accessed February 28, 2022, ‹https://blogs.ucl.ac.uk/researchers-in-museums/2015/03/02/old-age-in-ancient-egypt.›

[819] Ibid., 139.

CHAPTER 8 ROMAN INEQUALITY

8.1 Abstract

Welding Mediterranean lands into an empire, Roman elites amassed fortunes by plundering countryside and provinces. Inequality enlarged over time as the richest rose further above commoners. As they did in Southwest Asia, the Levant and Greece, and Egypt, slaves, freedmen, serfs, tenants, hirelings, and peons generated Rome's plenitude. Over 200 rebellions in the empire's first two centuries evinced the introduction's Newtonian system. Now a ruin, first century CE Herculaneum contrasted haves and have-nots.

8.2 Origin

Egypt fell in 31 BCE to the Romans, whose story began northwest of the Nile in Italy.[820] From a boot-shaped peninsula originating south of the Alps and extending into the sea, the Romans moved people, commodities, and ideas across the Mediterranean region. Through commerce and militarism, the Romans fashioned an empire, an achievement that may seem surprising for people who traced their lineage to shepherds on Rome's seven hills.[821] The location benefitted them because *Anopheles* mosquitoes, poor fliers, could not reach the hilltops to give them malaria.[822] Lowlanders suffering, highlanders shaped Rome.

---

[820] Robin W. Winks, Crane Brinton, John B. Christopher, and Robert Lee Wolff, *A History of Civilization, Vol. I: Prehistory to 1715*, 7th ed. (Englewood Cliffs, NJ: Prentice Hall, 1988), 75.

[821] Michael Kerrigan, *Ancient Rome and the Roman Empire* (London: Dorling Kindersley, 2001), 9.

[822] Robert Sallares, "Ecology," in *The Cambridge Economic History of the Greco-Roman World*, ed. Walter Scheidel, Ian Morris, and Richard Saller (Cambridge, UK: Cambridge University Press, 2007), 35.

The Romans entered Italy from elsewhere in Europe after 2000 BCE, settling Rome in the eighth century.[823] This location along the Tiber River put them in central Italy. To the south were Greek settlements and in the north the Etruscans, who governed Rome from 753 to 509, tradition held. They gave Rome an alphabet, demonstrated that mining, agriculture, and trade produced wealth, shaped its military ethos, and extolled urbanism.

Etruscan elites displayed status through ornate tombs, a practice chapter 4 traced to the Paleolithic Period. Roman patricians dwarfed these displays as empire enriched them. Transition from village to Mediterranean power began in Italy, where warfare and diplomacy made Rome master of the peninsula south of the Po River by 265.[824]

Conquest brought Rome near Sicily, which North Africa's Carthage controlled. Conflict was inevitable between the two Mediterranean commercial and military giants. Rome's victory against Carthage and others gave it Sicily, Sardinia, Corsica, Spain, Greece, and part of North Africa by 146.[825]

8.3 Empire and Inequality

8.3.1 Elites

Empire engorged elites. Among antiquity's richest, Roman land speculator and slave trader Marcus Crassus (115–53 BCE) had a fortune around 200 million sesterces and an annual income about 12 million sesterces.[826] For context, one sesterce purchased one cup of good wine.[827] Five hundred bought a mule.

Like other ambitious Romans, Crassus, believing the ability to buy an army defined one as rich, hoped to translate wealth into military and political glory.[828] A later section describes his role in crushing Roman slave and gladiator Spartcus' (c. 110–71 BCE) rebellion. His career culminated in elec-

---

[823] Joseph R. Strayer and Hans W. Gatzke, *The Mainstream of Civilization*, 3d ed. (New York: Harcourt Brace Jovanovich, 1979), 57-58; John P. McKay, Bennett D. Hill, John Buckler, Clare Haru Crowston, Merry E. Wiesner-Hanks, and Joe Perry, *Understanding Western Society: A Brief History* (Boston and New York: Bedford/St. Martin's, 2012), 116.

[824] Strayer and Gatzke, 59.

[825] Ibid., 65.

[826] Branko Milanovic, *The Haves and the Have-Nots: A Brief and Idiosyncratic History of Global Inequality* (New York: Basic Books, 2011), 42.

[827] Mary Beard, *SPQR: A History of Ancient Rome* (New York and London: Liveright Publishing, 2015), 461.

[828] Plutarch, *Fall of the Roman Republic: Six Lives: Marius, Sulla, Crassus, Pompey, Caesar, and Cicero*, trans. Rex Warner (Harmondsworth, UK: Penguin Books, 1986), 115.

tion as consul, the highest Republican office, in 70, though the Parthians executed him after a disastrous invasion of Iran.[829]

Other elites like statesman Marcus Cicero (106–43), "the most powerful man in Rome" in 63, and general, dictator, and Rome's "greatest soldier" Julius Caesar (100–44) also died violently, though the most successful combined stupendous wealth and longevity.[830] First emperor Augustus (63 BCE–14 CE), "wealthy on a new scale," descended from among Rome's oldest and richest families as Caesar's grandnephew and adopted son.[831] The family estate in 14 CE was worth roughly 250 million sesterces, which, calculated for the household, cannot compare with Crassus' individual fortune.[832] Comparing Roman and British empires, Augustus was roughly eightfold richer, adjusting for inflation, than George III (1738–1820).[833]

Augustus tapped riches unavailable to previous Romans. Egypt's conqueror, he, barring senators from visiting it without his permission, declared it his property.[834] Its wealth, flowing from last chapter's farm-workers to pharaoh, now enriched him as pharaoh's successor. He displayed his fortune through ostentation, writing in 14 CE that he transformed Rome from brick to marble at his expense.[835] He spent 860 million sesterces to reward loyal soldiers with land or a bonus upon retirement. He bragged about repairing 82 temples in one year and building a new forum, Senate building, theater, and over 12 temples. Flush with empire's spoils, Augustus gave the "people" 43.5 million sesterces upon his death, about $30 billion in 2009.[836] Additional donations to soldiers and the treasury raised the total to 2.4 billion sesterces, around $165.5 billion in 2009.[837]

These boasts ignored that workers created Augustus' riches. Parasitizing laborers who made Rome an empire, he mirrored elites throughout history by building nothing with his own hands yet taking credit for every achievement.

Wealth rose over time. Rome's largest fortune approximated 4 to 5 million sesterces in the second century BCE, 25 million in the early first

---

[829] Strayer and Gatzke, 74.

[830] Plutarch, *Fall of the Roman Republic*, 246, 334.

[831] Strayer and Gatzke, 75; Beard, 364.

[832] Milanovic, 42.

[833] Ibid., 47.

[834] Beard, 364.

[835] Ibid., 365-366; M. I. Finley, *The Ancient Economy* (Berkeley: University of California, 1999), 35; Augustus, *Res Gestae*, in *Understanding Western Society: A Brief History*, John P. McKay, Bennett D. Hill, John Buckler, Clare Haru Crowston, Merry E. Wiesner-Hanks, and Joe Perry (Boston and New York: Bedford/St. Martin's 2012), 142-143.

[836] Milanovic, 47.

[837] Finley, 35.

century BCE, 100 million in the 60s BCE, 200 million a decade later, 300 to 400 million in the first century CE, and 350 million in the early fifth century.[838] The richest 1.5 percent of Romans held between one sixth and one third of all wealth around 150 CE.[839]

Today's inequality is worse. The world's six richest magnates owned more than the poorest 4 billion people in 2017, as stated in the introduction. Yet Roman inequality permitted elites, as shown by Spartacus' rebellion, to crucify slaves.

Enhancing their status as gentry by purchasing land, Roman elites rejected chapter 6's gospel ambivalence toward wealth.[840] "But of all things from which one may acquire, none is better than agriculture, none more fruitful, none sweeter, none more fitting for a free man," wrote Cicero.[841] This sentiment may seem strange, but Americans may think of third U.S. president Thomas Jefferson (1743–1826) in these terms. Coveting profits and self-sufficiency, landowners, depending on nobody and needed neither government handout nor charity. Perverting Roman values by failing this test, paupers "aroused little sympathy and no pity throughout antiquity."[842]

Cicero and Jefferson did no labor. Slaves worked their estates, evincing the dichotomy between landowner and underling. Later chapters find this bifurcation in South and East Asia, the Americas, and medieval and modern Eurasia.

Olive oil, "the source of fabulous wealthy and power," and wine generated profits throughout the Mediterranean.[843] Emperor Hadrian (76–138 CE) was the scion of Spanish olive magnates. Emperor and stoic Marcus Aurelius (121–180) traced his paternal ancestry to Spanish olive tycoons. Emperor Septimius Severus (145–211) descended from prominent Libyan olive planters.

As in the Fertile Crescent, usury gave Roman oligarchs another path toward enrichment. Demonstrating elites' penchant for fleecing the provinces, senator and assassin Marcus Brutus (85–42 BCE) loaned money to Cyprian city Salamis at 48 percent interest.[844] When default loomed, Cicero tried to negotiate a reduction to 12 percent in hopes of preserving Brutus' profit while persuading Salamis' authorities that a better deal was not forth-

---

[838] Walter Scheidel, *The Great Leveler: Violence and the History of Inequality from the Stone Age to the Twenty-First Century* (Princeton, NJ and Oxford: Princeton University Press, 2017), 72.
[839] Ibid., 77-78.
[840] Finley, 36.
[841] Ibid., 42.
[842] Ibid., 39.
[843] Tom Mueller, *Extra Virginity: The Sublime and Scandalous World of Olive Oil* (New York and London: Norton, 2012), 43.
[844] Finley, 54.

coming. Roman lawyer and senator Pliny the Younger (61–c. 113 CE) wrote around 100 CE that interest averaged 9 percent.[845]

Wealth corrupted intellectuals who might have feigned disinterest in it. For example, Lucius Seneca (4 BCE–65 CE), philosopher, senator, and advisor to Nero (37–68 CE), was worth 300 million sesterces.[846] Entanglement with money was a Roman phenomenon that contradicted Greek philosopher Plato's (c. 428–c. 348 BCE) unease with greed, splendor, idleness, and inordinate inequality, treated in earlier chapters.

Rome's division into rich and poor pitted patrician against plebeian.[847] Belonging to Rome's oldest, richest families, patricians venerated the status quo that elevated them above everyone else. After expelling Etruscans from Rome, they established a republic and monopolized office, though they could not ignore plebeians, who formed most of the army needed to repulse invaders and conquer territory. Refusing conscription without reform, fifth century BCE plebeians won representation through a new office: the people's tribune, who could veto any patrician proposal. But wealth aligned rich plebeians, who alone could afford to campaign for office, with patricians, who absorbed them into the plutocracy. Indigents gained nothing.

"From the very beginning, kings have ruled the city of Rome," wrote Roman historian Publius Tacitus (c. 55–c. 120 CE) in acknowledging as much.[848] Similarly, Pliny the Younger's uncle, Roman naturalist Pliny the Elder (23–79), quoted in chapter 5, remarked that six men owned half Africa. Exaggeration aside for a moment, he did not mean the entire continent. The Romans neither controlled nor knew much about Africa south of the Sahara Desert. Roman Africa was North Africa: Libya, Tunisia, Algeria, and Morocco.[849]

If today's North Africa approximates the dimensions under Rome, a rough calculation is possible. The four modern nations approximate 1,172,400,000 acres.[850] If six men owned half this total in the first century, each approxi-

---

[845] Ibid., 118.

[846] Ibid., 56.

[847] Strayer and Gatzke, 58-61.

[848] Beard, 400.

[849] Milanovic, 51-52.

[850] Christina Dendy and Ellen Bailey, "Algeria," in *Countries, Peoples and Cultures: Middle East and North Africa*, vol. 5, ed. Michael Shally-Jensen (Ipswich, MA: Salem Press, 2015), 6; Michael Carpenter, Amy Whitherbee, and M. Lee, "Libya," in *Countries, Peoples and Cultures: Middle East and North Africa*, vol. 5, ed. Michael Shally-Jensen (Ipswich, MA: Salem Press, 2015), 186; Heidi Edsall, John Pearson, and M. Lee, "Morocco," in *Countries, Peoples and Cultures: Middle East and North Africa*, vol. 5, ed. Michael Shally-Jensen (Ipswich, MA: Salem Press, 2015), 208; Jennifer Carlson, Eric Badertscher, Micah Issitt, and Savannah Schroll Guz, "Tunisia," in *Countries, Peoples and Cultures: Middle East and North Africa*, vol. 5, ed. Michael Shally-Jensen (Ipswich, MA: Salem Press, 2015), 364.

---

mated 97,702,000 acres. Even were this amount incorrect by 100 percent, the impression would remain that Roman Africa maldistributed land and that these men operated as monarchs.

Other figures contradicted these numbers. Roman general Lucius Ahenobarbus (c. 98–48 BCE) promised each soldier 25 acres from his estate north of Rome.[851] His 4,000- to 15,000-man army implied a 100,000- to 375,000-acre plantation, though he probably owned more land because elites often had several properties, as shown by the example of Roman landowner and Christian saint Melania the Younger (383–439), treated later. But he surely held under 97.7 million acres.

A second example came from sixth century CE Egypt, near Roman rule's end, where the Apion family approximated 75,000 acres.[852] Chapter 7 emphasizing the lopsidedness of Egypt's land distribution, the Apions should have summited Roman inequality. Yet 75,000 acres badly trailed Pliny's figure. Either my estimate is grossly inaccurate, or he exaggerated.

The richest elites occupied the Senate. Although losing influence over time, it originally included only men from the 100 wealthiest families. By the early empire, a man needed 1 million sesterces to qualify for admission.[853] Three million per average senator yielded an annual income from rent and investment some 500 times beyond the average Roman. Their wealth, adjusted for inflation, made Rome's senators richer than today's U.S. senators.

Italy and the provinces had perhaps 200,000 to 400,000 magnates in a population of 50 to 55 million, making under 1 percent of Romans enormously rich.[854] By comparison, 3 to 5 percent of last chapter's Egyptians held great wealth.

8.3.2 Commoners

8.3.2.1 Penury

Far below the apex, without a middle class as buffer, was "abject poverty in the bottom."[855] This circumstance may surprise readers who think a large middle class typical. Yet Rome was no aberration; elites, monopolizing wealth, pauperized underlings. Negligible distance between middle and low incomes produced "equality in poverty."[856]

---

[851] Finley, 101.
[852] Ibid., 99.
[853] Milanovic, 49.
[854] Ibid., 50.
[855] Ibid., 46.
[856] Ibid., 50.

Roman cities resembled "Third World" encampments of "the nearly starving" and beggars.[857] These unfortunates left only their skeletons, trash, and coprolites for archaeologists to find later. Leaving the records that scholars study, elites disdained indigents. The adage that the victors write history reiterates that the past bifurcated into winners and losers, rich and poor. Among winners, Cicero, typifying elite contempt for labor, equated it with slavery.[858]

This attitude disadvantaged omegas. Rome's cities offered sporadic work in construction, crafts, taverns, and brothels.[859] Pay was inadequate, labor arduous, and undernutrition common. Mine owners employed children as young as four years. In Cartagena, Spain's second century BCE silver mines engaged around 40,000 slaves.[860] The homeless occupied tombs or propped anything resembling a windbreak against a building, arch, or aqueduct.[861] Condemning the practice, authorities sought their expulsion.

The countryside no better, Italian and provincial landowners reduced the laborer to tenant, serf, slave, peon, or hireling on plantations known as *latifundia*. Elites investing nothing in Britain's countryside, conditions stagnated circa 800 BCE to 1500 CE.[862]

8.3.2.2 Slavery

Heeding the advice of Greek philosopher Aristotle (384–322 BCE) cited in chapter 6, Rome empowered the homeowner, the *paterfamilias*, over all property including slaves.[863] Applying this scheme in the countryside, Roman authors from poets to agronomists linked bondage and farming.

Distilling attitudes toward omegas in *On Agriculture* (c. 160), Roman senator Cato the Elder (234–149 BCE) noted, "The owner of great plantations worked by slave labour."[864] Field hands were to receive more bread than was common in Egypt, implying an expectation that they worked harder or longer than customary.[865] Demanding that tasks be timely completed,

---

[857] Beard, 444.

[858] Ibid., 441; Sara C. Bisel and Jane F. Bisel, "Health and Nutrition at Herculaneum: An Examination of Human Skeletal Remains," in *The Natural History of Pompeii*, ed. Wilhelmina Feemster Jashemski and Frederick G. Meyer (Cambridge, UK: Cambridge University Press, 2002), 461.

[859] Beard, 446-449.

[860] Jean-Paul Morel, "Early Rome and Italy," in *The Cambridge Economic History of the Greco-Roman World*, ed. Walter Scheidel, Ian Morris, and Richard Saller (Cambridge, UK: Cambridge University Press, 2007), 505.

[861] Beard, 443-444.

[862] Ibid., 442.

[863] Finley, 19.

[864] "Introduction," in *On Agriculture*, Marcus Porcius Cato, trans. William Davis Hooper (Cambridge, MA: Harvard University Press, 1967), ix.

[865] Finley, 107.

overseers were to maximize workload even during corvée or bad weather.[866] "Remember that even though work stops, expenses run on none the less," he warned.[867] Slaves were to be chained in gangs, sold when old or infirm, and underfed when unable to work.[868] Receiving work no more than one day at a time, hirelings were to teeter near unemployment.[869] Greek historian and philosopher Plutarch's (46–124 CE) boast that "everybody admired Cato" ignored workers, who must have resented him.[870]

Like inequality, slavery was zero sum.[871] Freedom for some required others' enslavement as poverty offset wealth. Nobody gained an advantage without denying someone money and dignity. Indeed, freedom meant nothing unless its possessor trumped slaves, whose nature dehumanized them, an idea that echoed Aristotle.

Bondage was the primary coercion from the third century BCE to the third century CE.[872] British classicist Mary Beard (b. 1955) estimated Italy at 1.5 million to 2 million slaves, around one fifth of population, about 50 BCE.[873] Another reckoned Italy one third slave.[874] A third numbered Italy's slaves between 2 million and 6 million by 100 CE.[875] Owning over 200 slaves and believing he controlled even freedmen, Cicero revoked an ex-slave's freedom after he disappeared on a trip, though efforts at recapture failed.[876] When masters freed chattel, kindness was no motive. Manumission ended upkeep as slaves aged and productivity diminished.

Arising in the third century BCE from Etruria in the north to Campania in the south to produce food and ornamentals for Rome, *latifundia* demanded slaves, whom war supplied.[877] Between 58 and 51 BCE, for example, Caesar's Gallic wars yielded 1 million captives.[878] By then, hundreds of thousands of

---

[866] Marcus Porcius Cato, *On Agriculture*, trans. William Davis Hooper (Cambridge, MA: Harvard University Press, 1967), 7.

[867] Ibid., 57.

[868] Ibid., 9, 71.

[869] Ibid., 15.

[870] Plutarch, "The Life of Cato the Elder," in *Sources of the West: Readings from Western Civilization, Vol. I: From the Beginning to 1648*, ed. Mark A. Kishlansky (New York: HarperCollinsPublishers, 1991), 63.

[871] Tom Holland, *Rubicon: The Last Years of the Roman Republic* (New York: Anchor Books, 2004), 143.

[872] Finley, 69.

[873] Beard, 329.

[874] Alex Butterworth and Ray Laurence, *Pompeii: The Living City* (New York: St. Martin's Press, 2005), 65.

[875] Marjorie Gann and Janet Willen, *Five Thousand Years of Slavery* (Toronto, ON: Tundra Books, 2011), 13.

[876] Beard, 330-331.

[877] Morel, 507.

[878] Finley, 72.

slaves changed hands yearly in an empire with 4 million to 8 million slaves and serfs.[879] Delos, Greece, sold roughly 10,000 slaves daily.[880] Bondage and inequality increased as landholding concentrated among few.

Slaves produced wine, olive oil, grain, and ornamentals for urbanites during an agricultural intensification that enriched capital's owners, who protected and promoted their empire-wide interests.[881] All labor servile, smallholders and hirelings lost income because slaves did most work.[882]

Bondage persisted and perhaps enlarged under the emperors. Augustus' wife, Livia Drusilla (58 BCE–29 CE), owned over 1,000 slaves.[883] Freedmen outnumbered freeborn Romans by the first century CE.[884] As in the late Republic, farms used slaves year-round, hiring help at times like harvest that demanded extra labor. Almost all miners were slaves, and domestic servants were slaves or freedmen. Melania the Younger and her husband Roman nobleman and Christian saint Valerius Pinianus (c. 381–c. 420) owned roughly 24,000 slaves who worked farms in Italy, Sicily, Spain, North Africa, and Britain. "Slaves were still ubiquitous in late antiquity," inferred American British classicist Moses Finley (1912–1986) from this information.[885] Late imperial inequality grew as the wealthiest continued to amass land and slaves.[886]

Rome's maxim "all slaves are enemies" encapsulated elite attitudes toward them.[887] In this context, the words "Whipping Boy" designated an agricultural slave.[888] An owner could have beasts kill a slave, though by the early empire a judge's consent was necessary to inflict this punishment.[889] Such "sadism" defined the master-slave relationship.[890]

---

[879] William V. Harris, "The Late Republic," in *The Cambridge Economic History of the Greco-Roman World*, ed. Walter Scheidel, Ian Morris, and Richard Saller (Cambridge, UK: Cambridge University Press, 2007), 527, 532.

[880] Morel, 504.

[881] Bruce W. Frier and Dennis P. Kehoe, "Law and Economic Institutions," in *The Cambridge Economic History of the Greco-Roman World*, ed. Walter Scheidel, Ian Morris, and Richard Saller (Cambridge, UK: Cambridge University Press, 2007), 138.

[882] Morel, 505.

[883] Beard, 409.

[884] Finley, 72-73.

[885] Ibid., 84-85, 101-102.

[886] Willem M. Jongman, "The Early Roman Empire: Consumption," in *The Cambridge Economic History of the Greco-Roman World*, ed. Walter Scheidel, Ian Morris, and Richard Saller (Cambridge, UK: Cambridge University Press, 2007), 616.

[887] Beard, 330.

[888] Ibid., 329.

[889] David Graeber, *Debt: The First 5,000 Years* (Brooklyn and London: Melville House, 2014), 202.

[890] Beard, 330.

Fear of revolt justified cruelty.[891] Three upheavals—all rural, implying that slaves suffered more in countryside than city—convulsed Italy and Sicily from 140 to 71 BCE.[892] The most infamous involved Spartacus and roughly 70 slaves, who escaped gladiator training in Capua, around 15 miles north of Naples, in 73 BCE.[893] Up to 120,000 hirelings, serfs, and slaves joined them in a "slave rebellion and civil war."[894] They wanted freedom and perhaps to return home, though they may not have sought slavery's termination.[895]

After the rebels defeated five Roman armies, Crassus determined to crush the insurrection.[896] His and Spartacus clash concretized the conflict between Rome's wealthiest citizen and omegas. Spartacus' death proved triumph impossible when indigents retaliated against elites. Afterwards Rome crucified some 6,000 survivors along the Appian Way, which linked Rome with Brindisi in the southeast.[897]

The uprising anticipated over 200 revolts from the late first century BCE to the late second century CE, a period of ostensible peace and good governance.[898] This number may underreport the total because writers, ignoring the downtrodden, omitted what they thought unimportant. Peace, "the tranquility of exhaustion or complete annihilation," persisted because paupers feared destruction.[899]

8.3.3 Inequality in Herculaneum

8.3.3.1 The City

From southeastern Europe, Greeks began colonizing the Mediterranean in the eighth century BCE.[900] The Bay of Naples, whose harbor facilitated trade, led them to settle an Oscan village, naming it Herculaneum after the god Heracles: "Hercules" to the Romans.[901]

---

[891] Finley, 84.

[892] Ibid., 68.

[893] Beard, 248; Edward J. Watts, *Mortal Republic: How Rome Fell into Tyranny* (New York: Basic Books, 2018), 151-152; Gann and Willen, 11.

[894] Beard, 218; Holland, 141.

[895] Beard, 248-249.

[896] Watts, 162-164; Arthur E. R. Boak, *A History of Rome to 565 A.D.*, 4th ed. (New York: Macmillan, 1955), 208-209.

[897] Boak, 208-209; Gann and Willen, 12.

[898] Myles Lavan, "Writing Revolt in the Early Roman Empire," in The Routledge History Handbook of Medieval Revolt, ed. Justine Firnhaber-Baker and Dirk Schoenaers (London and New York: Routledge, 2017), 19.

[899] Mueller, 44.

[900] McKay, Hill, Buckler, Crowston, Wiesner-Hanks, and Perry, 62.

[901] Andrew Wallace-Hadrill, *Herculaneum: Past and Future* (London: Frances Lincoln Publishers, 2011), 91, 93.

Likewise promoting commerce, Rome conquered it about 310 BCE, thereafter seeking stability conducive to agriculture and trade rather than its micromanagement.[902] Admiring and copying Greek architecture, urban planning, and culture, Rome maintained rather than remade the town's economy, appearance, and customs.

The eruption of Mount Vesuvius in 79 CE, covered Herculaneum in rock and ash, preserving it for later study that illuminated Greek, Roman, and Mediterranean worlds. The town's rediscovery in 1709 came during an attempt to dig a well rather than careful excavation. Although nearby Pompeii attracted greater attention, Herculaneum detailed Roman inequality.

Vesuvius preserved skeletons beneath 22 yards of rock and ash at constant temperature, humidity, and pH.[903] Teeth and bones from 350 skeletons examined up to the year 2015 differentiated workloads, health, and nutrition, though Herculaneum cannot detail inequality's every aspect. Its destruction both enhanced and limited its economic, social, archaeological, anthropological, historic, demographic, and medical value. Although Vesuvius pinpointed the moment of preservation, demographers cannot quantify life expectancy because everyone died prematurely. Without this information, it remains less obvious that magnates outlived paupers as happens today.

8.3.3.2 Unequal Wealth

Elites cavorting at beachfront Herculaneum, Caligula (12–41 CE) was among the uberwealthy who owned a villa there.[904] Merchants inhabited "luxuriously appointed" homes.[905] Around this nucleus revolved a constellation of subordinates.

American archaeologist and "pioneer in forensic anthropology" Sara Bisel (1932–1996) judged four of 139 skeletons "privileged."[906] One woman wore "a lot of gold jewelry"—two rings, two bracelets, and earrings—and carried coins.[907] As any laborer whose ring causes blisters or callouses can appreciate, jewelry advertised the ancient wearer's retention of pristine hands by offloading toil. Having little wear, a second woman's teeth suggested only refined foods' consumption. Two of the three adults' robust bones implied excellent lifelong nutrition. They ate even when shortages priced food

---

[902] Michael Grant, *Cities of Vesuvius: Pompeii and Herculaneum* (London: Phoenix Press, 2005), 7.

[903] Bisel and Bisel, 451.

[904] Joanne Berry, *The Complete Pompeii* (London: Thames & Hudson, 2007), 89.

[905] Kerrigan, 39.

[906] Bisel and Bisel, 460-463; Cindy Visser, "Our List of 23 Famous Female Forensic Scientists," Crimes Lab, September 17, 2018, accessed September 25, 2022, ‹Our List of 23 Famous Female Forensic Scientists - Crimes Lab.›

[907] Bisel and Bisel, 461-463.

beyond workers. An eight-year-old girl wore a gold ring and glass bead neck-lace.

Bisel omitted whether these four were the lone elites among the 139 or brevity limited coverage. *Eternal Inequality* favors the first possibility. Even the four, almost 3 percent of 139, tripled the earlier estimate that under 1 percent of Romans owned fortunes. Attracting elites, Herculaneum likely had a larger proportion of them.

These few had servants, slaves, and space. As large as some houses, one apartment had bronze and silver decorations.[908] Its occupants afforded the spice pepper, represented by two peppercorns recovered from the sewer. Arriving from southwestern India, a voyage that wind permitted only once annually, pepper was expensive. The sewer also had date pits. Italy's barren palms necessitated Levantine and Egyptian imports. Additionally, the wealthy bought Spanish pickles, Gallic ham, Libyan pomegranates, and British oysters.[909]

Laborers "vastly outnumbered" the elite as chapter 2's worker bees crowded the queen.[910] The town's furniture memorializing them, 46 of 50 wood samples were maple, attractive enough to disguise poverty, or fir.[911] The 39 fir samples, a wood authors omitted as suitable for furniture, confirmed privation. Grown throughout Italy, the tree was the Model T rather than Mercedes-Benz of woods. Absent were expensive woods like ebony, which symbolized luxury and evoked Egypt, a virtue given Roman reverence for Egyptian civilization and its trappings.

8.3.3.3 Unequal Health and Reproduction

Herculaneum having perhaps 4,000 denizens in 79 CE, researchers, as mentioned, studied 350 skeletons, though only 139—almost 3.5 percent of population—thoroughly.[912] "A great melting pot of peoples," it surpassed 25 Irish settlements separated by time and place in diversity.[913] Inequality magnified this variability.

---

[908] Mark Robinson and Erica Rowan, "Roman Food Remains in Archaeology and the Contents of a Roman Sewer at Herculaneum," in A Companion to Food in the Ancient World, ed. John Wilkins and Robin Nadeau (Chichester, UK: Wiley Blackwell, 2105), 110, 114.

[909] Bisel and Bisel, 458.

[910] Ibid., 460.

[911] Stephan T. A. M. Mols, "Identification of the Wood Used in the Furniture at Herculaneum," in *The Natural History of Pompeii*, ed. Wilhelmina Feemster Jashemski and Frederick G. Meyer (Cambridge, UK: Cambridge University Press, 2002), 226, 228.

[912] Berry, 89.

[913] Bisel and Bisel, 454-455.

Among the four elites cited, a man and woman, both dying around age 46, had sturdy bones from good nutrition.[914] Large muscles moved him, likely an athlete by avocation.[915] All muscles were big whereas laborers enlarged only those necessary for work. Never exercising to exhaustion, his bones had not thickened where tendons attached, overuse that identified underlings. Underdeveloped hands implied that he dictated rather than writing letters. He delegated tasks because the rich avoided labor. Height evincing nutrition and rank, at 67.9 inches he stood over 1.2 inches above the average Herculaneum and Greek man. At 61.9 inches, the bejeweled woman was 0.9 inches over her average Herculaneum and Greek counterparts.

The other privileged woman, about age 36, had "virtually perfect" teeth with just one cavity's inception.[916] Sugar's absence and refined foods like bakery breads rather than paupers' coarse fare benefited her. She too had large muscles from excellent nutrition and exercise or household tasks.

The fourth elite, the eight-year-old girl, had five cavities unlike other decedents.[917] Without sugar, honey was probably the culprit, since elites, as in the Fertile Crescent, could afford it while indigents could not.

Far below these four were everyone else. Betraying toil while so young, a seven-year-old slave girl exhibited a humerus thickened where the deltoid attached.[918] Thin enamel indicated undernutrition, illness, or both between ages four and six. Undernutrition stunted her below three quarters of a modern sample her age from Denver, Colorado.

Another probable slave girl, around age 14, had a femur flattened, providing width for stout quadriceps, rather than rounded into a normal shape from overwork and undernutrition.[919] She might have enlarged them by repeatedly climbing and descending steps to do chores or fetch items. Thin enamel revealed undernutrition so severe that she lacked, or illness so grave that she could not absorb, calcium for about one month during childhood. The damage necessitated two teeth's extraction weeks before the eruption.

Excavators found few other juvenile skeletons, possibly because the investigation was incomplete.[920] Perhaps the town's unexplored parts entombed most youths, though this explanation requires the unlikelihood that residents segregated by age before death in a way that hindered chil-

---

[914] Ibid.
[915] Ibid., 461.
[916] Ibid., 463.
[917] Ibid., 456, 463.
[918] Ibid., 456, 464.
[919] Ibid., 464-465.
[920] Ibid., 453.

dren's discovery. Juveniles' paucity indicating low birthrate, 37 skeletons judged to have been adolescent and postpubescent women averaged 1.69 births per woman, too few to sustain even populations without infant mortality. The 18 skeletons identified as women over age 40 and so at or near menopause averaged 1.81 births per woman, still insufficient to perpetuate a population. Births had to average 4.5 to 6.5 per woman who reached menopause just to replace losses from antiquity's mortality.[921] Population growth required even greater birthrate.

Undernutrition may decrease fertility.[922] Excessive leanness impairing ovulation, Herculaneum's underfed women may have struggled to conceive, though inequality ensured elites ample food and fertility even if pauper reproduction declined.

Slavery may explain youths' dearth. Counting at least a quintile of ancient Italians as slaves, earlier estimates implied that Herculaneum had many unfree. Buyers likely purchased them in their twenties, when child mortality no longer threatened, and labor output was greatest.[923] The few young slaves represented a small population for Vesuvius to entomb.

8.4 Review and Preview

Making the Mediterranean an empire, Roman kleptocrats took the provinces' wealth, profited from cash crops like olive oil and wine, traded slaves, practiced usury, and burdened underlings with corvée, conscription, rent, and taxes. Rome traded as far east as the next two chapters' India and China.[924] Chapter 9's Indian peasantry enriched landowners. City parasitized farm as urban elites prospered without advancing the economy.

[921] Walter Scheidel, "Demography," in *The Cambridge Economic History of the Greco-Roman World*, ed. Walter Scheidel, Ian Morris, and Richard Saller (Cambridge, UK: Cambridge University Press, 2007), 41.

[922] E. A. Wrigley and R. S. Schofield, *The Population History of England, 1541-1871: A Reconstruction* (Cambridge, UK: Cambridge University Press, 1989), 309.

[923] Wallace-Hadrill, 129.

[924] Boak, 374-375; Strayer and Gatzke, 93.

Chapter 9 Indian Inequality

9.1 Abstract

Homo erectus began Indian prehistory and inequality before 1 million years ago. His successor *Homo sapiens* intensified inequality through pastoralism and agriculture. Plantations exploited tenants, hirelings, serfs, peons, and slaves. Combining early Indian ideas and Aryan racism, the caste system heightened inequality. Besides the countryside, inequality shaped cities, where elites occupied mansions whereas laborers inhabited workrooms. Grave goods' disparity evinced inequality. Flourishing outside, not within, India, Buddhism questioned caste and inequality.

9.2 Geography and Climate

India's northern mountains hindered invaders whereas its central Satpura and Vindhya mountains impeded unification by dividing north from south.[925] The northwest's Aravalli Mountains separate the Thar Desert from the rest of India. Desert and mountains isolate India from Pakistan. The northeast's Himalayas, including the world's tallest peak Mount Everest, divide India from the Qinghai-Tibetan plateau. Clouds rise as they move north into the mountains, cooling upon expansion.[926] Holding less water as

---

[925] Fritz Blackwell, *India: A Global Studies Handbook* (Santa Barbara, CA: ABC-CLIO, 2004), 5; Achala Punja, Kim Nagy, and Beverly Ballaro, "India," in *Countries, Peoples and Cultures: Central, South and Southeast Asia*, vol. 2, ed. Michael Shelly-Jensen (Ipswich, MA: Salem Press, 2015), 165.

[926] A. L. Basham, *The Wonder that Was India: A Survey of the History and Culture of the Indian Sub-Continent before the Coming of the Muslims* (Calcutta: Rupa, 1986), 1.

temperatures decrease, they shed it as rain, which joins summer snowmelt to form India's longest rivers. A later section overviews these rivers' importance to agriculture.

From the Himalayas, the Indus River flows southwest through Pakistan into the Arabian Sea.[927] Also beginning in the Himalayas, the northeast's Ganges River, the goddess *Mata Ganga* or "Mother Ganges," moves east and southeast through the Gangetic plain into the Bay of Bengal. Indians cleanse body and spirit by bathing in the Ganges, which symbolizes purity. To its north, the Brahmaputra River likewise starts in the Himalayas, meanders southeast through China, India, and Bangladesh, and joins the Ganges before entering the Bay of Bengal.[928]

From west to east, India borders Pakistan, Afghanistan, China, Nepal, Bhutan, Bangladesh, and Myanmar.[929] Movement south through India tapers the peninsula, which penetrates the Indian Ocean and ends at Indira Point roughly 580 miles north of the equator.[930] Within the Tropic of Cancer, the sultry peninsula yields to northernmost India's tundra and glaciers.[931] Temperatures are hottest from March to June, the monsoon spans July to October, and winter occurs November to February.[932] To India's southeast is Sri Lanka.

9.3 The First Inhabitants

The first human outside Africa stated chapter 3, *H. erectus* inaugurated Eurasia's prehistory, though scientists, having only his tools, fossils, and ash from fires, cannot detail his societies, which *H. sapiens* later modified. Readers may remember that *H. erectus* arose roughly 1.9 million years ago in Africa, from where he entered Sinai, which led north to the Levant, south to Arabia, east and southeast to South, Southeast, and East Asia, and east and northeast to Central Asia and Russia.

Eurasia's earliest *H. erectus*' fossils predate 1.8 million years ago in Dmanisi, Republic of Georgia.[933] The species entered Sinai earlier to walk over 1,400 miles to it. Between 1.6 million and 1 million years ago, he settled Indone-

---

[927] Blackwell, 5-6; Punja, Nagy, and Ballaro, 165.

[928] Punja, Nagy, and Ballaro, 167.

[929] Ibid., 165.

[930] "Geography of India—Chapter 1—Introduction of India," Shakti IAS Academy, April 30, 2019, accessed March 4, 2022, ‹Geography of India- Chapter 1- Introduction of India - Shakti IAS Academy.›

[931] Blackwell, 6-8.

[932] Punja, Nagy, and Ballaro, 167.

[933] Robert Jurmain, Lynn Kilgore, Wenda Trevathan, and Russell L. Ciochon, *Introduction to Physical Anthropology*, 2013-2014 ed. (Belmont, CA: Wadsworth Cengage Learning, 2014), 316-317.

sia's Java, though not from Georgia, whose specimens were shorter and had smaller brains than Javanese *H. erectus*. Rather, the biped twice entered Asia. First, small individuals reached Georgia and Central Asia. Second, large people populated Indonesia and next chapter's China.

Movement from Sinai to Java in under 1 mega-annum implies that *H. erectus* crossed Asia from southwest to southeast. Another route would have lengthened distance and time. *H. sapiens* hugged Indian Ocean coastline.[934] *H. erectus* probably did likewise.

Scant hair and numerous sweat glands adapted the tropical species for heat not cold, noted chapter 3, prompting colonization of the south before the north. Keeping to the coast, he reached Pakistan and India from the west. Acheulian stone tools placed him in southern India's Tamil Nadu before 1 million years ago.[935]

H. erectus invented them in Africa before 1.6 million years ago to butcher carcasses and unearth roots and tubers.[936] With only these artifacts at one site, scientists cannot detail his anatomy, diet, dispersal, or duration in India. Moreover, one set of tools cannot reveal whether Indian *H. erectus* modified technology. The subcontinent's pre-*H. sapiens* past remains poorly understood.

H. erectus heightened inequality, first, by organizing chapter 3's hunt. A leader or council probably aggregated neighbors into hunting parties and deployed them in a manner that improved prospects for success, readers may recall. Second, a leader or clique, evaluating talent at campsites, must have assigned nonhunters to fish, gather plants, rear children, or defend the campsite.

9.4 *Homo sapiens'* Arrival

Entering India perhaps 120,000 years ago, *H. sapiens* left diverse stone tools rather than fossils over the millennia.[937] Differences in type and age imply several migrations into India, where he probably mated with *H. erectus*. These couplings appear to have contributed no genes to today's Indians, descended from migrants who reached India around 63,000 BCE.

---

[934] Tom Hoogervorst, "The Indian Ocean," in *The World's Oceans: Geography, History, and Environment*, ed. Rainer F. Buschmann and Lance Nolde (Santa Barbara, CA and Denver, CO: ABC-CLIO, 2018), 37.

[935] Tiasa Adhya, "When Did Early Humans Reach India?" Down to Earth, May 15, 2011, accessed March 4, 2022, ‹When did early humans reach India? (downtoearth.org.in).›

[936] Ibid.

[937] Tony Joseph, "Who Were the Earliest Humans in India and What Did They Look Like?" Quartz India, December 26, 2018, accessed March 4, 2022, ‹Who were the first humans in India? — Quartz India (qz.com).›

With northern mountains a hindrance, the Indian Ocean, "the first ocean to facilitate human expansion," moved people, commodities, and ideas among India and its neighbors.[938] From China, likely Taiwan, Austronesian speakers moved east through the Pacific Ocean and west through the Indian Ocean circa 3000 BCE to 1250 CE.[939] Reaching Madagascar about 700 CE, they probably landed in India earlier, though the time is unknown, as they moved west from Indonesia.[940]

Arriving overland and from the Indian Ocean, early Indians hunted, gathered, and fished.[941] Between the Himalaya and Vindhya mountains, for example, they hunted elephant, horse, auroch, hippopotamus, crocodile, and turtle about 31,000 to 26,000 BCE.[942] Edible plants included progenitors of rice, barley, wheat, buckwheat, and millet including sorghum.[943]

Like *H. erectus*, these Indians likely perpetuated inequality whereby a chief or council outranked others, made decisions, and compelled subordinates' obedience. *H. sapiens* thus continued the stratification *H. erectus* began.

9.5 Pastoralism and Agriculture

9.5.1 Origin

Seventh millennium BCE Indians kept goat, sheep, water buffalo, and *Bos indicus*, a cattle species different from western Asia's *Bos taurus*.[944] Cattle and buffalo populated all India whereas sheep, goat, and camel, entering the Indus valley by 2300 BCE, occupied the northwest.[945] Stockmen favored sheep and goats on hills and arid land, and camels were unknown east of

---

[938] Hoogervorst, 35-37.

[939] Lance Nolde, "Austronesians," in *The World's Oceans: Geography, History, and Environment*, ed. Rainer F. Buschmann and Lance Nolde (Santa Barbara, CA and Denver, CO: ABC-CLIO, 2018), 182.

[940] Ibid.; Roger Blench, "Chapter 19: Evidence for the Austronesian Voyages in the Indian Ocean," in *The Global Origins and Development of Seafaring*, ed. Atholl Anderson, James H. Barrett, and Katherine V. Boyle (Cambridge, UK: McDonald Institute for Archaeological Research, 2010), 239; Marc Jason Gilbert, *South Asia in World History* (New York: Oxford University Press, 2017), 1.

[941] Gilbert, 1; Basham, 11.

[942] Shibani Bose, "Human-Plant Interactions in the Middle Gangetic Plains: An Archaeobotanical Perspective (From the Mesolithic up to c. Third Century BC)," in *Ancient India: New Research*, ed. Upinder Singh and Nayanjot Lahiri (Oxford and New York: Oxford University Press, 2009), 75-76.

[943] Ibid., 78, 82.

[944] Parth Chauhan, "Early Food Producers in the Indus Valley," in *World History Encyclopedia*, vol. 2, *Era 1: Beginnings of Human Society*, ed. Mark Aldenderfer (Santa Barbara, CA: ABC-CLIO, 2011), 140.

[945] John Reader, *Man on Earth: A Celebration of Mankind* (New York: Harper & Row, 1988), 183; Elizabeth A. Stephens, "Camels," in *The Cambridge World History of Food*, vol. 1, ed. Kenneth

---

the Aravalli Mountains.[946] Chickens, native to eastern India, and swine were ubiquitous after 2000 BCE.[947]

India's best soils border the Indus, Ganges, and Brahmaputra rivers.[948] Chapters 5 and 7 described the Tigris, Euphrates, and Nile rivers' alluvial deposition upon inundation. India's trio did likewise. Moreover, northern India's pedological recency, giving rain insufficient time to leach nutrients, has greater natural fertility than Africa, Australia, North America, and South America's older ground.[949] "India's civilization—ancient and modern—therefore is founded on the enduring fertility of its soils," enthused British anthropologist John Reader (b. 1937).[950]

India's transition from hunting and gathering to farming and herding was incomplete; farmers and pastoralists continued to eat wild plants and animals, including fish.[951] The staple was rice, whose importance grew over time and whose antiquity led nineteenth-century scholars to think India pioneered its cultivation.[952] Next chapter overviews its domestication in China. India's later domestication probably began near Mohenjo-Daro in today's Pakistan about 2500 BCE. During the next 500 to 1,000 years, rice spread along the upper and middle Ganges. Irrigation extended it from eastern India's Odisha south to Tamil Nadu by 300 BCE.

Barley, millets, wheat, and buckwheat followed rice as domesticates.[953] Wild rice, not closely related to the domesticate, remained a food even where rice was grown. Peninsular India's warmth permitted its double cropping whereas barley and wheat were secondary crops. Austronesian voyages gave India African millets and Southeast Asian sugarcane and banana after 2000 BCE. Rain sustained millet whereas rice was irrigated.

F. Kiple and Kriemhild Conee Ornelas (Cambridge, UK: Cambridge University Press, 2000), 477-478.

[946] Charles Keith Maisels, *Early Civilizations of the Old World: The Formative Histories of Egypt, the Levant, Mesopotamia, India, and China* (London and New York: Routledge, 1999), 190; Ilse Kohler-Rollefson, "The Raikas and Camels in Rajasthan," Sahapedia, November 22, 2018, accessed March 5, 2022, ‹Camel Cultures of India | Sahapedia.›

[947] Reader, 183; Roger Blench and Kevin C. MacDonald, "Chickens," in *The Cambridge World History of Food*, vol. 1, ed. Kenneth F. Kiple and Kriemhild Conee Ornelas (Cambridge, UK: Cambridge University Press, 2000), 496.

[948] Punja, Nagy, and Ballaro, 167.

[949] Reader, 183.

[950] Ibid., 184.

[951] Bose, 80.

[952] Te-Tzu Chang, "Rice," in *The Cambridge World History of Food*, vol. 1, ed. Kenneth F. Kiple and Kriemhild Conee Ornelas (Cambridge, UK: Cambridge University Press, 2000), 133-134.

[953] Bose, 78; Reader, 183-184.

Initially without the plow, rice, and irrigation, farmers expected the Indus' June through September flood to fertilize and wet soil.[954] October's recession permitted planting. Indus husbandmen favored wheat for bread and porridge, though barley better tolerated cold, salinity, drought, and excessive moisture, as chapter 5 remarked. Fearing crop failure and starvation, cautious peasants planted it, though cold seldom threatened away from the Himalayas, which blocked Central Asia's cool air from India.[955] Salinizing soil over time, irrigation made barley essential.

Second millennium BCE Gangetic people farmed, herded, hunted, gathered, and fished.[956] The consumption of legumes, which supply essential amino acids deficient in grains, increased.[957] Lentil, that millennium's chief legume, and pea were the earliest such domesticates, though Indians also grew mung bean and chickpea.

Fruits further diversifying diets, Indians after 1300 BCE ate grape, date, and jackfruit.[958] Before 600 BCE, they cultivated watermelon from Africa via the Indian Ocean.[959] Although fishing, hunting, and gathering rivaled farming and herding through much of the first millennium BCE, agriculture expanded after 300 BCE.[960]

9.5.2 Inequality

9.5.2.1 Pre-Aryan Rural Inequality

The countryside bifurcating into landowners and landless, agriculture intensified inequality by making most Indians tenants.[961] Creating nearly all wealth while paying rent and taxes, they remained "impoverished and exploited."[962] Expressing inequality's parasitism, an adage listed "three bloodsuckers in the world: the flea, the bug, and the Brahman."[963]

---

[954] Maisels, 206-207.

[955] "Climate of India," Vedantu, accessed March 5, 2022, ‹Climate of India - Introduction, Factors, Controls and FAQs (vedantu.com).›

[956] Bose, 83.

[957] Ibid.; Jimmy Louie, "Breads and Cereals," in *Essentials of Human Nutrition*, 5th ed., ed. Jim Mann and A. Stewart Trusell (Oxford: Oxford University Press, 2017), 274; Bernard Venn, "Legumes," in *Essentials of Human Nutrition*, 5th ed., ed. Jim Mann and A. Stewart Trusell (Oxford: Oxford University Press, 2017), 277.

[958] Bose, 85.

[959] Ibid., 87.

[960] Uthara Suvrathan, "Landscapes of Life and Death: Considering the Region of Vidarbha," in *Ancient India: New Research*, ed. Upinder Singh and Nayanjot Lahiri (Oxford and New York: Oxford University Press, 2009), 125-127, 136-137.

[961] Robert W. Strayer, Edwin Hirschmann, Robert B. Marks, Robert J. Smith, James J. Horn, and Lynn H. Parsons, *The Making of the Modern World: Connected Histories, Divergent Paths (1500 to the Present)* (New York: St. Martin's Press, 1989), 248.

[962] Ibid.

[963] Ibid.

Absent the large uprisings that convulsed chapters 10 and 19's China and chapter 18's Russia, the caste system, retarding class consciousness through fragmentation, pitted farmers against one another by dividing them into roughly 3,000 castes and over 25,000 subcastes, termed *jatis*.[964] Arising in prehistory, caste may have originated in children taking parents' occupation. Begun voluntarily to the extent that a rural economy supplied diverse employment, this practice became an expectation and hardened into a requirement over time. Upward mobility vanished as jobs became hereditary. Comprising people who shared resources, rank, and genes, caste confined marriage and reproduction to insiders.

9.5.2.2 Aryans and Inequality

Into this system intruded Aryan pastoralists who may have originated in Central Asia, whose earliest history is uncertain, and whose later association with Nazism is spurious.[965] From southern Russia, where grasslands fed their herds, some migrated south and west into western Asia and Europe about 2500 BCE whereas others penetrated south into India around one to two millennia later.[966]

Calling themselves *Arya*, meaning "noble" or "honorable," they disdained southern India's Dravidians.[967] Refusal to mate with them preserved purity, separateness, and hierarchy, with Aryans above "the numerous darker peoples around them."[968] Chapters 12 and 14 further examine racism as aspect of inequality.

Believing their pastoral and warrior existence trumped farm drudgery, Aryans avoided labor as inferiority's mark, delegated it to underlings, put themselves atop the hierarchy, and ranked everyone else near or at the bottom.[969] Initially oral tradition, these beliefs coalesced as Vedas, the oldest Hindu scriptures, around 1200 to 1100 BCE.[970] They imagined a past when the god Manu specified the proper gradations of people and the laws applicable to each by narrating the birth of the god Brahma, "grandfather of all the worlds."[971] Brahma populated earth with the first humans, the Brahmans,

---

[964] Ibid.; Reader, 184-185.

[965] Gilbert, 14.

[966] Karen Armstrong, *Fields of Blood: Religion and the History of Violence* (Waterville, ME: Thorndike Press, 2014), 60-61; Strayer, Hirschmann, Marks, Smith, Horn, and Parsons, 243.

[967] Armstrong, 60; Strayer, Hirschmann, Marks, Smith, Horn, and Parsons, 246-247.

[968] Strayer, Hirschmann, Marks, Smith, Horn, and Parsons, 246-247.

[969] Armstrong, 61.

[970] Ibid., 90; A. C. Grayling, *The History of Philosophy* (New York: Penguin Press, 2019), 519-520.

[971] Isabel Wilkerson, *Caste: The Origins of Our Discontents* (Waterville, ME: Thorndike Press, 2020), 163; Strayer, Hirschmann, Marks, Smith, Horn, and Parsons, 247; Reader, 186.

who, issuing from his mouth as intellectuals, priests, and teachers, preserved sacred learning, controlled access to the gods, and performed rituals that maintained stability and hierarchy. Second, Kshatriyas, born from Brahma's arms, defended India as warriors and nobles. Third, Vaishyas issued from his thighs as merchants. Fourth, craftspeople and laborers, Sudras, originating lower still at Brahma's feet, occupied the bottom rank.

Beneath these four, impurity disqualified untouchables from inclusion.[972] Their fate was biological because status was hereditary and occupational since the worst jobs—garbage collector, toilet cleaner, mortician, under-taker, shoemaker, or another worker with hides—confirmed debasement.[973] Their shadow corrupting anyone it shaded, they prostrated themselves when near a brahman to ensure they posed no danger to him; they walked with a bell to warn of their presence and with a broom to erase their footprints so nobody trod upon them.[974]

Karma, belief that actions in this life determine status and occupation upon rebirth, justified caste.[975] Acceptance of rank and performance of duties earned promotion upon rebirth whereas rejection of caste and duties caused demotion. Hindus sought elevation to nirvana: a state of oneness with the gods that ended desire, suffering, and rebirth.

Rigidity made caste "the most thoroughgoing attempt known in human history to introduce absolute inequality as the guiding principle in social relations."[976] This language exaggerates; all polities, not just India, preserved inequality by preventing upward mobility.[977] Elites always created hier-archy, enforced it, and feigned the possibility of upward mobility to dupe the underclass into toiling ceaselessly.

India's inequality was no more inflexible than what existed elsewhere. Shaping inequality, race was used the same way as caste in sorting people by skin color. As ratified in 1788, the U.S. Constitution counted each slave three fifths of a person and declined to enfranchise him or her (amid far from universal suffrage).[978] The Thirteenth Amendment, ratified in 1865, ended bondage "except as a punishment for crime."[979] Yet many black Africans, hereafter "blacks" for concision, struggle to attend good schools, own prop-erty in upscale neighborhoods, or join a profession.

---

[972] Reader, 186; Strayer, Hirschmann, Marks, Smith, Horn, and Parsons, 247.
[973] Wilkerson, 210.
[974] Ibid., 164, 183-184; Blackwell, 141.
[975] Gilbert, 18-20.
[976] Reader, 186.
[977] Strayer, Hirschmann, Marks, Smith, Horn, and Parsons, 248.
[978] U.S. Const. art. I, S 2.
[979] U.S. Const. amend. XIII, S 1.

9.5.2.3 Inequality, Race, and Intelligence

Among scholars and scientists attributing a racial underclass' persistence to innate differences in intelligence, American "towering figure in biology" and 1962 Nobel laureate in physiology or medicine James Watson (b. 1928) admitted in 2007 and 2018 his pessimism about blacks.[980] "All our social policies are based on the fact that their intelligence is the same as ours—whereas all the testing says not really," he stated.[981]

Defending Watson against critics, Canadian psychologist John Philippe Rushton (1943–2012) and American psychologist and "best-known hereditarian" Arthur Jensen (1923–2012) ranked East Asians, Europeans, and blacks from greatest to least intelligence.[982] Although environment influences intelligence, genes determine up to 80 percent of it.

His interest in individual and racial cognitive differences dating to 1969, Jensen challenged former U.S. president Lyndon Johnson's (1908–1973) War on Poverty because education conferred uneven benefits.[983] Return on investment diminishing as intelligence decreased, funding should target the brightest students to benefit them, society, and taxpayers.

Restating this thesis, American psychologist Richard Herrnstein (1930–1994) and American political scientist Charles Murray (b. 1943), repeatedly referencing Jensen, retained his ranking of East Asians, Europeans, and blacks.[984] Herrnstein and Murray documented a small intelligence gap between East Asians and Europeans and a chasm between Europeans and blacks.[985]

---

[980] J. G. Whitesides," Watson, James (1928-)," in *Research and Discovery: Landmarks and Pioneers in American Science*, vol. 1, ed. Russell Lawson (Armonk, NY: Sharpe Reference, 2008), 254; "James Watson: Scientist Loses Titles after Claims over Race," BBC, January 13, 2019, accessed December 3, 2022, ⟨James Watson: Scientist loses titles after claims over race - BBC News.⟩

[981] "James Watson: Scientist Loses Titles after Claims over Race."

[982] Stephen Jay Gould, The Mismeasure of Man, rev. ed. (New York and London: Norton: 1996), 347; J. Philippe Rushton and Arthur R. Jensen, "James Watson's Most Inconvenient Truth: Race Realism and the Moralistic Fallacy," Medical Hypotheses 71, no. 5 (November 2008): 629-640, accessed December 3, 2022, ⟨James Watson's most inconvenient truth: race realism and the moralistic fallacy - PubMed (nih.gov).⟩

[983] Richard J. Herrnstein and Charles Murray, The Bell Curve: Intelligence and Class Structure in American Life (New York: Free Press, 1994), 9.

[984] Ibid., 9-10, 13, 15, 283. 302-304, 408, 584-585, 628, 666, 687.

[985] Gould, 368-369.

The hereditarian hypothesis posited, first, that intelligence can be quantified as one number.[986] Jensen believed IQ the best measure of intelligence. Second, assigning an IQs to each person permitted his ranking in a population. Third, intelligence was as measurable and rankable among races as individuals. Fourth, education little improved IQ, which was largely uniform throughout life because biology fixed it.

The crucial belief credited genes with shaping intelligence in a linear and additive way.[987] Suppose for simplicity that 100 genes determine intelligence. A person with all 100 would top the population in intelligence and would be twice brighter than someone with 50 of the genes and tenfold smarter than a person with 10.

Watson, Jensen, Herrenstein, and Murray never claimed that genes alone determine intelligence, which results from genes and environment. As mentioned, Jensen typified hereditarians by prioritizing genes.

Conservatism popularized hereditarianism.[988] Jensen published his 1969 article after 1968's riots, assassinations, and the Tet offensive discredited Johnson and the Democratic Party and elevated U.S. Navy veteran, anticommunist, and former vice president Richard Nixon (1913–1994) to the presidency. Herrnstein and Murray published *The Bell Curve* (1994) while Republicans campaigned for Congress by publicizing a Contract with America as their governing plan.

Disputing hereditarianism, paleontologist Stephen Jay Gould (1941–2002), among "the most widely recognized American scientists," judged intelligence an abstraction incapable of reification as one number.[989] IQ thus revealed nothing about intelligence, whether of individuals or races. Even if hereditarians were correct, they still misjudged education. Just as eyeglasses sharpen vision, education raises intelligence.[990]

9.6 Urbanization, Religion, Empire, and Inequality

9.6.1 Urbanization and Inequality

Farming produced the reliable surplus necessary for cities after 4000 BCE.[991] The first civilization, known as Harappan, evinced inequality in

---

[986] Ibid., 35-36.

[987] Ibid., 33-34.

[988] Ibid., 30.

[989] Ibid., 22, 348; David Sepkoski, "Gould, Stephen Jay (1941-2002)," in *Research and Discovery: Landmarks and Pioneers in American Science*, vol. 1, ed. Russell Lawson (Armonk, NY: Sharpe Reference, 2008), 217.

[990] Gould, 186.

[991] Gilbert, 2-5.

today's eastern Afghanistan, Pakistan, and northwestern India after 2500 BCE. Building mansions, with luxuries like baths and toilets, on platforms some 10 feet above ground, the rich dwarfed underlings. Merchants and craftsmen lived at ground level. Laborers tenanted workrooms. Elites wore gold bracelets, merchants an alloy of gold and copper or tin, and everyone else clay or seashells. As implied, occupation defined status. Harappans adorned no graves, however, suggesting that death equalized everybody.

Harappan decline shifted urbanization to the Ganges Valley around 1500 BCE.[992] Inhabiting cities, nobles topped the hierarchy while "slaves and laborers" worked their estates.[993] This reality resembling chapter 8's Rome, American anthropologist David Graeber (1961–2020) equated ancient Indian and Mediterranean inequality.

Grave goods' disparity demonstrated inequality about 1000 BCE to 300 CE in central India's Vidarbha.[994] Boulders, whose placement must have required time and labor only magnates commanded, encircled one interment.[995] Another had over 2,200 carnelians. Others had gold, silver, copper, or their combination whereas most lacked ornamentation.

In a parallel development, Indian literature described first millennium BCE wealthy urbanites, including a "gold-digger" courtesan who selected only affluent lovers.[996] Eschewing labor, they enjoyed lavish meals, alcohol, parties, picnics, poetry readings, plays, music, gossip, and other recreation while contributing nothing to the economy. Full of them, ancient Indian cities, consuming the harvest, impoverished peasants through rent, taxes, peonage, slavery, serfdom, and corvée. Inequality thus pitted rich against poor and city against countryside.

9.6.2 Buddhist Critique of Wealth

Among the rich, cities housed those with leisure for philosophy, both ethics and epistemology, between the sixth and second centuries BCE.[997] Contemplation produced the Upanishads, Hindu scriptures critical of Brahmans. Their authorship is unknown, though urban Brahmans sympathetic

---

[992] Ibid., 12; David Graeber, *Debt: The First 5,000 Years* (Brooklyn and London: Melville House, 2014), 232.

[993] Graeber, 232; Armstrong, 110.

[994] Suvrathan, 125, 128-131.

[995] Meera Visvanathan, "Of Death and Fertility: Landscapes of Heroism in Ancient South India," in *Ancient India: New Research*, ed. Upinder Singh and Nayanjot Lahiri (Oxford and New York: Oxford University Press, 2009), 182.

[996] Shoneleeka Kaul, "Pleasure and Culture: Reading Urban Behaviour through Kavya Archetypes," in *Ancient India: New Research*, ed. Upinder Singh and Nayanjot Lahiri (Oxford and New York: Oxford University Press, 2009), 255-257, 266-267.

[997] Armstrong, 113-115.

to indigents may have written some. Urging Indians to access the gods without Brahmans' intercession and to spurn ritual and sacrifice as useless, Kshatriyas likely wrote most in hopes of replacing Brahmans as alphas.

Around this time, sannyasins, "renouncers," declared society evil and withdrew to purify themselves through asceticism and penury.[998] They abjured property, begged food, and embraced pacifism. Through self-denial, they hoped to approach the gods without Brahmans' help. Chapter 12 revisits this spirituality in late antiquity's monasticism.

Kshatriya prince Siddhartha Gautama (c. 563–c. 483 BCE), the Buddha, initially ignored the movement.[999] Like Greek philosopher Socrates (469–399 BCE) and Hebrew prophet Jesus (c. 5 BCE–c. 30 CE), he wrote nothing. Compiled long afterwards, hagiographies contain inaccuracies.[1000]

Born into wealth and shielded from suffering in youth, he married, had a child, and planned to succeed his father as king in Nepal, tradition held.[1001] Losing his complacency around age 29 after encountering a geriatric, an invalid, a corpse, and a monk, he left his family and home to study with Hindu scholars but disliked their guidance. Seeking solitude, like monks there and later in the West, he meditated until achieving enlightenment.

Buddha creating "among the most influential doctrines and institutions in human history," this chapter emphasizes his criticism of caste and inequality.[1002] Equalizing monks regardless of background, his monasteries may have been the first to admit women.[1003] Emphasizing universal brotherhood, he, traditional held, ate with paupers.[1004] Rejecting Brahmans, he advocated their demotion. Summarizing its desire for equality, Graeber thought Buddhism a type of communism.[1005]

Egalitarianism failed. First, Buddha vacillated about bondage.[1006] He opposed slaves' mistreatment, tradition averred, though early Buddhist texts

---

[998] Ibid., 117-118.

[999] Leo D. Lefebure, "Siddhartha Gautama," in *Berkshire Encyclopedia of World History*, vol. 4, ed. William H. McNeill, Jerry H. Bentley, David Christian, David Levinson, J. R. McNeill, Heidi Roupp, and Judith P. Zinsser (Great Barrington, MA: Berkshire Publishing Group, 2005), 1706.

[1000] Ingrid Fischer-Schreiber, Franz-Karl Ehrhard, Kurt Friedrichs, and Michael S. Diener, *The Encyclopedia of Eastern Philosophy and Religion: Buddhism, Taoism, Zen, Hinduism* (Boston: Shambhala, 1994), 332-333.

[1001] Lefebure; Blackwell, 120-121.

[1002] Jonathan C. Gold, "Life of the Buddha," in *World History Encyclopedia, Vol. 6, Era 3: Classical Traditions, 1000 BCE-300 CE*, ed. William E. Mierse, Kevin M. McGeough, Alfred J. Andrea, and Carolyn Neel (Santa Barbara, CA: ABC-CLIO, 2011), 593.

[1003] Lefebure, 1706-1707.

[1004] Joseph R. Strayer and Hans W. Gatzke, *The Mainstream of Civilization*, 3d ed. (New York: Harcourt Brace Jovanovich, 1979), 127.

[1005] Graeber, 235.

[1006] Gann and Willen, 129.

---

documented abuse despite owners' accepting his other teachings as Jews, Christians, and Muslims reconciled slavery with faith. Second, Buddhism permitted usury despite its complicity in inequality.[1007]

9.6.3 Indian Empires of Inequality

Indian slavery may have peaked in the fourth century BCE, when Macedonian general Alexander the Great (356–323), "one of the greatest generals in world history," invaded the Indus Valley and the Mauryan empire (321–185) was formed.[1008] War produced captives who augmented convicts on state plantations, where demand for labor prevented their sale elsewhere. The armies that confronted Alexander had servants and prostitutes, whose purchase made them state slaves.

The empire peaked under Asoka (c. 292–232), "a towering figure in India's national historical narrative" and grandson of Mauryan founder and "great conqueror" Chandragupta Maurya (r. 321–297).[1009] Taking power after murdering two brothers, Asoka established a cruel reputation. Affirming bondage and inequality as tools of statecraft, he, conquering eastern India's Odisha about 260, killed or enslaved several hundred thousand combatants and civilians.

Vanquishing all South Asia except southern allies, he renounced warfare, converted from Hinduism to Buddhism, and inaugurated India's tradition of monumental architecture, ordering stupas, monasteries, and pillars' erection throughout the empire.[1010] Involving corvée, such construction overburdened farmworkers who tilled imperial land and owed government "large shares" of the harvest.[1011] Taxes on trade were also onerous.

Although peasants and merchants resented taxes, corvée, conscription, and empire, British author and "creative artist" Herbert George Wells (1866–1946) rated Asoka history's greatest ruler, a judgement that affirmed the emperor's designation of himself as the "Beloved of the Gods."[1012] Less adula-

---

[1007] Graeber, 235.

[1008] Ibid., 233-234; Blackwell, 13; Abraham O. Mendoza, "The Military Career of Alexander the Great," in World History Encyclopedia, Vol. 6, Era 3: Classical Traditions, 1000 BCE-300 CE, ed. William E. Mierse, Kevin McGeough, Alfred J. Andrea, and Carolyn Neel (Santa Barbara, CA: ABC-CLIO, 2011), 507.

[1009] Armstrong, 131-132; Mandakini Arora, "Asoka," in Berkshire Encyclopedia of World History, vol. 1, ed. William H. McNeill, Jerry H. Bentley, David Christian, David Levinson, J. R. McNeill, Heidi Roupp, and Judith P. Zinsser (Great Barrington, MA: Berkshire Publishing Group, 2005), 197; Purushottam Lal Bhargava, Chandragupta Maurya (Lucknow: Upper India Publishing, 1935), 100.

[1010] Arora, 197; Punj, Nagy, and Ballaro, 173.

[1011] Strayer and Gatzke, 128-129.

[1012] Ibid.; Blackwell, 18; Armstrong, 131; George Sampson, "Introduction," in The Time Machine, The Island of Dr. Moreau, The Invisible Man, The First Men in the Moon, The Food of the Gods, In the

tory, American historian Fritz Blackwell criticized his attempt to create a "police state."[1013] The effort failed absent modern surveillance and communications technologies.

Centralism and urbanism weakened after Asoka.[1014] Graeber described India as a network of cities in antiquity but a collection of villages in the Middle Ages (c. 500–c. 1500 CE). *Eternal Inequality* disagrees; low yields, quantified elsewhere, made almost everyone farm in both periods. Agriculture underpinned Indian civilization over the millennia, Reader stated earlier.

Government waning, officials, struggling to collect taxes from farmers, looted Buddhist monasteries.[1015] Although Buddha made monks renounce property and live simply, as in the West, their reputation for holiness attracted donations of land and money. Hoarding gold, monasteries and temples cast it into idols.

Closing some 4,000 monasteries and temples, northern Indian king and "warrior" Harsha (606–647) recruited and provisioned an army with their gold.[1016] His assassination heightened instability. Buddhism and government weak, Brahmans reasserted control. In principle, a clique of elders managed the medieval village, though deference to Brahmans empowered them.[1017] India's largest landowners, they made Sudras farmhands. Those who dared hear the scriptures or learned discussions, violating caste, had molten lead poured into their ears. A second offense cost them their tongue.

Cities shrinking, urbanites became laborers on Brahman estates.[1018] Once funding cities, taxes now enriched rural Brahmans. Preoccupied with inequality, scholars debated laws attributed to Manu that divided slaves into seven castes depending on how they became enslaved. "The caste system became both more complicated and more unchangeable," wrote American medievalist Joseph Strayer (1904–1987) and German American historian Hans Gatzke (1915–1987).[1019]

Reinforcing the link among slavery, peonage, inferiority, and caste, bondage subsumed peonage as it became hereditary and as Indians lost the ability to indebt a superior.[1020] A direct relationship arose in the Middle

---

Days of the Comet, and The War of the Worlds, H. G. Wells (London: Octopus Books, 1985), [1].

[1013] Blackwell, 18.

[1014] Graeber, 253.

[1015] Ibid., 253-254.

[1016] Ibid., 254-255; Bidyut Kumar Sarkar, "Rajarshi: The Ethical Leadership Concept of India for the World," *Journal for Ethics in Social Studies* 4, no. 1 (2020): 109, ‹View of Rājarshi: The Ethical Leadership Concept of India for the World (lumenpublishing.com).›

[1017] Strayer and Gatzke, 322.

[1018] Graeber, 255-257.

[1019] Strayer and Gatzke, 324.

[1020] Ibid.

Ages between interest on a loan and difference in status between creditor and debtor, entrapping the latter in peonage. Encapsulating Indian hierarchy, French anthropologist Louis Dumont (1911–1998) doubted the words "unequal" and "inequality," presuming equality possible where it was not, applied to India.[1021]

9.6.4 India, Islam, and Slavery

Reaching India in the eighth century, Muslims joined the Indian Ocean slave trade, which violated Hinduism though the faith legalized bondage.[1022] Slaves captured or bought lacked rights whereas law, which authorities may have ignored, protected peons from assault and rape. Expanding as far west as Morocco and Spain and as far east as Indonesia in the Middle Ages, Muslims, enslaving and Islamizing many ethnicities, sold some in India. "From the day India became a target of Muslim invaders, its people began to be enslaved in droves to be sold in foreign lands or employed in various capacities on menial and not-so-menial jobs within the country," averred Indian historian Kishori Saran Lal (1920–2002).[1023]

Invading Pakistan in 712, Muslims, killing men, enslaved women and children in Debal, Rawar, Sehwan, Dhalila, Brahmanabad, and Multan.[1024] Rawar alone yielded some 60,000 slaves. Those India's economy could not absorb were sold west, for example to Iraqi landowners. The Koran permitting enslavement of women, single or married, as concubines, they provided sex and kept house, though an owner's income limited their number.[1025] Emulating the Prophet Muhammad (570–632), "the catalyst for a revolution in politics, economics, law, and civilization," India's Muslim rulers and nobles amassed slave harems.[1026] Seeking beautiful women and girls, these men humiliated Hindu elites by taking their wives and daughters.

Bondage persisted when Turkish armies entered India. Turkish general Mahmud of Ghazni (971–1030), "that ferocious and insatiable conqueror,"

[1021] Graeber, 257.

[1022] Marjorie Gann and Janet Willen, *Five Thousand Years of Slavery* (Toronto, ON: Tundra Books, 2011), 130.

[1023] K. S. Lal, *Muslim Slave System in Medieval India: Chapter II: The Origins of Muslim Slave System* (New Delhi: Aditya Prakashan, 1994), accessed March 5, 2022, ‹09272019090110_muslim_slave_system_in_medieval_india.pdf (vediclibrary.in).›

[1024] K. S. Lal, *Muslim Slave System in Medieval India: Chapter III: Enslavement of Hindus by Arab and Turkish Invaders* (New Delhi: Aditya Prakashan, 1994), accessed March 5, 2022, ‹09272019090110_muslim_slave_system_in_medieval_india.pdf (vediclibrary.in).›

[1025] K. S. Lal, *Muslim Slave System in Medieval India: Chapter XII: Sex Slavery* (New Delhi: Aditya Prakashan, 1994), accessed March 5, 2022, ‹09272019090110_muslim_slave_system_in_medieval_india.pdf (vediclibrary.in).›

[1026] Ibid.; Yahiya Emerick, *The Life and Work of Muhammad* (Indianapolis: Alpha, 2002), iv.

enslaved roughly 700,000 women and men from 1001 to 1003.[1027] Large numbers encouraged merchants to staff their shops with slaves. Others cleared jungle and built edifices and roads.

India's Muslims thought bondage part of Allah's plan to uplift inferiors.[1028] Owners "brought [savages] from the House of War to the House of Islam under the rule of slavery, which hides in itself a divine providence," Tunisian Egyptian philosopher, historian, and "founder of sociology" Ibn Khaldun (1332–1406) claimed.[1029]

Indians disagreed. Hiding in jungle or atop hills for fear of massacre or enslavement as an army approached, they counterattacked with spear and bow and arrow, both common among farmworkers.[1030] Muslims who pursued them found the fighting difficult as peasants preferred death to enslavement. Destroying empty villages while seeking food, frustrated generals stiffened resistance. No matter how many skirmishes Muslims won, their enemies rebounded.

Racism influencing slavery, Khaldun likened blacks to "dumb animals."[1031] The Arab word for slave, *abd*, initially generic, came to mean only blacks, whose "position was generally that of inferior species."[1032] Muslims may have imported more blacks into India than Europeans did into the western hemisphere. As chapter 14 demonstrates for tropical America, high mortality necessitated continual replacement in India.

9.7 Review and Preview

India's first inhabitant, *H. erectus*, introduced inequality whereby leaders, organizing and ranking members at campsites, managed the hunt. Heightening inequality through pastoralism and agriculture, *H. sapiens* exploited tenants, hirelings, peons, slaves, and serfs. India's cities also fostered inequality. Next chapter moves northeast to China, where *H. erectus* and *H.*

[1027] K. S. Lal, *Muslim Slave System in Medieval India: Chapter III: Enslavement of Hindus by Arab and Turkish Invaders.*

[1028] K. S. Lal, *Muslim Slave System in Medieval India: Chapter V: Slave-Taking during Muslim Rule* (New Delhi: Aditya Prakashan, 1994), accessed March 5, 2022, ‹09272019090110_muslim_slave_system_in_medieval_india.pdf (vediclibrary.in).›

[1029] Ibid.; Syed Farid Alatas, "Ibn Khaldun," in *The Wiley-Blackwell Companion to Major Social Theorists, Vol. 1: Classical Social Theorists*, ed. George Ritzer and Jeffrey Stepnisky (Malden, MA: Wiley-Blackwell, 2011), 12.

[1030] K. S. Lal, *Muslim Slave System in Medieval India: Chapter VI: Enslavement and Proselytization* (New Delhi: Aditya Prakashan, 1994), accessed March 5, 2022, ‹09272019090110_muslim_slave_system_in_medieval_india.pdf (vediclibrary.in).›

[1031] K. S. Lal, *Muslim Slave System in Medieval India: Chapter VII: Struggle for Power among Slave Nobles* (New Delhi: Aditya Prakashan, 1994), accessed March 5, 2022, ‹09272019090110_muslim_slave_system_in_medieval_india.pdf (vediclibrary.in).›

[1032] Ibid.

sapiens again perpetuated inequality. China's landowners oppressed the land-less. Furthering rather than reducing inequality, dynasties sought to weaken local elites and give peasants land to free them for corvée and conscription.

Chapter 10 Early Chinese Inequality

10.1 Abstract

From the south or west, chapters 3 and 9's *Homo erectus* began China's prehistory about 1.7 million years ago. Premodern and modern humans thereafter perpetuated inequality in "one of the cradles of world civilization."[1033] Transition from hunting and gathering to farming and herding worsened inequality. Elite opulence and commoner austerity characterized burial. Government exploited farmworkers through corvée and taxation. Cities housed magnates and beggars.

10.2 The Setting

"The first fact of Chinese history is geography," wrote British historian Michael Wood (b. 1948).[1034] About 2.4 billion acres, modern China spans one fifth Asia.[1035] This expanse a recent achievement, China's first dynasties ruled about half this territory.[1036] Manchuria in the northeast, Inner Mongolia in the north, Xinjiang in the northwest, and the Qinghai-Tibetan plateau in the west and southwest eluded control for millennia. The southernmost moun-

---

[1033] Tony Allan, Kay Celtel, Jacob F. Field, R. G. Grant, Philip Parker, and Sally Regan, *Imperial China: The Definitive Visual History* (London: DK, 2020), 11.

[1034] Michael Wood, *The Story of China: The Epic History of a World Power from the Middle Kingdom to Mao and the China Dream* (New York: St. Martin's Press, 2020), 19.

[1035] April Sanders, John Pearson, Micah L. Issit, and Amy Witherbee, "China," in *Countries, Peoples and Cultures: East Asia and the Pacific*, vol. 9, ed. Michael Shally-Jensen (Ipswich, MA: Salem Press, 2015), 4; John Tidey and Jackie Tidey, *China: Land, Life, and Culture* (New York: Marshall Cavendish, 2009), 4-5.

[1036] Paul S. Ropp, *China in World History* (Oxford: Oxford University Press, 2010), xii-xiv.

tains and jungle, with pathogens, insects, and parasites, impeded habitation and governance before 1000 CE.

Like Egypt, geography helped China develop without continual outside interference.[1037] The Gobi Desert kept Mongolia sparsely populated and less threatening to northern China than it otherwise might have been. The northeast's Siberian forests and Manchurian woodlands and mountains functioned likewise. The northwest's Taklamakan Desert buffered China against Central Asia. The arid west peaks at the Qinghai-Tibetan plateau, another barrier to invaders. China's neighbors underpopulated, underdeveloped, and an existential threat only when unified, northerners nonetheless raided often enough, a later section indicates, to prompt the Great Wall's construction.

Geography, climate, and hydrology shaped China's two agrarian systems.[1038] Aridity above 33 degrees North required crops that tolerated scant rainfall. Coolness shrank the growing season under six months. Increasing below this latitude, rainfall and temperature permitted multiple annual harvests. Affirming this division, two great rivers, the north's Yellow and the south's Yangtze, affected settlement and subsistence.

From the Qinghai-Tibetan plateau, the 3,300-mile Yellow River, the "cradle of China" and the "Mother River of China," nourished China's first civilization.[1039] Blown into the water by wind, Gobi Desert sand gave the river its color and name. Sand, dust, and other debris gave it the most sediment among the world's rivers.[1040] Like the Tigris and Euphrates, the Nile, and the Indus, Ganges, and Brahmaputra, the Yellow River, depositing silt upon flooding, created alluvium as deep as 500 feet over millennia.[1041]

Shallow and unpredictable from superabundant sediment, it shifted southeast about 2600 BCE only to resume the earlier channel around 600 years later.[1042] Farmers diked the river, which sometimes broke the embankment, causing them to name it "China's Sorrow."[1043] The 1887 flood, for example, destroyed villages and killed almost 1 million people.

China's longest river, the Yangtze stretches over 3,700 miles from the Qinghai–Tibetan plateau.[1044] Deeper than the Yellow, it enabled riverine

---

[1037] Ibid., xiii; Tidey and Tidey, 7.

[1038] Allan, Celtel, Field, Grant, Parker, and Regan, 18-19.

[1039] Tidey and Tidey, 13, 20; Ropp, xiii.

[1040] Ruth Mostern, "Erosion, Flooding and Climate in Yellow River History," Historical Climatology, December 14, 2020, accessed March 8, 2022, ‹Erosion, Flooding and Climate in Yellow River History - HISTORICALCLIMATOLOGY.COM.›

[1041] Cheryl Bardoe, *China: A History* (New York: Abrams Books, 2018), 3.

[1042] Allan, Celtel, Field, Grant, Parker, and Regan, 20-21.

[1043] Ibid.

[1044] Ibid., 21; Tidey and Tidey, 12.

transit and China's most productive agriculture since 1000 CE.[1045] Also perilous, its 1931 inundation slaughtered some 4 million Chinese.[1046]

While farming is a relatively recent invention in most of the world, hunter-gatherers colonized China nearly 2 mega-anna before becoming husbandmen. This duration gave it a long prehistory begun by *H. erectus*. *Homo sapiens* arrived later. The uncertain relationship between the two demonstrates that much remains contentious or unknown about earliest China.

10.3 The Original Inhabitants

The first human outside Africa, *H. erectus* entered Sinai and penetrated north to Dmanisi, Republic of Georgia. Movement east would have approached China, but this route seems unlikely because the Georgian specimens were shorter, slighter, and had smaller crania than Chinese *H. erectus*.[1047] A better match being chapter 3's Indonesian *H. erectus*, migrants probably hugged the Indian Ocean coastline from Sinai to Southeast Asia, then moved north into China.

Although Hebei province's Majuangou announced *H. erectus*' entrance into China about 1.7 million years ago, chapter 3's Zhoukoudian near Beijing was more famous.[1048] Its story resonated in the United States, whose money and physical anthropologists played a leading part, arguably for the first time, on an international stage. Chinese anecdotes mentioned old bones at Zhoukoudian, known locally as Dragon Bone Hill.[1049]

Dutch physician and anatomist Eugene Dubois (1858–1940), mentioned in chapter 3, discovered the first *H. erectus* specimen on the Indonesian island Java in 1890–1892, intensifying interest in Asia. Canadian physician and anthropologist Davidson Black (1884–1934), sure "that Asia had been the cradle and nursery of humankind," heard stories about "dragon bones" while in Peking, now Beijing.[1050] Identifying a fossil tooth, he secured funds from New York City's Rockefeller Foundation for an excavation, which in 1929 yielded the first skull of the *H. erectus* known as Peking Man. Journalists reported the find worldwide.

[1045] Ropp, xiv.

[1046] Allan, Celtel, Field, Grant, Parker, and Regan, 21.

[1047] Clark Spencer Larsen, *Our Origins: Discovering Physical Anthropology* (New York and London: Norton, 2008), 317.

[1048] Ibid.

[1049] Ruth Moore, *Evolution*, rev. ed. (New York: Time-Life Books, 1968), 132; Glenn C. Conroy, *Reconstructing Human Origins: A Modern Synthesis* (New York and London: Norton, 1997), 304.

[1050] F. Clark Howell, *Early Man*, rev. ed. (New York: Time-Life Books, 1968), 78-79; Moore, 132-133; Frank Spencer, "Black, Davidson (1884-1934)," in *History of Physical Anthropology, Vol. 1: A-L*, ed. Frank Spencer (New York & London: Garland Publishing, 1997), 180.

After Black's death, the foundation named German American physician and anatomist Franz Weidenreich (1873–1948) to direct the excavation.[1051] His team found fragments from roughly 45 adults and children, about which he published "a magnificent set of monographs," though Japan's 1931 invasion of China complicated his job.[1052] World War II's tension among Japan, China, and the United States forced him to suspend the excavation in 1941. A U.S. Marine base agreed to house the fossils. But the ship tasked with transporting them never arrived, and they disappeared.[1053] Fortunately Weidenreich had made casts of them before leaving China.

Zhoukoudian *H. erectus*, other animal remains, and over 100,000 stone tools fostered a narrative of him as a hunter whose mastery of fire enabled cooking and who ate deer, horse, bear, leopard, tiger, hyena, camel, boar, ostrich eggs, fruits, and vegetables including tubers.[1054] Combining "logical procedures and quantitative approaches," American archaeologist Lewis Binford (1931–2011) disagreed, believing *H. erectus* resembled his predecessors in scavenging rather than hunting.[1055] Moreover, Zhoukoudian lacked evidence of fire, noted chapter 3.

Yet an image of *H. erectus* sans fire contradicted his presence so far north. "Without fire, heat-adapted animals, including humans, simply cannot survive in regions of the globe where the temperature is cold much or all of the year," stated American anthropologist Clark Spencer Larsen (b. 1952), who credited meat "acquired from hunting" with enlarging *H. erectus'* body and brain beyond his forebears.[1056] Prey bones at Hubei province's Yunxian in central China, which he occupied 800,000 to 580,000 years ago, showed that he targeted young and old, the easiest kills, and so must have hunted.[1057]

Anthropologists once thought the species tenanted Zhoukoudian "for many thousands of years," though perhaps intermittently.[1058] But most fossils came as the remains of hyena meals, asserted American physician and anthropologist Noel Boaz (b. 1952).

[1051] Howell, 79; Moore, 134.

[1052] Robert Eckhardt, "Weidenreich, Franz (1873-1948)," in *History of Physical Anthropology, Vol. 2: M-Z*, ed. Frank Spencer (New York & London: Garland Publishing, 1997), 1107.

[1053] Larsen, 318; Moore, 135-136.

[1054] Robert Jurmain, Lynn Kilgore, Wenda Trevathan, and Russell L. Ciochon, *Introduction to Physical Anthropology*, 2013-2014 ed. (Belmont, CA: Wadsworth Cengage Learning, 2014), 320-321; Allan, Celtel, Field, Grant, Parker, and Regan, 25.

[1055] Jurmain, Kilgore, Trevathan, and Ciochon, 320-321; John Bintliff, "David Clarke & Lewis Binford," in *The Great Archaeologists*, ed. Brian Fagan (London: Thames & Hudson, 2014), 277.

[1056] Larsen, 318, 321.

[1057] Jurmain, Kilgore, Trevathan, and Ciochon, 322.

[1058] Ibid., 320.

Additional discoveries in Shaanxi province's Lantian county in central China dated the biped around 1.15 million years ago.[1059] Undated remains in Anhui province's Hexian county in eastern China probably postdated Zhoukoudian. Taken together, Chinese sites demonstrated that he inhabited large areas and persisted longer than in Africa or Europe.

10.4 From *Homo erectus* to *Homo sapiens* in China

Many Chinese anthropologists, identifying Chinese with *H. erectus* and modern traits 900,000 to 100,000 years ago, believed he evolved into Chinese *H. sapiens*.[1060] For example, a 100,000-year-old mandible and two teeth look modern, but their robusticity and the chin's absence resembled *H. erectus*. "Those fossils are a big mystery," remarked American anthropologist Russell Ciochon (b. 1948).[1061] "They clearly represent more advanced species than *H. erectus*, but nobody knows what they are because they don't seem to fit into any categories we know." Perhaps Chinese *H. erectus* mated with newcomers over millennia to produce today's population. Incremental transition from premodern to modern forms paralleled stone tools' gradual refinement 1.7 million years ago to 8000 BCE.

Others argued that *H. sapiens*, arising in Africa, colonized the rest of the world, including China. Rather than evolving in China, he replaced *H. erectus* there. This viewpoint noted that modern Chinese and Africans share 97.4 percent of genes.[1062] Chinese's remainder came from Denisovans and Neanderthals.

Named after Siberia's Denisova cave, site of the first discovery, Denisovans shared a common ancestor with Neanderthals about 400,000 years ago. They ranged from Siberia to Southeast Asia, becoming extinct around 28,000 BCE.[1063] A mandible put them in northwestern China's Gansu province before

---

[1059] Ibid., 321-323.

[1060] Ibid., 337; Jane Qiu, "How China is Rewriting the Book on Human Origins," *Scientific American*, July 13, 2016, accessed March 8, 2022, ‹https://www.scientificamerican.com/article/how-china-is-rewriting-the-book-on-human-origins/#.›

[1061] Qiu.

[1062] Ibid.

[1063] "First Look at the Face of Denisovans," Smithsonian National Museum of Natural History, May 1, 2019, last modified July 29, 2021, accessed March 8, 2022, ‹https://humanorigins.si.edu/research/whats-hot-human-origins/first-look-face-denisovans;› Michael Price, "Ancient DNA Puts a Face on the Mysterious Denisovans, Extinct Cousins of Neanderthals: From a Single Fossil, Researchers Use New Genomic Method to Predict Facial Anatomy," *Science*, September 19, 2019, accessed March 8, 2022, ‹https://www.science.org/news/2019/09/ancient-dna-puts-face-mysterious-denisovans-extinct-cousins-neanderthals.›

160,000 years ago.[1064] Adapting to altitude, they bequeathed Tibetans genes for efficient respiration.[1065]

Chinese ancestry may exclude *H. erectus*, though scientists, extracting none of its genes, cannot know whether it birthed today's Chinese.[1066] Heredity aside, fossils put *H. sapiens* in China 100,000 to 30,000 years ago.[1067]

10.5 Inequality

10.5.1 Paleolithic and Neolithic

Chapters 3 and 9 described *H. erectus'* inequality. *H. sapiens* intensified it through pastoralism and agriculture, which resulted from, rather than caused, sedentism.[1068] Collection of wild grain and fruit catalyzed China's first villages near the Yellow River circa 10,000 BCE. This development implied inequality whereby a leader or clique ranked and managed villagers. Farmers planted millet along the river by 7500 BCE and wheat by 5000 BCE.[1069] Northerners tamed or adopted the dog, pig, and chicken by the second date and sheep and cattle around 3000 BCE.[1070] Yangtze River farmers domesticated rice about 8000 to 6000 BCE.

The south, where warmth and rainfall permitted double cropping between the Yangtze and the West River to its south, outpopulated the north.[1071] Farmers harvested three rice crops in the West River delta. Rain leaching nutrients, farmland required human and other animal dung. Rice paddies intensified labor by requiring seedlings' transplantation.[1072] Although

[1064] "Ancient Denisovan DNA Found in Chinese Karst Cave," CGTN, Beijing, October 31, 2020, accessed March 8, 2022, ‹https://news.cgtn.com/news/2020-10-31/Ancient-Denisovan-DNA-found-in-Chinese-karst-cave--V2yLXz02zK/index.html.›

[1065] Matthew Warren, "Biggest Denisovan Fossil Yet Spills Ancient Human's Secrets: Jawbone from China Reveals that the Ancient Human Was Widespread across the World—and Lived at Surprising Altitude," *Nature* 569 (May 1, 2019): 16-17, accessed March 8, 2022, ‹https://www.nature.com/articles/d41586-019-01395-0.›

[1066] Qiu.

[1067] Allan, Celtel, Field, Grant, Parker, and Regan, 16; Jean-Jacques Hublin, "How Old Are the Oldest *Homo sapiens* in Far East Asia?" *Proceedings of the National Academy of Sciences* 118, no. 10 (February 18, 2021), accessed March 8, 2022, ‹https://www.pnas.org/content/118/10/e2101173118.›

[1068] Bardoe, 10-11; Marcie Flinchum Atkins, *Ancient China* (Minneapolis, MN: Essential Library, 2015), 17-18.

[1069] Allan, Celtel, Field, Grant, Parker, and Regan, 16; Ropp, xiii.

[1070] Allan, Celtel, Field, Grant, Parker, and Regan, 25; Bardoe, 11.

[1071] Ropp, xiv.

[1072] Te-Tzu Chang, "Rice," in *The Cambridge World History of Food*, vol. 1, ed. Kenneth F. Kiple and Kriemhild Coneè Ornelas (Cambridge, UK: Cambridge University Press, 2000), 140-141.

not thirsty enough to need inundation, rice, tolerating waterlogged soil, yields better in paddy with less competition from weeds for sunlight and nutrients than on dryland.

10.5.2 The Harvest and Hierarchy

Emphasizing status through ostentatious burial, middle and lower Yellow River Longshan culture magnates commissioned elaborate tombs after 3500 BCE.[1073] Six percent of burials in Shandong province's Chengtzu-yai cemetery, which segregated opulent interments from the rest, featured wooden caskets and numerous grave goods whereas the simplest graves were pits.[1074]

Longshan villages, China's first with walls, aimed to thwart outsiders from stealing the harvest.[1075] Demonstrating wealth's power as the chasm widened between classes, Longshan authorities compelled walls' construction through corvée.

Yangtze River Liangzhu society also unequal, rudimentary graves again housed just bones whereas 11 elite tombs approximated 1,100 jade ornaments.[1076] A seventh century BCE economist ranked the mineral, prized for hardness and luster, first in value above gold in second and copper in third.[1077] Elites alone commanded labor's skill, exertion, and tools to fashion it into decorations.

The richest burials contained tall black goblets so thin they could have held not liquid but the afterworld's ethereal beverages.[1078] Care must have been taken to place them intact into tombs. Others just sturdy enough for liquid had residues of alcohol from fermented rice, honey, and fruit, which elites probably imbibed to commemorate the decedent. No such ceremony launched commoners into eternity.

Like Egypt's pharaohs, Liangzhu kings claimed divinity, styled themselves peace and prosperity's preserver, and wielded political, religious,

---

[1073] Bardoe, 23-24; Bruce Owen, China: Longshan Horizon, Emergence of Civilizations/ Anthro 341, 2008, accessed May 21, 2022, ‹341-08s-20-ChinaLongshan (bruceowen. com)›, 1.

[1074] Owen, 5-6.

[1075] Ibid., 3; Bardoe, 25; Allan, Celtel, Field, Grant, Parker, and Regan, 17.

[1076] Bardoe, 23-24.

[1077] Ropp, 2; Allan, Celtel, Field, Grant, Parker, and Regan, 26; Xinru Liu, *The Silk Road in World History* (Oxford and New York: Oxford University Press, 2010), 2.

[1078] Bardoe, 23-24.

economic, and military authority.[1079] Religiosity peaked under them. Over time China secularized more than earlier chapters' polities.[1080]

10.5.3 From Farm to Government

China centralized more slowly than Mesopotamia, Egypt, and India.[1081] As noted, Longhan and Liangzhu authorities controlled villagers, who resented them as agents of compulsion. The drift toward centralism began in prehistory as families cooperated to ease drudgery. Cooperation enlarged for huge tasks like building and maintaining dikes and irrigation canals. Southern farms' double and triple cropping and rice seedlings' transplantation demanded the most labor.

This rationale linked centralization with movement south, but as mentioned, Yellow River settlements centralized first. Early texts originated imperialism around 2700 BCE, though the earliest kings were more legendary than real.[1082] Embellishment typified antiquity. For example, scholars challenged the historicity of Spartan archon Lycurgus (c. 800–c. 730) and Hebrew prophets Moses and Jesus (c. 5 BCE–c. 30 CE).

Chinese civilization arose with the creation of bronze.[1083] Invented in Southwest Asia, it reached Gansu province about 3000 BCE. The copper, tin, and lead alloy required identification and extraction of the metals from their ore, their proportional combination, and temperatures above 1,800 degrees Fahrenheit to melt them before casting into the desired shape. Widespread in China a millennium later, bronze coincided with the putative origin of the Xia dynasty (c. 2000–c. 1600 BCE), which may have been a regional power with larger unrealized aspirations.

Novelty and initial scarcity associated bronze with royalty. Eleven tons of ore produced 3,500 pounds of grave goods—460 mirrors, bells, weapons, and utensils—for the tomb of general and priestess Fu Hao (c. 1250–c. 1200), a wife of Shang emperor Wu Ding (r. c. 1215–c. 1190).[1084] The earliest dynasty in

---

[1079] "Liangzhu and Ancient China: The 5,000-Year Civilization Demonstrated by Jades," ed. Adam J. Ensign and Zhuang Ying, The Palace Museum, 2001-2020, accessed March 8, 2022, ‹Liangzhu and Ancient China: The 5,000-Year Civilization Demonstrated by Jades|The Palace Museum (dpm.org.cn).›

[1080] Ropp, 2; Joseph R. Strayer and Hans W. Gatzke, *The Mainstream of Civilization*, 3d ed. (New York: Harcourt Brace Jovanovich, 1979), 133-134.

[1081] Allan, Celtel, Field, Grant, Parker, and Regan, 16-18.

[1082] Edwin E. Moise, *Modern China: A History* (London and New York: Longman, 1986), 3, 5.

[1083] Ropp, 2-3; Allan, Celtel, Field, Grant, Parker, and Regan, 36.

[1084] Ropp, 5-6; Paul Bahn, *Ancient Civilizations Explained* (New York: Rosen Publishing, 2014), 50; Allan, Celtel, Field, Grant, Parker, and Regan, 42-43; Wu Mingren, "Lady Fu Hao and Her Lavish Tomb of the Shang Dynasty," Ancient Origins: Reconstructing the Story of Humanity's Past, last modified November 1, 2014, accessed May 21, 2022, ‹Lady Fu Hao and her Lavish Tomb of the Shang Dynasty | Ancient Origins (ancient-origins.net).›

China's archaeological record, the Shang (c. 1600–c. 1100) may have followed the Xia. Sixteen servants buried with her demonstrated her power over them. One was cut in half at the waist. Others were entombed alive, burned, or beheaded. Such behavior, evincing violence as innately human and unidirectional, belied the boast that "Our king of Shang brilliantly displayed his sagely prowess; for oppression he substituted his generous gentleness."[1085] The tomb also housed three ivory carvings, roughly 750 jade ornaments, 70 sculptures, 500 hairpins, and nearly 7,000 cowrie shells.

Shang inequality, evident in Fu's tomb, increased with population and the harvest.[1086] Slaves, servants, mistresses, and livestock were sacrificed when emperors died.[1087] Shang city Anyang's royal cemetery reserved the largest burials for them and kin.[1088] Nobles and officials also had sizable graves, whose expanse and inventory varied with status. Persisting into eternity, inequality required dead ancestors' ranking.

Urban mansions on hills or platforms overshadowed ordinary dwellings.[1089] One palace floor neared 98,000 square feet whereas a typical home approximated 130 square feet. "Privileged aristocrats...lived and died amid great wealth and splendor" whereas paupers inhabited a hole large enough for one person.[1090]

Outside cities, the masses "scraped by as peasants."[1091] At hierarchy's bottom, Shang China accrued slaves through warfare, criminal punishment, or default. Human sacrifice affirmed commoners' worthlessness.[1092]

10.5.4 The Dynastic Cycle

After the Shang, a succession of dynasties guided China into the twentieth century. Vigorous at the outset, each sought maximum wealth and power.[1093] A dynasty plateaued at its zenith, declined afterwards, and fell to a rival army, which established a new dynasty to repeat the cycle.

Seeking starkest inequality by monopolizing wealth and power, an emperor pushed Gini, a measure of inequality introduced in chapter 6,

---

[1085] Allan, Celtel, Field, Grant, Parker, and Regan, 41.

[1086] Bardoe, 33.

[1087] Ropp, 6-8.

[1088] Mu-Chou Poo, *Daily Life in Ancient China* (Cambridge, UK: Cambridge University Press, 2018), 20.

[1089] Poo, 26.

[1090] Ropp, 6.

[1091] Bardoe, 33.

[1092] Allan, Celtel, Field, Grant, Parker, and Regan, 43.

[1093] Robert W. Strayer, Edwin Hirschmann, Robert B. Marks, Robert J. Smith, James J. Horn, and Lynn H. Parsons, *The Making of the Modern World: Connected Histories, Divergent Paths (1500 to the Present)* (New York: St. Martin's Press, 1989), 248.

toward one. Far beneath him, farmers produced the harvest that under-pinned empire while lacking the wherewithal to challenge inequality. The attempt to achieve this bifurcation pitted an emperor against local land-owners able to raise an army against him.

The Qin (221–206 BCE) may have been the first dynasty to near this ambition. Its predecessor, the Zhou (c. 1100–256), had recruited ninth century Gansu province Qin kings to defend the northwest from invaders.[1094] Inculcating militarism, warfare sharpened Qin proficiency with chariot and crossbow. Its leaders adopted authoritarianism to thwart underlings' self-ishness and greed. Punishment, including castration, mutilation, and execu-tion, compelled obedience, which required subjects to prioritize state over family.

Qin prince Ying Zheng (259–210), "a very capable and tireless monarch," became king in 247, unified China in 221, and named himself Qin Shi Huangdi, First Emperor of China.[1095] Believing his authority gargantuan, he supposed his dynasty would last 10,000 generations.[1096] This aim elusive, he nonethe-less centralized China and amassed unprecedented wealth and power.

Desiring the above bifurcation, Qin Shi Huangdi, resettling the largest landowners in China's capital Xianyang in Shaanxi province, gave loyal-ists their property.[1097] He also opposed land concentration by freeing serfs and distributing small parcels to families. Through corvée, this peasantry built and maintained roads, canals, and palaces and expanded what would become the Great Wall. He instituted a uniform currency and standardized axle width so carts and wagons used the same ruts.

The assault on local elites inspiring plots against him, the emperor became preoccupied with his legacy and immortality.[1098] As early as 247, he ordered his tomb's construction. The tempo quickening when he became First Emperor, corvée poured some 700,000 laborers into the project. Upon completion, the mortuary complex near Xi'an, Shaanxi province's capital, covered 24,320 acres. His mausoleum topped a 165-foot mound. A 3.4-acre pit housed terra cotta representations of 8,000 warriors, 130 chariots, and 670 horses.[1099] Archaeologists have yet to excavate the mausoleum, though looting surely reduced its treasures.

[1094] Allan, Celtel, Field, Grant, Parker, and Regan, 78.
[1095] Ibid.; Ropp, 24.
[1096] Allan, Celtel, Field, Grant, Parker, and Regan, 81.
[1097] Ibid., 78-79.
[1098] Ibid., 81-82; Jacqueline Morley, *You Wouldn't Want to Work on the Great Wall of China!* (London: Franklin Watts, 2017), 8.
[1099] Allan, Celtel, Field, Grant, Parker, and Regan, 82; Ropp, 23.

Han (206 BCE–220 CE) elites were no less wealthy, demonstrated the tomb of Xin Bi (c. 212–c. 158 BCE), wife of a local official in south China's Hunan provincial capital Changsha.[1100] The grave's 1971 discovery made headlines because the contents were lavish and the corpse was intact. After the body and grave goods' transfer to Hunan Provincial Museum, tourists visited, including one who regretted her inability to question Xin about daily life.[1101]

Such fantasy presumed a counterfactual world of inconsequential inequality. No more reason exists to believe a wealthy woman would answer a commoner than former U.S. president Donald Trump (b. 1946) would want my opinion about anything. Inequality ordered relationships along class lines, excluding people above or below one's status, though exceptions occurred. For example, Byzantine emperor Justinian (482–565 CE) married a stripper, but such events scandalized onlookers.[1102]

Every aspect of Xin's tomb signaled privilege. Like Egyptian royalty, she had atherosclerosis, was obese and inactive, and likely perished from a heart attack.[1103] At a time when work required muscles, idleness distinguished her.

Despite inactivity, she ate numerous foods. Her grave held 30 baskets and 51 pots with grain, vegetables, fruit, meat, poultry, fish, spices, sweeteners, sauces, and beverages.[1104] Poultry alone included chicken, duck, goose, pheasant, crane, pigeon, quail, partridge, owl, and magpie, and sparrow eggs. Sweeteners included honey and sugar, the second unknown in earlier chapters' ancient Southwest Asia, Egypt, and Europe.

Another luxury was silk, whose manufacture from silkworms China hid from outsiders. Rome equated it with gold by weight.[1105] The fiber functioning as currency in China, 20 layers of it, fastened with nine silk bands, wrapped Xin's corpse. Her grave also had silk gowns, robes, curtains, pillows, skirts, gloves, socks, shoes, and belts, plus 46 rolls of silk and an 81-inch-long silk painting, unique in antiquity.

Intent on remaining idle in eternity, she equipped her tomb with 162 wood statues of servants.[1106] A zither and bamboo organ were to furnish

[1100] Allan, Celtel, Field, Grant, Parker, and Regan, 90; Christine Liu-Perkins, *At Home in Her Tomb: Lady Dai and the Ancient Chinese Treasures of Mawangdui* (Watertown, MA: Charlesbridge, 2014), 17.

[1101] Liu-Perkins, 4.

[1102] John P. McKay, Bennett D. Hill, John Buckler, Clare Haru Crowston, Merry E. Wiesner-Hanks, and Joe Perry, *Understanding Western Society: A Brief History* (Boston and New York: Bedford/St. Martin's, 2012), 192; Strayer and Gatzke, 160.

[1103] Liu-Perkins, 22; Allan, Celtel, Field, Grant, Parker, and Regan, 90.

[1104] Liu-Perkins, 36-37; Allan, Celtel, Field, Grant, Parker, and Regan, 90.

[1105] Liu-Perkins, 46-47.

[1106] Allan, Celtel, Field, Grant, Parker, and Regan, 90.

music, and nine boxes of cosmetics were to enhance her appearance. Impressive for a provincial, her wealth nonetheless underwhelmed the emperor and his family.

Against imperial aspirations, local elites, whose zero-sum acquisitions reduced smallholders to tenants, hirelings, servants, slaves, or serfs, augmented wealth and power by monopolizing land. Reduction to dependency worried emperors, who needed unencumbered people for corvée and conscription. As emperors feared, the richest landowners raised armies to guarantee independence, spurn taxes, and challenge a dynasty.

Battling them, government tried 11 times from 140 BCE to 2 CE to give farmhands land and resettle elites in the capital to break their control of the countryside.[1107] This repetition implied futility. As part of the plan, 7 BCE officials wanted to cap acreage and slaves per estate, but landowners objected. Between 9 and 23 CE, Emperor Wang Mang (45 BCE–23 CE), who "could almost be described as a socialist," tried to nationalize land, end the slave trade, shrink plantations, or enact some combination of these measures.[1108] Critics killed him.

Restored afterwards, the Han took one-thirtieth to one-fifteenth of crops as tax, rates below prior chapters' Sumer and Egypt.[1109] Rent was the greater burden. Corvée and conscription worsened poverty by reducing farm manpower. Low yields kept smallholders near subsistence. Debtors surrendered land, their children, and themselves upon default.

The largest Han cities, Chang'an and Luoyang, showcased luxuries that elites accumulated by parasitizing the countryside.[1110] Fancy garments and insignia elevated rich urbanites above everyone else. Their colossal tombs, like earlier elite burials, eternalized inequality. Inequality widening during the Han, ostentation increased as the rich, evading taxes, put the entire burden on workers.[1111]

10.5.5 The Great Wall

The Mongolian-Manchurian steppe supported pastoralists who raided northern China enough to necessitate walls. Efforts coalesced into the Great Wall, a United Nations World Heritage Site that extends over 4,500 miles

---

[1107] Walter Scheidel, *The Great Leveler: Violence and the History of Inequality from the Stone Age to the Twenty-First Century* (Princeton, NJ and Oxford: Princeton University Press, 2017), 63.

[1108] Ropp, 30; Michael Loewe, "Wang Mang and His Forebears: The Making of the Myth," *T'oung Pao* 80, no. 4/5 (1994): 197.

[1109] Poo, 38; Scheidel, 68.

[1110] Poo, 8-9; Liu, 4.

[1111] Ropp, 30.

from the east's Yellow Sea to the west's Gansu province.[1112] China's largest use of corvée, the construction of the Wall evinced the chasm between rich and poor as elites oppressed laborers. The earliest extant portion dating to 685 BCE, the wall began as a series of separate, local initiatives.

Upon declaring himself First Emperor, Qin Shi Huangdi commanded prisoners, farmers, soldiers, and slaves to unite the disparate walls and forts.[1113] In 215, he ordered an army, which settled some 30,000 families in the north, to repulse incursions and help build the wall. A workforce estimated near 1 million must in fact have been larger if over 1 million died during construction.[1114] Such mortality implied indifference toward commoners.

Death on this scale affected China's psyche. A man died while building the wall, one legend held.[1115] When he did not return home in autumn, his wife, unaware of his passing, took warm clothes to him. Learning of his demise, she cried so bitterly that her tears, dissolving part of the wall, revealed her husband and others' skeletons. Reburying them, she killed herself.

Authorities worked underlings to death, such stories emphasized. When one succumbed, another took his place while the First Emperor ordered the decedent's widow north as a substitute.[1116] Mourning no fatalities, overseers buried them in the wall, the above tale asserted. Live burial punished disobedience.

In truth, workers trenched the dead south of the wall in "the longest cemetery on earth."[1117] "Every stone is wet with the tears of the workers who suffered. Every brick is covered with the blood of those who died," wrote American author and editor Allison Lassieur.[1118]

In principle, corvée burdened all boys and men over four feet tall, though the rich hired substitutes.[1119] Penetrating the countryside, China's army made farmers walk up to eight weeks to the wall.[1120] Scavengers devoured decedents en route. Undermining agriculture, labor's diversion to the Great Wall doomed the Qin, which disintegrated after the First Emperor died.[1121]

[1112] Anita Ganeri, *Asia* (Chicago: Heinemann Library, 2007), 27; Allan, Celtel, Field, Grant, Parker, and Regan, 84; Sanders, Pearson, Issit, and Witherbee, 15.

[1113] Allan, Celtel, Field, Grant, Parker, and Regan, 85; Allison Lassieur, *Building the Great Wall of China: An Interactive Engineering Adventure* (North Mankato, MN: Capstone Press, 2015), 7-8.

[1114] Allan, Celtel, Field, Grant, Parker, and Regan, 84; Lesley A. DuTemple, *The Great Wall of China* (Minneapolis, MN: Lerner Publications, 2003), 6.

[1115] Lassieur, 37.

[1116] Ibid., 24; DuTemple, 31-32.

[1117] Lassieur, 22; DuTemple, 31; Morley, 15.

[1118] Lassieur, 11.

[1119] Ibid., 20.

[1120] Ibid., 39; Morley, 18.

[1121] DuTemple, 32.

Compulsion yielded 2,485 miles of wall and supply road in just seven years, but little is extant.[1122] Between 121 and 101, Han emperor Wu Di (156–87) added some 300 miles of wall east and west of the Qin achievement. To its north, the Northern Wei (386–534) erected a fifth century CE wall. The Sui (581–617) made over 1 million men repair and enlarge this wall and its forts a century later. South of the Qin ruin, most extant sections date to the fifteenth and sixteenth centuries.

10.5.6 Inequality's Ideology

The milieu that produced Chinese philosopher Confucius (551–479 BCE), whose "maxims and moral values became so influential that Confucianism can almost be regarded as religion," resembled that of Greek philosophers Plato (c. 428–c. 348 BCE) and Aristotle (384–322 BCE).[1123] Chapter 1 described upheavals, which Plato counteracted by seeking certitude through the comprehension of timeless truth. For his part, Confucius found certainty in hierarchy, which subordinated child to parent, wife to husband, and citizen to ruler.[1124]

Venerating rank and stasis, Confucius resembled Aristotle, who defended inequality and slavery.[1125] Playing "a central role in the development of Confucianism," Chinese philosopher Mencius (c. 372–289 BCE) likewise judged inequality natural and desirable.[1126] Hierarchy's rejection threatening chaos, order and stability necessitated respect for authority. Indeed, subordinates learned rectitude by emulating their wealthy and learned superiors. Prioritizing thinkers over doers, Mencius put scholars above farmers, craftspeople, merchants, and moneylenders.[1127] Influencing some dynasties, these ideas dominated Chinese scholarship for two millennia.

Favoring practicality over platitude, however, Qin Shi Huangdi disliked Confucianism.[1128] Detractors accused him of burning all books except agricultural and medical texts. Intolerant of criticism, he buried 460 Confucian scholars alive, an atrocity modern historians disbelieve.

[1122] Ibid., 47; Allan, Celtel, Field, Grant, Parker, and Regan, 85.

[1123] Martyn Oliver, *History of Philosophy: Great Thinkers from 600 B.C. to the Present Day* (New York: Barnes & Noble, 1999), 38-39.

[1124] Demi, *Confucius: Great Teacher of China* (New York: Shen's Books, 2018), [8].

[1125] Bardoe, 81-82.

[1126] Ropp, 13-14; Robert John Perrins, "Mencius," in *Berkshire Encyclopedia of World History*, vol. 2, ed. William H. McNeill, Jerry H. Bentley, David Christian, David Levinson, J. R. McNeill, Heidi Roupp, and Judith P. Zinsser (Great Barrington, MA: Berkshire Publishing Group, 2005), 1225.

[1127] Ropp, 14; Allan, Celtel, Field, Grant, Parker, and Regan, 100-101.

[1128] Allan, Celtel, Field, Grant, Parker, and Regan, 81.

Promoting stability through hierarchy, the Han revived Confucianism, cut funds to scholars who promoted alternatives, and established an academy, which required Confucian classics' memorization, to train officials.[1129] By 150 CE, it enrolled over 30,000 students who aimed to trump workers by becoming scholar-officials. Three Han emperors led this Confucian revival. Wu Di styled himself a patron of literature and scholarship. Guangwu (5 BCE–57 CE) deemed wisdom as worthy of reverence as gods or ancestors. Ming Di (28–75) visited Confucius' birthplace and debated scholars.

10.6 Review and Preview

Regressing China 1.7 million years, this chapter, treating its original inhabitant *H. erectus* and his successor *H. sapiens*, argues that both intensified inequality. Underpinning Chinese civilization, farming and herding widened the gulf between rich and poor. Crossing the Pacific Ocean, next chapter examines the precontact Americas, which, like the eastern hemisphere, ranked hunter-gatherers and farmers from the outset.

[1129] Ibid., 100-101.

Chapter 11 Precontact American Inequality

11.1 Abstract

If inequality characterized the eastern hemisphere, so it did the Americas, from the outset. Hunting, gathering, fishing, farming, and herding created wealth and intensified inequality. The harvest enriched urban plutocrats who managed the countryside. First millennium CE Belize elites inhabited homes, adorned with jade, obsidian, and seashells, tenfold larger than ordinary dwellings.[1130] About 200 to 1400, oligarchs controlled northwestern Mexican and American Southwest agriculture, turkey husbandry, trade, and labor.[1131] Eighth and ninth century Colorado's inequality increased with population.[1132] Ninth to thirteenth century Chaco Canyon, New Mexico's wealthy made laborers erect structures as massive as Egypt's pyramids.[1133] Killing slaves to placate gods and display power, royalty imposed tax, tithe, rent, corvée, conscription, serfdom, peonage, and bondage on farmworkers.

[1130] Will Dunham, "Maya Ruins in Belize Offer Peek at Ancient Wealth Inequality," Reuters, March 24, 2021, accessed March 11, 2022, ‹Maya ruins in Belize offer peek at ancient wealth inequality (yahoo.com).›

[1131] John A. Ware, "Foreword," in *Ancient Paquimé and the Casas Grandes World*, ed. Paul E. Minnis and Michael E. Whalen (Tucson: University of Arizona Press, 2015), xi.

[1132] Donna M. Glowacki, *Living and Leaving: A Social History of Regional Depopulation in Thirteenth-Century Mesa Verde* (Tucson: University of Arizona Press, 2015), 176.

[1133] Carrie C. Heitman, "The House of Our Ancestors: New Research on the Prehistory of Chaco Canyon, New Mexico, A.D. 800-1200," in *Chaco Revisited: New Research on the Prehistory of Chaco Canyon, New Mexico*, ed. Carrie C. Heitman and Stephen Plog (Tucson: University of Arizona, 2015), 235; Elizabeth Miller, "'As Close as the US Gets to Egypt's Pyramids': How Chaco Canyon Is Endangered by Drilling," *The Guardian*, November 8, 2017, accessed March 11, 2022, ‹As close as the US gets to Egypt's pyramids': how Chaco Canyon is endangered by drilling | Public lands | The Guardian.›

11.2 The First Inhabitants

American historian Robin Winks (1930–2003) and coauthors' insight that "our concepts of the distant past are changing much faster than our concepts of the periods closer to us in time" informs the western hemisphere's earliest prehistory.[1134] In 2005, for example, British anthropologists Chris Stringer (b. 1947) and Peter Andrews (b. 1940) stated, in 2008 American anthropologist Clark Spencer Larsen affirmed, and in 2013 American historians Nancy Hewitt and Steven Lawson reaffirmed, the consensus that migrants first entered the New World via Beringia around 13,000 BCE.[1135]

The route and time made sense. Earlier chapters emphasizing our tropical origin, *Homo erectus* and we colonized warm climates before cool ones. Arising in Africa's tropics perhaps 200,000 years ago, we may have entered temperate lands only when population pressure pushed us there. Migration beyond Africa put us in Asia. Competition for food drove us north after we filled the southwest, south, and southeast. Practically unliveable without fire and warm clothes, Siberia discouraged settlement for millennia. Movement from there to Alaska became possible during the last ice age, when glaciers, holding water as ice, lowered sea level enough to expose Beringia.[1136]

Migrants entered Alaska before warmth melted glaciers, causing the rising sea to reclaim Beringia about 10,000 to 9500 BCE.[1137] Some groups vanished, though the belief that all Amerindians descended from this northern peopling implies genetic continuity between them and northeastern Asians, notably Siberians and Mongolians.[1138]

Accurate for late migrations, this narrative no longer describes the first Americans. Two facts identified the Pacific Ocean, not land, as initial conduit between Asia and the Americas. First, genes connect some Amazon Amerindians with Papuans and aborigines, implying a long Pacific crossing likely

---

[1134] Robin W. Winks, Crane Brinton, John B. Christopher, and Robert Lee Wolff, *A History of Civilization, Vol. I: Prehistory to 1715*, 7th ed. (Englewood Cliffs, NJ: Prentice Hall, 1988), 2.
[1135] Chris Stringer and Peter Andrews, *The Complete World of Human Evolution* (London: Thames & Hudson, 2005), 142; Clark Spencer Larsen, *Our Origins: Discovering Physical Anthropology* (New York and London: Norton, 2008), 373, 376; Nancy A. Hewitt and Steven F. Lawson, *Exploring American Histories: A Brief Survey with Sources* (Boston and New York: Bedford/St. Martin's, 2013), 4-5.
[1136] Hewitt and Lawson, 5.
[1137] A. M. Mannion, "Introduction: The First Americans," in *World History Encyclopedia, Vol. 2, Era 1: Beginnings of Human Society*, ed. Alfred J. Andrea, Carolyn Neel, and Mark Aldenderfer (Santa Barbara, CA: ABC-CLIO, 2011), 204; Peter Jones, "Early Debates about the Peopling of the New World," in *World History Encyclopedia, Vol. 2, Era 1: Beginnings of Human Society*, ed. Alfred J. Andrea, Carolyn Neel, and Mark Aldenderfer (Santa Barbara, CA: ABC-CLIO, 2011), 205.
[1138] Alan Brinkley, *The Unfinished Nation: A Concise History of the American People*, 6th ed. (New York: McGraw Hill, 2010), 3.

in stages.[1139] Settlers reached South America, probably Chile or Peru, not the north.[1140] Second, skulls from Brazilian and Colombian natives resembled aborigines over other Amerindians.[1141]

These data lacked chronology. Archaeologists identified California's 130,000-year-old putative stone tools and broken animal bones, but nature rather than people likely produced them.[1142] Favoring later incursions, American historian Richard Morris (1904–1989), referencing "painfully thin" evidence, believed humans entered the Americas not before 48,000 BCE.[1143] Nature probably also yielded 37,000-year-old fractured New Mexican mammoth bones.[1144] Unlike contemporaneous Afro-Eurasian sites, New Mexico's location lacked stone tools. Later still, arrivals may have occupied Mexico's Chiquihuite Cave around 28,000 BCE, though genetic evidence excludes humans from the western hemisphere before roughly 13,000 BCE.[1145]

No precursor to chapter 14's transatlantic migrants, early arrivals included people related to Europeans who walked from Europe or western Asia east to Siberia, then crossed Beringia.[1146] Twenty-four-thousand-year-old Siberian DNA suggested that Europeans and western Asians bequeathed today's Native Americans one third of genes. East Asians supplied the remainder.

[1139] Helen Thompson, "A DNA Search for the First Americans Links Amazon Groups to Indigenous Australians: The New Genetic Analysis Takes Aim at the Theory that Just One Founding Group Settled the Americas," *Smithsonian Magazine*, July 21, 2015, accessed March 11, 2022, ‹A DNA Search for the First Americans Links Amazon Groups to Indigenous Australians | Science | Smithsonian Magazine.›

[1140] Brinkley, 3.

[1141] Thompson.

[1142] Christopher Joyce, "New Evidence Suggests Humans Arrived in the Americas Far Earlier than Thought," NPR, April 26, 2017, accessed March 11, 2022, ‹New Evidence Suggests Humans Arrived In The Americas Far Earlier Than Thought : The Two-Way : NPR.›

[1143] Richard B. Morris, *The New World, Vol. 1: Prehistory to 1774* (New York: Time-Life Books, 1963), 9.

[1144] Tom Metcalfe, "Mammoth Bones and 'Ghost' Footprints Add to Heated Debate about First Humans in North America," NBC News, August 4, 2022, accessed August 7, 2022, ‹Mammoth bones and 'ghost' footprints add to heated debate about first humans in North America (yahoo.com).›

[1145] Robby Berman, "Mexican Cave Contains Signs of Human Visitors from 30,000 Years Ago: Archaeologists Suggest This May Have Been the Americas' "Oldest Hotel"," Big Think, July 24, 2020, accessed August 7, 2022, ‹Mexican cave contains signs of human visitors from 30,000 years ago - Big Think.›

[1146] Brinkley, 3; Colin Schultz, "The Very First Americans May Have Had European Roots: Some Early Americans Came Not from Asia, It Seems, But by Way of Europe," *Smithsonian Magazine*, October 25, 2013, accessed March 11, 2022, ‹The Very First Americans May Have Had European Roots | Smart News | Smithsonian Magazine.›

In the Pacific Northwest before 6400 BCE, Kennewick Man complicated the debate over ethnicity and American origins.[1147] Although Washington and Oregon indigenes claimed descent from him, his cranial morphology resembled Europeans, North Africans, and western Asians whereas the post crania resembled Polynesians and Japan's indigenous Ainu.[1148] Genetic study vindicated Amerindians as his closest kin.

A July 2022 publication resurrected the Beringia route.[1149] Yunnan province Chinese with premodern and modern features, migrating east to the Pacific coast about 12,000 BCE, moved north into Siberia and east into the Americas, where their lineage died.

The New World's early colonization involving many groups over millennia by more than one route, Siberians and Mongolians may have outpopulated rivals.[1150] Although diverse, all settlers belonged to *H. sapiens*. Unlike the eastern hemisphere, the west lacked earlier chapters' premodern populations.

11.3 Inequality

11.3.1 America North of the Rio Grande

11.3.1.1 Early Subsistence

Early Americans hunted, gathered, and fished. Treated next section, Pacific Northwesterners fished. To their south, native Californians ate acorns, insects, fish, shellfish, seal, sea otter, and whale.[1151] Between California's Sierra Nevada Mountains to the west and the Rocky Mountains to the

---

[1147] "The Ancient One, Kennewick Man," Burke Museum, University of Washington, February 20, 2017, accessed August 7, 2022, ‹The Ancient One, Kennewick Man | Burke Museum.›

[1148] Sara E. Pratt, "July 28, 1996: Kennewick Man Is Discovered," Earth, The Science behind the Headlines, 2008-2021, accessed March 11, 2022, ‹July 28, 1996: Kennewick man is discovered (earthmagazine.org).›

[1149] Deniz Yildiran, "Native Americans May Have Had Roots in Southern China, Study Reveals," Interesting Engineering, July 15, 2022, accessed July 22, 2022, ‹Native Americans may have had roots in Southern China, study reveals (interestingengineering.com);› Jane Nam, "Native Americans May Have Originated from China, Says New Study on 14,000-Year-Old Human Fossils," Yahoo!News, July 21, 2022, accessed July 22, 2022, ‹Native Americans may have originated from China, says new study on 14,000-year-old human fossils (yahoo.com).›

[1150] Brinkley, 3.

[1151] David N. Dickel, Peter D. Schulz, and Henry M. McHenry, "Central California: Prehistoric Subsistence Changes and Health," in *Paleopathology at the Origins of Agriculture*, ed. Mark Nathan Cohen and George J. Armelagos (Orlando, FL: Academic Press, 1984), 449; Liz Sonneborn, *California Indians* (Chicago: Heinemann Library, 2012), 13; Brian Fagan, *The Great Warming: Climate Change and the Rise and Fall of Civilizations* (New York: Bloomsbury Press, 2008), 121-122.

---

east, hunters targeted wild camel, wild horse, bison, mammoth, and duck.[1152] East of the Rockies and west of the Mississippi River, Amerindians pursued bison, antelope, elk, deer, wolf, fox, bear, beaver, muskrat, mink, weasel, and raccoon, and collected plants.[1153] East of the Mississippi were deer, mastodon, caribou, raccoon, turtle, wild turkey, goose, bear, dog, squirrel, and snake.[1154] Lakes and rivers supplied fish and shellfish, and trees yielded acorn, walnut, hickory nut, hazelnut, and fruit. Wild marsh elder and wild goosefoot seeds were also eaten.

Shrinking food supply, over half North America's large mammals vanished around 38,000 to 8000 BCE.[1155] North Americans compensated by inventing, or borrowing from the south, agriculture, which postdated Southwest Asian, Egyptian, Indian, and Chinese farming.[1156] North Americans domesticated or adopted squash and sunflower around 3000 BCE, marsh elder and goosefoot a millennium later, and corn around 1000 CE. The dog and turkey were North America's lone domestic animals by the fifteenth century.[1157] Agriculture hardened the division between haves and have-nots.

11.3.1.2 Pacific Northwest

Entering continents without rivals, the first Americans were free in principle to create any arrangement between egalitarianism and steep inequality. Disproving egalitarianism among hunter-gatherers, chapter 1 noted inequality in the Pacific Northwest, which spanned the Pacific coast from northern California in the south to Alaska in the north.[1158] The region's Tlingit, Haida, Nootka, Chinook, Nuu-chah-nulth, Kwakwaka'wakw, and Yurok, "the People of the Totem Pole," fished rather than farmed.[1159] Practicing upward redistribution by taking paupers' food during shortage, nobles

---

[1152] Jake Page, *In the Hands of the Great Spirit: The 20,000-Year History of American Indians* (New York: Free Press, 2003), 46.

[1153] Jack L. Hofman and Russell W. Graham, "The Paleo-Indian Cultures of the Great Plains," in *Archaeology on the Great Plains*, ed. W. Raymond Wood (Lawrence: University Press of Kansas, 1998), 93; Joseph M. Prince and Richard H. Steckel, *Tallest in the World: Native Americans of the Great Plains in the Nineteenth Century* (Cambridge, MA: National Bureau of Economic Research, 1998), 5.

[1154] Bradley T. Lepper, *Ohio Archaeology: An Illustrated Chronicle of Ohio's Ancient American Indian Cultures* (Wilmington, OH: Orange Frazer Press, 2005), 38, 41, 63, 69, 86, 121, 203.

[1155] George Washington University, "Mass Extinction: Why Did Half of North America's Large Mammals Disappear 40,000 to 10,000 Years Ago?" Science Daily, November 27, 2009, accessed March 11, 2022, ‹Mass extinction: Why did half of N. America's large mammals disappear 40,000 to 10,000 years ago? -- ScienceDaily.›

[1156] Larsen, 386, 389.

[1157] Stanley J. Olsen, "Turkeys," in *The Cambridge World History of Food*, vol. 1, ed. Kenneth F. Kiple and Kriemhild Coneè Ornelas (Cambridge, UK: Cambridge University Press, 2000), 582.

[1158] Marjorie Gann and Janet Willen, *Five Thousand Years of Slavery* (Toronto, ON: Tundra Books, 2011), 54-57.

[1159] Ibid., 54.

shared it among peers to maintain a system whereby they never hungered and Gini, which chapter 6 introduced as a measure of inequality, must have neared one.[1160]

As in chapter 14, undernutrition increased Pacific Northwest slave mortality and kept population below the land's carrying capacity.[1161] Against this trend, the Yurok enslaved debtors. Poor parents sold children, each worth one or two dentalia, into bondage. Advertising owners' wealth, slaves collected plants, firewood, water, and shellfish, fished, hunted, made cloth and fishhooks, erected and repaired homes, and built and paddled canoes.[1162] A nineteenth century estimate valuing each Pacific Northwest slave at $200 to $1,000, a chief with up to 20 slaves owned as much as $20,000 in persons.

This sum would be more today. Englishmen reaching the region in 1803, this chapter uses the estimate that $1 in 1803 would be $26.22 in September 2022.[1163] A chief worth $20,000 in slaves in 1803 would have had $524,400 in September 2022. For comparison, the 2022 minimum hourly wage in Ohio, my residence, is $9.30, though employers may pay workers with physical or mental impairments less.[1164] A minimum wage Ohioan would in principle toil 56,387 hours to equal the chief, though expenses would preclude equality. A 2019 U.S. Federal Reserve System survey found that the average American aged 55 to 64—a population of more than menials that should include earners near or at their peak income—saved $57,800, just 11 percent of the chief's maximum, after decades in the workforce.[1165]

"Quite literally tons of food," notably fish like salmon, enriched the Pacific Northwest.[1166] Declaring them, rivers, and riverine land private property, nobles made underlings fence it. Amid plenitude's fluctuation during a year and from one year to another, the region's precontact population approximated 80,000. Disregarding shortage, chiefs and their retinue stole indigents' food, as mentioned. Underlings were disposable.

[1160] Wayne Suttles, "Coping with Abundance: Subsistence on the Northwest Coast," in *Man the Hunter*, ed. Richard B. Lee and Irven DeVore (Chicago: Aldine Publishing, 1968), 59.

[1161] Suttles, 65-66.

[1162] Ibid.; Gann and Willen, 55-56.

[1163] Gann and Willen, 56; Ian Webster, "$1 in 1803 Is Worth $26.22 Today," Official Data Foundation, last modified September 5, 2022, accessed September 9, 2022, ‹$1 in 1803 ⬜ 2022 | Inflation Calculator (officialdata.org).›

[1164] "State of Ohio 2022 Minimum Wage," Ohio Department of Commerce, accessed September 9, 2022, ‹2022-MW-Poster.pdf (ohio.gov).›

[1165] "What Is the Average Savings by Age?" SoFi Money, March 15, 2021, accessed March 10, 2022, ‹What is the Average Savings by Age? | SoFi.›

[1166] Suttles, 58; John Reader, *Man on Earth: A Celebration of Mankind* (New York: Harper & Row, 1988), 128-129.

Natives inhabited longhouses with a base up to 21,125 square feet.[1167] Rain from moist Pacific air sustained forest, which provided timber. Each village, with totem poles signaling identify, surpassed 1,000 residents.[1168] Insignia, fancy canoes, copper, slaves, and privilege put aristocrats, who exhibited "unabashed megalomania" and whose utterances were law, above common-ers.[1169]

Pacific Northwest southern tribes prohibited, whereas northerners permitted, slave rape and murder, which attended potlatch, a ceremony whereby chiefs showed their wealth was so great they could give it away without worry.[1170] Among chattel gifted to others, slaves were executed, often with a "slave killer" club, to reinforce the message of their disposability.[1171]

War generating slaves, the Nootka of Vancouver, Washington, gained them by raiding neighbors.[1172] During war, southeastern Alaska's Tlingit and the Haida of British Columbia, Canada, enslaved children and women, who kept house.[1173] Although kin might ransom captives, the enormous price and bondage's stigma discouraged intervention.

Only royalty owned slaves. "I have slaves who hunt for me, paddle me in my canoe, and have my wife to attend me. Why should I care to leave?" replied a Nootka king invited to England.[1174]

11.3.1.3 Eastern Woodlands

East of the Mississippi, southwestern Indiana's early archaic period (c. 8000–c. 6000 BCE) burials exhibited inequality.[1175] Elite graves had spear points, shells, and nonhuman canines probably fashioned into necklaces, nonhuman and human bones, and chapter 4's hematite. Encouraging late archaic period (c. 3000–c. 1000) sedentism, agriculture heightened inequality.[1176] Whereas nomadism prevented possessions' accumulation, late archaic elites amassed and displayed wealth, which others tried to seize through warfare.

The wealthy ordered burial mounds' construction after the late archaic.[1177] West Virginia's early woodland period (c. 800 BCE–c. 1 CE) Grave Creek Mound, for example, had many unadorned skeletons whereas elite inter-

---

[1167] Reader, *Man on Earth*, 126-127.
[1168] Suttles, 56.
[1169] Reader, *Man on Earth*, 130-131, 133.
[1170] Suttles, 65-66; Gann and Willen, 57.
[1171] Gann and Willen.
[1172] Ibid., 54-55.
[1173] Ibid., 59-60.
[1174] Ibid.
[1175] Lepper, 62.
[1176] Ibid., 71, 74.
[1177] Ibid., 90.

ments, possibly chiefs, warriors, and shamans, featured "lavish" shells acquired from distant trade, copper shaped into antlers, stone and ceramic pipes, spear points, and flint knives.[1178] Middle woodland period (c. 100 BCE–c. 500 CE) differentiation enlarged with inequality.[1179]

Two elaborate southwestern Ohio late prehistoric period (c. 900–c. 1600) Sunwatch Indian Village burials housed elites, perhaps a chief and a shaman, whereas 75 percent of graves lacked adornment.[1180] With large houses, graves, and food storage pits, Sunwatch's western neighborhood dwarfed its east.[1181]

This period overlapped the Mohawk, Oneida, Onondaga, Cayuga, and Seneca's sixteenth century formation of the Iroquois confederation.[1182] The Tuscarora joined around 1720, when Iroquois territory stretched from the Carolinas in the south to Canada in the north. Warfare again generated slaves, who replaced losses from disease, undernutrition, murder, and accidents, though the worst conflicts sought to annihilate enemies.

Iroquois abused chattel. They renamed them, as Europeans did to Africans. A seventeenth century Jesuit witnessed an owner stab slaves in the back and shoulders and amputate their fingers.[1183] Slaves who survived benefitted owners by farming and carrying loads in lieu of pack animals. Slave women again kept house. Adopting Christianity, one mother, fearing her deceased daughter would be unable to care for herself without her 20 slaves, asked a priest to baptize an ill slave so she could serve the daughter in heaven.

11.3.2 Mesoamerica

11.3.2.1 Settlement

South of these events, Siberian descendants colonized today's Mexico City about 21,000 BCE.[1184] The climate, cooler then, supported grass that fed herbivores they hunted and that ceded to jungle, where rainfall was plentiful, and to desert, where it was negligible after temperatures rose around 7000 BCE.

As prey diminished, Mesoamericans—Mexicans, Guatemalans, Belizeans, Hondurans, and Salvadorans—domesticated plants, notably corn

---

[1178] Ibid., 92-93.

[1179] Ibid., 129.

[1180] Ibid., 214.

[1181] Ibid., 210.

[1182] Gann and Willen, 57.

[1183] Ibid, 57-58.

[1184] Charles Phillips, *The Complete Illustrated History of the Aztec and Maya: The Definitive Chronicle of the Ancient Peoples of Central America and Mexico—including the Aztec, Maya, Olmec, Mixtec, Toltec, and Zapotec* ([London]: Hermes House, 2015), 28.

or maize, "the grain that built a hemisphere."[1185] These crops' inability to reproduce without aid demonstrates domestication's thoroughness. More productive than native edibles like sunflower, goosefoot, and marsh elder, corn supported villages and cities from Chile in the south to Canada in the north before 1400 CE.[1186] The Mayas, Aztecs, and Incas ate it, which today trails only wheat in world acreage.[1187] "Corn is life," remarked Hopi chief Don Talayesva (1890–1985) in summarizing its importance.[1188]

11.3.2.2 Olmec

Corn growers formed Mesoamerica's first villages about 2000 to 1500 BCE.[1189] Thereafter enlarging Gulf of Mexico villages into Mexico's first cities, Olmec nobles made commoners, moving boulders over 50 miles to reach the construction site, build monuments like pyramids. "Great armies of labourers were needed to build these vast ceremonial centres," wrote British historian Charles Phillips (b. 1948) in summarizing corvée's pervasiveness.[1190] Elites sacrificed underlings, violence later Mesoamericans copied. Peaking 1200 to 400 BCE, Olmec civilization spanned Mexico City in the northwest to El Salvador in the southeast.[1191]

11.3.2.3 Zapotec

Urbanizing around 1350 BCE, southern Mexico's Zapotec made Oaxaca state's Monte Alban the capital about 500 BCE.[1192] Aristocrats had workers build pyramids, temples, and palaces. Undernutrition's uncommonness in skeletons implied that commoners lived outside the city, shrinking the distance between Monte Alban's top and bottom.[1193] Inequality, whereby

---

[1185] Ibid.; Meredith Sayles Hughes, *Glorious Grasses: The Grains* (Minneapolis, MN: Lerner Publications, 1999), 51.

[1186] Larsen, 385; Robert W. Strayer, Edwin Hirschmann, Robert B. Marks, Robert J. Smith, James J. Horn, and Lynn H. Parsons, *The Making of the Modern World: Connected Histories, Divergent Paths (1500 to the Present)* (New York: St. Martin's Press, 1989), 210; Walton C. Galinat, "Domestication and Diffusion of Maize," in *Prehistoric Food Production in North America*, ed. Richard I. Ford (Ann Arbor: University of Michigan, Museum of Anthropology, Anthropology Papers No. 75, 1985), 245.

[1187] Ellen Messer, "Maize," in *The Cambridge World History of Food*, vol. 1, ed. Kenneth F. Kiple and Kriemhild Conee Ornelas (Cambridge, UK: Cambridge University Press, 2000), 97; Jeff Desjardins, "The World's Most Valuable Cash Crop," Visual Capitalist, November 10, 2014, accessed March 11, 2022, ‹The World's Most Valuable Cash Crop - Visual Capitalist.›

[1188] Betty Fussell, *The Story of Corn* (New York: Knopf, 1992), 167.

[1189] Phillips, 28-29.

[1190] Ibid., 29.

[1191] Ibid.; Paul Bahn, *Ancient Civilizations Explained* (New York: Rosen Publishing, 2014), 129.

[1192] Phillips, 30-31.

[1193] Mattha Busby, "Equality Was Key to Ancient Mexican City's Success, Study Suggests," *The Guardian*, March 16, 2022, accessed May 25, 2022, ‹Equality was key to ancient Mexican city's success, study suggests | Mexico | The Guardian.›

nobility managed farmworkers on nearby acreage, pitted city against countryside.

Believing rich and poor inhabited Monte Alban, American archaeologist
Gary Feinman (b. 1951) interpreted undernutrition's infrequency as evidence
that inequality was mild enough to permit most citizens adequate food.[1194]
Ornate tombs' absence and palaces' rarity strengthened this opinion, compli-
cating attempts to assign class, pinpoint class conflict, and gauge inequality.

Avoiding labor, Monte Alban elites parasitized the harvest. Feinman
attributed Zapotec post-800 CE decline to worsening inequality rather than
farmland's overexploitation.[1195]

11.3.2.4 Maya

Settling southern Guatemala in the second millennium BCE, the contemporaneous Maya spread northwest into southern and eastern Mexico and
northeast into Belize after 800 BCE.[1196] The most populous villages became
cities after 600 BCE. Again employing corvée, elites made farmers, battling
insects, mud, heat, and humidity, deforest land and erect temples, pyramids,
and palaces. Warfare added slaves to the workforce.[1197]

Possibly requiring 15 million man-days to complete, Mayan capital El
Mirador's La Danta pyramid outweighs, though it is shorter than, the Great
Pyramid.[1198] Roughly half a U.S. ton, each La Danta stone required 12 men to
drag some 700 yards from quarry to site. Draining swamps, clearing jungle,
and terracing hillsides, farmers planted corn, beans, squash, and cacao trees.
Soil depletion and inequality doomed El Mirador in the second century CE.

11.3.2.5 Pre-Aztecs and Aztecs

First century BCE Mesoamericans built Teotihuacan, the forerunner of
Aztec Tenochtitlan and today's Mexico City.[1199] "The Place of the Gods,"
with roughly 40,000 denizens about 1 CE and 100,000 to 200,000 half a

---

[1194] Ibid.

[1195] Ibid; Phillips, 30-31.

[1196] Phillips, 31.

[1197] Douglas J. Kennett, Marilyn Masson, Carlos Peraza Lope, Stanley Serafin, Richard J.
George, Tom C. Spencer, Julie A. Hoggarth, Brendan J. Culleton, Thomas K. Harper, Keith
M. Prufer, Susan Milbrath, Bradley W. Russell, Eunice Uc Gonzalez, Weston C. McCool,
Valorie V. Aquino, Elizabeth H. Paris, Jason H. Curtis, Norbert Marwan, Mingua Zhang,
Yemane Asmerom, Victor J. Polyak, Stacy A. Carolin, Daniel H. James, Andrew J. Mason,
Gideon M. Henderson, Mark Brenner, James U. L. Baldini, Sebastian F. M. Breitenbach,
and David A. Hodell, "Drought-Induced Civil Conflict among the Ancient Maya," *Nature
Communications* 13, no. 3911 (July 19, 2022), accessed August 8, 2022, ‹Drought-Induced
Civil Conflict Among the Ancient Maya | Nature Communications.›

[1198] Chip Brown, "El Mirador, the Lost City of the Maya: Now Overgrown by Jungle, the
Ancient Site Was Once the Thriving Capital of the Maya Civilization," *Smithsonian
Magazine*, May 2011, accessed March 11, 2022, ‹El Mirador, the Lost City of the Maya |
History | Smithsonian Magazine.›

[1199] Phillips, 32.

millennium later, surpassed London.[1200] Over 60,000 workers toiled a decade to erect Teotihuacan's first century CE Pyramid of the Sun.[1201] Government, overtaxing and overworking farmers, widened inequality. Famine may have emptied the city in the seventh or eighth century.

Ranking themselves aristocrats, commoners, serfs, or slaves, Aztecs encountered Teotihuacan's ruins in the fourteenth century.[1202] Thinking it too impressive to raze, they enlarged it into their capital Tenochtitlan, which Spaniards later judged as magnificent as Turkish port Istanbul and cleaner, better managed, and fivefold larger than London.[1203] Admiration vanished when over 100,000 sacrificial skulls were found.

Merchants bought slaves—Tenochtitlan was the principal market—for many purposes, including sacrifice.[1204] Buyers preferred an attractive slave who could entertain them by dancing or singing in the days beforehand. Ownership guaranteed them the corpse afterwards, which complemented corn at a feast.

Unlike other chapters' slaveowners, Aztecs declared slaves' children free.[1205] Default enslaved debtors. Satisfactory performance prevented their sale unless they consented. Poor performance justified sale after an owner rebuked them before witnesses and they failed to improve. Deemed incorrigible, peons sold thrice were sacrificed. Male slaves, foreign slaves, and peons constituted most sacrifices.

Slaves and serfs worked "vast estates."[1206] Landowners monopolizing wealth, power, and privilege, laborers, serfs, and slaves could not improve their lot. Recurring throughout *Eternal Inequality*, this pattern's independent emergence in eastern and western hemispheres implies an immutable impulse to hierarchize.

11.3.3 South America

11.3.3.1 Brazil

South of Mesoamerica, Panama's isthmus led to South America, which humans may have entered around 38,000 BCE.[1207] Colonized early, Brazil evinced inequality. Its Tupinamba, like Aztecs, combined slavery, human

---

[1200] Ibid.

[1201] Ibid., 34; Strayer, Hirschmann, Marks, Smith, Horn, and Parsons, 210.

[1202] Phillips, 36-37; Bahn, 133-134; Gann and Willen, 54; Hewitt and Lawson, 5-6.

[1203] Strayer, Hirschmann, Marks, Smith, Horn, and Parsons, 211.

[1204] Gann and Willen, 54; Phillips, 68.

[1205] Gann and Willen, 54.

[1206] Hewitt and Lawson, 5-6.

[1207] Hayden Chakra, "The First Settlement of the Americas (c. 15,000 Years Ago)," About History, March 10, 2021, accessed March 11, 2022, ‹The First Settlement Of The Americas (c. 15,000 Years Ago) - About History (about-history.com).›

sacrifice, and cannibalism.[1208] Warfare enslaved captives who, wearing a necklace with one bead per month of life left, were fed enough to stay healthy until sacrifice. An owner sometimes let slaves wed and live with him beforehand. When dared to escape, death, dismemberment, roasting, and consumption followed recapture. The uneaten head surmounted a pole.

11.3.3.2 The Andes Mountains

11.3.3.2.1 Early Habitation and Subsistence

West of Brazil, along the Pacific Ocean coastline and the Caribbean Sea, the Andes Mountains stretch some 4,500 miles from the south's Cape Horn to the north's Venezuela. The mountain range attracted Quechua hunter-gatherers about 10,000 BCE.[1209] They domesticated the potato, the region's "principal fuel of empire," around 8000 BCE.[1210] The only adequate producer above 2,500 yards altitude, it permitted agriculture in mountains where only 3 percent of land is arable (compared to 21 percent in the United States, over 30 percent in Europe, 57 percent in India, 58 percent in Mauritius, 62 percent in Denmark, 68 percent in Bangladesh, and 77 percent in Barbados).[1211] "Without it, nothing resembling Andean civilization could have arisen," wrote Canadian American "authority in world history" William McNeill (1917–2016).[1212] Andean farming, which human muscles enabled, was arduous without plow, draft animal, or wheel.[1213]

Precontact America, including the Andes, lacked eastern hemisphere livestock except possibly chickens. The Quechua tamed two camelids, the llama as the primary pack animal and the alpaca, which furnished excellent wool, by 4000 BCE.[1214] They ate both when past their prime. Although potatoes have many nutrients, including all essential amino acids, their protein is small and fat nil.[1215] Supplying both, camelid meat complemented them,

---

[1208] Gann and Willen, 53-54.

[1209] Erinn Banting, *South America* (New York: AV2, 2013), 8; John Reader, *Potato: A History of the Propitious Esculent* (New Haven, CT and London: Yale University Press, 2008), 7.

[1210] "White Potato," in *The Cambridge World History of Food*, vol. 2, ed. Kenneth F. Kiple and Kriemhild Conee Ornelas (Cambridge, UK: Cambridge University Press, 2000), 1878; William H. McNeill, "How the Potato Changed the World's History," *Social Research* 66, no. 1 (Spring 1999): 70.

[1211] Reader, *Potato*, 7, 57; Reader, *Man on Earth*, 183.

[1212] McNeill, 70; Patrick Manning, "William H. McNeill: Lucretius and Moses in World History," *History and Theory* 46, no. 3 (October 2007): 428.

[1213] Reader, *Potato*, 9.

[1214] Daniel W. Gade, "Llamas and Alpacas," in *The Cambridge World History of Food*, vol. 1, ed. Kenneth F. Kiple and Kriemhild Conee Ornelas (Cambridge, UK: Cambridge University Press, 2000), 555-557.

[1215] Reader, *Man on Earth*, 174; Stephanie Pedersen, *Roots: The Complete Guide to the Underground Superfood* (New York: Sterling 2017), 22.

---

though neither was milked. The larger llama preferred for meat, demand led herders to populate the Andes with both animals.

11.3.3.2.2 Early Governance

Pastoralism and agriculture underpinned Andean civilization.[1216] By 2800 BCE, Lima, Peru plutocrats made laborers build pyramids, temples, tombs, and forums. Occurring first in South America, New World centralization "subsumed [villages] into states under the control of a ruling elite."[1217]

Around 1 to 600 CE, the Moche united northwestern Peru's cities, which imported highland potatoes because aridity precluded agriculture.[1218] Moche decline coincided with Peruvian and Bolivian farmers' formation of Tiwa-naku state, which may have fought Moche armies or withheld the harvest to starve urbanites. Amassing potatoes and "vast numbers of llamas," Tiwa-naku elites made underlings elevate the polity to its peak from 800 to 1200 by building palaces, pyramids, temples, forums, and roads.[1219]

Drought circa 1100 to 1300 shrank Peru and Bolivia's Lake Titicaca to its smallest in over 500 years, hastened Tiwanaku decline, and provided an opportunity for Incas, originating about 1200 among the Quechua of Peru's Cuzco valley and making Cuzco their capital.[1220] Governing over 386,000 square miles, the Inca empire—the western hemisphere's largest before the sixteenth century—spanned the Pacific in the west to Amazonia in the east and Colombia in the north to central Chile and Argentina in the south.

Premodern agriculture is understood to have employed 90 percent of population; that would mean that 9 to 14.4 million of the Inca empire's 10 to 16 million inhabitants were needed for farming.[1221] Authorities trisected the harvest among farmers, government, and priests. Tax and tithe took two thirds, overburdening agriculture given the mere 10 percent surplus.

Inca confiscation was large by any measure. Sumer, discussed in chapter 5, demanded 48 percent of the harvest, though the amount collected must have been smaller. In Egypt, the Hebrews owed pharaoh 20 percent. China's tax decreased from 15–20 percent in the fourteenth century CE to 5 percent in the eighteenth century.

Besides tax and tithe, elites made commoners terrace hillsides, dig canals, build aqueducts, cut tunnels through mountains for aqueducts and roads, span swamps and rivers with bridges, and pave almost 25,000 miles

---

[1216] McNeill, 70; Reader, *Potato*, 51; Bahn, 137.

[1217] Reader, *Potato*, 51.

[1218] Ibid., 51-53.

[1219] Ibid., 53.

[1220] Ibid., 55-59.

[1221] Ibid., 56-57; Hewitt and Lawson, 7.

of roads.[1222] Mining and other exertions enriched nobles enough to pay the Spanish 11 tons of pure gold and silver in 1533.[1223]

The empire's capitulation to 160 Spaniards exposed as frail a system that severely oppressed underlings.[1224] Resenting government and temples, they had no incentive to defend inequality when the Spanish appeared. "The Incas...were not unseated by a handful of intrepid invaders alone, but by widespread discontent among the native populations, who saw the Spanish as a means of deliverance from the prevailing state of affairs," averred Peruvian historian Maria Rostworowski (1915–2016).[1225] The Inca collapse produced not equity but chapter 14's continuation of inequality.

11.4 Review and Preview

In principle free to create any economic and social system, Amerindians essentially produced in the western hemisphere the same inequality that prevailed in the Old World. Disagreeing that preagricultural people were egalitarian, this chapter, corroborating chapter 1, shows that Pacific Northwest inequality pitted nobles against slaves. Farmers furthered this aristocrat-slave dichotomy. Sacrificing slaves, elites imposed tax, tithe, rent, corvée, conscription, serfdom, peonage, and bondage on underlings. Chapter 11 presaging chapter 14's post-contact slavery, chapters 12 and 13 treat medieval inequality and the backlash against it.

[1222] Reader, *Potato*, 56; Kristen Rajczak Nelson, *Ancient Inca Culture* (New York: Rosen Publishing, 2017), 12, 14.

[1223] Reader, *Potato*, 59.

[1224] Ibid., 58; Nelson, 29.

[1225] Maria Rostworowski, "The Incas," in *The Inca World: The Development of Pre-Columbian Peru, A.D. 1000-1534*, ed. Laura Laurencich Minelli (Norman: University of Oklahoma Press, 2000), 187.

Chapter 12 Medieval Inequality

12.1 Abstract

Inequality shaped medieval farming, herding, mining, cities, banks, trade, and religion. As in antiquity, agriculture and pastoralism underpinned the economy. Creating wealth that enriched landowners and worsened inequality, farmworkers "sweated, starved, and died of plague."[1226] European towns and cities, home to paupers and elites, revived as loci of inequality after roughly 1000 CE.

12.2 Transition from Antiquity to the Middle Ages

Last chapter's Mayan classical period (c. 250–c. 900), Peru and Bolivia's Tiwanaku (c. 600–c. 1200), and the eastern woodlands' late prehistoric period (c. 900–c. 1600) overlapped the Middle Ages, traditionally an "Age of Belief" around 500 to 1500, which began in Asia about 400 and spread to Europe and Africa.[1227] Transition from antiquity to the Middle Ages occurred as landowners and warlords replaced centralism. English historian and "giant of the Enlightenment" Edward Gibbon (1737–1794) described Rome's "Decline and Fall," when German king Flavius Odoacer (c. 430–c. 493)

[1226] Richard O'Neill, *The Middle Ages: Turbulent Centuries* (New York and Avenel, NJ: Crescent Books, 1992), 11.

[1227] Anne Fremantle, "Introduction," in *The Age of Belief: The Medieval Philosophers*, ed. Anne Fremantle (Boston: Houghton Mifflin, 1955), ix–x; Marsha Groves, *Manners and Customs in the Middle Ages* (New York: Crabtee Publishing, 2006), 1; Allison Lassieur, *The Middle Ages: An Interactive History Adventure* (Mankato, MN: Capstone Press, 2010), 7; David Graeber, *Debt: The First 5,000 Years* (Brooklyn and London: Melville House, 2014), 255.

dethroned Romulus Augustulus (c. 460–c. 527), Rome's last emperor in the Latin-speaking West, in 476.[1228]

The event symbolized Rome's economic, military, and political ener-vation. Like chapter 10's China during periods of decline, imperial decay allowed landowners to rule the countryside whereas merchants and money-lenders governed cities. The north was more rural than Mediterranean lands, where, as in antiquity, ports profited from trade.

From the third to fifth centuries, landowners replaced government. Feudalism, strongest in the north and discussed next, defined relations between landholders, the lords, and those who needed their protection and access to land, crops, livestock, and timber. During the Middle Ages, there-fore, local elites topped the economic, social, religious, and political pyramid. Where it lingered, government could seldom compel their allegiance or tax the harvest.

12.3 Feudal Inequality

12.3.1 Feudalism and Serfdom

Feudalism arose as an alliance between landowner and warrior or knight.[1229] Following German tradition, a lord required warriors' loyalty in exchange for land, known as a fief or *feudum*, making them his vassal. He retained title to land, though the vassal managed its labor. Succeeding late antiquity's Frankish invaders, Europe's Merovingian and Carolingian rulers furthered feudalism in this way. Carolingian ninth century fragmentation strengthened secular and religious elites like bishops and abbots.[1230]

Feudalism centered on the manor: a village and adjacent farmland.[1231] The wealthy overburdened the farmhands, who were "part of the lord's perma-nent labor force."[1232] Bound to the soil, they became serfs. "Serfdom was not the same as slavery in that lords did not own the person of the serf," averred American historian of Europe John McKay (b. 1948) and coauthors.[1233]

[1228] Edward Gibbon, *The Decline and Fall of the Roman Empire*, abridged ed. (New York: Modern Library, 2003), 3; Arthur E. R. Boak, *A History of Rome to 565 A.D.*, 4th ed. (New York: Macmillan, 1955), 477-478; J. G. A. Pocock, *Barbarism and Religion, Vol. One: The Enlightenments of Edward Gibbon, 1737-1764* (Cambridge, UK: Cambridge University Press, 1999), 6.

[1229] John P. McKay, Bennett D. Hill, John Buckler, Clare Haru Crowston, Merry E. Wiesner-Hanks, and Joe Perry, *Understanding Western Society: A Brief History* (Boston and New York: Bedford/St. Martin's, 2012), 222-223; Joseph R. Strayer and Hans W. Gatzke, *The Mainstream of Civilization*, 3d ed. (New York: Harcourt Brace Jovanovich, 1979), 143.

[1230] McKay, Hill, Buckler, Crowston, Wiesner-Hanks, and Perry, 215.

[1231] Ibid., 223.

[1232] Ibid., 224.

[1233] Ibid.

Eternal Inequality judges this claim to be a distinction without a difference. Indeed, McKay and colleagues, describing serfs as unfree, stated that they could not leave the farm without the lord's consent as slaves could not leave the plantation without the master's permission.[1234] Moreover, serfdom, like bondage, was permanent and heritable.

12.3.2 Medieval Slavery

Some three fifths of Europeans were serfs by 800, though others were slaves generated by "extensive" trade.[1235] Present in antiquity, as earlier chapters noted, Mediterranean slavery persisted through the Middle Ages, when Europeans and Arabs traded unfortunates like war captives.[1236] Permitting bondage in general, Judaism, Christianity, and Islam opposed co-religionists' enslavement.

Tracing bondage to Prophet Muhammad's (570–632) ownership of slaves, Muslims outbid Europeans three or fourfold.[1237] Consequently, most European captives were taken across the Mediterranean Sea to North Africa, Egypt, East Africa, West Africa, and Southwest Asia. Trading in Africa and Asia as far east as India, Muslims made slaves mine gold in Nubia and salt in the Sahara Desert, where they survived less than five years.[1238] They grew sugarcane, cloves, and grain in East Africa and on Indian Ocean archipelago Zanzibar; dates, vegetables, and grain in Saharan oases; sugarcane and cotton in Iraq; and dates in Arabia.

The Umayyad Caliphate (661–750), headquartered in Syria and Mesopotamia, raided North Africa for slaves.[1239] Its successor, the Abbasid Caliphate (750–1258), bought slaves from the Khazar Qaghanate (c. 650–c. 967), which governed land north of the Black Sea in the west to Central Asia in the east.[1240] Training them as soldiers, Abbasid rulers conscripted or sold them. Originating in Afghanistan, the Samanid Empire (819–1005) enslaved Turks and eastern Europe's Slavs in war.[1241]

[1234] Ibid.

[1235] Ibid.

[1236] Ibid.; Marjorie Gann and Janet Willen, Five Thousand Years of Slavery (Toronto, ON: Tundra Books, 2011), 22–38.

[1237] McKay, Hill, Buckler, Crowston, Wiesner-Hanks, and Perry, 224.

[1238] Gann and Willen, 32, 38.

[1239] Fred M. Donner, "Muhammad and the Caliphate: Political History of the Islamic Empire up to the Mongol Conquest," in The Oxford History of Islam, ed. John L. Esposito (Oxford: Oxford University Press, 1999), 20.

[1240] Peter B. Golden, Central Asia in World History (Oxford: Oxford University Press, 2011), 64-65.

[1241] Ibid.; Donner, 39.

Muslims racialized bondage by paying more for whites.[1242] Favoring white over black women in harems, men thought the latter "vile" and "evil."[1243] Blacks resenting this prejudice, one remarked around 660 that he would have suffered less had he been white.

Inequality, slavery, and racism provoked a backlash east of Iraqi city Basra, where ninth century landowners made Nubian and Ethiopian slaves dig salt pans to expose soil suitable for sugarcane.[1244] Revolting against drudgery and desiring freedom and land, they joined the poorest peasants in 868 in class war against elites.[1245] Pitting black slaves against Arab masters, the Zanj rebellion (868–883) was also racial. Ninth century chroniclers, judging the uprising the period's worst, reported 300,000 deaths in a single battle.[1246] Rejecting this number, scholars estimated tens of thousands killed during turmoil that Abbasid and slaveowner mercenaries only managed to end in 883.

An estimate of slaves' worth comes from Moroccan city Marrakesh's patron saint Abu-al-Abbas-al-Sabti (c. 1129–c. 1204). Resembling next chapter's Italian founder of the Franciscan Order and Christian saint Francis of Assisi (c. 1182–1226) in almsgiving, he reconciled piety, inequality, and ownership of 32 slaves, allotting them, his wife, and children as much money as himself.[1247] For simplicity, this calculation equalizes all slaves, his wife, and children and assumes paternity of two children, totaling 35 recipients. These conditions valued each slave at 1/35 (2.9 percent) of al-Sabti, an amount that decreased with additional offspring or valuation of his wife and progeny above them, as seems probable.

Jutting into the Mediterranean, Italy bought slaves from many of its neighbors: Greece, Russia, Turkey, Crete, Arabia, Ethiopia, and central and eastern Europe.[1248] The trade quickened after the Black Death, covered in the next chapter, when urbanites like wealthy Florentines purchased slaves to offset free labor's dearth.

[1242] Ibid., 33, 37.

[1243] Ibid., 36.

[1244] Nigel D. Furlonge, "Revisiting the Zanj and Re-Visioning Revolt: Complexities of the Zanj Conflict (868–883 CE)," *Negro History Bulletin* 62, no. 4 (December 1999): 7; Mohammed Elnaiem, "What Was the Zanj Rebellion?: A Remarkable Episode of Medieval Muslim History That Often Goes Untold," JSTOR Daily, February 4, 2021, accessed August 10, 2022, ‹What Was the Zanj Rebellion? - JSTOR Daily.›

[1245] Furlonge, 10-11; Elnaiem.

[1246] Furlonge, 7, 9.

[1247] Vincent J. Cornell, "Fruit of the Tree of Knowledge: The Relationship between Faith and Practice in Islam," in *The Oxford History of Islam*, ed. John L. Esposito (Oxford: Oxford University Press, 1999), 98, 100.

[1248] Gann and Willen, 26-27.

To the north, Vikings, deeming blacks "swarthy" and "ugly," captured or bought slaves starting in the eighth century.[1249] Wales established a market to meet demand. Medieval Denmark permitted slaves' torture. Iceland allowed their whipping, mutilation, and execution. Norwegian owners could kill slaves without cause. Some Scandinavian slaves were sacrificed to serve their owner in the afterlife.

12.3.3 Landowners and Laborers

Recounting royal misbehavior, Frankish historian and bishop Gregory of Tours (538–593) described Frankish princess Rigunth's (c. 569–c. 589) difficulties with her mother, Queen Fredegund (545–597).[1250] In one episode, Fredegund, showing her daughter an enormous chest with jewels, pulled many handfuls from it. When her arms tired, she asked Rigunth to remove the rest. The daughter reaching into the chest, the queen tried to break her hand by slamming the lid. Later marrying a Spanish prince, Rigunth needed 50 chariots for her dowry. Even if Gregory exaggerated, she must have approached the apex of early medieval wealth and privilege.

Rigunth was a Merovingian, a Frankish dynasty named after King Meroweg (c. 411–458).[1251] Merovingian kings owned vast lands in today's France and parts of Germany, Switzerland, Austria, and northern Italy. Land ownership was, of course, the source of wealth in agrarian economies. Pre-Merovingian farms sought subsistence whereas, by about 650 to 850, stockmen raised pigs for pork and sheep for wool to export.[1252] Making wool an important wealth generator, Merovingian, Carolingian, and Anglo-Saxon monasteries spearheaded this development.

Affluence allowed Frankish royals and their successors to build palaces.[1253] French journalist Paul Lacroix (1806–1884) stopped counting at 15, signifying others with "etcetera."[1254] Royal estates collected rent and fees. French king Philip Augustus (1165–1223), for instance, had an annual income worth 72,000 pounds of silver.[1255]

[1249] Ibid., 22-25.

[1250] Paul Lacroix, *Manners, Customs, and Dress during the Middle Ages and during the Renaissance Period* (New York: Skyhorse Publishing, 2013), 58.

[1251] Strayer and Gatzke, 153.

[1252] Pam J. Crabtree, "Agricultural Innovation and Socio-Economic Change in Early Medieval Europe: Evidence from Britain and France," *World Archaeology* 42, no. 1 (March 2010): 122.

[1253] Lacroix, 60-61.

[1254] Ibid., 61.

[1255] Ibid., 312.

To the south, Byzantine secular and religious elites carved Sicily into *latifundia* on the Roman model between the sixth and eighth centuries.[1256] Based in Rome and Ravenna, Italy's Christian authorities were absentees who profited by exploiting the peasants of Sicily. Invading the island in 827, Muslims, like China's emperors, sought to break entrenched power by dividing *latifundia* into smaller units.[1257]

From Sicily southeast across the Mediterranean, Egypt's sixth and seventh century Coptic churchmen amassed land.[1258] Difficult to administer, their largest estates began to fragment around 700. About then, Muslims penetrated Upper Egypt, imposed corvée, and taxed the harvest and income. Replacing many Coptic landowners, they raised wheat and sheep. The caliph, kin, and senior military officers had the most acreage.[1259]

Apa Apollo, a Coptic monastery at Bawit, Egypt, owned "very extensive" property in the seventh and eighth centuries.[1260] Following secular custom, its monks cultivated some land, hired laborers for other tracts, and rented additional acres to tenants. Rentier and taxman, the monastery collected rent from religious and lay tenants, part of which went as taxes, presumably to the caliph.[1261] Although not requiring conversion to Islam, the caliphate surtaxed Jews and Christians who retained their faith.

Revisiting Europe, Les Dunes Abbey at Coxyde, Belgium, held some 25,000 acres.[1262] Sheep numbered roughly 18,000 in Yorkshire, England, at the Fountains Abbey, 14,000 at North Yorkshire's Rievaulx Abbey, and 12,000 at Yorkshire's Jervaulx Abbey. These institutions became "great

---

[1256] Annliese Nef *et* Vivien Prigent, *"Controle et xxploitation des campagnes en Sicile,"* in *Authority and Control in the Countryside: From Antiquity to Islam in the Mediterranean and Near East (6th-10th Century),* ed. Alaine Delattre, Marie Legendre, and Petra Sijpesteijn (Leiden and Boston: Brill, 2019), 314.

[1257] Robert Venosa, "Muslim Cultural Influences in Sicily," Stony Brook Press, December 20, 2008, accessed March 14, 2022, ‹Muslim Cultural Influences in Sicily | The Stony Brook Press (sbpress.com).›

[1258] Marie Legendre, "Landowners, Caliphs and State Policy over Landholdings in the Egyptian Countryside," in *Authority and Control in the Countryside: From Antiquity to Islam in the Mediterranean and Near East (6th-10th Century),* ed. Alaine Delattre, Marie Legendre, and Petra Sijpesteijn (Leiden and Boston: Brill, 2019), 404-405.

[1259] Ibid., 412.

[1260] Gesa Schenke, "Monastic Control over Agriculture and Farming: New Evidence from the Egyptian Monastery of Apa Apollo at Bawit," in *Authority and Control in the Countryside: From Antiquity to Islam in the Mediterranean and Near East (6th-10th Century),* ed. Alaine Delattre, Marie Legendre, and Petra Sijpesteijn (Leiden and Boston: Brill, 2019), 421-422.

[1261] Ibid., 424-425, 428.

[1262] Jean Gimpel, *The Medieval Machine: The Industrial Revolution of the Middle Ages* (New York: Penguin Books, 1976), 46-47.

---

corporations, thoroughly tied into the increasingly complex web of medieval economic life."[1263]

Enlarging the harvest with three or four extra weeks of warmth yearly, Europe around 800 to 1300 was 1 or 2 degrees Fahrenheit above twentieth century temperatures.[1264] Slowing tree growth, the drier climate eased the chore of replacing forest with farm. Central Europe's orchards and grain flourished. Viticulture spread north from the Mediterranean into England, where over 40 vineyards operated in 1086 and where agriculture advanced farther north than during World War II (1939–1945).[1265]

Adopting a plow suitable for heavy soils, northern Europe discarded Rome's scratch plow, which was unsatisfactory outside the Mediterranean.[1266] Fallowing fewer acres than in antiquity, experiments with crop rotation extended cultivation to two thirds arable land whereas half had been Rome's norm.

12.4 Urbanization and Inequality

12.4.1 Medieval Urbanization

The harvest's enlargement circa 800 to 1300 increased Europe's population, about 27 million around 700, to 73 million in 1300.[1267] With over 90 percent of medieval Europeans engaged in farming, most occupied villages.[1268] A rough calculation is possible by rounding to 90 percent, the figure American Australian historian David Christian (b. 1946) supplied in chapter 5. Ninety percent of 73 million persons put 65.7 million in the countryside and 7.3 million in towns and cities in 1300.

[1263] Robin W. Winks, Crane Brinton, John B. Christopher, and Robert Lee Wolff, *A History of Civilization, Vol. 1: Prehistory to 1715*, 7th ed. (Englewood Cliffs, NJ: Prentice Hall, 1988), 194.

[1264] Richard H. Steckel, *Health and Nutrition in the Preindustrial Era: Insights from a Millennium of Average Heights in Northern Europe* (Cambridge, MA: National Bureau of Economic Research, 2001), 18; Gimpel, 31-32; Alfred J. Andrea, "Environment and Population," in *World History Encyclopedia, Vol. 9, Era 5: Intensified Hemispheric Interactions, 1000-1500*, ed. Alfred J. Andrea and Carolyn Neel (Santa Barbara, CA: ABC-CLIO, 2011), 13.

[1265] Gimpel, 32; James L. Newman, "Wine," in *The Cambridge World History of Food*, vol. 1, ed. Kenneth F. Kiple and Kriemhild Coneè Ornelas (Cambridge, UK: Cambridge University Press, 2000), 732.

[1266] Strayer and Gatzke, 206.

[1267] Gimpel, 57; Mortimer Chambers, Raymond Grew, David Herlihy, Theodore K. Rabb, and Isser Woloch, *The Western Experience, Vol. II: The Early Modern Period*, 4th ed. (New York: Knopf, 1987), 395.

[1268] Gimpel, 29.

Cities rebounding after roughly 1000, Milan, Italy, approximating 200,000 inhabitants in 1300, was Europe's largest.[1269] Venice and Florence, Italy, and Paris, France, approximated 110,000 denizens, Belgium's Ghent 56,000, Bruges 27,000, and Tournai and Brussels 20,000. Medieval European cities trailed Rome in the first and second centuries, Constantinople, now Istanbul, Turkey, in the fourth and fifth centuries, and Beijing, China, in the thirteenth century, all with near 1 million citizens.[1270]

Venice imported into Europe spices, sugar, and silk that traveled the silk road to Constantinople, Aleppo, or another entrepot.[1271] Buying wool from local stockmen or in England, the Belgian cities of Bruges, Ghent, and Ypres made cloth for export and revived trade that had decreased in late antiquity. German, Bohemian, Italian, French, and English silver discoveries after 1160 increased coins in circulation, encouraged the profit motive, and fostered trade, urbanization, and capitalism.[1272]

12.4.2 Urban Inequality

Cities housed "fabulously wealthy merchants" who wore bright clothes, silk, expensive wool, and stylish hats.[1273] Sumptuary laws reserved velvet, satin, pearls, fur, and clothes stitched with gold thread or colored with costly dyes for elites.

Among them, Florence's Frescobaldi, Bardi, and Perruzzi families amassed fortunes through usury.[1274] The Frescobaldis loaned money to mine owners in Devon, England, while the Bardis and Perruzzis collected tithes for popes and loaned money to England's crown. Frescobaldi profits financed northern European textile manufacture. Purchasing wool two years before it was produced, the family eliminated merchants who lacked the capital to offer similar contracts and "effectively enslaved the majority of [Florence's] thirty thousand textile workers."[1275]

Northern Europe's magnates employed servants whereas wealthy Italians bought Balkan slaves, often young women.[1276] The richest had several servants or slaves who laundered clothes, reared children, delivered pack-

---

[1269] McKay, Hill, Buckler, Crowston, Wiesner-Hanks, and Perry, 291-292.

[1270] Ibid., 150; Annie Labatt, "Constantinople after 1261," Metropolitan Museum of Art, October 2004, accessed March 14, 2022, ‹Constantinople after 1261 | Essay | The Metropolitan Museum of Art | Heilbrunn Timeline of Art History (metmuseum.org)›; O'Neill, 14.

[1271] McKay, Hill, Buckler, Crowston, Wiesner-Hanks, and Perry, 294-295; O'Neill, 58.

[1272] McKay, Hill, Buckler, Crowston, Wiesner-Hanks, and Perry, 298.

[1273] Ibid., 299.

[1274] Gimpel, 102.

[1275] Ibid., 104.

[1276] McKay, Hill, Buckler, Crowston, Wiesner-Hanks, and Perry, 294, 300.

ages and letters, repaired dwellings, and afforded only the cheapest food. Especially powerless, cripples sought charity in cities. Toiling from youth, destitute children lacked even the chimera of upward mobility.

12.5 Medieval Christianity and Inequality

12.5.1 Christianity's Origin

Centralism's decline in late antiquity left Christianity to unite Europe. Chapter 6 treated the gospels, whose ambiguities shaped medieval opinions about poverty, affluence, inequality, sin, justice, and salvation. That chapter overviewing ideas, this one examines Christianity's institutional and economic roles.

It began within Judaism.[1277] Hebrew prophet Jesus (c. 5 BCE–c. 30 CE) emphasized faithfulness to Hebrew god Yahweh, chose Hebrews as apostles, preached to Hebrews, and may have favored reform over creation of a religion.[1278] Emphasizing Jewish apocalypticism, he attracted followers unhappy with Roman rule. After his death, the movement's earliest members defined themselves as Jews.

Jewish authorities disagreeing with their views, Christians were still a minority in the late first century amid Romans suspicious of their novelty.[1279] The actual magnitude of persecution is controversial. Those who emphasized Rome's cruelty sought sympathy through victimhood, though persecution was apparently infrequent enough to let Christianity grow without fearing annihilation.[1280] More than any contemporary, Jewish convert to Christianity Paul (c. 5–c. 65), directing growth toward gentiles, differentiated Christianity from Judaism.[1281]

By roughly 130, hundreds of adherents populated the west's Italy to the east's Mesopotamia.[1282] Christianity, the empire's largest faith by 284, pagans still outnumbered Christians.[1283]Affirming truth as timeless and promising an afterlife, third century turmoil made Christianity attractive amid uncer-

---

[1277] Strayer and Gatzke, 90.

[1278] William C. Placher, *A History of Christian Theology: An Introduction* (Philadelphia: Westminster Press, 1983), 28-30, 32; McKay, Hill, Buckler, Crowston, Wiesner-Hanks, and Perry, 158-161; Winks, Brinton, Christopher, and Wolff, 98, 101, 103.

[1279] McKay, Hill, Buckler, Crowston, Wiesner-Hanks, and Perry, 158-161; Strayer and Gatzke, 91.

[1280] Strayer and Gatzke, 106.

[1281] Ibid., 159; Placher, 32-33.

[1282] Placher, 32.

[1283] Strayer and Gatzke, 106; McKay, Hill, Buckler, Crowston, Wiesner-Hanks, and Perry, 161.

---

tainty. Some third century emperors, however, blamed it for economic and political woes.

Its illegality ended under Emperor Constantine I (c. 272–337), who allegedly saw a cross with the words "Conquer in this sign" before a battle in 312.[1284] He emblazoned the image on his standard, won the battle, credited God with the victory, and legalized Christianity. Expecting support, he hoped its structure and officials would help him govern.[1285] Although still worshiping the sun, he sought baptism and required anyone who had taken church land to return it. Decreeing Christianity Rome's only religion in 380, Emperor Theodosius I (347–395) outlawed the pre-Christian calendar and in 394 began persecuting pagans.[1286]

Medieval Christianity gained wealth, privilege, and power. Near hierarchy's summit, church authorities, benefiting from the status quo, urged Christians to accept their rank, however humble, rather than seek advancement.[1287] "Rising in society was a sign of pride; demotion was a shameful sin," averred French historian Jacques Le Goff (1924–2014).[1288] "The organization of society that God had ordained was to be respected, and it was based on the principle of hierarchy."

12.5.2 Monasticism

12.5.2.1 Origin

Recruiting the earliest Christians, Paul visited Mediterranean cities and sent them letters.[1289] With trade, coinage, and urbanism dwindling in late antiquity and the Early Middle Ages, as noted, Christianity targeted the countryside, where monks established monasteries. "In the absence of large cities and royal courts, monasteries provided the largest and most stable communities, and the leadership of Christianity fell increasingly to monks and nuns," stated American theologian William Placher (1948–2008).[1290]

Whether urban or rural, Christianity noted the divide between haves and have-nots. Luke (c. 90), for example, had Jesus exalt the poor and hungry while condemning the wealthy and overfed.[1291] German philosopher and philologist Friedrich Nietzsche (1844–1900) denounced this ideal as

---

[1284] Strayer and Gatzke, 107; Winks, Brinton, Christopher, and Wolff, 107.
[1285] Placher, 75.
[1286] McKay, Hill, Buckler, Crowston, Wiesner-Hanks, and Perry, 169.
[1287] Adam Woog, *The Late Middle Ages* (San Diego: Reference Point Press, 2012), 57.
[1288] Jacques Le Goff, "Introduction: Medieval Man," in *Medieval Callings*, ed. Jacques Le Goff, trans. Lydia G. Cochrane (Chicago: University of Chicago Press, 1990), 34.
[1289] Strayer and Gatzke, 90-91, 112.
[1290] Placher, 123.
[1291] Luke 6:20-25 (New American Bible).

life-negating despair and asceticism.[1292] Whatever the truth of his opinion, early monks were poor and lived simply. Embodying faith, they provided an example more powerful than any rhetorical defense of Christianity.

Preceding monasticism, Essenes, Jewish ascetics who lived in today's Israel and the West Bank, isolated themselves amid mountains and desert.[1293] Adherents may have included Jewish messianic precursor John the Baptist (c. 5 BCE–c. 30 CE). If Jesus was John's disciple, as seems likely because Mark (c. 70), Luke, and Matthew (c. 90) had John baptize him, Jesus may also have belonged to the group.[1294]

John's piety attracted followers. His sparse attire and diet of "grasshoppers and wild honey," quoted chapter 6, anticipated monasticism by marking him an ascetic and wealth's critic. Mark, Luke, and Matthew's description of him as "a herald's voice in the desert" suggested solitude.[1295] Jesus isolated for 40 days after baptism, stated these three.[1296]

These stories inspired the faithful to leave society. Egyptian and Syrian Christians unhappy with taxes, rent, corvée, poverty, disorder, and lack of upward mobility abandoned farms in late antiquity, as chapter 2 relates. . Occupying caves and tomb and temple ruins, they attracted followers who formed the first monasteries.[1297]

Egyptian ascetic, Christian saint, and "Father of Monasticism" Anthony (c. 251–c. 356), in 271 hearing commentary on Matthew's injunction that perfection required the donation of everything one had to indigents, renounced his inheritance and sought solitude on a hill east of the Nile River.[1298] Athanasius I (c. 298–c. 373), Christian saint and bishop of Alexandria, Egypt, who "received popular ovations greater than those given any military hero," wrote *Life of Anthony* (c. 360) after visiting him.[1299] Pitting Anthony against Satan, it challenged readers to battle their demons.

One passage, blaming Satan for beating him unconscious, underscored hermits' vulnerability.[1300] They aggregated for safety and to emulate a para-

---

[1292] Friedrich Nietzsche, *On the Genealogy of Morals*, trans. Walter Kaufman and R. J. Hollingdale (New York: Viking Books, 1969), 108-117.

[1293] Anthony C. Meisel and M. L. del Mastro, "Introduction," in *The Rule of St. Benedict*, trans. Anthony C. Meisel and M. L. del Mastro (New York: Doubleday, 1975), 12.

[1294] Mark 1:9; Luke 3:21; Matt 3:13-15.

[1295] Mark 1:3; Matt 3:3; Luke 3:4.

[1296] Mark 1:12-13; Matt 4:1-2; Luke 4:1-2.

[1297] Meisel and Mastro, 13.

[1298] Ibid., 15; Placher, 123; Matt 19:21; "St. Anthony of the Desert: Who Is Saint Anthony?" Orthodox Christian Mission, Las Cruces, New Mexico, accessed March 14, 2022, ‹Who is Saint Anthony? | St. Anthony (stanthonylc.org).›

[1299] Placher, 73-74, 123; Meisel and Mastro, 14-15.

[1300] "St. Anthony of the Desert."

gon.[1301] Anthony's holiness attracted followers and a letter from Constantine.[1302] After Anthony's death, they established the Monastery of Saint Anthony the Great about 200 miles southeast of Cairo.

His exploits led Roman soldier, Egyptian ascetic, and Christian saint Pachomius (c. 290–c. 346) to establish a monastery in Tabennisi.[1303] Prior cenobites acted as they thought best, but he established rules for novices, a practice common thereafter. Among regulations, he required everyone to labor for the community, a policy like corvée.

Founding a monastery in today's Turkey, bishop and Christian saint Basil (c. 329–c. 379), creating what Serbian American economist Branko Milanovic (b. 1953) termed "equality in poverty," required penury and almsgiving from all.[1304] Milanovic had antiquity in mind, suggesting that Basil, less an innovator than a realist, understood that almost everyone was poor. His directive, if achieved, equalized monks and produced a Gini, a measure of inequality, near zero.

12.5.2.2 Benedictine Monasticism and Inequality

From Egypt and Southwest Asia, monasticism entered Italy, where ascetic and Christian saint Benedict (c. 480–c. 543) was "the most important figure in monasticism in the West."[1305] Born to nobles, he attended a Roman academy but disliked other students' immorality.[1306] Disillusioned with secular knowledge, he renounced his patrimony and spent three years in a cave near Subiaco. A reputation for holiness led people to seek his advice. Nearby monks asked him to lead them when their abbot died.

Their management entailed his writing *The Rule of St. Benedict*, which "probably guided the details of more human lives than any other document," around 529, the year Byzantine emperor Justinian (482–565) closed Athens' last philosophy school.[1307] Christianity having surpassed philosophy as truth, Benedict quoted scripture 17 times in the prologue while omitting philosophy.[1308]

[1301] Meisel and Mastro, 15.

[1302] "St. Anthony of the Desert."

[1303] McKay, Hill, Buckler, Crowston, Wiesner-Hanks, and Perry, 173; Meisel and Mastro, 15-16.

[1304] McKay, Hill, Buckler, Crowston, Wiesner-Hanks, and Perry, 173; Placher, 125; Branko Milanovic, *The Haves and the Have-Nots: A Brief and Idiosyncratic History of Global Inequality* (New York: Basic Books, 2011), 50.

[1305] Placher, 125.

[1306] Meisel and Mastro, 25-26.

[1307] Placher, 125-126; McKay, Hill, Buckler, Crowston, Wiesner-Hanks, and Perry, 173.

[1308] *The Rule of St. Benedict*, trans. Anthony C. Meisel and M. L. del Mastro (New York: Doubleday, 1975), 43-45.

"The vice of private ownership must be uprooted from the monastery," he wrote in denying monks anything without an abbot's consent, a directive that intended "equality in poverty" indeed.[1309] Elevating the group above the individual, this requirement helped monasteries succeed as farms by precluding land's division through partible inheritance and profits' flow to shareholders.[1310] Settling the hinterland, monks cleared forests and drained swamps to establish farms that attracted admirers and donations.

"Equality in poverty" retained hierarchy. Addressed as "Abbot or My Lord," an abbot, a monastery's father, wielded authority just as Aristotle urged fathers to rule children.[1311] Urging an abbot to treat underlings alike, not to put free person above a serf, this advice came as near equality as Benedict ventured. Taking "counsel with himself," an abbot made a monastery more autocracy than oligarchy or democracy.[1312]

His absolute authority, displaying "the sternness of a master," compelled obedience.[1313] Disobedience's punishment, evoking the master–slave relationship, included whipping.[1314] A monastery resembling a plantation that required daily exertion, and field work when weather permitted, monks resembled slaves.[1315] "Monks have neither free will nor free body," emphasized Benedict, and were "truly monks when they must live by manual labor."[1316] Rather than innovate, monasteries replicated agrarian inequality.

12.5.2.3 Monastic Wealth and Inequality

Like wealth, poverty, and inequality, salvation was an economic matter. The rich gave monasteries land and money in hopes of buying God's favor.[1317] Affluence, connections, administrative skills, and literacy made abbots essential to government by the tenth century. As monastic power increased, spirituality waned. Hastening this change, the Franks embraced Christianity around 500 as the Benedictines were emerging as a movement.[1318] Funding monasteries and churches, Merovingian and Carolingian lords recruited their leaders as advisers and administrators.

Wealth, power, and privilege undermined restraint. Retaining Benedict's avoidance of meat, abbots and bishops nevertheless took two or three

---

[1309] Ibid., 76.
[1310] McKay, Hill, Buckler, Crowston, Wiesner-Hanks, and Perry, 173.
[1311] *Rule of St. Benedict*, 48-49, 99.
[1312] Ibid., 49.
[1313] Ibid., 49, 54.
[1314] Ibid., 50, 70, 73.
[1315] Ibid., 86.
[1316] Ibid., 76, 86.
[1317] Placher, 140.
[1318] Ibid., 154.

courses of fish at meals.[1319] Spurning labor, overfed monks were thrice fatter than commoners and became rentiers who supervised tenants, servants, and lay farmworkers.[1320] Overindulgence and sloth flouted Benedict's warning that "Nothing is more contrary to being a Christian than gluttony."[1321]

Aggravating problems, Vikings swept south from Scandinavia, destroyed monasteries and farms, and brought Carolingian rule to an end in the ninth century.[1322] Crossing the Mediterranean, Moors attacked Sicily and Italy north to Venice. Raiding as far west as Spain, Magyars from Russia settled Hungary after 950.

Absent Carolingians, monasteries sought protection from local land-owners.[1323] This alliance perpetuated the problem of spiritual decline amid secular control as the wealthy appointed themselves or kin abbots. Imposing vassalage, landowners required military service from monks. As noted, some elites gave monasteries land and money whereas others seized the harvest or monastic land.

12.5.2.4 Monastic Reform and Inequality

Impetus for reform came from atop the hierarchy as early as the sixth century, when monk, pope, and Christian saint Gregory I (c. 540–c. 604), known as Gregory the Great, warned against seven deadly sins, including greed, gluttony, sloth, and lust.[1324] Although we associate the fourth with sex, he meant to condemn all excesses and reinvigorate the gospel message of poverty and humility. The first monk to lead the church, Gregory, "the greatest pope of the early Middle Ages," epitomized reform, spent papal lands' revenues on the poor, and ate daily with 12 indigents.[1325]

Reform was difficult to implement. From the outset, monasticism attracted individuals who felt God's call to abandon society, its strictures, and authority. As noted, Benedict reimposed authority by emphasizing

---

[1319] *Rule of St. Benedict*, 80; C. Anne Wilson, *Food and Drink in Britain: From the Stone Age to the 19th Century* (Chicago: Academy Chicago Publishers, 1973), 31.

[1320] Jennifer Viegas, "Fat Jolly Monks Had Painful Secrets," ABC, July 26, 2004, accessed March 22, 2022, ‹http://www.abc.net.au/science/news/health/HealthRepublish_1161819.htm.›

[1321] *Rule of St. Benedict*, 80.

[1322] McKay, Hill, Buckler, Crowston, Wiesner-Hanks, and Perry, 215, 221, 280; Charles Homer Haskins, *The Renaissance of the Twelfth Century* (Cambridge, MA and London: Harvard University Press, 1927), 19.

[1323] McKay, Hill, Buckler, Crowston, Wiesner-Hanks, and Perry, 280.

[1324] U. Voll and A. Kenel, "Deadly Sins," in *New Catholic Encyclopedia, Vol. 4: Com-Dyn*, 2d ed., ed. Berard L. Marthaler, Gregory F. LaNave, Jonathan Y. Tan, Richard E. McCarron, Denis J. Obermeyer, and David J. McGonagle (Detroit: Thomson Gale, 2003), 565; Kevin Vost, *The Seven Deadly Sins: A Thomistic Guide to Vanquishing Vice and Sin* (Manchester, NH: Sophia Institute Press, 2015), 61, 64-66.

[1325] John Julius Norwich, *Absolute Monarchs: A History of the Papacy* (New York: Random House, 2011), 42, 48-49.

---

abbot as autocrat. Each abbot a law unto himself, independence trumped oversight.

From the tenth century, devout secular and religious leaders sought control of monasteries to improve quality and spirituality. Around 910, French nobleman William the Pious (875–918) established Burgundy's Cluny Abbey, which enforced Benedict's mandate that monks obey their superior.[1326] Opposing secular interference, William subordinated Cluny to the pope. Even after founding new monasteries, monks remained under Cluniac and papal sway.

Yet oversight diminished as they mushroomed and old problems recurred.[1327] Isolation and slow travel and communication made monasteries independent in fact if not intent. Cluny and its satellites achieved a reputation for holiness, attracted donations of land and money, and gained privilege and power as had earlier monasteries. Angering Pope Gregory VII (1015–1085) in 1076, for example, Holy Roman Emperor Henry IV (1050–1106) sought the abbot of Cluny's guidance.[1328]

Reform stalling, several monks, leaving Burgundy's Molesme Abbey in 1098 to found an independent monastery at Citeaux, created the Cistercian order.[1329] To ensure seclusion, they chose a swamp, which they reclaimed through labor, asceticism, and without slaves, serfs, hirelings, tenants, luxury, or profit.[1330] Unlike Cluny, each Cistercian monastery had an abbot. All met frequently to standardize policy.

Establishing Burgundy's Clairvaux Abbey in 1115, Cistercians named French monk and Christian saint Bernard (1090–1153) abbot.[1331] Despite seeking seclusion, he advised popes and rulers, helped organize the second crusade, and became "the most powerful churchman of the early twelfth century."[1332] "The walls of the church are aglow, but the poor of the church go hungry," he remarked.[1333] "The stones of the church are covered with gold, while its children are left naked. The food of the poor is taken to feed the eyes of the rich."[1334]

[1326] McKay, Hill, Buckler, Crowston, Wiesner-Hanks, and Perry, 280; Placher, 146; Winks, Brinton, Christopher, and Wolff, 192.

[1327] Placher, 146.

[1328] Strayer and Gatzke, 216; Winks, Brinton, Christopher, and Wolff, 187.

[1329] McKay, Hill, Buckler, Crowston, Wiesner-Hanks, and Perry, 280.

[1330] Strayer and Gatzke, 219; Placher, 146

[1331] Placher, 146; McKay, Hill, Buckler, Crowston, Wiesner-Hanks, and Perry, 280-281.

[1332] Strayer and Gatzke, 218.

[1333] Placher, 146-147.

[1334] Ibid.

The Saint-Denis Abbey of Paris corroborated Bernard.[1335] Aiming to erect the "crown of the kingdom," Abbot Suger (c. 1091–1152) rebuilt the church, "a monument to...his worldly pomp and glory, and his enlightened patronage of the arts," in the new Gothic style.[1336] Its chalice had 140 ounces of gold, and sapphires adorned the windows. Born to peasants, Suger left their problems for next chapter's fourteenth century.

12.6 Review and Preview

As in earlier millennia, the medieval economy enriched few and impoverished most. Racism influenced slavery; magnates oppressed underlings; serfs, slaves, tenants, and hirelings worked land they could never own; mining truncated lives; servants and slaves staffed spacious mansions while living in misery; and beggars crowded cities. Against inequality, monks, abandoning society and possessions as sinful, settled the hinterland only to become rich and unable to lessen economic and social ills. Absent religious remedy, famine, the Black Death, and inequality, inflaming next chapter's class conflict, pitted farmhands and urban poor against elites.

[1335] Strayer and Gatzke, 220.
[1336] Ibid.; Haskins, 255-256.

Chapter 13 Medieval Reactions against Inequality

13.1 Abstract

Late medieval Europeans confronted inequality, heresy, famine, pestilence, and revolt. The period was among history's most tumultuous. It began with heretics opposing, and Christian authorities abetting, inequality. Seeking to bridge the divide, Franciscans and Dominicans, following their founders and the gospels' asceticism, attracted adherents by embracing heretics' emphasis on poverty while avoiding condemnation by obeying church authorities. Unlike monks, these mendicants inhabited cities, had university degrees, and sought to combine penury with sophistication relevant to worldly merchants and bankers.[1337] Although unable to eradicate inequality, the friars avoided worsening it.

Heretics and Christians inhabited an unstable society. Killing paupers more than plutocrats, hunger weakened survivors. Possibly humankind's worst pandemic, the Black Death, slaughtering millions more, intensified class warfare that pitted workers against rural and urban elites. The Late Middle Ages thus exhibited the introduction's Newtonian backlash.

13.2 Christianity and Inequality

13.2.1 Heresy as Opposition to Inequality

Strengthening medieval Christianity, monasticism left unresolved last chapter's conflict between piety and profits. Churchmen powerless against

---

[1337] Joseph R. Strayer and Hans W. Gatzke, *The Mainstream of Civilization*, 3d ed. (New York: Harcourt Brace Jovanovich, 1979), 250.

inequality, heretics combatted it in ways that alarmed authorities. Arising in the Balkans, Catharism or Albigensianism combined Christianity, early heresies, and paganism.[1338] Contrasting light and darkness, the faith heeded Greek philosopher Plato (c. 428–c. 348 BCE) who described men imprisoned in a dim cave, where shadows deceived them.[1339] One freed himself, struggled up and out of the cave, and saw the sun's light. Now possessing truth, he rejoined the others in hopes of convincing them.

Borrowing this metaphor, Christianity made Jesus "the light of the world" who promised an end to darkness.[1340] Catharism agreed but contradicted dogma by denying his humanity.[1341] Averring that an evil god, the equivalent of Satan, created all matter including the body, they believed Jesus was never human but the good god's emanation. As such, he never experienced birth, pain, and death, an opinion contrary to the gospels. Condemning the Tanakh as inspired by the evil god, Cathars formed their own church to supplant corrupt Christianity.[1342]

Matter's rejection extended to wealth, luxury, and comfort.[1343] Denunciation of private property threatened landowners' monopoly on wealth, against which Cathars adopted early monasticism's asceticism. Zealous in their faith, some starved themselves. Before 1200, piety and austerity attracted followers, notably in southern France's Albi, where Christians hoped for a Cathar's blessing to guarantee salvation. Wealth and private property's criticism led Innocent III (1161–1216), "under whom the medieval Papacy reached its zenith," in 1207 to organize a crusade against Cathars, whose defeat doomed the movement.[1344]

Heeding German philosopher and philologist Friedrich Nietzsche's (1844–1900) insight that the powerful defined language, *Eternal Inequality* emphasizes that it was church authorities who defined heresy.[1345] Rather than expressions of objectivity, the words orthodoxy and heresy reflected

---

[1338] Ibid., 244.

[1339] Plato, *Republic*, in *The Great Dialogues of Plato*, trans. W. H. D. Rouse (New York and Scarborough, Ontario: New American Library, 1956), 312-315.

[1340] John 8:12 (New American Bible).

[1341] William C. Placher, *A History of Christian Theology: An Introduction* (Philadelphia: Westminster Press, 1983), 148; Willis Barnstone, "Introduction," in *The Gnostic Bible*, rev. ed., ed. Willis Barnstone and Marvin Meyer (Boulder, CO: Shambhala, 2009), 751; Robin W. Winks, Crane Brinton, John B. Christopher, and Robert Lee Wolff, *A History of Civilization, Vol. I: Prehistory to 1715*, 7th ed. (Englewood Cliffs, NJ: Prentice Hall, 1988), 208.

[1342] Placher, 148; Strayer and Gatzke, 244.

[1343] Placher, 148; Winks, Brinton, Christopher, and Wolff, 208; Strayer and Gatzke, 244.

[1344] John Julius Norwich, *Absolute Monarchs: A History of the Papacy* (New York: Random House, 2011), 171.

[1345] Friedrich Nietzsche, *On the Genealogy of Morals*, trans. Walter Kaufman and R. J. Hollingdale (New York: Viking Books, 1969), 25-29.

the outcome of competing claims to truth, which the winner defined. A victorious crusade enabled church apologists to brand Catharism an evil destined for damnation.

Besides Cathars, Italian monk and "tireless critic of abuses in the Church" Arnold of Brescia (c. 1094–1155) advocated that clerics own nothing.[1346] His near contemporary French merchant and moneylender Peter Waldo (c. 1140–c. 1218) "underwent a radical conversion experience."[1347] Like last chapter's Egyptian ascetic, Christian saint, and "Father of Monasticism" Anthony (c. 251–c. 356), he heard and obeyed Matthew's injunction to give indigents everything. Denouncing priestly wealth, he became a beggar. Echoing them, English theologian, philosopher, and "stalwart advocate of Church reform" John Wycliffe (c. 1320–1384) believed the church could regain purity only by surrendering all property.[1348]

13.2.2 Friars and Inequality

Attacking heresy, Innocent also sought reform. Despite the pope's eminence, Italian founder of the Franciscan Order and Christian saint Francis of Assisi (c. 1182–1226), "the Troubadour of God," embodied the thirteenth century longing for spirituality.[1349] His life coincided with economic revival that enriched Italian merchants, whose ostentation discomforted sincere Christians. A merchant's son, Francis indulged himself during his youth.[1350] Believing God required charity, however, he sold some of his father's belongings and gave paupers the money.

His father's anger drove him, demonstrating his commitment to destitution, to renounce his patrimony and strip naked in Assisi's marketplace.[1351] His literal fidelity to the gospels attracted followers. "Probably no other group of Christians has ever come closer to imitating the life of Jesus and the Apostles than did St. Francis and the early Franciscans," remarked American

---

[1346] John P. McKay, Bennett D. Hill, John Buckler, Clare Haru Crowston, Merry E. Wiesner-Hanks, and Joe Perry, *Understanding Western Society: A Brief History* (Boston and New York: Bedford/St. Martin's, 2012), 313; Marguerite Ragnow, "Arnold of Brescia (c. 1094-1155)," in *The Rise of the Medieval World, 500-1300: A Biographical Dictionary*, ed. Jana K. Schulman (Westport, CT and London: Greenwood Press, 2002), 42.

[1347] Robert E. Lerner, "Waldensians," in *Dictionary of the Middle Ages, Vol 12: Thaddeus Legend-Zwartnoc*, ed. Joseph R. Strayer (New York: Charles Scribner's Sons, 1982), 508.

[1348] Winks, Brinton, Christopher, and Wolff, 267; "Wycliffe, John," in *The Encyclopedia of the Middle Ages*, ed. Norman F. Cantor (New York: Viking, 1999), 450.

[1349] G. K. Chesterton, *St. Thomas Aquinas* (San Rafael, CA: Angelico Press, 2011), 9.

[1350] Placher, 149.

[1351] Strayer and Gatzke, 248-249; Liza Picard, *Chaucer's People: Everyday Lives in Medieval England* (London: Weidenfeld & Nicolson, 2017), 196-197.

medievalist Joseph Strayer (1904–1987) and German American historian Hans Gatzke (1915–1987).[1352]

Although a mystic, Francis understood power well enough to seek Innocent's approval.[1353] The decision entailed risk because Francis' penury implied criticism of the church. Before meeting him in 1210 the pope, who had condemned Waldo for spearheading a similar movement, reputedly had a dream whereby a man in a brown cloak prevented an unstable church from collapsing. Francis visited Innocent in this attire, won his blessing, and never questioned papal authority.

Francis' contemporary, Spanish founder of the Dominican Order and Christian saint Dominic de Guzman (c. 1170–1221), grasping "the essential connection between poverty of spirit and the effectiveness of the preached word," joined the crusade against the Cathars to convert, not kill, them.[1354] Admiring their devoutness and destitution, Dominic sought to win souls by emulating them. Like Francis, he renounced all possessions and demanded his followers do likewise. Francis winning devotees through the purity of his example, Dominic, adding the need to engage the intellect, aimed to persuade urbanites through logic and sensitivity to secular concerns.

13.3 Famine, Pestilence, and Inequality

13.3.1 Famine

Heretics and friars' opposition to wealth and inequality revolutionized neither economy nor society, both of which were supported by agriculture. The warm period around 800 to 1300 increased the harvest, as discussed, and European population grew to around 73 million in that period. This growth was remarkable for a continent with roughly 27 million people in about 700.

Reversing earlier gains, temperatures cooled roughly 1.8 to 3.6 degrees Fahrenheit after 1300 and heavy rainfall rotted crops.[1355] During the next 150 years the harvest was inadequate every fourth year on average.[1356] Afflicting Europe in 1312, 1315 to 1322, 1339, and 1340, famine presaged the next sections'

[1352] Strayer and Gatzke, 249.

[1353] Placher, 149; Picard, 197.

[1354] Strayer and Gatzke, 249; Picard, 200; Denys Turner, *Thomas Aquinas: A Portrait* (New Haven, CT and London: Yale University Press, 2013), 18.

[1355] Alfred J. Andrea, "Introduction: From the Great Warming to the Little Ice Age," in *World History Encyclopedia, Vol. 9, Era 5: Intensified Hemispheric Interactions, 1000-1500*, ed. Alfred J. Andrea and Carolyn Neel (Santa Barbara, CA: ABC-CLIO, 2011), 17; Christine Shearer, "How Cold Was Cold?: The Origins of Little Ice Age," in *World History Encyclopedia, Vol. 9, Era 5: Intensified Hemispheric Interactions, 1000-1500*, ed. Alfred J. Andrea and Carolyn Neel (Santa Barbara, CA: ABC-CLIO, 2011), 27.

[1356] McKay, Hill, Buckler, Crowston, Wiesner-Hanks, and Perry, 322.

Black Death (1347–1351).[1357] The decades afterwards were no better, with famine recurring in 1352, 1362, 1397, 1416, 1426, and 1467.[1358]

Inaugurating this misery, northern Europe's 1315 rainfall destroyed spring crops and prevented autumn's winter wheat sowing and spring 1316 plantings.[1359] Continuing into 1317, rain flooded fields and roads, shrank the harvest, starved cattle and swine, and impeded food's overland transit to the most desperate areas. Grain and legumes outpriced the masses.[1360] Markets lacked meat, poultry, and eggs.

The chief animal protein before 1300, fish were numerous in waters on western and northern Europe's continental shelf.[1361] Europeans ate several types, especially cod and herring, dried or salted for preservation. With continental shelf waters cooling faster than deep ocean after 1300, fish moved offshore, seeking warmth. Lengthening their time at sea by working farther from shore, fishers labored harder to catch fish. Disputing access to fisheries, they raided each other.

The hungry died in fields and streets. People allegedly consumed dogs, while prisoners, parents, and children practiced cannibalism; and others ate corpses.[1362] For example, Irish paupers exhumed corpses to eat in 1318, cannibalism pervaded 1319 Poland and Siberia, and Europeans attended executions to eat the victim before he could be buried, commentators lamented.

[1357] Mortimer Chambers, Raymond Grew, David Herlihy, Theodore K. Rabb, and Isser Woloch, *The Western Experience, Vol. II: The Early Modern Period*, 4th ed. (New York: Knopf, 1987), 395; H. J. Teutenberg, "The General Relationship between Diet and Industrialization," in *European Diet from Pre-Industrial to Modern Times*, ed. Elborg Forster and Robert Forster (New York: Harper Torchbooks, 1975), 74.

[1358] Teutenberg, 74; Alfred J. Andrea, "Environment and Population," in *World History Encyclopedia, Vol. 9, Era 5: Intensified Hemispheric Interactions, 1000-1500*, ed. Alfred J. Andrea and Carolyn Neel (Santa Barbara, CA: ABC-CLIO, 2011), 16; Steven Sams, "It Was Not All Wine and Roses—Incidents of Famine in Europe," in *World History Encyclopedia, Vol. 9, Era 5: Intensified Hemispheric Interactions, 1000-1500*, ed. Alfred J. Andrea and Carolyn Neel (Santa Barbara, CA: ABC-CLIO, 2011), 21.

[1359] Barbara A. Hanawalt, *The Middle Ages: An Illustrated History* (New York and Oxford: Oxford University Press, 1998), 130; Shearer, 27.

[1360] Andrea, "Introduction," 17-18; McKay, Hill, Buckler, Crowston, Wiesner-Hanks, and Perry, 322.

[1361] Jonathan H. L'Hommedieu, "Changes in Baltic and Atlantic Fishing Patterns," in *World History Encyclopedia, Vol. 9, Era 5: Intensified Hemispheric Interactions, 1000-1500*, ed. Alfred J. Andrea and Carolyn Neel (Santa Barbara, CA: ABC-CLIO, 2011), 30-31; Andrea, "Environment and Population," 16.

[1362] Hanawalt, 130; Andrea, "Introduction," 18; Abraham O. Mendoza, "Fourteenth-Century Famine in Europe," in *World History Encyclopedia, Vol. 9, Era 5: Intensified Hemispheric Interactions, 1000-1500*, ed. Alfred J. Andrea and Carolyn Neel (Santa Barbara, CA: ABC-CLIO, 2011), 28; Jean Gimpel, *The Medieval Machine: The Industrial Revolution of the Middle Ages* (New York: Penguin Books, 1976), 207-208.

Survivors likened the 1315 to 1322 catastrophe to Genesis' (c. 550 BCE) "seven years of famine."[1363]

Northern Europe's population being around 30 million in 1315, 3 to 7.5 million starved from 1315 to 1317.[1364] Famine killed some 2,800 Belgians, roughly a decile of population, in Ypres between May 1 and September 1, 1316.[1365] Mortality averaged around 190 fatalities weekly whereas 15 or 16 died in ordinary times. Intensifying inequality, famine killed mostly vagrants.[1366] Hunger and death tormented Europe from Britain in the west to Poland in the east.[1367]

Even the rich were hungry, tradition averred, with only the wealthiest 5 percent affording bread.[1368] King Edward II (1284–1327) toured England in 1315 to gauge the food supply, behavior that would have been unimaginable were only commoners unhappy.[1369] Angry elites required mollification lest they rebel.

Yet famine, exacerbating inequality, benefited them. Enlarging their property, landowners absorbed abandoned farms in Scotland, England, Belgium, the Netherlands, and Luxembourg.[1370] Holding grain to increase inflation and profits, a practice French and English kings unsuccessfully forbad, merchants worsened hunger.

England attempted to import food from Italy, but the long route from the Mediterranean Sea through the Strait of Gibraltar and then north through the Atlantic Ocean permitted pirates to steal the cargo.[1371] Ships carrying edibles lost them to looters. Shortage intensified desperation as a stampede for food killed 60 Londoners.

Desperation heightened antisemitism.[1372] Arresting Jews, authorities coerced confessions that caused other Jews and lepers' execution.

"Through hunger, malnutrition, and plague the hand of death was correcting the ledgers of life, balancing the numbers of people and the

---

[1363] McKay, Hill, Buckler, Crowston, Wiesner-Hanks, and Perry, 322; Gen. 41:27 (New American Bible).

[1364] Sams, 21; Adam Woog, *The Late Middle Ages* (San Diego: Reference Point Press, 2012), 66-67; Mendoza, 28.

[1365] Gimpel, 206.

[1366] Bas van Bavel, *Manors and Markets: Economy and Society in the Low Countries, 500-1600* (Oxford: Oxford University Press, 2010), 279.

[1367] Andrea, "Introduction," 17.

[1368] Ibid., 18; Woog, 67.

[1369] Andrea, "Introduction," 17.

[1370] McKay, Hill, Buckler, Crowston, Wiesner-Hanks, and Perry, 323.

[1371] Ibid.; Hanawalt, 130.

[1372] McKay, Hill, Buckler, Crowston, Wiesner-Hanks, and Perry.

resources that supported them," wrote American historian Mortimer Chambers (1927–2020) and coauthors, anticipating contagion's discussion next.[1373]

13.3.2 The Black Death

13.3.2.1 The Black Death's Origin, Spread, and Mortality

Undernutrition heightened vulnerability to diseases, the worst being the Black Death or the "Great Afro-Eurasian Pandemic."[1374] The seventeenth century moniker "Black Death" revealed little about symptoms.[1375] Fourteenth century accounts described a "great pestilence" or "great plague," language generic for a dreadful contagion.[1376]

Possibly originating in southern Russia, Central Asia, Mongolia—whether part of Central Asia or not—or China, all under Mongol rule, or in India or East Africa, the disease, appearing in 1331 in southwestern China, moved west, east, and south that decade, killing perhaps 25 million Asians, primarily Chinese and Indians.[1377] One account continued it west in 1347 to today's Istanbul, Turkey, whence merchants took it by ship to Italy's Naples and Genoa and France's Marseille.[1378] Another stated that in 1347 Mongols besieged today's Feodosiya, a Crimean port, which attracted merchants including Genoese, on the Black Sea. The Black Death struck Mongols who, catapulting corpses into the city, infected residents and merchants. Sailing through the Black Sea and into the Mediterranean, pre-symptomatic Genoese infected Messina, Sicily.

However it reached Europe, the Black Death entered Italy's Genoa, Pisa, and Venice by January 1348.[1379] From the north, it moved south to Florence and Rome. That June it traveled north to southern Germany and England and thereafter to Scandinavia. From Marseille, it penetrated north through France and southwest to Spain. By year's end, the Black Death engulfed islands throughout the Mediterranean and all Italy, France, and Spain. Overwhelming central and northern Europe in 1349, it afflicted Scotland and lands east of the Baltic Sea by 1351.

[1373] Chambers, Grew, Herlihy, Rabb, and Woloch, 395.

[1374] John Aberth, "The Great Afro-Eurasian Pandemic—Did It Originate in Inner Asia?" in *World History Encyclopedia, Vol. 9, Era 5: Intensified Hemispheric Interactions, 1000-1500*, ed. Alfred J. Andrea and Carolyn Neel (Santa Barbara, CA: ABC-CLIO, 2011), 79.

[1375] Joseph P. Byrne and Jo N. Hays, *Epidemics and Pandemics: From Ancient Plagues to Modern-Day Threats*, vol. 2 (Santa Barbara, CA and Denver, CO: Greenwood, 2021), 26.

[1376] Ibid.

[1377] Ibid., 25; Bruno Leone, *Disease in History* (San Diego: Reference Point Press, 2016), 50; McKay, Hill, Buckler, Crowston, Wiesner-Hanks, and Perry, 324; Aberth, "Great Afro-Eurasian Pandemic," 79.

[1378] McKay, Hill, Buckler, Crowston, Wiesner-Hanks, and Perry, 324; Gimpel, 209.

[1379] McKay, Hill, Buckler, Crowston, Wiesner-Hanks, and Perry, 324; Gimpel, 209-210.

Fragmentary data weaken attempts to quantify mortality. Cautious historians put losses around 30 to 40 percent of Europe's population by 1353.[1380] A review and extrapolation of pre- and post-pandemic numbers, however, estimated morality at 60 percent or 48 million deaths among 80 million Europeans by 1353. Another 100 million may have perished in North Africa, Egypt, and western Asia. World population, including Amerindians and others untouched by the pestilence, may have fallen from roughly 500 million in 1347 to 300 million in 1400.[1381]

"Tens of thousands of European villages literally disappeared from the face of the earth," wrote French historian Jean Gimpel (1918–1996).[1382] England, "a ghastly expanse of death," lost roughly a quintile, over 2,200, of villages by 1350.[1383] About 23 percent of German, and half Sicily and Sardinia's, villages vanished by then. Half to two thirds of Florentines died in 1348.[1384] Italy's San Gimignano may have suffered 70 percent mortality from famine and contagion by 1350.[1385]

Pestilence curbed Europe's population for decades. For example, 1427 Italy's Florence, San Gimignano, Prato, and Pistoia recorded populations 62 to 75 percent below pre-pandemic levels, implying that population shrank after, not just during, the calamity.[1386] Northern France reported even greater losses from 1347 to 1442.

Sparing nobody, it killed rich and poor alike, stated some writers.[1387] This claim ignored that the wealthy, owning urban and rural mansions, fled cities in hopes of escaping death. This evasion failed when the pathogen was in the body, though elites alone had the luxury of mobility. Indigents died in their hovels or in an alley. The Black Death thus evinced inequality in medieval villages, towns, and cities.

13.3.2.2 The Black Death's Cause

Unaware of pathogens, many doctors and laity blamed corrupt air.[1388] This belief, the miasma opinion, was understandable because putrid organic matter like corpses looked and smelled awful. Another held that Mars,

---

[1380] Byrne and Hays, 26.

[1381] Leone, 53.

[1382] Gimpel, 211.

[1383] Ibid., 211-213; Picard, 27.

[1384] McKay, Hill, Buckler, Crowston, Wiesner-Hanks, and Perry, 324.

[1385] Gimpel, 210-211.

[1386] John Aberth, "The Demographic Impact on Europe, 1347-1500," in *World History Encyclopedia, Vol. 9, Era 5: Intensified Hemispheric Interactions, 1000-1500*, ed. Alfred J. Andrea and Carolyn Neel (Santa Barbara, CA: ABC-CLIO, 2011), 92.

[1387] McKay, Hill, Buckler, Crowston, Wiesner-Hanks, and Perry, 325-327.

[1388] Ibid., 326-327; Winks, Brinton, Christopher, and Wolff, 259.

Jupiter, and Saturn's appearance in Aquarius, not decomposition, fouled air. Others speculated that earthquakes from 1345 to 1347 emitted toxins.

Originating with Greek physicians Hippocrates (c. 460–c. 370 BCE) and Galen (c. 129–c. 216 CE) and Arab physician and philosopher Ibn Sina (c. 980–c. 1037), another idea faulted bodily fluids' imbalance for diseases including the Black Death.[1389] Balance's restoration supposedly cured patients.

Christians killed Jews, vilified during famine and now suspected of poisoning wells.[1390] Without evidence, some accused outcasts of causing illness through witchcraft or an alliance with Satan. Advocating prayer and donations to churches and monasteries, others thought God was punishing sinners. The most extreme penitents, the flagellants whipped themselves as penance in towns and cities.

Scientists and scholars disputed the Black Death's cause, likely the bacterium *Yersinia pestis*, which inhabits over 30 flea species that colonize rodents including Europe's black or house rat and brown or common rat.[1391] Preferring them to humans, however, the flea transmitted the bacterium to people only if it became so numerous, and rodents so scarce, that it jumped or crawled onto humans.[1392] The infestation must have been gargantuan to kill millions of people.

Yet this scenario probably occurred. A medieval cemetery in Central Asia's Kara-Djigach, Kyrgyzstan accumulated inordinate burials in 1338 and 1339.[1393] Ten tombstones identified pestilence as the killer. Three of seven skeletons had harbored *Y. pestis*, likely from last chapter's silk road, in the blood. Grave goods, including pearls and shells from the Indian or Pacific Ocean, coral from the Mediterranean Sea, silk from China, and coins from Iran and Afghanistan, evinced trade's breadth but not the bacterium's direction. The above 1331 report of contagion, however, implies origin in or

---

[1389] Winks, Brinton, Christopher, and Wolff, 258.

[1390] McKay, Hill, Buckler, Crowston, Wiesner-Hanks, and Perry, 327; Strayer and Gatzke, 280.

[1391] Byrne and Hays, 25; Leone, 43-45; C. J. Duncan and S. Scott, "What Caused the Black Death?" *Postgraduate Medical Journal* 81 (May 5, 2005), accessed May 31, 2022, ‹315.full.pdf (bmj.com),› 316.

[1392] McKay, Hill, Buckler, Crowston, Wiesner-Hanks, and Perry, 324; Chambers, Grew, Herlihy, Rabb, and Woloch, 395.

[1393] Anna Salleh, "Black Death Pandemic Originated in Kyrgyzstan, Ancient DNA from Plague Victims' Teeth Suggests," Australian Broadcasting Corporation News, June 15, 2022, accessed June 15, 2022, ‹Black Death pandemic originated in Kyrgyzstan, ancient DNA from plague victims' teeth suggests - ABC News;› Ewen Callaway, "Ancient DNA Traces Origin of Black Death," *Nature* News, June 15, 2022, accessed June 15, 2022, ‹Ancient DNA traces origin of Black Death (nature.com).›

near southwestern China and movement west to Kara-Djigach by 1338 and Europe by 1347.

In other ways, Y. *pestis* made sense as the cause. Multiplying inside the flea, bacteria filled the gut and caused regurgitation with every bite.[1394] Entering the victim, they swelled lymph glands into buboes that witnesses described and that named bubonic plague, which may have killed 60 to 90 percent of victims amid undernutrition. Entering blood, bacteria may cause sepsis, which is nearly always fatal. But transmission required the rarity that one person absorb a victim's blood.

The Black Death's contagiousness indicated easy transmission. Travelling through blood to the lungs, Y. *pestis* caused pneumonia, the deadliest plague.[1395] Coughing ejected bacteria that caregivers inhaled. Winter confinement would have spread pneumonia by crowding people, but most died in summer and fewest in winter. Fleas most numerous in summer, bubonic plague fit this pattern better than pneumonia.

Rejecting Y. *pestis*, British zoologist Christopher Duncan (1932–2005) and British biologist Susan Scott, favoring a filovirus like Ebola or Marburg, believed fourteenth-century symptoms better matched these infections, which, endemic to Africa, originated the Black Death not in Eurasia but Ethiopia, where modern humans probably arose, where they had longest contact with other animals, and where they were likeliest to contract zoonoses like the great pestilence.[1396] From Ethiopia, it travelled down the Nile River to the Mediterranean, which moved commodities, people, and pathogens among Egypt, North Africa, Southwest Asia, and southern Europe.

But this hypothesis makes sense only if a local outbreak unrelated to the Black Death killed Kara-Djigach's unfortunates. Heeding Occam's rule, *Eternal Inequality* judges this possibility less likely than a single pathogen, Y. *pestis*, not a virus, as culprit.

13.4 Reactions against Inequality

13.4.1 Inequality and Class Antagonism

Like earlier periods, the Late Middle Ages provided opportunities to enlarge wealth. Specialization in cash crops over subsistence enriched Belgian, Dutch, and Luxembourgian large landowners.[1397] Rivaling them,

---

[1394] Leone, 44-45; McKay, Hill, Buckler, Crowston, Wiesner-Hanks, and Perry, 324.
[1395] Ibid., 45-46; Chambers, Grew, Herlihy, Rabb, and Woloch, 395.
[1396] Duncan and Scott, 319-320.
[1397] Bavel, 324.

wealthy merchants profited from local and distant trade. Far below, the underclass had only its labor to sell.

To the west, landowners opposed labor in England, where the Black Death threatened to deprive them of farmhands.[1398] Against this danger, in 1349 King Edward III (1312–1377), aiming to reimpose serfdom and protect landowners' feudal privileges, forbad wages to exceed pre-pandemic levels and workers to leave jobs or the land.

The 1351 Statute of Laborers affirming Edward, Parliament in 1371 funded war against France through new taxes on each parish, leaving local authorities to collect them.[1399] Evasion led Parliament to impose the 1379 poll tax, which tripled the next year and which commoners decried as regressive, on Englishmen at least age 16. Those most unhappy were not vagrants whom Parliament exempted but people with some property, for example a few sheep or cattle on rented land or a small business.

13.4.2 Peasant Uprisings

These grievances actuated the English Peasants' Revolt "during a period of keen unrest almost everywhere in the West."[1400] One leader, English priest John Ball (1338–1381), "a foolish fanatic to many," amplified discontent as an itinerant preacher who asserted from 1366 that nature and God equalized humans, that Christians were to oppose inequality for contradicting God, and that workers created all wealth, which enriched elites, whose privilege was unworthy of preservation.[1401] Like Cathars, Arnold of Brescia, Peter Waldo, and John Wycliffe, he thought Christianity, corrupted by wealth, should restore purity by dividing church lands among peasants.

These ideas displeased elites. "The poor and small folk...demand to be better fed than their masters," complained English landowner and poet John Gower (c. 1330–1408), who supplied neither evidence for this claim nor awareness that, exertion depleting the body, workers needed more food than idle employers.[1402]

Anticipating chapter 17's socialism and communism, Ball expressed "aspirations unknown to the classical world."[1403] British historian Rodney Hilton (1916–2002) contextualized the revolt and other medieval upris-

[1398] Picard, 27.

[1399] Ibid., 27-30; McKay, Hill, Buckler, Crowston, Wiesner-Hanks, and Perry, 340; Strayer and Gatzke, 282.

[1400] Guy Fourquin, *The Anatomy of Popular Rebellion in the Middle Ages*, trans. Anne Chesters (Amsterdam: North-Holland Publishing, 1978), 139.

[1401] Picard, 32; Gimpel, 217; "Ball, John," in *The Encyclopedia of the Middle Ages*, ed. Norman F. Cantor (New York: Viking, 1999), 61.

[1402] Gimpel, 214.

[1403] Ibid., 217.

ings within peasants' perennial "revolutionary struggles."[1404] Chambers and colleagues averred that the fourteenth century aroused "class warfare."[1405] American historian of Europe John McKay (b. 1948) and coauthors located the revolt within "a wider revolution of poor against rich."[1406]

His beliefs causing repeated imprisonment and excommunication, Ball won release just before joining the revolt's other leader, Wat Tyler (c. 1341–1381),[1407] an enigma whose very name is uncertain. Tyler, joining Kent's anti-taxers in 1381, may have been an archer against French troops during the Hundred Years' War (1337–1453).[1408] Parliament required Kent authorities to report their progress collecting the tax that May. Kent city Canterbury, appointing tax collectors around May 20, angered farmhands and workmen unhappy with serfdom and corvée.

Inflaming tensions that month, Kent landowner Simon Burley (c. 1336–1388) sent men to arrest an escaped serf, whose imprisonment caused Tyler and Ball to storm the jail.[1409] Freeing prisoners, their group, with bows and arrows, billhooks, pitchforks, and spades, killed Canterbury landowners and destroyed property, including tax records. Amassing hundreds of supporters against secular and church landowners, serfdom, corvée, the tithe, the poll tax, taxmen, and other officials, Tyler and Ball marched toward London.

Meanwhile, Essex commissioner Thomas Brampton announced on June 1 his intention to collect the poll tax from everyone in nearby townships.[1410] Many refused, claiming prior payment, but Brampton raised a military escort to force compliance. Although he escaped to London after a skirmish, villagers, decapitated three soldiers and carried their heads while searching for lawyers and officials to murder. Attracting roughly 50,000 partisans, they burned estates before also seeking redress in London.

Petitioners wanted Richard II (1367–1400), Edward III's grandson, to end the poll tax, corvée, the tithe, feudal fees, serfdom, and slavery and reduce an acre's annual rent to four pence.[1411] They may have expected the king, just 14 years old in June 1381, to sympathize with them. With few troops for defense because most were fighting in France or Scotland, Richard was fortunate that Ball, Tyler, and their men bypassed opportunities to kill him and his mother Joan (c. 1328–1385), countess of Kent.

[1404] Rodney Hilton, *Bond Men Made Free: Medieval Peasant Movements and the English Rising of 1381*, 3d ed. (London and New York: Routledge, 2005), xvi.

[1405] Chambers, Grew, Herlihy, Rabb, and Woloch, 401.

[1406] McKay, Hill, Buckler, Crowston, Wiesner-Hanks, and Perry, 340.

[1407] "Ball, John," 61.

[1408] Picard, 31–32.

[1409] Ibid., 32; Hilton, 138.

[1410] Picard, 31.

[1411] Ibid., 33, 35; Chambers, Grew, Herlihy, Rabb, and Woloch, 402.

Before reaching London, a detachment destroyed archbishop of Canterbury and chancellor of England Simon Sudbury's (1316–1381) tax records.[1412] Entering the city, insurgents camped along the Thames River, where some Londoners joined them upon Ball's urging. Stealing nothing, they killed bureaucrats, freed prisoners, burned tax records and razed the palace of Richard's uncle John of Gaunt (1340–1399), duke of Lancaster, on June 13.

Joan, Sudbury, and English friar William Appleton (d. 1381) wanted Richard to delay and dissemble in hopes of persuading the rebels to return home, where crown loyalists could assassinate them.[1413] Accordingly the king had the rebels submit their demands in writing, feigned sympathy for their plight, and promised "justice" and serfdom's termination.[1414]

Convincing many to leave, these assurances weakened Ball and Tyler, though others killed Sudbury and Appleton upon discovering them in the Tower of London.[1415] Richard, with London's mayor William Walworth (1322–1385) and some soldiers, meeting the rebels again on June 15, killed Tyler and arrested Ball. Dictating and signing a pledge to resolve their grievances, the king dispersed the rest. Ending the threat, he declared them traitors on July 2 and required each to pay 25 shillings to 4 pounds sterling for a pardon. King and Parliament abandoned, without repealing, the poll tax.

The revolt's failure supports the contention that inequality is permanent. Ball's quest for equality, unsuccessful from start to finish, ended in his execution.[1416] Pursuing and murdering rebels through October, England's elites enforced inequality.[1417]

13.4.3 Urban Revolts

As noted, medieval cities were models of inequality. After roughly 1250, commerce and banking enriched French, Belgian, Dutch, and Luxembourgian magnates, whose ostentation angered laborers.[1418] Although modern workers strike for better pay and working conditions, medieval Europeans invented the strike around 1275 to protest rent, food prices, and taxes.

Strikes were risky because authorities outlawed them.[1419] In 1280, for instance, officials in Douai, France, jailed or executed strikers. Despite the threat of punishment, in Barcelona, Spain, the poor protested unafford-

---

[1412] Picard, 33-34.
[1413] Ibid., 33.
[1414] Ibid., 35.
[1415] Ibid., 35-37; Fourquin, 143.
[1416] Gimpel, 219.
[1417] Fourquin, 143.
[1418] Ibid., 148-149.
[1419] Ibid., 149-150.

able food in 1334. Italy's Venice, Bologna, Florence, and Siena followed this example in the decade before the Black Death. Florentine workers withheld taxes in 1343.

Northern European and Italian textile workers having become "a real proletariat bound to a capitalist system," labor had weakened since roughly 1275, when wool-producing England increased the fiber's price by taxing it.[1420] Suspending exports to France after 1290, England made wool scarce throughout Europe, eliminating textile jobs. Near starvation by 1297, jobless French and Belgian urbanites begged food.

Last chapter's Frescobaldi, Bardi, and Peruzzi families, entering the wool market before 1300 and eliminating competition, targeted wages, which totaled three fifths the cost of producing cloth.[1421] To them, rather than an asset worthy of investment, labor was an expense that eroded profit. Decreasing pay, employers lessening the work hours needed to offset a laborer's maintenance and captured the proceeds of all work beyond this threshold as "surplus value."[1422]

Hostility engulfed Florence, where textile workers, among the industry's poorest, accumulated debt and could neither join a guild nor influence government.[1423] Wool carders, the *ciompi*, attacked plutocrats in June 1378. Broadening violence, workers in other occupations demolished convents and killed foreigners.

Like other cities, Florence segregated by income. The chasm between rich and poor neighborhoods intensified revolution.[1424] An agitator's July arrest caused workers and the unemployed to incinerate "patrician palaces."[1425] Looting and fires spread on July 22. Storming the Palazzo Vecchio, the seat of government, rioters demanded amnesty and abolition of debt imprisonment.

The leaders, small businessmen and merchants rather than workers, formed a government to represent everybody.[1426] But the original problems, unemployment and unaffordable food, persisted. Although desire for reform was widespread, the new government, betraying the revolution by enfranchising only one sixth of taxpayers, collapsed in 1382 when the richest families, proving Plato's remark that the strong rule, reasserted authority.

[1420] Gimpel, 99-100.

[1421] Ibid., 104-105.

[1422] V. I. Lenin, "Karl Marx: Part Three," International Communist League, October 2, 2015, accessed March 16, 2022, ‹"Karl Marx" by V.I. Lenin (icl-fi.org).›

[1423] Fourquin, 151-152.

[1424] Ibid., 152.

[1425] Ibid., 153.

[1426] Ibid., 153-154.

Although a failure, the revolt began a half decade of "large number of disturbances and rebellions in the West."[1427] Uprisings swept France's Paris, Rouen, Amiens, and Orleans in 1379 and 1380.[1428] Laborers opposed government for taxing but not benefiting them.

Taxation provoked rebellion after 1380 in Lubeck, Germany, where butchers challenged families that had governed for generations without aiding workers.[1429] Revolt spread to Brunswick and Cologne, where labor weakened entrenched power. Unrest subsided after 1450 as governments grew strong enough to silence protest. Taxes remained inordinate and often increased despite dissatisfaction.

Elites reigned amid worker impotence. Extending entrepreneurialism into the sixteenth century, for example, Belgian businessman Gilbert van Schoonbeke (1519–1556) built and sold homes on Antwerp's formerly empty land, financed construction of over 20 city streets from 1542 to 1553, and bribed officials to lower his taxes and give him municipal contracts.[1430] An advantageous marriage increased his fortune, which he invested in brewing beer. Magnates like Schoonbeke guided Europe from feudalism to capitalism.

13.5 Review and Preview

Famine and contagion killing millions in the Late Middle Ages, class antagonism pitted survivors against rural and urban elites. If the fourteenth century intensified socialism and communism, as Gimpel believed, it also advanced capitalism, modernity's dominant, and inherently unequal, economic system. Leaving Afro-Eurasia aside, , next chapter treats post-contact American slavery and the slave trade.

[1427] Ibid., 150.
[1428] Ibid., 155-158.
[1429] Ibid., 158-159.
[1430] Bavel, 322.

CHAPTER 14 POST-CONTACT AMERICAN SLAVERY, THE SLAVE TRADE, AND INEQUALITY

14.1 Abstract

Africans, hereafter blacks for concision, worked post-contact American plantations. Demand for slaves increased toward the equator, where pathogens, parasites, insects, and exhaustion weakened or killed them, requiring continual replacement, and where tropical crops like sugarcane—which Italian mariner Christopher Columbus (1451–1506) planted on Caribbean island Hispaniola, now Haiti and the Dominican Republic, in 1493 or 1494—and coffee demanded year-round care.[1431] Profiting colonial and antebellum tobacco, rice, indigo, sugarcane, and cotton planters, bondage provoked a Newtonian backlash through rebellion.

14.2 Europe Discovers the Americas

Closing the Middle Ages, last chapter examined the fourteenth century reaction against inequality. Description of the factors that guided that period into modernity transcends our focus on one facet of this transition: Europe's extension west across the Atlantic Ocean into the Americas and slavery's continuation there.

[1431] Henry Hobhouse, *Seeds of Change: Six Plants That Transformed Mankind* (Washington, DC: Shoemaker & Hoard, 2005), 54; Deborah Jean Warner, *Sweet Stuff: An American History of Sweeteners from Sugar to Sucralose* (Washington, DC: Smithsonian Institution Scholarly Press, 2011), 5.

This development originated in Europe's demand for spices from the Molucca Islands, now part of Indonesia.[1432] In the easternmost Indian Ocean, Indonesia is over 8,500 miles from westernmost Europe's Portugal and Spain. For centuries, Europe got spices through distant, expensive overland routes. Prices rose after 1453,when Turks conquered Byzantine capital Constantinople, whose control let them price spices and other commodities that transited it for Europe.

Eager to bypass the Turks, Portugal and Spain hoped to defy ancient geography by sailing to the Moluccas. The Mediterranean Sea permitted movement no farther east than the Levant. No sea route let Europe into the Indian Ocean, which Africa separated from the Atlantic by extending south to encircle southernmost earth, believed Greek scientist, mathematician, philosopher, and "father of modern geography" Claudius Ptolemy (c. 100–c. 170 CE).[1433]

If an eastern trek was impossible, westward movement across the Atlantic was uncertain, though knowledgeable people understood no ship would fall off an edge. They heeded fifth century BCE Greeks, who knew the world was a sphere, not a plane, but were unsure where such a journey led, though earth's roundness implied that travel west from Europe should reach Asia.[1434] Greek polymath Eratosthenes (c. 276–c. 195 BCE), among "the greatest minds of antiquity," had calculated earth's circumference, permitting estimation of the oceanic distance between Europe and Asia, but few medieval Europeans consulted his figure.[1435]

Eschewing westward travel, fifteenth century Portugal moved south along Africa's western coast to disprove Ptolemy.[1436] Blown by a storm, Portuguese explorer Bartholomeu Dias (1450–1500) rounded southernmost Africa in 1487 or 1488. Portuguese explorer Vasco da Gama (c. 1460–1524)

[1432] John P. McKay, Bennett D. Hill, John Buckler, Clare Haru Crowston, Merry E. Wiesner-Hanks, and Joe Perry, *Understanding Western Society: A Brief History* (Boston and New York: Bedford/St. Martin's, 2012), 422; Robert B. Marks, *The Origins of the Modern World: A Global and Environmental Narrative from the Fifteenth to the Twenty-First Century*, 4th ed. (Lanham, MD: Rowman & Littlefield, 2020), 62-64; Joseph R. Strayer and Hans W. Gatzke, *The Mainstream of Civilization*, 3d ed. (New York: Harcourt Brace Jovanovich, 1979), 395-396; R. R. Palmer and Joel Colton, *A History of the Modern World to 1815*, 5th ed. (New York: Knopf, 1978), 101.

[1433] Daniel J. Boorstin, *The Discoverers* (New York: Random House, 1983), 97, 153.

[1434] Ibid., 94-96; Arthur Beiser, *The Earth*, rev. ed. (New York: Time-Life Books, 1968), 10-11.

[1435] Boorstin, 95; Beiser, 10-11; Nicholas Nicastro, *Circumference: Eratosthenes and the Ancient Quest to Measure the Globe* (New York: St. Martin's Press, 2008), ix.

[1436] Robin W. Winks, Crane Brinton, John B. Christopher, and Robert Lee Wolff, *A History of Civilization, Vol. I: Prehistory to 1715*, 7th ed. (Englewood Cliffs, NJ: Prentice Hall, 1988), 374, 378; McKay, Hill, Buckler, Crowston, Wiesner-Hanks, and Perry, 425; Terri Koontz, Mark Sidwell, and S. M. Bunker, *World Studies*, 2d ed. (Greenville, SC: BJU Press, 2000), 138.

repeated the feat a decade later, sailed east to India, and opened the Indian Ocean to European merchants.

Portugal's efforts left rival Spain to fund Columbus, who sought "a shorter, less expensive, safer route to Asia."[1437] In 1492, crossing the Atlantic, he reached Hispaniola. The West Indies' European discovery and settlement would intertwine sugarcane and slavery. His third voyage found Venezuela in 1498.

The claim that he discovered the Americas requires qualification. Humans entered the New World millennia before Columbus, who was not even the first European there.[1438] His achievement was visiting it four times and popularizing his finds. By his death, nobody could plausibly deny the existence of lands, absent from the bible, between Europe and Asia.

14.3 Greed, Coercion, Slavery, and Inequality

14.3.1 Greed and Coercion

Greed motivated Columbus and his successors, who compelled labor no matter the danger.[1439] Conquest of the Aztecs in 1521 and the Incas in 1532 gave Spaniards gold and silver, intensifying avarice. Silver deposits included Bolivia's Potosi, discovered in 1545. The world's largest mine of its kind, Potosi produced half the New World silver from 1503 to 1660, over 32 million pounds. The western hemisphere also yielded 360,000 pounds of gold then.

Some 8 million natives perished by 1645—deaths German economist Karl Marx (1818–1883), who "had more impact on actual events, as well as on the minds of men and women, than any other intellectual in modern times," attributed to greed—while enriching Spain with these metals.[1440] Seldom surviving seven years, miners deemed Potosi "the mouth of hell."[1441]

[1437] McKay, Hill, Buckler, Crowston, Wiesner-Hanks, and Perry, 425-427; Richard Kurin, *The Smithsonian's History of America in 101 Objects* (New York: Penguin Press, 2013), 46.

[1438] McKay, Hill, Buckler, Crowston, Wiesner-Hanks, and Perry, 428-429; J. William T. Youngs, *American Realities: Historical Episodes: Vol. 1: From the First Settlements to the Civil War*, 3d ed. (HarperCollins College Publishers, 1993), 17; Nancy A. Hewitt and Steven F. Lawson, *Exploring American Histories: A Brief Survey with Sources* (Boston and New York: Bedford/St. Martin's, 2013), 14-15.

[1439] Marks, 81-82; Nicolas Wey Gomez, *The Tropics of Empire: Why Columbus Sailed South to the Indies* (Cambridge, MA and London: MIT Press, 2008), 69.

[1440] Marks, 81; Karl Marx, *Capital: A Critique of Political Economy*, vol. 1, trans. Ben Fowkes (London: Penguin Books, 1990), 915; Paul Johnson, *Intellectuals* (New York: Harper & Row, 1988), 52.

[1441] Marks, 81; Marjorie Gann and Janet Willen, *Five Thousand Years of Slavery* (Toronto, ON: Tundra Books, 2011), 71.

Greed exhausted the mines. After silver and gold enriched sixteenth century Spain, decline thereafter compelled it to seek wealth through agri-culture.[1442] Earlier chapters examined Southwest Asian, Egyptian, Roman, Indian, and Chinese slavery. Sugarcane spurred it in the New World, though native labor shrank as Old-World diseases massacred Amerindians.[1443] The solution was blacks' enslavement.

14.3.2 Black Slavery

14.3.2.1 The Encounter with Africa

Promoting Mediterranean trade, Rome facilitated interaction among southern Europeans, Egyptians, and North Africans, the last two of more Mediterranean than black ancestry. This chapter applies the word "black" to sub-Saharan Africans, though skin color does not bifurcate into black and white but varies on a continuum. Egypt's second century CE death portraits, for example, reveal numerous hues, some most viewers would probably consider black.[1444]

Egypt enslaved blacks before 500 BCE, though Europeans seldom encountered them before the fifteenth century. Greek historian Herodotus (c. 485–c. 425 BCE) described Egyptians with "black skins and kinky hair," perhaps implying Nubian lineage.[1445] Either from ignorance or disinterest, European art omitted blacks before Dutch painter and "fantastical visionary" Hieronymus Bosch (c. 1450–1516), whose life overlapped Portugal's move-ment south along Africa's Atlantic coast.[1446]

Like others, Europeans conflated color, race, and inequality. Greek philosopher Aristotle's (384–322 BCE) elevation of persons in temperate lands above those in the tropics put Europeans above Africans and others in hot climates.[1447] This opinion influenced Columbus, who landed "where the aspect of the solar rays is too strong," darkening indigenes to shades not as "black as in Guinea" but still too swarthy.[1448]

[1442] Strayer and Gatzke, 403; Marks, 85-88.

[1443] McKay, Hill, Buckler, Crowston, Wiesner-Hanks, and Perry, 435, 439-441.

[1444] Anthony de Feo, "The Lifelike Fayum Death Portraits of Roman Egypt," *Daily Art Magazine*, November 21, 2020, accessed March 20, 2022, ‹The Lifelike Death Fayum Portraits of Roman Egypt | DailyArt Magazine;› "Fayum Death Portraits," Microsoft Bing Images, accessed March 20, 2022, ‹fayum death portraits - Bing images.›

[1445] "The Story of Africa: Nile Valley," BBC World Service, accessed March 20, 2022, ‹The Story of Africa| BBC World Service.›

[1446] Roy T. Matthews and F. DeWitt Platt, *The Western Humanities*, 3d ed. (Mountain View, CA: Mayfield Publishing, 1998), 270; Stefan Fischer, *Hieronymus Bosch: The Complete Works*, trans. Karen Williams (Koln: Taschen, 2016), 13.

[1447] Gomez, 70.

[1448] Ibid., 18.

Infrequent encounters made blacks curiosities displayed as entertainment.[1449] Bigotry grew with enslavement. Depicting them as nearly nude brutes more like apes than whites, Europeans disliked their religions, libido, and morals. A Jamaican master judged them "unjust, cruel, barbarous, half-human, treacherous, deceitful thieves, drunkards, proud, lazy, unclean, shameless, jealous to fury, and cowards."[1450] A West Indian law described their "wild, barbarous and savage nature, to be controlled only with strict severity."[1451]

These beliefs undercut English planter John Davies' (1625–1693) claim that his compatriots, replacing Africa's wars and privation with stability, benefited blacks, who preferred bondage to freedom.[1452] Were this true, "strict severity" would have been unnecessary. Enjoying their new status, they would have obeyed whites, who need not have feared rebellion and armed themselves.

The post-contact Americas justified slavery and racism on utilitarian grounds. Europeans like Davies styled themselves blacks' benefactors by claiming to protect and civilize them. Even the bible seemingly condoned their enslavement. Hebrew patriarch Noah enslaved his grandson Canaan, whom Europeans deemed black.[1453]

14.3.2.2 Tropical American Slavery

14.3.2.2.1 Portugal and Brazil

Enslaving blacks after 1420, Portugal sold perhaps 150,000 within Europe from 1450 to 1500, as Muslims and other underlings became scarce and expensive.[1454] Internal demand warranted no larger numbers, though tropical plantations were another matter. Near Africa's northwestern coast, enslaved Guanches cleared Madeira and Canary Islands' forest for sugarcane. When diseases struck, Portugal turned to blacks.

This pattern helped Portugal pair sugarcane and slavery in Brazil. The 1494 Treaty of Tordesillas divided much of the world between Portugal and Spain, with Brazil, claimed by Portuguese aristocrat and explorer Pedro

---

[1449] Hewitt and Lawson, 12-13; McKay, Hill, Buckler, Crowston, Wiesner-Hanks, and Perry, 444.

[1450] Gann and Willen, 68.

[1451] Ibid., 72.

[1452] Richard S. Dunn, *Sugar and Slaves: The Rise of the Planter Class in the English West Indies, 1624-1713* (Chapel Hill: University of North Carolina Press, 1972), 246.

[1453] Gen. 9:24-27 (New American Bible); Hewitt and Lawson, 12.

[1454] Marks, 86; McKay, Hill, Buckler, Crowston, Wiesner-Hanks, and Perry, 439-440; Robert W. Strayer, Edwin Hirschmann, Robert B. Marks, Robert J. Smith, James J. Horn, and Lynn H. Parsons, *The Making of the Modern World: Connected Histories, Divergent Paths (1500 to the Present)* (New York: St. Martin's Press, 1989), 137.

Cabral (c. 1468–c. 1520) in 1500, as Portugal's only New World colony.[1455] As in the islands, Portugal subjugated the native population, in this case Tupi, who hid in the rainforest.[1456] Those unable to escape often died of diseases, leaving blacks the default in hot, unhealthy environments.

Brazil and the rest of tropical America suffered. Yellow fever and malaria were absent before 1500, and the western hemisphere even lacked yellow fever's vector, *Aedes aegypti*.[1457] *Anopheles* mosquitoes, able to host malarial plasmodia, were present, though the parasites were not. The shipment of Blacks to the Americas brought *Aedes aegypti*, yellow fever virus, and malarial slaves. Upon biting them, *Anopheles* species acquired plasmodia with which to infect the next target. Having evolved amid malaria and yellow fever, blacks were less susceptible than whites and Amerindians.

It is said that some 10 to 15 million slaves were shipped to the Americas.[1458] Deriving from incomplete data, these numbers underreport the total. At the low end, U.S. historian Stephan Thernstrom (b. 1934) estimated western hemisphere imports at 9.4 million from 1526 to 1810.[1459] With 3.6 million, Brazil approached 40 percent of the whole. Under 1.7 million imports, England's West Indies ranked second. Another estimate allotted Brazil over 5 million slaves by the 1860s while all other colonies combined for 6 million.[1460]

Five to 20 percent transatlantic mortality shrank deliveries to planters while "frightfully high" mortality from undernutrition, overwork, diseases, accidents, suicide, execution, and other causes led tropical America to enlarge imports.[1461] Paying roughly the same for women and men despite differences in strength and productivity, owners "stood to earn hundreds, and perhaps thousands, of dollars in capitalized rent from producing new slaves."[1462] "A woman who brings a child every two years is more profit than

[1455] Gann and Willen, 67; Strayer and Gatzke, 399.

[1456] Marks, 86.

[1457] Ibid., 86-87.

[1458] Ibid., 87-88; Gann and Willen, 61; McKay, Hill, Buckler, Crowston, Wiesner-Hanks, and Perry, 441; Koontz, Sidwell, and Bunker, 190.

[1459] Stephan Thernstrom, *A History of the American People, Vol. I: To 1877*, 2d ed. (San Diego: Harcourt Brace Jovanovich, 1989), 73.

[1460] Gann and Willen, 63.

[1461] Kahalil Gibran Muhammad, "Sugar," in *The 1619 Project: A New Origin Story*, ed. Nikole Hannah-Jones, Caitlin Roper, Ilena Silverman, and Jake Silverstein (New York: One World, 2021), 78; Dunn, 301.

[1462] Jeremy Atack and Peter Passell, *A New Economic View of American History: From Colonial Times to 1940*, 2d ed. (New York and London: Norton, 1994), 350; Thernstrom, 88.

the best man on a farm," remarked U.S. president and slaveowner Thomas Jefferson (1743–1826).[1463]

Misery and death pointed tropical America toward the future. For example, Brazil about 2010 ranked among the world's most unequal countries with a Gini, which chapter 6 introduced as a measure of inequality, around 0.6.[1464]

14.3.2.2.2 England's West Indies

Although Spanish gold and silver and Portuguese sugar, "white gold," dominated the sixteenth century, England, whose slaves produced tobacco in Virginia, rice in the Carolinas and Georgia, and sugar in the Caribbean, commanded the next century.[1465] Although sugarcane never guaranteed affluence because agriculture was, and remains, risky, only its planters rivaled England's aristocrats, whose families monopolized land for centuries. England supported its Caribbean magnates by surtaxing rivals' sugar.

Once a luxury, the sweetener seduced commoners throughout Europe as American plantations boomed. Sustaining prices amid expanding supply, robust demand enticed planters to produce even more. Adding sugar to coffee, Europeans increased the market for the tropical duo of lowland sugarcane and hillside coffee trees.[1466]

As elsewhere in the tropics, Caribbean slaves died from malaria, yellow fever, dysentery, edema, elephantiasis, leprosy, yaws, hookworm, undernutrition, overwork, accidents, suicide, and execution.[1467] Women ate so little that perhaps half were infertile.[1468] Carelessness worsening contagion, Barbadians, for example, polluted once potable water by putting corpses from a 1647 yellow fever outbreak in swamps. Mortality was greatest in the first year or two after importation, a period of adjustment termed "seasoning."[1469] Slaves' inability to multiply fast enough to outpace death underscored bond-

---

[1463] Thernstrom; Thomas Jefferson, "'Laws' (Query XIV) (1781-1782)," in *The Nature of Difference: Sciences of Race in the United States from Jefferson to Genomics*, ed. Evelynn M. Hammonds and Rebecca M. Herzig (Cambridge, MA and London: MIT Press, 2008), 25.

[1464] Branko Milanovic, *The Haves and the Have-Nots: A Brief and Idiosyncratic History of Global Inequality* (New York: Basic Books, 2011), 30-31.

[1465] Dunn, 188; Atack and Passell, 29-30, 33-34; Te-Tzu Chang, "Rice," in *The Cambridge World History of Food*, vol. 1, ed. Kenneth F. Kiple and Kreimhild Conee Ornelas (Cambridge, UK: Cambridge University Press, 2000), 139; Muhammad, 73.

[1466] Steven C. Topik, "Coffee," in *The Cambridge World History of Food*, vol. 1, ed. Kenneth F. Kiple and Kreimhild Conee Ornelas (Cambridge, UK: Cambridge University Press, 2000), 642, 648.

[1467] Dunn, 302-303, 317, 320.

[1468] Gann and Willen, 71.

[1469] Dunn, 323.

age's harshness near the equator. "It is in tropical culture...that negro life is most recklessly sacrificed," wrote Marx.[1470]

Unable to work, the young and old were underfed, as chapter 8's Roman senator and slaveowner Cato the Elder (234–149 BCE) had advocated. "Systematic semistarvation and a stupefying round of brute chores" degraded slaves.[1471] Barbados authorities admitted in 1688 that starvation made slaves steal food.[1472] When food was scarce, liquid from sugarcane stems, known as cane juice, was the lone intake.[1473] Although brief, such privation undermined health. One hundred one Barbadian slave skeletons revealed malocclusion, enamel growth on teeth roots, and enamel thinning severe enough to indicate starvation. These defects in infant skeletons implied starvation at weaning, when cane juice, exacerbating hypoproteinemia and emaciation, substituted poorly for mother's milk.

Importing some 264,000 slaves from 1640 to 1700, Barbados, Jamaica, and the Leeward Islands approximated 100,000 blacks in 1700.[1474] Barbados bought about 85,000 slaves from 1708 to 1735 to increase the black population just 4,000. Barbados, Jamaica, and the Leeward Islands purchased over 1.2 million, but had only 387,000, slaves by 1790. Death outstripping reproduction, owners, taking whatever shippers had, bought replacements rather than tried to breed new generations.[1475]

Profit lured Dutch and English carriers from 1640 to 1672, after which England granted a monopoly to investors who formed the Royal African Company, history's "single most successful transatlantic slave-trading institution."[1476] Unable to enforce a monopoly, Parliament in 1689 reopened the trade to all.

This commerce perpetuated African slavery that began in prehistory. As mentioned, Egypt enslaved blacks. Latecomers to the continent, ninth century CE Arabs documented bondage.[1477] Europeans grafted themselves onto the system as an extra layer of buyers.

For example, Englishmen bought slaves from Nigerian sellers. Over generations, one such Nigerian family, adopting English garb, manners, and language to ease business, never approached equality with buyers who,

---

[1470] Marx, 377.

[1471] Ibid., 324.

[1472] Ibid., 242.

[1473] Jerome S. Handler and Robert S. Corruccini, "Plantation Slave Life in Barbados: A Physical Anthropological Analysis," *Journal of Interdisciplinary History* 14, no. 1 (Summer 1983): 74-75, 79.

[1474] Dunn, 314.

[1475] Ibid., 301.

[1476] Ibid., 230-231; Muhammad, 75.

[1477] Gann and Willen, 43.

kidnapping two of its men in 1767, sold them in Caribbean island Dominica.[1478] Seven months later they secretly arranged return home, but the shipper instead sold them in Virginia. The owner dying five years later, they, trying again to escape, ended up in England, where a court freed them. Returning home in 1774, one of the two, impervious to the harm he suffered and continued to cause others, resumed the trade.

At their destination, slaves, like worker bees, shortened their lives through toil.[1479] Year-round heat and humidity, permitting no respite, made slaves work nearly naked.[1480] Worsening the ordeal, owners denied them anything that lessened labor. Without plows, for instance, they broke ground with hoes.[1481]

The worst chore, manuring soil, made slaves carry 75-pound buckets of dung on their head to the field.[1482] Buckets full and balance imperfect, excrement dripped onto the face, which a slave could not wipe because they occupied both hands.

More dangerous was the mill, which operated round the clock to process sugarcane stalks within hours of harvest to avoid spoilage.[1483] A frantic tempo, insufficient sleep, and a moment's inattention caught fingers, a hand, or an arm in a roller. To save the machine, supervisors axed the unfortunate body part.

14.3.2.3 Mainland North America and Slavery

14.3.2.3.1 Early Settlements' Failure

South American and Mexican gold and silver led Europeans to covet similar riches to the north.[1484] Several nations establishing northern colonies, England and France clashed throughout the eighteenth century. The 1763 Treaty of Paris ended the Seven Years' War (1756–1763), expelled France from North America, and gave England all French possessions east of the Mississippi River while giving Spain the Louisiana Territory.[1485]

As mentioned, North America's slave colonies included Virginia, which Englishmen settled from 1607 and which imported slaves 12 years later.[1486]

[1478] Ibid., 63-64.
[1479] Dunn, 317.
[1480] Ibid., 264.
[1481] Ibid., 191, 200.
[1482] Ibid., 191; Gann and Willen, 70.
[1483] Dunn, 191; Gann and Willen, 69-70.
[1484] Koontz, Sidwell, and Bunker, 188-189; Thernstrom, 23.
[1485] McKay, Hill, Buckler, Crowston, Wiesner-Hanks, and Perry, 538.
[1486] Hewitt and Lawson, 43; Atack and Passell, 29: Thernstrom, 76.

Identifying this event as formative, *The 1619 Project* (2021) argued that bondage and racism defined, and still influence, the United States.[1487]

Although the book faced criticism, *Eternal Inequality* affirms the premise. Slavery and racism complicated inequality, which many Americans perceived along racial, not class, lines, though both prohibited talent and effort from transcending poverty.

Sixteen nineteen marking a milestone, the English floundered in North America without slaves. Before 1580, English explorer Martin Frobisher (c. 1535–1594) claimed gold in Canada.[1488] The announcement filled 11 ships with Englishmen who joined the search, but the mineral turned out to be pyrite or fool's gold. In 1583 English nobleman, soldier, and explorer Humphrey Gilbert (c. 1539–1583) sailed for Newfoundland, Canada, to find gold, but everyone died when his ship sank.

Two years later Queen Elizabeth I (1533–1603), promoting "trade, exploration, and eventually colonization as vital to the interests of a secure and prosperous England," authorized Gilbert's half-brother, English aristocrat, soldier, and explorer Walter Raleigh (c. 1552–1618), "a spider of hell," to detractors, to colonize North America, govern it, and keep one fifth its gold and silver.[1489] Claiming all land north of Spanish Florida, he named it Virginia after "Virgin Queen" Elizabeth.[1490] Never visiting the region, he dispatched soldiers to colonize North Carolina's Roanoke Island in 1585. After the settlement's desertion, a second attempt landed 117 adults and children on Roanoke in 1587, but a supply ship found nobody three years later.

Jamestown, Virginia, England's first permanent North American colony, was a "fiasco" early on.[1491] Prior failures dissuaded the crown from funding the venture. Instead, English landowners and merchants, hoping to equal East India Company investors who sextupled their outlay by 1607, formed the Virginia Company.

Jamestown, "a nightmare for all concerned," disappointed expectations.[1492] Despising the requirement to perform physical labor, nobles formed the settlement's nucleus. Their servants, goldsmiths, and jewelers were no

---

[1487] Nikole Hannah-Jones, "Origins," in *The 1619 Project: A New Origin Story*, ed. Nikole Hannah-Jones, Caitlin Roper, Ilena Silverman, and Jake Silverstein (New York: One World, 2021), xix-xxi.

[1488] Thernstrom, 24.

[1489] Anna Beer, *Patriot or Traitor: The Life and Death of Sir Walter Ralegh* (London: Oneworld, 2018), 47; Mary K. Pratt, *Elizabeth I: English Renaissance Queen* (Edina, MN: ABDO, 2012), 92; Peter Ackroyd, *Rebellion: The History of England from James I to the Glorious Revolution* (New York: Thomas Dunne Books/St. Martin's Press, 2014), 4.

[1490] Hewitt and Lawson, 23; Richard B. Morris, *The New World, Vol. 1: Prehistory to 1774* (New York: Time-Life Books, 1963), 37.

[1491] Thernstrom, 24.

[1492] Ibid., 25.

readier to toil. Rather than farm, everyone depended on ships for food while searching for gold and silver. Hunger abetting mortality, 66 of 104 arrivals died the first year. Investors sent replacements, but half perished the second winter, termed the "starving time."[1493]

14.3.2.3.2 Virginia, Tobacco, Slaves, and Elites

The colony suffered other problems beyond this book's scope and likely would have perished but for the realization that tobacco could be grown profitably, asserted American economists Jeremy Atack (b. 1949) and Peter Passell (b. 1944).[1494] Although insightful, this conjecture omits slaves' contribution. Unwilling to work, nobles did not elevate tobacco to prominence.

Investors named English aristocrat and soldier Thomas Dale (1570–1619) Virginia governor in 1610.[1495] Under martial law, Jamestown became a labor camp, though hunger persisted because commoners evaded compulsion by escaping to live among the natives. Those captured were executed rather than returned to labor. Nothing could compel the elite to do the necessary work, but the use of slaves made tobacco profitable. Jamestown succeeded because omegas, unable to resist coercion, rescued it.

The "bewitching vegetable," tobacco may have seemed an unlikely cash crop.[1496] Native to Virginia, it was unknown to Africans, Europeans, and Asians until the sixteenth century, when Spaniards witnessed the Amerindian practice of smoking.[1497] English king James I (1566–1625), "the wisest fool in Christendom," abhorred the habit, declared tobacco "that stinking weed," and opposed cultivation and use.[1498] The condemnation may have emboldened his subjects. Absent freedom of speech, smoking may have been the least risky noncompliance with government.

Virginia exported 500,000 pounds of tobacco in 1627, one million in 1635, and 15 million by 1670.[1499] Only sugar generated greater seventeenth century profits.[1500] Unlike tropical sugarcane, tobacco grew nearly anywhere, causing supply to overwhelm demand as price per pound, 27 cents in 1619, sank below a penny in 1660.[1501]

[1493] Ibid.
[1494] Atack and Passell, 29.
[1495] Thernstrom, 27-28.
[1496] Morris, 52.
[1497] Thernstrom, 32.
[1498] Ibid., 33; Ackroyd, 92.
[1499] Thernstrom, 33.
[1500] Dunn, 188.
[1501] Atack and Passell, 34.

Volatility ruined smallholders, whose land plantations absorbed. Before 1700, large landowners dominated Virginia.[1502] Atop the colony they shaped the movement toward independence and governed the early republic. Of the first five presidents, only John Adams (1735–1826) was not a Virginia slaveowner.[1503] American historian Comer Vann Woodward (1908–1999) declared them "men of enormous prestige and formidable integrity [who] held rigid standards of conduct and scrupulous regard for the Constitution," which permitted slavery as ratified in 1788.[1504] Of presidents six through 14, only Adams' son John Quincy Adams (1767–1848) never owned slaves.[1505]

14.3.2.3.3 Rice and Slaves

The slave trade opened a market for rice, which African women prepared for crew and slaves aboard ship. Viable in the Americas, uncooked grains brought rice agriculture and cuisine to the West Indies and Mexico after 1520, Brazil and Uruguay about 1570, the Gulf of Mexico north of Mexico by 1579, Virginia in 1609, and Carolina, which would split into north and south in 1712, around 1685.[1506]

Carolina imported Caribbean and African slaves to grow rice.[1507] Expertise was obtained after 1700 by purchasing slaves from West Africa's rice-growing areas. Their knowledge and exertions expanded and intensified cultivation south from coastal South Carolina through northern Florida and north to North Carolina's Cape Fear River.[1508]

Unusual among grains, rice yields well in waterlogged soil. Among their contributions, slaves devised the tidal flow system, which South Carolina planter McKewn Johnstone popularized around 1750 and which used the Atlantic's tide to inundate paddies.[1509] Pushing water upriver, the tide opened a gate, which closed upon recession to trap water for paddies.

Landowners like Johnstone, becoming a plantocracy that shaped regional and transatlantic policies, profited as slaves produced rice for

---

[1502] Morris, 64.

[1503] Alan Brinkley, *American History: A Survey, Vol. I: To 1877*, 9th ed. (New York: McGraw-Hill, 1995), A-24; Tim McGrath, *James Monroe* (New York: Dutton, 2020), 584.

[1504] C. Vann Woodward, "The Conscience of the White House," in *Presidential Misconduct: From George Washington to Today*, ed. James M. Banner Jr. (New York and London: New Press, 2019), xxvi.

[1505] McGrath, 584.

[1506] C. Wayne Smith, *Crop Production: Evolution, History, and Technology* (New York: Wiley, 1995), 228, 232; Henry C. Dethloff, *A History of the American Rice Industry, 1685-1985* (College Station: Texas A & M University Press, 1988), 4.

[1507] Jill Dubisch, "Low Country Fevers: Cultural Adaptations to Malaria in Antebellum South Carolina," *Social Science and Medicine* 21, no. 6 (February 1985): 643.

[1508] Bill Laws, *Fifty Plants that Changed the Course of History* (Buffalo, NY and Richmond Hill, ON: Firefly Books, 2015), 145.

[1509] Smith, 232.

domestic consumption and export to Europe, where it was eaten, fermented into alcohol, and processed into paper.[1510] Portuguese and Spanish Catholics, eating it with fish on meatless days, were steady buyers. Importing American rice, England sold it in Europe and India.

Rice pitted black against white, noted French American soldier, diplomat, traveler, and author Hector St. Jean de Crevecoeur (1735–1813), whose *Letters from an American Farmer* (1782), despite condemning bondage, earned first U.S. president and slaveowner George Washington's (1732–1799) praise.[1511] Contrasting "a people enjoying all that life affords...without labor, without fatigue" against slaves required "to toil, to starve, and to languish," Crevecoeur toured Charleston, South Carolina, a resort whose landowners, lawyers, and merchants enjoyed power, leisure, and privilege, displayed opulence and ennui, and attended churches where sermons, exploring abstractions, ignored slavery.[1512]

As late as 1680, before rice's ascent, the colony was 80 percent white.[1513] But by 1708 slaves, too conspicuous to disregard, totaled over half the population. By 1740 they, doubling whites overall, approached nine tenths of plantation residents near Charleston.

Plantations were "virtual labor camps, where thousands of slaves worked under harsh conditions with no hope of improvement."[1514] Kneeling in mud, they were vulnerable to snakes, alligators, and insects.[1515] A visitor described the labor as the harshest she witnessed. Mentioned earlier and endemic upon transition to rice, malaria and yellow fever killed blacks and whites.[1516]

14.3.2.3.4 Cotton and Louisiana Sugarcane

After pollination, a cotton flower produces a boll with fiber.[1517] Under genetic control, fiber length varies by cultivar. Eighteenth century farmers

---

[1510] Laws, 145; Gann and Willen, 97.

[1511] Hector St. Jean de Crevecoeur, "From *Letters from an American Farmer*," in *The Norton Anthology of American Literature*, 2d ed., Nina Baym, Francis Murphy, Ronald Gottesman, Hershel Parker, Laurence B. Holland, William H. Pritchard, and David Kalstone (New York and London: Norton, 1986), 207-212; Nina Baym, Francis Murphy, Ronald Gottesman, Hershel Parker, Laurence B. Holland, William H. Pritchard, and David Kalstone, *The Norton Anthology of American Literature*, 2d ed. (New York and London: Norton, 1986), 195.

[1512] Crevecoeur, 207-209.

[1513] Gary B. Nash, Julie Roy Jeffrey, John R. Howe, Peter J. Frederick, Allen F. Davis, and Allan M. Winkler, *The American People: Creating a Nation and a Society, Vol. 1: to 1877*, 2d ed. (HarperCollins*Publishers*, 1990), 58; Thernstrom, 82.

[1514] Hewitt and Lawson, 87.

[1515] Thernstrom, 82; Gann and Willen, 97.

[1516] Nash, Jeffrey, Howe, Frederick, Davis, and Winkler, 58; Gann and Willen, 97.

[1517] "How a Cotton Plant Grows," Texas A & M Agrilife Research and Extension Center at San Angelo, accessed June 4, 2022, ‹https://sanangelo.tamu.edu/extension/agronomy/

grew two types. Long fiber cotton made excellent cloth, commanded a higher price, and thrived on Georgia's coast and nearby islands.[1518] Inland, however, insects, fungi, intolerance of all but sandy soil, and early frost diminished yield. Tolerating diverse soils and shorter growing seasons, hardier short fiber cotton fetched a lower price.

Political geography restricted it by confining the American colonies to easternmost North America. Ending the American Revolution, the 1783 Treaty of Paris gave the new nation all land east of the Mississippi River except Canada and Florida.[1519] Geography no longer impeding cotton, seeds' extraction from lint required inordinate labor, which American inventor Eli Whitney (1765-1825) mechanized with his 1793 cotton gin.[1520] From 1810 to 1835 the crop penetrated west through South Carolina, Georgia, Tennessee, Alabama, Mississippi, and Louisiana.[1521] From 1810 to 1820 Alabama, Mississippi, and Louisiana bought roughly 120,000 slaves to grow it.[1522] The Panic of 1837 tightening credit, acreage and slavery enlarged afterwards, especially in Louisiana, Texas, and Arkansas.

Before sugarcane, which Jesuits planted in 1751, Louisiana grew corn, rice, and indigo.[1523] Afterwards, the sugarcane-slave dyad shaped the economy under French and U.S. rule. As in the tropics, mortality outstripped births. Louisiana and Jamaica having similar longevity, Louisiana imported roughly 21,000 slaves from 1763 to 1812. Earlier sections treating Brazilian and West Indian sugarcane and slaves, additional details are unnecessary.

14.4 Rebellion as Newtonian Backlash

14.4.1 The West Indies

The West Indies, where Columbus had introduced sugarcane, spearheaded defiance. Seven insurrections, six in Jamaica, mobilized at least 50 slaves each in England's Caribbean from 1640 and 1713.[1524] In July 1685, for example, roughly 150 slaves killed 11 whites before escaping to the mountains. Recruiting another 105 slaves, rebels killed 15 more whites by March

---

agronomy-publications/how-a-cotton-plant-grows.›

[1518] Atack and Passell, 300; Stephen Yafa, *Big Cotton: How a Humble Fiber Created Fortunes, Wrecked Civilizations, and Put America on the Map* (New York: Viking, 2005), 14.

[1519] Hewitt and Lawson, 181-182.

[1520] Ibid., 243.

[1521] Atack and Passell, 300-301.

[1522] Gann and Willen, 106.

[1523] Muhammad, 73, 81-83; Sanjida O'Connell, *Sugar: The Grass that Changed the World* (London: Virgin Books, 2004), 74.

[1524] Dunn, 256-261.

1686. Order having been restored late that year, some 400 slaves renewed the offensive in 1691 and again destroyed plantations, killed owners and their families, and succumbed to the militia. Divulging plots, blacks loyal to the owners enabled them to quash the uprisings.

To the east, Saint-Domingue, the richest Caribbean sugar producer and "jewel of French colonies," ranked free blacks who had a European ancestor and had never been enslaved above manumitted slaves, known as freedmen, and slaves.[1525] Heightening tension, authorities diminished or eliminated free blacks' rights after 1760.

Discussed in France, Enlightenment ideals of freedom and equality pervaded the colony after 1780. The French Revolution's 1789 outbreak, a chapter 16 topic, led slaves to hope France might end bondage. These hopes dashed, biracial nobleman Vincent Oge (1755–1791), raising an army in July 1790, defeated French troops before his capture and execution.[1526] Free blacks fought whites throughout 1791. Instigating a colony-wide insurrection on August 22, slaves, numbering 10,000 men within five days, destroyed hundreds of plantations by late November.[1527]

Sensing vulnerability, Britain blockaded the coast as prelude to an invasion.[1528] Aiming to unify the island, Spain in adjacent Santo Domingo, now the Dominican Republic, invaded Saint-Domingue. Hoping to weaken the revolution, France freed the colony's slaves in October 1793 and all French slaves in February 1794.

At this juncture, Spanish officer and freedman Toussaint Louverture (c. 1743–1803), "a heroic symbol of black emancipation from colonial rule for African Americans and the African Diaspora," joined France, commanding all its Saint-Domingue forces in May 1796.[1529] Raising an army in the southwest, rival general and free black Andre Rigaud (1761–1811) hoped to keep free blacks above freedmen. Louverture's 1799 victory fleeting, French general, emperor, and "war-lover" Napoleon Bonaparte (1769–1821) in 1802 sent an army to arrest him, reconquer Saint-Domingue, and reimpose slavery.[1530] Defeating it, general and emperor Jean Jacques Dessalines (1758–1806), the

---

[1525] McKay, Hill, Buckler, Crowston, Wiesner-Hanks, and Perry, 595-596; Thomas Piketty, *Capital and Ideology*, trans. Arthur Goldhammer (Cambridge, MA and London: Belknap Press of Harvard University Press, 2020), 214.

[1526] McKay, Hill, Buckler, Crowston, Wiesner-Hanks, and Perry, 596.

[1527] Ibid., 601.

[1528] Ibid., 603.

[1529] Ibid., 603, 607; Philippe R. Girard, "Louverture, Toussaint Breda (ca. 1743-1803)," in *Africa and the Americas: Culture, Politics, and History*, vol. 2, ed. Richard M. Juang and Noelle Morrissette (Santa Barbara, CA: ABC-CLIO, 2008), 710.

[1530] Alan Strauss-Schom, *The Shadow Emperor: A Biography of Napoleon III* (New York: St. Martin's Press, 2018), 425.

"most flamboyant of Toussaint's senior military officers," declared an independent Haiti January 1, 1804.[1531]

14.4.2 Mainland North America

Fearing similar misfortune at home, President Jefferson refused to recognize Haiti.[1532] In 1739, four years before his birth, 20 slaves had seized guns from a store near the Stono River southwest of Charleston.[1533] Marching along the river, beating drums, chanting "liberty," recruiting another 30 to 100 slaves, destroying plantations, and killing almost 30 whites, they may have hoped to reach Florida, then Spanish territory, where authorities promised runaways freedom. But their beating a drum, announcing not concealing them, contradicted this possibility. A two-day battle with militia killed dozens, and authorities executed about 40 captives.

The revolt deepened white anxiety in Charleston, where in 1783 captain Joseph Vesey (1747–1835) settled with his slave Denmark Vesey (1767–1822) who, purchasing his freedom in 1799, established a carpentry business downtown.[1534] A philanthropist, he aided churches and attended the African Methodist Episcopal (AME) church, headquarters of a putative plot to burn the city, kill whites, and flee to Haiti. Details emerged during a month of coerced confessions possibly fabricated to frame others. Vesey executed with 34 other supposed conspirators, authorities demolished the AME church.

North of these events, in Southampton County, Virginia, slave Nat Turner (1800–1831) interpreted a February 1831 solar eclipse and a vision of black and white spirits fighting amid thunder as God's command to kill his owners.[1535] He and six associates accomplished this aim on August 21, recruited more slaves, and attacked nearby plantations. Using knives and axes, they avoided gunfire that would have alerted authorities and killed around 60 whites before militia confronted them on August 22 and 23 with artillery. Hiding in a swamp over two months before his capture, Turner,

---

[1531] Sudhir Hazareesingh, *Black Spartacus: The Epic Life of Toussaint Louverture* (New York: Farrar, Straus and Giroux, 2020), 85; Laurent Dubois, *Avengers of the New World: The Story of the Haitian Revolution* (Cambridge, MA and London: Belknap Press of Harvard University Press, 2004), 1.

[1532] McKay, Hill, Buckler, Crowston, Wiesner-Hanks, and Perry, 607.

[1533] Gann and Willen, 98; Hewitt and Lawson, 87; Brinkley, 80; Leslie Alexander and Michelle Alexander, "Fear," in *The 1619 Project: A New Origin Story*, ed. Nikole Hannah-Jones, Caitlin Roper, Ilena Silverman, and Jake Silverstein (New York: One World, 2021), 105.

[1534] Hewitt and Lawson, 274; Walter C. Rucker, "Vesey, Denmark," in *Encyclopedia of African American History*, vol. 2, ed. Leslie M. Alexander and Walter C. Rucker (Santa Barbara, CA: ABC-CLIO, 2010), 565-566.

[1535] Hewitt and Lawson, 302; Gann and Willen, 109-110; Zoe Trodd, "Turner, Nat," in *Encyclopedia of African American History*, vol. 2, ed. Leslie M. Alexander and Walter C. Rucker (Santa Barbara, CA: ABC-CLIO, 2010), 557-558.

whose hanging emboldened mobs to kill nearly 200 blacks, compared himself to Hebrew prophet Jesus (c. 5 BCE–c. 30 CE).[1536]

Abolitionists exalting Vesey and Turner, the Thirteenth Amendment, ratified in 1865, was part of a movement whose details transcend this chapter to end western hemisphere bondage and the slave trade.[1537]

14.5 Review and Preview

Amerindian and black slaves worked post-contact American mines and plantations. Next chapter heeds Marx and Trinidadian historian and prime minister Eric Williams (1911–1981), who asserted that bondage financed the Industrial Revolution. Like plantations, factories perpetuated inequality.

[1536] Alexander and Alexander, 111.

[1537] "Denmark Vesey," National Park Service, last modified July 17, 2020, accessed March 20, 2022, ‹Denmark Vesey (U.S. National Park Service) (nps.gov)›; Trodd, 558-559; Gann and Willen, 78-93; Hewitt and Lawson, A-14.

Chapter 15 Industrial Inequality

15.1 Abstract

Substituting machines for muscles, industrialization marked a watershed. After 1770 England launched the first industrial revolution, which produced garments, iron, coal, and the steam engine. After 1850 Belgian, French, German, and U.S. industries negated England's early advantage. This second industrial revolution produced steel, chemicals, electricity from coal's combustion, petroleum, and automobiles. Like agriculture and pastoralism, industry perpetuated rather than revolutionized inequality.

15.2 Trade and Capitalism as Industrial Prerequisites

15.2.1 Trade

15.2.1.1 European Trade

Industrialization harnessed developments in technology, agriculture, trade, and ideology. The moniker Industrial Revolution implies it was as consequential as the Neolithic Revolution. Farming and herding benefited elites whereas the masses subsisted amid prosperity and perished during famine, epidemics, war, and other disruptions, earlier chapters emphasized.

Retaining this pattern of plenitude for few and privation for everyone else, the economy industrialized after moving from risk-averse subsistence to entrepreneurialism. This change occurred first in Europe, where commerce and capitalism, a Hobbesian "economic war of all against all" that

American author Jack London (1876–1916) criticized as "blind and greedy," underpinned industry.[1538]

Europe's preindustrial economy was agrarian, an orientation capitalism initially retained. Indeed, merchants arose not to displace the farmer, but to sell his produce. They inhabited cities, growing in antiquity and again after roughly 1000 CE mentioned chapter 12, where money and trade expanded opportunities for profit.

15.2.1.2 West African Trade as Comparison with European Trade

Europe's economy resembled those in China and Muslim lands until around 1700.[1539] Before Islam, West African farming and herding supported commerce and urbanism from the first millennium BCE.[1540] Unsuitable for aridity, oxen as pack animals hobbled trans-Saharan trade before the camel, which reached Lower Egypt and North Africa around the first century BCE.[1541] Migrating south into Upper Egypt by 300 CE, it became the Sahara's beast of burden when Arabs conquered Egypt and North Africa in the seventh and eighth centuries.

Early West African commerce featured dates, rice, cattle, butter, and milk.[1542] Distant trade moved slaves despite high mortality and durables like copper, bronze, iron, gold, leather, and cotton. Perhaps 3,000 to 5,000 slaves yearly crossed the Sahara north to the Mediterranean for shipment to Eurasia.[1543] European slaves trickled south to West African elites.

Arabs Islamized West Africa between the tenth and twelfth centuries.[1544] The faith penetrating cities, the countryside retained traditional religions.

[1538] Robert W. Strayer, Edwin Hirschmann, Robert B. Marks, Robert J. Smith, James J. Horn, and Lynn H. Parsons, *The Making of the Modern World: Connected Histories, Divergent Paths (1500 to the Present)* (New York: St. Martin's Press, 1989), 64; David McLellan, "Introduction," in *The Condition of the Working Class in England*, Friedrich Engels, ed. David McLellan (Oxford: Oxford University Press, 2009), xv; Jack London, "Revolution," in *The Radical Jack London: Writings on War and Revolution*, ed. Jonah Raskin (Berkeley: University of California Press, 2008), 151.

[1539] Strayer, Hirschmann, Marks, Smith, Horn, and Parsons, 64.

[1540] Jonathan T. Reynolds, "Horses, Salt, Manufactured Goods, Islamic Books, Gold, and Slaves—What Was Traded across the Sahara and Why?" in *World History Encyclopedia, Vol. 10, Era 5: Intensified Hemispheric Interactions, 1000-1500*, ed. Alfred J. Andrea and Carolyn Neel (Santa Barbara, CA: ABC-CLIO, 2011), 489.

[1541] Ibid.; Ralph A. Austen, "Trading Patterns, Trans-Saharan," in *Berkshire Encyclopedia of World History*, vol. 5, ed. William H. McNeill, Jerry H. Bentley, David Christian, David Levinson, J. R. McNeill, Heidi Roupp, and Judith P. Zinsser (Great Barrington, MA: Berkshire Publishing Group, 2005), 1883.

[1542] Austen, 1883; Strayer, Hirschmann, Marks, Smith, Horn, and Parsons, 436; Mary Quigley, *Ancient West African Kingdoms: Ghana, Mali, and Songhai* (Chicago: Heinemann Library, 2002), 14.

[1543] Reynolds, 490.

[1544] Robert B. Marks, *The Origins of the Modern World: A Global and Environmental Narrative from the Fifteenth to the Twenty-First Century*, 4th ed. (Lanham, MD: Rowman & Littlefield, 2020), 58.

Unlike Mesopotamia, Egypt, Rome, India, China, Mesoamerica, South America, and Europe, West African Muslims taxed only trade.[1545] West Africa bifurcated into rich and poor as taxation supported "a very wealthy court."[1546]

Among its cities, Timbuktu became an entrepôt around 1100.[1547] North of the Niger River at the Sahara's southern fringe, it facilitated trade between the Mediterranean and lands south of the desert. From the Mediterranean, Egyptians and Italians brought cloth, salt, and spices and took slaves, gold, ivory, and ostrich shells and feathers north.[1548]

Enlarging commerce, Arabs brought Timbuktu cotton from India, silk from China, and horses, glass and ceramic vessels, weapons, paper, books, beads, mirrors, and salt from elsewhere in Asia.[1549] Caravans with up to 25,000 camels took Timbuktu slaves and gold, financing trade among West Africa, North Africa, Egypt, Europe, Southwest Asia, India, Southeast Asia, and China, to the Mediterranean.

After 1200, the Mali empire made the capital Timbuktu, where King Mansa Musa I (r. c. 1307–1337), "the most famous person in all of the western Sudan," prioritized art and scholarship, built mosques, schools, and libraries, and fostered the book trade.[1550] Intensifying inequality, taxation enriched his 1324 visit to Egypt and Arabia with roughly 100 camels, each carrying 300 pounds of gold.[1551] His profligacy in Cairo depreciated the metal by one tenth to one fifth. Royal affluence came from enslaving captives during war, settling them in villages near Timbuktu and other cities, and assigning them quotas. For example, 200 slaves supplied the capital 1,000 bags of rice and another 100 furnished 700 bags of millet.

"Commerce turned Timbuktu into a great center, attracting scholars, architects, poets, and astronomers to its university, and Muslim theologians went there to the more than 100 schools established to study the Quran," wrote American historian Robert Marks (b. 1949).[1552] With perhaps 25,000

[1545] Strayer, Hirschmann, Marks, Smith, Horn, and Parsons, 436.

[1546] Ibid.; Terri Koontz, Mark Sidwell, and S. M. Bunker, *World Studies*, 2d ed. (Greenville, SC: BJU Press, 2000), 124.

[1547] Koontz, Sidwell, and Bunker.

[1548] Koontz, Sidwell, and Bunker; Reynolds, 490.

[1549] Marks, 58; Austen, 1884.

[1550] Justin Corfield, "Mali," in *Africa and the Americas: Culture, Politics, and History*, vol. 2, ed. Richard M. Juang and Noelle Morrissette (Santa Barbara, CA: ABC-CLIO, 2008), 724; Koontz, Sidwell, and Bunker, 124; Reynolds, 488; Willie F. Page, *Encyclopedia of African History and Culture, Vol. II: African Kingdoms (500-1500)* (New York: Facts on File, 2001), 161.

[1551] Roland Oliver and Brian M. Fagan, *Africa in the Iron Age, c. 500 B.C. to A.D. 1400* (Cambridge, UK: Cambridge University Press, 1975), 171-172, 174.

[1552] Marks, 58.

citizens by the fifteenth century, it surpassed Rome's 17,000.[1553] A century later roughly 60,000 inhabitants, 180 schools, and thousands of students populated Timbuktu.

15.2.1.3 Europe's Divergence from Africa and Asia

It and West Africa overall were as eager to trade as Europe, which diverged from Africa and Asia.[1554] Medieval European government weak, merchants accrued wealth and status beyond those possible elsewhere. Their values—thrift, work, and profit—overshadowed aristocratic leisure, ostentation, and militarism after 1700.[1555]

This shift affected agriculture, which after 1400 increasingly valued land for its productivity rather than as status indicator.[1556] Whereas the medieval village let farmworkers access land, after roughly 1650 landowners, especially in England, Belgium, the Netherlands, and Luxembourg, began to enclose it for livestock.[1557] Animals needing less labor than crops, landlords expelled workers, who accelerated urbanization by seeking city jobs.

This transition was ethical as well as economic. The village prioritized community above individual and cooperation over competition, but the new ethos reversed this order.[1558] Everyone now being responsible for self, not community, competition defined human interactions, produced winners and losers, and made inequality unassailable. Nobody owed another charity as greed trumped generosity.

Farmers and herders aside, mariners and merchants created a global economy after 1500, a development Europeans led by exploring and settling the Americas.[1559] Profiting from globalism, businessmen sought to maximize sales and minimize wages. Bypassing urban guilds, a medieval holdover, for aiming to maximize members' wages, entrepreneurs exploited cheap rural labor through the "putting-out system," whereby they gave countryfolk linen, wool, or cotton to make into cloth.[1560] After 1770 businessmen organized labor in factories to ease oversight.

[1553] Strayer, Hirschmann, Marks, Smith, Horn, and Parsons, 436-437; Koontz, Sidwell, and Bunker, 124; Quigley, 36.
[1554] Strayer, Hirschmann, Marks, Smith, Horn, and Parsons, 64-65.
[1555] Ibid., 71.
[1556] Ibid., 68-69.
[1557] John P. McKay, Bennett D. Hill, John Buckler, Clare Haru Crowston, Merry E. Wiesner-Hanks, and Joe Perry, *Understanding Western Society: A Brief History* (Boston and New York: Bedford/St. Martin's, 2012), 523-524.
[1558] Strayer, Hirschmann, Marks, Smith, Horn, and Parsons, 64-65.
[1559] McKay, Hill, Buckler, Crowston, Wiesner-Hanks, and Perry, 442-443.
[1560] Ibid., 528-529; Strayer, Hirschmann, Marks, Smith, Horn, and Parsons, 70.

Textile scion German economist Friedrich Engels (1820–1895) considered the putting-out system "a passably comfortable existence."[1561] Working together, a family maintained a pace that prevented exhaustion, kept a garden for recreation and wholesome food, inhaled "fresh country air," and "led moral lives."[1562] Glamorizing the years just before industrialization, he contrasted them against the factory system, though both oppressed underlings. Conceding as much, Engels deemed peasants "toiling machines in the service of the few aristocrats who had guided history down to that time."[1563]

Clothmaking required a loom which occupied most of a hovel's one room. The husband or a mature son operated it while the women and children fed it thread.[1564] Men who worked long and fast earned satisfactory wages, paid per finished cloth's weight, but employers decreased them to require constant effort for the total to suffice; illness or lulls meant hunger. Justifying stinginess, employers described workers as idlers who would slacken pace were pay generous. Theft's accusation permitted imprisonment and whipping.

To these "horrendous injustices," Engels' associate German economist Karl Marx (1818–1883) added last chapter's U.S. plantations, without which England could not have industrialized, as cotton suppliers.[1565] Demand for the fiber led masters to buy and breed slaves.[1566] Marx overrating the United States, England imported cotton primarily from the Levant and Caribbean.[1567]

Marx and Trinidadian historian and prime minister Eric Williams (1911–1981) believed England's profits from slavery and the slave trade fueled industrialization, mentioned the introduction and last chapter. Bondage thus anticipated Europe's "veiled slavery of the wage workers."[1568]

15.2.2 Adam Smith and Capitalism

Scottish economist and "patron saint of capitalism" Adam Smith (1723–1790) promoted the free market, *laissez faire* in French, which alone, and thus absent guilds, unions, and governments, should price commodities, including

---

[1561] Friedrich Engels, *The Condition of the Working Class in England*, ed. David McLellan (Oxford: Oxford University Press, 2009), 16.

[1562] Ibid.

[1563] Ibid., 17.

[1564] McKay, Hill, Buckler, Crowston, Wiesner-Hanks, and Perry, 530-531.

[1565] Marks, 120; Karl Marx, *Capital: A Critique of Political Economy*, vol. 1, trans. Ben Fowkes (London: Penguin Books, 1990), 924-925.

[1566] Marx, 571.

[1567] Marks, 109.

[1568] Marx, 925.

labor.[1569] This rationale completed workers' transition from individuals to machines whose purpose was to produce value at lowest cost.

Capitalism thus removed government from the economy, which employers, not officials, were competent to manage, though this posture was rhetoric over actuality because corporations wanted government to mold the economy to suit them. U.S. history is replete with state and federal use of soldiers to crush strikes and unions. Moreover, the policy of open borders has always attracted immigrants, who reduce wages by competing for jobs.[1570]

Nullifying Christian animus toward greed and selfishness, the free market encouraged egoism because the sum of all wants supposedly yielded the best economy and society.[1571] Pursuing their interest by seeking the best and cheapest product, for example, buyers forced businesses to comply or lose sales. Satisfying consumers by producing affordable quality, manufacturers benefited everyone. But chapter 17's socialism and communism opposed capitalism and industrialism for intensifying inequality.

Capitalism, whereby "the stronger treads the weaker under foot," empowered employers over employees.[1572] Rejecting slavery as wasteful for requiring chattel's provision, capitalism made pay the only compensation.[1573] Slashing costs, employers discharged underlings during downturns, a practice impossible in bondage, though earlier chapters' owners underfed slaves to economize.

15.3 The Machine Age

15.3.1 First Industrial Revolution

With capitalism as foundation, industry harnessed energy. Scientists define energy as capacity for work and work as application of force to move a load over distance.[1574] The greater the load, distance, or both the more energy is necessary. Humans long expended energy. For example, a farmer goaded an ox, using energy from digested grasses, to pull a plow.

[1569] Brian Duignan, ed., *Economics and Economic Systems* (New York: Britannica, 2013), 79-82; Jonathan Levy, *Ages of Capitalism: A History of the United States* (New York: Random House, 2021), 9.

[1570] Jeremy Atack and Peter Passell, *A New Economic View of American History*, 2d ed. (New York and London: Norton, 1994), 538-539.

[1571] Strayer, Hirschmann, Marks, Smith, Horn, and Parsons, 80.

[1572] Engels, 37.

[1573] Ibid., 92.

[1574] James E. Brady and Gerard E. Humiston, *General Chemistry: Principles and Structure*, 3d ed. (New York: Wiley, 1982), 26.

The preindustrial economy exploiting animals, industry prioritized machines over muscles. Fossil plant remains and "man's prime source of power," coal actuated machines.[1575] Plants absorbed the sun's energy by photosynthesis. Scientists term stored energy, having potential to do work, potential energy.[1576] Coal's energy is also chemical because plants store energy in chemical bonds.[1577] Plants' conversion into coal took millions of years, though combustion released energy in hours.

England's large population cleared land for farms, factories, and homes. Wood enabled construction and cooking and heated the home.[1578] Deforestation increased reliance on coal, which supplied half England's energy by 1700.[1579] The country in 1800 yielded around 10 million tons of coal, perhaps 90 percent of world output. About 70 percent of English coal heating homes, the rest powered industry. Led by England, global coal output increased 55 times from 1800 to 1900.

The demand for coal stimulated mining, so that employers hired men, women, and children.[1580] Children and small women pulled heavy carts along narrow shafts. The mine's warmth plus the body's exertion overheating them, many worked seminude. Ignoring toil and injuries but fearing orgies, conservatives convinced Parliament in 1842 to ban women and children under age 10. The law excluding factories, some employers made female workers a "harem."[1581]

Engineers boiled water by burning coal. Water's rapid expansion upon conversion from liquid into steam supplied kinetic energy, the energy of motion, to move a piston in a steam engine or spin a turbine to generate electricity.[1582] English engineer Thomas Savery (c. 1650–1715) invented the steam engine, "the Industrial Revolution's most fundamental advance in technology," in 1698.[1583] English inventor Thomas Newcomen (1664–1729) patented his model, the first with a piston, in 1705. Scottish engineer and chemist James Watt (1736–1819) patented his version in 1769. Large models,

---

[1575] Arthur Beiser, The Earth, rev. ed. (New York: Time-Life Books, 1968), 93.

[1576] Brady and Humiston, 26.

[1577] J. R. McNeill and William H. McNeill, The Human Web: A Bird's-Eye View of World History (New York and London: Norton, 2003), 230.

[1578] Marks, 121.

[1579] David Christian, Origin Story: A Big History of Everything (London: Allen Lane, 2018), 253-255.

[1580] McKay, Hill, Buckler, Crowston, Wiesner-Hanks, and Perry, 635-637.

[1581] Engels, 158.

[1582] Brady and Humiston, 26.

[1583] McKay, Hill, Buckler, Crowston, Wiesner-Hanks, and Perry, 619-620; Robert Ergang, Europe: From the Renaissance to Waterloo (Boston: D. C. Heath, 1967), 561-562.

whose connection to shafts and belts rooted them to the spot, were immobile.

The steam engine powered looms in England's textile mills, which, proliferating after 1770 to satisfy domestic demand for woolen and cotton garments, totaled 22 percent of English industrial output by 1831.[1584] Before industrialization, England imported cotton clothes from India, which made them for centuries.[1585] Afterwards England, seeking to export its handiwork throughout its colonies, taxed imports out of existence and flooded India with English textiles to destroy its producers.

The steam engine also powered the locomotive, which English engineer George Stephenson (1781–1848) invented in 1825 and which sped overland transit and enlarged cities.[1586] Five years later his *Rocket* completed the inaugural Liverpool to Manchester trip. France opening its first railway in 1832, Belgium and Germany followed three years later. Exceeding 6,000 miles of track in 1850, England more than doubled France and Germany combined. Linking Pacific and Atlantic Oceans with a transcontinental line in 1869, the United States laid another 100,000 miles of track by 1894 to surpass all other nations.[1587] Chapter 1 described management and railroad workers' disparate wealth, status, privilege, and power.

Luddites attacked factories, which, replacing workers with machines, cut jobs and wages.[1588] In 1718, for instance, English merchant Thomas Lombe (1685–1739) opened a textile mill with roughly 300 workers, though his second factory's larger looms halved the workforce.[1589] The trend continues. While over 90 percent of Americans were farming in 1790, for example, machines shrank the percentage to below 2 in 2000.[1590]

[1584] McKay, Hill, Buckler, Crowston, Wiesner-Hanks, and Perry, 618.

[1585] Marks, 106; McNeill and McNeill, 236.

[1586] McKay, Hill, Buckler, Crowston, Wiesner-Hanks, and Perry, 620; Albert M. Craig, William A. Graham, Donald Kagan, Steven Ozment, and Frank M. Turner, *The Heritage of World Civilizations, Vol. II: Since 1500* (New York: Macmillan, 1986), 854.

[1587] Joshua Freeman, Nelson Lichtenstein, Stephen Brier, David Bensman, Susan Porter Benson, David Brundage, Bret Eynon, Bruce Levine, and Bryan Palmer, *Who Built America?: Working People and the Nation's Economy, Politics, Culture, and Society* (New York: Pantheon Books, 1992), 9.

[1588] McKay, Hill, Buckler, Crowston, Wiesner-Hanks, and Perry, 630-631; Engels, 145, 147.

[1589] Ergang, 558.

[1590] Statistical Reporting Service, *The Story of U.S. Agricultural Estimates* (Washington, DC: USDA, 1969), 1; Daniel Gross, "U.S. Farms Still Feed the World, But Farm Jobs Dwindle," Strategy + Business, August 2, 2016, accessed March 23, 2022, ‹U.S. farms still feed the world, but farm jobs dwindle (strategy-business.com).›

15.3.2 Second Industrial Revolution

England peaking around 1850 at roughly one fifth of global goods and services, Belgian, French, German, and U.S. industries ended its early advantage during a second industrial revolution.[1591] Steel supplanted iron in construction; coal's combustion generated electricity, which replaced steam for power after 1910; petroleum rivaled coal as a fossil fuel; and chemistry created products for agriculture, industry, and home.[1592] U.S. factories produced more wealth by 1894 than England, Germany, and France combined.[1593]

This phase of industrialization multiplied consumer products, none more popular than the automobile. Conceiving it a status symbol for the wealthy, German engineer Gottlieb Daimler (1834–1900) patented the invention in 1885.[1594] Reducing the price from $850 in 1908 to $290 in 1924 through standardization and mass production, American automaker Henry Ford (1863–1947), mechanization's "commanding general," made it a mass commodity, thereby stimulating demand for petroleum distillates gasoline and diesel.[1595]

Confirming America's might, U.S. automakers produced 1.9 million cars in 1920 and nearly 4.5 million in 1929.[1596] The United States in 1920 had 8.1 million registered vehicles, one for every third household, and in 1929 23.1 million, one per 1.3 households. The United States produced 2 million automobiles in 1946 and 8 million in 1955.[1597] Aiding the automobile, Congress allocated $26 billion in 1956 to lay over 40,000 miles of highways.

Besides petroleum, the automobile needed steel. Around 1850, British engineer Henry Bessemer (1830–1898) decreased steel's manufacturing cost through the Bessemer process, which England, Belgium, France, and Germany used to raise production from 125,000 tons in 1860 to over 32

[1591] Christian, 254-255; Craig, Graham, Kagan, Ozment, and Turner, 904-908.

[1592] Ibid.; Tim Harford, "Why Didn't Electricity Immediately Change Manufacturing?" BBC News, August 21, 2017, accessed March 23, 2022, ‹Why didn't electricity immediately change manufacturing? - BBC News.›

[1593] Freeman, Lichtenstein, Brier, Bensman, Benson, Brundage, Eynon, Levine, and Palmer, 7.

[1594] Craig, Graham, Kagan, Ozment, and Turner, 908.

[1595] George Brown Tindall and David E. Shi, *America: A Narrative History*, vol. II, 4th ed. (New York and London: Norton, 1996), 1133-1134; John M. Blum, Edmund S. Morgan, Willie Lee Rose, Arthur M. Schlesinger, Jr., Kenneth M. Stampp, and C. Vann Woodward, *The National Experience: A History of the United States Since 1865*, vol. 2, 4th ed. (New York: Harcourt Brace Jovanovich, 1977), 593.

[1596] Atack and Passell, 578.

[1597] Gary B. Nash, Julie Roy Jeffrey, John R. Howe, Peter J. Frederick, Allen F. Davis, and Allan M. Winkler, *The American People: Creating a Nation and a Society, Vol 2, Since 1865*, 2d ed. (New York: HarperCollinsPublishers, 1990), 923.

million tons in 1913.[1598] Although the glut reduced prices and profits, the average American mill produced roughly $2.5 million of steel in 1920.[1599]

15.4 Factory, Management, and Labor

15.4.1 Employer as Oppressor

Unable to go to workers, the steam engine gathered them at England's textile mills, the world's first factories.[1600] Before the engine was , owners situated mills along rivers, which powered looms by waterwheel. Circumventing guilds, their rural location sought to attract cottagers, who despised factories as unnatural, loud, dirty, crowded, and regimented. Emphasizing their unpleasantness, English "prophetic poet, apocalyptic humanist, proletarian rebel, and visionary" William Blake (1757–1827) called them "dark satanic mills."[1601]

Although farming was arduous, factories demanded labor keep pace with a machine, repeat the same task *ad nauseam*, and adjust to the clock by working a shift, typically 12 hours in 1800.[1602] Having the poorhouse's appearance, stigma, and regimentation, they displeased employees.

Alienating workmen, factories reduced them to machines, misfortune Marx and Engels, designating them "slaves," attributed to management's power and workers' impotence.[1603] Struggling to hire adults, employers contracted churches to supply orphans, who worked from age five or six for 14 hours daily without pay, abuse Marx designated "child slavery."[1604] Locked inside dormitories, they could not escape hardship. Beatings subdued them.

Factories' long hours caused children rickets from inadequate sunshine.[1605] Stunting Manchester's workers, undernutrition disqualified them for military service.[1606] Slums proliferating, Dublin, Ireland's were "among the most hideous and repulsive to be seen in the world."[1607]

[1598] Craig, Graham, Kagan, Ozment, and Turner, 906.

[1599] Freeman, Lichtenstein, Brier, Bensman, Benson, Brundage, Eynon, Levine, and Palmer, 11; Atack and Passell, 474.

[1600] McKay, Hill, Buckler, Crowston, Wiesner-Hanks, and Perry, 632-633.

[1601] Ibid., 630; Harold Bloom, *Take Arms against a Sea of Troubles: The Power of the Reader's Mind over a Universe of Death* (New Haven, CT and London: Yale University Press, 2020), 110.

[1602] McKay, Hill, Buckler, Crowston, Wiesner-Hanks, and Perry, 632-633; McNeill and McNeill, 248.

[1603] Karl Marx and Friedrich Engels, *Communist Manifesto*, trans. Samuel Moore (Chicago: Great Books Foundation, 1955), 17.

[1604] McKay, Hill, Buckler, Crowston, Wiesner-Hanks, and Perry, 617; Marx, 925.

[1605] Ibid., 112-113; Fogel, "Nutrition and the Decline in Mortality Since 1700," 471.

[1606] Engels, 168.

[1607] Ibid., 46.

These problems thrived amid industrial and capitalist inequality. Connecting capitalism, industry, and inequality, *Eternal Inequality* heaps all blame on neither capitalism nor industry because inequality, thriving everywhere always, is innately human. As noted, while capitalism rewards selfishness and greed, these attributes are conspicuous throughout time, place, and circumstance.[1608]

15.4.2 Labor and Destitution

English economist David Ricardo's (1772–1823) "iron law of wages" blamed poverty on population growth for shrinking pay to subsistence by increasing competition for jobs.[1609] Although chapter 13's fourteenth century decreased population, last chapter's European exploration and colonization of the western hemisphere gave the eastern hemisphere new foods. Especially important for Europe were potatoes and corn.

Chapter 11's potato doubled England and Wales from 9 million inhabitants in 1801 to 18 million in 1850.[1610] Leaving farm for city, the surplus staffed factories and worsened the labor glut that worried Ricardo.[1611] Industrialism linked potatoes and penury among English and Irish workers, noted Engels.[1612] "Low-cost provisions enabled industrialists to keep wages low," wrote American anthropologist Ellen Messer (b. 1948).[1613] After roughly 1750, the tuber, whose consumers were "politically powerless and economically exploited," sustained inequality wherever grown and eaten.[1614]

Women worked alongside men on farms that yielded edibles like potatoes, but by 1850 industrialization, favoring men, relegated women to the home.[1615] Those who worked were paupers with children. Their "dead-end jobs" centered on domestic service, England's largest employer after agriculture in 1850, when 90 percent of domestics were women.[1616]

[1608] Emory Elliott, "Afterword," in *The Jungle*, Upton Sinclair (New York: Signet Classic, 1990), 343.

[1609] McKay, Hill, Buckler, Crowston, Wiesner-Hanks, and Perry, 622.

[1610] "History of the Potato," Klondike Brands, 2022, accessed March 22, 2022, ‹http://www.klondikebrands.com/potato-history.›

[1611] William H. McNeill, "How the Potato Changed the World's History," *Social Research* 66, no. 1 (Spring 1999): 81-82.

[1612] Engels, 31, 84.

[1613] Ellen Messer, "Potatoes (White)," in *The Cambridge World History of Food*, vol. 1, ed. Kenneth F. Kiple and Kriemhild Conee Ornelas (Cambridge, UK: Cambridge University Press, 2000), 192.

[1614] Ibid.

[1615] McKay, Hill, Buckler, Crowston, Wiesner-Hanks, and Perry, 634-635.

[1616] Ibid.

Across the Atlantic, U.S. factories favored women and children as cheaper than men.[1617] Massachusetts mills paid women 30 to 37 percent men's wages around 1815. Women narrowed the gap to half men's pay by 1850, to three fifths by 1920, and to 70 percent in the 1990s. Women still trail men.

Advocating women and children's factory employment, first U.S. treasury secretary and "prophet of the capitalist revolution" Alexander Hamilton (c. 1757–1804) believed they, underemployed in agriculture, could augment family income in industry.[1618] Waltham, Massachusetts' Boston Manufacturing Company in 1814 recruited rural women, preferring those single, childless, and unburdened by obligations outside work, to operate looms.[1619] Over three fifths U.S. textile workers were women in 1850.[1620]

Another option was prostitution. Rich businessmen married to enhance status.[1621] Those in dull marriages pursued poor girls who viewed prostitution as an activity they endured for some time and hoped to escape through marriage. Most, aware that adulterers would never leave their wives for an inferior, courted men in their own class. Class thus resembled caste in confining reproduction to insiders.

Immigrants were also attractive hires. After 1830 factories employed the Irish, whose poverty compelled work without complaint.[1622] Later immigrants likewise inhabited cities and staffed factories. Hiring them as scabs, employers intensified xenophobia.[1623]

Attracting labor, factories decreased farm population. For example, Massachusetts counted roughly 87,800 farmers in 1840 and 55,700 a decade later.[1624] The transition to industry upsetting them, they criticized the economy and government during the remainder of the nineteenth century.

Industry "created a gulf between the owners and managers of industrial enterprises and the men, women, and children who worked for them," averred British editor Brian Duignan.[1625] *Eternal Inequality* emphasizes that industry continued rather than created inequality. The agrarian economy bifurcated into few landowners and many indigents, demonstrated earlier chapters. Industry provided a new way of exploiting workers, not a new magnitude of inequality.

[1617] Atack and Passell, 531.
[1618] Ibid., 179; Ron Chernow, *Alexander Hamilton* (New York: Penguin Press, 2004), 6.
[1619] Atack and Passell, 181.
[1620] Ibid., 191.
[1621] McKay, Hill, Buckler, Crowston, Wiesner-Hanks, and Perry, 687.
[1622] Atack and Passell, 185.
[1623] Ibid., 236.
[1624] Ibid., 178.
[1625] Duignan, xiii.

"The living conditions and poverty of the poorer classes in the cities—particularly London—cannot be exaggerated," asserted American historian Robert Ergang (1898–1978).[1626] From 1750 to 1800, its poorest were shorter than Caribbean island Trinidad's slaves and over 99 percent of all English laborers.[1627] London's slums housed "puny children and half-starved, ragged women."[1628] Its 2.5 million residents in 1844 included 50,000 homeless.[1629] These figures put homelessness at 2 percent compared to 0.03 percent in 2018 Tokyo, Japan, 0.2 to 0.5 percent in 2018 Johannesburg, South Africa, 1 percent in 2019 San Francisco, California, and 6.5 percent in 2019 Buenos Aires, Argentina.[1630]

Slums exacerbated overcrowding and contagion that in the 1840s killed over half Manchester's newborns before age five.[1631] Almost 60 percent of them were born to workers and 20 percent to elites.[1632] Liverpool's life expectancy at birth (e0) in 1840 was 15 years for workers and 35 years for the wealthy.

This difference shrank over time but never vanished. The 2016 Massachusetts Institute of Technology study cited in the introduction showed that the richest centile of U.S. men outlived the poorest centile nearly 15 years on average. The gap exceeded 10 years for the same centiles of U.S. women.

By comparison, two New Mexican precontact settlements yielded a life expectancy at birth (e0) of 21.5 and 22.2 years.[1633] Four Mexican precontact

[1626] Ergang, 569.

[1627] Robert William Fogel, "Nutrition and the Decline in Mortality Since 1700: Some Preliminary Findings," in *Long-Term Factors in American Economic Growth*, ed. Stanley L. Engerman and Robert E. Gallman (Chicago and London: University of Chicago Press, 1986), 471-474.

[1628] Engels, 41.

[1629] Ibid., 36, 43-44.

[1630] Emily Kil, "Why Don't You See Homeless People in Japan?" Eco Bear, June 12, 2018, accessed March 23, 2022, ‹Why Don't You See Homeless People in Japan? | Eco Bear Biohazard Cleaning Company;› Lucille Davie, "Slaying the Homelessness Giant," Johannesburg Homeless Network, March 17, 2021, accessed March 23, 2022, ‹Johannesburg Homeless Network - The Johannesburg Inner City Partnership (jicp. org.za);› Nicole Karlis, "One Percent of San Franciscans Are Now Homeless," Salon, July 10, 2019, accessed March 23, 2022, ‹One percent of San Franciscans are now homeless | Salon.com;› Morgan Harden, "Addressing Homelessness in Argentina," Borgen Project, October 12, 2019, accessed March 23, 2022, ‹Addressing Homelessness in Argentina - Global Poverty - The Borgen Project.›

[1631] McLellan, xv.

[1632] Engels, 118.

[1633] Ann L. W. Stodder, Debra L. Martin, Alan H. Goodman, and Daniel T. Reff, "Cultural Longevity and Biological Stress in the American Southwest," in *The Backbone of History: Health and Nutrition in the Western Hemisphere*, ed. Richard H. Steckel and Jerome C. Rose (Cambridge, UK: Cambridge University Press, 2002), 491.

settlements had e0s of 20, 21, 37, and 40.[1634] Chapter 7 estimated Egyptian e0 at 19 years. In nineteenth century Belleville, Canada, prosperous English colonists achieved an e0 of 21 years.[1635] Between Neanderthal prehistory and roughly 1900 CE, e0 was typically 20 to 30 years.[1636] Liverpool workers being below the nadir of these e0s, elites neared the top.

Truncating workers' lives, employers committed murder, believed Engels.[1637] This outcome making laborers' deaths a capital crime, they would evince a Newtonian backlash by retaliating more than during next chapter's French Revolution, he predicted.[1638]

Taller than Brits on average by 1750, preindustrial Americans, evincing nourishment equal to recent times, reached twentieth century developed world heights.[1639] Stature and longevity rose until about 1790, when industry reversed gains.[1640] As in England, inequalities widened, management underpaid workers, and their nutrition, height, and longevity deteriorated. These measures rebounding after roughly 1880, industry deserved no credit. Pasteurization, clean water, sewage treatment and disposal, antisepsis in hospitals, and hygiene in the home improved health.

In 1900 Europe and the United States, "the gap between rich and poor remained enormous."[1641] The poorest 80 percent of Europeans and Americans then totaled less income than the top 20 percent. The poorest 30 percent earned under 10 percent of overall income. The richest 5 percent amassed one third, and the wealthiest quintile half to three fifths, of income.

The business cycle perpetuated inequality, destitution, and desperation. The Panic of 1837 led Cincinnati's unemployed to burn two Ohio River steamships that year in hopes of being hired to build new ones.[1642] Some 33,000 businesses lost around $500 million by 1841 while real estate

---

[1634] Lourdes Marquez Morfin, Robert McCaa, Rebecca Storey, and Andres Del Angel, "Health and Nutrition in Pre-Hispanic Mesoamerica," in *The Backbone of History: Health and Nutrition in the Western Hemisphere*, ed. Richard H. Steckel and Jerome C. Rose (Cambridge, UK: Cambridge University Press, 2002), 312-315.

[1635] Shelley R. Saunders, Ann Herring, Larry Sawchuk, Gerry Boyce, Rob Hoppa, and Susan Klepp, "The Health of the Middle Class: The St. Thomas' Anglican Church Cemetery Project," in *The Backbone of History: Health and Nutrition in the Western Hemisphere*, ed. Richard H. Steckel and Jerome C. Rose (Cambridge, UK: Cambridge University Press, 2002), 146.

[1636] Edward S. Deevey Jr., "The Human Population," *Scientific American* 203, no. 3 (September 1, 1960), 200, 202.

[1637] Engels, 106-107.

[1638] Ibid., 31.

[1639] Fogel, "Nutrition and the Decline in Mortality Since 1700," 466.

[1640] Robert William Fogel, *The Escape from Hunger and Premature Death, 1700-2100: Europe, America, and the Third World* (Cambridge, UK: Cambridge University Press, 2004), 17-19.

[1641] McKay, Hill, Buckler, Crowston, Wiesner-Hanks, and Perry, 681.

[1642] Alasdair Roberts, *America's First Great Depression: Economic Crisis and Political Disorder after the Panic of 1837* (Ithaca, NY and London: Cornell University Press, 2012), 18-19.

and stocks plummeted $1 billion to $6 billion.[1643] Six New Orleans banks failed in January 1842. Its markets unable to sell crops and livestock that year, Chicago hotels and streets emptied out.[1644] British novelist Charles Dickens in 1842 (1812–1870) judged Cairo, Illinois, disappointing hopes for a great metropolis at the Ohio and Mississippi rivers' confluence, "an ugly sepulchre."[1645]

The post-Civil War (1861–1865) years were no better. Roughly 1 million Americans, many reduced to vagrancy, lost work from 1873 to 1878.[1646] Wages and jobs shrinking during depressions from 1882 to 1885 and 1893 to 1898, the economy contracted roughly half the years between 1873 and 1900.

Destitution made laborers rent cellars with 11 occupants per room.[1647] New York City pioneered the tenement, whose "fouler and dreadfuller poverty-smell" American author and editor William Dean Howells (1837–1920), examining "class conflict" and criticizing "poverty and injustice," criticized in 1896.[1648] Visiting a room, he saw "the work-worn look of mothers."[1649] Without toilets, outdoor workers urinated and defecated in vacant spaces.[1650]

Also disenchanted, American author, activist, and "literary lion" Upton Sinclair (1878–1968) wrote almost 100 books without exhausting his critique.[1651] Denouncing the American Dream for duping immigrants into drudgery in the illusion that capitalism rewarded work, he decried "an economic and social system that destroyed millions of lives every year through disease, poverty, and mental torture."[1652]

15.5 Review and Preview

Producing commodities unknown or uncommon in the agrarian era, industry perpetuated inequality. Agricultural and urban inequality intensi-

---

[1643] Ibid., 8, 21-22.

[1644] Ibid., 19.

[1645] Ibid., 14-15.

[1646] Freeman, Lichtenstein, Brier, Bensman, Benson, Brundage, Eynon, Levine, and Palmer, 9-10.

[1647] Alan M. Kraut, *The Huddled Masses: The Immigrant in American Society, 1880-1921* (Arlington Heights, IL: Harlan Davidson, 1982), 70.

[1648] Ibid.; Levy, 295-296; Barbara Ryan, "Howells, William Dean," in *Historical Dictionary of the Gilded Age*, ed. Leonard Schlup and James G. Ryan (Armonk, NY and London: M. E. Sharpe, 2003), 242.

[1649] Kraut, 70.

[1650] Ibid., 71.

[1651] Helis Sikk, "Sinclair, Upton (1878-1968)," in *Reforming America: A Thematic Encyclopedia and Document Collection of the Progressive Era*, vol. 2, ed. Jeffrey A. Johnson (Santa Barbara, CA and Denver, CO: ABC-CLIO, 2017), 592; Anthony Arthur, *Radical Innocent: Upton Sinclair* (New York: Random House, 2006), 3.

[1652] Elliott, 345.

fying class antagonism, next chapter pits French peasants, combating taxes, tithe, and corvée, against secular and ecclesiastic landowners. Urban poor opposing high food prices, the French Revolution executed king, queen, taxmen, landowners, and other elites without ending inequality.

CHAPTER 16 CLASS CONFLICT AND FRENCH REVOLUTION

16.1 Abstract

Hundreds of insurrections predated the French Revolution (1789–1799), which, releasing tensions from centuries of inequality, "challenged the old order of monarchs and aristocrats."[1653] A gulf separating rich and poor, taxes overburdened farmhands and laborers. France dividing citizens into nobility, clergy, and everyone else, only the third paid yearly taxes. No less burdensome, the third had to tithe money or produce to churches and monasteries. Peasants opposing taxes, tithe, and corvée and urbanites denouncing high food prices, the revolution executed elites like king, queen, taxmen, and landowners, though inequality persisted.

The French Revolution typified the Newtonian backlash through "class struggle."[1654] Although German economists Karl Marx (1818–1883) and Friedrich Engels (1820–1895) viewed class conflict as urban because factories impoverished workers, France's tumult engulfed the countryside, where farmworkers resented landowners. Like chapter 18's Russian Revolution and chapter 19's Chinese Revolution, it involved peasants over workmen.

[1653] Myles Lavan, "Writing Revolt in the Early Roman Empire," in *The Routledge History Handbook of Medieval Revolt*, ed. Justine Firnhaber-Baker and Dirk Schoenaers (London and New York: Routledge, 2017), 19; John Watts, "Conclusion," in *The Routledge History Handbook of Medieval Revolt*, ed. Justine Firnhaber-Baker and Dirk Schoenaers (London and New York: Routledge, 2017), 371; John P. McKay, Bennett D. Hill, John Buckler, Clare Haru Crowston, Merry E. Wiesner-Hanks, and Joe Perry, *Understanding Western Society: A Brief History* (Boston and New York: Bedford/St. Martin's, 2012), 582.
[1654] Mortimer Chambers, Raymond Grew, David Herlihy, Theodore K. Rabb, and Isser Woloch, *The Western Experience, Vol. III: The Modern Era*, 4th ed. (New York: Knopf, 1987), 731.

16.2 Revolutionary Discontent

16.2.1 Inequality as Basis for Discontent

16.2.1.1 The Poor

France's economy before and during the cataclysm was agrarian, like those reviewed in chapters 5 to 14. Grievances concerned food production, distribution, price, taxation, and ownership. Landowners, publicans, and churchmen oppressed farmhands. Urbanites were harmed by inflation, speculators, and *laissez faire* indifference to their plight.

Europe's most populous polity, France added 5 to 6 million people around 1720 to 1789. Meanwhile, grain output stagnated and sometimes diminished[1655] and job openings stagnated as well.[1656] The situation was a Malthusian trap, an illustration of the problem identified by English demographer and cleric Thomas Malthus (1766–1834) who argued that humans produce more children than farms can feed.[1657] War, famine, and disease kill excess.[1658]

France avoided chapter 13's famine and pandemic that depopulated Europe in the fourteenth century, though food prices rose 65 percent whereas wages increased 22 percent as population grew from 1764 to 1789.[1659] By the second date, wheat bread, which only the wealthy afforded, devoured 60 to 80 percent of income. Most Frenchmen subsisted on less expensive rye, often mixed with barley.

Cheaper options included potatoes,. As elsewhere in Europe, France was slow to adopt the tuber. Erroneously fearing leprosy, seventeenth century Burgundy outlawed it.[1660] Against fear and irrationality, French pharmacist Antoine-Augustin Parmentier (1737–1813) promoted its healthfulness, though France heeded him only in the nineteenth century.[1661]

Chestnuts sustained France's poorest on hills too steep to plow. Mountains on the border with Spain and in the center and east had trees whose

---

[1655] McKay, Hill, Buckler, Crowston, Wiesner-Hanks, and Perry, 582; Olwen Hufton, "Social Conflict and the Grain Supply in Eighteenth-Century France," *Journal of Interdisciplinary History* 14, no. 2 (Autumn 1983): 303.

[1656] Chambers, Grew, Herlihy, Rabb, and Woloch, 731.

[1657] Thomas Malthus, *An Essay on the Principle of Population* (Amherst, NY: Prometheus Books, 1998), 13-14.

[1658] Ibid., 100, 139-140; Peter Farb, *Ecology*, rev. ed. (New York: Time, 1967), 167-169.

[1659] Hufton, 304.

[1660] "White Potato," in *The Cambridge World History of Food*, vol. 2, ed. Kenneth F. Kiple and Kriemhild Conee Ornelas (Cambridge, UK: Cambridge University Press, 2000), 1879.

[1661] Sylvia A. Johnson, *Tomatoes, Potatoes, Corn, and Beans: How the Foods of the Americas Changed Eating around the World* (New York: Atheneum Books, 1997), 76-77; Ellen Messer, "Potatoes (White)," in *The Cambridge World History of Food*, vol. 1, ed. Kenneth F. Kiple and Kriemhild Conee Ornelas (Cambridge, UK: Cambridge University Press, 2000), 191-192.

chestnuts, added to flour to extend bread, sustained families up to half a year.[1662] This meager diet produced the shortest, ricketiest, least suitable men for conscription.[1663]

Eighteenth century undernutrition replacing fourteenth century starvation, harvests were inadequate in the 1760s, early 1770s, and after 1785.[1664] In 1772, for example, over 82 percent of Brittany's population subsisted on cabbage stalks and grass.[1665] During the 1780s, around one third of Frenchmen consumed under 1,800 calories daily, intake below current U.S. recommendations for men, even when the harvest was satisfactory.[1666] Without labor-savers like automobiles, the eighteenth century demanded more exertion and food. Undernutrition sentenced the masses to lifelong hunger and resentment toward the few who ate well.

16.2.1.2 The Rich

Among these few, "Sun King" Louis XIV (1638–1715) epitomized plenitude.[1667] A typical supper featured four soups, pheasant, partridge, mutton, ham, salad, pastry, fruit, and confection. Emulating him, other elites hosted feasts with "hundreds of dishes."[1668] Queen Marie Antoinette (1755–1793), "icon of an exquisite but doomed social order," traveled with chefs and husband Louis XVI (1754–1793), "awkward, secluded and retiring," was overweight from youth.[1669]

The divide between mass privation and elite satiation grew after roughly 1750 as officials, landowners, and merchants, abandoning belief in food as communal resource, adopted last chapter's capitalism, which commodified everything.[1670] Affording food, the rich ate while the rest hungered. Food's

---

[1662] Antoinette Fauve-Chamoux, "Chestnuts," in *The Cambridge World History of Food*, vol. 1, ed. Kenneth F. Kiple and Kriemhild Conee Ornelas (Cambridge, UK: Cambridge University Press, 2000), 359; Hufton, 305.

[1663] Hufton, 308.

[1664] Ibid., 327.

[1665] Robert Ergang, *Europe: From the Renaissance to Waterloo* (Boston: D. C. Heath, 1967), 629.

[1666] Hufton, 305; "Estimated Calorie Needs Per Day by Age, Gender, and Physical Activity Level," USDA, November 30, 2011, accessed August 25, 2022, ‹EstimatedCalorieNeedsPerDayTable.pdf (azureedge.us).›

[1667] Albert M. Craig, William A. Graham, Donald Kagan, Steven Ozment, and Frank M. Turner, *The Heritage of World Civilizations, Vol. II: Since 1500* (New York: Macmillan, 1986), 654; Meaghan Trewin, "Cuisine, Customs and Character: Culinary Tradition and Innovation in Eighteenth Century France" (master's thesis, Queen's University, 2009), accessed March 27, 2022, ‹UVic Thesis Template,› 15.

[1668] Trewin, 3.

[1669] Dana Meachen Rau, *Who Was Marie Antoinette?* (New York: Grosset & Dunlap, 2015), 2, 26; Simon Schama, *Citizen: A Chronicle of the French Revolution* (New York: Knopf, 1989), 213; Caroline Weber, *Queen of Fashion: What Marie Antoinette Wore to the Revolution* (New York: Henry Holt, 2006), 2.

[1670] Hufton, 315.

commodification began not around 1750, however, but millennia earlier when Neolithic cities separated consumer from producer.

Abjuring responsibility to curb inflation, the crown irked consumers by endorsing *laissez faire* in 1764, 1774, and 1776.[1671] Refusal to tame the market presaged revolution by depriving government of popular support as Frenchmen, perceiving government as speculators' abettor, hated both.

16.2.2 Inequality as Product of Elite Oppression of the Masses

Inequality and unhappiness were not happenstance but inevitable wherever elites oppressed underlings. Like other agrarian economies, France bifurcated into few landowners and the destitute multitude.[1672] Many Frenchmen thought God decreed hierarchy, which only malcontents or atheists dared subvert.

Secular and religious landowners parasitized farmworkers, 60 to 85 percent of whom rented insufficient land for subsistence.[1673] The problem worsening over time, four Basse Auvergne villages in south-central France, for example, had 490 farms under 2.5 acres in 1700 and 870 in 1792 while rent tripled.[1674] Poverty made villagers seek extra work on large estates, migrate to cities during winter to toil for wealthy families, or join last chapter's putting-out system.

By the revolution, Basse Auvergne and central France, surrendering one quarter of the harvest as rent, lost the entire surplus, which previous chapters estimated at 10 percent during premodern times, plus 15 percent.[1675] Peasants had to borrow food at interest from landowners who had taken it. Under 0.4 percent of population, churchmen took 8 percent of grain as tithe, which, varying throughout France, averaged 7.5 rather than 10 percent of the harvest.[1676] "Taxpayers hated the tithe," emphasized American historian Robin Winks (1930–2003) and colleagues.[1677] Rather than dirty their hands, bishops and abbots farmed collection to secular landowners and merchants. Rent, tithe, and tax takers sold grain amid inflation while peasants hungered.

In northern and Mediterranean France, inequality was manifest as landowners, specializing in grapes for wine and olives for oil, hired day laborers

---

[1671] Ibid., 318.

[1672] Karen Diane Haywood, *The French Revolution: The Power of the People* (New York: Lucent Press, 2017), 16.

[1673] Hufton, 311.

[1674] Ibid., 308.

[1675] Ibid., 311.

[1676] Ibid., 310; Ergang, 625.

[1677] Robin W. Winks, Crane Brinton, John B. Christopher, and Robert Lee Wolff, *A History of Civilization, Vol. II: 1648 to the Present*, 7th ed. (Englewood Cliffs, NJ: Prentice Hall, 1988), 484.

who earned only wages, had to buy food, feared inflation, and joined urbanites in attacking tax, tithe, and rent collectors and speculators.[1678] For example, southwestern France's Riberac rioted in 1739 upon learning a woman was selling grain to nearby Nontron amid shortage that raised prices there.[1679] Riots recurred in 1770 under similar circumstances.[1680]

Promising to pay their court challenges, large farmers organized medium and smallholders against the tithe after 1760.[1681] Animus against the church, which amassed wealth during the Middle Ages and whose bishops and abbots avoided privation, thus permeated all classes.

16.3 Hierarchy and Taxation

16.3.1 Commoners

As discussed in chapter 12, in late antiquity Franks settled Gaul, part of which became France during the Middle Ages, when their descendants, beginning to centralize, divided into three groups, termed orders or estates, corresponding to medieval society's division into worshipers, fighters, and workers.

The third and largest estate, commoners, about 27.5 million of France's 28 million denizens in 1789, funded state and church through taxes and tithe.[1682] Taxes, tithe, and feudal fees took three fifths of the harvest, averred American historian Robert Ergang (1898–1978), though in some regions corvée replaced these payments.[1683] This estimate ruinous given 10 percent surplus, *Eternal Inequality* doubts "primitive" French farming could have survived this confiscation.[1684] Sixty percent of the harvest's seizure exceeded the 48 percent tax rate in Sumer and the 20 percent Hebrews were levied by pharaoh. China's taxes decreased from 15–20 percent of the harvest in the fourteenth century CE to 5 percent in the eighteenth century. France surely struggled to collect taxes, tithe, and feudal fees amid evasion. With different occupations, education, and outlook, commoners were no class. Although most farmed, a few were urban lawyers, merchants, and officials who often had more education and income than farmworkers.

[1678] Hufton, 306-307, 309.
[1679] Ibid., 314.
[1680] Ibid., 324.
[1681] Ibid., 328.
[1682] Ibid., 331; McKay Hill, Buckler, Crowston, Wiesner-Hanks, and Perry, 584.
[1683] Ergang, 630.
[1684] Ibid., 628.

16.3.2 Nobles and Clergy

The second and second largest estate, nobles approximated 400,000 members in 1789, owned 20 to 25 percent of land, and seldom paid taxes.[1685] Provoking opposition, desperate kings sometimes tried to tax them to fund their opulence and wars. Like commoners, aristocrats, whose wealth and outlook varied, were no class. Traditionalists retained the premodern emphasis on land as status symbol, though others, investing in mining and trade, held mercantile values.

The first and smallest estate, clergy approximated 100,000 members— under 1,000 being bishops and abbots—and 10 to 15 percent of land in 1789.[1686] Although sixteenth century Protestantism won converts, Catholicism remained France's state religion. Absent land confiscation, churches and monasteries, paying government a "voluntary gift" every fifth year, remained rich.[1687] Their ostentation angered commoners, whose tithe enriched institutions that needed no help. Like the first two groups, the clergy was heterogeneous. Privileged from birth, bishops and abbots lived well whereas parish priests, having humble origins, shared parishioners' dislike of luxury and idleness.

Dividing people within each group, riches and rank united those atop the aristocracy and clergy because nobles filled senior church offices.[1688] Uninterested in serving God and humanity, they owned vast acreage, socialized with king, queen, and other royals, and collected "fat incomes."[1689]

16.3.3 Divide and Rule

Disunity within each estate benefited elites, who avoided widespread backlash while exploiting everyone else by keeping their opponents too suspicious of one another to unify. Divide and rule failing, however, the monarchy's opponents united against taxation and absolutism.[1690] The two intertwining, kings claimed absolute power to tax. But authoritarianism failed without other elites' consent.

Weaker and less successful than the English crown in raising revenues, medieval French kings struggled against nobles who opposed taxes, a recur-

---

[1685] McKay, Hill, Buckler, Crowston, Wiesner-Hanks, and Perry, 584; Haywood, 17; Winks, Brinton, Christopher, and Wolff, 484.
[1686] McKay, Hill, Buckler, Crowston, Wiesner-Hanks, and Perry, 584; Haywood, 17; Winks, Brinton, Christopher, and Wolff, 484.
[1687] McKay, Hill, Buckler, Crowston, Wiesner-Hanks, and Perry, 584.
[1688] Ergang, 625-626.
[1689] Haywood, 17.
[1690] Ibid.

rent problem.[1691] The Hundred Years' War (1337–1453) belatedly led French sovereigns to create an agency to collect taxes and manage the treasury.

They thereafter made progress. Victory in the war strengthening nationalism, the sixteenth century crown gave to the papacy the first year's income of French bishops and abbots in exchange for the right to appoint them.[1692] Withstanding the Reformation and religious wars, the state–church alliance benefited kings under administrators like Cardinal Armand Jean du Plessis, Duke of Richelieu (1585–1642).[1693] Royal power peaked under Louis XIV despite extravagance and war.[1694] He never convened the Estates General, whose three groups were overviewed in the last section, France's national debt exceeded 3 billion livres at his death.[1695]

His successors aimed to emulate him. Refusal to share power excluded the Estates General, though it was conservative by design. Although most numerous, commoners had one vote.[1696] The clergy and nobility, each with one vote despite representing far fewer Frenchmen, together outvoted commoners. The Estates General thus favored stasis, which benefited monarch, nobles, bishops, and abbots.

Moreover, it was conservative because members, all men, had wealth, connections, and status to win election.[1697] Absent from the Estates General, farmhands, workmen, and vagrants could not shape its agenda, though they were the most numerous commoners, suffered the worst inequality, and needed forums for expressing discontent.

Historians once considered the revolution a reaction against feudalism whereby wealthy commoners favored capitalism and resented nobles' refusal to deem them equals.[1698] No matter how rich, merchants and professionals remained commoners unable to enter the aristocracy.

This viewpoint ceded to the recognition that rich commoners and nobles shared values that allied them.[1699] The former bought land, lived as nobles had for centuries, and became indistinguishable from them. Seeking power, rich commoners and aristocrats united against royal aspirations to autocracy.

[1691] McKay, Hill, Buckler, Crowston, Wiesner-Hanks, and Perry, 233-234.
[1692] Ibid., 334, 377.
[1693] Ibid., 458.
[1694] Craig, Graham, Kagan, Ozment, and Turner, 654.
[1695] Ergang, 616.
[1696] Haywood, 30.
[1697] Ibid., 23.
[1698] McKay, Hill, Buckler, Crowston, Wiesner-Hanks, and Perry, 584-585.
[1699] Ibid.

16.4 Debt

Absolutism required frugality or enough income that a despot needed nothing from the wealthiest citizens. Neither happened, and wars' expense burdened Louis XIV's successors. Taxes unpopular, France borrowed money; by the 1780s half government revenues paid interest on the debt.[1700]

Needing money, the monarchy might have broadened the tax base. Increasing debt, the War of Austrian Succession (1740–1748) spurred Louis XV (1710–1774), Louis XIV's great grandson, down this path.[1701] Like his predecessors, Louis XV believed he needed consult nobody before imposing taxes. In 1748 he announced 5 percent tax on everyone, a variant of chapter 13's poll tax.

The king backtracked when nobles, bishops, abbots, and Paris Parlement, the city's highest court, objected, though, raising taxes during the Seven Years' War (1756–1763), he tried to continue them afterwards, again irritating elites.[1702] Parlement forbade new taxes without its consent. Gaining the advantage in 1768, lawyer and chancellor Rene de Maupeou (1714–1792) replaced contrary judges with loyalists and taxed everyone.

When Louis died, son Louis XVI became king. Marie Antoinette welcomed "the tenderness and eagerness of the poor people, who, in spite of the taxes which oppress them, were carried away with joy on seeing us."[1703] Popularity waned as wastefulness made her "Madame Deficit," though she, probably not especially prodigal, behaved as elites always had.[1704] Tradition blaming her for urging Parisians unable to afford bread to eat cake, Louis XIV's wife may have uttered the remark.[1705] Paupers downgraded to potatoes or chestnuts rather than upgraded to cake.

Marie's husband dismissed Maupeou to placate advisers.[1706] Against England, France supported colonial America during the American Revolution (1775–1783). The treasury empty, Louis XVI's finance minister, hoping to tax land, urged his convening an assembly of notables to gain support for the initiative.[1707] It instead urged approval from the Estates General, which last met in 1614. Louis rejected the recommendation, decreed the tax, and disbanded the assembly and Parlement when they objected.

[1700] Ibid., 588.
[1701] Ibid., 585-586; Ergang, 616-617.
[1702] McKay, Hill, Buckler, Crowston, Wiesner-Hanks, and Perry, 586.
[1703] Rau, 44.
[1704] Haywood, 18.
[1705] Rau, 72.
[1706] McKay, Hill, Buckler, Crowston, Wiesner-Hanks, and Perry, 586.
[1707] Ibid., 588.

16.5 Revolution

16.5.1 Estates General

Nationwide indignation led Louis in July 1788, however, to announce elections for the Estates General, which would meet in spring 1789.[1708] Although unhappy, he expected neither reform nor revolution.[1709] Moreover, he and other elites ignored the dismal 1788 harvest, one of several before the revolution, as noted.

Paris authorities requisitioned grain but the Seine River froze, that winter, preventing shipment.[1710] Marie Antoinette enjoyed sleigh rides "while the vast majority of the city's inhabitants shivered and starved."[1711] Bread prices, doubling by spring 1789, slashed demand for nonessentials. Businesses responded by discharging workers. Workers and the jobless, targeting elites in April attacked Réveillon, a wallpaper maker with wealthy clients. Smoldering in the countryside since the 1760s, class warfare divided Paris, other cities, and towns as consumers protested inflation into May.[1712]

Inflaming tensions, "priest, political theorist, and major figure in the revolution" Emmanuel Joseph Sieyès (1748–1836) denounced nobles as "a foreign parasite" in a January 1789 pamphlet that circulated roughly 30,000 copies by May.[1713] France's backbone, commoners created wealth and paid taxes, tithe, and rent, he wrote.

That month the Estates General met in Versailles, where king and queen resided.[1714] Disdaining bishops and abbots, clergy had elected parish priests as delegates.[1715] About two thirds of nobles favored stasis whereas the rest wanted reform. Commoners electing lawyers and officials, nobody represented beggars and farmworkers.

This mix of conservatives, progressives, and no obvious champion of paupers presaged neither reform nor revolution. Delegates could not even

---

[1708] Ibid.

[1709] Winks, Brinton, Christopher, and Wolff, 487.

[1710] Ibid.

[1711] Nancy Goldstone, *In the Shadow of the Empress: The Defiant Lives of Maria Theresa, Mother of Marie Antoinette, and Her Daughters* (New York: Little, Brown, 2021), 328-329.

[1712] McKay, Hill, Buckler, Crowston, Wiesner-Hanks, and Perry, 590-591.

[1713] Ibid., 590; Emmanuel Joseph Sieyès, "The Middle Class Sought Increased Political Rights," in *The French Revolution*, ed. Laura K. Egendorf (San Diego: Greenhaven Press, 2004), 47; Jennifer Llewellyn and Steve Thompson, "Emmanuel Sieyès," Alpha History, last modified March 24, 2022, accessed March 27, 2022, ‹Emmanuel Sieyès (alphahistory.com).›

[1714] Winks, Brinton, Christopher, and Wolff, 487.

[1715] McKay, Hill, Buckler, Crowston, Wiesner-Hanks, and Perry, 588.

agree on voting.[1716] Most priests and nobles favored the tradition of one vote per estate, though commoners wanted one vote per delegate. Deadlock led them in June to refuse discussions until priests and nobles accepted their demand.

16.5.2 National Assembly

Sieyès urged commoners on June 17 to proclaim themselves the National Assembly and invite the others to join.[1717] Most priests acceded while nobles refused. When Louis denied the assembly its room, members, meeting at a tennis court on June 20, vowed not to dissolve before writing a constitution that required everybody, including elites, to obey the same laws and that granted everyone basic rights.[1718] Such reforms would fulfill the Enlightenment, an eighteenth century philosophical, literary, and scientific movement, and align France with England.

Promising reform on June 23, the king, intending to dismiss the assembly, recalled 18,000 to 20,000 troops.[1719] Four days later, doubting soldiers' loyalty, he instead encouraged holdouts to join the other delegates. Louis' inability to crush reformers marked the revolution's birth, asserted Winks and coauthors. Rather than an event or date, this chapter originates the revolution in farm and urban grievances.

From Versailles, revolution revisited Paris. Fearing soldiers were approaching to kill demonstrators, Parisians, gathering weapons, stormed the Bastille prison on July 14 for gunpowder and more arms.[1720] Guards slaughtering 98 attackers, survivors broke the gate and killed the warden. Next day, officer, aristocrat, and "Hero of Two Worlds" Marquis de Lafayette (1757–1834), who had joined the American Revolution, assumed command of Paris.[1721]

Like chapter 13's English Peasants' Revolt, French farmhands destroyed chateaux and tax and tithe records in summer 1789, refused to pay taxes and tithe, and seized land that owners wanted to enclose.[1722] The assembly ended feudal fees, tithe, and corvée on August 4. Its Declaration of the Rights of

---

[1716] Ibid., 589; Haywood, 30.

[1717] Winks, Brinton, Christopher, and Wolff, 487.

[1718] McKay, Hill, Buckler, Crowston, Wiesner-Hanks, and Perry, 588-599.

[1719] Ibid., 590; Chambers, Grew, Herlihy, Rabb, and Woloch, 734; Winks, Brinton, Christopher, and Wolff, 488.

[1720] McKay, Hill, Buckler, Crowston, Wiesner-Hanks, and Perry, 591-592; Rau, 76.

[1721] JoAnn A. Grote, *Lafayette: French Freedom Fighter* (Philadelphia: Chelsea House Publishing, 2001), 63.

[1722] McKay, Hill, Buckler, Crowston, Wiesner-Hanks, and Perry, 592; Ergang, 629; Chambers, Grew, Herlihy, Rabb, and Woloch, 734.

Man and of the Citizen (1789) stated that all men were born free with equal rights.

Like the U.S. Declaration of Independence (1776), France's statement expressed aspiration over actuality, ignored blacks and women, and benefited neither poor nor hungry as unemployment increased.[1723] Freeing no slaves, it sparked chapter 14's Haitian Revolution (1791–1804).

Without the tithe, churches and monasteries rebuffed the poor, hungry, and jobless.[1724] Some 7,000 women with scythes, pikes, pitchforks, guns, and sticks marched 12 miles from Paris to Versailles on October 5 to demand royal help.[1725] Entering the assembly, one silenced the delegates. Parisians wanted bread not rhetoric. Exhibiting class antagonism, this confrontation exposed the assembly's inability or unwillingness to institute meaningful reform.

Intent on murdering the queen, the women, killing guards who challenged them, searched the palace for her.[1726] She might have perished without intervention from Lafayette, an aristocrat unwilling to sacrifice a peer. With the king, queen, and assembly moving to Paris, delegates established a constitutional monarchy, ended nobility as a legal status, nationalized church property, and abolished monasteries.[1727]

These changes, while long overdue, still excluded women, who could neither vote nor hold office.[1728] Moreover, church land's nationalization ignored farmworkers because government sold it in units too large for them to afford. Buying land, speculators divided it into small plots for resale. Only this step accommodated peasants.

Louis accepting these reforms in September 1791, "the Incorruptible" lawyer and delegate Maximilien Robespierre (1758–1794) declared the revolution done.[1729] Resigning an early judicial appointment because he opposed capital punishment, Robespierre would lead the revolution during a bloody period.[1730] Advocating rights for women, Jews, and free blacks, he remained

---

[1723] Ian Davidson, *The French Revolution: From Enlightenment to Tyranny* (New York and London: Pegasus Books, 2016), 36.

[1724] McKay, Hill, Buckler, Crowston, Wiesner-Hanks, and Perry, 592.

[1725] Ibid.; Rau, 80-81.

[1726] McKay, Hill, Buckler, Crowston, Wiesner-Hanks, and Perry, 593-594.

[1727] Ibid.; Rau, 84.

[1728] McKay, Hill, Buckler, Crowston, Wiesner-Hanks, and Perry, 594.

[1729] Ibid., 596; Tom McGowen, *Robespierre and the French Revolution in World History* (Berkeley Heights, NJ: Enslow Publishers, 2000), 68.

[1730] Ergang, 670.

silent about slavery.[1731] This imperfect progressivism vanished during the revolution as violence consumed the "apostle of terror."[1732]

16.5.3 Legislative Assembly

Convening in October, the Legislative Assembly faced threats. Initially welcoming upheaval for weakening a rival, European and American plutocrats became uneasy as violence escalated. Their concern intensified in June 1791, when peasants apprehended the king and queen as they fled France.[1733] Marie Antoinette's Austrian birth and lineage led Austria, with ally Prussia, that August to declare Louis France's rightful ruler. That winter the queen begged Europe's royalty to rescue her and him by invading France.

Eager to strike first, the assembly declared war against Austria in April 1792.[1734] Honoring its alliance, Prussia reinforced Austria against French troops, who fled the battlefield. Had the two advanced, they might have captured Paris, where the assembly called everyone to arms. Prussia and Austria halting, Parisians attacked the Tuileries palace August 10, killed guards and servants, destroyed furnishings, took jewels, and discarded royal belongings in the street.[1735]

King and queen fled to the assembly, which, jailing them, scheduled elections for the National Convention, which would convene September 21 to form a new government.[1736] Anarchy pervading the interim, lawyer, orator, and "revolutionary hothead" Georges Danton (1759–1794) advocated "boldness, more boldness, always boldness."[1737]

Parisians created informal courts from September 2 to 7 to sentence and execute over 1,000 unfortunates.[1738] Many were prostitutes and priests whose transgressions were trifling or imaginary. Others were aristocrats whose death class warfare demanded. Savagery reached its nadir at the torture, rape, execution, and corpse mutilation of an Italian noblewoman and ally of Marie Antoinette.[1739]

[1731] Chambers, Grew, Herlihy, Rabb, and Woloch, 749.

[1732] Ergang, 670.

[1733] McKay, Hill, Buckler, Crowston, Wiesner-Hanks, and Perry, 597; Rau, 88-91.

[1734] McKay, Hill, Buckler, Crowston, Wiesner-Hanks, and Perry, 597-598.

[1735] Ibid.; Rau, 91-92.

[1736] McKay, Hill, Buckler, Crowston, Wiesner-Hanks, and Perry, 598; Winks, Brinton, Christopher, and Wolff, 492.

[1737] Winks, Brinton, Christopher, and Wolff, 493; Jeremy D. Popkin, *A New World Begins: The History of the French Revolution* (New York: Basic Books, 2019), 302.

[1738] Winks, Brinton, Christopher, and Wolff, 493.

[1739] Ibid.; Melanie Clegg, "The Death of the Princess de Lamballe," Madame Guillotine, September 3, 2012, accessed June 12, 2022, ‹The death of the Princesse de Lamballe - Madame Guillotine.›

16.5.4 National Convention

Elections empowered two groups: Girondins and the Mountain.[1740] Both prosecuting Louis for treason, only the Mountain, led by Robespierre and Danton, favored his execution. Guillotining king and queen in 1793, class warfare intensified violence against crises, real or illusory.

Outside France, its army encouraged revolution, ended feudalism, and exiled plutocrats.[1741] Victory over Prussia in September 1792's Battle of Valmy put the French on offense. Europe's peasantry initially welcoming them as liberators, their practice of taking food stoked hatred. With enemies throughout Europe by February 1793, France conscripted farmhands, who resisted, especially in the west.

External foes and domestic unrest heightened tension between Girondins and Mountain, which encouraged workers to disrupt the convention that June.[1742] Using the disturbance to arrest 29 Girondins, the Mountain governed. Controlling the Committee of Public Safety, Robespierre, implementing "an embryonic emergency socialism," gave indigents bread and jobs, mostly in armaments manufacture.[1743] Besides these measures, the convention in 1794 ended slavery, though general and emperor Napoleon Bonaparte (1769–1821), "an alien monster" to critics, would reinstate it.[1744]

Labeling opponents "enemies of the nation" and defining "terror [as] nothing more than prompt, severe inflexible justice," Robespierre jailed up to 400,000 men and women and killed some 40,000.[1745] Western France's Nantes drowned hundreds of prisoners and priests in the Loire River. Despite contrary claims, the revolution executed more farmhands and workmen than nobles, bishops, and abbots.[1746]

Enlarging the search for enemies, Robespierre purged anyone whose loyalty might waver.[1747] The decapitation of Danton in April 1794 disquieted other delegates. In May, the Reign of Terror beheaded "chemist of genius,"

[1740] McKay, Hill, Buckler, Crowston, Wiesner-Hanks, and Perry, 598; Winks, Brinton, Christopher, and Wolff, 492-493.

[1741] McKay, Hill, Buckler, Crowston, Wiesner-Hanks, and Perry, 598.

[1742] Ibid., 599.

[1743] Ibid., 600.

[1744] Thomas Piketty, *Capital and Ideology*, trans. Arthur Goldhammer (Cambridge, MA and London: Belknap Press of Harvard University Press, 2020), 213; Adam Zamoyski, *Napoleon: A Life* (New York: Basic Books, 2018), xiv.

[1745] McKay, Hill, Buckler, Crowston, Wiesner-Hanks, and Perry, 600-601; Chambers, Grew, Herlihy, Rabb, and Woloch, 751.

[1746] Alexander Mikaberidze, "The Reign of Terror," in *World History Encyclopedia, Vol. 15, Era 7: The Age of Revolutions, 1750-1914*, ed. James H. Overfield, Alfred J. Andrea, and Carolyn Neel (Santa Barbara, CA: ABC-CLIO, 2011), 429.

[1747] Winks, Brinton, Christopher, and Wolff, 497.

aristocrat, and taxman Antoine Lavoisier (1743–1794).[1748] "It took but a moment to cut off that head, though a hundred years perhaps will be required to produce another like it," stated Italy's Joseph-Louis Lagrange (1736–1813), "the greatest mathematician of the eighteenth century," in expressing the dismay of intellectuals and class war's opponents.[1749]

Denouncing and executing Robespierre in July's Thermidorian reaction, conservatives let priests celebrate mass, though without tithe or government funding.[1750] Committed to *laissez faire*, conservatives, ending price controls, caused inflation to approach 1,000 percent. Hungry indigents protested inflation throughout 1795. Banning demonstrations, government ordered soldiers to kill protestors.[1751] Abandoning activism, the underclass reengaged during next chapter's revolutions.

16.5.5 Directory and Napoleon

Defeating the backlash against elites and inequality, the 1795 constitution moved right. Its five-member executive, termed the directory, disenfranchised the poorest quartile of population.[1752] Only wealthy landowners held office.

Conservatives having proved no better than moderates or progressives at assuaging hunger, the 1795 harvest, worse than in 1788, 1789, and 1793, threatened famine.[1753] Exposing the revolution's failure to uplift the downtrodden and reduce inequality, suicide and overall mortality rose.

Sick of unrest, elites, wanting stability through absolutism, abolished the directory and appointed Napoleon first consul of the republic in 1799.[1754] The title alluded to chapter 8's Roman Republic, whose highest office was consul. The position combining lawgiver and executive, Rome denied one man total authority by annually electing two, each able to veto the other. Pretending to honor this precedent, Napoleon consulted two other consuls, but they lacked power.[1755] Believing "effective government required a dictator," he crowned himself emperor in 1804.[1756]

[1748] Henry Guerlac, "Lavoisier, Antoine-Laurent," in *Dictionary of Scientific Biography, Vol. 8: Jonathan Homer Lane-Pierre Joseph Macquer*, ed. Charles Coulson Gillispie (New York: Charles Scribner's Sons, 1981), 66.

[1749] Bernard Jaffe, *Crucible: The Story of Chemistry: From Ancient Alchemy to Nuclear Fission*, 4th ed. (New York: Dover Publications, 1976), 71; W. W. Rouse Ball, *A Short Account of the History of Mathematics* (New York: Dover Publications, 1960), 330-331.

[1750] Winks, Brinton, Christopher, and Wolff, 497.

[1751] McKay, Hill, Buckler, Crowston, Wiesner-Hanks, and Perry, 604.

[1752] Winks, Brinton, Christopher, and Wolff, 497.

[1753] Chambers, Grew, Herlihy, Rabb, and Woloch, 759-760.

[1754] McKay, Hill, Buckler, Crowston, Wiesner-Hanks, and Perry, 605.

[1755] Winks, Brinton, Christopher, and Wolff, 500-501.

[1756] Zamoyski, 244.

His legal reforms, the Code Napoleon, feigned legal equality for all, though he despised equality while styling himself "the 'father of the poor.'"[1757] "Aristocracy always exists," he stated.[1758] "Destroy it in the nobility, it removes itself to the rich and powerful houses of the middle class." Private property being inviolable, he tried to reimpose slavery, as mentioned. Outlawing free speech, press, and expression, he permitted torture, executed innocent people, banned strikes and labor unions, and let management coerce labor.[1759] Despite wanting to rid agriculture of government, he conscripted peasants for endless wars.

16.6 Review and Preview

The French Revolution originating in rural distress, misery intensified when poor harvests priced food beyond commoners. Attacking feudal privileges, despotism, aristocracy, corvée, tithe, rent, and taxes, the revolution, leaving inequality for next chapter's nineteenth century revolutions and revolutionary thought, anticipated twentieth century revolutions in chapter 18's Russia and chapter 19's China.

[1757] McKay, Hill, Buckler, Crowston, Wiesner-Hanks, and Perry, 605; D. M. G. Sutherland, *France, 1789-1815: Revolution and Counterrevolution* (New York and Oxford: Oxford University Press, 1986), 435.

[1758] Winks, Brinton, Christopher, and Wolff, 501.

[1759] Ibid.; Chambers, Grew, Herlihy, Rabb, and Woloch, 768; Robert W. Strayer, Edwin Hirschmann, Robert B. Marks, Robert J. Smith, James J. Horn, and Lynn H. Parsons, *The Making of the Modern World: Connected Histories, Divergent Paths (1500 to the Present)* (New York: St. Martin's Press, 1989), 78.

Chapter 17 Revolutions and Revolutionary Thought

17.1 Abstract

The French Revolution (1789–1799) influenced revolutions in 1830 and 1848. Paris' government between 1789 and 1795 inspired the 1871 commune. Workers and intellectuals challenged wealth, power, privilege, monarchy, and capitalism. Learning from the French Revolution, intellectuals promoted socialism and communism. German economist Friedrich Engels (1820–1895) expected the proletarian upheaval to be deadlier than the French Revolution. Opposing socialism and communism, Social Darwinists defended inequality as natural, inevitable, and desirable.

17.2 Socialism

17.2.1 Early Socialism

Chapter 15's capitalists defended inequality, which critics thought unfair. Chapters 12 and 13's medieval reformers criticized wealth as unchristian. Secularists grappled with inequality as religion waned in modernity. Socialists and communists blamed inequality on private property, which profited owners whereas workers, with only their labor to sell, remained poor.

American historian John McKay (b. 1948) and coauthors thought socialism, "the radical new doctrine after 1815," an outgrowth of the French Revolution and dissatisfaction with capitalism and industry.[1760] This chro-

---

[1760] John P. McKay, Bennett D. Hill, John Buckler, Clare Haru Crowston, Merry E. Wiesner-Hanks, and Joe Perry, *Understanding Western Society: A Brief History* (Boston and New York: Bedford/St. Martin's, 2012), 652.

nology omitted chapter 6's Greek philosopher Plato (c. 428–c. 348 BCE), who advocated in *Republic* (c. 380 BCE) socialism's central feature, communal property. Chapter 12's Essenes and monks also held property in common. Besides them, Jerusalem's Christians, selling property, gave indigents the money.[1761]

From these origins, socialism entered modernity. In *Utopia* (1516), English chancellor, lawyer, Christian saint, and "above all a social reformer" Thomas More (1478–1535), fretting about inequality's increase during his life, combined Platonism and Christianity.[1762] Borrowing from Plato, he faulted greed for inequality and offered egalitarianism as an alternative.[1763] The book's title, meaning a nonexistent place, implies More knew such a society was impossible.

Equality being so elusive, German eschatologist and Protestant reformer Thomas Muntzer (c. 1490–1525), believing himself "inspired by God," declared the apocalypse near and exhorted farmhands, as God's elect, to seize property in a 1524 and 1525 "proletarian revolution."[1764] Initially sympathetic, German theologian and Protestant reformer Martin Luther (1483–1546), supposing "God had called him to be his prophet," branded Muntzer "the arch-devil" and urged their obliteration.[1765] Denouncing peasant, but encouraging elite, violence, Luther proved chapter 1's assertion of its unidirectionality. Despite execution, Muntzer influenced Engels and German economist Karl Marx (1818–1883), treated later.

17.2.2 Nineteenth Century Socialism

Advocating the "greatest happiness of the greatest number," socialist French nobleman Henri de Saint-Simon (1760–1825) traced his ancestry to Carolingian king and "Father of Europe" Charlemagne (c. 747–814).[1766]

[1761] Acts 2:44-45.

[1762] Thomas Fleming, *Socialism* (New York: Marshall Cavendish, 2008), 23; Daniel W. Hollis III, *The ABC-CLIO World History Companion to Utopian Movements* (Santa Barbara, CA: ABC-CLIO, 1998), 252; Thomas Cahill, *Heretics and Heroes: How Renaissance Artists and Reformation Priests Created Our World* (New York: Doubleday, 2013), 212.

[1763] Fleming, 23; Plato, *Phaedo*, in *Great Dialogues of Plato*, trans. W. H. D. Rouse (New York and Scarborough, ON: New American Library, 1956), 469.

[1764] Fleming, 21; Heiko A. Oberman, *Luther: Man between God and the Devil*, trans. Eileen Walliser-Schwarzbart (New Haven, CT and London: Yale University Press, 1989), 64; Eric Metaxas, *Martin Luther: The Man Who Rediscovered God and Changed the World* (New York: Viking, 2017), 331; Eric Vuillard, *The War of the Poor*, trans. Mark Polizzotti (New York: Other Press, 2019), 52.

[1765] Robert Ergang, *Europe: From the Renaissance to Waterloo* (Boston: D. C. Heath, 1967), 192; Oberman, 18; Heinz Schilling, *Martin Luther: Rebel in an Age of Upheaval*, trans. Rona Johnston (Oxford: Oxford University Press, 2017), 1.

[1766] Robin W. Winks, Crane Brinton, John B. Christopher, and Robert Lee Wolff, *A History of Civilization, Vol. II: 1648 to the Present*, 7th ed. (Englewood Cliffs, NJ: Prentice Hall, 1988),

Although this background might have made him elitist, Saint-Simon wanted to uplift indigents. Plato, Christianity, More, and the American Revolution as inspiration, he envisioned a society with a parliament of improvements led by industrialists, artists, scientists, philosophers, and mathematicians. *Republic* identified philosophers as worthy of ruling a city and mathematics as integral to their training.[1767] Christianity's golden rule required that parliament benefit paupers.[1768] Logic persuading people to adopt his reforms without coercion, Saint-Simon expected transition to equality would be rapid and peaceful.

Saint-Simon's compatriot, philosopher Charles Fourier (1772–1837), favoring cooperation over competition, deemed capitalism "chaotic anarchy" after observing a Lyon textile mill's noise and squalor.[1769] Noting an apple cost one hundredfold more in Paris than the countryside, he experienced insight he likened to English polymath and "most influential figure in the history of Western science" Isaac Newton's (1643–1727) intuition of the law of gravity when an apple supposedly fell on him from a tree.[1770]

Aiming to be socialism's Newton, Fourier advocated land's division into 400-acre plots, each with 500 to 2,000 people.[1771] Workers receiving five twelfths of the land's wealth, managers four twelfths (one third), and investors the rest (one fourth), this allocation gave labor the most for creating wealth and investors the least for contributing only capital. The hardest, most dangerous jobs would command greatest pay. Promoting chapter 2's sociality, Fourier wanted everyone to inhabit one dormitory per plot.

Saint-Simon and Fourier's contemporary Welsh businessman and "founder of British socialism" Robert Owen (1771–1858) bought a Scottish textile mill in 1800.[1772] Like Fourier, Owen disliked industry's impoverishment of workers. Determined to correlate profit with worker satisfaction, he raised pay, shortened the workday to 10.5 hours, improved housing, closed the town's worst taverns, and lowered alcohol's price and potency. Prefer-

---

559-560; Keith Taylor, *The Political Ideas of the Utopian Socialists* (London: Frank Cass, 1982), 54; Dominique T. Hoche, "Charlemagne," in *Icons of the Middle Ages: Rulers, Writers, Rebels, and Saints*, vol. 1, ed. Lister M. Matheson (Santa Barbara, CA: Greenwood Press, 2012), 144.

[1767] Plato, *Republic*, in *Great Dialogues of Plato*, trans. W. H. D. Rouse (New York and Scarborough, ON: New American Library, 1956), 173, 323-324.

[1768] Winks, Brinton, Christopher, and Wolff, 560.

[1769] Ibid; Taylor, 110; Hollis, 258.

[1770] John Simmons, *The Scientific 100: A Ranking of the Most Influential Scientists, Past and Present* (Secaucus, NJ: Citadel Press, 1996), 3.

[1771] Winks, Brinton, Christopher, and Wolff, 560.

[1772] Winks, Brinton, Christopher, and Wolff, 561; Alan Ebenstein, William Ebenstein, and Edwin Fogelman, *Today's Isms: Socialism, Capitalism, Fascism, Communism, and Libertarianism*, 11th ed. (Upper Saddle River, NJ: Prentice Hall, 2000), 4-5.

ring gradualism over revolution, he wanted employees to take pride in their work rather than stoke class warfare.

Hiring nobody under age 10 whereas the former owner employed orphans at six, Owen let children attend school and study at home.[1773] He favored self-guided study, as had the introduction and chapter 1's Swiss philosopher Jean-Jacques Rousseau (1712–1778), and vocational training. Funding education, not managing the economy, government made graduates masters of their fate. Education thus spared its creating jobs or dispensing welfare, a proposal that combined socialism and *laissez faire*.

Revisiting France, historian, reformer, and "philosopher of socialism" Louis Blanc (1811–1882) criticized a society whose newspapers reported that children froze to death without sparking outrage at such neglect.[1774] Since only government had the authority and wealth to spare paupers this fate, he urged it to buy factories and equipment and pay fair wages. Once a factory was stabilized, government would transfer ownership to workers, who would share profits. Outcompeting capitalist firms, these businesses would create socialism over time. As these factories came to dominate society, workers would constitute nearly the entire population and inequality and classes would disappear.

A compatriot of Blanc, socialist and anarchist Pierre-Joseph Proudhon (1809–1865), understanding that "class conflict was rife" and attacking private property as theft, declared it "physically and mathematically impossible."[1775] This opinion, which he tried to make a geometric proof, resembles an attempt to deny malaria's existence, though unpleasantries cannot be wished away.

17.3 The 1830 Revolution

As noted, socialism infiltrated France, where general and emperor Napoleon Bonaparte (1769–1821) ended the French Revolution. Austria, Prussia, Russia, Spain, and Britain defeated his armies in 1814 and 1815, reinstated the monarchy, and appointed Louis XVIII (1755–1824), a younger brother of

---

[1773] Winks, Brinton, Christopher, and Wolff, 561.; Ebenstein, Ebenstein, and Fogelman, 4-5.

[1774] Winks, Brinton, Christopher, and Wolff, 561-562; Leo A. Loubere, *Louis Blanc: His Life and His Contribution to the Rise of French Jacobin-Socialism* (Westport, CT: Greenwood Press, 1961), 31.

[1775] P. J. Proudhon, *What Is Property?: An Inquiry into the Principle of Right and of Government, Chapter IV: That Property Is Impossible*, Project Gutenberg, last modified February 4, 2013, accessed March 31, 2022, ‹What is Property?, by P. J. Proudhon (gutenberg.org);› Paul Kelly, Rod Dacombe, John Farndon, A. S. Hodson, Jesper Johnson, Niall Kishtainy, James Meadway, Anca Pusca, and Marcus Weeks. *The Little Book of Politics* (London: DK, 2020), 115.

Louis XVI (1754–1793), king without French input.[1776] Under him, fewer than 100,000 of France's roughly 30 million citizens could vote.[1777]

Louis XVIII's death made younger brother Charles X (1757–1836) king.[1778] More undemocratic than Louis, he denied freedom of the press, disbanded the legislature, and shrank the franchise on July 25, 1830. Parisians stormed city hall from July 27 to 29 while farmhands declared the right to graze livestock on royal land. Charles fleeing to England, revolutionary leaders tried to govern.

Wanting a republic with universal suffrage, the most democratic reformers supported last chapter's officer and aristocrat Marquis de Lafayette (1757–1834).[1779] Opposite them, conservatives proposed a constitutional monarchy that enfranchised only the wealthy. Between the two, moderates esteemed aristocrat Louis Philippe (1773–1850), who had commanded an army division during last chapter's Battle of Valmy (1792). Feigning enthusiasm for a republic, he secured Lafayette's endorsement, became king in 1830, and disappointed reformers by enfranchising only about 166,000 men in 1831.

Northeast of France, Brussels students protested Dutch rule of Belgium in August 1830.[1780] Underpaid, underemployed, and unemployed factory workers joined them. Declaring independence that November, Belgium enfranchised a larger proportion of the population than had France and Britain. The Netherlands, Britain, France, Prussia, Austria, and Russia recognized Belgian independence and neutrality in 1839.

Belgian success led Poles to seek independence from Russia.[1781] Warsaw army cadets revolting in November 1830, leadership passed to Polish landowners less intent on independence than on oppressing serfs. A September 1831 cholera epidemic weakened rebellion that, absent serfs, had shallow support. Imposing martial law and closing universities, Russia ended dissent.

To the southwest, Italy's secret societies, termed *Carbonari*, hoped to unify a peninsula disunited since the Middle Ages.[1782] Controlling northern Italy's Parma and Modena and part of the papal states in 1831, they begged French aid. Without it, their uprising was crushed by Austria. Two years later Austria and Prussia jailed students who hoped to unite Germany.

[1776] Joseph R. Strayer and Hans W. Gatzke, *The Mainstream of Civilization*, 3d ed. (New York: Harcourt Brace Jovanovich, 1979), 542; Winks, Brinton, Christopher, and Wolff, 510.
[1777] Winks, Brinton, Christopher, and Wolff, 527-528.
[1778] Ibid., 528-529; Strayer and Gatzke, 557.
[1779] Winks, Brinton, Christopher, and Wolff, 529.
[1780] Ibid., 529-530.
[1781] Ibid., 530.
[1782] Ibid., 530-531; Strayer and Gatzke, 557-558.

17.4 Communism

17.4.1 Tenets

Germany's fragmentation led Marx and Engels to believe people felt greater allegiance to class than nation.[1783] Whereas chapter 2 grounded sociality in biology, these men thought class aggregated people.[1784] Workers united in awareness of their exploitation by capitalists, whose unity derived from consciousness that they owned the means of production and thus the right to control labor.[1785] Crossing political boundaries, both realizations made the state irrelevant to class conflict, which Marx and Engels regressed into the past. "The history of all hitherto existing society is the history of class struggles," their *Communist Manifesto* (1848) announced.[1786] "Freeman and slave, patrician and plebian, lord and serf, guild-master and journeyman, in a word; oppressor and oppressed, stood in constant opposition to one another."

Obeying chapter 15's "iron law of wages," capitalism pauperized employees, whose wages covered only subsistence plus reproduction to ensure an employer future laborers.[1787] He achieved this aim through laws that protected his interests.[1788] "Political power...is merely the organized power of one class for suppressing another," wrote Marx and Engels.[1789] Fueling class warfare, tension between haves and have-nots propelled humankind toward a final upheaval whereby workers would overthrow capitalists and create a "dictatorship of the proletariat" to nationalize property and abolish class and inequality.[1790]

17.4.2 Communism and Richard Wright

"There'll be no white and no black; there'll be no rich and no poor," the fictional Marxist Jan Erlone said,[1791] predicting a revolution to confiscate

---

[1783] Karl Marx and Friedrich Engels, *Communist Manifesto*, trans. Samuel Moore (Chicago: Great Books Foundation, 1955), 48; Strayer and Gatzke, 590.
[1784] Henry D. Aiken, *The Age of Ideology: The 19th Century Philosophers* (New York: New American Library, 1956), 192.
[1785] Ibid., 188.
[1786] Marx and Engels, 8.
[1787] Ibid., 16, 22; Winks, Brinton, Christopher, and Wolff, 563.
[1788] Marx and Engels, 28.
[1789] Ibid., 34.
[1790] Strayer and Gatzke, 589.
[1791] Richard Wright, *Native Son* (New York: Harper Perennial/Modern Classics, 2005), 68.

wealth. But neither his interlocutor or the actual author of the book was persuaded, judging communism "too simple for belief."[1792]

Yet Wright admired communists for understanding workers better than other reformers did.[1793] Reading Marxist magazines, he learned that the best chance laborers had to surmount misery was by uniting everywhere.[1794] Penury and hunger kept him in the underclass, where an agitator urged everybody to "Read Karl Marx and get the answer, boys."[1795] Wright complied.

The Great Depression (1929–1939) further impoverished him and others.[1796] "Unemployed men loitered in doorways with blank looks in their eyes," he wrote.[1797] Desperation drove Wright to a company that sold burial insurance. It sent him, a literate black, to black neighborhoods to rewrite policies to deny protection while deceiving policyholders into thinking they were receiving an upgrade. Illiterates would detect fraud only upon trying to file a claim.

Such dishonesty pushed Wright toward communism despite believing it oversimplified, an opinion that underrated the *Communist Manifesto*, which made history, a coherent, lawlike narrative rather than a welter, the outcome of class antagonism.[1798] This conviction evinced Marx's debt to German philosopher and historian Georg Wilhelm Friedrich Hegel (1770–1831), who asserted that the "law of history is that the past proceeds rationally."[1799] Making history the stage upon which class conflict unfolded, Marx and Engels predicted capitalism's overthrow, a classless society's creation, and history's end as story of class warfare.[1800] Marxism was thus as utopian as socialism.

17.4.3 Communism v. Socialism

Although some scholars subsume communism within socialism, differences exist. First, socialists wanted government to hold property in common whereas Engels believed the state would "wither away."[1801] Second, as

---

[1792] Richard Wright, *Black Boy (American Hunger): A Record of Childhood and Youth* (New York: HarperCollins, 2005), 296.
[1793] Ibid., 371.
[1794] Ibid., 317–318.
[1795] Ibid., 287.
[1796] Ibid., 287–294.
[1797] Ibid., 288.
[1798] Marx and Engels, 8.
[1799] G. W. F. Hegel, *Reason in History: A General Introduction to the Philosophy of History*, trans. Robert S. Hartman (Indianapolis and New York: Bobbs-Merrill, 1953), 11.
[1800] Marx and Engels, 34.
[1801] Fleming, 15; Strayer and Gatzke, 589.

mentioned, Saint-Simon anticipated peaceful transition to socialism whereas Marx and Engels understood that humans are innately competitive, hierarchical, and violent.

Emphasis on strife aligned with English philosopher Thomas Hobbes (1588–1679) and British naturalist Charles Darwin (1809–1882).[1802] Chapter 1 overviewed Hobbesian inequality and consequent "war of every one against every one."[1803] A later section introduces Darwin. The two emphasized discord between individuals whereas Marx and Engels focused on classes, which shaped behavior and thus group conflict.

17.4.4 Karl Marx and Georg Hegel

Elaborating the manifesto's ideas in *Kapital* (1867), Marx completed only the first of three volumes before his death.[1804] Like its predecessor, *Kapital* applied Hegel's dialectic to history. As noted, Hegel believed reason actuated history. In responding to circumstances, people generated ideas, each of which led critics to formulate an antithesis.[1805] Wanting to resolve contradiction, onlookers harmonized opposites with a new thesis.

Marx replaced this emphasis on ideas with the reality of wealth and destitution. The thesis, magnates generated and exploited their antithesis, workers who owned only their labor, as mentioned.[1806] Only revolution could reconcile these opposites by creating a classless society.

Kapital detailed labor's exploitation. Affirming English economist David Ricardo (1772–1823), Marx believed labor created all wealth.[1807] Like Proudhon, Marx defined profit as "surplus value" that employers took from workers.[1808]

Besides labor, management took what employees produced.[1809] Like labor, a product belonged to workers because they created it, averred English philosopher John Locke (1632–1704).[1810] Alienating them from work and from

---

[1802] Aiken, 188.

[1803] Thomas Hobbes, *Leviathan* (Oxford and New York: Oxford University Press, 1998), 86.

[1804] Mortimer Chambers, Raymond Grew, David Herlihy, Theodore K. Rabb, and Isser Woloch, *The Western Experience, Vol. III: The Modern Era*, 4th ed. (New York: Knopf, 1987), 933.

[1805] Robert S. Hartman, "Introduction," in *Reason in History: A General Introduction to the Philosophy of History*, G. W. F. Hegel, trans. Robert S. Hartman (Indianapolis and New York: Bobbs-Merrill, 1953), xii.

[1806] Winks, Brinton, Christopher, and Wolff, 562.

[1807] McKay, Hill, Buckler, Crowston, Wiesner-Hanks, and Perry, 654.

[1808] Ibid.; Chambers, Grew, Herlihy, Rabb, and Woloch, 935; V. I. Lenin, "Karl Marx: Part Three," International Communist League, October 2, 2015, accessed March 31, 2022, ‹"Karl Marx" by V.I. Lenin (icl-fi.org).›

[1809] Ebenstein, Ebenstein, and Fogelman, 102.

[1810] Ibid., 3.

---

what they fashioned, this theft deprived laborers of what was theirs and made them "slaves" and "an appendage of the machine."[1811] As this language suggests, autonomy and pleasure's loss dehumanized them and made work drudgery. Intensifying inequality, the factory contrasted management's wealth and power against labor's penury and impotence.[1812]

This knowledge prompted Marx to join the 1848 Paris revolution, examined next.[1813] Its failure led him next year to London, where his reputation discouraged employers from hiring him.[1814] Privation beset Marx and killed three of his children. Undeterred, he helped found the 1864 First International Workmen's Association, which disbanded in 1876.

17.5 The 1848 Revolution

17.5.1 Overview

Conveying energy and urgency, the manifesto announced, coincided with, but little influenced the 1848 revolution, asserted American historian Robin Winks (1930–2003) and colleagues.[1815] Russian American scholar Serge Levitsky, however, credited it with "driving people to the barricades."[1816]

Misfortune afflicted the 1840s.[1817] Ireland's potato crop failing in 1845 and 1846, at least 1 million denizens starved.[1818] Hunger stalked northern Europe's poorest, who afforded little but potatoes. The inadequate 1846 grain harvest exacerbated undernutrition. Trouble spreading beyond agriculture, around 500,000 French railroad employees lost work in 1847.[1819] Mines and factories also shed laborers. Those employed resented inability to unionize or protest poor wages and working conditions.

[1811] Ibid., 102; Marx and Engels, 16-17.

[1812] Marx and Engels, 17.

[1813] Aiken, 185.

[1814] Winks, Brinton, Christopher, and Wolff, 564; Jacques Barzun, *Darwin, Marx, Wagner: Critique of a Heritage*, 2d ed. (Chicago and London: University of Chicago Press, 1981), 130.

[1815] Winks, Brinton, Christopher, and Wolff, 564; Marx and Engels, 7.

[1816] Serge L. Levitsky, "Introduction," in *Das Kapital: A Critique of Political Economy*, Karl Marx, ed. Frederick Engels (Washington, DC: Regnery Gateway, 1996), xv.

[1817] Winks, Brinton, Christopher, and Wolff, 532.

[1818] Gail L. Schumann and Cleora J. D'Arcy, *Hungry Planet: Stories of Plant Diseases* (St. Paul, MN: American Phytopathological Society, 2012), 12; Jessie I. Wood, "Three Billion Dollars a Year," in *Plant Diseases: The Yearbook of Agriculture, 1953*, ed. Alfred Stefferud (Washington, DC: GPO, 1953), 6.

[1819] Winks, Brinton, Christopher, and Wolff, 532.

17.5.2 France

Despite a ban against demonstrations, Parisians rioted February 22 and 23, 1848.[1820] Troops killed or wounded over 50 protestors, enraging workers, the jobless, journalists, and activists. Philippe abdicating February 24, the provisional government created a position for Blanc in hopes of placating reformers as unemployment and unrest worsened. Attempting to reduce unemployment by creating jobs, government increased the number of desperate people by drawing vagrants to Paris.

France's April 1848 election, Europe's first to enfranchise all men, disappointed reformers.[1821] France's sizable rural population made peasants the largest voting bloc. Opposing socialists' desire for communal property, those who owed, or aspired to own, land elected conservatives.

Repudiating the election, reformers disrupted the national assembly, which arrested them and required the jobless to join the army or accept farm work.[1822] From June 23 to 26, Paris' poorest, including unemployed railroad men and dockworkers, rioted in modernity's first widespread "class warfare," stated Winks and coauthors.[1823]

General Louis-Eugene Cavaignac's (1802–1857) soldiers killed or wounded over 10,000 protestors and sent another 10,000 to North African colony Algeria.[1824] Declaring an emergency, he outlawed all socialist organizations and newspapers. That November the assembly, upholding private property, rejected reformers' demand that government hire all jobless. Next month, voters elected Napoleon Bonaparte's nephew Charles Louis Napoleon Bonaparte (1808–1873) president. Disappointing reformers, he declared himself emperor Napoleon III in 1852.

17.5.3 Germany

Revolutionaries promoted nationalism in Italy and Germany, neither a nation then.[1825] German peasants disliking feudal obligations, urbanites feared competition for jobs. Having adopted the potato, Germans hungered when blight struck. Newspapers advised consumption of insects and stale bread, which sated better than fresh.[1826] Farmhands, workmen, businessmen,

---

[1820] Ibid., 533; McKay, Hill, Buckler, Crowston, Wiesner-Hanks, and Perry, 664-665.
[1821] Winks, Brinton, Christopher, and Wolff, 533.
[1822] Ibid.
[1823] Ibid.
[1824] Ibid., 533-534; McKay, Hill, Buckler, Crowston, Wiesner-Hanks, and Perry, 666.
[1825] Winks, Brinton, Christopher, and Wolff, 534-535.
[1826] Martin Gregor-Dellin, *Richard Wagner: His Life, His Work, His Century*, trans. J. Maxwell Brownjohn (San Diego: Harcourt Brace Jovanovich, 1983), 147.

and professors pursued diverse aims. Not all pitying indigents, for example, businessmen hoped to end internal tariffs by unifying Germany.

Demonstrations began March 1848 in western Germany, where reformers monitored French events.[1827] Mid-March protests spread east to Prussia's capital Berlin. Skirmishes between soldiers and protestors killing over 200, Prussian king Frederick William IV (1795–1861) urged calm. Entering the royal palace, survivors made him pledge reforms, including a constitution. That May delegates, representing the rich and intellectuals, met in Frankfurt on the Main River and modeled a draft after the U.S. Constitution. Frederick rejected it despite his promise.

In Saxony, German composer Richard Wagner (1813–1883), "the single most important phenomenon in the artistic life of the latter nineteenth century," was an erratic revolutionary.[1828] Initially fearing revolution might jeopardize government funding of the theater, he, changing course in June 1848, published a poem against landowners and laws that protected them.[1829] Although he may not have read the *Communist Manifesto*, he condemned equality and communism later that month, denounced greed and usury as misery's causes, and proposed to eliminate money and nobility while preserving the crown.

A newspaper anonymously published these ideas, which Wagner disavowed when suspicion pinpointed him as author, though by July he hoped revolution might reinvigorate art, music, and drama, all of which he aimed to unite.[1830] An anonymous essayist for a progressive newspaper in October, he faulted inequality for impoverishing peasants and workers.[1831] Befriending Russian anarchist Mikhail Bakunin (1814–1876), "the smoldering-eyed revolutionary," in May 1849 and aiming "to bring revolution wherever I go," Wagner made bombs for detonation in Saxony's capital Dresden, reported soldiers' deployment for the revolution's leaders, and fled a warrant to Switzerland.[1832]

17.5.4 Habsburg Empire

South of Germany, Habsburg kings confronted protests in Austria, Hungary, Bohemia, and northern Italy.[1833] Hungarian peasants disliked

---

[1827] Winks, Brinton, Christopher, and Wolff, 535.

[1828] Joseph Machlis, *The Enjoyment of Music: An Introduction to Perceptive Listening* (New York: Norton, 1955), 220.

[1829] Gregor-Dellin, 146-149.

[1830] Ibid., 149, 153; Machlis, 226.

[1831] Gregor-Dellin, 158.

[1832] Ibid., 163, 166; Barzun, 230; Ted Libbey, *The NPR Listener's Encyclopedia of Classical Music* (New York: Workman Publishing, 2006), 940.

[1833] Winks, Brinton, Christopher, and Wolff, 536-537; Strayer and Gatzke, 563-565.

corvée, taxes, and serfdom. Ending the third in March 1848, Hungary required taxes from everyone irrespective of rank.

Monitoring Hungary, university students and the jobless in Vienna, Austria, revolted March 12.[1834] Ending corvée that September, Vienna lawmakers weakened reform as peasants, achieving their aim, withdrew from activism. In October Austria's army killed Viennese protestors and their leaders.

June 1848 demonstrations racking Prague, now the Czech Republic's capital. Authorities declared martial law, and Austrian soldiers shelled the city.[1835] Sending troops to Hungary and offering to reinforce Austria's army, Russian czar and "stern defender of monarchical legitimacy" Nicholas I (1796–1855) boasted "of delivering Europe from constitutional governments."[1836]

17.6 Social Darwinism

17.6.1 Overview of Darwinism

During these events, England incubated revolution. Studying animals and plants while circumnavigating earth from 1831 to 1836, Darwin came to reject the longstanding belief that species remain constant.[1837] Instead, they evolve by natural selection.[1838] As organisms compete for scarce resources, those best adapted to their surroundings have the greatest chance of amassing enough to sustain themselves and offspring. Maladapted organisms are at a disadvantage. This "struggle for existence" modifies populations through differential survival and reproduction to create new species over time.[1839]

17.6.2 Social Darwinism

17.6.2.1 Overview

Darwinism complemented Marxism, capitalism, and industry. Admiring Darwin, Marx and Engels believed their rigor, making communism "scientific socialism," elevated them above "social quacks" who misunderstood

---

[1834] Winks, Brinton, Christopher, and Wolff, 537.
[1835] Ibid.
[1836] Ibid.; Rosina Beckman, ed., *The History of Russia from 1801 to the Present* (New York: Britannica, 2019), 13.
[1837] Ernst Mayr, *The Growth of Biological Thought: Diversity, Evolution, and Inheritance* (Cambridge, MA and London: Belknap Press of Harvard University Press, 1982), 397-398.
[1838] Charles Darwin, *The Origin of Species by Means of Natural Selection or the Preservation of Favored Races in the Struggle for Life* (New York: Modern Library, 1993), 87-108.
[1839] Ibid., 90-91.

workers and perpetuated inequality.[1840] Designating Marx "the Darwin of sociology," Engels expected their dialectic to revolutionize history as natural selection had biology.[1841]

Despite widespread interest in his ideas, Darwin never applied them outside biology. Reluctant even to extend natural selection to humankind for fear of religious backlash, he allotted us one sentence in *The Origin of Species* (1859), "one of the most famous and influential books of all time," but the implications became obvious as Darwinism merged with capitalism after 1880.[1842] Winning the competition for wealth, plutocrats outranked everyone else such that inequality was natural, inevitable, and desirable. Conservatives cautioned government against derailing progress by helping paupers.

17.6.2.2 Herbert Spencer and Social Darwinism

These ideas transcending Darwinism, German American biologist Ernst Mayr (1904–2005), "one of the founders of modern neo-Darwinism," replaced the label Social Darwinism with "social Spencerism" to identify their originator, British philosopher and "apostle of evolution" Herbert Spencer (1820–1903).[1843] "The individuals best adapted to the conditions of their existence shall prosper most, and the individuals least adapted to the conditions of their existence shall prosper least," wrote Spencer.[1844] Opposing socialism and welfare, he believed "the ultimate result of shielding men from folly is to fill the world with fools."[1845]

Yet he judged compassion and love evolutionary products that put humans above other animals.[1846] These qualities complementing Darwinism, the individual rather than government should practice them. Most Social Darwinists, however, omitted them from their vision of economy and society, leaving only "unmerciful competition" to define human interactions.[1847]

[1840] Robert W. Strayer, Edwin Hirschmann, Robert B. Marks, Robert J. Smith, James J. Horn, and Lynn H. Parsons, *The Making of the Modern World: Connected Histories, Divergent Paths (1500 to the Present)* (New York: St. Martin's Press, 1989), 58-59; Strayer and Gatzke, 589; Friedrich Engels, "Preface," in *Communist Manifesto*, Karl Marx and Friedrich Engels, trans. Samuel Moore (Chicago: Great Books Foundation, 1955), 4-5.

[1841] Engels, 5; Barzun, 169.

[1842] Darwin, 647; Robert Jurmain, Lynn Kilgore, Wenda Trevathan, and Russell L. Ciochon, *Introduction to Physical Anthropology*, 2013-2014 ed. (Belmont, CA: Wadsworth Cengage Learning, 2014), 37; Mayr, 598; Peter H. Raven and George B. Johnson, *Biology*, 2d ed. (St. Louis: Times Mirror/Mosby College Publishing, 1989), 7; Stephen Jay Gould, *Ever Since Darwin: Reflections in Natural History* (New York and London: Norton, 1977), 24-27.

[1843] Mayr, 883; Aiken, 16; Simmons, 304.

[1844] Winks, Brinton, Christopher, and Wolff, 570.

[1845] Ibid.; Aiken, 167-168.

[1846] Winks, Brinton, Christopher, and Wolff, 570.

[1847] Mayr, 883.

Extending Mayr's critique of the appellation Social Darwinism, the adjective "economic" might replace "social" to yield economic Spencerism because capitalism is an economic system. Yet Spencer included morality, politics, and epistemology in economics.[1848] This breadth acknowledged that economic matters transcend economics. His opinion that science was the only path to knowledge defined and circumscribed his epistemology. His belief that philosophy could reconcile science and religion offered hope to a skeptical age. Although Social Darwinism is an imperfect name, no other moniker better encapsulates the modification and movement of Darwin's ideas beyond biology.

17.6.2.3 Social Darwinism and Racism

Shaping Europe and the United States, Social Darwinists identified competition between not only individuals but races.[1849] As a construct, race may be configured many ways, including by skin color.

Social Darwinists considering war the supreme competition, Europeans supposedly demonstrated superiority by vanquishing Africans, Amerindians, Asians, and Australians and creating colonies.[1850] Endorsing South Africa's apartheid and blacks' "serf-like status," British "imperialist and capitalist adventurer" Cecil Rhodes (1853–1902), ranking Anglo-Saxons the best race, envisioned their world domination.[1851]

Disagreeing that a master race was sure to triumph, French nobleman Joseph-Arthur de Gobineau (1816–1882), judging only whites "capable of creative thinking and civilization building," warned that brown and black people outbred them.[1852] Ranking Scandinavians first, he dreaded their replacement by underlings who would doom civilization. Especially sinister, miscegenation allegedly tainted Nordic blood. Civilization required inequality to prevent such contamination.

These opinions influenced Latin America, especially Mexico and Brazil, where Europeans governed darker people.[1853] Fearing further darkening, authorities encouraged European immigration to lighten and supposedly

---

[1848] Aiken, 162-164.

[1849] Winks, Brinton, Christopher, and Wolff, 570-571; Robert B. Marks, *The Origins of the Modern World: A Global and Environmental Narrative from the Fifteenth to the Twenty-First Century*, 4th ed. (Lanham, MD: Rowman & Littlefield, 2020), 171-172; Robert M. Crunden, *A Brief History of American Culture* (Armonk, NY and London: North Castle Books, 1994), 129-131.

[1850] Winks, Brinton, Christopher, and Wolff, 571.

[1851] Ibid., 571; Brian Roberts, *Cecil Rhodes: Flawed Colossus* (New York and London: Norton, 1987), xiii, 194-195.

[1852] Winks, Brinton, Christopher, and Wolff, 571; John P. Jackson Jr. and Nadine M. Weidman, *Race, Racism, and Science: Social Impact and Interaction* (New Brunswick, NJ and London: Rutgers University Press, 2006), 107.

[1853] Marks, 172.

improve future generations. Sketched later, eugenics—a pseudo-science invented by Darwin's cousin British polymath Francis Galton (1822–1911), who envisioned "a genetic utopia"—attempted to guide human reproduction and future evolution.[1854]

17.6.2.4 Social Darwinism in the United States

Social Darwinism fused with puritanism and capitalism in the United States.[1855] As a sign of success, wealth indicated God's favor and adaptation to the environment. Inequality his will, stated chapter 1's English lawyer and first Massachusetts Bay Colony governor John Winthrop (1588–1649), desire for egalitarianism disobeyed him. Taxation should not transfer income from the elect to failures who deserved God's disfavor. Charity was equally misguided. Like nature, the economy, purging weaklings, vindicated the strong.

"Light came in as a flood and all was clear," remarked Scottish American industrialist and "staunch social Darwinist" Andrew Carnegie (1835–1919) upon reading Spencer.[1856] Carnegie was not alone in embracing Social Darwinism. "To make money honestly is to preach the gospel," enthused American Baptist minister Russell Conwell (1843–1925), who believed the United States afforded unprecedented opportunities.[1857] Loathing "the inequities and injustices in the American socioeconomic system," however, American author Jack London (1876–1916) likened Social Darwinism to *laissez faire* callousness.[1858]

17.6.2.5 Social Darwinism, Eugenics, and Their Critics

Even in the nineteenth century, inequality's pseudo-scientific defense faced opposition as Social Darwinism merged with eugenics.[1859] Galton hoped to spare indigents lifelong misery by breeding them out of existence. If only winners reproduced, inequality would diminish or disappear by eliminating losers. Society could thereby lessen or eradicate underemployment, unemployment, starvation, poverty, stupidity, sloth, insanity, and crime. Because failures seldom choose chastity, government must prevent their

---

[1854] Ibid., 134; Mayr, 623; Nicholas Wright Gillham, *A Life of Sir Francis Galton: From African Exploration to the Birth of Eugenics* (Oxford: Oxford University Press, 2001), 1.

[1855] Crunden, 129-133.

[1856] Harold C. Livesay, *Andrew Carnegie and the Rise of Big Business* (New York: HarperCollins*Publishers*, 1975), 74; Charles F. Howlett, "Carnegie, Andrew," in *Historical Dictionary of the Gilded Age*, ed. Leonard Schlup and James G. Ryan (Armonk, NY and London: M. E. Sharpe, 2003), 79.

[1857] Crunden, 133.

[1858] Jack London, *War of the Classes* (New York: Regent Press, 1905), 18; Earle Labor, *Jack London: An American Life* (New York: Farrar, Straus and Giroux, 2013), xiii.

[1859] Winks, Brinton, Christopher, and Wolff, 570; Mayr, 623.

reproduction. This logic led Britain, the United States, and Germany to sterilize criminals, the mentally ill, and idiots. The holocaust discredited eugenics.

17.7 Paris Commune

Attempting to replicate Paris' 1789 to 1795 government, the 1871 commune followed the Franco–Prussian War (1870–1871), which originated in Prussian statesman Otto von Bismarck's (1815–1898) desire to strengthen Prussia.[1860] Possibly not intending to unify Germany, he, "a colossal chess player capable of the most daring combinations," confederated lands north of the Main River by 1866.[1861]

Fearing Prussia, Napoleon III's opponents criticized him for not thwarting Bismarck.[1862] Hoping to appease them, Napoleon sought territory in western or southern Germany. Failure led him to declare war on Prussia in 1870, though he, "an incompetent military officer," surrendered himself and his army that September.[1863]

Angry in defeat, Parisians demanded a new government, which continued war with Prussia and its allies.[1864] Besieging Paris, Prussia forced France's January 1871 surrender. Refusing capitulation, Parisians formed a commune. Marx thought it the first successful workers' revolution, though most Parisians, advocating neither socialism nor communism, endorsed private property. Having fought Prussia, they now faced a French army, which ended the commune by killing some 20,000 Parisians in May 1871. Marxism would await the next century.

17.8 Review and Preview

Like last chapter's farmworkers and urbanites, nineteenth century farmhands, workmen, and intellectuals opposed inordinate wealth, power, and privilege. Intellectuals advocating socialism and communism, revolutions erupted in 1830 and 1848, when Marx and Engels described class conflict as inevitable. Although ignoring agrarian class war, they influenced the Russian and Chinese revolutions. As in France and China, next chapter's Russian Revolution was more rural than urban.

[1860] Winks, Brinton, Christopher, and Wolff, 588.
[1861] McKay, Hill, Buckler, Crowston, Wiesner-Hanks, and Perry, 711; Strayer and Gatzke, 608-609; Alan Strauss-Schom, *The Shadow Emperor: A Biography of Napoleon III* (New York: St. Martin's Press, 2018), 360.
[1862] Strayer and Gatzke, 609-610.
[1863] Strauss-Schom, 425.
[1864] Winks, Brinton, Christopher, and Wolff, 587-588.

Chapter 18 Class Conflict and Russian Revolution

18.1 Abstract

The Volga River provided an important trade route in the Middle Ages, connecting the Baltic Sea to the Caspian, enabling commerce between the Scandinavian Varangians in the north and the Byzantine Empire in the south, and the agrarian or semi-nomadic peoples in between. This region, then known as Rus', evolved into the heart of the Russian Empire. Agrarian elites owned land, livestock, crops, slaves, and serfs. Peter the Great converted slaves to serfs in 1723 and serfdom was officially abolished in 1861, although, as elsewhere, the formal change did not translate into an egalitarian system.

A revolution in 1905 failed, but the unrest remained. Ill prepared for war, when World War I (1914–1918) broke out Russia sent peasant soldiers to the front without boots or rifles. They deserted, returned home, and joined the growing tide of discontent. A revolution and a civil war began in 1917. Millions died in the violence and chaos.

Marxists seized government. Women's rights and minority rights were proclaimed, and literacy rates were improved steadily. But Soviet communism continued Russia's authoritarianism and inflamed class warfare.

In the following decades enormous progress was made in industrial and economic growth; but this came at enormous social cost. British author and socialist George Orwell (1903–1950) and Russian American author, philosopher, and *laissez faire* exponent Ayn Rand (1905–1982) criticized the Soviet

Union (USSR) from the left and right. An elitist and "relentless self-server," Rand loathed the USSR's advocating equality.[1865]

Before the revolution, inequality here was modest by global standards and it diminished under communism; it rose again sharply after Gorbachev's "reforms" and the institution of post-USSR capitalism while corruption rose to levels worse than before the revolution.

18.2 Earliest Inequality

Migrating south and east along the Volga River after 700 CE, Scandinavians encountered Finno-Ugric tribes and further south, Turkic farmers and herders.[1866] Appropriating sparsely populated land between the Black Sea in the south and the Baltic Sea in the north, these peoples became a polity known as Rus' around 862 CE, and expanded thereafter east across Eurasia toward the Pacific just as the United States would later elongate west across North America toward the same ocean.

All across European Russia, Siberia and its neighbors, the transition from hunting and gathering to farming and pastoralism perpetuated inequality as it did around the world.

18.3 Rural Inequality

18.3.1 Slavery and Serfdom

Slavery was practiced in the region before Russia became a state.[1867] It antedated the eighth century CE, when Scandinavians identified slaves, a word whose etymology revealed that many were Slavs, as the chief commercial item. Paupers became slaves by surrendering to landowners during famine or unrest.[1868]

Over 34 dismal eighteenth century Russian harvests enslaved 10 percent of population.[1869] Into the nineteenth century one harvest in five was inadequate and one tenth failed. Owners favored men over women 2:1 because farming was arduous.

[1865] William F. Buckley, Jr., *A Torch Kept Lit: Great Lives of the Twentieth Century*, ed. James Rosen (New York: Crown Forum, 2016), 299.

[1866] Robin W. Winks, Crane Brinton, John B. Christopher, and Robert Lee Wolff, *A History of Civilization, Vol. I: Prehistory to 1715*, 7th ed. (Englewood Cliffs, NJ: Prentice Hall, 1988), 160-161; Mark A. Galeotti, *A Short History of Russia: How the World's Largest Country Invented Itself, from the Pagans to Putin* (Toronto, ON: Hanover Square Press, 2020), 22, 24-25.

[1867] Galeotti, 11, 24-25.

[1868] Richard Hellie, "Women and Slavery in Muscovy," *Russian History* 10, no. 2 (1983): 213.

[1869] Ibid., 214-215; Jerome Blum, "Russian Agriculture in the Last 150 Years of Serfdom," *Agricultural History* 34, no. 1 (January 1960): 5.

Slaves outnumbered serfs because landowners could not fix farmhands to land.[1870] Sparse population and abundant land made migration easy. Moreover, Russians moved every few years to find fertile soil, using swidden agriculture or shifting cultivation. In England, France, Germany, and Poland serfs outnumbering slaves after roughly 900 CE; Russia transitioned about three centuries later.[1871]

Evincing bondage's persistence, Kazan, now Tatarstan Republic's largest city, exceeded 60,000 slaves in 1552, though after 1200 owners, requiring corvée and part of the harvest, shackled peasants to land.[1872] Oppression worsening over time, corvée occupied farmworkers four to six days weekly after roughly 1750.[1873]

Russian fur trader Boris Tarasov, American medievalist Joseph Strayer (1904–1987), German American historian Hans Gatzke (1915–1987), American authors Marjorie Gann and Janet Willen, and British scholar Mark Galeotti (b. 1965) equated Russian slavery and serfdom.[1874] Their status hereditary, both could be sold or transferred.[1875] American historian Richard Hellie (1937–2009) judged Russian serfdom "near-slavery" by the eighteenth century.[1876] "The peasant serf was little more than a slave," stated American historian John McKay (b. 1948) and coauthors.[1877] Inflicting injury or death, owners enforced discipline by beating serfs.[1878]

Government, which landowners controlled, made serfdom "the basis of the entire social order."[1879] Russia's "peculiar institution," it resembled U.S. slavery.[1880] "Intensifying serfdom to meet the demand for army recruits, labor,

[1870] Richard Hellie, "Russian Slavery and Serfdom, 1450-1804," in *The Cambridge World History of Slavery*, vol. 3, ed. David Eltis and Stanley L. Engerman (Cambridge, UK and New York: Cambridge University Press, September 28, 2011), accessed April 3, 2022, ‹Russian Slavery and Serfdom, 1450–1804 (Chapter 11) - The Cambridge World History of Slavery.›

[1871] Marjorie Gann and Janet Willen, *Five Thousand Years of Slavery* (Toronto, ON: Tundra Books, 2011), 30; Robert Ergang, *Europe: From the Renaissance to Waterloo* (Boston: D. C. Heath, 1967), 443.

[1872] Galeotti, 80; Ergang, 443; Blum, 3.

[1873] Boris Tarasov, "Serf Russia, the History of People's Slavery," LitNet, last modified November 18, 2020, accessed April 3, 2022, ‹Tarasov Boris. Serf Russia, the history of people's slavery. (samlib.ru.).›

[1874] Ibid.; Gann and Willen, 30; Strayer and Gatzke, 513; Galeotti, 119.

[1875] Galeotti, 119; John P. McKay, Bennett D. Hill, John Buckler, Clare Haru Crowston, Merry E. Wiesner-Hanks, and Joe Perry, *Understanding Western Society: A Brief History* (Boston and New York: Bedford/St. Martin's, 2012), 714.

[1876] Hellie, "Russian Slavery and Serfdom."

[1877] McKay, Hill, Buckler, Crowston, Wiesner-Hanks, and Perry, 714.

[1878] Gann and Willen, 30; Tarasov.

[1879] Blum, 3.

[1880] Roger Bartlett, "Serfdom and State Power in Imperial Russia," *European History Quarterly* 33, no. 1 (2003): 29-64, accessed August 1, 2022, ‹ "Serfdom and State Power in Imperial

and tax revenues," Peter the Great (1672–1725) and his successors, enserfing millions, increased its severity and ubiquity.[1881] He made some 500,000—up to 100,000 died of undernutrition and disease—build St. Petersburg, now Russia's second largest city, in the early eighteenth century.

Among "the most important leaders in Russia's history," Catherine the Great (1729–1796) owned roughly 500,000 serfs while perhaps 2.8 million tilled public lands.[1882] Admiring philosophy and progressivism as abstractions, she widened inequality, exempted landowners from taxes after 1785, and put the entire burden on serfs.[1883] Allowing landowners complete authority, she encouraged "the forces that were making Russia a state built on slavery."[1884] Some 34 million of Russia's 36 million residents were serfs at her death. They exceeded 46 million of Russia's 60 million inhabitants by 1850.[1885]

18.3.2 Emancipation

Symbolizing Russian backwardness, inefficiency, and inequality, serfdom provoked a backlash.[1886] Proclaiming himself czar in 1773, Russian soldier Emelian Pugachev (c. 1740–1775), "a righter of social wrongs," tried to end it, taxation, corvée, and conscription.[1887] Roughly 25,000 serfs, miners, and indigents joined him in "the greatest popular rising of early modern Europe" to ravage southwestern Russia before Catherine amassed an army to obliterate them in 1775.[1888]

Russia" by Roger Bartlett - chriscumo1995@gmail.com - Gmail (google.com).›

[1881] Galeotti, 96; Ergang, 455-456; Lindsey Hughes, "Peter the Great," in *Berkshire Encyclopedia of World History*, vol. 4, ed. William H. McNeill, Jerry H. Bentley, David Christian, David Levinson, J. R. McNeill, Heidi Roupp, and Judith P. Zinsser (Great Barrington, MA: Berkshire Publishing Group, 2005), 1466.

[1882] Galeotti, 129; Lori Feldstein, "Catherine the Great," in *Berkshire Encyclopedia of World History*, vol. 1, ed. William H. McNeill, Jerry H. Bentley, David Christian, David Levinson, J. R. McNeill, Heidi Roupp, and Judith P. Zinsser (Great Barrington, MA: Berkshire Publishing Group, 2005), 309.

[1883] McKay, Hill, Buckler, Crowston, Wiesner-Hanks, and Perry, 512.

[1884] Strayer and Gatzke, 513.

[1885] Galeotti, 156.

[1886] Ibid., 148.

[1887] McKay, Hill, Buckler, Crowston, Wiesner-Hanks, and Perry, 512; Ergang, 527-528; Roger Bartlett, "The Russian Peasantry on the Eve of the French Revolution," *History of European Ideas* 12, no. 3 (1990): 407.

[1888] McKay, Hill, Buckler, Crowston, Wiesner-Hanks, and Perry, 512; Ergang, 527-528; Bartlett, "Serfdom and State Power in Imperial Russia;" Bartlett, "The Russian Peasantry on the Eve of the French Revolution," 406.

Serfs not only paid all taxes but rendered them to landowners whom government made collectors.[1889] Taking taxes, rent, fees, and corvée from serfs, elites were as unpopular as their peers in earlier chapters.

Discussing emancipation with advisors, Nicholas I (1796–1855) concluded it would aggravate not solve problems though, after millennia of unfree labor, it was inevitable in a century that abolished chapter 14's western hemisphere slavery.[1890] Sharing Nicholas' opinion of serfdom's unsustainability, son Alexander II (1818–1881), "the 'Tsar Liberator'" had at age nineteen visited serf hovels.[1891] Combating six revolts monthly on average upon becoming czar in 1855, he granted emancipation in 1861 rather than risk nationwide rebellion, as almost befell Catherine.

The edict pleased nobody. Landowners abhorring any inkling of freedom, serfs resented, first, having to buy land in installments over 49 years.[1892] Second, thinking any price unfair, they believed centuries of drudgery earned them land. Third, wanting all arable land, they decried landowners keeping half. Fourth, serfs disliked village control for stymieing them. Fifth, they had to wait two to five years for freedom.

Revolts throughout 1862 required the army to suppress over one rebellion daily on average.[1893] Rather than solve Russia's rural problems, emancipation perpetuated grievances that fueled future unrest, including the Bolshevik revolution.

18.4 Urban Inequality and Unrest

Like India and China, Russia remained agrarian in modernity. Roughly 97 percent of Russians farmed in 1724, 96 in 1796, and 92 in 1861.[1894] Russia had fewer cities and factories than Britain, France, Germany, Belgium, and the United States, though after 1880 mines increased output of coal to burn

---

[1889] Richard Pevear and Larissa Volokhonsky, "Translator's Note," in Dead Souls, Nikolai Gogol, trans. Richard Pevear and Larissa Volokhonsky (New York: Vintage Classics, 1996), xxiii.

[1890] Galeotti, 154-157.

[1891] David Warnes, Chronicle of the Russian Tsars: The Reign-by-Reign Record of the Rulers of Imperial Russia (London: Thames and Hudson, 1999), 177; James E. Strickler, Russia of the Tsars (San Diego: Lucent Books, 1998), 57.

[1892] Galeotti, 156-157; McKay, Hill, Buckler, Crowston, Wiesner-Hanks, and Perry, 714.

[1893] Galeotti, 157.

[1894] Ibid., 119; Blum, 3.

for heat, the steam engine, and electricity.[1895] Stimulating industry, railroad mileage doubled from 1894 to 1904 to over 35,000.[1896]

Russia industrializing with cheap labor, real wages fell in the 1890s while the economy expanded 5 percent annually.[1897] Killing perhaps 500,000 Russians, the 1891 to 1892 famine spiked food prices. Slums, where violence frightened police, swelled cities. Hungry, angry urbanites wanted revolution. Snubbing them, government supported an 11-hour workday in 1897 whereas laborers sought reduction to eight.[1898]

These problems led St. Petersburg intellectuals, including lawyer Vladimir Lenin (1870–1924) who "developed Marxism in a practical context and changed the course of the 20th century," in 1898 to form the Social Democratic Party, which issued a newspaper two years later.[1899] Heeding German economists Karl Marx (1818–1883) and Friedrich Engels (1820–1895), they organized urbanites to lead the revolution.

Non-Marxists organized farmhands, that is, almost all Russians.[1900] Understanding rural aspirations, these revolutionaries advocated land redistribution. Pursuing domestic terrorism, they assassinated several officials from 1902 to 1907.

Government hoped war would unite Russia, but defeat against Japan sparked the 1905 revolution, which Lenin deemed prelude to 1917.[1901] Moderates hoped to petition Nicholas II (1868–1918) for a constitution that guaranteed civil rights, including legal equality. Denouncing reform, Nicholas planted a secret police officer in a St. Petersburg factory to weaken workers' rights by organizing a sham union. Instead, he led them in January 1905 to the winter palace. Loyal to country, church, and czar, protestors carried icons and photographs of Nicholas. Soldiers nonetheless killed roughly 1,000 demonstrators.

Reform's failure intensified tension between peasants and workmen at one pole and elites at the other.[1902] Aiming to govern St. Petersburg through the first workers' assembly (soviet), printers struck in October to halt

---

[1895] Robin W. Winks, Crane Brinton, John B. Christopher, and Robert Lee Wolff, *A History of Civilization, Vol. II: 1648 to the Present*, 7th ed. (Englewood Cliffs, NJ: Prentice Hall, 1988), 622.

[1896] Ibid.; McKay, Hill, Buckler, Crowston, Wiesner-Hanks, and Perry, 715.

[1897] Galeotti, 160-161

[1898] Winks, Brinton, Christopher, and Wolff, *A History of Civilization, Vol II*, 622; Martyn Oliver, *History of Philosophy: Great Thinkers from 600 B.C. to the Present Day* (New York: Barnes & Noble, 1999), 108.

[1899] Winks, Brinton, Christopher, and Wolff, *A History of Civilization, Vol II*.

[1900] Ibid.

[1901] Ibid., 623-624; Galeotti, 161-162.

[1902] Winks, Brinton, Christopher, and Wolff, *A History of Civilization, Vol II*, 624-625.

newspaper publication and cripple communication. Joining them, railroad workers stopped traffic. St. Petersburg's isolation from the rest of Russia made Nicholas promise civil rights and a national legislature, the duma.

18.5 The Duma, Reform, and World War I

Although Nicholas disbanded the duma in July 1906 when it demanded reform, "highly intelligent and conservative" nobleman and interior minister Peter Stolypin (1862–1911) grasped the need to appease farmhands.[1903] As mentioned, emancipation empowered villages rather than individuals, a policy he ended in 1906. Roughly one quarter of farmworkers, about 9 million people, detached land from village authority by 1917. This success worried Lenin, who feared content peasants would abandon revolution.

Opposing further reform, Nicholas dissolved the second duma in June 1907 and weighted future dumas against peasants and toward landowners.[1904] The conservative third duma (1907–1912) and fourth (1912–1917) supported the czar against reformers who, gaining nothing more from government, could revolt or acquiesce.

Hoping to stimulate nationalism and salvage his popularity, Nicholas, understanding "next to nothing about military matters," entered World War I in 1914.[1905] As in previous wars, the army tried to maintain order by elevating landowning officers over peasant conscripts. Class antagonism dividing them, the second, without boots or rifles, began deserting in 1915. Tens of thousands returned home the next year hungry and angry.

Wages stagnated from 1914 to 1917 while prices quintupled.[1906] Shortages afflicted the 1916 and 1917 winter as conscription, taking farmworkers, reduced the harvest. Petrograd—St. Petersburg before 1914—urbanites rioted March 1917. Disobeying Nicholas' order to kill them, peasant soldiers joined the demonstrations. The revolution intensified then because farmworkers prevented his behaving as elites always had by enforcing inequality. Nicholas abdicated March 15, 1917.

The czar gone, Russia pursued egalitarianism more than the war's other belligerents.[1907] Opposing conscription, farmhands wanted land, urbanites demanded better wages and food, and nationalists hoped to continue a disas-

---

[1903] Ibid., 625-626.
[1904] Ibid., 626.
[1905] McKay, Hill, Buckler, Crowston, Wiesner-Hanks, and Perry, 783-784; Galeotti, 169; Orlando Figes, *A People's Tragedy: A History of the Russian Revolution* (New York: Viking, 1996), 270.
[1906] McKay, Hill, Buckler, Crowston, Wiesner-Hanks, and Perry, 784; Galeotti, 169.
[1907] Walter Scheidel, *The Great Leveler: Violence and the History of Inequality from the Stone Age to the Twenty-First Century* (Princeton, NJ and Oxford: Princeton University Press, 2017), 214.

trous war.[1908] The provisional government neither redistributed land nor ended conscription. Allying with peasants, Petrograd's soviet denounced the government, which ordered the army forward against the Germans in July 1917. Peasants instead returned home to take land from secular landholders and the Russian Orthodox Church in "a great agrarian upheaval."[1909]

Applauding peasants and workmen, Lenin enlarged his Bolshevik party.[1910] Attacking the government as capitalism's stooge, he urged its overthrow. The November 1917 election giving Bolsheviks just 23 percent of delegates, he ordered soldiers loyal to the revolution to disband the legislature. Nationalizing land, he attacked rich landowners and church, not smallholders, to reduce inequality.[1911] He solidified urbanites' support by authorizing them to manage factories.

The revolution destroyed the aristocracy, around 500,000 of Russia's 90 million people.[1912] For example, though his father dissipated most of the family estates, nobleman Sergey Rachmaninov (1873–1943), among "the most formidable pianists of all time and the last truly great composer in the Russian Romantic tradition," retained 46 acres about 340 miles southeast of Moscow as a summer home.[1913] Among the first rural Russians with an automobile, "a large—and expensive—coupe," he preferred to drive with his chauffeur as passenger.[1914] This idyll ended in 1917 when farmhands looted the property, revolutionary forces seized it, and Rachmaninov fled Russia the next year for Sweden and then the United States.[1915]

Absent nobility, Lenin extracted revenue from merchants and professionals, another 125,000 Russians.[1916] More could come only from peasants, who held some 97 percent of arable land by 1919, though resistance to collec-

---

[1908] McKay, Hill, Buckler, Crowston, Wiesner-Hanks, and Perry, 784-786.

[1909] Ibid., 786.

[1910] Ibid., 786-788.

[1911] Scheidel, 215.

[1912] Ibid., 216; Sergey Bobylev, "How Russia's Population Changed over the Years: Key Facts about Russia's Population Since the Year 1897," TASS Russian News Agency, January 24, 2019, accessed April 3, 2022, ‹How Russia's population changed over the years - Society & Culture - TASS.›

[1913] Ted Libbey, *The NPR Listener's Encyclopedia of Classical Music* (New York: Workman Publishing, 2006), 657; Robert Matthew-Walker, *Rachmaninoff* (London: Omnibus Press, 1980), 7-11; Michael Rodman, Robert Cummings, Steven Coburn, Adrian Corleonis, Sol Louis Siegel, Roger Dettmer, Joseph Stevenson, Timothy Dickey, James Reel, and James Leonard, "Sergey Rachmaninov," in *All Music Guide to Classical Music: The Definitive Guide to Classical Music*, ed. Chris Woodstra, Gerald Brennan, and Allen Schrott (San Francisco: Backbeat Books, 2005), 1054.

[1914] Matthew-Walker, 73.

[1915] Ibid., 82-84; Peter Gammond, *Classical Composers* (Surrey, UK: CLB Publishing, 1995), 140.

[1916] Scheidel, 216-218.

tivization left under 1 percent collectively farmed by 1921. Lenin hoped to take the harvest by heightening class antagonism against supposedly prosperous farmers, termed kulaks. Propaganda created an illusion of wealth though, obeying chapter 6's maxim "equality in poverty," they had little more than the poor. Treated later, Soviet dictator Joseph Stalin (1878–1953), inflicting "decades of misery upon many Soviet people," massacred them.[1917]

18.6 Marxism in Russia and the Soviet Union

18.6.1 Leninism

Intellectual and doer, Lenin adapted Marxism to Russian circumstances, human nature, and global economics, politics, and demography.[1918] First, he doubted Marx and Engels' faith in progress, an eighteenth-century anachronism. Aware of oppression, workers, embracing communism, would overthrow capitalism and industry, the two supposed. But Lenin believed workers, unable to advance on their own, required intellectuals to educate, organize, and lead them in revolt.

This insight discrediting last chapter's "dictatorship of the proletariat," the communist party would rule workers to further their aims.[1919] Lenin's colleague Ukrainian Marxist Leon Trotsky (1879–1940), whose "legacy has been the most enduring of all the intellectual leaders of the Russian Revolution," foresaw that this authoritarianism would devolve into Stalinism.[1920]

Second, Lenin rejected Marx and Engels' Eurocentrism.[1921] Supposing Europe the theater of class conflict, these Germans reduced the rest of the world to European appendage. Focusing instead on poor, populous Asia as the continent where Marxism should most appeal, Lenin "was the first important political figure in the twentieth century to see the world as more than Europe."[1922]

Third, appreciating Russia's countless desperate peasants, he repudiated last chapter's Marxist expectation that communism would triumph first in

---

[1917] Linda Cernak, *Joseph Stalin: Dictator of the Soviet Union* (Minneapolis: Essential Library, 2016), 89.

[1918] Alan Ebenstein, William Ebenstein, and Edwin Fogelman, *Today's Isms: Socialism, Capitalism, Fascism, Communism, and Libertarianism*, 11th ed. (Upper Saddle River, NJ: Prentice Hall, 2000), 104-108; Winks, Brinton, Christopher, and Wolff, *A History of Civilization, Vol II*, 562; McKay, Hill, Buckler, Crowston, Wiesner-Hanks, and Perry, 786.

[1919] Ebenstein, Ebenstein, and Fogelman, 107-108.

[1920] Oliver, 110.

[1921] Ebenstein, Ebenstein, and Fogelman, 106-107.

[1922] Ibid., 107.

cities.[1923] The previous section mentioning his support for land redistribution, Lenin's slogan "Bread, Land, and Peace" encapsulated peasant yearnings.[1924]

Fourth, concentrating on Russia, Lenin challenged Marx and Engels' prediction of worldwide revolution.[1925] His geographic precision undermined their confidence that ideas could change the world. Politicians must tailor ideas, impotent on their own, to specific circumstances to triumph.

Fifth, emphasizing Asia, Russia, and the countryside and discarding Marx and Engels' assumption that communism would prevail where capitalism was strongest, Lenin targeted its underbelly.[1926] Appreciating that Asian, African, and Latin American governments controlled large rural populations with a small army and police, he believed an equally small force, winning mass allegiance, would overthrow them.

Honoring his promise of peace, Lenin exited the war with the 1918 Brest-Litovsk Treaty that gave Germany Russia's western lands and roughly one third its population.[1927] Furious at this humiliation and his repudiation of the 1917 election, his opponents provoked civil war. Leading an army against them, Trotsky reconquered by 1920 most land ceded Germany.

The Bolsheviks nationalized all banks and factories, seized grain, rationed food and other resources, and abolished private property.[1928] Like chapter 16's Committee of Public Safety, Lenin's secret police, the Cheka, executed thousands as "enemies of the people," including the czar and his family.[1929]

Igniting rural riots, grain confiscation caused famine in 1921.[1930] Hunger, unemployment, and disease besetting Russia, Lenin, replacing communism with the 1921 New Economic Policy (NEP), restored privatization by letting peasants sell part of the harvest, though they owed taxes in kind. Helping farms and factories recover by 1926, the NEP offered farmers permanent land occupancy in lieu of ownership. Small businesses kept profits, though banks, industry, and railroads remained public.

18.6.2 Stalinism

Trotsky and Stalin contesting power upon Lenin's death, Stalin became party leader in 1927, unveiled his modernization plan "Socialism in One

[1923] Ibid., 106-107.

[1924] McKay, Hill, Buckler, Crowston, Wiesner-Hanks, and Perry, 786.

[1925] Ebenstein, Ebenstein, and Fogelman, 105.

[1926] Ibid., 106-107.

[1927] McKay, Hill, Buckler, Crowston, Wiesner-Hanks, and Perry, 788.

[1928] Ibid., 788-789.

[1929] Ibid.; Tom Firme, *Russian Revolution of 1917* (Chicago: World Book, 2018), 100.

[1930] McKay, Hill, Buckler, Crowston, Wiesner-Hanks, and Perry, 837; Winks, Brinton, Christopher, and Wolff, *A History of Civilization, Vol II*, 739-740.

Country" the next year, and expelled Trotsky from the USSR in 1929.[1931] Pursuing collectivization more than had Lenin, he angered farmers who burned crops, refused to cultivate land, destroyed plows, and killed livestock.[1932] The resulting famine killed around 6 million in Ukraine alone in 1932 and 1933.[1933]

Worsening famine by exporting grain, Stalin intensified class hatred by pitting farmworkers against kulaks.[1934] Sure that kulaks hoarded food, he ordered farmhands to find it in exchange for work on collective farms with access to kulak tools and machines, an unappealing prospect to those who wanted land. He killed perhaps 10 million kulaks from 1929 to 1939 and sent 1 million to labor camps in 1931 and another 12 million to Siberia.[1935] Collectivizing 93 percent of farmland by 1937, he sought to mechanize agriculture to reduce dependence on labor, free it for industry, and thereby increase rural and urban production.[1936] Aiming to increase factory output in five-year increments, Stalin set unachievable goals he nonetheless declared fulfilled.[1937]

Imagining enemies everywhere, he ordered the murder of three quarters of delegates to the 1934 communist party congress, 90 percent of generals in 1937, and Trotsky in 1940.[1938] Devoting his life to advancing agriculture worldwide, Soviet agronomist and geneticist Nikolai Vavilov (1887–1943), among "the greatest scientists of the twentieth century," starved in prison because a Stalin sycophant envied him.[1939] Stalin censured Soviet composers Sergey Prokofiev (1891–1953), Aram Khachaturian (1903–1978), and Dmitry Shostakovich (1906–1975) because their music was somehow decadent.[1940]

18.6.3 Backlash against Soviet Communism

18.6.3.1 George Orwell

[1931] McKay, Hill, Buckler, Crowston, Wiesner-Hanks, and Perry, 837-838; H. Stuart Hughes, *Contemporary Europe: A History*, 5th ed. (Englewood Cliffs, NJ: Prentice-Hall, 1981), 258; Strayer and Gatzke, 748; Galeotti, 176-177.

[1932] Winks, Brinton, Christopher, and Wolff, *A History of Civilization, Vol II*, 742-743.

[1933] McKay, Hill, Buckler, Crowston, Wiesner-Hanks, and Perry, 838-839.

[1934] Ibid; Winks, Brinton, Christopher, and Wolff, *A History of Civilization, Vol II*, 743.

[1935] Winks, Brinton, Christopher, and Wolff, *A History of Civilization, Vol II*, 743; Albert M. Craig, William A. Graham, Donald Kagan, Steven Ozment, and Frank M. Turner, *The Heritage of World Civilizations, Vol. II: Since 1500* (New York: Macmillan, 1986), 1130.

[1936] Scheidel, 219; Craig, Graham, Kagan, Ozment, and Turner, 1132; Strayer and Gatzke, 751.

[1937] Winks, Brinton, Christopher, and Wolff, *A History of Civilization, Vol II*, 744.

[1938] Galeotti, 178; Strayer and Gatzke, 750.

[1939] Vadim Birstein, "Famed Biologist Lost to Stalin's Terror," *Nature Genetics* 40, no. 8 (August 2008): 930; Peter Pringle, *The Murder of Nikolai Vavilov: The Story of Stalin's Persecution of One of the Great Scientists of the Twentieth Century* (New York: Simon & Schuster, 2008), 1-2, 4.

[1940] Libbey, 646.

Hating "any system in which power was used by the strong to domi-nate and intimidate the weak," Orwell opposed Stalinism.[1941] Collectiviza-tion's excesses convinced him around 1931 that Stalin, betraying the revolu-tion, denied Soviets their humanity and freedom.[1942] Embracing democratic socialism and aligning Marxism with the gospel concern for paupers, Orwell advocated "fairer income distribution," free elections, and land, mines, banks, industry, and railroads' nationalization.[1943]

Although rooting for the USSR while fearing its collapse would dispirit workers everywhere, Orwell rejected propaganda that the USSR was constructing a classless society, disputed intellectuals who believed this untruth, and wanted the novella *Animal Farm* (1945) to inaugurate "a liter-ature of disillusionment about the Soviet Union."[1944] Describing a Leninist revolution organized and led by pigs, the narrative recounted paradise won and lost as livestock overthrew owner Mr. Jones, tried to institute equality, and relapsed into inequality.[1945] The pig Old Major inciting revolt, his death left conspecifics Napoleon, Snowball, and Squealer in charge.[1946]

Expelling Jones, livestock celebrated with a double ration.[1947] This exper-iment in equality failed almost immediately as some animals loafed. The mare Mollie arrived late for work and quit early.[1948] Pigs supervised others rather than toiled whereas the horse Boxer volunteered for extra duties, shouldered most of the load, and confronted every problem by vowing to "work harder."[1949] Originally as strong as two horses, he worked as hard as three, and eventually equaled all others' aggregate exertions.[1950]

Demanding ever more from underlings while reducing rations, the pigs, fattening from plenitude, commandeered all milk, then part of the apple harvest, thereafter all apples, and finally the barley crop too.[1951] Inequality and autocracy growing, Napoleon banished Snowball, executed putative

[1941] Tanya Agathocleous, *George Orwell: Battling Big Brother* (New York and Oxford: Oxford University Press, 2000), 24.

[1942] Paul Kirschner, "The Dual Purpose of Animal Farm," in *George Orwell*, updated ed., ed. Harold Bloom (New York: Chelsea House Publishers, 2007), 150-151.

[1943] Ibid., 150.

[1944] Ibid., 147; Tea Obreht, "Introduction," in *Animal Farm: A Fairy Story*, George Orwell (Boston: Berkley/Houghton Mifflin Harcourt, 2020), v; Russell Baker, "Afterword," in *Animal Farm: A Fairy Story*, George Orwell (Boston: Berkley/Houghton Mifflin Harcourt, 2020), 107.

[1945] Obreht, xi; George Orwell, *Animal Farm: A Fairy Story* (Boston: Berkley/Houghton Mifflin Harcourt, 2020), 5.

[1946] Orwell, 12-13.

[1947] Ibid., 14-16.

[1948] Ibid., 21-23.

[1949] Ibid., 22.

[1950] Ibid., 4, 22, 45.

[1951] Ibid., 26-27, 54, 80-82.

traitors, trained dogs to menace anyone who questioned him, occupied Jones' former house, enjoyed luxuries forbidden subordinates, and lengthened the workday and workweek while remaining idle.[1952]

Typifying the animals' disillusionment, the mare Clover understood that Napoleon and other pigs, ending neither hunger nor inequality, had betrayed the revolution.[1953] The strong should have protected weaklings, not emulated Jones by oppressing them. Mollifying disappointment, the raven Moses promised everyone an afterlife with rewards unattainable on earth.[1954] Orwell here affirmed Marx's view of religion as "the *opium* of the people."[1955]

Underscoring his indifference toward workers, Napoleon sold Boxer, collapsing one month before retirement, for slaughter.[1956] Nobody thereafter pretended the revolution benefitted anyone but pigs. Like all pledges, retirement was illusory. Planting barley on ground promised as pasture for retired livestock, Napoleon, prospering without exertion, demanded travail and austerity from others.[1957]

18.6.3.2 Ayn Rand

Orwell criticizing inequality, Ayn Rand attacked egalitarianism. Like Rachmaninov, she suffered during the revolution. Inhabiting the bourgeoisie Marx disdained, she hated Bolsheviks for expropriating her father's pharmacy.[1958] Also like Rachmaninov, she escaped to the United States, capitalism's bastion, which she judged insufficiently pitiless for her individualism.[1959]

Individualism and competition venerated last chapter's Social Darwinism. Like chapter 15's Scottish economist Adam Smith (1723–1790), Rand believed government imperiled the economy by doing more than operate an army, police, and courts.[1960] Taxation erred by transferring resources from producers to "welfare recipients," who sapped the economy.[1961] Downward redistribution promoted egalitarianism, "so evil—and so silly—a doctrine

---

[1952] Ibid., 40, 44, 49, 60-61.

[1953] Ibid., 62.

[1954] Ibid., 83-84.

[1955] Sven-Eric Liedman, *A World to Win: The Life and Works of Karl Marx*, trans. Jeffrey N. Skinner (London and New York: Verso, 2018), 99. The italicized *opium* duplicates the original.

[1956] Orwell, 85-87.

[1957] Ibid., 91-92.

[1958] Gary Weiss, *Ayn Rand Nation: The Struggle for America's Soul* (New York: St. Martin's Press, 2012), 12.

[1959] Ayn Rand, *Philosophy: Who Needs It* (New York: Signet Book, 1982), 162-163, 180, 288-289.

[1960] Ibid., 180.

[1961] Ibid., 176.

that it deserves no serious study or discussion," she averred.[1962] Desire for equality weakened civilization over the last two centuries.

Rand attacked not just equality, which ruined the USSR and kindred nations, but the notion that society should aid paupers at all.[1963] "After half a century of total dictatorship, Soviet Russia is begging for American wheat and for American industrial 'know-how,'" she stated in 1974.[1964] Writing Soviet grandmaster Boris Spassky (b. 1937) that year, Rand praised chess' hierarchy. King, queen, rook, bishop, and knight outrank pawns, which represent the masses.[1965] The game would degenerate into chaos were pawns thought superior to the rest. Moreover, chess attracted Spassky and others by rewarding excellence. Nobody would play if it honored losers.

Hating equality and communist "maggots," Rand branded "Marxism...a dismal failure as far as the people are concerned: Americans cannot be sold on any sort of class war."[1966] Communism's defeat vindicated capitalism, which alone obviated oppression and guaranteed freedom.

18.6.4 Post Stalinist Policies

Condemning Stalinism in 1956, communist party secretary Nikita Khrushchev (1894–1971) closed some labor camps and allowed writers, scholars, and artists greater freedom of expression.[1967] Nineteen sixties' living standards rose as government prioritized agriculture and consumer goods over heavy industry and the military.[1968] Emulating Americans, Russians bought automobiles and televisions. Full employment, paid vacation, pensions, and subsidized healthcare, childcare, housing, and transit reduced inequality, though ordinary Russians resented elite privilege and ostentation.[1969]

Before the revolution, Russia's 1905 Gini—chapter 6 introduced this measure of inequality—approximated 0.36, a value below those in today's Brazil, South Africa, Malaysia, the Philippines, most of Africa and Latin America, China, and the United States.[1970] Readers may remember from chapter 1 that current inequality, as before World War I, is enormous. The USSR beginning with less inequality than many other nations, Soviet poli-

---

[1962] Ibid., 162-163, 176.
[1963] Ibid., 183.
[1964] Ibid.
[1965] Ibid., 73-74.
[1966] Ibid., 12, 288.
[1967] Galeotti, 182; Firme, 105.
[1968] McKay, Hill, Buckler, Crowston, Wiesner-Hanks, and Perry, 886.
[1969] Branko Milanovic, *The Haves and the Have-Nots: A Brief and Idiosyncratic History of Global Inequality* (New York: Basic Books, 2011), 54-55, 58.
[1970] Ibid., 30-31; Scheidel, 221.

cies decreased it, with nonfarm Gini at 0.23 in 1967. Soviet farm and nonfarm Gini approximated 0.27 to 0.28 from 1968 to 1991.

Inequality lessened as the gap between blue- and white-collar wages shrank and sometimes reversed.[1971] For example, labor paid better than engineering and similar jobs from 1945 to 1985. Government managed inequality by setting wages, which were three quarters of 1988 income. Eliminating private property, the USSR abolished rent, which had benefited the rich.[1972] Full employment ended poverty from joblessness.

18.6.5 Soviet Communism's End and Legacy

The economy slowed in the 1960s and in the next decade suffered high fuel prices as chapter 20 relates.[1973] Central planning proved less efficient and less innovative than capitalism. Although the satellite Sputnik's 1957 launch amplified fears that the United States trailed the USSR in technology, the opposite was true because Soviet pursuit of egalitarianism discouraged productivity, education, and innovation.

Seeking prosperity in the 1980s, communist party secretary Mikhail Gorbachev (1931–2022), turning "Marxism-Leninism on its head," shifted planning from government to factories and farms, encouraged private enterprise, and permitted profit.[1974] Dissatisfaction intensified in the USSR and its dependents as stagnation persisted. Strikes and inflation racked Poland in 1988 and spread throughout eastern Europe, which abandoned communism the next year.[1975] The USSR fragmented in December 1990.

Inequality spiking with communism dead, capitalism ascendant, and corruption rife, Russia's 1980s Gini ballooned from 0.26 to 0.27, to 0.51 in 1995.[1976] Typifying all former Soviet states, Ukrainian Gini leapt from 0.25 in 1992 to 0.45 next year.

The richest quintile of Russians gained wealth at the rest's expense from 1988 to 1994.[1977] With 34 percent of 1988 national wealth, this quintile held 54 percent in 1994 while poverty, tripling between 1991 and 1994, tormented over one third of population. Russia's 111 billionaires owned 20 percent of

---

[1971] Scheidel, 221.

[1972] Branko Milanovic, *Global Inequality: A New Approach for the Age of Globalization* (Cambridge, MA and London: Belknap Press of Harvard University Press, 2016), 100-101.

[1973] Ibid., 101-102; Firme, 107; McKay, Hill, Buckler, Crowston, Wiesner-Hanks, and Perry, 887.

[1974] Brian Duignan, ed., *Economics and Economic Systems* (New York: Britannica, 2013), 108; William Taubman, *Gorbachev: His Life and Times* (New York and London: Norton, 2017), 2.

[1975] McKay, Hill, Buckler, Crowston, Wiesner-Hanks, and Perry, 927-928.

[1976] Milanovic, *The Haves and the Have-Nots*, 54; Scheidel, 222.

[1977] Scheidel, 222.

2014 national wealth. The richest decile monopolized 85 percent three years later.

The wealthiest magnate, entrepreneur Mikhail Khodorkovsky (b. 1963), worth some $24 billion by 2003, could negotiate contracts with China and the United States as though he were a state.[1978] Surpassing 0.4, Russia's 2011 Gini approximated those for the Roman Republic and 2011 China, the United States, and parts of the European Union.[1979] Over two millennia since Rome's republic, part of the world's Gini values remain static, confirming both inequality's persistence despite countervailing efforts and *Eternal Inequality*'s demonstration that it is durable and innately human.

18.7 Review and Preview

The Newtonian backlash against inequality, heightening during the French Revolution, peaked in Russia and China. Lenin and Trotsky violently reduced inequality. Stalin's atrocities ranked among humanity's worst in egalitarianism's pursuit; then Soviet collapse reinvigorated capitalism and inequality. Another peasant upheaval engulfed China, where, as in Russia, inequality was moderated at great cost, then enlarged in recent decades.

[1978] Milanovic, *The Haves and the Have-Nots*, 43-44.
[1979] Ibid., 31.

CHAPTER 19 CLASS CONFLICT AND CHINESE REVOLUTION

19.1 Abstract

Like the French and Russians, Chinese farmhands revolted against inequality, poverty, taxes, rent, corvée, and government inability or unwillingness to benefit them. Paupers, coolies, and jobless urbanites joined them in demanding reform or the old order's destruction. Among insurrections, the Taiping Rebellion (1850–1865) nearly achieved the second. The Boxer Rebellion (1899–1901) put the Qing (1644–1912) on its final descent toward oblivion.

Its demise, ending dynasticism, advantaged communism, which sought to modernize China along Marxist lines. Chinese communism, like its Russian predecessor, was a peasant movement that nationalized land, banks, and factories, though results were mixed. Although inequality decreased markedly into the 1980s, agriculture and industry alternated periods of growth and retrenchment. Now among the world's most inegalitarian nations, China, where inequality rose after 1985, resembles former Soviet countries in being more unequal than before the revolution.

19.2 Widespread Poverty

19.2.1 Rural Poverty

Chapter 10 described agrarian China, where farmworkers enriched landowners. Feeding everyone, agriculture underpinned Chinese civilization, which inequality destabilized as dynasties rose, plateaued, and fell.

Farming persisted amid dynastic transience. Gauging oppression through taxation, peasants seemingly benefited between the fourteenth and eighteenth centuries, when their contribution diminished from 15–20 percent of the harvest to 5 percent. Yet population, quadrupling from 1200 to 1800, threatened the land's carrying capacity, caused its division into smaller units as in eighteenth century France, and shrank per person surplus.[1980]

Despite these problems, the planting of one rice seed averaged 20 seeds (1:20) at harvest around 1700.[1981] By comparison, Russia's best lands produced 1:18 of rye, oats, barley, or wheat in the best years from 1750 to 1800, though the national average was 1:3 to 1:6.[1982] Circa 1800 to 1850, grain approximated 1:14 in Belgium and the Netherlands, 1:13 in Britain and parts of Germany, 1:10 in Austria, 1:9 in France, Sweden, Prussia, and Italy, 1:7 in Norway, and 1:6 in Russia, Spain, and Greece.

Eschewing fallow, China—harvesting two rice crops annually between the Yangtze and West rivers and three in the West River delta, as stated in chapter 10—kept more farmland in cultivation than Europe or western Asia.[1983] Visiting China's countryside, French botanist Pierre Poivre (1719–1786) lauded its bounty.

Producing more mouths to feed instead of raising living standards, "prolific abundance" neared Malthusian crisis by 1800.[1984] Some landowners worsened the problem by planting trees over rice as population growth demanded more wood, whose shortage forced the poor to burn rice straw for heat.[1985] Overcrowded by 1800, China had little spare land to bring into cultivation. Production could increase only by working harder on each acre.

As in Europe, Chinese farmers increased specialization in modernity.[1986] Cotton, tea, sugarcane, and mulberry trees for silkworms and thus silk took land from grain, legumes, vegetables, and fruits. Prioritizing tea shrubs over subsistence to meet eighteenth century demand, specialists bought food and, like urbanites, were vulnerable to inflation. Government compounding the danger by following England and France toward *laissez faire*, food became less communal resource than commodity that fed the rich.

[1980] Robert W. Strayer, Edwin Hirschmann, Robert B. Marks, Robert J. Smith, James J. Horn, and Lynn H. Parsons, *The Making of the Modern World: Connected Histories, Divergent Paths (1500 to the Present)* (New York: St. Martin's Press, 1989), 350.

[1981] Robert B. Marks, *The Origins of the Modern World: A Global and Environmental Narrative from the Fifteenth to the Twenty-First Century*, 4th ed. (Lanham, MD: Rowman & Littlefield, 2020), 111-112.

[1982] Jerome Blum, "Russian Agriculture in the Last 150 Years of Serfdom," *Agricultural History* 34, no. 1 (January 1960): 5-6.

[1983] Marks, 111-112.

[1984] Ibid., 127.

[1985] Ibid., 115-118.

[1986] Ibid., 114, 126-127.

19.2.2 Urban Poverty

As chapter 10 indicated for ancient China, inequality pervaded cities, where elites dwarfed everyone else. For example, China's financial center and ancient capital Nanjing in Jiangsu province housed the emperor, his family, senior officials, wealthy merchants, and landowners who managed farms from the comfort of mansions.

Beijing grew opulent after Ming emperor Zhu Di (1360–1424) moved the capital there in 1403.[1987] He gathered roughly 100,000 artisans and countless laborers—amassed and controlled, as during construction of chapter 10's Great Wall, through corvée—to enlarge "the link between Earth and Heaven."[1988] Workers dragged heavy marble blocks to Beijing from a quarry 45 miles distant during the coldest months so frozen ground minimized friction.[1989] Creating a metropolis with some 960,000 residents by 1440, these exertions benefited only elites, who restricted access to the Forbidden City.

Urbanization accelerated after 1550, though agriculture overshadowed the nonfarm economy, which, just 3 percent of eighteenth-century GDP, included dockworkers, sailors, miners, metalworkers, potters, cloth makers, and coolies who did jobs usually reserved for livestock in Europe.[1990] Its large population needing almost all land for crops, China had few such animals.

Inflation imperiled urban poor. Vulnerability worsened after 1550 as cities and slums grew. Cold weather diminished the harvest after 1600.[1991] After centuries of growth, China's population decreased during famine from 1615 to 1618 and in the 1630s. Taxation amid inflation and famine irked rural and urban workers.

Trade with Europe after 1680, discussed later, shifted commerce from southern China north to Shanghai. Coolies who had packaged tea and silk and loaded them on ships in Guangdong province's Guangzhou lost work.[1992] Those who pulled ships along canals lost their jobs to European steamships.

[1987] Tony Allan, Kay Celtel, Jacob F. Field, R. G. Grant, Philip Parker, and Sally Regan, *Imperial China: The Definitive Visual History* (London: DK, 2020), 214.

[1988] Ibid.

[1989] Ibid., 216-217.

[1990] Ibid., 225; Robert W. Strayer, Edwin Hirschmann, Robert B. Marks, Robert J. Smith, James J. Horn, and Lynn H. Parsons, *The Making of the Modern World: Connected Histories, Divergent Paths (1500 to the Present)* (New York: St. Martin's Press, 1989, 351.

[1991] Allan, Celtel, Field, Grant, Parker, and Regan, 229, 238; Strayer, Hirschmann, Marks, Smith, Horn, and Parsons, 348.

[1992] Strayer, Hirschmann, Marks, Smith, Horn, and Parsons, 366-367.

19.3 Rebellion, Change, and Late Dynastic China

19.3.1 Li Zicheng

As in France and Russia, government, whose ostentation and corruption emptied the treasury after 1570, mismanaged discontent.[1993] Power devolved to local landowners, who increased their estates at smallholders' expense, noted chapter 10.

Sparking rebellion after 1628, famine turned central China's Shaanxi province unemployed postal worker Li Zicheng (c. 1605–1645), typifying the region's "rootless, violent men," against the Ming dynasty (1368–1644).[1994] Raising an army, he promised farmworkers taxation's abolition and land. His men and other peasant forces held parts of China by 1634 and appeared capable of greater conquests. But a 1642 battle, destroying Yellow River dikes, unleashed flood, famine, and a smallpox epidemic. Many Chinese, especially intellectuals and landowners, hated these rebels for destabilizing China. Deposing the last Ming emperor in 1644, Li, unaware his rebellion had lost broad support, declared a new dynasty.

19.3.2 Qing Dynasty and Commerce

Rather than accept peasant governance, elites cooperated with a Manchu army north of the Great Wall.[1995] Sweeping south, Manchus crushed peasants, founded the Qing, reunited China about 1680, and conquered peripheral lands to double the empire beyond its Ming domain.

Like previous rulers, the Qing prioritized agriculture, promoting corn, potato, sweet potato, and peanut, all crops that arrived from the western hemisphere before 1600 and that enlarged population with their calories and nutrients.[1996] Profits from trade, discussed next, stimulated investment in land and specialization in cash crops, especially in the Yangtze River delta.[1997] Becoming an important export, tea joined silk and porcelain as a luxury attractive to Europeans.

Before the 1680s, Chinese–European trade, making Europe the buyer, gained China the New World silver mentioned in chapter 14.[1998] From 1600

[1993] Ibid., 348.

[1994] Allan, Celtel, Field, Grant, Parker, and Regan, 238; Paul S. Ropp, *China in World History* (Oxford and New York: Oxford University Press, 2010), 95; Jonathan D. Spence, *The Search for Modern China* (New York and London: Norton, 1990), 21.

[1995] Strayer, Hirschmann, Marks, Smith, Horn, and Parsons, 349.

[1996] Ropp, 90.

[1997] Strayer, Hirschmann, Marks, Smith, Horn, and Parsons, 349.

[1998] Ibid., 359.

to 1630, half this silver bought luxuries like spices, tea, and silk.[1999] Absorbing three quarters of silver from 1500 to 1800, China became the world's richest nation.[2000] Trade quickened after roughly 1680, though in 1759 China restricted Europeans to one port, where they resented paying fees and bribes.

Disliking this situation, Europe sought a product to sell China. The search ended with opium, the source of morphine which relieves pain but is addictive.[2001] China had used it sparingly for centuries as medicine. Then the British East India Company (BEIC), managing trade with China, began growing the opium poppy in colonial India and sold the opium to China. Although the Qing outlawed it, the BEIC smuggled the drug, paying officials to ignore the illegality.

The BEIC in 1815 and 1834 reduced prices to increase sales.[2002] After the second year, the United States, entering the trade, became China's second largest supplier. The BEIC in 1835 sold China nearly 3.6 million pounds of opium for 17 million ounces of silver. Once silver rich, China now watched the metal flow to Britain and the United States.

The Qing trying to end smuggling in 1838 and 1839, the BEIC urged the royal navy to force resumption by attacking China.[2003] Steam power advantaged the navy over China's fleet, still in the age of sail. Entering the Yangtze River in 1840 and shelling Nanjing, British warships compelled the Qing to beg peace. The 1842 Nanjing Treaty gave Britain the equivalent of $21 million, Hong Kong, and access to five Chinese ports. The second opium war (1856–1858) opened another 11 ports.

19.3.3 Taiping Rebellion

Before, during, and after the second debacle, the Taiping Rebellion, engulfing China's 18 provinces, threatened the Qing.[2004] Rural and urban grievances found a revolutionary in civil service aspirant Hong Xiuquan (1814–1864). Born to prosperous farmers, he hoped to become an official by passing the exams, which required mastery of texts attributed to chapter 10's Chinese philosopher Confucius (551–479 BCE) and his adherents. Repeated failure turned Hong against Confucianism.

[1999] Ibid., 349.

[2000] Ropp, 91.

[2001] Strayer, Hirschmann, Marks, Smith, Horn, and Parsons, 359; Edwin E. Moise, *Modern China: A History* (London and New York: Longman, 1986), 29.

[2002] Strayer, Hirschmann, Marks, Smith, Horn, and Parsons, 359.

[2003] Ibid., 360-362.

[2004] Ibid., 366-367; Ropp, 106.

An 1836 encounter with a Guangzhou missionary after his third exam introduced him to Christianity.[2005] Undermining his health, two additional failures caused hallucinations, which Hong interpreted in 1843 as visions of heaven, where he met God and learned he was Jesus' brother. Believing God wanted him to eradicate sin in preparation for an eternal kingdom, he fashioned an apocalyptic message that attracted indigents, beggars, farm-hands, coolies, and jobless urbanites who believed they could succeed only by destroying the status quo.

Announcing in 1851 China's impending transition from the Qing to *Taiping Tianguo*, "the Heavenly Kingdom of Great Peace," Hong, believing "the Manchus were demons fighting against the true God," led a peasant army from south China's Guangdong and Guangxi provinces north to conquer Hubei province's Wuhan in 1852 and Nanjing in 1853.[2006] By then, recruiting Hunan province's farmhands, his army approximated 500,000.

Operating as a polity, this army named Nanjing its capital in 1855.[2007] Hong expected a thrust farther north would capture Beijing and end the Qing. History seemingly supported him because landowners had for centuries increased their power and weakened or destroyed centralism, completing chapter 10's dynastic cycle, through revolt.

But they abhorred this rebellion because, first, Hong and his followers, espousing communism, wanted to abolish private property and hold all wealth in common for distribution to the neediest.[2008] Second, the revolt undermined Confucian respect for authority and hierarchy, which privileged landowners. Third, the Taiping call for gender equality further affronted Confucianism. Fourth, the movement advocated industrialization, which landowners feared would create a managerial elite to rival them.

The Qing unable to defeat Taiping forces, landowners, deciding survival necessitated alliance with it, gathered mercenaries to overwhelm them.[2009] Hong killing himself in June 1864, mercenaries next month captured Nanjing and slaughtered 100,000 residents. The rebellion confirming landowners as richer and more powerful than the Qing, they thereafter ignored the emperor, promulgated and enforced laws on their estates, and collected taxes. Communism awaited the twentieth century.

[2005] Strayer, Hirschmann, Marks, Smith, Horn, and Parsons, 367.

[2006] Ibid., 367-368; Spence, 172.

[2007] Strayer, Hirschmann, Marks, Smith, Horn, and Parsons, 368.

[2008] Ibid., 368-370; Albert M. Craig, William A. Graham, Donald Kagan, Steven Ozment, and Frank M. Turner, *The Heritage of World Civilizations, Vol. II: Since 1500* (New York: Macmillan, 1986), 1017.

[2009] Strayer, Hirschmann, Marks, Smith, Horn, and Parsons, 370-371.

19.3.4 Qing Decline and Demise

Britain's opium war victories empowered foreigners to travel and trade throughout China, buy land, sell opium, and demand government protect them and their investments.[2010] Perceiving frailty, the French, attacking Chinese protectorate Vietnam in 1884 and 1885, gained the Southeast Asian colony French Indochina. A decade later Japan, striking Chinese protectorate Korea, sank half China's navy. The 1895 Shimonoseki Treaty gave Japan 200 million ounces of silver, Korea, Taiwan, the Pescadores Islands, and permission to establish factories in Chinese ports.

Amid Qing decline, landowners, setting the national agenda, aimed to reinvigorate agriculture after Taiping's depredations, restore Confucian emphasis on hierarchy, tradition, and obedience to authority, and create a strong army.[2011] Agricultural advancement required corvée's enlargement1

Militarism, however, led modernizers to defy traditionalists by urging that China adopt European weapons and tactics.

Although China remained agrarian, industrialization, quickening after 1860, pitted workmen against management.[2012] Assailing countryside and city, the 1876 to 1879 famine starved 9 million to 13 million Chinese.[2013] The 1887 Yellow River flood slaughtered over 900,000 people.

Drought in 1899 and xenophobia, which Europe's ruthlessness toward China intensified, provoked the Boxer Rebellion.[2014] The Righteous and Harmonious Fists—the Boxers—attacked European missionaries and converts from 1899 to 1901, killing roughly 250 foreigners.[2015] Despite distrusting Boxers, empress dowager Cixi (1835–1908), among "history's wickedest women," in summer 1900 allied with them in hopes of expelling foreigners after officials deceived her that magic protected the rebels from bullets.[2016]

Moving north from east China's Shandong province, Chinese troops and Boxers destroyed churches and other property en route to Beijing in June 1900.[2017] Next month Japan, the United States, Britain, France, Germany, Russia, Italy, and Austria-Hungary sent 55,000 troops against the rebellion.

[2010] Ibid, 362.

[2011] Ibid., 371-372.

[2012] Ibid., 372.

[2013] Allan, Celtel, Field, Grant, Parker, and Regan, 247.

[2014] Ropp, 110-111.

[2015] Allan, Celtel, Field, Grant, Parker, and Regan, 299; Terri Koontz, Mark Sidwell, and S. M. Bunker, *World Studies*, 2d ed. (Greenville, SC: BJU Press, 2000), 371.

[2016] Michael Wood, *The Story of China: The Epic History of a World Power from the Middle Kingdom to Mao and the China Dream* (New York: St. Martin's Press, 2020), 433; Ropp, 111; Sean Stewart Price, *Cixi: Evil Empress of China?* (New York: Franklin Watts, 2009), 118.

[2017] Allan, Celtel, Field, Grant, Parker, and Regan, 299; Ropp, 111.

Entering Beijing in August, they forced Cixi into the countryside, where she witnessed penury and misery for the first time. When the eight powers restored her in 1901, she promoted modernization she had previously scorned. That year's truce executed all Boxers, required China to pay 400 ounces of silver—more than $60 billion today—over 45 years to the eight powers, and kept their troops in China.[2018] Japan maintained the largest force.

With the Qing moribund, China could venerate tradition and its agrarian past and present, an untenable approach, or modernize through industry and militarism, an option incompatible with Confucianism and dynasticism.[2019] During the dynasty's last decade, warlords strengthened their grip on the provinces, peasants opposed tax increases to pay the indemnity, and intellectuals and students criticized China's backwardness.[2020] The 1911 army rebellion and student protests ended the Qing in February 1912.

19.4 Chinese Communism

19.4.1 To 1949

Among 1911 protestors, Mao Zedong (1893–1976), "a leading architect of China's twentieth-century Communist revolution," was the son of Hunan province prosperous farmers.[2021] A Peking University librarian under chief librarian, Chinese communist party (CCP) cofounder, "great Marxist and revolutionary" Li Dazhao (1889–1927), Mao was an early convert.[2022] His upbringing sensitizing him to agrarian concerns, he, like last chapter's revolutionaries knew communism needed rural support.

"The present upsurge of the peasant movement is a colossal event," stated his 1926 CCP report.[2023] In a Newtonian backlash, Mao believed hundreds of millions of farmhands, soon to revolt, would kill landowners, corrupt offi-

---

[2018] Allan, Celtel, Field, Grant, Parker, and Regan, 299; Wood, 436.

[2019] Wood, 436; Strayer, Hirschmann, Marks, Smith, Horn, and Parsons, 373.

[2020] Strayer, Hirschmann, Marks, Smith, Horn, and Parsons, 380-381.

[2021] Ibid., 390; Dorothea A. L. Martin, "Mao Zedong," in *Berkshire Encyclopedia of World History*, vol. 3, ed. William H. McNeill, Jerry H. Bentley, David Christian, David Levinson, J. R. McNeill, Heidi Roupp, and Judith P. Zinsser (Great Barrington, MA: Berkshire Publishing Group, 2005), 1186; Zheng Yibing, "Li Dazhao, Co-Founder of CPC, Remembered in China," China Global Television Network, last modified June 16, 2021, accessed September 2, 2022, ‹Li Dazhao, co-founder of CPC, remembered in China - CGTN.›

[2022] Strayer, Hirschmann, Marks, Smith, Horn, and Parsons, 390; Ropp, 126; "Mao Zedong," Peking University Library, accessed April 6, 2022, ‹Mao Zedong | Peking University Library (pku.edu.cn).›

[2023] Strayer, Hirschmann, Marks, Smith, Horn, and Parsons, 390.

---

cials, and other oppressors. Everyone must choose to support or oppose the revolution.

By that year intellectual, Marxist, and anarchist Peng Pai (1896–1929), pioneering "the Chinese peasant movement," organized farmworkers throughout Guangdong province's Haifeng county, where he had been born to wealthy landowners.[2024] This background might have prejudiced him against farmhands. Instead, he was among China's first to understand their revolutionary potential.[2025] Demanding rent reduction and then land redistribution, Peng criticized a system that impoverished laborers and enriched rentiers.[2026] Only workers earned the right to enjoy the wealth they created.

Unlike Mao, Peng never achieved his vision. Attacking the CCP in 1927, Chinese general Chiang Kai-shek (1887–1975), "aggressive, resourceful, and brimming with ambition," targeted Shanghai, Nanjing, Hangzhou, Fuzhou, and Guangzhou.[2027] The offensive, termed the white terror, killed thousands of Marxists including Peng and forced the CCP to abandon cities for the countryside, a move that saved and strengthened it. On a mountain in southeastern China's Jiangxi province in 1928, Mao organized the Red Army to protect villages against Chiang and Japanese soldiers, present since the Boxer Rebellion, as mentioned.

Ruthless and egalitarian, Mao, executing landowners, equally divided their property among farmworkers.[2028] These actions sought to reduce the Gini, which chapter 6 introduced as a measure of inequality, to zero. But no government could micromanage affairs to ensure everyone lifelong identical wealth, that chapter noted.

Understanding their inability to defeat superior numbers in conventional warfare, his guerrillas eluded Chiang, who tried five times from 1931 to 1934 to destroy them. Nearly succeeding, the fifth assault forced them between October 1934 and October 1935 northwest on the Long March, among "the truly heroic chapters in military history."[2029] Over nine-tenths of the 86,000 to 100,000 troops died or deserted while fighting one battle every other day on average. As this army traversed over 6,000 miles across 12 provinces,

---

[2024] Yong-Pil Pang, "Peng Pai: From Landlord to Revolutionary," *Modern China* 1, no. 3 (July 1975): 297, 300.

[2025] Strayer, Hirschmann, Marks, Smith, Horn, and Parsons, 390.

[2026] Pang, 319.

[2027] Strayer, Hirschmann, Marks, Smith, Horn, and Parsons, 390-391; Ropp, 126; Laura Tyson Li, *Madame Chiang Kai-shek: China's Eternal First Lady* (New York: Atlantic Monthly Press, 2006), 63; Richard Baum, "The Reign of White Terror in China," Wondrium Daily, May 15, 2021, accessed April 6, 2022, ‹The Reign of White Terror in China (thegreatcoursesdaily.com).›

[2028] Strayer, Hirschmann, Marks, Smith, Horn, and Parsons, 391-393; Ropp, 126-128.

[2029] Strayer, Hirschmann, Marks, Smith, Horn, and Parsons, 391; Ropp, 127.

18 mountains, and 24 rivers, the CCP defied last chapter's Soviet dictator Joseph Stalin (1878–1953) by elevating Mao to leader. More than anyone else, he spearheaded CCP successes and atrocities.

The 8,000 survivors in October 1935 reached Shaanxi province, where they inhabited caves.[2030] Japan's army swarming China in 1937, the onslaught may have prevented Chiang from obliterating them. Although he and Mao feigned a united front against Japan, the two fought almost immediately, prompting Mao to declare a "people's war" against the general, Japan, and landowners.[2031]

Swelling to 1 million soldiers, the Red Army controlled 1 million square miles with 100 million people by 1945.[2032] Young recruits made the average enlistee 19 years old and the average officer 24. Ostensibly neutral, the United States gave Chiang money and weapons after World War II (1939–1945).[2033] Appearing to be a U.S. puppet, he watched his dismal popularity vanish. Negotiations allowed Mao, doubling his army, to overpower the general, who fled to Taiwan in 1949.

19.4.2 1949–1956

Unifying China after decades of turmoil, the CCP continued to pursue egalitarianism. "Land reform in a population of over 300 million people is a vicious war," admitted Mao, who expected class conflict to kill at least one person per village throughout China.[2034] "This is the most hideous class war between peasants and landlords. It is a battle to the death."

The CCP aimed to equalize all land, money, livestock, crops, and tools and to execute or imprison recalcitrant rentiers.[2035] Everyone who had aided Japan lost property. Initially requiring rent reduction, the CCP in 1947 outlawed tenancy and peonage. Property remaining private after redistribution, these actions stopped short of communism.

American historian Robert Strayer (b. 1942) and coauthors inferred "substantial leveling of a very unequal society," though Austrian American historian Walter Scheidel (b. 1966) cautioned that prerevolutionary China was less unequal than communists asserted.[2036] Although the CCP estimated that the richest decile of landowners owned 70 to 80 percent of land

---

[2030] Strayer, Hirschmann, Marks, Smith, Horn, and Parsons, 391-393; Ropp, 128.

[2031] Strayer, Hirschmann, Marks, Smith, Horn, and Parsons, 394-395.

[2032] Ibid.

[2033] Ibid., 397.

[2034] Walter Scheidel, *The Great Leveler: Violence and the History of Inequality from the Stone Age to the Twenty-First Century* (Princeton, NJ and Oxford: Princeton University Press, 2017), 225.

[2035] Ibid., 224; Strayer, Hirschmann, Marks, Smith, Horn, and Parsons, 404.

[2036] Strayer, Hirschmann, Marks, Smith, Horn, and Parsons, 405; Scheidel, 223.

before 1949, a survey of 16 provinces' 1,750,000 farms put its 1920s and 1930s' ownership at half the land. The richest 10 to 15 percent held one third to half the land in the most egalitarian areas. Poor and middling farmers owned 70 percent of land in northern Chinese village Zhangzhuangcun.

Intensifying hatred against even modest wealth as last chapter's Soviet authorities targeted kulaks, the CCP disliked middling farmers and landlords.[2037] The staunchest partisans wanted to make them a permanent underclass by taking all their property whereas Mao, favoring equality, envisioned them neither above nor below anyone else.

Killing 500,000 to 1 million rentiers in 1950, seizing over 10 million farms by 1952, and redistributing over 40 percent of land at a cost of 1.5 million to 2 million additional deaths, the CCP shrank China's Gini.[2038] The richest 5 to 7 percent of landowners held 7 to 10 percent of land. Ninety percent of Zhangzhuangcun's least poor villagers held 90.8 percent of land in 1952.

The nonpoor defeated, the CCP, anticipating at least a decade of effort, began collectivization in 1953.[2039] American historian Edwin Moise (b. 1946) described a multistage process.[2040] The first year, roughly six families shared labor, though each retained land allotted during equal division and its harvest. The second year, some 20 families, sharing all land, apportioned the harvest by how much labor, equipment, money, and livestock each contributed. The third year, at least 100 families, pooling land, labor, equipment, money, and livestock, distributed the harvest solely by amount of labor. The CCP allowed minorities extra time to comply; yet the transition took just one year. Fourteen percent of peasants farming collectively in 1955, the percentage surpassed 90 the next year, when China's 100 million peasant families worked 485,000 collective farms.[2041]

Although some CCP officials thought the change too abrupt, Mao, believing privatization impeded whereas collectivization boosted productivity, opposed delay.[2042] Applying this surmise to industry, he aimed to close the gap with Europe and the United States. Rentiers' disappearance freeing money, industrial investment rose from 5 percent of GDP in 1933 to over 25 percent in 1953.[2043]

The CCP in 1949 nationalized factories and banks that had helped Japan or Chiang and in 1952, attacking the urban middle class, encouraged laborers

---

[2037] Scheidel, 223-224.
[2038] Ibid., 225-226.
[2039] Strayer, Hirschmann, Marks, Smith, Horn, and Parsons, 407.
[2040] Moise, 136.
[2041] Scheidel, 227; Strayer, Hirschmann, Marks, Smith, Horn, and Parsons, 407.
[2042] Moise, 136.
[2043] Strayer, Hirschmann, Marks, Smith, Horn, and Parsons, 404.

to drive hundreds of thousands of supervisors and professionals to suicide.[2044] Killing 1 million urbanites and sending another 2.5 million to labor camps, the CCP expected metropolitan population to decrease 1 percent. Adopting Stalin's five-year plans in 1953, China sought to match Soviet industrialization. Nationalizing all factories and banks by 1957, government advocated efficiency, centralization, science, technology, and generous pay for engineers and scientists. A wealth disparity, with white collar employees above workmen, disappointed Mao, who distrusted those who avoided labor, especially intellectuals.

19.4.3 1957–1976

Believing the revolution complete, the CCP granted free expression during the Hundred Flowers Movement (1957–1958).[2045] Intellectuals responded by criticizing the party, which silenced them, revoked any inkling of freedom, and launched the Great Leap Forward (1958–1960) to tap China's greatest resource, its vast population. Intent on increasing farm and factory output but not wages, Mao wanted people to work harder out of patriotism.

Expecting gains from economies of scale, he consolidated China's 750,000 collective farms into 24,000 huge units, each with 30,000 workers.[2046] Nationalizing even pots and pans, Mao pursued absolute egalitarianism—a Gini of zero—by equally dividing the harvest irrespective of effort. The decision disincentivized work, which he compelled through corvée. Building 7.5 million rural factories in hopes of matching United Kingdom (UK) industrial output within 15 years, Mao expected farmers to produce food, farm equipment, and steel.

These demands overburdened them as drought, flood, and famine killed 15 million to 45 million Chinese by 1962.[2047] The disasters forcing him to re-privatize agriculture as Russian lawyer and Marxist Vladimir Lenin (1870–1924) had during last chapter's New Economic Policy, Mao neglected daily management of affairs amid CCP criticism.

Eager to strengthen farming, CCP reformers encouraged fertilizer use, closed rural factories so peasants could farm, and reduced the grain tax from 15 to 10 percent of the harvest.[2048] Grain production grew from 195 million

---

[2044] Ibid., 405-409; Scheidel, 226.

[2045] Strayer, Hirschmann, Marks, Smith, Horn, and Parsons, 409-410.

[2046] Ibid., 410-411.

[2047] Ibid., 411-412; Paul Kelly, Rod Dacombe, John Farndon, A. S. Hodson, Jesper Johnson, Niall Kishtainy, James Meadway, Anca Pusca, and Marcus Weeks, *The Little Book of Politics* (London: DK, 2020), 161.

[2048] Strayer, Hirschmann, Marks, Smith, Horn, and Parsons, 412.

tons in 1961 to 240 million tons in 1965. Raising wages, the CCP increased factory output 11 percent annually from 1961 to 1965.

This growth widening inequality, Mao rejected what he deemed capitalism and unfairness.[2049] Opposing a system that gave only the richest 15 percent of urbanites medical care, he urged students to destroy capitalism and inequality during the Great Proletarian Cultural Revolution (1966–1976). Exceeding his expectations, they beat or killed putative capitalists including officials, teachers, professors, journalists, factory supervisors, and farmers. Buddhist temples' destruction horrified onlookers. Overthrowing city authorities, Shanghai workers emulated chapter 17's Paris Commune and last chapter's St. Petersburg Soviet. Closing schools, universities, and factories, the Cultural Revolution killed 6 million to 10 million Chinese and sent 50 million, 40 percent of whom died, to labor camps.[2050]

Repudiating this disaster as GDP plummeted from 1967 to 1969, the CCP urged farmers to plant grains, legumes, vegetables, and fruits over cotton and sugarcane.[2051] Against inequality, the party ordered peasants to farm collectively at least 95 percent of land. Intent on reviving industry, the CCP reopened rural factories in another attempt to make farmers support the entire economy. Those in northeastern China's Manchuria, for example, grew food and extracted and refined petroleum. Stretching resources and personnel, the party trained farmers in preventive medicine. It sent the army wherever disorder persisted.

These actions reduced inequality. Although prerevolutionary Gini is unknown, Scheidel estimated it around 0.4 in the 1930s.[2052] It diminished to 0.31 at Mao's death and fell further into the 1980s.

19.5 Chinese Capitalism and Inequality

Mao's death left pragmatist Deng Xiaoping (1904–1997), "doing whatever was necessary to strengthen the state and enrich the people," to lead China.[2053] Embracing communism at age 15, he survived the Long March.[2054] Demoted during the Cultural Revolution, he won reinstatement in 1977.[2055] "Wherever I see a communist economy I see poverty. Wherever I see the

---

[2049] Ibid., 412-413.

[2050] Scheidel, 227.

[2051] Strayer, Hirschmann, Marks, Smith, Horn, and Parsons, 414-415.

[2052] Scheidel, 227.

[2053] Orville Schell and John Delury, *Wealth and Power: China's Long March to the Twenty-First Century* (New York: Random House, 2013), 260.

[2054] Wood, 499-500.

[2055] Ibid., 502; Strayer, Hirschmann, Marks, Smith, Horn, and Parsons, 414.

American system I see people's lives enriched," he said in expressing the paradox of building socialism through capitalism.[2056]

Ending collectivism in 1979, Deng leased land to families for 15 years.[2057] Leases later became lifetime with ability to pass land to heirs. Families could grow what they wanted provided they sold government some of the harvest, with the lease specifying the portion and price. They could use the remainder as they wished. Inequality would enlarge as some farmers outperformed others, the CCP acknowledged. China's grain harvest rising from 300 tons in 1978 to 400 tons in 1984, food production increased 9 percent annually during these years.

After 1984, businesses competed and pegged pay to productivity.[2058] That decade, low wages attracted domestic and foreign investment, which China encouraged through low tax zones. The economy largely capitalist by 1990, government still owned banks and energy firms.

Enabling production and export of inexpensive consumer goods, cheap labor reestablished China's historic role as seller over buyer.[2059] Each month in the 1990s, Chinese exports surpassed imports by $18 billion, and by March 2019 the country had a $3 trillion trade surplus. Investment and low wages made China's economy, growing fastest worldwide since the 1980s, earth's largest, though the United States retained the greatest per person income.

Inexpensive labor attracted employers. In 2013, for example, automakers Nissan and Honda paid the average Wuhan worker $333 monthly whereas Detroit's poorest autoworker earned $560 weekly.[2060] The difference enticed automakers, worsening next chapter's U.S. inequality and poverty, to move jobs to China.

Having suffered under communism, Deng permitted its criticism until reversing course in 1979 as dissatisfaction mounted.[2061] Thereafter the CCP banned opposition to socialism, Marxism, Leninism, Maoism, and chapter 17's "dictatorship of the proletariat." Intolerance led Chinese soldiers in 1989 to kill 400 to 3,000 protestors and wound 10,000 in Beijing's Tiananmen Square.

This prosperity was China and the world's key development from 1950 to 2000,[2062] as judged by American historian Paul Ropp (b. 1944). China's GDP

[2056] Wood, 501.

[2057] Strayer, Hirschmann, Marks, Smith, Horn, and Parsons, 417; Ropp, 146.

[2058] Strayer, Hirschmann, Marks, Smith, Horn, and Parsons, 417, 418; Marks, 216; Ropp, 146.

[2059] Marks, 216.

[2060] Richard D. Wolff, *Capitalism's Crisis Deepens: Essays on the Global Meltdown, 2010-2014* (Chicago: Haymarket Books, 2016), 42.

[2061] Ropp, 147-150; Wood 520.

[2062] Ropp, 150-151.

quadrupled between 1978 and 2004, when its universities, quintupling U.S. production, graduated 325,000 engineers.

However, it came at the cost of conformity, brutally enforced, and inequality grew along with the economy. Desperate women turned to prostitution.[2063] Slums swelled after 2000; over 100 million countryfolk, sought city jobs, which would have required the economy to grow at least 8 percent annually. The jobless became beggars. China spent $586 billion, roughly 7 percent of 2008 and 2009 GDP, to hire the unemployed to build and repair roads and bridges.

Decreasing into the 1980s, as mentioned, inequality reached a nonfarm Gini of 0.16 in 1980 and 0.23 overall in 1984.[2064] By comparison, chapter 20's worldwide Gini values exceeded 0.25. Inequality widened after 1985 as China's wealthiest became richer.[2065] Around 1985, China's richest centile, like their peers in Sweden, Norway, Finland, Denmark, and Iceland, received under 5 percent of national income. By 2010, these Chinese had 10 to 11 percent of national income. By comparison, the wealthiest centile received 12 to 14 percent of national income in India, Indonesia, the UK, and Canada, 16 to 18 percent in South Africa and Argentina, 20 percent in Colombia, and over 20 percent in the United States when capital gains are included. Trailing Europe and the United States in 1980, Chinese inequality, greater than that in countries with similar per person wealth, surpassed Europe and roughly matched the United States in 2020.[2066] As unequal as Malaysia, the Philippines, and most of Africa and Latin America, China increased Gini from 0.51 in 2000 to 0.55 in 2017.[2067] Only Brazil and South Africa surpassed Chinese inequality.

Despite China's rising Gini, poverty decreased after 1978, especially in the countryside, and the middle class grew.[2068] Some 745 million indigents escaped penury from 1990 to 2020.[2069]

[2063] Ibid., 152-153.

[2064] Scheidel, 227.

[2065] Thomas Piketty, *Capital in the Twenty-First Century*, trans. Arthur Goldhammer (Cambridge, MA and London: Belknap Press of Harvard University Press, 2014), 326-327.

[2066] Thomas Piketty, *Capital and Ideology*, trans. Arthur Goldhammer (Cambridge, MA and London: Belknap Press of Harvard University Press, 2020), 617, 623; Scheidel, 227.

[2067] Piketty, *Capital and Ideology*, 623; Scheidel, 227; Branko Milanovic, *The Haves and the Have-Nots: A Brief and Idiosyncratic History of Global Inequality* (New York: Basic Books, 2011), 30-31.

[2068] Fang, Conlong, Qingen Gai, Chaofei He, and Qinghau Shi, "The Experience of Poverty Reduction in Rural China," SAGE Open 10, no. 4 (December 24, 2020), ‹The Experience of Poverty Reduction in Rural China - Conglong Fang, Qingen Gai, Chaofei He, Qinghua Shi, 2020 (sagepub.com).›

[2069] Jack Goodman, "Has China Lifted 100 Million People out of Poverty?" BBC, February 28, 2021, accessed December 26, 2022, ‹Has China lifted 100 million people out of poverty? - BBC News.›

19.6 Review and Preview

As in Russia, communists combatted inequality, which decreased from 1949 to 1985 at the cost of countless lives but thereafter enlarged, in China. This increase paralleled next chapter's growth in global inequality during the last half century. Even revolution violent enough to overthrow government only temporarily reduced inequality, as indicated in chapters 16, 18, and 19. Never disappearing, it enlarged over the long term to corroborate *Eternal Inequality*'s contention that it is innate and permanent.

Chapter 20 Globalism and Recent Inequality

20.1 Abstract

Global inequality increased since the 1970s, when rising energy prices worsened inflation.[2070] Businesses responded by cutting wages and jobs. Defending corporate privilege, conservatives reduced taxes, government benefits, and services to the needy. Inequality provoked a backlash. International protest movement Occupy Wall Street (OWS), for example, criticized the world's wealthiest centile for greed and plutocracy. Yet ten years later, inequality was still larger.

20.2 Global Inequality Since the 1970s

20.2.1 Inequality's Enlargement

Although enduring mega-anna, inequality seems recent from a U.S. perspective. World War II (1939–1945) created jobs, as armaments production ended the Great Depression (1929–1939).[2071] Destroying European and Asian factories, the war, leaving the United States to supply much of the world, continued to stimulate growth.[2072] Sixty percent of Americans middle

---

[2070] Matthew P. Drennan, *Income Inequality: Why It Matters and Why Most Economists Didn't Notice* (New Haven, CT and London: Yale University Press, 2015), 111.

[2071] Joshua Freeman, Nelson Lichtenstein, Stephen Brier, David Bensman, Susan Porter Benson, David Brundage, Bret Eynon, Bruce Levine, and Bryan Palmer, *Who Built America?: Working People and the Nation's Economy, Politics, Culture, and Society* (New York: Pantheon Books, 1992), 443, 445.

[2072] Ibid., 503; Albert M. Craig, William A. Graham, Donald Kagan, Steven Ozment, and Frank M. Turner, *The Heritage of World Civilizations, Vol. II: Since 1500* (New York: Macmillan, 1986), 1163.

class from 1945 to 1960, U.S. real income rose more than it had during the previous half century.[2073] The middle class bridged opulence and poverty as incomes for the wealthiest 5 percent of Americans diminished from 21.3 percent of national income in 1947 to 19 percent in 1960   and the poor declined from 34 percent of population in 1947 to 22.1 percent in 1960.

Inequality's reduction ended with the era of cheap energy for the United States and other nations dependent on foreign oil. The Organization of Petroleum Exporting Countries' 1973 embargo halted postwar prosperity and transitioned the United States from industry to a service economy as factory output, profits, and wages decreased.[2074] Gasoline's price, 30 cents per gallon in the United States in 1970, more than quadrupled by 1980. U.S. factories economized by cutting wages and jobs. Some moved to Mexico while others occupied the U.S. south and southwest, where wages were lower and unions weaker than in the northeast and Midwest.

Absent unions, workers accepted meager pay, few benefits, and few protections against termination. Accompanying this adjustment, high energy prices exacerbated inflation.[2075] The typical U.S. home more than doubled in price from 1974 to 1980 and the average new car rose from $3,900 to $5,770. Economists coined the term "stagflation" to describe high inflation and high unemployment, both above 8 percent in 1975.[2076] Rather than reduce spending, Americans, borrowing on high interest credit cards, increased debt.

Retrenchment haunted decrepit cities. Whereas 1920s Cleveland, Ohio, produced steel, refined petroleum, and offered employment with adequate pay, benefits, and security, whites, fearing "the impoverished, jealous, and disorderly factions that have arisen among the people in the city and elsewhere in the United States, who are without a job now that industry has moved on," fled to suburbs as 1970s Cleveland lost 24 percent of population.[2077] By the 1980s, joblessness reduced neighborhoods to "derelict and decaying residential properties."[2078]

[2073] Nancy A. Hewitt and Steven F. Lawson, *Exploring American Histories: A Brief Survey with Sources* (Boston and New York: Bedford/St. Martin's, 2013), 791.

[2074] Robert B. Marks, *The Origins of the Modern World: A Global and Environmental Narrative from the Fifteenth to the Twenty-First Century*, 4th ed. (Lanham, MD: Rowman & Littlefield, 2020), 213; Jonathan Levy, *Ages of American Capitalism: A History of the United States* (New York: Random House, 2021), 544.

[2075] Hewitt and Lawson, 868.

[2076] Levy, 548.

[2077] Ibid., 562; John Reader, *Man on Earth: A Celebration of Mankind* (New York: Harper & Row, 1988), 235, 238.

[2078] Reader, 239.

Inequality widening, the richest centile of Americans more than doubled their income after 1980 while the poorest 90 percent earned stagnant wages.[2079] U.S. CEO pay jumping 940 percent, the average worker earned 12 percent more. Whereas the average 1960s CEO earned 20 times more than the typical worker, the 2019 difference was three hundredfold. Whereas the richest 0.1 percent of Americans had under 10 percent of 1980 national wealth, they owned 20 percent forty years later, or as much as the poorest 90 percent of Americans. Only the United States and Russia concentrated so much wealth at the top.

Money's flow to alphas pauperized omegas. The poorest half of Americans totaled 1.3 percent of U.S. wealth in 2020.[2080] Low wages, part time work, and job insecurity put the United States atop the Organisation for Economic Co-operation and Development's 38 nations in percentage of poor.[2081] Antiunionism disempowers U.S. workers; 10 percent belongs to a union against 26 percent in Canada, 34 percent in Italy, and 90 percent in Iceland.[2082] Employees' impotence makes the United States the lone modern economy without a labor party.

20.2.2 Globalism's Contribution to Recent Inequality

Inequality affected more than the United States. Regulations weakened worldwide on banks, easing money's late twentieth century transnational movement.[2083] Managing investments, a financial elite arose in London, Moscow, New York City, and Hong Kong. Multinational corporations in these cities and elsewhere lacked allegiance to any worker, city, country, or continent.

Hardship became ubiquitous. Thailand, Indonesia, South Korea, and Japan's 1997 banking crisis engulfed the world and destabilized Russian and Latin American economies in 1997 and 1998.[2084] The 2008 and 2009 recession, treated later, was the worst since the Great Depression. Governments rescued corporations while unemployment persisted. Supporting businesses, Ireland and Latvia reduced benefits to workers, retirees, and the

---

[2079] Robert B. Reich, *The System: Who Rigged It, How We Fix It* (New York: Knopf, 2020), 15-16.
[2080] Ibid.
[2081] Matthew Desmond, "Capitalism," in in *The 1619 Project: A New Origin Story*, ed. Nikole Hannah-Jones, Caitlin Roper, Ilena Silverman, and Jake Silverstein (New York: One World, 2021), 166-167, 185.
[2082] Ibid., 181-182.
[2083] John P. McKay, Bennett D. Hill, John Buckler, Clare Haru Crowston, Merry E. Wiesner-Hanks, and Joe Perry, *Understanding Western Society: A Brief History* (Boston and New York: Bedford/St. Martin's, 2012), 945.
[2084] Ibid., 945, 947.

jobless. Amid debt and protests, the United Kingdom (UK), Spain, Portugal, and Greece cut social programs in 2010.

While continuing to extol free trade, western Europe lost jobs to low wage eastern Europe, South America, and East Asia.[2085] For example, from 1973 to 2004 factory laborers decreased from 40 to 24 percent of France's workforce while those in services rose from 24 to 72 percent. Service work, especially retail, restaurants, and tourism, paid less while offering fewer benefits and less security than factories. Around one third of Europe's employees staffed factories in 2005.

Discontent ailed French cities, where Muslim adolescents and men, especially ages 13 to 23, lacked opportunity.[2086] Their grandfathers' genera-tion had left French North Africa after World War II to rebuild France. By the time their sons came of age, these jobs had disappeared and the current generation has no prospect of work Nonetheless, the tempo of migration into France has quickened. Their names disqualified them on applications because of prejudice. Unable to fulfill traditional notions of work and gender, they felt emasculated and resented Muslim women who excelled in school and found jobs. Arson, especially where unemployment exceeded 40 percent for the youngest men, flared in 2005, 2007, and 2009.[2087]

Atop the economic pyramid, executives and professionals, about one quarter of Europe's population, managed information and money.[2088] Below them, expectations, wealth, and living standards diminished for the middle class in services after losing a factory job. At bottom, a racial and economic underclass, another one quarter of Europe, performed jobs that required the least skill and education.

By 1980, the world's richest nations exhibited inequality unknown since 1913.[2089] After 1980, the world's richest centile amassed the greatest gains. The richest tenth took 56 percent, and the wealthiest 5 percent captured 37 percent, of 2005 global income.[2090] The poorest tenth had 0.7 percent, with the poorest 5 percent under 0.2 percent. Most countries' richest decile owned 60 to 90 percent of 2010 wealth, the 40 percent below it had 5 to 35 percent, and the rest held under 5 percent.[2091]

[2085] Ibid., 945-946.

[2086] William Pfaff, "The French Riots: Will They Change Anything?" *The New York Review of Books* 52, no. 20 (December 15, 2005): 88-89.

[2087] McKay, Hill, Buckler, Crowston, Wiesner-Hanks, and Perry, 956.

[2088] Ibid., 946.

[2089] Marks, 211-212.

[2090] Branko Milanovic, *The Haves and the Have-Nots: A Brief and Idiosyncratic History of Global Inequality* (New York: Basic Books, 2011), 152.

[2091] Marks, 211.

The uberwealthy dwarfed underlings. The richest 1.75 percent had as much wealth as the poorest 77 percent around 2010.[2092] The world's six richest magnates owned more than the poorest 4 billion people in 2017, stated the introduction. "Inequality...is today probably as high as it has ever been," remarked Serbian American economist Branko Milanovic (b. 1953).[2093]

American investor and "Oracle of Omaha" Warren Buffett (b. 1930) attributed this reality to class antagonism, stating that "There's class warfare all right. But it's my class, the rich class, that's making war, and we're winning."[2094] This conflict, chapter 1 noted its uni-directionality, shaped tension between haves and have-nots throughout this book. Elites' triumph eternalized inequality, an *Eternal Inequality* leitmotif.

20.2.3 Inequality's Geography

As implied, inequality was geographic as well as hereditary and occupational.[2095] Northern Italy, southern Germany, and Austria joined London, Moscow, New York City, and Hong Kong in housing a financial elite. Poorer were rural southern Italy and Spain and the UK north of London, where empty factories deteriorated. Trailing Europe, the United States, and Canada in wealth, Africa and South America became a global south.

The gap between rich and poor nations more than doubled from 1960 to 1995.[2096] The wealthiest countries had per person incomes 55 times greater than the poorest by 1990. Indigents, many in India, China, Southeast Asia, and Africa, totaled half the world's population. Thirty-four of the world's most indebted countries occupied sub-Saharan Africa, where roughly 30 percent of people were undernourished and paupers more than doubled from 1981 to 2001.[2097]

[2092] Milanovic, 161.

[2093] Ibid.

[2094] MHProNews, "Warren Buffett Declared "Class Warfare," Buffett Says Fellow Billionaires—"We're Winning,"" Manufactured and Modular Housing News, June 29, 2020, accessed September 21, 2022, ‹Warren Buffett Declared "Class Warfare," Buffett Says Fellow Billionaires - "We're Winning" (manufacturedhomepronews.com);› Tom Huddleston Jr., "How Warren Buffet Made His Billions and Become the 'Oracle of Omaha,'" CNBC Disruptor, August 30, 2020, accessed September 21, 2022, ‹https://www.cnbc.com/2020/08/30/how-warren-buffett-made-billions-became-oracle-of-omaha.html.›

[2095] McKay, Hill, Buckler, Crowston, Wiesner-Hanks, and Perry, 946-947.

[2096] Marks, 207.

[2097] Ibid., 210.

20.2.4 The Gini Scale as Measure of Inequality

The most unequal countries in 2010, Brazil and South Africa had a Gini, which chapter 6 introduced as a measure of inequality, around 0.6.[2098] Below them, Malaysia, the Philippines, China, and most of Africa and Latin America were between 0.5 and 0.6. In the third tier, Russia and the United States hovered between 0.4 and 0.5. Inequality rose steeply in both after roughly 1990. Fourth, most of the European Union (EU) was between 0.3 and 0.35. At bottom, the Czech Republic, Slovakia, Sweden, Denmark, Norway, Finland, and Iceland were least unequal at 0.25 to 0.3.

By continent, South America, Africa, and Asia in that order exhibited the highest Gini.[2099] Of them, as implied, Africa was poorest.[2100] Indian and Chinese growth lessened Asian destitution. The juxtaposition of slums and posh neighborhoods concretized inequality in South America, whose colonial past still curtails opportunities.[2101]

20.3 Conservatism v. Reform

20.3.1 Defenders of Privilege and Inequality

Causing conservative backlash, the two world wars enlarged government management of the economy. Attracting voters, conservatism, labelled neoliberalism in Europe, empowered politicians like U.S. president Ronald Reagan (1911–2004), UK prime minister Margaret Thatcher (1925–2013), and West German chancellor Helmut Kohl (1930–2017).[2102] The word "neoliberalism" was unhelpful given the imprecision of "liberalism," which may mean government spending to uplift the needy, a definition incongruous with conservatism. Neoliberals lionized chapter 15's Scottish economist Adam Smith (1723–1790).

Smith advocating *laissez faire*, government, rather than manage the economy, should create the stability it needed through a strong military. Combining entrepreneurialism, patriotism, and militarism, conservatives glorified *laissez faire* as abstraction but wanted government's help controlling

---

[2098] Milanovic, 30-31; Walter Scheidel, *The Great Leveler: Violence and the History of Inequality from the Stone Age to the Twenty-First Century* (Princeton, NJ and Oxford: Princeton University Press, 2017), 227.

[2099] Milanovic, 31.

[2100] Ibid., 101.

[2101] Arianna Smith, "Addressing the Causes of Poverty in South America," Borgen Project, February 12, 2018, accessed April 8, 2022, ‹Addressing the Causes of Poverty in South America (borgenproject.org).›

[2102] McKay, Hill, Buckler, Crowston, Wiesner-Hanks, and Perry, 913-914; Hewitt and Lawson, 873.

---

labor. Abhorring aid to indigents as wealth's downward redistribution, they favored upward redistribution via subsidies.

Of the three politicians, Thatcher, becoming prime minister in 1979, "represented everything wrong with capitalism" to detractors.[2103] She persuaded Parliament to sell public businesses, reduce taxes—the rich's fell over 50 percent—and cut public housing, education, and health care.[2104] Subsidies decreased to steel and textile mills and coal mines while 1980s unemployment, poverty, inequality, crime, strikes, protests, and riots increased.

Two years after Thatcher became prime minister, Reagan, a "fervent believer in supply-side economics," assumed the U.S. presidency.[2105] Following her agenda, he asked Congress to cut income taxes 30 percent over three years and social programs over $40 billion.[2106] Congress reduced taxes, especially on the rich, and food stamps—now the Supplemental Nutrition Assistance Program (SNAP)—school lunches, Aid to Families with Dependent Children, and Medicaid. But thrift never resulted, first, because Congress increased the military budget to counter chapter 18's Soviet Union, which Reagan labelled the "evil empire."[2107] Second, Congress, reversing course, increased spending on unemployment and Medicaid during an early 1980s recession. Tax cuts plus robust spending tripled the debt between 1981 and 1990.

Reaganomics, "voodoo economics" to critics, enlarged inequality.[2108] Defense contracts enriching corporations, the number of millionaires doubled from 1981 to 1990, when the richest centile of Americans owned 42 percent of national wealth and 60 percent of the stock market. Opposite them, poverty rose from 11.7 percent of population in 1981 to 13.5 percent in 1990, homelessness grew, and the middle class shrank.

[2103] Claire Berlinski, *"There Is No Alternative:" Why Margaret Thatcher Matters* (New York: Basic Books, 2008), 206.

[2104] H. Stuart Hughes, *Contemporary Europe: A History*, 5th ed. (Englewood Cliffs, NJ: Prentice-Hall, 1981), 573; McKay, Hill, Buckler, Crowston, Wiesner-Hanks, and Perry, 914; Hewitt and Lawson, 876.

[2105] McKay, Hill, Buckler, Crowston, Wiesner-Hanks, and Perry, 914; Mary Beth Norton, David M. Katzman, Paul D. Escott, Howard P. Chudacoff, Thomas G. Patterson, and William M. Tuttle, Jr., *A People and a Nation: A History of the United States, Vol II: Since 1865*, 4th ed. (Boston: Houghton Mifflin, 1994), 1034.

[2106] Hewitt and Lawson, 876.

[2107] Gary B. Nash, Julie Roy Jeffrey, John R. Howe, Peter J. Frederick, Allen F. Davis, and Allan M. Winkler, *The American People: Creating a Nation and a Society, Vol. 2: Since 1865*, 2d ed. (HarperCollinsPublishers, 1990), 1052.

[2108] Hewitt and Lawson, 876-877; Norton, Katzman, Escott, Chudacoff, Patterson, and Tuttle, 1034; Levy, 610-611.

That decade Illinois and Indiana steel mills closed because profits were insufficient.[2109] Ninety thousand steelworkers in these states lost employment in 1980 alone. Bethlehem Steel shut its Lackawanna, New York, factory in 1982. United States Steel Corporation was "no longer in the business of making steel," announced CEO David Roderick (1924–2019).[2110] Eliminating Homestead, Pennsylvania's mill and Pittsburgh jobs, it was "in the business of making profits."[2111]

In 1982, Kohl, "the genius of the present" to admirers, became chancellor of what was then West Germany.[2112] Tax and spending cuts increased joblessness and shifted medical and dental costs to patients, though these changes never persuaded Thatcher of his conservatism.

Initially taking a different path, French socialist, president, and "technician of power" François Mitterrand (1916–1996) in 1981, appointing four communists to his cabinet, formed a coalition with the French Communist Party.[2113] Unable to spend France into prosperity, he retreated after 1983, privatized public businesses, and cut government benefits. Rather than advance progressivism, France aped conservatism.

20.3.2 The Challenge to Privilege and Inequality

20.3.2.1 2008 and 2009 Recession

The 2008 and 2009 recession aggravated inequality.[2114] Above 14,000 points at its October 2007 peak, the Dow Jones Industrial Average, tracking 30 companies' stock price, fell below 6,600 in March 2009.[2115] The drop, the largest by percentage since 1931, obliterated trillions of dollars.[2116] The fourth largest U.S. investment bank, Lehman Brothers, lost over $2 billion and declared bankruptcy in 2008, when GDP fell 6 percent, consumer spending decreased, some 10 million Americans lost their home, and unemployment rose from 4.9 percent in January 2008 to 7.6 percent a year later. Home values

---

[2109] Levy, 604.

[2110] Ibid.

[2111] Ibid.

[2112] McKay, Hill, Buckler, Crowston, Wiesner-Hanks, and Perry, 914; Karl Hugo Pruys, "Introduction," in *Kohl, Genius of the Present: A Biography of Helmut Kohl*, ed. Karl Hugo Pruys, trans. Kathleen Bunten (Chicago: Edition Q, 1996), viii.

[2113] Ibid., 916; Robin W. Winks, Crane Brinton, John B. Christopher, and Robert Lee Wolff, *A History of Civilization, Vol. II: 1648 to the Present*, 7th ed. (Englewood Cliffs, NJ: Prentice Hall, 1988), 826; David S. Bell, *François Mitterrand: A Political Biography* (Cambridge, UK: Polity, 2005), 173.

[2114] Hewitt and Lawson, 944.

[2115] Kimberly Amadeo, "The Stock Market Crash of 2008," The Balance, last modified January 8, 2022, accessed April 8, 2022, ‹Stock Market Crash 2008: Dates, Causes, Effects (thebalance.com).›

[2116] Hewitt and Lawson, 943; Reich, 43-45.

---

declining, homeowners lost $11.1 trillion in 2008. Averaging losses across the population, the Great Recession cost each American roughly $70,000.

Anecdotes conveyed despair. For example, an anonymous woman reported in 2011 that she and her husband, both U.S. Navy veterans and college graduates, received medical, but no dental, care through the Veterans Administration absent private insurance.[2117] The state insured their two children, who qualified for SNAP, though wife and husband were ineligible because they worked under 32 hours weekly. Without steady income, both tried to improve employability by pursuing master's degrees. Their combined debt exceeding $140,000, additional loans would be necessary to complete the programs.

Most banks and corporations avoided disillusionment. During George W. Bush's (b. 1946) presidency, Congress loaned or gave financial institutions $700 billion.[2118] J. P. Morgan, the largest credit card company and provider of automobile loans, received $25 billion in 2008.[2119] Its CEO Jamie Dimon (b. 1956) earned $20 million that year while roughly 8.7 million Americans lost work. Prospering thereafter, the company owned $2.6 trillion and managed $25 trillion in 2019.[2120]

Also benefiting, General Motors (GM) took $50 billion in loans in 2009.[2121] Demanding privation during recession, GM hired employees at half the prevailing wage. Temporary workers earned even less while GM offshored jobs. Like J. P. Morgan, GM, receiving $600 million in government contracts and $500 million in tax breaks from 2017 to 2019, profited after the recession. Pocketing $22 million in 2017, GM CEO Mary Barra (b. 1961) announced five factories' closure and 14,000 jobs' elimination the next year. Among victims was the Lordstown, Ohio, plant, which President Donald Trump (b. 1946) had promised to save.

Beyond the United States, recession imperiled UK banks.[2122] The EU loaned money to Greece, Spain, and Ireland, provided they reduced government spending and the minimum wage, to prevent collapse. Businesses failed in China as spending dropped and unemployment rose.

"Eleven years after Wall Street's near meltdown, not a single major financial executive has been convicted or even indicted for crimes that wiped out the savings of countless Americans. Contrast this with a teenager who is

---

[2117] Hewitt and Lawson, 949.
[2118] Ibid., 943.
[2119] Reich, 43-44.
[2120] Ibid., 20.
[2121] Ibid., 48.
[2122] Hewitt and Lawson, 944.

imprisoned for years for selling an ounce of marijuana," wrote attorney and former U.S. Labor Secretary Robert Reich (b. 1946) in 2020.[2123]

20.3.2.2 Occupy Wall Street as Backlash against Greed and Inequality

Previous chapters examined earlier backlashes whereas this chapter, integrating the United States into the narrative, contextualizes OWS as protest against decades of worsening inequality. Like other backlashes, it never eliminated inequality.

Following Tunisia's December 2010 demonstrations that engulfed North Africa, Egypt, Southwest Asia, and Europe, Canadian online magazine Adbusters in July 2011 urged readers to gather in New York City's financial district on September 17, international Anti-Banks Day, against inequality, greed, and plutocracy.[2124] The Great Recession motivated demonstrators to criticize inadequate funding for public education, social programs, and infrastructure; inordinate student debt and pollution; overreliance on fossil fuels; and climate change.[2125]

Adbusters hoped to attract 20,000 activists to One Chase Manhattan Plaza, once home to Chase Manhattan Bank, but police fenced it and an alternative, Bowling Green Park, which displays the Wall Street bull statue.[2126] Protestors instead gathered at private Zuccotti Park. Police could not overrule the owner's decision to host peaceful demonstrators. New York City mayor Michael Bloomberg (b. 1942) on September 17 affirmed the right of peaceful assembly.

The crowd, initially about 1,000 mostly young, middle-class whites who feared living standards' erosion, never surpassed 15,000 despite organizers' attempt to attract attendees by hiring a public relations firm.[2127] Autumn's coolness may have diminished attendance.

Designating Wall Street "the financial Gomorrah of America" and referencing chapter 6's Hebrews' escape from Egypt, Adbusters amplified protestors' demand for equality and justice.[2128] Evincing both, they made Zuccotti

---

[2123] Reich, 52.

[2124] Elisabetta Cangelosi, "Occupy Movement," in *Ideas and Movements that Shaped America: From the Bill of Rights to "Occupy Wall Street," Vol. 2: F through O*, ed. Michael S. Green and Scott L. Stabler (Santa Barbara, CA and Denver, CO: ABC-CLIO, 2015), 745; Andrew C. Worthington, "Occupy Wall Street," in *The SAGE Encyclopedia of Economics and Society*, vol. 3, ed. Frederick F. Wherry and Juliet Schor (Los Angeles: SAGE Reference, 2015), 1202-1203; Sarah van Gelder, "Introduction: How Occupy Wall Street Changed Everything," in *This Changes Everything: Occupy Wall Street and the 99% Movement*, ed. Sarah van Gelder and the Staff of *Yes! Magazine* (Oakland, CA: Berrett-Koehler Publishers, 2011), 1.

[2125] Hewitt and Lawson, 947.

[2126] Worthington, 1203.

[2127] Ibid.

[2128] Ibid; Gelder, 8.

Park, renamed Liberty Square, an egalitarian tent city.[2129] Sharing food and labor, they resembled chapter 12's Essenes and monks and chapter 17's first century Christians, though OWS lacked Christianity's centralism.

Against politicians and journalists too craven to acknowledge capitalism's defects and police who protected elites over commoners, the movement's slogan, "we are the 99%," concretized the tussle between proletarians and "the super-rich."[2130] This struggle gained urgency from the realization that the masses lacked upward mobility wherever hard work plus education yielded poverty.[2131]

"A group of people started camping out in Zuccotti Park, and all of a sudden the conversation started being about the right things," stated American economist and 2008 Nobel laureate in economics Paul Krugman (b. 1953).[2132] "It's kind of a miracle." Praise also came from U.S. senator and former presidential candidate Bernie Sanders (b. 1941).[2133]

Krugman and Sanders could not save OWS. Citing hazardous, unsanitary conditions, police on November 15, 2011 evicted demonstrators, who took their crusade to banks, corporations, government offices, colleges, and universities.[2134] Besides New York City, the movement reached Boston, Chicago, Los Angeles, Portland, Atlanta, San Diego, San Francisco, and hundreds of smaller U.S. cities.[2135] With some 3,000 protestors at its peak, Oakland hosted the largest occupation outside New York City. Around 25,000 marchers energized Oakland's November 2, 2011 strike. Over 100,000 activists occupied more than 1,500 cities from Madrid, Spain south to Cape Town, South Africa and from Buenos Aires, Argentina east to Hong Kong, China.

"The 99% are no longer sitting on the sidelines of history—we are making history," enthused American author, editor, and activist Sarah van Gelder, though OWS ended in 2012 without thwarting inequality.[2136] French economist Thomas Piketty (b. 1971) credited the movement with highlighting "the spectacular growth of inequality," but neither rhetoric nor action averted COVID-19's enlargement of inequality, examined next.[2137]

[2129] Gelder; Worthington, 1203; Cangelosi, 746-747.

[2130] Cangelosi, 745; Gelder, 2.

[2131] Gelder, 4.

[2132] Ibid., 11.

[2133] Worthington, 1202.

[2134] Ibid., 1203.

[2135] Gelder, 2; Cangelosi, 745.

[2136] Gelder, 12; Cangelosi, 749.

[2137] Thomas Piketty, *Capital in the Twenty-First Century*, trans. Arthur Goldhammer (Cambridge, MA and London: Belknap Press of Harvard University Press, 2014), 254.

20.4 The Business Cycle and Twenty-First Century Inequality

20.4.1 COVID-19 Downturn

20.4.1.1 Wealth, Misery, and Inequality

Overviewing the Black Death, chapter 13 demonstrated that contagion affected our past and inequality, a fact this chapter confirms by examining the latest pandemic, caused by a coronavirus identified in 2019 and named COVID-19.[2138] Scientists, physicians, journalists, economists, and policymakers discussing its ramifications, this book considers only inequality.

More than doubling Great Recession losses, the pandemic shed around 20.6 million U.S. jobs from March 15 to April 30, 2020.[2139] Partly rebounding, U.S. net losses approximated 10 million jobs by December 2020.[2140] U.S. unemployment that year reached 14.7 percent, the highest since the Great Depression.

Some 114 million jobs vanished worldwide in 2020.[2141] Employees' hours diminishing, Geneva, Switzerland's World Economic Forum estimated 2020 losses equivalent to 255 million full-time jobs. COVID cost global workers that year roughly $3.7 trillion, losses fourfold worse than the Great Recession.

Paupers, some 88 million to 114 million having incomes under $1.90 daily from March to October 2020, swelled to some 700 million worldwide and 8 million Americans fell below the federal poverty line.[2142] From March 2020 to January 2022, the poorest 99 percent of the world lost income while the richest 10 men more than doubled their collective wealth from roughly

---

[2138] "Coronavirus Disease 2019 (COVID-19)," Centers for Disease Control and Prevention, last modified December 21, 2021, accessed April 8, 2022, ‹Coronavirus Disease 2019 (COVID-19) | Disease or Condition of the Week | CDC.›

[2139] Stephanie Soucheray, "US Jobs Loses Due to COVID-19 Highest Since Great Depression," University of Minnesota Center for Infectious Disease Research and Policy, May 8, 2020, accessed April 8, 2022, ‹US job losses due to COVID-19 highest since Great Depression | CIDRAP (umn.edu).›

[2140] Ryan Ansell and John P. Mullins, "COVID-19 Ends Longest Employment Recovery and Expansion in CES History, Causing Unprecedented Jobs Losses in 2020," U.S. Bureau of Labor Statistics, Monthly Labor Review, June 2021, accessed June 21, 2022, ‹COVID-19 ends longest employment recovery and expansion in CES history, causing unprecedented job losses in 2020 : Monthly Labor Review: U.S. Bureau of Labor Statistics (bls.gov).›

[2141] Felix Richter, "COVID-19 Has Caused a Huge Amount of Lost Working Hours," World Economic Forum, February 4, 2021, accessed April 8, 2022, ‹How many jobs were lost in 2020 due to COVID-19? | World Economic Forum (weforum.org).›

[2142] Igor Derysh, "Billionaire Wealth Rises to More Than $10 Trillion for First Time Ever amid Pandemic: Analysis," Salon, October 17, 2020, accessed April 8, 2022, ‹Billionaire wealth rises to more than $10 trillion for first time ever amid pandemic: analysis | Salon. com.›

$700 billion to $1.5 trillion.[2143] By the second date, these 10 had sixfold more wealth than the poorest 3.1 billion persons. Were the decemvir to lose 99.999 percent of their wealth, they would remain richer than the poorest 99 percent. "For billionaires, this is a heads-we-win, tails-you-lose economy," remarked American author and scholar Chuck Collins (b. 1959).[2144]

Yet COVID inaugurated no recession. A downturn must persist two consecutive quarters or six months to be a recession, whereas the COVID setback lasted just March and April 2020.[2145]

20.4.1.2 The American Dream as Myth

COVID amplified doubts about the American dream, which American linguist, philosopher, and "world's leading public intellectual" Noam Chomsky (b. 1928) defined as upward mobility.[2146] Entering the United States in 1913 and funding his education through sweatshop labor, his father Zeev Chomsky (1896–1977) earned a Ph.D. and became middle class. Like other immigrants, he fled opportunity's absence for the American dream.

Today, fewer Americans than Europeans transcend poverty.[2147] "Inequality is really unprecedented," Noam Chomsky stated.[2148] "If you look at total inequality today, it's like the worst periods of American history." This appraisal indicates that the American dream, if it ever existed, perished before COVID. All that remains is propaganda.

[2143] Kalila Sangster, "Musk and Bezos among World's 10 Richest Men Who Doubled Their Wealth in Pandemic," Yahoo!Finance, January 17, 2022, accessed April 8, 2022, ‹World's 10 richest men double their wealth in pandemic (yahoo.com)›; Huileng Tan, "The World's 10 Richest Men Have Made So Much Money during the Pandemic that a One-Time 99% Tax on Their Gains Could Pay for All COVID-19 Vaccine Production and More: Oxfam," Insider, January 17, 2022, accessed April 8, 2022, ‹World's 10 Richest Men's Fortunes More Than Doubled in Pandemic: Oxfam (businessinsider.com)›; Max Zahn with Andy Serwer, "Billionaire Charlie Munger: Critics of the Ultra-Rich 'Motivated by Envy'," Yahoo!Finance, February 16, 2022, accessed April 8, 2022, ‹Billionaire Charlie Munger: Critics of the ultra-rich 'motivated by envy' (yahoo.com)›; Nabil Ahmed, *Inequality Kills: The Unparalleled Action Needed to Combat Unprecedented Inequality in the Wake of COVID-19* (Oxford: Oxfam International, 2022), 10.

[2144] Derysh.

[2145] David Rodeck and Benjamin Curry, "What Is a Recession?" Forbes Advisor, last modified March 24, 2022, accessed April 8, 2022, ‹Recession Definition: What Is A Recession?–Forbes Advisor›; Jeff Cox, "It's Official: The COVID Recession Lasted Just Two Months, the Shortest in U.S. History," CNBC, last modified July 19, 2021, accessed April 8, 2022, ‹It's official: The Covid recession lasted just two months, the shortest in U.S. history (cnbc.com).›

[2146] C. J. Polychroniou, "Introduction," in *Optimism over Despair: On Capitalism, Empire, and Social Change*, Noam Chomsky and C. J. Polychroniou (Chicago: Haymarket Books, 2017), 1; Noam Chomsky, *Requiem for the American Dream: The 10 Principles of Concentration of Wealth and Power* (New York: Seven Stories Press, 2017), x–xi; Jack Holmes, "The American Dream is Collapsing. Are We Too Angry to Fix It?" Esquire, April 15, 2020, accessed April 8, 2022, ‹Why Americans Are Too Angry to Fix The American Dream (esquire.com).›

[2147] Chomsky, x–xi.

[2148] Ibid., x–xi.

Upward mobility being myth, onlookers struggle to locate it. American historian Gary Nash (1933–2021) and coauthors situated it between 1870 and 1900, when industrialization and the rise of professions created middle-class jobs.[2149] Believing the United States offered more opportunity for advancement than Europe, Americans celebrated U.S. oilman John Rockefeller (1839–1937) and Scottish American industrialist Andrew Carnegie (1835–1919) as "rags-to-riches" icons.[2150]

Piketty positioned the American dream in the early nineteenth century, when European Americans moved west to settle former Native American lands.[2151] Like Noam Chomsky, he acknowledged that upward mobility happened less in the United States than Europe despite contrary belief.

American historian Robert Crunden (1940–1999) located the American dream even earlier in Puritan work, thrift, and piety.[2152] Secularizing and popularizing Puritanism, Americans like "many-sided genius" Benjamin Franklin (1706–1790), who "came from the ranks of common men and never lost touch with them," believed American exceptionalism let anyone succeed through effort and integrity.[2153]

As myth, the American dream needed proselytizers like American author Horatio Alger (1832–1899) whose 119 novels, describing "America as the land of opportunity," sold over 20 million copies.[2154] The myth's durability despite contradictory evidence proved Alger's effectiveness and required that lawyer and politician Harry Reid (1939–2021), rising from penury to U.S. Senate majority leader, lie in state at the Capitol.[2155] Americans venerate those who vivify the grandest fiction.

[2149] Nash, Jeffrey, Howe, Frederick, Davis, and Winkler, 624-625.

[2150] Ibid.

[2151] Piketty, 484.

[2152] Robert M. Crunden, *A Brief History of American Culture* (Armonk, NY and London: North Castle Books, 1994), 131-132.

[2153] John M. Blum, Edmund S. Morgan, Willie Lee Rose, Arthur M. Schlesinger, Jr., Kenneth M. Stampp, and C. Vann Woodward, *The National Experience: A History of the United States Since 1865*, vol. 1, 4th ed. (New York: Harcourt Brace Jovanovich, 1977), 68; Mark G. Spencer, "Franklin, Benjamin (1706-1790)," in *Research and Discovery: Landmarks and Pioneers in American Science*, vol. 1, ed. Russell Lawson (Armonk, NY: Sharpe Reference, 2008), 27.

[2154] Nash, Jeffrey, Howe, Frederick, Davis, and Winkler, 625; Alan Brinkley, *American History: A Survey, Vol. II: Since 1865*, 9th ed. (New York: McGraw-Hill, 1995), 489; C. Edward Balog, "Alger, Horatio, Jr.," in *Historical Dictionary of the Gilded Age*, ed. Leonard Schlup and James G. Ryan (Armonk, NY and London: M. E. Sharpe, 2003), 9.

[2155] Lisa Mascaro, "Biden Pays Silent Tribute as Reid Lies in State at Capitol," AP News, January 12, 2022, accessed April 9, 2022, ‹Biden pays silent tribute as Reid lies in state at Capitol | AP News.›

20.4.2 A K-Shaped Recovery

Economic recovery is k-shaped when one group prospers while others suffer.[2156] Outcomes diverge, an *Eternal Inequality* leitmotif whereby underlings languish despite enriching elites. Beginning May 2020, the COVID recovery followed this pattern.[2157] For example, a Columbus, Ohio realtor sold a home for $4.5 million in October 2020.[2158] Several offers, all cash, evinced prospective buyers' affluence. Commission from its sale and others helped her buy a $645,000 three-story home.

Fourteen miles to the southeast, a mother and two children, without natural gas for heat because of nonpayment, huddled near an electric oven that month, though electricity was likewise scheduled for disconnection.[2159] Unable to afford $840 monthly rent, she feared eviction. Full-time work as a medical assistant without benefits was inadequate because a creditor garnished one quarter of her wages for a 22 percent interest car loan. Nonpayment after the car broke accumulated fees, penalties, and interest over $10,000.

Another Columbus resident, her husband, and three children also struggled.[2160] A U.S. Army veteran, she received an honorable discharge after having a seizure. Even with an associate degree and medical assistant certification, she, lacking steady work from March to October 2020, subsisted by washing cars, cutting lawns, and demolishing hovels. Despite these efforts, her income was inadequate for veterans' assistance. Typifying a nation where hunger tripled from July 2019 to July 2020, wife and husband fasted three days in October so their children could eat.

The downturn spared Kroger, the largest U.S. grocer and fourth largest employer, which profited $4.1 billion in 2020.[2161] CEO Rodney McMullen (b. 1961) pocketed over $22 million that year, some 909 times Kroger's average

[2156] "K-Shaped Recovery," Corporate Finance Institute, 2015-2022, accessed April 9, 2022, ‹K-Shaped Recovery - Overview, How It Works, Example (corporatefinanceinstitute.com).›

[2157] Cox.

[2158] Michelle Conlin, "The Great Divergence: U.S. COVID-19 Economy Has Delivered Luxury Homes for Some, Evictions for Others, Reuters, October 31, 2020, accessed April 9, 2022, ‹https://news.yahoo.com/great-divergence-u-covid-19-110716520.html?fr=sycsrp_catchall.›

[2159] Ibid.

[2160] Jackie Mader, "With Help Slow to Come from Washington, A Veteran's Family Gets by Washing Cars, Skipping Meals," The Hechinger Report, October 17, 2020, accessed April 9, 2022, ‹Seven months into the pandemic, many families are struggling with poverty (hechingerreport.org).›

[2161] Jason Lalljee, "Kroger Workers Experienced Hunger, Homelessness, and Couldn't Pay Their Rent in 2021. Its CEO Made $22 Million the Previous Year," Insider, January 14, 2022, accessed April 9, 2022, ‹Kroger workers experienced hunger, homelessness, and couldn't pay their rent in 2021. Its CEO made $22 million the previous year. (yahoo.com).›

pay. Fourteen percent of employees, whose real wages fell 11 to 22 percent after 1990, were homeless in 2021, over one third struggled with rent, and 78 percent reported hunger.

20.5 Final Statement

Examining the last 4 million years, this book ends where it began by deeming inequality our fundamental constant. Like English polymath Isaac Newton's (1643–1727) law of gravitation, inequality operated, and continues to operate, in all times, places, and circumstances, shaping our past and present and making our existence predictable and stable. Reformers like German economists Karl Marx (1818–1883) and Friedrich Engels (1820–1895) hoped to negate the past by creating an egalitarian future, but this idealism failed because inequality remains the default.

Their classless society disregarded hierarchy's inviolability. Even after killing his father and marrying his mother, Theban king Oedipus, epitomizing "the extraordinary man or woman who separates himself or herself from the group," never surrendered status.[2162] The final chorus acknowledged him as "the king" and "most powerful of men."[2163] Worthy of rank even amid catastrophe, he "towered" over underlings.[2164]

Greek philosopher Aristotle (384–322 BCE) praised Oedipus' wealth and eminence.[2165] His fall from hierarchy's summit was too consequential to ignore. "The heroes of classical tragedy are always members of the nobility," remarked American poet and scholar David Bergman (b. 1950) and American poet and playwright Daniel Mark Epstein (b. 1948).[2166] "Their fates are terrifying to us, for we sense that if these great, privileged figures are vulnerable, then none of us is safe."

[2162] "Greek Drama and Oedipus Rex," in The Heath Guide to Literature, ed. David Bergman and Daniel Mark Epstein (Lexington, MA and Toronto: D. C. Heath, 1984), 920.

[2163] Sophocles, Oedipus Rex, in The Heath Guide to Literature, ed. David Bergman and Daniel Mark Epstein (Lexington, MA and Toronto: D. C. Heath, 1984), 960.

[2164] Ibid.

[2165] Aristotle, Poetics, trans. Malcolm Heath (London: Penguin Books, 1996), 21.

[2166] "Fear and Pity," in The Heath Guide to Literature, ed. David Bergman and Daniel Mark Epstein (Lexington, MA and Toronto: D. C. Heath, 1984), 1013.

Selected Bibliography

"Aggression and Violence in Man—A Dialogue." L. S. B. Leakey Foundation for Research Related to Man's Origin, November 1971. Accessed April 25, 2022, 1-27. ‹https://authors.library.caltech.edu/25660/1/Munger_Africana_Library__Notes.9.pdf.›

Ahmed, Nabil. *Inequality Kills: The Unparalleled Action Needed to Combat Unprecedented Inequality in the Wake of COVID-19.* Oxford: Oxfam International, 2022.

Aiken, Henry D. *The Age of Ideology: The 19th Century Philosophers.* New York: New American Library, 1956.

Allan, Tony, Kay Celtel, Jacob F. Field, R. G. Grant, Philip Parker, and Sally Regan. *Imperial China: The Definitive Visual History.* London: DK, 2020.

Allee, W. C. *The Social Life of Animals.* Ann Arbor: University of Michigan Libraries, 1958. Accessed April 21, 2022. ‹https://babel.hathitrust.org/cgi/pt?id=mdp.39015064489134&view=1up&seq=2&skin=2021.›

Allen, Robert C. *Global Economic History: A Very Short Introduction.* Oxford and New York: Oxford University Press, 2011.

Ardrey, Robert. *African Genesis: A Personal Investigation into the Animal Origins and Nature of Man.* New York: Atheneum, 1970.

Ardrey, Robert. *The Hunting Hypothesis: A Personal Conclusion Concerning the Evolutionary Nature of Man.* New York: Atheneum, 1976.

Ardrey, Robert. *The Territorial Imperative: A Personal Inquiry into the Animal Origins of Property and Nations.* New York: Atheneum, 1966.

Aristotle. *Politics,* trans. Benjamin Jowett. New York: Modern Library, 1943.

Armstrong, Alan. *Farmworkers in England and Wales: A Social and Economic History, 1770-1980.* Ames: Iowa State University Press, 1988.

Armstrong, Karen. *Fields of Blood: Religion and the History of Violence.* Waterville, ME: Thorndike Press, 2014.

Atack, Jeremy and Peter Passell. *A New Economic View of American History: From Colonial Times to 1940,* 2d ed. New York and London: Norton, 1994.

Austen, Ralph A. "Trading Patterns, Trans-Saharan." In *Berkshire Encyclopedia of World History.* Vol. 5, ed. William H. McNeill, Jerry H. Bentley, David Christian, David Levinson, J. R. McNeill, Heidi Roupp, and Judith P. Zinsser, 1883-1886. Great Barrington, MA: Berkshire Publishing Group, 2005.

Bardoe, Cheryl. *China: A History.* New York: Abrams Books, 2018.

Bartlett, Roger. "The Russian Peasantry on the Eve of the French Revolution." *History of European Ideas* 12, no. 3 (1990): 395-416.

Bartlett, Roger. "Serfdom and State Power in Imperial Russia." *European History Quarterly* 33, no. 1 (2003): 29-64.

Barzun, Jacques. *Darwin, Marx, Wagner: Critique of a Heritage,* 2d ed. Chicago and London: University of Chicago Press, 1981.

Basham, A. L. *The Wonder that Was India: A Survey of the History and Culture of the Indian Sub-Continent before the Coming of the Muslims.* Calcutta: Rupa, 1986.

Bavel, Bas van. *Manors and Markets: Economy and Society in the Low Countries, 500-1600.* Oxford: Oxford University Press, 2010.

Beard, Mary. *SPQR: A History of Ancient Rome.* New York and London: Liveright Publishing, 2015.

Beckman, Rosina, ed. *The History of Russia from 1801 to the Present.* New York: Britannica, 2019.

Bellah, Robert N. *Religion in Human Evolution: From the Paleolithic to the Axial Age.* Cambridge, MA and London: Belknap Press of Harvard University Press, 2011.

Benedict of Nursia. *The Rule of St. Benedict,* trans. Anthony C. Meisel and M. L. del Mastro. New York: Doubleday, 1975.

Bergounioux, F. M. "Notes on the Mentality of Primitive Man." In *Social Life of Early Man,* ed. Sherwood L. Washburn, 106-118. Chicago: Aldine Publishing, 1961.

Bisel, Sara C. and Jane F. Bisel. "Health and Nutrition at Herculaneum: An Examination of Human Skeletal Remains." In *The Natural History of Pompeii,* ed. Wilhelmina Feemster Jashemski and Frederick G. Meyer, 451-475. Cambridge, UK: Cambridge University Press, 2002.

Blackwell, Fritz. *India: A Global Studies Handbook.* Santa Barbara, CA: ABC-CLIO, 2004.

Blum, Jerome. "Russian Agriculture in the Last 150 Years of Serfdom." *Agricultural History* 34, no. 1 (January 1960): 3-12.

Boak, Arthur E. R. *A History of Rome to 565 A.D.*, 4th ed. New York: Macmillan, 1955.

Boatwright, Mary T., Daniel J. Gargola, and Richard J. A. Talbert. *The Romans: From Village to Empire.* New York and Oxford: Oxford University Press, 2004.

Boaz, Noel T. and Russell L. Ciochon. *Dragon Bone Hill: An Ice-Age Saga of Homo erectus.* Oxford: Oxford University Press, 2004.

Boix, Carles. "Origins and Persistence of Economic Inequality." *Annual Review of Political Science* 13 (2010): 489-516. Accessed April 19, 2022. ‹Origins and Persistence of Economic Inequality | Annual Review of Political Science (annualreviews.org).›

Bowlby, John. *Charles Darwin: A New Life.* New York and London: Norton, 1990.

Braudel, Fernand. *Capitalism and Material Life, 1400-1800*, trans. Miriam Kochan. New York: Harper Colophon Books, 1973.

Brewer, Douglas J. *Ancient Egypt: Foundations of a Civilization.* Harlow, UK: Pearson Longman, 2005.

Brier, Bob and Hoyt Hobbs. *Ancient Egypt: Everyday Life in the Land of the Nile.* New York: Sterling, 2009.

Brinkley, Alan. *American History: A Survey, Vol. I: To 1877*, 13th ed. New York: McGraw-Hill, 2009.

Brinkley, Alan. *American History: A Survey, Vol. II: Since 1865*, 13th ed. New York: McGraw-Hill, 2009.

Brinkley, Alan. *The Unfinished Nation: A Concise History of the American People*, 6th ed. New York: McGraw Hill, 2010.

Brumbaugh, Robert S. *The Philosophers of Greece.* Albany: State University of New York Press, 1981.

Bunn, Henry T. "Meat Made Us Human." In *Evolution of the Human Diet: The Known, the Unknown, and the Unknowable*, ed. Peter S. Ungar, 191-211. Oxford and New York: Oxford University Press, 2007.

Byrne, Joseph P. and Jo N. Hays. *Epidemics and Pandemics: From Ancient Plagues to Modern-Day Threats.* Vol. 2. Santa Barbara, CA and Denver, CO: Greenwood, 2021.

Cannadine, David. *The Decline and Fall of the British Aristocracy.* New York: Vintage Books, 1999.

Cannadine, David. "The Landowner as Millionaire: The Finances of the Dukes of Devonshire, c. 1800-c. 1926." *Agricultural History Review* 25, no. 2 (1977): 77-97.

Cascio, Elio Lo. "The Early Roman Empire: The State and the Economy." In *The Cambridge Economic History of the Greco-Roman World*, ed. Walter Scheidel, Ian Morris, and Richard Saller, 619-648. Cambridge, UK: Cambridge University Press, 2007.

Casson, Lionel. *Everyday Life in Ancient Egypt*, rev. ed. Baltimore and London: Johns Hopkins University Press, 2001.

Cato, Marcus Porcius. *On Agriculture*, trans. William Davis Hooper. Cambridge, MA: Harvard University Press, 1967.

Ceplair, Larry. *Revolutionary Pairs: Marx and Engels, Lenin and Trotsky, Ghandi and Nehru, Mao and Zhou, Castro and Guevara.* Lexington: University Press of Kentucky, 2020.

Chambers, Mortimer, Raymond Grew, David Herlihy, Theodore K. Rabb, and Isser Woloch. *The Western Experience, Vol. II: The Early Modern Period*, 4th ed. New York: Knopf, 1987.

Chambers, Mortimer, Raymond Grew, David Herlihy, Theodore K. Rabb, and Isser Woloch. *The Western Experience, Vol. III: The Modern Era*, 4th ed. New York: Knopf, 1987.

Chase, Ivan D. "Models of Hierarchy Formation in Animal Societies." *Behavioral Science* 19, no. 6 (November 1974): 374-382.

Chomsky, Noam. *Requiem for the American Dream: The 10 Principles of Concentration of Wealth and Power.* New York: Seven Stories Press, 2017.

Chomsky, Noam and C. J. Polychroniou. *Optimism over Despair: On Capitalism, Empire, and Social Change.* Chicago: Haymarket Books, 2017.

Christian, David. "Acceleration: The Agrarian Era." In *Berkshire Encyclopedia of World History.* Vol. 1, ed. William H. McNeill, Jerry H. Bentley, David Christian, David Levinson, J. R. McNeill, Heidi Roupp, and Judith P. Zinsser, TWF15-TWF35. Great Barrington, MA: Berkshire Publishing Group, 2005.

Christian, David. "Beginnings: The Era of Foragers." In *Berkshire Encyclopedia of World History.* Vol. 1, ed. William H. McNeill, Jerry H. Bentley, David Christian, David Levinson, J. R. McNeill, Heidi Roupp, and Judith P. Zinsser, TWF1-TWF14. Great Barrington, MA: Berkshire Publishing Group, 2005.

Christian, David. *Origin Story: A Big History of Everything.* London: Allen Lane, 2018.

Clark, Stephen R. L. *Plotinus: Myth, Metaphor, and Philosophical Practice.* Chicago and London: University of Chicago Press, 2016.

Coates, Ta-Nehisi. *We Were Eight Years in Power: An American Tragedy.* New York: One World, 2017.

Conlin, Michelle. "The Great Divergence: U.S. COVID-19 Economy Has Delivered Luxury Homes for Some, Evictions for Others." Reuters, October 31, 2020. Accessed April 9, 2022. ‹https://www.yahoo.com/news/great-divergence-u-covid-19-110903275.html.›

Conneller, Chantal. "Power and Society." In *The Oxford Handbook of the Archaeology of Death and Burial*, ed. Sarah Tarlow and Liv Nilsson Stutz, 347-358. Oxford: Oxford University Press, 2013.

Cornell, Vincent J. "Fruit of the Tree of Knowledge: The Relationship between Faith and Practice in Islam." In *The Oxford History of Islam*, ed. John L. Esposito, 63-105. Oxford: Oxford University Press, 1999.

Crabtree, Pam J. "Agricultural Innovation and Socio-Economic Change in Early Medieval Europe: Evidence from Britain and France." *World Archaeology* 42, no. 1 (March 2010): 122-136.

Craig, Albert M., William A. Graham, Donald Kagan, Steven Ozment, and Frank M. Turner. *The Heritage of World Civilizations, Vol. II: Since 1500*. New York: Macmillan, 1986.

Crevecoeur, Hector St. Jean de. "From *Letters from an American Farmer*." In *The Norton Anthology of American Literature*, 2d ed., Nina Baym, Francis Murphy, Ronald Gottesman, Hershel Parker, Laurence B. Holland, William H. Pritchard, and David Kalstone, 195-212. New York and London: Norton, 1986.

Crunden, Robert M. *A Brief History of American Culture*. Armonk, NY and London: North Castle Books, 1994.

Culbertson, Laura. "A Life-Course Approach to Household Slaves in the Late Third Millennium B.C." In *Slaves and Households in the Near East*, ed. Laura Culbertson, 33-48. Chicago: Oriental Institute of the University of Chicago, 2011.

Dahl, Jacob L. "Revisiting Bala." *Journal of the American Oriental Society* 126, no. 1 (January-March 2006): 77-88.

Dart, Raymond A. "The Predatory Transition from Ape to Man." *International Anthropological and Linguistic Review* 1, no. 4 (1953). Accessed April 25, 2022. ‹the-predatory-transition-from-ape-to-man.pdf (wordpress.com).›

Darwin, Charles. *The Descent of Man, and Selection in Relation to Sex*. London: Penguin Books, 2004.

Darwin, Charles. *The Origin of Species by Means of Natural Selection or the Preservation of Favored Races in the Struggle for Life*. New York: Modern Library, 1993.

Daunton, Martin. *Wealth and Welfare: An Economic and Social History of Britain, 1851-1951*. Oxford and New York: Oxford University Press, 2007.

Davidson, Ian. *The French Revolution: From Enlightenment to Tyranny*. New York and London: Pegasus Books, 2016.

Derricourt, Robin. "The Enigma of Raymond Dart." *The International Journal of African Historical Studies* 42, no. 2 (2009): 257-282.

Derysh, Igor. "Billionaire Wealth Rises to More Than $10 Trillion for the First Time Ever Amid Pandemic: Analysis." Salon, October 17, 2020. Accessed April 8, 2022. ‹https://www.salon.com/2020/10/17/billionaire-wealth-rises-to-more-than-10-trillion-for-first-time-ever-amid-pandemic-analysis-2.›

Desmond, Matthew. "Capitalism." In in *The 1619 Project: A New Origin Story*, ed. Nikole Hannah-Jones, Caitlin Roper, Ilena Silverman, and Jake Silverstein, 165-185. New York: One World, 2021.

Diamond, Jared. *The Third Chimpanzee for Young People: On the Evolution and Future of the Human Animal.* New York and Oakland, CA: Seven Stories Press, 2014.

Diamond, Jared. "The Worst Mistake in the History of the Human Race." *Discover Magazine*, May 1, 1999. Accessed May 3, 2022. ‹https://www. discovermagazine.com/planet-earth/the-worst-mistake-in-the-history-of-the-human-race.›

Dizikes, Peter. "New Study Shows Rich, Poor Have Huge Mortality Gap in U.S." MIT News, April 11, 2016. Accessed July 3, 2022. ‹http://news.mit. edu/2016/study-rich-poor-huge-mortality-gap-us-0411.›

Donner, Fred M. "Muhammad and the Caliphate: Political History of the Islamic Empire up to the Mongol Conquest." In *The Oxford History of Islam*, ed. John L. Esposito, 1-61. Oxford: Oxford University Press, 1999.

Drennan, Matthew P. *Income Inequality: Why It Matters and Why Most Economists Didn't Notice.* New Haven, CT and London: Yale University Press, 2015.

Dubois, Laurent. *Avengers of the New World: The Story of the Haitian Revolution.* Cambridge, MA and London: Belknap Press of Harvard University Press, 2004.

Duignan, Brian, ed. *Economics and Economic Systems.* New York: Britannica, 2013.

Dunham, Will. "Maya Ruins in Belize Offer Peek at Ancient Wealth Inequality." Reuters, March 24, 2021. Accessed March 11, 2022. ‹Maya ruins in Belize offer peek at ancient wealth inequality (yahoo.com).›

Dunn, Richard S. *Sugar and Slaves: The Rise of the Planter Class in the English West Indies, 1624-1713.* Chapel Hill: University of North Carolina Press, 1972.

Ebenstein, Alan, William Ebenstein, and Edwin Fogelman. *Today's Isms: Socialism, Capitalism, Fascism, Communism, and Libertarianism*, 11th ed. Upper Saddle River, NJ: Prentice Hall, 2000.

Elnaiem, Mohammed. "What Was the Zanj Rebellion?: A Remarkable Episode of Medieval Muslim History That Often Goes Untold." JSTOR Daily, February 4, 2021. Accessed August 10, 2022. ‹What Was the Zanj Rebellion? - JSTOR Daily.›

Emerick, Yahiya. *The Life and Work of Muhammad.* Indianapolis: Alpha, 2002.

Engels, Friedrich. *The Condition of the Working Class in England*, ed. David McLellan. Oxford: Oxford University Press, 2009.

Engels, Friedrich. "Preface." In *Communist Manifesto*, Karl Marx and Friedrich Engels, trans. Samuel Moore, 1-6. Chicago: Great Books Foundation, 1955.

Ergang, Robert. *Europe: From the Renaissance to Waterloo.* Boston: D. C. Heath, 1967.

Faust, Katharine. "Animal Social Networks." In *The SAGE Handbook of Social Network Analysis*, ed. John Scott and Peter J. Carrington, 148-166. Los Angeles: SAGE, 2011.

Ferguson, Niall. *The Ascent of Money: A Financial History of the World.* New York: Penguin Press, 2008.

Figes, Orlando. *A People's Tragedy: A History of the Russian Revolution.* New York: Viking, 1996.

Finley, Moses. *The Ancient Economy.* Berkeley: University of California Press, 1999.

Finley, Moses. *Slavery in Classical Antiquity: Views and Controversies.* Cambridge, UK: W. Heffer, 1960.

Finley, Moses. "Was Greek Civilization Based on Slave Labour?" *Historia: Zietschrift fur alte geschichte* 8, no. 2 (April 1959): 145-164.

Fogel, Robert William. *The Escape from Hunger and Premature Death, 1700-2100: Europe, America, and the Third World.* Cambridge, UK: Cambridge University Press, 2004.

Fogel, Robert William. "Nutrition and the Decline in Mortality Since 1700: Some Preliminary Findings." In *Long-Term Factors in American Economic Growth*, ed. Stanley L. Engerman and Robert E. Gallman, 439-556. Chicago and London: University of Chicago Press, 1986.

Fourquin, Guy. *The Anatomy of Popular Rebellion in the Middle Ages*, trans. Anne Chesters. Amsterdam: North-Holland Publishing, 1978.

Freedman, Paul. "A Dossier of Peasant and Seigneurial Violence." In *The Routledge History Handbook of Medieval Revolt*, ed. Justine Firnhaber-Baker and Dirk Schoenaers, 267-278. London and New York: Routledge, 2017.

Freeman, Joshua, Nelson Lichtenstein, Stephen Brier, David Bensman, Susan Porter Benson, David Brundage, Bret Eynon, Bruce Levine, and Bryan Palmer. *Who Built America?: Working People and the Nation's Economy, Politics, Culture, and Society.* New York: Pantheon Books, 1992.

Frier, Bruce W. and Dennis P. Kehoe. "Law and Economic Institutions." In *The Cambridge Economic History of the Greco-Roman World*, ed. Walter Scheidel, Ian Morris, and Richard Saller, 113-143. Cambridge, UK: Cambridge University Press, 2007.

Furlonge, Nigel D. "Revisiting the Zanj and Re-Visioning Revolt: Complexities of the Zanj Conflict (868-883 AD)." *Negro History Bulletin* 62, no. 4 (December 1999): 7-14.

Galeotti, Mark A. *A Short History of Russia: How the World's Largest Country Invented Itself, from the Pagans to Putin.* Toronto, ON: Hanover Square Press, 2020.

Gann, Marjorie and Janet Willen. *Five Thousand Years of Slavery.* Toronto, ON: Tundra Books, 2011.

Garnsey, Peter. *Food and Society in Classical Antiquity.* Cambridge, UK: Cambridge University Press, 1999.

Gelder, Sarah van. "Introduction: How Occupy Wall Street Changed Everything." In *This Changes Everything: Occupy Wall Street and the 99% Movement,* ed. Sarah van Gelder and the Staff of *Yes! Magazine,* 1-12. Oakland, CA: Berrett-Koehler Publishers, 2011.

Gibbon, Edward. *The Decline and Fall of the Roman Empire,* abridged ed. New York: Modern Library, 2003.

Gilbert, Marc Jason. *South Asia in World History.* New York: Oxford University Press, 2017.

Gimpel, Jean. *The Medieval Machine: The Industrial Revolution of the Middle Ages.* New York: Penguin Books, 1976.

Glowacki, Donna M. *Living and Leaving: A Social History of Regional Depopulation in Thirteenth-Century Mesa Verde.* Tucson: University of Arizona Press, 2015.

Goff, Jacques Le. "Introduction: Medieval Man." In *Medieval Callings,* ed. Jacques Le Goff, trans. Lydia G. Cochrane, 1-35. Chicago: University of Chicago Press, 1990.

Golden, Peter B. *Central Asia in World History.* Oxford: Oxford University Press, 2011.

Gomez, Nicolas Wey. *The Tropics of Empire: Why Columbus Sailed South to the Indies.* Cambridge, MA and London: MIT Press, 2008.

Gorer, Geoffrey. "Ardrey on Human Nature: Animals, Nations, Imperatives." In *Man and Aggression,* 2d ed., ed. Ashley Montagu, 159-167. New York: Oxford University Press, 1973.

Graeber, David. *Debt: The First 5,000 Years.* Brooklyn and London: Melville House, 2014.

Grayling, A. C. *The History of Philosophy.* New York: Penguin Press, 2019.

Gregor-Dellin, Martin. *Richard Wagner: His Life, His Work, His Century,* trans. J. Maxwell Brownjohn. San Diego: Harcourt Brace Jovanovich, 1983.

Green, Paul. *Hymn to the Rising Sun.* New York: Samuel French, 1936.

Greenspan, Alan and Adrian Woodridge. *Capitalism in America: A History.* New York: Penguin Press, 2018.

Guthrie, R. Dale. *The Nature of Paleolithic Art.* Chicago and London: University of Chicago Press, 2005.

Haarmann, Harald. "Foraging to Farming—The Neolithic Revolution." In *World History Encyclopedia, Vol. 2, Era 1: Beginnings of Human Society,* ed. Alfred J. Andrea, Carolyn Neel, and Mark Aldenderfer, 129-131. Santa Barbara, CA: ABC-CLIO, 2011.

Hammond, Michael. "The Expulsion of the Neanderthals from Human Ancestry: Marcellin Boule and the Social Context of Scientific Research." *Social Studies of Science* 12, no. 1 (February 1982): 1-36.

Hanawalt, Barbara A. *The Middle Ages: An Illustrated History.* New York and Oxford: Oxford University Press, 1998.

Handler, Jerome S. and Robert S. Corruccini. "Plantation Slave Life in Barbados: A Physical Anthropological Analysis." *Journal of Interdisciplinary History* 14, no. 1 (Summer 1983): 65-90.

Hannah-Jones, Nikole. "Origins." In *The 1619 Project: A New Origin Story,* ed. Nikole Hannah-Jones, Caitlin Roper, Ilena Silverman, and Jake Silverstein, xvii-xxxiii. New York: One World, 2021.

Harris, David R. "Origins and Spread of Agriculture." In *The Cultural History of Plants,* ed. Ghillean Prance and Mark Nesbitt, 13-26. New York and London: Routledge, 2005.

Harris, William V. "The Late Republic." In *The Cambridge Economic History of the Greco-Roman World,* ed. Walter Scheidel, Ian Morris, and Richard Saller, 511-539. Cambridge, UK: Cambridge University Press, 2007.

Harvey, Alun. "Ancient Burial Practices at Sunghir in Russia." Hunebed Nieuwscafe, February 2019. Accessed February 19, 2022. ‹https://www.hunebednieuwscafe.nl/2019/02/ancient-burial-practices-at-sunghir-in-russia/?cn-reloaded=1.›

Haskins, Charles Homer. *The Renaissance of the Twelfth Century.* Cambridge, MA and London: Harvard University Press, 1927.

Hazareesingh, Sudhir. *Black Spartacus: The Epic Life of Toussaint Louverture.* New York: Farrar, Straus and Giroux, 2020.

Hegel, G. W. F. *Reason in History: A General Introduction to the Philosophy of History,* trans. Robert S. Hartman. Indianapolis and New York: Bobbs-Merrill, 1953.

Heitman, Carrie C. "The House of Our Ancestors: New Research on the Prehistory of Chaco Canyon, New Mexico, A.D. 800-1200." In *Chaco Revisited: New Research on the Prehistory of Chaco Canyon, New Mexico,* ed. Carrie C. Heitman and Stephen Plog, 215-248. Tucson: University of Arizona, 2015.

Hellie, Richard. "Russian Slavery and Serdom, 1450-1804." In *The Cambridge World History of Slavery.* Vol. 3, ed. David Eltis and Stanley L. Engerman, 275-296. Cambridge, UK and New York: Cambridge University Press, September 28, 2011. Accessed April 3, 2022. ‹Russian Slavery and Serfdom, 1450–1804 (Chapter 11) - The Cambridge World History of Slavery.›

Hellie, Richard. "Women and Slavery in Muscovy." *Russian History* 10, no. 2 (1983): 213-229.

Herman, Arthur. *The Cave and the Light: Plato Versus Aristotle, and the Struggle for the Soul of Western Civilization.* New York: Random House, 2013.

Hewitt, Nancy A. and Steven F. Lawson. *Exploring American Histories: A Brief Survey with Sources.* Boston and New York: Bedford/St. Martin's, 2013.

Hilton, Rodney. *Bond Men Made Free: Medieval Peasant Movements and the English Rising of 1381,* 3d ed. London and New York: Routledge, 2005.

Hobbes, Thomas. *Leviathan.* Oxford and New York: Oxford University Press, 1998.

Hobhouse, Henry. *Seeds of Change: Six Plants That Transformed Mankind.* Washington, DC: Shoemaker & Hoard, 2005.

Holland, Tom. *Rubicon: The Last Years of the Roman Republic.* New York: Anchor Books, 2004.

Hollis III, Daniel W. *The ABC-CLIO World History Companion to Utopian Movements.* Santa Barbara, CA: ABC-CLIO, 1998.

Holloway, Ralph. "Territory and Aggression in Man: A Look at Ardrey's *Territorial Imperative.*" In *Man and Aggression,* 2d ed., ed. Ashley Montagu, 176-182. New York: Oxford University Press, 1973.

Holmes, Jack. "The American Dream is Collapsing. Are We Too Angry to Fix It?" Esquire, April 15, 2020. Accessed April 8, 2022. ‹Why Americans Are Too Angry to Fix The American Dream (esquire.com).›

Hovers, Erella and Anna Belfer-Cohen. "Insights into Early Mortuary Practices of *Homo.*" In *The Oxford Handbook of the Archaeology of Death and Burial,* ed. Sarah Tarlow and Liv Nilsson Stutz, 631-642. Oxford: Oxford University Press, 2013.

Howell, F. Clark. *Early Man,* rev. ed. New York: Time-Life Books, 1968.

Hufton, Olwen. "Social Conflict and the Grain Supply in Eighteenth-Century France." *Journal of Interdisciplinary History* 14, no. 2 (Autumn 1983): 303-331.

Hughes, H. Stuart. *Contemporary Europe: A History,* 5th ed. Englewood Cliffs, NJ: Prentice-Hall, 1981.

Hunt, James L. Review of *The Great Industrial War: Framing Class Conflict in the Media, 1865-1950,* by Troy Rondinone. *The Historian* 73, no. 3 (Fall 2011): 579-580.

Jackson Jr., John P. and Nadine M. Weidman, *Race, Racism, and Science: Social Impact and Interaction.* New Brunswick, NJ and London: Rutgers University Press, 2006.

Johnson, Paul. *Intellectuals.* New York: Harper & Row, 1988.

Jongman, Willem M. "The Early Roman Empire: Consumption." In *The Cambridge Economic History of the Greco-Roman World,* ed. Walter Scheidel, Ian Morris, and Richard Saller, 592-618. Cambridge, UK: Cambridge University Press, 2007.

Jurmain, Robert, Lynn Kilgore, Wenda Trevathan, and Russell L. Ciochon. *Introduction to Physical Anthropology,* 2013-2014 ed. Belmont, CA: Wadsworth Cengage Learning, 2014.

Kaul, Shoneleeka. "Pleasure and Culture: Reading Urban Behaviour through Kavya Archetypes." In *Ancient India: New Research*, ed. Upinder Singh and Nayanjot Lahiri, 254-281. Oxford and New York: Oxford University Press, 2009.

Kemp, Barry, Anna Stevens, Gretchen R. Dobbs, Melissa Zabecki, and Jerome C. Rose. "Life, Death and beyond in Akhenaten's Egypt: Excavating the South Tombs Cemetery at Amarna." *Antiquity* 87, no. 335 (March 1, 2013): 64-78.

Kerrigan, Michael. *Ancient Rome and the Roman Empire*. London: Dorling Kindersley, 2001.

Kleinman, Paul. *Philosophy 101: From Plato and Socrates to Ethics and Metaphysics, An Essential Primer on the History of Thought*. New York: Adams Media, 2013.

Kotlikoff, Laurence J. "The Structure of Slave Prices in New Orleans, 1804 to 1862." *Economic Inquiry* 17, no. 4 (October 1979): 496-518.

Kraut, Alan M. *The Huddled Masses: The Immigrant in American Society, 1880-1921*. Arlington Heights, IL: Harlan Davidson, 1982.

Lacroix, Paul. *Manners, Customs, and Dress during the Middle Ages and during the Renaissance Period*. New York: Skyhorse Publishing, 2013.

Lal, K. S. Muslim *Slave System in Medieval India*. New Delhi: Aditya Prakashan, 1994). Accessed March 5, 2022. ‹09272019090110_muslim_slave_system_in_medieval_india.pdf (vediclibrary.in).›

Lalljee, Jason. "Kroger Workers Experienced Hunger, Homelessness, and Couldn't Pay Their Rent in 2021. Its CEO Made $22 Million the Previous Year." Insider, January 14, 2022. Accessed April 9, 2022. ‹Kroger workers experienced hunger, homelessness, and couldn't pay their rent in 2021. Its CEO made $22 million the previous year. (yahoo.com).›

Larsen, Clark Spencer. *Our Origins: Discovering Physical Anthropology*. New York and London: Norton, 2008.

Lavan, Myles. "Writing Revolt in the Early Roman Empire." In *The Routledge History Handbook of Medieval Revolt*, ed. Justine Firnhaber-Baker and Dirk Schoenaers, 19-38. London and New York: Routledge, 2017.

Leakey, Richard E. *The Making of Mankind*. New York: E. P. Dutton, 1981.

Leakey, Richard and Roger Lewin. *Origins Reconsidered: In Search of What Makes Us Human*. New York: Anchor Books/Doubleday, 1992.

Legendre, Marie. "Landowners, Caliphs and State Policy over Landholdings in the Egyptian Countryside." In *Authority and Control in the Countryside: From Antiquity to Islam in the Mediterranean and Near East (6th-10th Century)*, ed. Alaine Delattre, Marie Legendre, and Petra Sijpesteijn, 392-419. Leiden and Boston: Brill, 2019.

Lenin, V. I. "Karl Marx: Part Three." International Communist League, October 2, 2015. Accessed March 31, 2022. ‹"Karl Marx" by V.I. Lenin (icl-fi.org).›

Levy, Jonathan. *Ages of Capitalism: A History of the United States.* New York: Random House, 2021.

Liedman, Sven-Eric. *A World to Win: The Life and Works of Karl Marx*, trans. Jeffrey N. Skinner. London and New York: Verso, 2018.

Littman, Robert J. *The Greek Experiment: Imperialism and Social Conflict, 800-400 BC.* New York: Harcourt Brace Jovanovich, 1974.

Liu, Xinru. *The Silk Road in World History.* Oxford and New York: Oxford University Press, 2010.

Liu-Perkins, Christine. *At Home in Her Tomb: Lady Dai and the Ancient Chinese Treasures of Mawangdui.* Watertown, MA: Charlesbridge, 2014.

Livesay, Harold C. *Andrew Carnegie and the Rise of Big Business.* New York: HarperCollinsPublishers, 1975.

Locke, John. *An Essay Concerning Human Understanding*, ed. Roger Woolhouse. London: Penguin Books, 2004.

Loewe, Michael. "Wang Mang and His Forebears: The Making of the Myth." *T'oung Pao* 80, no. 4/5 (1994): 197-222.

London, Jack. "Revolution." In *The Radical Jack London: Writings on War and Revolution*, ed. Jonah Raskin, 139-156. Berkeley: University of California Press, 2008.

London, Jack. *War of the Classes.* New York: Regent Press, 1905.

Loubere, Leo A. *Louis Blanc: His Life and His Contribution to the Rise of French Jacobin-Socialism.* Westport, CT: Greenwood Press, 1961.

Luft, Friedrich C. "Rudolf Virchow and the Anthropology of Race." *Hektoen International: A Journal of Medical Humanities* 14, no. 1 (Winter 2022), ‹Rudolf Virchow and the anthropology of race (hekint.org).›

Machiavelli, Nicolo. *The Prince*, trans. Luigi Ricci. Chicago: Great Books Foundation, 1955.

Mader, Jackie. "With Help Slow to Come from Washington, A Veteran's Family Gets by Washing Cars, Skipping Meals." The Hechinger Report, October 17, 2020. Accessed April 9, 2022. ‹Seven months into the pandemic, many families are struggling with poverty (hechingerreport.org).›

Magdalene, F. Rachel and Cornelia Wunsch. "Slavery between Judah and Babylon: The Exilic Experience." In *Slaves and Households in the Near East*, ed. Laura Culbertson, 113-134. Chicago: Oriental Institute of the University of Chicago, 2011.

Maisels, Charles Keith. *Early Civilizations of the Old World: The Formative Histories of Egypt, the Levant, Mesopotamia, India and China.* London and New York: Routledge, 1999.

Malthus, Thomas. *An Essay on the Principle of Population.* Amherst, NY: Prometheus Books, 1998.

Marks, Robert B. *The Origins of the Modern World: A Global and Environmental Narrative from the Fifteenth to the Twenty-First Century*, 4ᵗʰ ed. Lanham, MD: Rowman & Littlefield, 2020.

Marx, Karl. *Capital: A Critique of Political Economy*. Vol. 1, trans. Ben Fowkes. London: Penguin Books, 1990.

Marx, Karl and Friedrich Engels. *Communist Manifesto*, trans. Samuel Moore. Chicago: Great Books Foundation, 1955.

Mattison, Siobhan M., Eric A. Smith, Mary K. Shenk, and Ethan E. Cochrane. "The Evolution of Inequality." *Evolutionary Anthropology Issues, News and Reviews* 25, no. 4 (July 2016): 184-199.

Mayhew, Robert J. *Malthus: The Life and Legacies of an Untimely Prophet*. Cambridge, MA and London: Belknap Press of Harvard University Press, 2014.

Mayr, Ernst. *The Growth of Biological Thought: Diversity, Evolution, and Inheritance*. Cambridge, MA and London: Belknap Press of Harvard University Press, 1982.

McKay, John P., Bennett D. Hill, John Buckler, Clare Haru Crowston, Merry E. Wiesner-Hanks, and Joe Perry. *Understanding Western Society: A Brief History*. Boston and New York: Bedford/St, Martin's, 2012.

McNeill, J. R. and William H. McNeill. *The Human Web: A Bird's-Eye View of World History*. New York and London: Norton, 2003.

McNeill, William H. "How the Potato Changed the World's History." *Social Research* 66, no. 1 (Spring 1999): 67-83.

Mendoza, Abraham O. "Fourteenth-Century Famine in Europe." In *World History Encyclopedia, Vol. 9, Era 5: Intensified Hemispheric Interactions, 1000-1500*, ed. Alfred J. Andrea and Carolyn Neel, 28-29. Santa Barbara, CA: ABC-CLIO, 2011.

Mertz, Barbara. *Red Land, Black Land: Daily Life in Ancient Egypt*, 2d ed. New York: William Morrow, 2008.

Messer, Ellen. "Potatoes (White)." In *The Cambridge World History of Food*. Vol. 1, ed. Kenneth F. Kiple and Kriemhild Conee Ornelas, 187-201. Cambridge, UK: Cambridge University Press, 2000.

Midant-Reynes, Beatrix. *The Prehistory of Egypt: From the First Egyptians to the First Pharaohs*, trans. Ian Shaw. Oxford, UK and Malden, MA: Blackwell, 2000.

Milanovic, Branko. *Global Inequality: A New Approach for the Age of Globalization*. Cambridge, MA and London: Belknap Press of Harvard University Press, 2016.

Milanovic, Branko. *The Haves and the Have-Nots: A Brief and Idiosyncratic History of Global Inequality*. New York: Basic Books, 2011.

Milanovic, Branko. "Pareto to Piketty CUNY 15 Spring," 2015. Accessed April 19, 2022. ‹https://www.scribd.com/document/256716727/Pareto-to-Piketty-Cuny-15-Spring.›

Miller, Naomi F. and Wilma Wetterstrom. "The Beginnings of Agriculture: The Ancient Near East and North Africa." In *The Cambridge World History of Food*. Vol. 2, ed. Kenneth F. Kiple and Kriemhild Conee Ornelas, 1123-1139. Cambridge, UK: Cambridge University Press, 2000.

Mingren, Wu. "Lady Fu Hao and Her Lavish Tomb of the Shang Dynasty." Ancient Origins: Reconstructing the Story of Humanity's Past. Last modified November 1, 2014. Accessed May 21, 2022. ‹Lady Fu Hao and her Lavish Tomb of the Shang Dynasty | Ancient Origins (ancient-origins. net).›

Mohamed, Theron. "'No One Ever Makes a Billion Dollars. You Take a Billion Dollars': Alexandria Ocasio-Cortez Slams Billionaires for Exploiting Workers." Markets Insider, January 24, 2020. Accessed October 30, 2022. ‹https://markets.businessinsider.com/news/stocks/aoc-accuses-billion-aires-exploiting-workers-paying-slave-wages-2020-1.›

Moise, Edwin E. *Modern China: A History*. London and New York: Longman, 1986.

Mols, Stephan T. A. M. "Identification of the Woods Used in the Furniture at Herculaneum." In *The Natural History of Pompeii*, ed. Wilhelmina Feemster Jashemski and Frederick G. Meyer, 225-234. Cambridge, UK: Cambridge University Press, 2002.

Morel, Jean-Paul. "Early Rome and Italy." In *The Cambridge Economic History of the Greco-Roman World*, ed. Walter Scheidel, Ian Morris, and Richard Saller, 487-510. Cambridge, UK: Cambridge University Press, 2007.

Morfin, Lourdes Marquez, Robert McCaa, Rebecca Storey, and Andres Del Angel. "Health and Nutrition in Pre-Hispanic Mesoamerica." In *The Backbone of History: Health and Nutrition in the Western Hemisphere*, ed. Richard H. Steckel and Jerome C. Rose, 307-338. Cambridge, UK: Cambridge University Press, 2002.

Muhammad, Kahalil Gibran. "Sugar." In *The 1619 Project: A New Origin Story*, ed. Nikole Hannah-Jones, Caitlin Roper, Ilena Silverman, and Jake Silverstein, 71-87. New York: One World, 2021.

Nash, Gary B., John R. Howe, Allen F. Davis, Peter J. Frederick, Julie Roy Jeffrey, Allan M. Winkler, Charlene Mires, and Carla Gardina Pestana. *The American People: Creating a Nation and a Society, Vol. 1: to 1877*, 8th ed. New York: Pearson, 2017.

Nash, Gary B., John R. Howe, Allen F. Davis, Peter J. Frederick, Julie Roy Jeffrey, Allan M. Winkler, Charlene Mires, and Carla Gardina Pestana. *The American People: Creating a Nation and a Society, Vol 2: Since 1865*, 8th ed. New York: Pearson, 2017.

Nef, Annliese et Vivien Prigent. *"Controle et xxploitation des campagnes en Sicile."* In *Authority and Control in the Countryside: From Antiquity to Islam in the Mediterranean and Near East (6th-10th Century)*, ed. Alaine Delattre, Marie Legendre, and Petra Sijpesteijn, 313-366. Leiden and Boston: Brill, 2019.

Nemet-Nejat, Karen Rhea. *Daily Life in Ancient Mesopotamia.* Westport, CT and London: Greenwood Press, 1998.

Neumann, Hans. "Slavery in Private Households toward the End of the Third Millennium B.C." in *Slaves and Households in the Near East,* ed. Laura Culbertson, 21-32. Chicago: Oriental Institute of the University of Chicago, 2011.

Nietzsche, Friedrich. *The Birth of Tragedy,* trans. Douglas Smith. Oxford and New York: Oxford University Press, 2000.

Nietzsche, Friedrich. *On the Genealogy of Morals,* trans. Walter Kaufmann and R. J. Hollingdale. New York: Viking Books, 1969.

Nietzsche, Friedrich. *Human, All Too Human, I,* trans. Gary Handwerk. Stanford, CA: Stanford University Press, 1995.

Norton, Mary Beth, David M. Katzman, Paul D. Escott, Howard P. Chudacoff, Thomas G. Patterson, and William M. Tuttle, Jr. *A People and a Nation: A History of the United States, Vol II: Since 1865,* 4th ed. Boston: Houghton Mifflin, 1994.

O'Connell, Sanjida. *Sugar: The Grass that Changed the World.* London: Virgin Books, 2004.

Oliver, Martyn. *History of Philosophy: Great Thinkers from 600 B.C. to the Present Day.* New York: Barnes & Noble, 1999.

Oliver, Roland and Brian M. Fagan. *Africa in the Iron Age, c. 500 B.C. to A.D. 1400.* Cambridge, UK: Cambridge University Press, 1975.

O'Neill, Richard. *The Middle Ages: Turbulent Centuries.* New York and Avenel, NJ: Crescent Books, 1992.

Ortner, Donald J. and Gretchen Theobald. "Paleopathological Evidence of Malnutrition." In *The Cambridge World History of Food.* Vol. 1, ed. Kenneth F. Kiple and Kriemhild Conee Ornelas, 34-44. Cambridge, UK: Cambridge University Press, 2000.

Orwell, George. *Animal Farm: A Fairy Story.* Boston: Berkley/Houghton Mifflin Harcourt, 2020.

Page, Jake. *In the Hands of the Great Spirit: The 20,000-Year History of American Indians.* New York: Free Press, 2003.

Page, Willie F. *Encyclopedia of African History and Culture, Vol. II: African Kingdoms (500-1500).* New York: Facts on File, 2001.

Palmer, R. R., Joel Colton, and Lloyd Kramer. *A History of the Modern World to 1815,* 9th ed. New York: Knopf, 2002.

Pang, Yong-Pil. "Peng Pai: From Landlord to Revolutionary." *Modern China* 1, no. 3 (July 1975): 297-322.

Perrin, Porter G. "'Pecking Order' 1927-54." *American Speech* 30, no. 4 (December 1955): 265-268.

Peters, Scott J. and Paul A. Morgan. "The Country Life Commission: Reconsidering a Milestone in American Agricultural History." *Agricultural History* 78, no. 3 (Summer 2004): 289-316.

Petrou, Karen. *Engine of Inequality: The Fed and the Future of Wealth in America.* Hoboken, NJ: Wiley, 2021.

Pettitt, Paul. *The Palaeolithic Origins of Human Burial.* London and New York: Routledge, 2011.

Pettitt, Paul, M. Richards, R. Maggi, and V. Formicola. "The Gravettian Burial Known as the Prince ("Il Principe"): New Evidence for His Age and Diet." *Antiquity* 77, no. 295 (March 2003): 15-19. Accessed April 28, 2022. ‹https://dro.dur.ac.uk/5846/1.›

Phillips, Charles. *The Complete Illustrated History of the Aztec and Maya: The Definitive Chronicle of the Ancient Peoples of Central America and Mexico—including the Azetc, Maya, Olmec, Mixtec, Toltec, and Zapotec.* [London]: Hermes House, 2015.

Phillips, Delisa L., Jerome C. Rose, and Willem M. van Haarlem. "Bioarchaeology of Tell Ibrahim Awad." *Egypt and the Levant* 19 (December 2009): 157-210.

Picard, Liza. *Chaucer's People: Everyday Lives in Medieval England.* London: Weidenfeld & Nicolson, 2017.

Piketty, Thomas. *Capital and Ideology*, trans. Arthur Goldhammer. Cambridge, MA and London: Belknap Press of Harvard University Press, 2020.

Piketty, Thomas. *Capital in the Twenty-First Century*, trans. Arthur Goldhammer. Cambridge, MA and London: Belknap Press of Harvard University Press, 2014.

Plath, O. E. "Insect Societies." In *A Handbook of Social Psychology.* Vol. 1, ed. Carl Murchison, 83-141. New York: Russell & Russell, 1935.

Plato. *Apology.* In *Great Dialogues of Plato*, trans. W. H. D. Rouse, 423-446. New York and Scarborough, ON: New American Library, 1956.

Plato. *Meno.* In *Great Dialogues of Plato*, trans. W. H. D. Rouse, 28-68. New York and Scarborough, ON: New American Library, 1956.

Plato. *Phaedo.* In *Great Dialogues of Plato*, trans. W. H. D. Rouse, 460-521. New York and Scarborough, ON: New American Library, 1956.

Plato. *Republic.* In *Great Dialogues of Plato*, trans. W. H. D. Rouse, 118-422. New York and Scarborough, ON: New American Library, 1956.

Plavcan, J. Michael. "Body Size, Size Variation, and Sexual Size Dimorphism in Early *Homo*." *Current Anthropology* 53, Supplement 6 (December 2012): S409-S423.

Plutarch. *Fall of the Roman Republic: Six Lives: Marius, Sulla, Crassus, Pompey, Caesar, and Cicero*, trans. Rex Warner. Harmondsworth, UK: Penguin Books, 1986.

Plutarch. "The Life of Cato the Elder." In *Sources of the West: Readings from Western Civilization, Vol. I: From the Beginning to 1648*, ed. Mark A. Kishlansky, 61-64. New York: HarperCollins*Publishers*, 1991.

Poo, Mu-Chou. *Daily Life in Ancient China*. Cambridge, UK: Cambridge University Press, 2018.

Popkin, Jeremy D. *A New World Begins: The History of the French Revolution*. New York: Basic Books, 2019.

Postma, Johannes. *The Atlantic Slave Trade*. Westport, CT and London: Greenwood Press, 2003.

"The Prince of Arene Candide." Ligurian Archaeological Museum. Accessed February 19, 2022. ‹https://www.museidigenova.it/en/prince-arene-candide.›

Proudhon, P. J. *What Is Property?: An Inquiry into the Principle of Right and of Government, Chapter IV: That Property Is Impossible*. Project Gutenberg. Last modified February 4, 2013. Accessed March 31, 2022. ‹What is Property?, by P. J. Proudhon (gutenberg.org).›

Qiu, Jane. "How China is Rewriting the Book on Human Origins." *Scientific American*, July 13, 2016. Accessed March 8, 2022. ‹https://www.scientificamerican.com/article/how-china-is-rewriting-the-book-on-human-origins/#.›

Rathbun, Ted A. and Richard H. Steckel. "The Health of Slaves and Free Blacks in the East." In *The Backbone of History: Health and Nutrition in the Western Hemisphere*, ed. Richard H. Steckel and Jerome C. Rose, 208-225. Cambridge, UK: Cambridge University Press, 2002.

Reader, John. *Man on Earth: A Celebration of Mankind*. New York: Harper & Row, 1988.

Reader, John. *Potato: A History of the Propitious Esculent*. New Haven, CT and London: Yale University Press, 2008.

Reich, David. *Who We Are and How We Got Here: Ancient DNA and the New Science of the Human Past*. New York: Pantheon Books, 2018.

Reich, Robert B. *The System: Who Rigged It, How We Fix It*. New York: Knopf, 2020.

Reynolds, Jonathan T. "Horses, Salt, Manufactured Goods, Islamic Books, Gold, and Slaves—What Was Traded across the Sahara and Why?" In *World History Encyclopedia, Vol. 10, Era 5: Intensified Hemispheric Interactions, 1000-1500*, ed. Alfred J. Andrea and Carolyn Neel, 489-490. Santa Barbara, CA: ABC-CLIO, 2011.

Riel-Salvatore, Julien and Claudine Gravel-Miguel. "Upper Palaeolithic Mortuary Practices in Eurasia." In *The Oxford Handbook of the Archaeology of Death and Burial*, ed. Sarah Tarlow and Liv Nilsson Stutz, 303-346. Oxford: Oxford University Press, 2013.

Robb, Greg. "The Harsh Truth about Economic Inequality, Based on Thousands of Years of Evidence." Market Watch, September 19, 2017. Accessed April 19, 2022. ⟨https://www.marketwatch.com/story/want-to-level-income-inequality-so-far-only-war-and-disease-have-worked-2017-09-18.⟩

Roberts, Alasdair. *America's First Great Depression: Economic Crisis and Political Disorder after the Panic of 1837.* Ithaca, NY and London: Cornell University Press, 2012.

Robinson, Mark and Erica Rowan. "Roman Food Remains in Archaeology and the Contents of a Roman Sewer at Herculaneum." In A Companion to Food in the Ancient World, ed. John Wilkins and Robin Nadeau, 105-115. Chichester, UK: Wiley Blackwell, 2105.

Ronen, Avraham. "The Oldest Burials and Their Significance." In *African Genesis: Perspectives on Hominin Evolution*, ed. Sally C. Reynolds and Andrew Gallagher, 554-570. Cambridge, UK: Cambridge University Press, 2012.

Ropp, Paul S. *China in World History.* Oxford and New York: Oxford University Press, 2010.

Rose, Jerome C. and Melissa Zabecki. "The Commoners of Tell el-Amarna." In *Beyond the Horizon: Studies in Egyptian Art, Archaeology and History in Honour of Barry J. Kemp.* Vol. 2, ed. Salima Ikram and Aidan Dodson, 408-422. Cairo: Supreme Council of Antiquities, 2009.

Rostworowski, Maria. "The Incas." In *The Inca World: The Development of Pre-Columbian Peru, A.D. 1000-1534,* ed. Laura Laurencich Minelli, 143-192. Norman: University of Oklahoma Press, 2000.

Rousseau, Jean-Jacques. *A Discourse on Inequality*, trans. Maurice Cranston. London: Penguin Books, 1984.

Russell, Bertrand. *A History of Western Philosophy: And Its Connection with Political and Social Circumstances from the Earliest Times to the Present Day*, 14th ed. New York: Simon & Schuster, 1964.

Rutherford, Adam. *Humanimal: How Homo sapiens Became Nature's Most Paradoxical Creature.* New York: The Experiment, 2019.

Sabbahy, Lisa. "A Decade of Advances in the Paleopathology of the Ancient Egyptians." In *Egyptian Bioarchaeology: Humans, Animals, and the Environment*, ed. Salima Ikram, Jessica Kaiser, and Roxie Walker, 113-119. Leiden: Sidestone Press, 2015.

Safina, Carl. *Beyond Words: What Animals Think and Feel.* New York: Henry Holt, 2015.

Sams, Steven. "It Was Not All Wine and Roses—Incidents of Famine in Europe." In *World History Encyclopedia, Vol. 9, Era 5: Intensified Hemispheric Interactions, 1000-1500*, ed. Alfred J. Andrea and Carolyn Neel, 21-22. Santa Barbara, CA: ABC-CLIO, 2011.

Sandle, Tim. "Pharaohs and Mummies: Diseases of Ancient Egypt and Modern Approaches." *Journal of Infectious Diseases and Preventive Remedies* 1, no. 4 (November 2013). Accessed April 28, 2022. ‹https://www.researchgate.net/publication/258842087_Pharaohs_and_Mummies_Diseases_of_Ancient_Egypt_and_Modern_Approaches.›

Sangster, Kalila. "Musk and Bezos among World's 10 Richest Men Who Doubled Their Wealth in Pandemic." Yahoo!Finance, January 17, 2022. Accessed April 8, 2022. ‹World's 10 richest men double their wealth in pandemic (yahoo.com).›

Saunders, Shelley R., Ann Herring, Larry Sawchuk, Gerry Boyce, Rob Hoppa, and Susan Klepp. "The Health of the Middle Class: The St. Thomas' Anglican Church Cemetery Project." In *The Backbone of History: Health and Nutrition in the Western Hemisphere*, ed. Richard H. Steckel and Jerome C. Rose, 130-161. Cambridge, UK: Cambridge University Press, 2002.

Schama, Simon. *Citizen: A Chronicle of the French Revolution.* New York: Knopf, 1989.

Scheidel, Walter. *Death on the Nile: Disease and the Demography of Roman Egypt.* Leiden: Brill, 2001.

Scheidel, Walter. "Demography." In *The Cambridge Economic History of the Greco-Roman World*, ed. Walter Scheidel, Ian Morris, and Richard Saller, 38-86. Cambridge, UK: Cambridge University Press, 2007.

Scheidel, Walter. *The Great Leveler: Violence and the History of Inequality from the Stone Age to the Twenty-First Century.* Princeton, NJ and Oxford: Princeton University Press, 2017.

Schell, Orville and John Delury. *Wealth and Power: China's Long March to the Twenty-First Century.* New York: Random House, 2013.

Schenke, Gesa. "Monastic Control over Agriculture and Farming: New Evidence from the Egyptian Monastery of Apa Apollo at Bawit." In *Authority and Control in the Countryside: From Antiquity to Islam in the Mediterranean and Near East (6th-10th Century)*, ed. Alaine Delattre, Marie Legendre, and Petra Sijpesteijn, 420-431. Leiden and Boston: Brill, 2019.

Schjelderup-Ebbe, Thorleif. "Social Behavior of Birds." In *A Handbook of Social Psychology*. Vol. 2, ed. Carl Murchison, 947-972. New York: Russell & Russell, 1935.

Scott, James C. *Against the Grain: A Deep History of the Earliest States.* New Haven, CT and London: Yale University Press, 2017.

Seeskin, Kenneth. *Thinking about the Prophets: A Philosopher Reads the Bible.* Philadelphia: Jewish Publication Society, 2020.

Sieyes, Emmanuel Joseph. "The Middle Class Sought Increased Political Rights." In *The French Revolution*, ed. Laura K. Egendorf, 47-54. San Diego: Greenhaven Press, 2004.

Simpson, George Gaylord. *Biology and Man.* New York: Harcourt, Brace & World, 1969.

Smith, Arianna. "Addressing the Causes of Poverty in South America." Borgen Project, February 12, 2018. Accessed April 8, 2022. ‹Addressing the Causes of Poverty in South America (borgenproject.org).›

Smith, Eric Alden, Kim Hill, Frank Marlowe, David Nolin, Polly Wiessner, Michael Gurven, Samuel Bowles, Monique Borgerhoff Mulder, Tom Hertz, and Adrian Bell. "Wealth Transmission and Inequality among Hunter-Gatherers." *Current Anthropology* 51, no. 1 (February 2010): 19-34.

Snape, Steven. *Ancient Egypt: The Definitive Visual History.* London: DK, 2021.

Solomon, Robert C. and Kathleen M. Higgins. *A Short History of Philosophy.* New York and Oxford: Oxford University Press, 1996.

Soucheray, Stephanie. "US Jobs Loses Due to COVID-19 Highest Since Great Depression." University of Minnesota Center for Infectious Disease Research and Policy, May 8, 2020. Accessed April 8, 2022. ‹US job losses due to COVID-19 highest since Great Depression | CIDRAP (umn.edu).›

Spence, Jonathan D. *The Search for Modern China.* New York and London: Norton, 1990.

Spodek, Howard. "Urbanization." In *World History Encyclopedia, Vol. 1: An Introduction to World History*, ed. Carolyn Neel and Alfred J. Andrea, 221-237. Santa Barbara, CA: ABC-CLIO, 2011.

St. Pierre, Maurice. *Eric Williams and the Anticolonial Tradition: The Making of a Diasporan Intellectual.* Charlottesville and London: University of Virginia Press, 2015.

Starmans, Christina, Mark Sheskin, and Paul Bloom. "Why People Prefer Unequal Societies." *Nature Human Behaviour* 1 (April 7, 2017), 1-7. Accessed October 30, 2022. ‹http://starlab.utoronto.ca/papers/2017%20Starmans%20Sheskin%20Bloom%20Inequality.pdf.›

Steckel, Richard H. *Health and Nutrition in the Preindustrial Era: Insights from a Millennium of Average Heights in Northern Europe.* Cambridge, MA: National Bureau of Economic Research, 2001.

Steinkeller, Piotr. "Corvee Labor in Ur III Times." In *From the 21st Century B.C. to the 21st Century A.D.: Proceedings of the International Conference on Sumerian Studies Held in Madrid 22-24 July 2010*, ed. Steven Garfinkle and Manuel Molina, 347-424. Winona Lake, IN: Eisenbrauns, 2013.

Stevenson, Robert Louis. *Strange Case of Dr. Jekyll and Mr. Hyde*, 1-78. In *Dr. Jekyll and Mr. Hyde and Other Stories.* New York: Knopf, 1992.

Stodder, Ann L. W., Debra L. Martin, Alan H. Goodman, and Daniel T. Reff. "Cultural Longevity and Biological Stress in the American Southwest." In *The Backbone of History: Health and Nutrition in the Western Hemisphere*, ed. Richard H. Steckel and Jerome C. Rose, 481-505. Cambridge, UK: Cambridge University Press, 2002.

Strayer, Joseph R. and Hans W. Gatzke. *The Mainstream of Civilization.* 4th ed. New York: Harcourt Brace Jovanovich, 1984.

Strayer, Robert W., Edwin Hirschmann, Robert B. Marks, Robert S. Smith, James S. Horn, and Lynn H. Parsons. *The Making of the Modern World: Connected Histories, Divergent Paths (1500 to the Present),* 2d ed. New York: St. Martin's Press, 1995.

Stringer, Chris and Peter Andrews. *The Complete World of Human Evolution.* London: Thames & Hudson, 2005.

Surugue, Lea. "Why This Paleolithic Burial Site Is So Strange (and So Important)." *Sapiens Anthropology Magazine,* February 22, 2018. Accessed February 19, 2022. ‹https://www.sapiens.org/archaeology/paleolithic-burial-sunghir.›

Sutherland, D. M. G. *France, 1789-1815: Revolution and Counterrevolution.* New York and Oxford: Oxford University Press, 1986.

Suttles, Wayne. "Coping with Abundance: Subsistence on the Northwest Coast." In *Man the Hunter,* ed. Richard B. Lee and Irven DeVore, 56-68. Chicago: Aldine Publishing, 1968.

Suvrathan, Uthara. "Landscapes of Life and Death: Considering the Region of Vidarbha." In *Ancient India: New Research,* ed. Upinder Singh and Nayanjot Lahiri, 124-173. Oxford and New York: Oxford University Press, 2009.

Swift, Jonathan. "A Modest Proposal for Preventing the Children of Poor People in Ireland from Being a Burden to Their Parents or Country, and for Making Them Beneficial to the Public." In *Student's Book of College English,* ed. David Skwire, Frances Chitwood, Raymond Ackley, and Raymond Fredman, 197-202. Beverly Hills, CA: Glencoe Press, 1975.

Szreter, Simon and Graham Mooney. "Urbanization, Mortality, and the Standard of Living Debate: New Estimates of the Expectation of Life at Birth in Nineteenth-Century British Cities." *The Economic History Review* 51, no. 1 (February 1998): 84-112.

Tan, Huileng. "The World's 10 Richest Men Have Made So Much Money during the Pandemic that a One-Time 99% Tax on Their Gains Could Pay for All COVID-19 Vaccine Production and More: Oxfam." Insider, January 17, 2022. Accessed April 8, 2022. ‹World's 10 Richest Men's Fortunes More Than Doubled in Pandemic: Oxfam (businessinsider.com).›

Tarasov, Boris. "Serf Russia, the History of People's Slavery." LitNet. Last modified November 18, 2020. Accessed October 29, 2022. ‹Tarasov Boris. Serf Russia, the history of people's slavery. (samlib.ru.).›

Taylor, Keith. *The Political Ideas of the Utopian Socialists.* London: Frank Cass, 1982.

Thernstrom, Stephan. *A History of the American People, Vol. I: To 1877*, 2d ed. San Diego: Harcourt Brace Jovanovich, 1989.

Thompson, R. C., A. H. Allam, G. P. Lombardi, L. S. Wann, M. L. Sutherland, J. D. Sutherland, M. A. Soliman, B. Frohlich, D. T. Mininberg, J. M. Monge, C. M. Vallodolid, S. L. Cox, G. Abd el-Maksoud, I. Badr, M. I. Miyamoto, A. el-Halim Nur el-Din, J. Narula, C. E. Finch, and G. S. Thomas. "Atherosclerosis across 4000 Years of Human History: The Horus Study of Four Ancient Populations." *Lancet* 381 (April 6, 2013): 1211-1222. Accessed May 10, 2022. ‹https://www.ncbi.nlm.nih.gov/pubmed/23489753.›

Trewin, Meaghan. "Cuisine, Customs and Character: Culinary Tradition and Innovation in Eighteenth Century France." Master's thesis, Queen's University, 2009. Accessed March 27, 2022. ‹UVic Thesis TemplateH .›

Trinkaus, Erik and Alexandra P. Buzhilova. "Diversity and Differential Disposal of the Dead at Sunghir." *Antiquity* 92, no. 361 (February 9, 2018): 7-21. Accessed April 28, 2022. ‹https://www.cambridge.org/core/journals/antiquity/article/diversity-and-differential-disposal-of-the-dead-at-sunghir/B7672FB594E94A505A35E10C869F3808.›

Turner, Michael. "Agriculture, 1860-1914." In *The Cambridge Economic History of Modern Britain, Vol. II: Economic Maturity, 1860-1939*, ed. Roderick Floud and Paul Johnson, 132-160. Cambridge, UK: Cambridge University Press, 2004.

Visvanathan, Meera. "Of Death and Fertility: Landscapes of Heroism in Ancient South India." In *Ancient India: New Research*, ed. Upinder Singh and Nayanjot Lahiri, 174-204. Oxford and New York: Oxford University Press, 2009.

Vuillard, Eric. *The War of the Poor*, trans. Mark Polizzotti. New York: Other Press, 2019.

Waal, Frans De. "Bonobo Sex and Society: The Behavior of a Close Relative Challenges Assumptions about Male Supremacy in Human Evolution." *Scientific American*, June 1, 2006. Accessed April 22, 2022. ‹https://www.scientificamerican.com/article/bonobo-sex-and-society-2006-06/#.›

Waal, Frans De. *Mama's Last Hug: Animal Emotions and What They Tell Us about Ourselves*. New York and London: Norton, 2019.

Wallace-Hadrill, Andrew. *Herculaneum: Past and Future*. London: Frances Lincoln Publishers, 2011.

Watts, Edward J. *Mortal Republic: How Rome Fell into Tyranny*. New York: Basic Books, 2018.

Watts, John. "Conclusion." In *The Routledge History Handbook of Medieval Revolt*, ed. Justine Firnhaber-Baker and Dirk Schoenaers, 370-380. London and New York: Routledge, 2017.

Weidman, Nadine. "Popularizing the Ancestry of Man: Robert Ardrey and the Killer Instinct." *Isis* 102, no. 2 (June 2011): 269-299.

Wickham, Chris. "Looking Forward: Peasant Revolts in Europe, 600-1200." In *The Routledge History Handbook of Medieval Revolt*, ed. Justine Firnhaber-Baker and Dirk Schoenaers, 155-167. London and New York: Routledge, 2017.

Wilkerson, Isabel. *Caste: The Origins of Our Discontents.* Waterville, ME: Thorndike Press, 2020.

Williams, Eric. *Capitalism and Slavery*, 3d ed. Chapel Hill: University of North Carolina Press, 2021.

Wilson, Edward O. *On Human Nature.* Cambridge, MA and London: Harvard University Press, 2004.

Wilson, Edward O. *The Social Conquest of Earth.* New York and London: Liveright Publishing, 2012.

Wilson, Edward O. *Sociobiology: The New Synthesis*, 25th anniversary ed. Cambridge, MA and London: Belknap Press of Harvard University Press, 2000.

Winks, Robin W., Crane Brinton, John B. Christopher, and Robert Lee Wolff. *A History of Civilization, Vol. I: Prehistory to 1715.* 7th ed. Englewood Cliffs, NJ: Prentice Hall, 1988.

Winks, Robin W., Crane Brinton, John B. Christopher, and Robert Lee Wolff. *A History of Civilization, Vol. II: 1618 to the Present.* 7th ed. Englewood Cliffs, NJ: Prentice Hall, 1988.

Winston, Mark L. *Bee Time: Lessons from the Hive.* Cambridge, MA and London: Harvard University Press, 2014.

Winthrop, John. "From *A Model of Christian Charity*." In *The Norton Anthology of American Literature*, 2d ed. Nina Baym, Francis Murphy, Ronald Gottesman, Hershel Parker, Laurence B. Holland, William H. Pritchard, and David Kalstone, 11-15. New York and London: Norton, 1986.

Wolff, Richard D. *Capitalism's Crisis Deepens: Essays on the Global Meltdown, 2010-2014.* Chicago: Haymarket Books, 2016.

Wood, Michael. *The Story of China: The Epic History of a World Power from the Middle Kingdom to Mao and the China Dream.* New York: St. Martin's Press, 2020.

Woodham-Smith, Cecil. "The Great Hunger: Ireland, 1845-1849." In *European Diet from Pre-Industrial to Modern Times*, ed. Elborg Forster and Robert Forster, 1-18. New York: Harper Torchbooks, 1975.

Woolf, Virginia. *A Room of One's Own.* San Diego: Harcourt Brace Jovanovich, 1981.

Worthington, Andrew C. "Occupy Wall Street." In *The SAGE Encyclopedia of Economics and Society.* Vol. 3, ed. Frederick F. Wherry and Juliet Schor, 1202-1204. Los Angeles: SAGE Reference, 2015.

Wragg Sykes, Rebecca. *Kindred: Neanderthal Life, Love, Death and Art.* London: Bloomsbury Sigma, 2020.

Wrangham, Richard and Dale Peterson. *Demonic Males: Apes and the Evolution of Human Aggression.* Boston: Houghton Mifflin, 1996.

Wright, Joshua. "Land Ownership and Landscape Belief: Introduction and Contexts." In *The Oxford Handbook of the Archaeology of Death and Burial*, ed. Sarah Tarlow and Liv Nilsson Stutz, 405-419. Oxford: Oxford University Press, 2013.

Wright Richard. *Black Boy (American Hunger): A Record of Childhood and Youth.* New York: HarperCollins, 2005.

Wright Richard. *Native Son.* New York: HarperPerennial/Modern Classics, 2005.

"The Young Prince of the Arene Candide." *Museo Diffuso del Finale*, 2019. Accessed July 13, 2022. ‹https://www.mudifinale.com/en/il-giovane-principe.›

Yafa, Stephen. *Big Cotton: How a Humble Fiber Created Fortunes, Wrecked Civilizations, and Put America on the Map.* New York: Viking, 2005.

Index

Engels, Friedrich, 8, 14, 16, 26, 27, 236, 239-242, 244-247, 251, 267, 268, 272-275, 278, 282, 288, 291, 330

England, 1, 22, 23, 44, 50, 63, 67, 138, 177, 190-192, 203, 206-208, 211-214, 222-226, 228, 230, 235, 236, 238, 239, 241-243, 245, 247, 248, 258, 260, 271, 278, 285, 300

English Peasants' Revolt, 211, 260

Enlightenment, the, 72, 73, 150, 185, 231, 260, 261

Entrepreneurialism, 215, 235, 320

Eratosthenes, 218

Essenes, 194, 268, 324

Estates General, 257-259

Ethiopia, 49, 59, 66, 112, 188, 210

Etruscans, 126, 129

Euphrates River, 49, 84, 85, 111, 112, 143, 156

Eurasia, 65, 71, 75, 78, 82, 128, 140, 210, 236, 284

Eurocentrism, 291

Europe, 49, 50, 63, 64, 68, 70-72, 74, 79, 126, 134, 145, 159, 165, 173, 182, 185-192, 204-210, 212, 214, 215, 217-219, 221, 223, 228, 235-239, 241, 244, 248, 252, 253, 262, 263, 268, 275, 276, 278, 279, 285, 286, 291, 292, 297, 300-303, 305, 309, 313, 317-320, 323, 327, 328

Exodus, 4, 94, 97, 98, 120

F

Factories, 8, 26, 233, 238, 241-246, 251, 270, 275, 287, 290, 292, 297, 299, 305, 309-311, 315, 316, 318, 319, 323

Famines, 4, 25, 26, 32, 33, 88, 91, 97, 98, 181, 200, 201, 204-206, 208, 209, 215, 235, 252, 264, 284, 287, 292, 301, 302, 305, 310

Fertile Crescent, 84, 85, 111, 128, 137

Feudalism, 186, 215, 257, 263

Fire, 7, 62-64, 67, 68, 158, 172

First International Workmen's Association, 275

Fishing, 82, 85, 144, 171, 205

Florence, Italy, 32, 188, 191, 192, 207, 208, 213, 214

Ford, Henry, 243

Fourier, Charles, 269

France, 12, 13, 57, 72, 75, 79, 121, 189, 191, 202, 207, 208, 211-214, 225, 231, 242, 243, 251-264, 270, 271, 275, 276, 282, 285, 287, 300, 302, 305, 318, 322

Francis of Assisi/Franciscans/Franciscan Order, 188, 201, 203, 246, 280

Franklin, Benjamin, 328

Freedmen, 125, 132, 133, 230, 231

French Communist Party, 322

French Revolution, 1789, 231, 251, 259, 260, 264, 267

French Revolution, 1830, 267, 270, 282

French Revolution, 1848, 242, 267, 272, 274, 275, 277, 282

Frescobaldi family, 192, 214

Frobisher, Martin, 226

Fu Hao, 162

G

Ganges River, 140

Gautama, Siddhartha (Buddhism), 139, 150-152

General Motors, 323

Genesis, 3, 4, 20, 45, 49, 51, 54, 56, 73, 97, 206

German Peasants' War, 276

Germany, 18, 67, 75, 189, 207, 215, 242, 243, 271, 272, 276, 277, 281, 285, 287, 292, 300, 305, 319, 322

Gibbons, 185, 186

Gibbon, Edward, 185, 186

Gilbert, Humphrey, 226

Gilded Age, 11, 12, 249, 281, 328

Gimpel, Jean, 190, 205, 208

Gini, Corrado, 98

Gini index, 98, 109-111, 163, 176, 196, 223, 296, 297, 307, 309-311, 313, 319, 320

Index

Printed in the United States
by Baker & Taylor Publisher Services